Other nonfiction books by Vincent Bugliosi

Helter Skelter (with Curt Gentry)

Till Death Us Do Part (with Ken Hurwitz)

And the Sea Will Tell (with Bruce Henderson)

The Phoenix Solution: Getting Serious About Winning America's Drug War

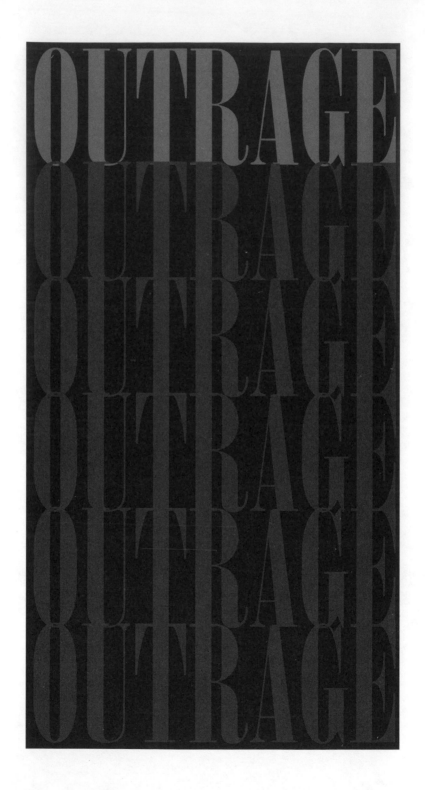

OUTRAGE

The Five Reasons Why O. J. Simpson Got Away with Murder

VINCENT BUGLIOSI

W · W · Norton & Company

New York   London

Excerpt from "Co-Workers Paint Different Portrait of Mark Fuhrman"
by Greg Krikorian from *Los Angeles Times* (November 8, 1995).
Copyright © 1995, *Los Angeles Times*. Reprinted by permission.

A portion of this book has previously appeared in *Playboy* magazine.

For information about permission to reproduce selections
from this book, write to Permissions,
W. W. Norton & Company, Inc.
500 Fifth Avenue, New York, New York 10110.

The text of this book is composed in 11/13 Electra
with display set in Monotype Onyx.
Manufacturing by Quebecor Printing, Fairfield, Inc.

Library of Congress Cataloging in Publication Data
Bugliosi, Vincent.
Outrage : the five reasons why O. J. Simpson got away with murder
/ Vincent Bugliosi
p. cm.
ISBN 0-393-04050-X
1. Murder—California—Los Angeles—Case studies. 2. Simpson, O. J., 1947–
—Trials, litigation, etc. 3. Trials (Murder)—California—Los Angeles—Case studies.
4. Criminal justice, Administration of—California—Los Angeles—Case studies.
I. Title
HV6534.L7B84   1996
364.1'532'0979494—dc20   96–7936
CIP

W. W. Norton & Company, Inc.
500 Fifth Avenue, New York, N.Y. 10110
http://web.wwnorton.com

W. W. Norton & Company Ltd.
10 Coptic Street, London WC1A 1PU

4 5 6 7 8 0

to the memory of
Nicole Brown Simpson and Ronald Goldman
and their surviving loved ones

OUTRAGE
OUTRAGE
OUTRAGE
OUTRAGE
OUTRAGE
OUTRAGE

Contents

OUTRAGE
OUTRAGE
OUTRAGE
OUTRAGE
OUTRAGE
OUTRAGE

Editor's Note

It may be useful to the reader, as background or context for the uncomfortable truths contained in this book, to know why I felt so strongly that Vincent Bugliosi was the only author in America who could write a truly meaningful account of the Simpson murder trial, and why I persisted until I finally persuaded him to write it, if not against his will, at least against his initial inclination.

Vincent Bugliosi should be on any knowledgeable person's short list of the great lawyers in America, but as a *prosecutor* he stands alone, in a class by himself. His record in the Los Angeles District Attorney's office speaks for itself: 105 convictions out of 106 felony jury trials; more importantly, 21 murder convictions without a single loss, including the prosecution of Charles Manson in the Tate-LaBianca murder case, which was to be the basis of his true-crime classic, *Helter Skelter*, the book that established him as the most celebrated true-crime author in America.

But perhaps a more substantive measure of Bugliosi's stature is the judgment of his peers, and here again the weight of evidence is overwhelming. Alan Dershowitz says simply, "Bugliosi is as good a prosecutor as there ever was." Harry Weiss, a veteran criminal defense attorney who has gone up against Bugliosi in court, makes this comparison: "I've seen all the great trial lawyers of the past thirty years and none of them are in Vince's class." Robert

11

Tannenbaum, for years the top prosecutor in the Manhattan District Attorney's office, says, "There is only one Vince Bugliosi. He's the best." Perhaps most telling of all is the comment by Gerry Spence, who squared off against Bugliosi in a televised, scriptless "docu-trial" of Lee Harvey Oswald, in which the original key witnesses to the Kennedy assassination testified and were cross-examined. After the jury returned a guilty verdict, in Bugliosi's favor, Spence said, "No other lawyer in America could have done what Vince did in this case."

The question I asked myself at the outset was this: What would the nation's foremost prosecutor have done with the evidence in the Trial of the Century? I think you will find the answers in this book as surprising and as compelling as I have. Bear in mind that while Bugliosi's analysis is unsparing, it is also objective, for he owes nothing to the myth of Simpson's innocence and has no need, unlike many other writers on this subject, to protect his own tarnished performance in the case.

—Starling Lawrence

OUTRAGE

Introduction

Well, here I go again. These are the words I am saying to myself after once again (by writing this book) being drawn back into the Simpson case after vigorously trying to remove myself from any association with it for well over a year. The initial shock was indeed overwhelming: to think that O. J. Simpson, famous and admired by millions of Americans, a Heisman Trophy winner who had carried the Olympic torch, could have committed two of the most horrendous murders imaginable. . . . But once I got past this reaction of disbelief, I found I had very little interest in the case itself. Certainly I was extremely interested in what the verdict was going to be, and if Simpson had testified I would have been interested in the cross-examination of him, but other than that, the case held little fascination for me. The reason is simple. How do you sustain your interest in a case, or in anything, when you already know what happened? And we all know what happened here. Simpson committed these murders. They just played a game during the trial, and I had minimal interest in the game.

The same was true of the Rodney King case. When Stephen Brill, president of Court TV, called me and asked me to commentate the first trial in Simi Valley for Court TV, I declined, telling him I was too busy with other commitments. That was certainly true, but the other reason is that the case held no fascination for me. It was a very important case sociologically, but again, we already know what happened. The crime was captured on film. So too with the Damian Williams case here in Los Angeles during the South-Central riots following the not-guilty Simi Valley verdicts. The crime was captured on film. In the Menendez case, the brothers admitted killing their parents. Where is the mystery? We already know what happened. The only type of criminal case that really appeals to me is a true murder mystery, and the interest is in the mystery, not the murder. But there was no mystery in the Simpson case. Anyone who says this case is a mystery and Simpson might actually be innocent is either being disingenuous—a euphemistic way of saying he or she is lying—or is suffering from a severe intellectual hernia, or is just not aware of the evidence. I know of no fourth option.

Yet many of the media referred to this case as a "true murder mystery." One writer for a national paper took it a step further and called it "one of the biggest murder mysteries of our time." The real mystery is how people with IQs no higher than room temperature can write for major publications. But actually, it's not IQ. It's a lack of common sense. One thing I have seen over and over again in life is that there is virtually no correlation between intelligence and common sense. IQ doesn't seem to translate that way.

Other reporters called the case a "classic whodunit," another way of calling it a mystery. But we all know what a whodunit is. That's a case where there is evidence pointing to four, five, or six suspects, and the question is, whodunit? But here, not just some of the evidence but all of the evidence pointed to one person and one person only, O. J. Simpson. Not one speck pointed to anyone else. I realize that sometimes in life the truth is an elusive fugitive. That wasn't the situation with the Simpson case.

Few reporters could resist the observation that the case against Simpson was "based entirely on circumstantial evidence," the implication being that this was an infirmity. But the reason for this implication is that the reporters, even though it is their job to know better, had no more knowledge of the nature and power of circumstantial evidence than the man on the street. Circumstantial evidence has erroneously come to be associated in the lay mind and vernacular with an anemic case. But nothing could be further from the truth. It depends on what type of circumstantial evidence one is talking about. In a case like the Simpson case, where the prosecution presented physical, scientific evidence connecting Simpson to the crime, it couldn't be stronger.

The true circumstantial evidence case, and the only kind that is difficult to try, is one in which not only are there no eyewitnesses—only eye-witness testimony, which is notoriously problematic, is direct evidence—but there are no bullet, blood, hair, semen, or skin matchups; in fact, no physical evidence of any kind whatsoever, such as clothing or glasses, connecting the defendant to the crime. That's the classic, textbook type of circumstantial evidence case, in which you have to put one speck of evidence—an inappropriate remark, a suspicious bank transaction, a subtle effort to deflect the investigation, things like that—upon another speck until ultimately there is a strong mosaic of guilt. But the Simpson case was something entirely different: O. J. Simpson might just as well have gone around with a large sign on his back declaring in bold letters that he had murdered these two poor people. In other words, the case was cir-cumstantial in name only.

Another reason why I sought to remove myself from the case is that I have been trying for some time now to complete my book on the assas-sination of President John F. Kennedy, the most important murder case in American history. Contemporaneously, I was updating my 1991 book, *Drugs in America: The Case for Victory*, which was republished this year as *The Phoenix Solution: Getting Serious About Winning America's Drug War*. I view the drug problem as the most serious crisis facing our coun-try, and I see this book as my magnum opus. When the media would call for a TV or radio appearance I had a choice: make the appearance, which required the expenditure of several hours out of my day which I didn't have, or decline, which is never pleasant, but which I did with 95 percent of the requests. Even declining, with any semblance of civility, can take up a lot of time when one is dealing with so many requests, not only from network TV, but from radio stations and newspapers all over the country.

Despite my efforts, I was only partially successful in staying away from the Simpson case. Reporters and talk show hosts are incredibly persistent, and occasionally I would agree to appear on national TV to comment on the Simpson case, every time telling myself it was the last time. But it never was. And since I never do anything, even appear on television, with-out doing my homework, I kept sufficiently current with the case to know what was going on.

Because I am a writer of true-crime books, during the past year many people suggested to me that I write a book on the case. My invariable response, without giving a second of reflection, was no. The first time I felt the faintest glimmer of interest was when my editor, Starling Lawrence, called me a few weeks after the outrageous verdict and suggested I do a book based on how I would have prosecuted the case, calling it "The

Second Trial of O. J. Simpson." That titillated me somewhat, because I knew the first trial had not been handled properly at all. The problem is that since, among other things, I would have presented much more evidence of guilt than the prosecutors in this case did, I would have had to invent the cross-examination of the witnesses testifying to this evidence, and I had no desire to get into fiction. Also, I was just too busy with my other books to take on a third major book.

But my editor, like the media, was persistent, and he called back a week later to suggest I write not an all-encompassing book on the case, but a book with a narrower focus—why did the prosecution lose this case? The book could be short, he said, almost an informal discussion and "personal conversation" with the reader, an extension of the interviews I've given on the case over radio and television, not the in-depth true-crime book I typically write, trying to nail down every date, name, and event with particularity. Because I was just about completing my drug book update, and because I feel very confident I know why this case was lost, I agreed to do the current book.

The reader should know that this book will not be a detailed recitation of all the facts of the case or the testimony and evidence at the trial (although there will be a meaningful amount of both). I assume the reader of this book, if interested enough to buy it, is already reasonably familiar with the case. In terms of heinousness and brutality, on a scale of one to ten, these murders were a ten. A veteran LAPD detective, one of the first officers to arrive at the scene, said, "It was the bloodiest crime scene I have ever seen." Nicole Brown Simpson, in a fetal position, and Ron Goldman, slumped over a few feet away, were found literally lying in a pool of blood, their clothing drenched in blood. The autopsies, conducted on June 14, 1995, showed that Nicole was stabbed seven times in her neck and scalp. The fatal wound was a vicious five-and-a-half-inch slash from left to right across her neck that severed both the left and right carotid arteries, virtually severed the left jugular vein, cut into the right jugular vein, and actually penetrated "for a depth of 1/4 inch into the bone of the 3rd cervical vertebra." The neck wound, the report says, was so severe, "it is gaping [2 1/2 inches wide] and exposes the larynx and cervical vertebral column." Goldman was stabbed thirty times on his scalp, face, neck, chest, abdomen, and left thigh. His fatal wounds were the severing of his "left internal jugular vein" and "stab wounds of the chest and abdomen causing intrathoracic and intra-abdominal hemorrhage." Many of his wounds were a "combination of stabbing and cutting." Both victims had defensive wounds to their hands, incurred trying to ward off the deadly assault.

How did it come to pass that someone we know—not believe, but know—committed these two savage murders is now out walking among us, enjoying life with a smile on his face? That's what this book is all about. For those who *are* looking for a discussion of everything that happened in this case, they will be able to find it in books to be published on the case by prominent authors like Joe McGinniss (*Fatal Vision*), Jeffrey Toobin, Joe Bosco, and others. Dominick Dunne (*The Two Mrs. Grenvilles*) reportedly is writing a novel about the case.

This book sets forth five reasons why the case was lost. But even these five can be distilled down to two: the jury could hardly have been any worse, and neither could the prosecution. In fact, as bad as this jury was, if the prosecution had given an A rather than a D- performance (discussed in Chapters 4 and 5 of this book), the verdict most likely would have been different. (Let's not forget that even with a dreadfully poor prosecution, on the first ballot, which the jury took within an hour after it commenced its deliberations, two of the jurors, a black and a white, voted guilty.) Even before I saw any of the jurors or heard or read what they had to say, I felt this way. And in listening to the Simpson jurors in posttrial interviews, and reading a book jointly written by three of them, my feelings in this respect have been strengthened. I got no sense at all from them that they didn't care if Simpson was guilty or not, no sense that their state of mind back in the jury room had been "Even though O.J. is obviously guilty, we like O.J., so let's give him two free murders," or "Even though we know O.J. is guilty, blacks have been discriminated against by whites for centuries, so let's pay back whitey and give O.J. a couple of freebies." I didn't sense that, nor do I believe it for one moment.

What I saw was jurors who (1) clearly did not have too much intellectual firepower and (2) were biased in Simpson's favor, most likely from the start. But a powerfully presented case and summation, in which you put bibs on the jury and spoon-feed them, can virtually always be counted on to overcome both of these problems. And this jury wasn't quite as dense as some have felt. In posttrial interviewing, nearly all have proved to be fairly articulate, two having college degrees. The only kind of juror you can't turn around would be one who was determined to let Simpson get away with these murders even if he or she had no doubt at all Simpson was guilty. But it would be an extremely rare occurrence for even one juror to have this attitude, much less all twelve. If the case had been properly prosecuted, not only would a conviction have been likely, but any hung jury would almost assuredly have been no worse than 10–2 or 9–3 for conviction.

All of the above, of course, presupposes Simpson's guilt for these two murders. But about that there can be no doubt. As I said in a *Playboy* magazine interview before the trial commenced: "No matter the outcome of the trial, O. J. Simpson is guilty. There can be no doubt in the mind of any reasonable person." In fact, the question in the Simpson case has never been whether he is guilty or not guilty but, given the facts and circumstances of this case, whether it is possible for him to be innocent. And the answer to that question has always been an unequivocal no. In all my years, other than in cases where the killer has been apprehended during the perpetration of the homicide, I have never seen a more obvious case of guilt.

To distill this case down to its irreducible minimum (and temporarily ignoring all the other evidence pointing inexorably to Simpson's guilt), if your blood is found at the murder scene, as Simpson's was conclusively proved to be by DNA tests, that's really the end of the ball game. There is nothing more to say. (And in this case, not only was Simpson's blood found at the murder scene, but the victims' blood was found inside his car and home.) I mean, to deny guilt when your blood is at the murder scene is the equivalent of a man being caught by his wife *in flagrante* with another woman and saying to her (quoting comedian Richard Pryor), "Who are you going to believe? Me or your lying eyes?"

At the crime scene there were five blood drops leading away from the slain bodies of Nicole Brown Simpson and Ronald Goldman toward the rear alley, four of which were immediately to the *left* of bloody size-12 shoe prints (Simpson's shoe size). This indicated, of course, that the killer had been wounded on the left side of his body. And the morning after the murders, Simpson was observed by the police to be wearing a bandage on his left middle finger. When the bandage was removed that afternoon, it was seen that he had a deep cut on the knuckle of the finger.

DNA (deoxyribonucleic acid) is the genetic material found in all human cells that carries the coded messages of heredity unique (with the exception of identical twins) to each individual. DNA, then, is our genetic fingerprint. Each of the approximately 100 trillion cells in a human body contains twenty-three pairs of chromosomes—one of each pair coming from one's father, the other from the mother—which contain DNA molecules. In criminal cases, DNA can be extracted from samples of blood, semen, saliva, skin, or hair follicles found at a crime scene and then compared to DNA drawn from a suspect to determine if there is a "match." DNA testing is a new forensic science, first used in Great Britain in 1985 and in the United States in 1987.

DNA tests on all five blood drops and on three bloodstains found on the rear gate at the crime scene showed that all of this blood belonged to Simpson. Two DNA tests were used, PCR (polymerase chain reaction) and RFLP (restrictive fragment length polymorphism). The PCR test is less precise than the RFLP, but can be conducted on much smaller blood samples as well as samples that have degenerated ("degraded") because of bacteria and/or exposure to the elements. PCR tests were conducted on four out of the five blood drops. Three showed that only one out of 240,000 people had DNA with the markers found in the sample. (A marker is a gene that makes up one portion of the DNA molecule, and the more markers in the sample, the more comparison tests can be conducted, and hence the greater the exclusion of other humans.) The fourth blood drop had markers which one out of 5,200 people could have. Simpson was one of these people. The fifth blood drop had sufficient markers for an RFLP test, and showed that only one out of 170 million people had DNA with those markers. Again, Simpson's blood did. The richest sample was on the rear gate, and an RFLP test showed that only one out of 57 *billion* people had those markers. Simpson was one of them. In other words, just on the blood evidence alone, there's only a one out of 57 billion chance that Simpson is innocent. Fifty-seven billion is approximately ten times the current population of the entire world.

Now I realize that Igor in Kiev, Gino in Naples, Colin down Johannesburg way, and Kartac on Pluto might have the same DNA as O. J. Simpson. If you're a skeptic I wouldn't blame you if you checked to see if Igor, Gino, Colin, or Kartac was in Brentwood on the night of the murders, used to beat Nicole within an inch of her life, had blood all over his car, driveway, and home on the night of the murders, had no alibi, and, if charged with the murders, would refuse to take the witness stand to defend himself. Who knows—maybe Simpson isn't the murderer after all. Maybe Igor or one of the others is. You should definitely check this out. And while you're checking it out, someone should be checking you in to the nearest mental ward.

To elaborate on the irreducible minimum mentioned earlier, there are only three possible explanations other than guilt for one's blood being found at the murder scene, and all three are preposterous on their face. One is that Simpson left his blood there on an earlier occasion. When Simpson was interrogated by LAPD detectives on the afternoon after these murders, he said he had not cut himself the last time he was at the Bundy address a week earlier. But even without that, how can one believe that on some prior occasion Simpson bled, not just on the Bundy premises, but at the precise point on the premises where the murders occurred? In fact, so far-fetched is this possibility that even the defense attorneys, whose stock-in-trade during the trial was absurdity, never proffered it to the jury.

And here, not only was Simpson's blood found at the murder scene, but there were the four drops of Simpson's blood found just to the left of the killer's bloody shoe prints leaving the murder scene. If there is someone who isn't satisfied even by this, I would suggest that this book is perhaps not for you, that you think about pursuing more appropriate intellectual pursuits, such as comic strips. When I was a kid, one of my favorites was *Mandrake the Magician*. You might check to see if Mandrake is still doing his thing.

The second possibility is that Simpson cut himself while killing Ron Goldman and Nicole Brown in self-defense—that is, either Ron or Nicole or both together unleashed a deadly assault on Simpson, and he either took out a knife he had on his own person or wrested Ron's or Nicole's knife away, and stabbed the two of them to death. This, of course, is just too insane to talk about. Again, even the defense attorneys, who apparently possess the gonads of ten thousand elephants, never suggested this possibility. It should be added parenthetically that if such a situation had occurred, Simpson wouldn't have had any reason to worry, since self-defense is a justifiable homicide, a complete defense to murder.

The third and final possibility is that the LAPD detectives planted Simpson's blood not just at the murder scene but to the left of the bloody shoe prints leaving the scene. This is not as insane a proposition as the first two, but only because there are degrees of everything in life. It is still an insane possibility, and if any reader is silly enough to believe that the LAPD detectives decided to frame someone they believed to be innocent of these murders (Simpson) and actually planted his blood all over the murder scene (and, of course, planted the victims' blood in Simpson's car and home), again, this book is probably not for that reader. This book is for people who are very angry that a brutal murderer is among us—with a smile on his face, no less—and want to know how this terrible miscarriage of justice could have occurred. In any event, a thorough discussion of the defense's allegation of an LAPD conspiracy to frame Simpson (and why such a charge is absurd) is in Chapters 4 and 5.

Let me point out to those who believe in the "possible" existence of either of the aforementioned three innocent possibilities for Simpson's blood being found at the murder scene, that the prosecution only has the burden of proving guilt beyond a *reasonable* doubt, not beyond all possible doubt. So it isn't necessary to have all possible doubts of guilt removed from one's mind in order to reach a conclusion of guilt. Only reasonable doubts of guilt have to be removed. Of course, in this case, *no* doubt remains of Simpson's guilt.

In discussing the five reasons why the Simpson case was lost, the reader should know that I have very little good to say about anyone associated with this case, because of either their offensive conduct and/or their abject incompetence. The choice I had was either to be candid or not to write the book at all. The reader should also know that I am, by nature, a critical person. I'd find fault with a beautiful morning sunrise. (I am also one who finds it easy to compliment.) However, where I do find fault I don't simply make the allegation, thereby setting up a burden for myself, and not make a solid effort to meet the burden. That's not my style, as it is that of so many people. While there will be interludes of calm in the pages that follow, when you couple my critical nature with the fact that for several weeks after the verdict I was so angry I could have eaten nails—and I'm *still* angry—the reader should be prepared for an almost unremitting scathing indictment of what took place in this case.

The biggest problem by far, of course, is that a brutal murderer was set free. But the straw that broke the camel's back was Simpson's demeanor throughout the case and in the wake of the verdict. I've seen many murderers in my life, but none even approached Simpson for audacity, which he has taken to previously unimaginable heights. Let me give you a few examples of what I mean. Although he had administered several terrible physical beatings to Nicole, causing her to fear for her life, and although he eventually killed her, in his farewell letter before his arrest he referred to himself as "a battered husband." Going on, there is a way for a guilty defendant to plead not guilty at his arraignment. You know what it is? To say "not guilty." That's what 999 out of 1,000 guilty defendants say. And when they do, it doesn't bother me. I expect them to plead not guilty, to deny guilt. But that wasn't good enough for Simpson. He had to say "absolutely, one hundred percent not guilty." Since he knew what he had done, that bothered me, a lot.

Throughout the trial, his knowing what he had done in no way inhibited him from showing disgust and contempt for the prosecutors whenever they did anything at all which he perceived to be even slightly improper or unfair. In fact, his entire demeanor and body language indicated that he felt he was being put out by the trial, the trial being an interference with his very pleasant and enjoyable lifestyle. It was as if he felt that this one little messy incident on the night of June 12, 1994, shouldn't be held against him. After all, he was *still* O. J. Simpson, wasn't he?

His lead lawyer, Johnnie Cochran, almost matched Simpson's audacity, and in one instance may have exceeded it. In mid-trial there were rumors that a plea bargain was being negotiated between the defense team and the Los Angeles County District Attorney's Office. Cochran denied this, and to disabuse everyone, including the public, of any idea that Simpson was going to plead to a lesser charge, told Judge Ito in open court that there would be no plea bargain in the case. Then, outside of court, when the media continued to inquire about the possibility, he told them (and the remark was undoubtedly heard by the grieving survivors, since it was on television, radio, and in the newspapers), "Are you kidding? Absolutely not. *The only thing we'll accept is an apology* and O.J. goes home today." Can you imagine that? Simpson is entitled to an apology. The question I have—and no one has been able to give me an answer—is: Where do you get guts like this? Are some people just born with them? Can you buy them?

At the defense's celebration party at Simpson's home on the night of the verdict, while two precious human beings were decomposing in their graves, Simpson, with a broad smile on his face, held a Bible up in the air with his outstretched right hand. A Bible. The word "unbelievable," a tired adjective, doesn't really describe this type of audacity. Suffice it to say that Simpson has elevated audacity to symphonic and operatic levels. And as if the not-guilty verdict was not painful enough to all right-thinking people, Simpson immediately attempted to profit from his murders. He tried to make more money than he has ever made in his career (it was said his people hoped for $30 million to $40 million) by giving a pay-per-view television interview. Fortunately, instant vocal opposition from outraged Americans squelched this crass endeavor. He did succeed, however, in getting paid a reported $3 million for filming a two-hour $29.95 mail-order video declaring his innocence.

And during the trial, he published a book of photographs and letters from supporters titled *I Want to Tell You* that made him more than $1 million. Unbelievably, and shamelessly, Simpson exploited the person he had murdered for money, putting many pictures of Nicole in the book.

And it wasn't enough for Simpson to walk out of court a free man with a smile on his face when the LAPD and DA's office knew he was guilty. He had to rub their noses in their defeat by actually demanding that they now go out and look for the real killer or killers, adding that it would be his "primary goal in life" to search for the person or persons who had killed his Nicole. One courthouse wag remarked: "Doesn't he have a mirror in his home?" (A month or so after his arrest, Simpson had offered reward money for the capture of the killer or killers. Since he committed the murders, he could have offered his entire net worth and it would have been an utterly risk-free offer.) Within days of the verdict he was also seen smiling and soaking up the sun on golf courses. In an interview he gave to the Associated Press, he said about himself: "The only thing that endures is character. Fame and wealth—all that is illusion. All that endures is character."

After the verdict, Simpson challenged Marcia Clark to get in a room with him and debate the case — you know, *mano a mano*. And he wanted to really lay it all out in an interview with NBC's Tom Brokaw and Katie Couric (called off by his civil lawyer). And, of course, the title of his book was *I Want to Tell You*. All of this showed he was a real stand-up guy. No B.S. He wanted to tell everyone what really went down, "tell it like it is." But he didn't want to tell it like it is to the jury at his trial, *the only* twelve people who held his life in their hands, the twelve people who could have convicted him of first-degree murder and sent him to prison for life. In over nine months of trial, he had no desire to say one single word to them. But after the trial he wanted to talk to everyone *else* about what happened.

No sound in any courtroom is as loud as the defendant's silence when he is accused of the most serious crime of all, murder, and he chooses not to deny it from the witness stand. When a person is falsely accused of a murder, it should take a team of wild horses to keep him from the witness stand. Simpson didn't testify, of course, because he was guilty. There is no other truly valid reason in this case for his not doing so. H. L. Mencken once said that no one ever went broke underestimating the intelligence of the American people. Simpson obviously subscribes to this, because he has tried to con us into accepting a friendly out-of-court chat with a TV commentator, or a rehearsed video as a legitimate and satisfactory substitute for his refusal to testify at his own trial.

Now for why this case was lost.

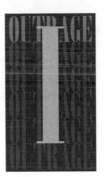

In the Air

What the Jurors Probably Knew

From the moment O. J. Simpson became a suspect in this double murder case, it was "in the air," perhaps as in no other case within memory, that he might get off despite the conclusive evidence of his guilt. In fact, even before the murders, it was in the air, Nicole presciently telling her close female friends that "O.J. is going to kill me someday and he's going to get by with it."

It was *in the air* from the day (June 17, 1994) when mental midgets stood atop the freeway overpasses holding "Go O.J., Go" signs during the slow-speed chase prior to his arrest. Everywhere one looked, it was *in the air*. People saying confidently, "This jury will never convict Simpson—they wouldn't convict him even if they were shown a film of him committing the murders." People carrying signs outside the courtroom during the trial declaring "Free O.J.," "Save the Juice," and even "Whether you did it or not, we still love you, O.J." The incessant jokes and tasteless comedy routines on TV and radio about the case, which could only serve to subliminally trivialize the murders of the victims. U.S. Senate Chaplin Richard Halverson beginning the Senate's day on June 23, 1994, with a "prayer for O. J. Simpson." The first juror called for questioning in the case happening to be juror number 32, the number Simpson wore throughout most of his football career, prompting Judge Ito to say, "I don't know if this is an omen," and Simpson to smile and nod his head in agreement. Marcia Clark, during jury selection, making one of the most ill-advised statements ever made to a jury by a prosecutor: "You may not like me for bringing this case. I'm not winning any popularity contests for doing so." Chris Darden's almost equally incredible and ill-advised statement to the jury in his summation at the end of the case: "Nobody wants to do anything to this man. We don't. There is nothing personal about this, but the law is the law." (Can you imagine being almost apologetic to a jury when you believe the person you're prosecuting committed a brutal double murder?)

To this day, virtually everyone refers to Simpson only as "O.J.," a friendly nickname that implies the speaker still likes Simpson or at most views him as one would an errant friend or relative, certainly not a brutal murderer. "How's O.J. doing?" Larry King would solicitously ask any guest of his who was a Simpson intimate and who had visited Simpson recently at the jail. These and many other small signs of respect, or awe, or affection, indicated that Simpson, even if guilty, might be given some break tantamount to a papal dispensation. In the absence of a powerful prosecution, it became almost a self-fulfilling prophecy that he would be found not guilty.

This feeling, this sense, which permeated every segment of our society, was obviously known to the jurors before they were selected, even manifesting itself during the trial. Because when something is in the air, it reaches everyone, by osmosis, by accident, or, if by no other means, by the weekly conjugal visits to the sequestered jurors. Surely, no one can doubt that the jurors were speaking to those loved ones who visited them in the privacy of their quarters. Everyone knew this. You don't have to take my word for it. What conceivable reason would Marcia Clark have had to beg Judge Ito not to let Simpson make a statement near the end of the case, when Simpson wanted to do so outside the presence of the jury, if she didn't virtually know that what Simpson said would get back to the jury?

This "in the air" phenomenon couldn't help but contribute, in some way, to the eventual not-guilty verdict. It made it so much easier, either consciously or subconsciously, for the jury to give Simpson every benefit he was legally entitled to, and then some. In such an atmosphere a not-guilty verdict would no longer seem to the jury like the very worst thing that any jury could do—let a brutal murderer walk out the door a free man. They were just doing what everyone had already *predicted* they were going to do, and apparently what most people *wanted* them to do. Wasn't that really what prosecutor Darden himself was suggesting when he said, "Nobody wants to do anything to this man"?

I've been asked to explain more than once why, right from the beginning, I was saying publicly that there was no question Simpson was guilty. I take no pride in having been the first public personality to come out publicly against Simpson. It just happened that way. I was asked by the media how I felt about the case way back in the early summer of 1994, and I decided to be candid. Before I tell you why I did, I should point out that some people objected to my having done so. One reason was the presumption of innocence in our society. Also, they felt that as a member of the bar, I should, therefore, not have spoken of Simpson's guilt before the verdict.

Contrary to common belief, the presumption of innocence applies only inside a courtroom. It has no applicability elsewhere, although the media do not seem to be aware of this. Even the editorial sections of major American newspapers frequently express the view, in reference to a pending case, that "we" — meaning the editors and their readers — have to presume that so-and-so is innocent. To illustrate that the presumption does not apply outside the courtroom, let's say an employer has evidence that an employee has committed theft. If the employer had to presume the person were innocent, he obviously couldn't fire the employee or do anything at all. But of course he not only can fire or demote the employee, he can report him to the authorities.

Actually, even in court there are problems with the presumption of innocence. The presumption of innocence, we all know, is a hallowed doctrine that separates us from repressive regimes. It's the foundation, in fact, for the rule that is the bedrock of our system of justice — that a defendant can be convicted of a crime only if his guilt has been proved beyond a reasonable doubt. However, legal presumptions are based on the rationale of probability. Under certain situations, experience has shown that when fact "A" is present, the presence of "B" should be presumed to exist unless and until an adverse party disproves it. For example, a letter correctly addressed and properly mailed is presumed to have been received in the ordinary course of mail delivery. But when we apply this underlying basis of probability for a legal presumption to the presumption of innocence, the presumption, it would seem, should fall. Conviction rates show that it is ridiculous to presume that when the average defendant is arrested, charged with a crime, and brought to trial, he is usually innocent. But obviously, the converse presumption that a defendant is presumed to be guilty would be far worse and, indeed, intolerable. Our system, for readily apparent reasons, is far superior to those in nations, mostly totalitarian, which presume an arrested person is guilty and place the burden on the accused to prove his innocence.

The solution would seem to be simply to eliminate the presumption-of-innocence *instruction* to the jury, keeping those two necessary corollaries of the presumption which do have enormous merit: first, the fact that the defendant has been arrested for and charged with a crime is no evidence of his guilt and should not be used against him; and second and more important, under our system of justice the prosecution has the burden of proving guilt. The defendant has no burden to prove his innocence. It is one thing to say that the defendant does not have to prove his innocence, and that in the absence of affirmative proof of guilt he is entitled to a not-guilty verdict even if he presented no evidence of his innocence at all. To go a step further, however, and say that he is legally presumed to be innocent when he has just been brought to court in handcuffs or with a deputy sheriff at his side seems to be hollow rhetoric. One day a defendant is going to stand up in court and tell the judge, "Your Honor, if I am legally presumed to be innocent, why have I been arrested for this crime, why has a criminal complaint been filed against me, and why am I now here in court being tried?"

As any seasoned criminal trial lawyer will attest, most juries see through the transparent fiction of the presumption of innocence. Whether they verbalize it or not, as reasonable human beings they know that if the defendant seated at the counsel table in front of them were truly presumed to be innocent in the eyes of the law, they would not have been empaneled to hear and adjudicate the charges brought against the defendant *by* the law. It is even possible that the articulation of the presumption of innocence by the judge to the jury may, on balance, work to the detriment of the accused. If the jury knows the presumption of innocence is a legal fiction, yet the judge intones the presumption to them in a very sober manner, and with the straightest of countenances, could it be that he thereby loses a speck of credibility in their eyes? And when he subsequently instructs them on those matters which *are* legally sound and designed by the law to protect the rights of the defendant (e.g., the doctrine of reasonable doubt), they may not take his words as seriously as they should?

With respect to the supposed inappropriateness of my speaking out because I am a member of the bar, the Rules of Professional Conduct of the American Bar Association, specifically Rule 3.6, provide that the prosecutor and defense attorney on a case should not make any statement outside of court as to whether the defendant is guilty or not guilty. Yet, the defense attorneys in the Simpson case consistently voiced their opinion to the media that Simpson was innocent. I don't have any problem with that. I think Rule 3.6 is unrealistic and unduly restrictive. But the point I want to make is that if lawyers *on the Simpson case* who were not supposed to state their opinion did so, certainly someone like me who was not involved was entitled to do so. The First Amendment to the United States Constitution allows this.

However, even given the fact that I was not prohibited by Rule 3.6, or by the presumption of innocence, I would normally have felt it unseemly and in poor taste for me, a member of the bar, or for any public official to speak out on an accused's guilt before the verdict, and this was the very first time I ever did so. I had objected when President Nixon (also a lawyer, by the way), during the Manson trial, said to reporters in Denver he believed Manson to be guilty. That statement made headlines throughout the country and almost caused a mistrial.

I spoke out in the Simpson case for two reasons. The main reason should be self-evident to the reader by now. The "in the air" phenomenon attending the Simpson case was, at least to my recollection, unprecedented for any criminal case. Because this was a highly unusual situation, I departed from my customary policy. There was no doubt in my mind that the "in the air" phenomenon had the potential of having a prejudicial impact on the prosecution's case, since the jury couldn't help but be aware of it and probably be adversely influenced in the process, and I was trying to counter what was happening. I obviously was unsuccessful.

There was another related reason I spoke out early on, months before the trial. I was disgusted by the tremendous groundswell of support for Simpson, even though two human beings had been brutally murdered, and *all* the evidence pointed to Simpson as the perpetrator. He had received 350,000 letters of support at the time, and although each revelation of his guilt the media learned of was clinically and dispassionately reported in the news, nearly all of the commentators on television nonetheless treated Simpson as if he were a very special human being, and not one of them dared to say one negative word about him. He was being given special treatment at the Los Angeles County Jail; thousands of people were calling in on radio talk shows asserting his innocence; some, unbelievably, stating or strongly implying that even if he was guilty, he's O.J., let him go, he has suffered enough. As I've indicated, even today, everyone still calls him O.J. You know, O.J. this and O.J. that. Well, he's no longer O.J. to me. He's Simpson. Someone who carves up two human beings like sides of beef forfeits his right to any endearing nicknames, at least in my view. Again, why there was this enormous support for someone who had obviously committed two of the worst murders imaginable I don't know, but I personally found it repulsive and repugnant.

In addition to Simpson's astonishing, and to me incomprehensible, popularity, there were two other dynamics at play in this case which were very much "in the air" and inuring to the detriment of the prosecution in the eyes of the jury: the media hype that converted the defense lawyers into "the Dream Team," and the phenomenon of the "talking heads" who made a cottage industry out of their daily and nightly television commentaries on the events in the courtroom.

Let's start with lawyers, specifically lawyers in criminal cases before a jury, which is the only area of the law I feel I'm qualified to talk about. I start out with the assumption that a lawyer in a criminal case is going to be incompetent, substantially so. I find my assumption to be rarely wrong. Yet society starts out with the very opposite assumption. I happen to know society is wrong, dead wrong. The reason I say this is that not only do the facts and the evidence show society is wrong, but common sense does. Here's why. Incompetence is rampant in our society, from presidents on down. It is everywhere. In fact, it is so prevalent and so bad that the only adjective I've ever been able to come up with in the lexicon that adequately describes it is "staggering."

It is not my purpose in this book to give examples of incompetence. If the reader isn't aware of the prevalence of incompetence, I certainly won't be able to disabuse him of his sheltered view in a few paragraphs. But people can't do the simplest things right. For instance, I travel a lot, and I always assume that room service is going to forget something, whether it is water, cream for my coffee or butter for my bread, a knife, fork, or spoon, part of the order, etc. And room service is a simple, repetitive, day-in-and-day-out task that people with an IQ of 60 should be able to perform. But the people making these errors, many of whom are students working their way through college, don't have low IQs. There is no reason to believe, in fact, that their IQs are any lower than those of people going to law school.

How often have you been in a parking garage and found that the signs directing you to the exit are grossly inadequate? They're too small, or partially obstructed, or not in the obvious place they should be in. Or after one exit sign, the next one is so far ahead that you have already taken a wrong turn where there was no sign to guide you. And so forth. Putting adequate signs up has to be fairly simple, and the person has all the time in the world to do it. And does anyone really think that those who are responsible for putting up these signs (or highway signs, which also are so often very bad, and undoubtedly have contributed to many, many deaths throughout the years) are mentally retarded? No, they're just incompetent. Normal people.

Have you ever moved into a brand-new home? Aren't there one hundred defective things, many of which require your calling the workers out three or four times to fix once and for all? Do you really believe all these carpenters, plumbers, electricians, etc. are morons? Of course not. They are perfectly normal, incompetent people. It is just too much for them to do their job well, even though the work they do is relatively simple work they do every working day, and it's almost mechanical, necessitating very little thinking.

How about all the consumer products that are difficult to operate because whoever manufactured them was too incompetent to make it easy? Or the instructions that are hopelessly confusing and sometimes flat-out wrong? How about the large office buildings either without street numbers on them or with numbers located on the building in such a way they are difficult to see from the street? Or floors and room numbers at some hotels which require an Indian guide to find? Or the recorded voice in the shuttles at some airports that are virtually impossible to hear or understand? Do you really believe the airport administrator has a much lower IQ than the average lawyer? How about the incompetents at the telephone company who decided a few years back to improve the perfectly adequate and easy-to-use touch keys on public pay telephones by adding a metal cusp on each side of them, making it actually difficult to punch the numbers? In fact, it is virtually impossible to punch the keys fast without hitting at least one or two cusps instead of the keys. Do you really think that all the people involved in this multimillion-dollar project at the telephone company are certifiable idiots, with IQs lower than those of trial lawyers? If you think so, you are wrong. There are of course countless other examples of incompetence. These are but a few.

If incompetence is so endemic in our society, even among people doing simple, repetitive things with a lot of time in which to do them, doesn't common sense tell you that the incompetence is going to be even more common and pronounced with trial lawyers who deal with different witnesses in every case, with different facts and evidence, who are constantly forced to think on their feet under pressure of time, and who have an opponent who is trying to thwart and negate their every move? Yes, common sense tells you this. But this is not the way society sees it.

The reason is the extremely strong myth in our society—the genesis, I imagine, being from novels and films—that criminal defense attorneys, particularly those on big cases, are brilliant, great, high-powered, silver-tongued; that they're magicians, able to pull rabbits out of hats, etc. Although there is incredible incompetence everywhere in our society, for some curious reason, because of this myth, defense lawyers are perceived to be an exception.

The reality is that the vast, overwhelming majority of trial lawyers in criminal jury trials are either incompetent or operating at a very low level of competence. And if most prominent trial lawyers met their reputations out on the street, they wouldn't recognize each other.

In addition to novels and the screen, the media have been very complicit in perpetuating the myth. For example, cross-examination as bland as pablum is routinely reported to be "rigorous" or "withering." Why? Because cross-examination is *supposed* to be rigorous and withering.

Similarly, there are some easy ways to destroy the credibility of an adverse witness that even a relatively unskilled cross-examiner can manage—introducing prior inconsistent or contradictory statements, showing the witness's bias or vested interest, his poor character for truth, etc. It's always amusing to me when I see laypeople and the media being so impressed when a lawyer does these simple, obvious things in court, things an average person would instinctively know to do. Here is how ingrained the myth is: How many times have you heard a layperson, talking about a weakness in a case, say, "A *clever* lawyer would . . ." and then proceed to tell you what the layperson thought to do himself? Why? Because lawyers are *supposed* to be clever.

For example, in the June 27, 1994, edition of *Newsweek*, the writer, referring to the apparently delirious behavior of Simpson during the slow-speed chase, wrote: "A *clever* defense lawyer might try to turn his bizarre ride around the L.A. freeways into evidence that he was mentally unhinged." The writer, of course, was not tactless enough to be complimenting himself here for his own idea. He was unconsciously playing into the myth, and once he furnished the lawyer with his, the writer's idea, he praised the lawyer's cleverness. Again, why? Because the criminal defense attorney, not the writer, is supposed to be clever, even if, as here, the idea required no intelligence at all.

Let's look at the Simpson case and Simpson's lawyers, and I will then tie it all in to the damage the above myth most likely caused the prosecution's case. It's not going to be a pretty or flattering picture I paint of the trial abilities of the main lawyers for the defense. (Specific examples of their incompetence are found in the Epilogue.) If any of you are thinking, "Well, they won, didn't they?" my reply is that surely no intelligent person can assess someone's performance simply by looking at the final result. The result can frequently be traceable to factors and dynamics that have nothing at all to do with the abilities of the victor. I intend to demonstrate throughout this book that the defense won this case because of the terrible jury that heard it and the incredible incompetence of the prosecutors, not because of anything special at all done by the main lawyers for the defense.

Right from the very beginning, the media immediately started referring to the lawyers for the defense (at that time, the lead defense attorney was Robert Shapiro) as "the best that money could buy." Why? Because they immediately assumed that if your life or liberty is on the line and you have a lot of money, you automatically get the best. Because that is the way it should be (which presupposes, erroneously, that the defendant would have any idea at all what trial lawyer to employ, or if he sought the advice of lawyer friends of his, that they would have any idea who the best criminal trial lawyers were, or had ever seen any of them in action), these simpletons unthinkingly assume that's the way it actually is, *totally ignoring the backgrounds and records of the lawyers involved.*

The reality is that most celebrity defendants are extremely unknowledgeable, naïve, and vulnerable, and if they get into trouble they usually call their lawyer friends who handle criminal cases, and if they don't know any, they call their business lawyers, who then refer them to lawyer friends of theirs. It's very incestuous, and that's apparently what happened with Simpson.

The first lawyer he called was a close friend of his, a celebrity lawyer named Howard Weitzman, who I don't believe has ever handled a murder case in his life. What had Weitzman done recently in the legal arena? The actress Kim Basinger had called him to represent her when she was sued for her backing out of a film, *Boxing Helena,* in which she had originally agreed to star. The strong consensus in the entertainment industry was that this was a highly winnable case for Ms. Basinger, since she backed out when she learned there were nude scenes, and the central character was too unsympathetic. Perhaps even more important, there had been only an oral agreement between her and the plaintiff producers, not a written contract, and in Hollywood, backing out of oral agreements is so common it's rarely the subject of a suit. Samuel Goldwyn, the master of malaprop, once said, "A verbal contract isn't worth the paper it's written on." And the further consensus was that if she did happen to lose, the damages would be very negligible. Weitzman not only lost, but the jury returned an award against his client that was so great, $8.1 million, that Ms. Basinger was forced into bankruptcy.

Weitzman's only big successful criminal case was the drug-trafficking case of John DeLorean. In the DeLorean case, DeLorean is seen engaging in a cocaine transaction on film, yet he was found not guilty. That indeed would be pulling a rabbit out of the hat if Weitzman and his co-counsel Donald Re had convinced the jury that DeLorean did not, in fact, engage in the transaction. But that wasn't the issue. The issue was whether DeLorean had been entrapped, and since there was consider-able evidence he had been, this was a relatively easy case for the defense. You don't even reach the issue of entrapment in a criminal case unless the jury concludes that the defendant *did* commit the crime.

How did Weitzman do during the brief period he represented Simpson? I was on *Larry King Live* with Johnnie Cochran before Simpson even was arrested. It was long before Cochran became a member of the defense team, and Cochran said during the show that if he were Simpson's lawyer he wouldn't let him talk with the police. I interjected that his first lawyer (Weitzman) already had, and that it was a monumental blunder, an enor-mous gift to the prosecution. Even if Simpson was innocent, in the emo-tionally traumatic state he was in on the afternoon after the murders he could have said things deleterious to his interests. But if he was guilty, it would have been virtually impossible for him to be grilled by detectives for over half an hour, trying to walk between raindrops, without telling one provable lie after another, without making one inconsistent or con-flicting statement after another, all of which could be used by the DA to show a consciousness of guilt.

A few days after I said this on national TV, and others started to criti-cize him, Weitzman said he had tried to stop Simpson from talking with the police. But it would seem that the only reason Simpson would have had for consenting to be questioned by the police is that if he refused he'd look guilty. However, if his lawyer was advising him not to talk and, if necessary, insisting that he not do so, he had a way out. "Look, guys, I had nothing to do with these murders, and I'd love to talk with you, but my lawyer won't let me." That would have been the end of it. Period. Whether or not Weitzman advised Simpson not to be interviewed, we do not know. What we do know is that Simpson made sufficiently incriminating state-ments in the interview alone to convict him of murder, but because of the remarkable incompetence of the DA's office, the jury never heard the statement. I will have much more to say about this later.

And astonishingly, while Weitzman's client, Simpson, was being inter-rogated by the LAPD about a double murder for which he was the prime suspect, Weitzman chose not to be at his client's side. Even a first-year law student, even laypeople reading this book, would know the advisability of Simpson's lawyer being present during the interrogation. But you have to realize that Weitzman was considered to be one of the premier criminal defense attorneys in town, and brilliant, high-powered lawyers do things like this, right?

Detective Philip Vannatter testified at the trial that Weitzman had elected to go out to lunch rather than sit in on the interview, his only request to the detectives being that they record the interview. Weitzman has since come up with an allegation I have never heard before in Los Angeles law enforcement, one that is absurd on its face. In defense of his conduct, he told the media that "when Mr. Simpson chose to be interviewed by the police, contrary to my advice, he and I were told that there would be no interview if he wanted an attorney present." No one, but no one, could possibly believe an allegation like that. As Will Rogers once said, "It's the most unheard of thing I ever heard of." At no time anywhere near the interview did Weitzman complain publicly (as he would be expected to do) or privately to the LAPD or DA's office that he wasn't allowed to be present during the interrogation of his client. What we do know is that Weitzman walked outside Parker Center during the interview, and when waiting reporters approached him, he said: "O.J. is upstairs trying to get his wits about him, and is answering whatever questions he can to help law enforcement investigate this case." Not even Simpson, Weitzman's client at the time, supports Weitzman's story. The detectives gave Simpson his Miranda rights at the start of the interrogation, which included (I've heard the audio of the interview) telling him, "You have the right to speak to an attorney *and to have an attorney present during the questioning*." Simpson said he understood all his rights, and when they then asked him, "Do you give up your right to have an attorney present while we talk?" he responded, "Mmm-hmm. Yes."

My guess is that Simpson had convinced Weitzman of his innocence, and Weitzman had assumed no great harm could come to Simpson as a result of the interview. Weitzman either quit or was fired as Simpson's lawyer, and Robert Shapiro, another celebrity lawyer like Weitzman, became the lead lawyer.

Shapiro has always been a well-respected lawyer in the legal community, but he has never distinguished himself as a trial lawyer. He has been known mostly as a plea bargainer. In my *Playboy* interview, which as I've said came out before the trial started, I pointed out that the Simpson case was apparently Shapiro's first murder *trial*. (He did represent Christian Brando, Marlon's son, in a homicide case a few years earlier, but he pled Brando guilty and Brando was sentenced to ten years.) That revelation in the interview shocked a lot of people. There were 1,159 journalists credentialed to cover the upcoming trial, with very little to do except do research on the case and its participants, as well as interview witnesses who were expected to testify in the trial, yet to my knowledge not one of them had learned that Simpson's chief defense attorney, in a case they had already christened "the trial of the century," had never tried a murder case before.

It wasn't too long after the preliminary hearing in July 1994 that Johnnie Cochran joined the defense team and soon emerged as Simpson's lead trial lawyer. I had tried a few criminal jury cases with him years earlier when I was down at the DA's office and recalled him to be above average, which, of course, isn't saying anything. Cochran was one of those people who (prior to the Simpson case) it had always been hard not to like. He has a ready smile and warm, jovial manner with everyone, rolls with the punches, and doesn't project arrogance or pomposity. Cochran's motto seems to be "Live and let live." He has always been very well liked and respected in the legal community and is particularly known and respected in the black community. Prior to the Simpson case, however, although he may have done so, I had never heard of Cochran ever winning a murder case before a jury. (He's claimed to reporters that he has won a great many, but not one reporter has ever thought to ask him to name just one of these cases.) In fact, in his thirty-two-year career as a lawyer in Los Angeles, the only murder case I'd ever heard of his trying before a jury that even got minimal coverage in the newspapers was when he defended a Black Panther named Elmer "Geronimo" Pratt in 1972 for having murdered a white schoolteacher on a Santa Monica tennis court. Cochran lost that case and Pratt was sentenced to life imprisonment.

Cochran had mostly made a name for himself as a civil lawyer, not a criminal lawyer, successfully representing several black plaintiffs in police brutality cases against the LAPD and L.A. Sheriff's Department. Cochran was also a friend of Simpson's and had been for years, going back to when Simpson was married to his first wife, Marguerite. Along with former law school dean Gerald Uelman, who hadn't tried a case for years and years, Shapiro and Cochran were the only lawyers representing Simpson in court during most of the court proceedings prior to the trial.

I had commented in the *Playboy* piece that for all of Simpson's money, it was nothing short of remarkable that he still didn't have one lawyer representing him in court who had demonstrated any real competence in murder cases. But if you were to listen to the media throughout this period, one would never have known this. Their reasoning was that if Shapiro and Cochran were on this big celebrity case, and presumably charging a lot of money, they must be the best. Who am I to quarrel with such powerful logic? When Mike Tyson was on trial, the media said the same thing—that he had the best defense team money could buy. You know, of course, where Mike spent the past several years. This is what one national magazine said later about Tyson: "He watched as his $5,000-a-day attorney fumbled his way through a closing argument."

F. Lee Bailey, an experienced and savvy trial lawyer who *had* distinguished himself in several murder cases, hadn't yet appeared in court, and no one knew what his role was going to be. Lee's last big case had been the Patti Hearst bank robbery case over twenty years earlier in San Francisco. Because the prosecution had conceded that Hearst had, in fact, been kidnapped by the SLA and she had no prior history of criminality, many in the legal community thought this was a very winnable case. But among other things, Lee gave a very short and weak final summation, and his client was convicted, propelling Lee's career into a seemingly irreversible decline since that time. He and Shapiro had been associated for years in the practice of law, each appearing on the other's letterhead, and Bailey was the godfather to one of Shapiro's sons. It was believed that Shapiro wanted to bring Bailey aboard, albeit in a limited way, to resuscitate Bailey's career and at the same time avail himself of Lee's considerable intelligence and experience.

Harvard Law professor Alan Dershowitz was also aboard. Alan has certainly distinguished himself in the legal profession, but it has been as a prominent appellate lawyer, not a trial lawyer. He is someone you go to *after* you've been convicted, though it took months for the media to finally figure this out. To almost all of them, in fact, Dershowitz was routinely reported at the time to be another name criminal defense attorney representing Simpson in his upcoming trial, one who had successfully defended, they would write, Claus von Bülow in his trial for attempted murder. But Dershowitz had not defended von Bülow, had not handled a single witness at von Bülow's trial. His involvement, admittedly critical, had been in securing a reversal, on appeal, of von Bülow's earlier conviction so there could *be* a second trial. To the media this was too much of a subtlety for their minds to digest without very substantial reflection.

The two DNA lawyers from New York, Barry Scheck and Peter Neufeld, had not yet appeared in court and were rarely, if ever, referred to by the media. But it was unnecessary. The media already had Shapiro and Cochran in court, and Lee Bailey in the wings. It had become holy writ— and to my knowledge, virtually all members of the media accepted the apparently unassailable verity—that Shapiro, Cochran, and Bailey were the very best lawyers in the country that money could buy. They were "the Dream Team," as almost all of the media started to call them, and no one was going to change that. It had become official.

The question I had at the time—and the trial only confirmed my need to ask it—was, how do you take a lawyer who has never tried a murder case before (Shapiro), another who isn't even primarily a criminal lawyer but a civil lawyer who may have never won a murder case before a jury in his career (Cochran), and another who lost the last big case he tried over twenty years ago, and convert them into the Dream Team, the best that money can buy? Under what bizarre, convoluted logic or theory do you do this? I'll tell you folks the theory. It's called the willy-nilly theory. Only the media people could come up with nonsense like "Dream Team" to describe these lawyers.

The term "Dream Team" is only properly used to describe the best in the field, like the 1994 Olympic basketball Dream Team consisting of players like Michael Jordan, Larry Bird, and Magic Johnson. The NBA itself has the best basketball players, by far, in the world, and the Olympic Dream Team was the best of these great players who night in and night out perform at an incredible level of skill above their contemporaries. The 1995 U.S. Davis Cup tennis team was called the Dream Team, but the team consisted of Pete Sampras and Andre Agassi, the two top tennis players in the world. It wouldn't bother me as much if the media who called these lawyers the Dream Team used the term tongue-in-cheek. But they were very serious about it. Dead serious.

Even an editorial in the *Los Angeles Times* referred to the defense lawyers as "the best that money could buy." Can you imagine that? This is the intellect of people sitting on the editorial board of one of the major papers of the world, the opinion-makers of our society. Wouldn't you think that at least one of these geniuses would say to another: "George, I understand this Cochran fellow has been practicing law in Los Angeles for thirty-two years. We've had countless murder cases throughout the years, many we've covered in fair depth. I can't recall ever seeing his name associated with even one of these cases. Have you?" I realize that thinking is hard work. That's why, as they say, so few people engage in it. But how much thinking is required to produce this type of question?

The point is, no one had to check. Being on a big case was enough. To hell with one's record. Don't confuse me with the facts, I've already made up my mind. On those occasions when reporters decided to do puff profiles on the backgrounds of Cochran and the others, they committed a cardinal error that is exasperatingly common among professional writers. How many times have you read a magazine or newspaper article with a dramatic or bold assertion in the caption or opening paragraph, only to search vainly for the support in the piece? Isn't it just common sense that when you set up a burden for yourself you at least have the decency to try to meet it? In a January 29, 1995, cover story on Cochran in the *Los Angeles Times Sunday Magazine*, the *Times* reporter typically and predictably and breathlessly described Cochran as a "brilliant" lawyer, and said that, "his effect upon a jury seems to be magical." He quoted unnamed lawyers as saying, "Cochran has an approach with the jury that is unbeatable," and "If Johnnie tells the jury that a turkey can pull a freight train, they'll look for a rope." Fine. But unless you're an incompetent writer, don't you say to yourself: "Since I'm accepting all of these candied observations as true, I had better get the evidence to support all of this."

But the writer proceeded to name only one—let me repeat, *only one*—felony jury trial Cochran had ever won (I'm sure he's won other felony jury trials), the acquittal of actor Todd Bridges in 1989 for an attempted murder inside a "rock house" in the South-Central section of Los Angeles. Bridges, who was using about fourteen grams of cocaine a day at the time, testified at his trial that he was so intoxicated after a four-day cocaine binge that he could not remember shooting the victim. Most of the article was about Cochran's civil cases (two are mentioned, one of which he lost), the Pratt murder case, which he lost, his representation of Michael Jackson on the child-molestation civil lawsuit, which was settled, and the well-connected life he led. And that was it. The writer felt he had met his burden of proof.

Time magazine, which almost consistently was more mature, disciplined, and sensible than its competitor *Newsweek* in its reportage on the Simpson case, fell down in its January 30, 1995, edition. In another puff piece on Cochran, after the author made her obligatory reference to Cochran's legal "brilliance," she spoke of his "extraordinary" talent in the courtroom, but only cited one case to support what she was saying—again, the Todd Bridges case. Then the writer really outdid herself, telling how "extraordinary" Cochran's successful representation of Michael Jackson was. I don't know if any of you readers recall, but the Michael Jackson child-molestation case was a five-month jury trial, and the evidence was overwhelming against Jackson, but Cochran gave a brilliant four-hour summation, turning the jury completely around and gaining an acquittal for Jackson. If you don't recall this it's because the brilliant and extraordinary way Cochran got his client off in this case was *not* by winning in a court of law (I was just being facetious earlier, of course) but by having Jackson pay the young lad reportedly around $20 million. Yes, you read right—$20 million. This requires, of course, the ability of a top-notch trial lawyer before a jury.

Listen to *Newsweek's* early (July 11, 1994) puff piece on Simpson's main lawyers at the time, Shapiro, Dershowitz, and Bailey. These were "powerhouse" lawyers, *Newsweek* proclaimed to its readers, and to support its point (finally, with *Newsweek*, we're in the big leagues now; it knows it has to meet the burden it sets up for itself) said the three had defended such clients as Claus von Bülow (Dershowitz, as indicated, did not defend von Bülow at his trial), Patti Hearst (lost by Bailey), Leona Helmsley (not defended by Dershowitz, who did represent her on appeal and lost), Marlon Brando's son (pled guilty by Shapiro, and up until recently was eating prison food), and the Boston Strangler (who was never prosecuted for the eleven murders he was suspected of committing; he was prosecuted, instead, for several felony sexual assaults, Bailey defended him, and Albert DeSalvo, the Boston Strangler, was convicted). Some support. So much for quality of research and reporting by one of the two leading national news magazines in America.

I realize that even if you lose a case, it may not be attributable to anything wrong you did, i.e., you may have been "brilliant in defeat." But I assure you the writers of the *Newsweek* piece did not have this on their minds, any more than did the media reporters who *immediately* called the lawyers on the Simpson case "the best that money can buy" and "the Dream Team." The only thing they knew was that these lawyers had been "on" or somehow associated with these big cases. That was enough for them. Again, who am I to quarrel with such powerful logic? I know when I'm out of my league.

It should be noted that I wouldn't be making so much out of this if such shoddy research were confined to the Simpson case. But it's not. It's typical. If any of you readers want to see how little the opinion-makers of our society know whereof they speak, become very knowledgeable about a subject (as I have about the drug problem in America), and then read the articles they write on the subject. You'll be shocked to learn they rarely know their posteriors from a hole in the ground.

Now that we know from their backgrounds and records that to call the defense attorneys in the Simpson case the best that money can buy is not only silly but approaching a sacrilege, how did they perform, nonetheless, at the trial? In my *Playboy* interview before the trial, I said, "I'll guarantee you this. If the outcome of the trial ends up being favorable to the defense—such as a hung jury—the result will have nothing to do with anything special the *principal* lawyers for the defense did. And the favorable result for them will have to be traceable to dynamics other than Simpson's innocence, since he is quite obviously guilty." I said these other factors could be things like "race, celebrity, and bogus allegations of police misconduct." I stand by that original assessment.

Whatever substantive yardage the defense made in this case during the trial (I'm excluding final summation, which I will discuss later) was achieved almost exclusively by the two lawyers from New York in their attack on the reliability of the prosecution's scientific evidence, particularly the DNA evidence. Also, because the defense team had almost unlimited funds, they could vigorously contest every issue, split every hair, and then proceed to split the split hair (almost all of this done by the New York lawyers), as well as hire expensive forensic experts, one of whom, Dr. Michael Baden, they paid in excess of $100,000.

But setting aside the two DNA lawyers (top-flight technicians rather than top-flight lawyers), as far as the principal lawyers for the defense were concerned (Cochran, Shapiro, and Bailey), they were spectacularly ordinary throughout the trial. If I were to grade their performance on a relative basis, i.e., vis-à-vis other defense attorneys, I'd give them a B. But were I to grade them on an absolute basis I'd have to be in a very generous and magnanimous mood (you know, the sun is shining brightly in the morning and the orange juice is good) to give them any higher than a D or C-. In fact, the only thing they did (with Shapiro's alleged disapproval; more on this later) was to improperly and fraudulently inject race into the case. Believe it or not, several of the inane talking heads thought this tactic was "brilliant." But thugs out on the street with IQs of 80 play the race card. I will have much more to say on the actual performance of the defense lawyers in the Epilogue.

And what did the media say about the prosecutors in the Simpson case? They depicted them in the same, stereotypical way that prosecutors are always depicted by the media. The almost automatic adjective to describe a prosecutor is "tough," that for a defense attorney, "brilliant." In this case, even *before* the trial, when Clark was at her best arguing in front of Judge Ito during pretrial hearings, and clearly outshone Cochran, over and over the media described Cochran as "brilliant," Clark "tough and steely." They attributed to the defense lawyers star-celebrity qualities, while treating the prosecutors dismissively. Two representative examples from right at the beginning of the trial. In the February 6, 1995, edition of *Time* magazine, the prosecutors were described (again by the same silly writer referred to earlier) as "scrappy, overworked state employees who appear to be just that when set against the silver-tongued [of course], moneyed and remarkably personable defense lawyers." Here's the *Los Angeles Daily News*, in its January 29, 1995, edition: "The trial puts the high-priced, smooth, charismatic and experienced defense lawyers, the legal Dream Team, against the workmanlike, civil-servant prosecutors." The prosecutors, in fact, were much more experienced in criminal homicide cases than Cochran and Shapiro, though not Bailey.

How is all of this relevant to the verdict in this case? It contributed to it on two levels. One, the most obvious level, is that people, particularly relatively simple and uneducated people, as most of the Simpson jurors were, lionize celebrities. In fact, I think we all know that if Simpson weren't who he is—a football star and legend—nothing about this otherwise mundane case would have been the same, including, most likely, the verdict. And the media had made the defense attorneys in this case celebrities in their own right, though only Bailey was prior to the trial. Implicit in the lionization of celebrities is wanting to be near them, to talk to them, and if ever lucky enough to be afforded the opportunity, to treat them specially, to help them. One manifestation of this childish but extremely common idolatry of celebrities, even though there may not be an ounce of substance behind the fame, is the interview of TV or motion picture stars on television by the station's Hollywood reporters. Watch for the virtually incessant obsequious grin on the interviewer's face throughout the interview. We're a nation of celebrity and hero worshipers, so much so that we make heroes out of those who aren't, such as John Wayne, a patriotic, red-blooded, two-fisted American who spent the Second World War in the trenches on the movie lots of Hollywood. In our passion for heroes we have bastardized the meaning of the word beyond recognition. The word "hero" has always implied courage to me, and courage, in turn, implies a choice. When the young American fighter pilot Scott O'Grady was shot down over Bosnian Serb territory last June and hid in a Bosnian forest for six days until he was rescued, under what conceivable definition does this fine young man's effort to survive qualify as the conduct of a hero? Yet he was treated like one by this country and feted by the president at the White House.

When Captain O'Grady, eschewing the hero status he had suddenly achieved, told a gaggle of reporters that "all I was was a scared little bunny rabbit, trying to survive," the media would have none of it. What did the pilot know? We know a hero when we see one, they said to themselves. "An American hero came home to an emotional Main Street welcome," the Los Angeles Times and other papers gushed. "He is an American hero," President Clinton proclaimed. Time, Newsweek, and U.S. News & World Report all had cover stories on the incident. "One Amazing Kid" and "The Right Stuff," U.S. News and Newsweek trumpeted on their covers.

But a hero, I always thought, was someone who had risked his life to help another. The four American helicopter pilots and their crews who flew into enemy territory and withstood deadly enemy ground fire to rescue Captain O'Grady were the real heroes in this piece, but hardly a word was said about them.

Most of the Simpson jurors, of course, knew about the "Dream Team" before they were selected to serve, and undoubtedly continued to hear of this nonsense through conjugal visits and, as I've suggested, osmosis. And consciously or unconsciously, people want to be on the side of the celebrity, the side of glamour. That's just the way it is.

There's another related but more subtle phenomenon at play here, and it's that usually, people see what they expect to see or want to see, not what they are actually seeing. I don't think I'm a particularly bright individual, but there are two qualities I long ago learned I did possess. One is the ability to separate the wheat from the chaff and see through to the core of a problem, usually very quickly. The second related quality (one which I have found is even more rare, and again has nothing to do with intelligence) is that when I read, see, or hear anything, for some reason I am totally uninfluenced by what has previously been said or written about the subject. I am able to form impressions simply on the basis of what I see taking place in front of me.

Here is just one example among a great many that come to mind. President Reagan has been called the great communicator, but the first time I heard him being interviewed years ago, it was immediately obvious to me he was not a good extemporaneous speaker, and that he was an effective communicator only when he was reading his lines from a TelePrompTer. His staff, of course, knew this, and this is the precise reason they kept presidential press conferences down to an absolute minimum, shielding him, whenever possible, from having to answer reporters' questions. I picked up on the difference between Reagan speaking without a TelePrompTer and *with* one within a few minutes of the first time I saw him interviewed. What I had heard and read previously about Reagan's supposedly superb oratorical skills meant absolutely nothing to me, having no influence on the opinion I formed about whether he was or was not an effective speaker and communicator. Yet the fact (it's not an opinion) that Reagan without a TelePrompTer was not a good communicator was lost on millions of people, including columnists and the media, for many years. It has only been in recent years that it has become much better known.

In Reagan's first debate with President Carter, Reagan was inarticulate and unknowledgeable. Moreover, he squirmed a lot and appeared nervous. In fact, there were moments when I felt embarrassed for him, as we all do when someone performing before us is not doing well. Carter, on the other hand, was organized, articulate, and very knowledgeable. There was no question in my mind he had won the debate on both substantive and stylistic levels. Immediately after the debate the networks interviewed the staffs of both Carter and Reagan. Carter's people were ebullient, and although they tried to hide it, Reagan's were clearly morose. But about half an hour or so later, the results of television surveys started coming in from the folks back home in Des Moines, Omaha, Amarillo, Tampa, and elsewhere around the country. Reagan had won the debate hands down, according to the American public. And the survey respondents didn't say it was because they simply liked Reagan more than Carter. No, they thought he performed better, knew what he was talking about more than Carter. What these people saw, of course, was not the actual debate. They saw what they expected to see. In their eyes, at least for debate purposes, they saw a peanut farmer from a one-stoplight town in rural Georgia against a famous Hollywood movie star. Obviously, the movie star is going to know how to perform and talk better than his opponent. That only stands to reason. I remember reading William Safire's account of the debate a day or two later in the *New York Times* and I was happy to learn that he, too, was aware of Reagan's dismal and embarrassing performance.

How could this tendency to see what we expect to see contribute to the verdict in the Simpson case? It is likely that the Simpson jury perceived the courtroom performances of the defense attorneys as being more effective than they were because they saw what they expected to see. And what they expected to see was the defense lawyers scoring a lot of points in their questioning of witnesses (whether they were doing so or not) *because* they were the Dream Team. If they were the Dream Team, they must be scoring a lot of points, and this all helps add up to reasonable doubt.

I saw the potential pernicious influence of the above phenomenon early on in the Simpson case, and it's one of the reasons why, in the *Playboy* interview, I pointed out the absurdity of the media's announcing that Simpson's attorneys were the best that money could buy. As of the moment of writing this book, I have yet to read or hear any other commentator on the case scoffing at the idea that Simpson's lawyers were the Dream Team and pointing out, instead, just how ordinary they really were. In fact, as I write these very words on my kitchen table, this is from today's (December 31, 1995) editorial in the *Los Angeles Daily News*: "Simpson's considerable personal wealth allowed him to hire *the best defense attorneys in the country.*"

There perhaps is no better example of the phenomenon of people seeing what they expect to see working to the prosecution's very definite disadvantage than the situation with one of the defense's expert witnesses, Dr. Henry Lee. Lee, director of the Connecticut State Forensic Science Laboratory, is reputed to be the preeminent dean of American forensic scientists, the "top forensic sleuth," as it were. But I think we all know by now how suspect reputations can be, and if Lee's testimony in the Simpson case is any indication at all of his abilities, he is nothing short of incompetent. At best, he's an example of how Mark Twain once described an expert: "Just some guy from out of town." The problem is that the jury couldn't see through the bloated reputation of Dr. Lee, and the prosecution, in its summation, never exposed Lee so the jurors could see the emperor without his clothing on.

There were two particular areas in which Lee's testimony, if believed by the jury, was very damaging to the prosecution. One, he testified that he found four small bloodstains on a paper bindle enclosing seven cotton swatches containing blood removed from one of the blood drops (Item 47) to the left of a bloody shoe print leaving the Bundy murder scene (later identified as Simpson's blood by DNA testing). Lee couldn't figure out how the blood could have leaked onto the paper when the swatches had been left out to dry overnight prior to their being packaged. The fact that there was no assurance the blood on all seven swatches had dried completely by the time they were wrapped, or that the subsequently frozen swatches did not leak the blood later in the summer when they were thawed out for DNA testing, or that there was not some other innocent explanation (in virtually every case there are questions, the innocent answers to which are simply never learned) did not deter Lee from saying there was "something wrong," a term that resonated with the jurors during their deliberations. The implication the defense sought to convey, of course, was that the answer lay in evil LAPD conspirators who crept into the LAPD lab in the middle of the night and planted and tampered with the blood evidence

Lee also testified that he found three key "imprints" on the terra-cotta walkway at the crime scene which he himself photographed when he went to the scene on June 25, 1994. They did not match the many size-12 Bruno Magli bloody shoe prints at the scene which the prosecutors said belonged to Simpson. One was definitely a shoe print, he testified, one was a "parallel line imprint," and the other he simply called an "imprint." The latter two "could be" shoe prints, he said, all of which raised the inference of a second assailant. This, of course, challenged the prosecution's position that Simpson was the lone killer, and hence challenged their conception of the entire case against him.

Lee also found bloody "parallel line imprint" patterns on the envelope found at the murder scene containing the glasses belonging to Nicole's mother which she had left at the Mezzaluna restaurant earlier in the evening and which Ron Goldman was returning when he was murdered, on a small, triangular piece of paper near the bodies, and on Ron Goldman's jeans. Lee testified that all of these imprints could possibly be partial shoe prints, and since he concluded they were not from the Bruno Maglis or Ron Goldman's shoes, the defense suggested they came from the shoe of the second assailant.

But William Bodziak, the FBI's senior expert on shoe prints, and the former chairman of the footwear and tire section of the International Association for Identification, later debunked all of Lee's conclusions. Bodziak told me he went back to the Bundy crime scene with copies of photographs Lee had taken on June 25 to examine the shoe print and the other two imprints on the walkway which Lee said "could be" shoe prints. What he found was astonishing. With blown-up color photographs, he pointed out to the jury that one of the imprints (the parallel line one) on the walkway Lee had photographed and testified to was actually tool (trowel) marks made by the workers in the laying of the cement years earlier, and the other imprint was a shoe print from one of these workers which was a permanent indentation in the concrete (ridges, depressions) that Bodziak felt with his own hands!

As to the bloody "parallel line imprint" patterns on the envelope, paper, and jeans Lee had suggested could possibly have come from the shoes of a second assailant, Bodziak said that none of them were shoe prints. The parallel line imprints on the right leg of Ron Goldman's blue jeans were too erratic to be shoe prints and also had no borders representing the edge of any heel or sole. They appeared to be consistent with having been made by a swiping or brushing motion against the jeans by a sleeve from Goldman's long-sleeved shirt, which was thick and roughly textured. Bodziak testified that he found a "striking similarity between the ribbed design on the shirt [taken from test impressions]" and the bloody imprint on the shirt. (FBI special agent Douglas Deedrick, an expert on fiber evidence, had previously testified that the bloody imprint on the jeans appeared to have come from fiber such as that on Goldman's shirt.) As to the small ("half the size of one's thumb") bloody imprint on the envelope, it too was not a part of a shoe print, again having no borders, being too erratic, and the patterns being so fine and small as to be uncharacteristic of any shoe sole or heel Bodziak had ever seen. Bodziak testified that the parallel lines were consistent with a "fabric" pattern, and could have come from the jeans or shirt of Goldman. Bodziak also testified that the bloody imprint on the piece of paper wasn't a shoe print, and even if it had been, it would have had to come from the shoe of a tiny child.

Lee demonstrated further incompetence in the forensic technique he employed to reach his conclusions. He made no test impressions of Ron

Goldman's Levi jeans and shirt (although photographs were taken of the small piece of paper, the LAPD criminalists did not collect it). This was shocking to Bodziak. He testified: "You could look at the fabric on my sleeves with a magnifying glass, but because of its three-dimensional quality, you could not determine what the exact pattern would look like in a test impression. It is absolutely essential to make test impressions for comparison purposes. It is the *only* way that you can make a valid comparison."

Lee, stung and wounded by the obvious repudiation of his conclusions by the FBI's shoe print expert (Lee's specialty is not shoe prints), told reporters from his laboratory in Connecticut that although he stuck to his conclusions, "I'm sorry I ever got involved in the Simpson case," and said he would probably resist any defense subpoena to return to Los Angeles to defend himself and his conclusions.

As it turned out, he didn't have to defend or rehabilitate himself. His reputation was enough for the jury, which should have been skeptical of every single one of his conclusions once his shoe print and imprint testimony was proved to be claptrap. The foreperson of the jury, Armanda Cooley, said in the book she coauthored on the case, *Madam Foreman*: "Dr. Henry Lee was a very impressive gentleman. Highly intelligent, *world-renowned*. I had a lot of respect for Dr. Lee." Lee's discredited testimony hadn't lessened his stature in Cooley's mind one iota. Juror Lionel (Lon) Cryer told the *Los Angeles Times* right after the verdict that the jury viewed Lee as "the most credible witness" of all at the trial. Cryer repeated Lee's statement that "there was something wrong," saying the jury took these words back to the jury room with them. "Dr. Lee had a lot of impact on a lot of people," he added.

Lee's reputation didn't just have an impact on the members of the jury. Remarkably, after Lee testified for the defense on direct examination, Judge Ito looked down at Hank Goldberg, the deputy district attorney scheduled to cross-examine Lee, and said: "Frankly, if I were in your shoes I would cross-examine Dr. Lee for no more than half an hour. Accentuate the positive in a friendly and professional manner, *given his reputation, and then get out*." Can you imagine that? Even David Margolick, the *New York Times* reporter who covered the trial in an expert fashion, and who should have known better, told his readers (before Bodziak testified) that Lee was "largely unassailable."

Ito and Margolick, at least for the moment, apparently forgot that all things and all people in life have to sink or swim on their own merits, not their reputation; that just as a wise man can say a foolish thing, a fool can say something wise.

In effect, Ito told Goldberg not even to bother cross-examining Lee because, as Margolick said, he was essentially "unassailable." (Oh, yes. *Newsweek*'s assessment of Dr. Lee, even after he had been discredited by William Bodziak? "The best witness money can buy.") So in an indirect, insidious way, because the much greater part of mankind only hears the music, not the lyrics, of human events, the jury's viewing the defense attorneys as stars, the Dream Team, the best in the legal profession (as they viewed Dr. Lee to be the best in his profession), most likely contributed to their perception of the evidence and what was taking place before their eyes.

The other significant influence that was not only "in the air" but "on the air" was the outlandish spectacle of the TV talking heads. This influence came into play not before but during the trial, and if it reached the jury, as it almost undoubtedly did (osmosis and conjugal visits), it could only have been harmful to the prosecution's case. These commentators, nearly all of whom were also quoted in the print media, were always talking about the enormous problems the prosecution was having, frequently suggesting their case was falling apart. But if you look at things *objectively*, how could the DA's case be falling apart—which means the prosecution couldn't win, doesn't it?—when the evidence put Simpson's blood at the murder scene and the victims' blood inside his car and home? Unless the defense was able to remove that blood, which it never did, objectively speaking you have the strongest case in the world. Yet the talking heads, as well as (though to a lesser degree) the print media, never looked at the case in its totality. Instead they looked at each day's testimony and events as if they were entire trials unto themselves, and were sending out a steady stream of distress signals about the prosecution's case. "Lots of seeds of doubt *have* been planted" was the *USA Today* headline after Cochran's opening statement on January 26, 1995, before even one witness had been called by either side—which is like saying that unless the prosecution does something about it, the case is already a reasonable-doubt case.

To me, the whole premise of the talking heads discussing the case throughout the day and on evening shows made no sense. Television coverage of the trial, while I was opposed to it, at least allowed anyone who was interested in the trial to watch it and see what was actually happening. And certainly, for those who wanted to watch the trial but couldn't because of work, commentary on the evening news describing what took place that day in court is not only an established practice and custom, but it makes sense. That's what the news is: someone telling you what happened that day in the courtroom, in Congress, in Bosnia, etc. But what conceivable purpose was there in having these silly talking heads sitting around the campfire every night chatting about the case? People didn't need the talking heads to tell them what happened that day, because they could get that on the news. All these legal commentators did was argue with one another over their interpretation and analysis of the significance of what had taken place that day in court. However, since their interpretation and analysis were for the most part only speculation and theorizing, and because their remarks, by definition, couldn't change what had taken place, these shows amounted to nothing but light entertainment for Simpson addicts. But needless to say, these shows were never presented as such, being offered as serious exercises.

Moreover, the whole notion of using these particular talking heads for legal analysis on the Simpson case was ludicrous on its face. In those situations where analysts are used to discuss a newsworthy event, the analysts almost always are or have been at the top of their profession. For instance, who are the analysts for professional football games? Ex-players like Terry Bradshaw and Joe Montana, among the greatest quarterbacks to have ever played the game, each winning four Super Bowls. Or Mike Ditka and John Madden, former coaches of NFL teams. At the U.S. Open or Wimbledon, the commentators are people like John McEnroe and Martina Navratilova, tennis legends who are members of the sport's pantheon of all-time greats.

What type of qualifications, on the other hand, did the talking heads of the Simpson trial have? At least nine out of every ten I had never seen or heard of before this case. Indeed, many had never even been on national television before, many not even on local television, yet suddenly they were fixtures on the evening shows. Although it was, of course, a great opportunity for them to get their faces on television night after night, the problem was that the majority of them didn't know what the hell they were talking about.

Look at it this way. If I can demonstrate to you, as I think I can in the Epilogue, that the members of the Dream Team, who were supposed to be the best in the legal profession, were in many instances incompetent, what does that tell you about lawyers whom no one had ever heard of before, and who were not considered by anyone to be the leading lights of their profession? The incongruous sideshow of these "experts" pontificating on how to try a criminal case was downright laughable. And listen to this. Many had never tried a murder case in their entire career. In fact, several of them, believe it or not, *weren't even criminal lawyers*. They were civil lawyers who had never handled any kind of criminal case in their lives. One would think, under the circumstances, that they would have been embarrassed to serve as analysts. But to the contrary, this didn't inhibit them at all from trying to come across like Delphic oracles to millions of people. Yet they couldn't go more than two or three minutes without saying something utterly ridiculous, but how would a lay listener ever know?

Even most of those analysts who were *ostensibly* qualified to discuss the intricacies of a murder trial were, in fact, rarely so. For instance, two former Los Angeles district attorneys were network commentators. But one had never distinguished himself as a prosecutor in any way, and had the most mediocre of records as a deputy district attorney before the governor of California, a close personal friend, helped secure his appointment as DA. And the other, who ran for the office of DA, had never prosecuted one single felony case of any kind in his entire career! But one would never know this to listen to them talk.

And then there were the law school professors. Before this case, I had never heard that law school professors, who teach dry law out of casebooks, were supposed to be authorities on how to try a criminal case before a jury. But suddenly, these unknown law professors were experts on the trial of a case. The fact that they *weren't*, and most, if not all, had never even tried a murder case themselves, was immaterial. They were law school professors, weren't they? The professors who commented on the Simpson trial are perfectly intelligent people, as I'm sure most of the talking heads are. But intelligence is hardly the key ingredient of either being a top-flight trial lawyer or being capable of sagacious comments on a criminal jury trial. As a trial lawyer, intelligence is important only in the sense that it allows you to play the game, if you will. Without it, you don't even have a ticket into the competitive arena. But beyond that, it doesn't get you very far at all. If it did, out of the close to one million lawyers in this country, we'd have a tremendous number of great trial lawyers, but the reality is that great trial lawyers are about as rare as fishermen who don't exaggerate. I could give you endless examples of the insipid remarks made by these talking heads ("The prosecution has no case without the domestic violence evidence"; "Johnnie Cochran bringing out that the LAPD hadn't found the murder weapon was just superb cross-examination"; "O.J.'s elderly mother is sitting in the courtroom, and I doubt the prosecution's evidence will be able to overcome that type of emotional pull with the jury toward O.J."; etc.). In fact, they seemed to have a sweet tooth for silliness.

One story I would like to relate is of a conversation I had with one of the law professors near the start of the case. I was pointing out to the professor how Simpson's having bled all over his car and home on the night of the murders made his guilt obvious. The professor, with the innocence of a child in its crib and without batting an eye, brushed my observation aside with these words: "Oh," the professor said, "the defense has that covered. They're going to say O.J. cut himself on his cellular phone." To the professor, as long as the defense had *some* answer for the blood, that was all that was needed to solve the problem. Whether the story was believable or not (that Simpson innocently cut himself very badly around the very same time of the murders) apparently never entered the professor's mind. Yet the professor, with this quality of thinking, was on radio and TV, and was quoted in the newspapers as much as or more than any other analyst during the entire Simpson trial.

One of the amusing things about the talking heads as well as the print analysts (some talking heads did both) was that everything happening in court was "critical," "devastating," "pivotal," or "disastrous." And they trotted out these adjectives (and continued to use them) from the very beginning of the trial. Listening to these people, if this had been a professional fight, both fighters would have been knocked out by the middle of the first round. I also found it amusing that although jurors for the most part sit wooden in the jury box during a trial, believing, like participants in a black-tie poker game, that they are never supposed to change their expressions, the talking heads were reading the jurors' minds almost every night.

Before we move on, let me present what I believe will prove the utter incompetence of the talking heads. As I've indicated, most were previously known only by their immediate families. Among those who were known, at least in the legal community, was a former prosecutor and U.S. attorney from back east who was on constantly and was quite passionate about his views. Near the beginning of the trial, when all we had seen of Cochran was his completely improper and inferior opening statement (see the Epilogue), as well as his nonexistent cross-examination skills, this lawyer was opining on what a superb lawyer Cochran was and about all the concerns he'd have over facing Cochran in court. What that instantly told me, of course, was this was a .200 hitter being impressed by a .250 hitter. Not that I needed one more speck of confirmation, but after the verdict, when the *L.A. Times* asked me and three other prosecutors, including this former prosecutor, to write a statement on how we would have handled the case differently, I set forth some of what I say in Chapters 4 and 5 of this book, where I point out the absolutely astounding, shocking, and incredible errors made by the prosecutors in this case. But this prosecutor wrote: "I don't have an answer for that question." He later added: "I think they did a damn good job under horrible circumstances." In other words, as far as this former prosecutor was concerned, the prosecutors in the Simpson case did all they could. I didn't have to read what he wrote to convince me he was a .200 hitter. I already knew. Yes, to that former prosecutor, Cochran *was* a hell of a lawyer. And this particular talking head was one of the stars of the talking head cottage industry. For the most part, it was downhill from him. After you read Chapters 4 and 5, think back to this prosecutor's assessment of the district attorney's performance in the Simpson case.

Why should I care if these talking heads were babbling and ranting on TV almost around the clock? Actually, I wouldn't have cared if Simpson had been convicted. But I feel confident—although I can't be positive— that they contributed, even if not in a major way, to the not-guilty verdict in this case. The majority of them were criminal defense attorneys who, whenever possible, usually offered a pro-Simpson, pro-defense interpretation to what was happening in court, magnifying defense points far beyond their worth and muting important points made by the prosecution. Like the print media, they were constantly finding problems and weaknesses with the prosecution's evidence that either did not exist or that they exaggerated. They loved to expound on how the prosecution's case was unraveling. "The DA has no chance of winning," one of the former Los Angeles district attorneys, who has been a defense attorney most of his career, said. "Their case is in rubbles." These negative interpretations of the prosecution's case were "in the air" every day and every night, and so they became the conventional wisdom, the party line, as it were.

If the jury somehow inferred that the consensus of the community was that the prosecution's case was full of holes and falling apart, how could this not help but push them, consciously or otherwise, in the direction of reasonable doubt, and hence a not-guilty verdict?

Before I get into the next chapter, I'd like to restate an important point. If any reader is wearying of my fairly constant criticism of everyone associated with this case, I'd like to remind that reader of what I said in the Introduction: that I'm still angry and upset about the verdict, and unquestionably this has affected my tone. If Simpson had been convicted, this book obviously wouldn't have been written. Even with the not-guilty verdict, if the defense hadn't injected the bogus issues of race and a police frame-up into the case, and if Simpson hadn't elevated, as I've indicated, audacity to a Zen art, my tone would be somewhat softer. But the conduct of virtually everyone associated with this case was deplorable, and as a result, we continue to be reminded of the horror of it all by the smiling face of Simpson frolicking somewhere in the sun, or by a disturbed Simpson, scolding his detractors. And in mid-December 1995, Johnnie Cochran threw a lavish celebration party for all the jurors in the Simpson case. Can you imagine the smiles, jokes, and celebratory toasts that took place? Picture Simpson with his sharp knife viciously stabbing Nicole and Ron to death while imagining the festive party-goers dining on the best food, laughing and enjoying themselves. It's so goddamn obscene there are no words for it.

The Change of Venue
Garcetti Transfers the Case Downtown

There can be little question—though no one could expect any of the Simpson jurors to admit it—that most members of the Simpson jury were biased against the prosecution and in favor of Simpson. If nothing else, the jury's outrageous verdict and the lightning speed with which they reached it, demonstrate this point. How dare Judge Ito tell this jury after the verdict that society owed them a "debt of gratitude" when they came back with a verdict that not only was incompatible with the evidence but had been reached after an inexcusably brief three and a half hours? (The guilt phase of the Manson case lasted close to seven and a half months, yet the jury deliberated seven days, and *that* was considered a relatively short time for a trial of such length. The entire Manson trial, including the penalty phase, lasted nine and a half months.) Ito could have thanked the jurors for their time without adding the absurd comment that society owed them a "debt of gratitude."

There also can be little question that the Simpson jurors unfortunately were the embodiment of what one English barrister said about juries in general, that a jury is "twelve people of average ignorance." Although it's hard to imagine how this particular jury could have been too much worse, I have never agreed with this description of juries as a general proposition. I look at juries as representing upward of five hundred years of collective human experience. Also, the knowledge of one juror is the knowledge of all twelve—that is, if one juror, because of experience or insight, sees something in the evidence the other eleven do not, as soon as he or she brings this fact, observation, or inference to the attention of the other jurors, the entire jury profits from the perception. When you look at juries in this light, it is easy to see why they normally reach the verdict called for by the evidence. But in this case, there certainly was no "collective" wisdom. The sum was no greater than the individual parts.

A few examples will suffice. One juror, a seventy-two-year-old black woman who originally had been an alternate, said during the jury selection process that she never read newspapers, magazines, or books. The only publication she subscribed to was the racing form, but she said she didn't really understand it. This juror, after the verdict, said: "I didn't understand the DNA stuff at all. To me, it was just a waste of time. It was way out there and carried absolutely no weight with me." Another black female juror felt that the domestic violence evidence the prosecution introduced, showing that Simpson severely beat Nicole and she was in fear of her life at his hands, had no place at the trial. This benighted soul informed us that "this was a murder trial, not domestic abuse. If you want to get tried for domestic abuse, go in another courtroom and get tried for that." Simpson's history of physical brutality and violence against Nicole was completely irrelevant, according to this juror. Syndicated columnist Kathleen Parker observed that this juror's reasoning was "akin to saying obesity is unrelated to eating. If it's eating you want to talk about, go somewhere else. This discussion is about fat."

A younger black female juror, we were told by court observers, appeared to be one of the brightest of the jurors. The juror, who had a college degree, was reasonably articulate and had some elementary knowledge of DNA. When she appeared on *Nightline* and was asked who she thought was the most impressive witness at the trial, she said she felt Dr. Henry Lee was. When asked why, she pointed out that when Dr. Lee approached the witness stand to testify, he had turned to face the jurors and smiled warmly to them.

So we know the jury was a problem. The seminal question is whether this murder trial had to be cursed with this jury. The answer is no. I don't think I can discuss the issue any more clearly than I did in my December 1994 *Playboy* interview, which was on the stands on November 1, 1994, before the trial started.

PLAYBOY: You've found considerable fault with the defense in this case [referring to my assessment of the defense's performance at the preliminary hearing as well as the quality of written motions it had filed, etc]. Has the prosecution done anything wrong?

BUGLIOSI: Actually, the prosecution may have made the biggest error by far in this case—dwarfing anything the defense has done. I have no doubt that the DA and his staff are not prejudiced or antiblack in any way. However, because Simpson is black and every survey shows that blacks are overwhelmingly sympathetic to him, it's common knowledge the DA's office fears that blacks may hang up the jury—though the office can't acknowledge this. If this fear—that the sympathy blacks have for Simpson at this point may override the evidence at the trial—is justified, and I'm not at all sure it is, the DA's office is responsible for its own problem.

PLAYBOY: How? In what way?

BUGLIOSI: Well, these murders happened in Brentwood. It's the practice in Los Angeles County to file a case in the superior court of the judicial district where the crime occurred, in this case, Santa Monica, which is where the Menendez case was filed. In Santa Monica, there would have been a small percentage of blacks in the jury pool. Instead, the DA filed the case downtown, where the percentage of blacks in the jury pool will be much higher, thereby—assuming the DA's fears are correct—multiplying the likelihood of a hung jury. If the DA tried to transfer the case out of downtown now, there would be an enormous hue and cry that he was prejudiced against blacks. But if he had filed the case where it should have been filed, and where he had every right to file it, who could have complained?

PLAYBOY: Has the DA's office given any reasons for filing the case downtown?

BUGLIOSI: Yes, but they are all weightless. A member of the DA's press office said that the reason was that the Special Trials section handling the case is located downtown. In other words, we'd rather have a hung jury than have our two prosecutors drive an extra fifteen miles each morning. The DA's office has also mentioned that the downtown court is set up to handle protracted cases and to accommodate the media better than the Santa Monica court. But there is absolutely nothing prohibiting the Santa Monica court from hearing this case. Whatever arrangements that would be necessary to allow this could easily have been made. I think what happened here is that when the DA's office filed the case downtown they simply weren't thinking of the ramifications of their decision.

Curiously, to my knowledge, this was the first public criticism of the DA's office for having transferred the case downtown. The only thing I had seen prior to this was a few one-paragraph newspaper references to the various explanations given by the DA's office for the transfer, without any accompanying criticism.

Los Angeles County district attorney Gil Garcetti, obviously concerned that I was speaking publicly about an alleged serious error of his, called me on the morning of November 4, 1994, three days after the article hit the stands. "Vince, I want to congratulate you on a great interview. The only thing I would like to point out to you is the reason this case is going to be tried downtown. I don't know how it was when you were in the office, but the way it's been for years now is that once you take the case to the grand jury [there is only one grand jury in Los Angeles County, and it's located in the Criminal Courts Building near downtown Los Angeles], the case has to stay downtown. [This was an explanation the DA's office had not given before.] So this case could not have been tried in Santa Monica."

"Gil," I told him, "not only wasn't it that way when I was in the office, but it still isn't that way. Just because you take a case to the grand jury definitely does not preclude you from trying the case in the judicial district where the crime occurred. If you don't believe me, call Jerrianne Hayslett [spokesperson for the Los Angeles County Superior Court]. I have already spoken to her and confirmed this."

At that point Gil immediately retreated and said, "Well, I was under the impression that we were stuck downtown." A momentous decision like this, and the DA was basing his decision on impressions as opposed to demanding and receiving definitive information from his staff on this very critical issue?

We terminated the phone conversation amiably, without my telling him something which he already knew, and which would only have served to embarrass him further. There are two ways for a case to reach the superior court for trial in the State of California. One is by grand jury indictment (forty or fifty felony cases a year, a fraction of one percent of California cases, proceed this way), and the second is the way 99.9 percent of cases reach the trial level, by the DA's filing a criminal complaint followed by a preliminary hearing in which the magistrate concludes there is sufficient evidence for the defendant to be bound over for trial. (This, in fact, is the way the Simpson case eventually reached the superior court, after the release of Nicole Simpson's 1993 911 tape aborted the grand jury proceedings.) I didn't bother to tell Garcetti that if, indeed, he was operating under the erroneous assumption that once he took the case to the grand jury he was "stuck downtown," he could have avoided the grand jury completely by simply starting the case with the filing of a criminal complaint out in Santa Monica. And if the case had been tried in Santa Monica, the likelihood of a conviction would have been immeasurably enhanced.

Since the not-guilty verdict, the DA's office, buffeted by criticism for the loss, particularly for failing to try the case in Santa Monica, has continued to tell an uninformed public that it had no choice but to try the case downtown, and has continually offered new reasons. None of the reasons, except one, have any merit to them. And that reason is not solid. It was known from the beginning that the Simpson case would be a protracted case (called a "long-cause" case in the L.A. Superior Court, meaning a case that is expected to last in excess of one month), and long-cause cases frequently are, indeed, transferred downtown. But they don't have to be—there is no superior court rule requiring it—and many criminal and civil trials which have lasted far in excess of one month have been tried in Santa Monica and other outlying courts.

One new spin Garcetti has put on the now infamous transfer is that even had the case been tried in Santa Monica, the composition of the jury would not have been any different from that of the jury which actually heard the Simpson case, because such a large jury pool was needed (one thousand prospective jurors) that jurors from the Simpson trial were chosen from the entire County of Los Angeles. He told the *Los Angeles Daily News* on October 29, 1995: "If the case had been tried in Santa Monica you would not have had the normal West Los Angeles jury pool— you would have had most of Los Angeles." He said the Simpson jury was chosen "from throughout the county."

Gil, I wrote off your erroneous belief that the case was stuck downtown as being attributable simply to a lack of knowledge on your part. But how can it be you did not even know where the jury pool came from in the biggest-publicity case your office has ever handled? To confirm my memory of events, I called Gloria Gomez, juror service manager for Los Angeles County. She told me that other than the fact that there were a greater number of jurors in the pool, absolutely nothing was different about the recruitment of jurors in the Simpson case. Jurors in the Simpson case were chosen under the "Bullseye system," a computer program used by Los Angeles County for assigning jurors in all cases. The computer calculates the distance from the courthouse for jurors in the eleven superior court judicial districts of the county, and, she said, "those jurors living outside a twenty-mile radius from the courthouse are not even contacted. Nothing was done differently in the Simpson case."

The Bullseye system, Ms. Gomez explained, tries to assign jurors in the district who live closest to the courthouse. But jurors can live in a surrounding district as long as their home isn't located more than twenty miles from the courthouse. In the Simpson case, seven out of the final twelve jurors resided either in the central district or in areas of contiguous districts with a predominantly black population. None lived more than twenty miles from the downtown court where the case was tried.

Gomez told me there is "no question" that if the Simpson case had been tried in Santa Monica, the racial composition of the jury would have been substantially different. This is so because the percentage of blacks in the central district (where the case was tried), according to the most recent census, is 31.3 (whites are 29.8), whereas in the West Judicial District (Santa Monica), the percentages are 78.8 white and 7 black.

And despite my informing Garcetti way back in November of 1994 that the case wasn't stuck downtown because the DA had taken it to the grand jury, and telling him whom he could contact for verification, Garcetti (an otherwise dedicated public servant), to justify his office's enormous blunder, has continued to tell the public that the die had been cast when the Simpson case was taken to the grand jury. One of the last people he told this to was Katie Couric on NBC's *Today* on November 1, 1995. So as to make double and triple sure that it was I, not Garcetti, who was correct, on that very same day, November 1, 1995, I called Los Angeles County deputy district attorney Stephen Licker (one of Garcetti's deputies), who is the DA's grand jury legal adviser. When I asked Licker if, once a case is taken to the grand jury, it is stuck downtown, he responded, "Oh no, it is common for it to go back for trial to the judicial district where the crime was committed."

For the purposes of this book, I did not have the time to get the documentation on all the cases that were taken to the Los Angeles County Grand Jury, and after the indictment (as we've seen, the Simpson case didn't even get to the stage of an indictment), the case was transferred back for trial to the judicial district where the crime occurred. But here are a few: *People v. Owen, Galvez, Leno and White*, Los Angeles Superior Court BA#099502, a burglary and rape case, was transferred back to Pomona in 1994. *People v. Guy Bouck*, BA#105867, a murder case, was transferred back to Van Nuys in 1995. In fact, on June 20, 1994, *People v. Salazar*, BA#096515, an eighty-one-count case of burglary, rape, and child molestation, was being presented to the Los Angeles County Grand Jury by Deputy District Attorney Gail Huttenbrauck when to her consternation she was "booted out" by the Simpson case's coming in. After the Simpson proceedings were aborted, she returned to the grand jury to finish the presentation of her case, and after she got an indictment the case was transferred back to Norwalk for trial.

Wherever I turned, the statements of Garcetti or his public affairs office proved to be either deliberately false or simply in error. The office continues to say that the Santa Monica courthouse didn't have a courtroom large enough to accommodate the media. Although the Santa Monica courthouse is, in fact, much smaller than the downtown one, the twelve courtrooms are not. Department C, the master calendar court in Santa Monica (where arraignments—pleas of guilty and not guilty—and assignment of cases to trial courts are made), has 104 seats. Department C could have been used as the trial court in the Simpson case by simply transferring the master calendar to another court for the length of the trial. If they didn't want to do that, Department M, a trial court in Santa Monica, has eighty seats, the same number of seats, in fact, as Department 103 downtown, where the Simpson trial took place.

Garcetti has also said that the January 1994 earthquake in Northridge (the northwest section of Los Angeles County) had damaged the Santa Monica Superior Court building to the point where the case could not have been tried there, but I verified with the administrator of the Santa Monica court that the courthouse had been repaired by the time Garcetti transferred the Simpson case downtown. And the argument he has also made that Santa Monica could not provide adequate security is ridiculous. The courthouse there is already equipped with a metal detector and staffed with security guards.

Nothing, however, is more personally odious to me than the DA's office saying that one of the factors considered in transferring the case downtown was that the downtown courthouse could better accommodate the media. Apart from the fact that there is just as much space near the Santa Monica courthouse for the TV trailers and their apparatus as downtown, since when is justice not the *only* concern? Since when should justice be jeopardized in any way at all by media considerations? If our society doesn't take *murder*, the ultimate crime, seriously, what do we take seriously anymore?

Many have said Garcetti wanted the case transferred downtown because his own office is there, and being a politician running for reelection who never met a TV camera he didn't like, he knew he wouldn't get the same radio and TV exposure if all the cameras and reporters were out at the Santa Monica court. My guess on this view is that it is wrong.

You may wonder why I am devoting so much time to this procedural matter. Even with the terribly incompetent handling of this case by the prosecution (see Chapters 4 and 5), since it nonetheless did prove Simpson's guilt beyond a reasonable doubt, if the case had been tried before a *normal* jury in Santa Monica, the very strong likelihood is that the verdict would have been guilty. The Simpson jury was not a normal jury. If it was, we should start packing our bags for Madagascar. Our jury system is perhaps the most priceless legacy we inherited from our legal ancestors, the British. The Simpson jury was a disgrace to that legacy.

One final point before we get into the next reason for the not-guilty verdict in the Simpson case. Those with a smattering of legal knowledge (a smattering is always a dangerous amount in any area of human endeavor) have assured anyone who will listen that even if the Simpson case had been filed in Santa Monica, the defense would have made a change of venue motion to have it transferred downtown. Such a motion, the argument goes, would have had to be granted by the court, because Santa Monica would not have been a representative cross section of the Los Angeles community, which is required by law.

In *Williams v. Superior Court,* 49 C 3d 738 (1989), the defendant, Edward Williams, a black man, was charged with the first-degree murder of one Bruce Horton, a white man. The DA filed the case in Santa Monica (West District), because it was the locus in which the crime had been committed, and the defendant sought to have it transferred to the Central District in downtown Los Angeles on the ground that only 5.6 percent of the presumptively eligible jurors in the West District at the time were black, while 11.4 percent of the presumptively eligible jurors of Los Angeles County were black. Williams argued that the community from which a cross section of jurors should be chosen was the entire county of Los Angeles. The people argued that "the community" means the judicial district. The California Supreme Court accepted the people's interpretation, affirming a lower appellate court's ruling denying the defendant's motion for a change of venue. The court said that "the [California Government] code sections relating to the establishment of superior court judicial districts and the sections relating to jury selection and management are easily harmonized. Read together, the statutes manifest an unmistakable legislative intent *that the courts of the district serve the population within its boundaries.* Use of the superior court judicial district as the appropriate 'community' in Los Angeles County effectuates this legislative purpose." The court also found no federal constitutional limitation on the California legislature's right to create its own communities for "representative cross section of the community" purposes, adding that having a judicial district serve as a community was particularly appropriate in dealing with "the practical problems posed by a far-flung megalopolis—Los Angeles County."

If the Simpson case had been filed in Santa Monica, the presiding judge of the county's criminal courts would have had the ultimate discretion to grant or deny the inevitable defense motion for a change of venue to downtown Los Angeles. But the consensus in the legal community is that he would have denied the motion, not just because of the *Williams* precedent, but because the presiding judge rarely disturbs the district attorney's decision on where to file a case in the county. Here, not only did the crime occur in the Santa Monica judicial district, but it is where Simpson lives. Moreover, Santa Monica being a much more affluent area than downtown, those sitting on a jury in Santa Monica would have been much closer, other than in race, to being Simpson's peers than the jury which ultimately heard the case.

"The case belonged in Santa Monica," says retired superior court judge Leonard Wolf, presiding judge in Santa Monica from 1986 to 1989. "And to say the case couldn't have been tried in Santa Monica is simply wrong— it could have been tried there. A number of major criminal cases have been tried in Santa Monica." Los Angeles County deputy district attorney Harvey Giss, a veteran prosecutor, says, "Anytime you have a tactical advantage, you're a damned fool to give it up. You argue like crazy to remain in a particular locale if you think it is to your advantage. It's like baseball. You play your percentages."

One footnote to all of this. The wrongful-death civil action by the Goldman and Brown families against Simpson will undoubtedly take several months to try and will generate considerable media attention. This case is scheduled to be tried in Santa Monica. The Michael Jackson child molestation civil lawsuit two years ago was also filed in Santa Monica. Pretrial motions had already been heard in the Santa Monica court, and, absent the settlement that terminated it, the case was scheduled to be tried there. Another major case that was tried in Santa Monica was the Billionaire Boys Club murder case in 1987, which received considerable publicity and lasted several months. I return to the original statement I made in the *Playboy* interview that when the DA's office transferred the case downtown it probably just wasn't thinking of the enormous ramifications of its decision. It was a monumental blunder, one that all by itself was a reason for the miscarriage of justice in the Simpson case.

A Judicial Error

Judge Ito Allows the Defense to Play the Race Card

A July 25, 1994, *Newsweek* poll, a month and a half after the murders, found that a minuscule 12 percent of American blacks felt that Simpson had been framed by the LAPD because of his race. Close to 90 percent of all blacks, then, did not feel that racism was an issue in the case. And the reason they didn't was that it was obvious to virtually everyone that race had nothing to do with this case. Yet near the end, after the defense had fabricated the race issue at the trial, poll after poll showed the majority of American blacks, including Simpson's jury, felt Simpson had been framed by the police because of his race. A *Los Angeles Times* poll of blacks in Los Angeles County showed that an astonishing 75 percent of them believed Simpson was framed. Although the defense attorneys, primarily Johnnie Cochran, were responsible for improperly injecting race into the case, I blame Judge Ito 100 percent for allowing it to happen, for permitting race to be a big issue at the Simpson trial. In considerable part because of it, and because the prosecutors were totally inept at dealing with it once it became an issue, Simpson is now a free man.

It wasn't as if Judge Ito hadn't been warned. I thought Chris Darden did an excellent job of forewarning Ito. In a January 13, 1995, pretrial hearing to determine whether the defense should be allowed to ask Detective Mark Fuhrman if he had ever used the word "nigger" in the previous ten years (this was months before the now infamous Fuhrman tapes surfaced), Darden, although overstating his case somewhat, nonetheless made this eloquent appeal to Ito: "[The word 'nigger'] is the filthiest, dirtiest, nastiest word in the English language. It has no place in this case or in this courtroom. It will do nothing to further the court's attempt at seeking the truth in this case. It will do one thing. It will upset the black jurors. It will . . . give them a test, and the test will be, whose side are you on, the side of the white prosecutors [a partial misstatement, since Darden himself is black] and the white policeman, or are you on the side of the black defendant and his very prominent and capable black lawyer? That's what it's going to do. Either you are with the man or with the brothers. . . .

"There is a mountain of evidence pointing to this man's guilt, but when you mention that word to this jury or to any African-American, it blinds people. It will blind the jury . . . to the truth . . . it will impair their ability to be fair and impartial. . . . Mr. Cochran wants to play the ace of spades and play the race card . . . *but you shouldn't allow him* to play that card. . . . It's the prosecution's position that if you allow Mr. Cochran to use this word and play this race card, not only does the direction and focus of the case change, but the entire complexion of the case changes. It's a race case then. It's white versus black, African-American versus Caucasian, us versus them, us versus the system. It's not an issue of simple guilt or inno-cence, or proof beyond a reasonable doubt. It becomes an issue of color. Who's the blackest man up here? Who are the real brothers?"

(Cochran, naturally, disputed this, telling Ito that it was "demeaning" to the mostly black jury to suggest that "African-Americans, who have lived under oppression for 200-plus years in this country . . . cannot hear these offensive words. African-Americans live with offensive looks, offen-sive treatment every day of their lives. But yet they still believe in this country. . . . To say they can't be fair is absolutely outrageous.")

Although Darden clearly overstated his case—the jury's hearing that a prosecution witness used the word "nigger" obviously doesn't automati-cally guarantee, as he suggested, a not-guilty verdict—there can be little question that Ito's permitting the defense to ask Fuhrman whether he had ever used the word in the previous ten years did, as Darden predicted, change the complexion of the trial. Based on the law, as well as on com-mon sense (which time and time again at the trial Judge Ito showed he had precious little of), Ito should have precluded the defense from intro-ducing race into the case.

First let's look at the law, which the prosecution argued to Ito, and of which he was already well aware. Section 352 of the California Evidence Code reads: "The court in its discretion may exclude evidence if its probative value [i.e., relevance] is substantially outweighed by the probability that its admission will . . . (b) create substantial danger of undue prejudice [to the opposing side]."

Although a defendant in a criminal trial has the *absolute* right—under the Confrontation Clause of the Sixth Amendment to the United States Constitution—to cross-examine witnesses against him, the nature and extent of that cross-examination is *not* absolute. Section 352, which is representative of nearly identical statutes throughout the land, provides a limitation on that right. In ruling that the defense could cross-examine Fuhrman on whether he had used the word "nigger" in the past ten years, Ito relied heavily on an obscure lower appellate court case in California, *In Re Anthony P.*, 167 CA 3rd 502 (1985), which held that where an answer to a question has "any tendency in reason" to affect the credibility of a witness, the question has to be allowed, apparently regardless (if we're to believe the ruling of the court) of Section 352, which the *Anthony* court failed to even mention. But that is not the law in California. (Fuhrman's using a racial epithet within the past ten years, by the way, wouldn't even satisfy the *Anthony* test.) For instance, in *People v. Jennings*, 53 Cal. 3rd 372 (1991), defense counsel sought to impeach certain prosecution witnesses with the fact that they had failed to reveal their incomes as prostitutes when applying for county welfare benefits. The California Supreme Court ruled that because the evidence in question was "only slightly probative of [the witnesses'] veracity, the application of Evidence Code Section 352 to exclude the evidence did not infringe the defendant's constitutional right to confront the witnesses against him. . . . The proffered evidence must have more than slight relevancy to the issues presented."

And, more specifically, in *Delaware v. Van Arsdall*, 475 U.S. 673 (1986), the United States Supreme Court held that with respect to a defense counsel's inquiring into the "potential bias of a prosecution witness" (the defense's argument regarding Fuhrman in the Simpson case), although the discovery "of a witness' motivation in testifying *is* a proper and important function of the constitutionally protected right of cross-examination," this did *not* include "interrogation that is . . . only marginally relevant."

If ever a case existed where the relevance of offered evidence was substantially outweighed by its probability of prejudice to the opposing side, this was it. It wasn't even a close call. Here, the relevance of Fuhrman's using the racial epithet "nigger" within the previous ten years was extremely remote, at best, from the issue of whether Simpson was guilty or not guilty of murdering Nicole Brown Simpson and Ronald Goldman. I mean, it's a non-sequitur and broad jump of Olympian proportions to conclude that just because Mark Fuhrman used such a racial slur, or is a racist, he is likely to have framed Simpson for these murders. This proposition, all by itself, is self-evident. What made the relevance of Fuhrman's use of the word "nigger" even more remote than it already was is the fact that at the time (January 1995) Ito ruled that the defense could ask Fuhrman if he had used the epithet in the last ten years, they had no evidence he had done so more recently than 1985 or 1986 (through witnesses Kathleen Bell and Andrea Terry—see later discussion), which was at the outer limits of the ten-year period. Also, a judge, in exercising his discretion under Section 352, does not resolve such an issue as if it existed in a vacuum. He naturally has to view it in the context of the case and the evidence. And here, by the time the cross-examination of Fuhrman commenced exactly two months later (March 13, 1995), two LAPD officers had already testified that they had arrived at the murder scene before Fuhrman and saw only one glove there. So even assuming Fuhrman had wanted to frame Simpson by planting one of the murder gloves at Simpson's Rockingham estate, Ito knew there was no such second glove at the crime scene for Fuhrman to have seized and deposited there. It doesn't take a genius to see why the relevance to this case of Fuhrman's use of the racial slur was extremely remote, perhaps nonexistent. Yet the prejudice to the prosecution was more than the requisite "substantial." It was monumental. Nonetheless, Ito, in an egregiously erroneous ruling which thumbed its nose at Section 352 as well as the law enunciated by the California and U.S. Supreme Courts, opened the door for the defense to let race become a central issue at the trial.

With Ito's fateful and improvident words on January 23, 1995, "I will allow cross-examination on that issue," the entire complexion of the trial was irrevocably changed to the prosecution's severe detriment. It should be noted that in addition to the "substantial danger of undue prejudice" ground for excluding the racial slur testimony, Section 352 provides additional, independent grounds for Ito to have excluded it—the fact that such testimony and evidence would predictably cause an "undue consumption of time," and also the "substantial danger of [its] confusing the issues, or . . . misleading the jury."

Even if Ito didn't want to follow the law, simple common sense should have told him how wrong it was to allow the defense to inquire of Fuhrman if he had used the word "nigger" in the preceding ten-year period. Every day in America, literally thousands of white police officers arrest or investigate black suspects. Does anyone really believe that when these thousands upon thousands of cases go to trial it's proper to ask every one of these officers if he has ever used that racial slur, and if he denies it and there is evidence he did, to have a satellite trial (which is what in effect happened in the Simpson case) on that issue? That's crazy. Ito couldn't have been more off-base here, and the prosecution had to pay dearly for Ito's sins.

An indication of the degree to which Fuhrman became the vortex of a satellite trial was the massive publicity surrounding Fuhrman and the Fuhrman tapes. Fuhrman, after the tapes surfaced and on the advice of his attorney, invoked the Fifth Amendment outside the presence of the jury and refused to answer questions on his racism or any other matter.

During this period, when the issues were whether the judge would allow the defense to force Fuhrman to invoke the Fifth before the jury and how much of the tapes Ito would allow the jury to hear, there were these types of headlines: "Trial Within a Trial Begins Today" (USA Today, September 1, 1995), "Who's on Trial Now?" (Newsweek, August 28, 1995), etc.

"Ron and Nicole were butchered by this man [Simpson]," Ron's father, Fred, said in a courthouse news conference, his eyes filling with tears. "This is not now the Fuhrman trial. This is a trial about the man who murdered my son." Nicole's father, Louis Brown, said on Rivera Live: "They [the defense] have got the trial so far off base it's pitiful. . . . To let them get away with this is murderous in itself."

In fact, even though it was Simpson who was on trial for double murder, the terribly misguided media treated Fuhrman's invocation of the Fifth Amendment as a far bigger story than Simpson's invoking the Fifth Amendment and sitting as silent as a cigar-store Indian, refusing to defend himself or answer any of the many allegations against him. "Fuhrman Takes the Fifth" was the September 7, 1995, banner, front-page headline story in the L.A. Daily News. "Fuhrman Invokes 5th Amendment, Refuses to Testify" was that day's main headline in the paper of record for the trial, the crosstown Los Angeles Times. Even the staid New York Times couldn't resist a front-page headline story (though not, as in the Los Angeles Times and Daily News, the main one) on September 7, 1995. In fact, at no time during the trial was there one, main, front-page headline story in either the Los Angeles Times or the Daily News on the fact that Simpson had invoked the Fifth Amendment. Again, the big story was Fuhrman's, not Simpson's, taking the Fifth.

We can thank Judge Ito for all of this. If he hadn't made his inexcusable ruling (which was incompatible with the law and did violence to all conventional notions of common sense), the Fuhrman tapes would have been irrelevant. Indeed, since Fuhrman's racism wouldn't have been an issue, they probably wouldn't have even surfaced.

A note about Fuhrman. For years he was an avowed racist, and I'm no apologist for him and his type. In fact, I wrote an article a few years ago severely criticizing the Los Angeles DA's Office, and other DA's offices around the country, for virtually never prosecuting police brutality cases against blacks and other minorities. If you think the Rodney King case was an exception to the DA's policy, it wasn't. The DA deserves no credit for prosecuting the police in the King case. Giving credit implies the DA had a choice. Because of private citizen George Holliday's eighty-one-second home videotape of the beating, he had no choice. If there had been no tape, there would have been no prosecution. No one would have ever heard the name Rodney King. In fact, the Christopher Commission, which was formed a month after the King beating to conduct a comprehensive review of police brutality by the LAPD, learned that the day after the beating—before the police knew the video existed—King's brother, Paul King, went to the LAPD's Foothill Station (the area where the beating occurred) to file a complaint. Instead, he was told by a sergeant that his brother was in "big trouble" for leading police on a dangerous high-speed chase. He left the station knowing he hadn't started an investigation. In his daily log, the sergeant reported that no further action was necessary. (If any reader at this point is thinking that I am speaking out of both sides of my mouth when I categorically reject the notion of a frame-up of Simpson by the LAPD because he was black, and also indict some members of the LAPD for police brutality against blacks, see my long discussion in the Epilogue on this point. They will be the first such words, among the millions published on this case about the matter, and I think you will be surprised.)

There's a small percentage (some say 5 percent, some even slightly higher) of officers in the LAPD—they're not representative at all—with a neofascist mentality. These officers hurt the reputation and stain the blue uniform of the LAPD, which, along with the L.A. Sheriff's Department, is one of the finest, least corrupt police agencies in the country. I'm very aware of these racist officers and I've been one of the few relatively well-known whites who have publically spoken out against them.

So no black person who knows me or knows about me can accuse me of being antiblack and insensitive to what blacks have gone through for over two centuries here in America. During my years at the DA's office, blacks, in fact, used to call me "bad," meaning good. With that long preface, let me tell you that Mark Fuhrman is a victim in this case. Here is someone who is awakened in the middle of the night to go to a crime scene. He goes there and does absolutely nothing wrong at all, and yet his life may be destroyed. And to that extent (much more on Fuhrman in the following chapters), I'm speaking out in this book in defense of Mark Fuhrman.

Before I continue my criticism of Judge Ito's performance at the Simpson trial, let me state the positive. Ito is intelligent, conscientious, and fairly experienced. I also sense he is a decent human being who tried very hard to be fair to both sides during the trial. But none of these favorable qualities was enough to prevent him from turning in a substandard performance at the trial and being a poor judge for this case.

Somehow it became the conventional wisdom at the trial that although Judge Ito had his faults and peculiarities, his legal rulings were almost always "legally sound." "Legal experts gave Judge Ito good marks for his specific evidentiary rulings during the trial," Newsweek said in a posttrial wrap-up story. Although I would agree that Ito's pretrial rulings were sound, I am at a total loss to see how anyone could possibly say his legal rulings during the trial were. Even if allowing the defense to ask Fuhrman if he had used the word "nigger" in the past ten years had been his only flagrant mistake, this was so devastating to the prosecution that all alone it would stand as a condemnation of Ito's judicial performance.

The plain fact is that Ito specialized in making patently erroneous rulings, one after another. Not only was his original ruling in the Fuhrman matter incorrect, but he kept compounding it and making it much worse. For instance, there were sixty-one excerpts from the Fuhrman tapes which the defense sought to have the jury hear, in forty-one of which Fuhrman used the word "nigger." To impeach Fuhrman's testimony that he had not used that word in the past ten years, Ito allowed the jury to hear Fuhrman's voice uttering the racial epithet on only one of the excerpts (speaking of women police officers: "They don't do anything. They don't go out there and initiate a contact with some six-foot-five nigger that's been in prison for seven years pumping weights"), and to have read to them a transcript from another ("We have no niggers where I grew up"). But he also allowed the screenwriter, Laura McKinny, to testify before the jury that during her tape-recorded conversations with Fuhrman he had used the word "nigger" thirty-nine other times.

Then Ito did something that was inexcusable and for which there wasn't any possible legal argument to be made in support of it. On August 29, 1995, Ito decided, over the strenuous objections of the prosecutors, to play all sixty-one excerpts in open court (outside the jury's presence) for a vast TV audience to hear. Since he had ruled the jury could not hear fifty-nine out of the sixty-one excerpts, what conceivable reason was there to play them for millions of people who weren't on the jury? It served no purpose other than to enrage and inflame the black community and millions of others. And with conjugal visits (once a week on Saturday evenings for five hours at the jurors' hotel, the Hotel Intercontinental, just a few blocks from the courthouse), there was the likelihood that the jury would hear about the contents of all the other excerpts.

Ito knew there was no legal basis for what he did, but he came up with the nonlegal justification that he did not want to be accused of "suppressing information of vital public interest." If that was his concern, he could have accomplished his purpose by simply releasing the tapes to the public *after the trial* (the end was just one month away). As reporter Tony Mauro said in *USA Today*: "Judge Lance Ito has repeatedly criticized participants in the O. J. Simpson trial for playing to the public instead of to the jury. Yet in deciding to air racially charged taped comments by retired detective Mark Fuhrman at a televised hearing without the jury present on Tuesday, Ito said he was doing it for no other reason but to satisfy public interest."

Then Ito really decided to take a smiling leap into the world of illogic and irrationality. Perhaps just as much as Fuhrman's use of the word "nigger," the defense wanted the jury to hear Fuhrman's remarks to McKinny about eighteen incidents of misconduct (things like picking a scab on a heroin addict's arm to produce evidence of a fresh needle puncture, justifying an arrest for being under the influence; ripping up the driver's license of a suspect who was belligerent because "if he's got that attitude, he's probably gotten several tickets he hasn't taken care of," so because the suspect didn't have any identification left, this was cause to bring him in to the police station; "If I was pushed into saying why [I had detained someone who did not belong in an area], I'd say suspicion of burglary," etc.) because this type of conduct obviously went in the direction of the main thrust of their case—that Fuhrman, with the help of his colleagues, had framed Simpson. But remarkably, Ito excluded all statements of alleged misconduct by Fuhrman on the tapes because, he said, "the underlying assumption [that Fuhrman planted the Rockingham glove] for the purpose of placing blame for two brutal and savage murders upon the defendant requires a leap in both law and logic too broad to be made based on the evidence before the jury." He said that "incidents of Fuhrman's alleged misconduct [on the tapes] as prior bad acts [and therefore] evidence of custom and habit" were only a "theory without factual support."

But if statements on the tapes, as weak as they were, suggesting Fuhrman was the type who may have framed people in the past didn't mean he tried to frame Simpson, why would his using the word "nigger" mean he did it? (Note that the only relevance of letting the defense inquire, on cross examination of Fuhrman, whether he had used the word "nigger" was to further their inference that it showed he was a racist *and therefore framed Simpson.* Just showing he was a racist, all by itself and *without* the following inference of a frame-up, would obviously have no relevance.) How, in Ito's mind, could Fuhrman's mere use of the word "nigger" in the past suggest he was more apt to have framed Simpson than if he claimed to have set up other criminal defendants in the past? Such a notion is too absurd even to discuss. Insofar as the Fuhrman affair was concerned, Ito didn't know whether he was coming or going.

To demonstrate even further what a thick fog he was operating in, Ito proceeded virtually to parrot Darden by proclaiming, on August 31, 1995, that the word "nigger" was "perhaps the single most insulting, inflammatory and provocative term in use in modern day America." But if he believed that, then in view of the fact that this was a predominantly black jury, how could he possibly have ruled earlier that the relevance of using this word was not substantially outweighed by the prejudice to the prosecution? And assuming Ito's description of the word "nigger" was correct, when had he come to realize this fact? And how?

Ito's illogic over the Fuhrman matter knew no bounds. He started to act and talk like a man who had just been roused out of a fire in the middle of the night and hadn't gotten his bearings yet, apparently even losing the capacity to read the clear and explicit language of the California Evidence Code.

When Fuhrman invoked the Fifth Amendment as to *all* questions (a witness can't pick and choose, an answer to one question being a waiver of the witness's right under the Fifth to refuse to answer any others), Ito agreed that existing law prohibited him from informing the jury, as the defense had urged, that Fuhrman had taken the Fifth. But what Ito did decide to do was almost as bad. Once again over the vigorous objection of the prosecution, he succumbed to pressure from the defense and said he intended to give the jury the following instruction: "Detective Mark Fuhrman is not available for further testimony as a witness in this case. His unavailability for further testimony on cross-examination is a factor *which you may consider in evaluating his credibility as a witness.*" The only problem, as the prosecution pointed out to Ito, is that this instruction flew straight into the teeth of existing case and statutory law in the State of California. Section 913 of the California Evidence Code provides, unambiguously, that when a witness invokes the Fifth Amendment, "the presiding officer [judge] . . . and the trier of fact [jury] *may not draw any inference therefrom as to the credibility of the witness."*

Yet Ito nonetheless intended to ignore the law and give his instruction. When the prosecution sought an emergency writ in the appellate court to stop Ito, Ito himself, as well as virtually every legal analyst covering the case, said it would be a futile effort inasmuch as the appellate courts rarely intervene in the middle of a trial (usually only about seven or eight times a year in California). The former Los Angeles district attorney, who had been elected DA, went even further, suggesting that the prosecution didn't even have a sound legal basis for its appeal. The prosecution's appellate argument, he declared, *"is very thin* and there's zero possibility the court of appeal will entertain an emergency writ." I wondered how the court could help but intervene when Ito was clearly wrong. On September 7, 1995, just three hours after the prosecution filed its appeal, the Court of Appeal for the Second District ruled: "The proposed instruction regarding the unavailability of Detective Fuhrman is not to be given." The court did give Ito until Sunday afternoon (it had ruled on Friday) an opportunity to draft a legal defense for his judicial apostasy, but Ito, without a legal leg or even cane to stand on, never even made the attempt.

Almost from the beginning of the trial right to the end, many of Ito's rulings were bad, sometimes bizarre. One of the first witnesses at the trial was Ronald Shipp, a black former LAPD officer who had been a close friend of Simpson's for years, serving as a loyal "gofer." Over defense objections, Ito permitted the prosecutors to elicit from Shipp his testimony that on the day following the murders, Simpson told Shipp at Simpson's Rockingham estate that "you know, to be honest, Shipp, I've had some dreams of killing her." Quite apart from why the prosecution would even want to present extremely weak dream evidence when it had a Himalayan mountain of other very solid evidence against Simpson, the decided weight of authority in the United States is against the admissibility of such evidence, since the medical profession has not yet been able to establish, through empirical studies, an unmistakable connection between dreams and actual conduct. Yet Ito nonetheless allowed this evidence to be heard by the jury, undoubtedly bringing a smile to the face of Alan Dershowitz, who felt that if there was an eventual conviction, Ito's incorrect ruling in allowing the jury to hear the dream evidence would be one of the stronger grounds on appeal seeking a reversal of the conviction.

And at the end of the trial, when Simpson waived his right to testify in his own defense, instead of simply taking the waiver, Ito permitted Simpson to address the court. "It is inappropriate and the defense is deliberately trying to do it for a clear purpose," prosecutor Clark had forewarned Ito, knowing what the defense was up to and what was coming. "This is an attempt to get testimony before the jury without cross-examination. Please don't do this, Your Honor. I beg you, I beg you." Ito never explicitly ruled on Clark's objection, and instead let Simpson make a self-serving state-ment which, as a member of the defense team later acknowledged, de-fense lawyers had been working on with Simpson for three weeks. With the television cameras in the courtroom, millions heard it. It played very heavily in all the media that night and the next day, and the defense obvi-ously hoped it would reach the jury via conjugal visits.

This was Simpson's statement to the court, meant only for the jurors' ears, the defense hoping it would be the equivalent of his testifying to the jury without being cross-examined. Judge Ito, who had to know he was being taken, didn't interrupt Simpson until the very end, when Simpson had just about run out of his rehearsed lines anyway.

> The Court: Mr. Simpson, good morning, sir.
> Simpson: Good morning, Your Honor. As much as I would like to address some of the misrepresentations made about myself and my Nicole concern-ing our life together, I'm mindful of the mood and stamina of the jury. I have confidence, a lot more it seems than Ms. Clark has, of their integrity, and that they will find, as the record stands now, that I did not, could not, and would not have committed this crime. I have four kids — two kids I haven't seen in a year. They ask me every week, "Dad, how much longer?"
> Court: All right.
> Simpson: I want this trial over. Thank you.
> Court: All right. Thank you, Mr. Simpson. You do understand your right to testify as a witness?
> Simpson: Yes, I do.
> Court: And you choose to waive your right to testify?
> Simpson: I do.
> Court: All right.

District Attorney Gil Garcetti pointed out that Ito's decision allowing Simpson to give his speech was "grossly inappropriate." Fred Goldman, Ron's father, said that Ito's decision was "outrageous. If he [Simpson] had a statement to make he should have gotten on the damn stand to make it, not be a coward."

One of Ito's dreadful rulings and decisions at the trial may, in fact, have been responsible for nothing less than depriving the prosecution of a guilty verdict, or an attempt by Simpson to plead guilty to some degree of crimi-nal homicide below first-degree murder. Following Simpson's arrest, former NFL defensive lineman Rosey Grier, who had become an ordained minis-ter, became a frequent visitor of Simpson's at the Los Angeles County Jail.

On November 13, 1994, a Sunday afternoon, a deputy sheriff seated close to where Simpson and Grier were talking (three-quarter-inch-thick glass separated Simpson from Grier, and they communicated by telephone) heard Simpson blurt out a loud exclamation which the deputy construed as a highly incriminating remark.

The deputy, Jeff Stuart, wrote out a report of the incident for his superiors at the sheriff's department, and on November 28, 1994, the department, in turn, submitted a report to Ito on the matter. (To this day, this report has been sealed by the court.) The very next day, November 29, 1994, Ito and representatives of the prosecution and defense visited the jail area where the alleged incident took place.

To determine the admissibility of the statement, Ito subsequently took testimony from Stuart and Grier outside the presence of the jury as to the circumstances surrounding the overheard remark, but not on the remark itself. Stuart testified he had been doing homework in a control booth about ten feet from Simpson when he heard a loud bang—the sound of Simpson slamming his phone down. He said Simpson then shouted out two short sentences to Grier. Asked to describe Simpson's tone of voice by prosecutor William Hodgman, Stuart replied: "He was yelling. It was very loud, in a raised voice. He appeared to be very upset." Grier, who carried a Bible with him to the witness stand, denied that Simpson had raised his voice above normal speaking levels during his visit that day. He testified about his jailhouse visits with Simpson: "We go over scriptures, we pray. We discuss various people in the Bible, problems they had, talk about who God is . . . what is sin. We talk about all kinds of things in the Bible."

Although the prosecutors did not know the words of Simpson's statement, they assumed it had to be incriminating, and this is why they argued to Judge Ito that they should hear it and, if they elected to do so, introduce it to the jury at the trial. The defense, naturally, was on its hind legs, trying to keep it out by arguing that whatever Simpson said, it was confidential and entitled to legal protection.

The main legal issue was whether Simpson's remark was protected by the "clergyman-penitent privilege," one of many privileged communications (husband-wife, attorney-client, physician-patient, etc.) which are designed by the law to protect personal relationships or other interests where the protection of confidentiality, from a public policy standpoint, is thought to be more important than the need for the communication to be received as evidence. However, there are several exceptions to the privilege; for instance, when the communication is used to contemplate—not defend against—a crime or fraud.

Moreover, the holder of the privilege (client, patient, penitent) can "waive" the privilege, which usually occurs when he makes the statement in the known presence of a third party not necessary (as an attorney's secretary) to the communication. Thus, in *People v. Poulin*, 27 C.A.3d 54 (1972), the victim of a bomb blast drew a diagram of the instrument while he was testifying. The bailiff, who was seated next to the jury box, heard the defendant, who was denying responsibility for the blast, say to his attorney, who was seated next to him, "It wasn't like that." The bailiff testified to what he heard, and the appellate court held that the bailiff's testimony had been properly admitted, since the defendant made the statement within earshot of the bailiff and the latter was not eavesdropping.

The Simpson case, of course, is an even more obvious case of waiver, since Simpson shouted out his statement knowing the deputy sheriff, whom he could see, was only a few feet away. On December 19, 1994, Ito ruled, in fact, that Simpson *had* waived the privilege, but remarkably kept Simpson's statement out on a totally nonlegal ground: "Counsel for Simpson now argue [after Ito held there had been a waiver] Simpson was lulled into a false sense of security in regard to the confidentiality of his communications in the visiting area. The argument is well taken," Ito said in his ruling, disallowing the prosecution from presenting the guard's testimony.

The only problem was that if there was a waiver, as Ito virtually had to rule there was, there was no *legal* basis for excluding the statement. If one were to accept Ito's nonlegal justification for excluding the statement, I guess it wouldn't have made any difference how loudly or how often Simpson shouted out his confession or incriminating statement, it would be inadmissible because he had been "lulled into a false sense of security."

What had Simpson allegedly said? For months, the media quoted unidentified sources as saying Simpson had shouted out, "Okay, I did it," or some variation thereof, but that stripped of its context, it couldn't be considered an outright confession. In the January 9, 1996, edition of *Globe* magazine (months after the trial), the guard told enterprising reporter Craig Lewis, who had been pursuing the story for months, what Simpson had said. This is the relevant excerpt from the *Globe* article:

> "In order for O.J. and Rosey to speak, they had to use a special telephone. With the glass between them, they couldn't touch, hug or even shake hands," Deputy Sheriff Stuart said.
> "From where I was sitting, if O.J. looked over Rosey's shoulder, he could see me. When they were inside the room they had complete privacy. And

under the law, no one is allowed to intentionally listen in on what might be a religious confession. The way the room is secured, as long as the two of them were talking in a normal tone of voice, I couldn't hear a thing. But that's not what happened."

On that particular Sunday, at around 4:30 p.m., he [Stuart] says the two ex-NFL stars were shouting—and what the jailer says he unintentionally overheard shocked him.

"Rosey had his bible opened in front of him and he and O.J. had been talking for about half an hour," Stuart recalls. "All of a sudden, O.J. slammed the telephone down on the counter and yelled: 'I didn't mean to do it! I'm sorry!' Rosey leaned forward, looked him in the eye and yelled back: 'O.J., you gotta come clean. You gotta tell somebody!'

"O.J. just sat there staring at the ceiling for several moments. I don't know if he was talking to his maker, asking for forgiveness or what. Rosey started tapping on the glass that separated them. He was trying to get O.J.'s attention, to get him to pick up the telephone. Then O.J. buried his head in his hands.

"O.J. looked like a man who had been totally wiped out. His shoulders were slumped over, his head hanging low. Rosey and O.J. talked a few more minutes and then it was time to go. The sergeant came to get O.J. and he shuffled silently back to his cell. Rosey passed me wearing his usual poker-face and said simply: 'Have a nice evening.'"

Simpson told Grier what we already knew, of course. With that extremely incriminating statement before the jury, Simpson's choices would have been not only limited, but about as pleasant for him as staring into the noonday sun: either try to plea-bargain or take the witness stand (which he was trying to avoid at all costs) and deny that he made the statement. But if Grier, who reportedly never visited Simpson again after this incident, confirmed the statement—which we don't know that he would have done—then Simpson's denial would not have been plausible. It should be noted that Stuart would have to be crazy to testify under oath and penalty of perjury that Simpson made the statement if he knew Simpson hadn't and Grier would confirm this fact. Finally, Simpson might have taken the stand and said the statement was misunderstood, that when he said "I didn't mean to do it! I'm sorry," to Grier, he was actually referring to eating another inmate's helping of dessert. I'm being facetious, of course, but whatever misconstruction he claimed took place over what he said, he'd need the testimony of Grier to say he and Simpson were talking about the inmate's dessert or what-have-you, not the murders of Ron and Nicole.

However it played out, it would have been exceedingly damaging, perhaps fatal, to Simpson, and if it didn't induce a termination of the trial by way of a plea bargain, it would have been up to the jurors to hear the guard's testimony and give it whatever weight or significance they felt it was entitled to. But Judge Ito, in his inimitable fashion, made another bad ruling, this one of pivotal and momentous consequences. Yet the great bulk of legal analysts felt that from a legal standpoint, Ito's rulings were excellent.

Among the other problems I had with Ito at the trial was that he lacked a sense of grandness, for lack of a better word, in how to behave in a case of this immense visibility and, because race became an issue, importance. Nowhere was that better demonstrated than in the "thousands of objections" (Ito's own words) he sustained to what he erroneously thought were argumentative questions. It should be added that I have never seen a jury trial where both sides objected anywhere near as much as this—an incredible sixteen thousand objections, seven thousand of which were sustained. In fact, it's even considered poor jury trial technique to object excessively. If one constantly interrupts proceedings, one can only irritate the jury that must sit there in weary forbearance. Moreover, if the jury concludes from a lawyer's objections that he is trying, by technicalities, to keep out relevant evidence, this has to hurt him. But in the Simpson case, *both* sides were constantly objecting, so the jury may have concluded it was perfectly normal behavior. It wasn't. It was aberrational.

And to exacerbate the situation, Ito, almost as often as not, sustained the improper and frivolous objections. He apparently didn't see the absurd incongruity and inappropriateness in a trial for a brutal double murder of making sure that every question asked was sufficiently dainty and delicate. If any question was in the least bit aggressive, Ito almost always reflexively sustained the objection on the ground it was argumentative. But a trial is not a tea party on the back lawn of some Bel Air estate on a Sunday afternoon. Argumentative questions are perfectly proper on cross-examination if they are asked to elicit the truth, as opposed to badger the witness. Apparently, Ito wasn't experienced enough to be aware of this distinction, which has been made by appellate courts.

I mentioned earlier how little common sense Ito exhibited during the trial. I will give a few examples. When Faye Resnick (Nicole's close friend) came out with her book on Nicole and Simpson in October 1994, Ito went ballistic. He actually suspended jury selection for two entire days while he read the book. Then, in an effort to prevent others—including prospective Simpson jurors—from reading the book, and to limit publicity generated by the book's release, he sent out feverish letters to the president of CBS News, as well as to talk show hosts Larry King and Maury Povich, beseeching them not to go through with their scheduled interviews with Ms. Resnick on the book. (Only one, Larry King, complied.)

All of this was reported on heavily in the media. A child would know that publicly treating the book like forbidden fruit could only serve to titillate people's interest in it and get them to buy it. The book, in fact, immediately shot up to number one on the *New York Times* best-seller list. Although the book turned out to be substantive in its own right and helpful to the prosecution, Ito was any publisher's dream, and arguably should have shared in the royalties.

Although everyone was complaining about the slowness of the trial, and the Los Angeles County Board of Supervisors was alarmed by the escalating cost, in late February 1995, Ito remarkably decided to shorten every court day to 3:00 p.m., with entire Friday afternoons off (Ito eventually went back to a normal schedule). His explanation was the grueling pace of the trial; the lawyers therefore needed more off-time. Shortening court days is very unusual, and if the hours are changed, they almost invariably are lengthened. Furthermore, if there ever was a case where there was no justification for shortening the court day, this was it. Since the jury was sequestered (a highly unusual situation—only three or four juries in California history have been sequestered during the whole trial) and getting stir-crazy, any shortening of the court day necessarily extended the length of the jury's sequestration. Moreover, there was an uncommonly large number of lawyers working for the prosecution and defense (eleven defense attorneys made speaking appearances in court, nine prosecutors). I have never seen such a compartmentalization of responsibility. A lawyer like Bailey would handle a witness, and then literally disappear from the courtroom for a month. The trial lasted over nine months, yet Shapiro examined only a small handful of witnesses. Marcia Clark, the lead prosecutor, actually went three entire months without handling one single witness. So the lawyers had time to burn, all the time in the world to work on the few witnesses they handled. Yet silly Judge Ito decided to shorten the court day.

In other words, Ito did several things at the trial I can only characterize as irrational, almost goofy, and because of this, throughout the trial I had an ongoing sense of unease that he might do something seriously bizarre.

Because so many jurors were excused, there was a frequently expressed fear that the case might run out of alternate jurors, and if one of the remaining twelve was excused for any reason, only eleven would be left, and without the consent of both sides, there would be a mistrial. Right in the middle of all of this, to entertain the jurors, Ito decided on May 20, 1995, to give them a ride in a Goodyear blimp. Yeah, you heard me right. A blimp ride. According to the *L.A. Times*, just a few days later, the blimp (called the *Eagle*) "suffered a mishap while attempting to take off with another load of passengers. A gust of wind blew it across its landing strip in Carson, breaking its tail and tearing a nine foot gash in the blimp's fabric skin. No one was injured, but with Ito's luck he must feel fortunate there were no jurors aboard that day."

To me, nothing demonstrated that the good judge may have been keeping time to a different drummer more than his announcing, near the very end of the trial, that he wanted to take a few days' vacation he had scheduled before he was assigned to the case. Closing arguments commenced on September 26, 1995, and with September having only thirty days, and two days being lost for the weekend, the arguments were expected to continue until October 5 or 6, after which the jury would immediately be instructed on the law and they would commence their deliberations. With interest in the case having reached a fever pitch and more media converging on L.A. for the trial than ever before, Ito announced that *right in the middle* of these closing arguments he was definitely going to suspend trial proceedings and take September 29 and October 2nd off because this was a mini-vacation he had planned a year earlier. Come hell or high water he wasn't about to postpone it even for a few days. For those who weren't left completely speechless, the only words that could be heard in the courtroom hallway, I'm told, were "incredible" and "unbelievable." Dominick Dunne, the widely respected writer and author who covered the trial with wit and insight for *Vanity Fair*, called Ito's decision to take his mini-vacation "disgraceful. Everyone in this case has made personal sacrifices. And as the leader, no matter how long ago he made his plans, he should obviously change them." Under mounting pressure from both the prosecution and the defense, and undoubtedly from fellow judges, who probably sat him down in his chambers and took his temperature, Ito changed his mind and agreed to postpone his vacation for a few days.

Changing his mind during the trial, by the way, became Ito's signature, his rulings having all the permanence of a breath upon a mirror. A small sampling: In August 1994, Ito ruled that all motions by the prosecution and defense had to be filed under seal, then quickly reversed himself. He held a hearing in mid-October 1994 to find out who had leaked information on DNA results to local television station KNBC, even subpoenaing many witnesses, then, with witnesses in his courtroom, he suddenly called the hearing off. Because of media misconduct during jury selection later that month, he barred all reporters from the courtroom, then reversed himself shortly thereafter. In considering a defense motion to impose sanctions on prosecutors for delaying the submission of DNA evidence for analysis, he convinced everyone, including the prosecutors (whom he told to "expect" the sanctions), that he would impose them, but to a startled courtroom, and without explanation, he announced that he would not do so.

But it was not Ito's changeable and irrational behavior that disturbed me the most, since no serious harm resulted from these idiosyncrasies. In addition, of course, to his fateful and very injurious ruling on the Fuhrman matter already discussed, two things in particular made me disapprove of Ito: allowing cameras in the courtroom, and the way he treated all the lawyers, particularly the prosecutors, right in front of the jury.

With respect to cameras in the courtroom, in my opinion they don't belong, not in this case, not in *any* case. Televising the trial turned it into a national soap opera. Without the cameras, the nation wouldn't have been exposed to the absurd spectacle of the talking heads (since they couldn't talk about something they weren't watching), with the resultant "in the air" harm to the prosecution effort. But there is an even more substantive objection to having cameras in the courtroom.

A trial is a serious and solemn proceeding that determines whether a person's liberty, and sometimes his life, should be taken away from him. Anything that interferes, or even has the slightest potential of interfering, with this determination should be automatically prohibited. Most people are self-conscious about speaking in public, even before a small audience. With cameras in the courtroom, sometimes millions of people are watching. Even if we make the doubtful assumption that most witnesses will not be affected, certainly, at least here and there, some are not going to be as natural. They are going to be more shy and hesitant, or perhaps they will put on an act, not just in their demeanor, but much worse, in the words they use in their testimony. When this happens, the fact-finding process and the very purpose of a trial have been compromised.

Witnesses aren't the only ones affected. The *Los Angeles Daily News* reported in the late summer of 1994 that as a result of a murder trial then being televised on Court TV, "the defense attorney bought two new suits, the judge's wife makes sure his hair is properly gelled before he leaves for work in the morning, and the court clerk makes an effort to keep her pen out of her mouth." Is it unreasonable to suggest that if people alter their physical appearance because of the camera, they may alter their words?

We know from the mouths of the lawyers on the Simpson case that the TV cameras were having a harmful influence on them, encouraging theatrics and posturing. Gerald Uelman, the scholarly former dean of the Santa Clara University School of Law, who argued most of the defense team's legal motions, said in June 1995, while the trial was still in progress, that he originally favored TV cameras in the courtroom because they would "open the walls of a tiny courtroom and allow everyone who was interested to come in to observe and learn." But he said he now shudders "at how naive and idealistic I was. The unprecedented public scrutiny of this case has intruded to alter the behavior of all the participants in many ways, some subtle, some not so subtle."

Also in June, Chris Darden told reporters: "I dislike having cameras in the courtroom. The lawyers cater to the cameras. That's been proven time and time again." Shortly after the trial, Barry Scheck made similar comments. But why did we have to learn this from the trial? Common sense would have told us. I set forth these arguments when I was interviewed by *Playboy* magazine in the late summer of 1994, months before the trial started.

What about the argument frequently used by the media that televising trials educates the public? It's transparent sophistry. The media's only motivation, though not an improper one, is commercial. Although televising trials may indeed educate the public, that obviously is not the principal reason why people watch trials such as the Menendez and Simpson cases on television. It's a form of entertainment for them, pure and simple. Televise a breach of contract or automobile collision lawsuit and see how many people watch. The entertainment aspect of the Simpson trial became so ludicrous that time and time again, the talking heads, and those who called in on these shows, actually complained that certain lawyers and witnesses, as well as certain evidence, were too boring and dull for their tastes—which is to say they wanted, were almost demanding, better and more scintillating entertainment.

Even given the ancillary benefit of being educational, the *sole* purpose of a criminal trial is to determine whether or not the defendant is guilty of the crime. It is not to educate the public.

But although the cameras could only have a negative effect, if any, upon the trial proceedings, they stayed, right to the very end. And they stayed, of course, because of one person and one person only, the only person who had the discretion and authority, under Rule 980 of the California Rules of Court, to pull the plug: Judge Lance Ito. Why didn't he? Even assuming he had what he believed to be valid reasons for keeping the cameras, one of his reasons was most assuredly improper—Ito loved to perform in front of these cameras. At least that seems to be the consensus of virtually all the reporters who covered the trial. Reporters called him "Judge Ego." He seems to "relish the presence of the television cameras. He likes the limelight," *Newsweek* said.

I knew for sure that Ito was out of his depth in this trial when early on he started inviting celebrities visiting the proceedings back to his chambers, particularly talk show hosts whose programs covered the trial. I don't have anything against these talk show hosts, but it was unseemly and undignified behavior for a judge presiding over an important murder trial. What conceivable reason could Ito possibly have had for being so eager to play host to these celebrities other than that he was concerned with what they might say about him on the air? (The only other possibility that occurs to me is almost equally damning—that Ito lionizes celebrities, like so many of his fellow citizens. But if he does, this is at least one piece of circumstantial evidence that he did not possess the intellectual maturity to preside over a case of this magnitude.)

"I was very disappointed with Judge Ito," defense attorney Peter Neufeld told *Time* magazine, "the fact that he was so concerned about his status as a celebrity, his willingness to entertain personalities in chambers, to show the lawyers little videotapes of skits on television." One day, Neufeld said, Ito brought all the lawyers into chambers to show them a clip of the "Dancing Itos" from Jay Leno's *Tonight Show*. "He had thought it was great and loved it and wanted all of us to see it in chambers. You may find that amusing on a personal level," Neufeld said, "but I can assure you that on a professional level it is so unacceptable for a judge who's presiding over a murder trial to bring the lawyers into chambers to show them comic reviews." Ito also told the lawyers Simpson jokes he had heard. Said Neufeld: "As someone who has tried cases for twenty years, I found it deplorable, and I was shocked." One such joke, as reported in the *New York Times*, may have been an Ito original. Near the beginning of the proceedings, Ito told Johnnie Cochran he had bad and good news for him. The bad news was that the authorities had found Cochran's client's blood at the murder scene. The good news, Ito said, was that Simpson's cholesterol was low.

The aspect of Ito's conduct that bothered me the most during the trial, however, was his demeaning, overbearing treatment of the lawyers, particularly the prosecutors. He wasn't as pompous, arrogant, and dictatorial as many judges are, but he was bad enough. The common complaint against Ito was that he gave too much leash to the lawyers on both sides, that he didn't rein them in, and that he let them take charge of the courtroom. But from what I saw of the trial, I don't agree. Ito has a reputation of being a judge who gives both sides a full and reasonably unrestricted opportunity to present their cases fully, not setting time limits on questioning, arguments, etc. Apart from monetary considerations (and we can't put a price tag on justice), up to a certain point I think this is commendable, not bad. This is the way he is in all his cases, not just the Simpson case, as some people assumed. I saw no lawyer or lawyers taking charge of the courtroom in any way whatsoever. Ito, at least to me, always seemed in charge, brooking no challenge to his authority. What I saw, instead, was a judge who had something of a tough-guy sneer on his face and a virtually constant intimidating tone to his voice. The tone was not as pronounced as it is in so many judges, but there was an unmistakable edge to his voice and his words that always implied the lawyers were on the brink, or within shouting distance, of being held in contempt of court.

The very slightest offense, real or imagined, was apt to set him off. In a February 23, 1995, sidebar conference called to discuss the prosecution's objections to a line of questions by Cochran, Cochran said: "They [the prosecutors] obviously haven't tried any cases in a long time and obviously don't know how, but this is cross-examination."

Darden said, "Who is he talking about, doesn't know how to try a case?"
Ito: "Wait, Mr. Darden."
Darden: "Is he the only lawyer that knows how to try a case?"
Ito: "I'm going to hold you in contempt."

After Ito excused the jury, he suggested to Darden that if Darden apologized, he might set aside his finding of contempt. But Darden, who had done nothing wrong, and therefore had said nothing to apologize for, refused, and asked Ito to schedule a hearing on the propriety of the contempt.

Ito said, "[I gave counsel] an opportunity to get up and say 'Gee, I'm sorry, I lost my head there. I apologize to the court. I apologize to counsel [Cochran]' . . . You want to fight some more with the court, you're welcome to do so." Eventually, Darden apologized to the court, saying he meant no disrespect, and Ito then also apologized for overreacting.

All of this took place in front of millions of TV viewers. Obviously, there were only two villains to this piece, Cochran and Ito. Cochran had been insulting to Darden, and Darden would have been completely justified in responding in kind to him. Instead, under the circumstances he was very mild in his response. Yet simply because he continued talking ("Is he the only lawyer that knows how to try a case?") after Ito had said "Wait, Mr. Darden," Ito held him in contempt of court, and then compounded it by demanding that Darden, the victim, apologize in front of millions to Cochran, who had insulted him, and to Ito, the overbearing judge with a hair-trigger sensitivity who improperly held him in contempt. Note that the one-sided exchange between Cochran and Darden at the sidebar was outside the hearing of the jury, so absolutely no harm was done to either side. Moreover, in jury trials, particularly murder cases where more is at stake, tempers frequently become frayed, and counsel lash out at each other, often even before the jury. But the super-prickly Ito would have none of it, even in the privacy of a sidebar, and even though Darden had simply defended himself, as opposed to lashing back at Cochran.

On July 20, 1995, Marcia Clark was a few minutes late for an early-morning court session outside the presence of the jury, for which she immediately apologized, explaining the reason for her tardiness. Ito, unimpressed, fined the DA's office $250. Clark responded: "Excuse me, Your Honor, may I remind the court that Mr. Shapiro kept the court waiting for twenty minutes—showing up at twenty after nine when it was his witness on the stand—and suffered no sanctions?"

Ito glowered back and said: "Thank you. The fine will be one thousand dollars." In other words, how dare Clark have the temerity to offer any kind of defense whatsoever to one of his rulings. (Consistent with his vacillating nature, Ito later reset the figure at $250 when DA Gil Garcetti publicly denounced the high fine.) Just another example of a thin-skinned judge who was offended by the slightest transgression, real or perceived.

Although I can't be sure, I have the very distinct feeling that because of Ito's snippy and thin-skinned judicial manner, Marcia Clark was intimidated by Ito, and as a direct consequence thereof, did not perform as well as she was capable of performing during the Simpson trial. The consensus of courtroom watchers is that Ito did not like Marcia, nor she him, and it showed in the strained and highly formal interchanges they had. It is also the consensus that Ito treated the defense, particularly Cochran, with a little more respect, since Cochran, for two years in the late seventies, had been Ito's superior in the district attorney's office. (As a sop to the black community, the incumbent DA, for political purposes, had appointed Cochran, who had never spent a day in the office and never prosecuted a felony in his career, assistant district attorney, the number three man in the office. It was solely an administrative position, and he handled no cases in the courtroom.)

Here's where the problem comes in. There are two main ways a lawyer can lose his credibility with the jury. One is when the jury forms the opinion that the lawyer is not being honest with them and is trying to win at all costs. The other way, which is rarely talked about, surely not in the reporting of this case, is when the judge demeans the lawyer in court and the lawyer lets him get away with it. In this case, on several occasions, Judge Ito crisply told Ms. Clark, right before the jury, "Sit down," as if he were talking to a child. Clark always complied immediately, without a whimper or the slightest indication of recalcitrance. Nothing could be worse for the prosecutor than to lose stature in the jurors' eyes. At one point in the trial when Clark had used the word "matched" for hair and fiber evidence purportedly being connected to Simpson and his Ford Bronco—a term which Ito had disallowed because hair and fiber evidence isn't as conclusive as DNA evidence—Ito snapped at her: "If I hear that word again [it's a word prosecutors are accustomed to using], somebody is going to be in jail over the weekend." Ito's threat to put Clark in jail was all over the news for the jurors' spouses and loved ones to hear and possibly pass on to them during conjugal visits. Can you imagine how it would sound for a juror to hear, "The judge almost put Marcia Clark in jail today for something she did"?

And when Clark, in cross-examining the defense's EDTA expert, Dr. Fredric Reiders, was seeking to show the jury that Reiders was not a reliable forensic scientist by the provably erroneous and incompetent testimony he had given in another murder case, Ito, instead of calling Clark to the bench, angrily snapped at her in front of the jury: "Let's wind this up. Let's try the Simpson case sometime today," thereby telling the jury in so many words that Clark was wasting everybody's time.

A word about judges. The American people have an understandably negative view of politicians, public opinion polls show, and an equally negative view of lawyers. David Kennedy, professor of history at Stanford University, in writing about politicians, says: "With the possible exception of lawyers, we hold no other professionals in such contempt. Who among us can utter the word 'politician' without a sneer?" Conventional logic would seem to dictate, then, that since a judge is normally both a politician and a lawyer, people would have an opinion of them lower than a grasshopper's belly. But on the contrary, a $25 black cotton robe elevates the denigrated lawyer-politician to a position of considerable honor and respect in our society, as if the garment itself miraculously imbued the person with qualities not previously possessed. As an example, judges have, for the most part, remained off-limits to the creators of popular entertainment, being depicted on screens large and small as learned men and women of stature and solemnity who are as impartial as sunlight. This depiction ignores reality.

As to the political aspect of judges, the appointment of judgeships by governors (or the president in federal courts) has always been part and parcel of the political spoils or patronage system. For example, 97 percent of President Reagan's appointees to the federal bench were Republicans. Thus in the overwhelming majority of cases there is a nexus between the appointment and politics. Either the appointee has personally labored long and hard in the political vineyards, or he is a favored friend of one who has, often a generous financial supporter of the party in power. Roy

Mersky, professor at the University of Texas Law School, says: "To be appointed a judge *to a great extent* is the result of one's political activity." Consequently, lawyers entering courtrooms are frequently confronted with the specter of a new judge they've never heard of and know absolutely nothing about. The judge may never have distinguished himself in the legal profession, but a cursory investigation almost invariably reveals a political connection. (Of course, just because there is a political connection does not mean that the judge is not otherwise competent and qualified to sit on the bench. Many times he is.) Incredibly, and unfortunately, the political connection holds true all the way up to the U.S. Supreme Court, where, for instance, the last three chief justices—Earl Warren, Warren E. Burger, and to a lesser extent William Rehnquist—have all been creatures of politics, like so many of their predecessors in history.

Although there are many exceptions, by and large the bench boasts undistinguished lawyers whose principal qualification for the most important position in our legal system is the all-important political connection. Rarely, for instance, will a governor seek out a renowned but apolitical legal scholar and proffer a judgeship.

It has been my experience and, I daresay, the experience of most veteran trial lawyers that the typical judge has little or no trial experience as a lawyer, or is pompous and dictatorial on the bench, or worst of all, is clearly partial to one side or the other in the lawsuit. Sometimes the judge displays all three infirmities.

It's always a great relief and pleasure to walk into court and find a judge who has had trial experience, knows the law, is completely impartial, and hasn't let his judgeship swell his head. There are, of course, many such admirable judges in this country, but regrettably they are decidedly in the minority.

For whatever reasons—undoubtedly the threat of being held in contempt of court ranks high—the great run of lawyers are intimidated by judges and continue to be outwardly respectful even when publicly humiliated by them. Lawyers' complaints are made in private to one another and to their families. Commonly heard at any watering hole for the courthouse crowd is one lawyer crying to another over his first drink of the evening: "The judge is *killing* me in court." No lawyer is exempt. For example, only a very few lawyers in the history of the legal profession have practiced law in as grand a fashion or sown more new legal ground (particularly in the area of tort law) than the celebrated San Francisco lawyer Melvin Belli. Yet, despite his considerable legal stature and characteristically gentlemanly behavior in court, he was treated with so much disrespect by a small-town judge a few years ago that he mournfully observed:

"The judge is riding me so hard in front of the jury I've got spur marks on my back." Predictably, the judge was a political animal, having run for the office a few years earlier. The judge's campaign theme was to "end the reign of arrogance" of the incumbent judge.

Fortunately, in my career I've had only one instance where the issue of the judge's conduct potentially affecting the result of the trial arose. It was in 1966, only two years after I had become a prosecutor at the L.A. District Attorney's Office. That year there had been a record 367 bus robberies in Los Angeles. The situation had gotten so bad that many of the drivers refused to drive without an LAPD officer present on the bus. Finally, a seventy-one-year-old driver who was due to retire within one month was shot and killed when he resisted two robbers, surprisingly the first homicide that the Rapid Transit District bus line in Los Angeles had ever had. It was an important case in the office, and we were seeking the death penalty against the two defendants.

The judge obviously felt that since I hadn't been in the DA's office long, I was a relative rookie and could be pushed around. On the first day of trial testimony, I made an objection while sitting down (a very common practice). The judge ordered me to stand up to make the objection. I did, after which he told me to sit down. I asked to approach the bench. These were my words, and it was obvious to him I was angry: "Judge, I represent the people of the state of California, twenty million people [it was only twenty million back then, now it's thirty-two million], and when I stand up in front of the jury in my final summation, I have to have stature and credibility with them. If you tell me to stand up and sit down like a yo-yo in this courtroom, I'm not going to have it. From now on, I'll stand up and sit down in this courtroom when I want to, not when you want me to." Whereupon I stalked back to my seat. You can believe it or not, but from that point on in the trial, I made all my objections sitting down, not standing up, and the judge never said a word.

While Judge Ito did not go so far as to humiliate the prosecutors in the Simpson Case, I nonetheless feel he was sufficiently disrespectful that when they stood up to give their summations, they had little stature with the jurors. What the prosecutors should have done to Ito right after the first sharp and abusive "Sit down" (Ito was democratic about his surliness: he also told several, but not all, of the defense attorneys to sit down) was to ask for a recess. Back in chambers he should have been told, first in a very civil way, but if this was unavailing, much more assertively, that although he had the right to speak, if he chose, in a condescending way to the prosecutors outside the presence of the jury, he did not have the right to hurt the prosecutors' clients, the people of the State of California, in any way whatsoever in front of the jury, and they therefore not only wouldn't permit him to do so, but had an obligation to ensure that he did not. Therefore, if he had anything negative to say to them, it had to be *outside* the presence of the jury. In front of the jury he had to show them the same, identical respect they showed him, nothing more, nothing less.

If necessary, Ito should also have been reminded that although he was an extremely important person at the trial, it was they, not he, who represented some thirty-two million people. Finally, *and most important*, he'd have to be told in so many words that if he did not treat the prosecutors with the same respect they showed for him, he himself would have to pay a price right in front of the jury and the millions watching the case. An example for you readers of a statement to the judge in front of the jury? "Judge, you apparently don't know, but that's not the way to talk to lawyers in front of the jury. I expect you to ask me politely to please sit down in the future." A stronger example? "Judge, a few years ago you were one of us, a deputy district attorney. You were appointed to the bench by the governor because you were a friend of a friend of the governor. If you think that your black robe entitles you, under the law, to treat us disrespectfully in front of this jury, I am here to inform you that you are wrong."

But it is my opinion that even the first example wouldn't have been necessary. The situation wouldn't have gotten that far. My sense of Judge Ito is that he just let his robe go to his head a bit. (Some judges think they are three steps closer to God when they ascend the courtroom bench — others don't even recognize that limitation.) He forgot who he was, and all he needed was someone to remind him, put him in his place, as it were.

Ito, who was so very concerned about his public image, would not have wanted to be demeaned before millions of people. What if he surprised everyone by not backing down? What if the prosecutors addressed him in open court as I suggested and he held them in contempt? Big deal. The prosecutor could handle any fine or sanction he might have imposed. But most important, I assure you that the prosecutors would have not only retained but perhaps even elevated their stature, and hence credibility, in the eyes of the jury.

The Trial

The Incredible Incompetence of the Prosecution

Syndicated columnist William Rusher, a Distinguished Fellow of the Claremont Institute for the Study of Statesmanship and Political Philosophy, writes: "I simply cannot imagine the prosecution's overwhelming case against Simpson being presented better than it was presented by Marcia Clark and Christopher Darden. They lost for reasons that were certainly no fault of theirs." If you say so, Will. Of course, saying someone did a good job presupposes that the declarant knows what a good job is.

The prosecution of O. J. Simpson was the most incompetent criminal prosecution I have ever seen. By far. There have undoubtedly been worse. It's just that I'm not aware of any. Anyone who knows me will tell you that it hurts me to say this, since right from the very beginning no one was more supportive of the prosecutors in this case than I. (Although I no longer am a prosecutor, and if I try a case today it's as a defense attorney, I still identify myself much more with the prosecutorial side of the table than the defense side, and my public image continues to be that of a prosecutor.) They are also good people, they fought hard for justice, and I was proud of the ethical and professional way they conducted themselves. I was 100 percent behind them. To pump them up and help inspire them, I even sent them a telegram on the morning of their summations telling them that all right-thinking people were behind them and

91

they had done a terrific job proving Simpson's guilt beyond a reasonable doubt. (Even though their prosecution was woefully incompetent, I certainly did not want to tell them this right before their summations; moreover, by the scientific evidence they presented putting Simpson's blood at the murder scene, they had, indeed, proved his guilt beyond all doubt.) I closed by saying, "Now go get 'em in your summations."

A word about Marcia Clark, the lead prosecutor. My image of a prosecutor has never been that of a woman, and that's primarily because in my day female prosecutors were about as rare as hair on a bald man. But the moment I saw Marcia Clark, I was impressed. She had a good look about her. She looked like a prosecutor. It was also obvious to me that she was very bright, spoke well and persuasively (I hadn't seen her yet before a jury), and could think on her feet. She also has a certain charisma about her. In short, I felt she was special. In retrospect I can only say that her performance in this case was a disappointment, a blighting of that early promise, and no one regrets this more than I do.

Like the calm before the storm, I had a sense there might be a serious problem with the prosecution in this case by the fact that the original prosecutors (Marcia Clark and David Conn at the time), long before the trial, didn't seem to be taking charge of the case. For instance, in a big-publicity case, it's DA 101 that the prosecution has to instruct all of its witnesses right off the top that they are not to talk to the media, particularly for money. My distinct impression is that this wasn't done here until later, after some of them already had talked. This created problems for the prosecution, resulting in its decision not to call certain witnesses to the stand because it felt the credibility of the witnesses had been damaged.

Also, the moment a decision is made to bring felony charges, the DA has to make all important decisions having an impact on the case. Again, this wasn't done here. Remarkably, David Conn (subsequently replaced by William Hodgman and then Chris Darden) actually told the LAPD—which properly called the DA's office for guidance—to follow the advice of the Los Angeles City Attorney's Office on whether the October 25, 1993, 911 tape of Nicole should be released to the media, which were clamoring for it. The city attorney's office improvidently and unfortunately told the police to release the tape. The tape saturated the news, and when the presiding judge of the Los Angeles County Superior Court personally confirmed that members of the grand jury who were hearing evidence in the case heard it, he aborted the grand jury proceedings, and there was no indictment. (As I recounted in Chapter 2, the DA then filed a criminal complaint against Simpson instead.)

And months before the trial (August 1994), the prosecution embarrassingly admitted in court that without its knowledge the LAPD had disregarded the DA's request and had not sent all of the blood samples to Cellmark Diagnostics Inc. in Maryland for DNA analysis, instead sending some of them to the California State Department of Justice lab at Berkeley. When the LAPD knows the DA is calling the shots on a case, this type of thing normally doesn't happen.

As far as the selection of a jury, we've already discussed Gil Garcetti's terrible blunder in transferring the case downtown. But once it was downtown, there is evidence that the prosecution only made a bad situation much worse.

On December 1, 1995, I met at the old-line and conservatively elegant California Club in downtown Los Angeles with Dr. Donald Vinson. Dr. Vinson is recognized as a national authority in the field of litigation support. He has written or contributed to several books and articles on litigation strategy and trial techniques. He holds a B.A. in economics, an M.S. in marketing research, an M.A. in sociology, and a Ph.D. in marketing and consumer behavior. He has taught courses in consumer behavior and marketing research at LSU and UCLA and was at one time chairman of the marketing department at the University of Southern California. Currently, Dr. Vinson is chairman of the board of DecisionQuest, Inc., which specializes in jury research and trial consulting. The firm, headquartered in Torrance, California, also maintains offices in New York, Washington, D.C., Boston, Chicago, Atlanta, and Houston. Over the last twenty years, Vinson and his firm have worked with hundreds of attorneys throughout the country in more than three thousand cases. Some of their high-profile cases have included *Pennzoil v. Texaco*, the Agent Orange case, the MGM Grand Hotel case, and *USFL v. NFL*. His office is presently assisting the prosecution in the Oklahoma City bombing case.

Vinson, fifty, is one of these public-spirited guys who have made "a bundle," he acknowledges, in the private sector and feel the need to give a little back. After the first hung jury in the Menendez trial, along with many others he was very disappointed, feeling that something was happening in our society that was bad, and he wanted to help the good guys out. So he volunteered his services, *pro bono*, to Gil Garcetti for the second Menendez trial.

When the Simpson case broke, Vinson also offered his firm's services free to Garcetti, and Garcetti accepted. DecisionQuest actually did provide all of the prosecution's elaborate electronic displays and exhibits (graphics) throughout the entire Simpson trial. He says the cost for these services, if paid for, would have been close to $1 million. But in the more important area of assisting in jury selection, he says that although Garcetti was amenable, Marcia Clark was not. Vinson says that from the very beginning, Clark and William Hodgman (the latter was named the 1992 prosecutor of the year in the state of California), particularly Clark, looked askance, as so many trial lawyers still do, at the emerging field of jury consultants. After the second day of jury selection, she told him she didn't feel there was any need for his services (jury consultation, not the preparation of exhibits, which continued).

His dismissal was reported in the media. The October 30, 1995, edition of *Newsweek* said: "Hired by Robert Shapiro just two months after the murders of Nicole Brown and Ron Goldman, Jo-Ellan Dimitrius [who used to work for Vinson] quickly became a member of the defense team. By contrast, prosecutors tried to hide their consultant, Donald Vinson, of DecisionQuest, and then banished him, and his research, from jury selection after only two days."

What is much more interesting and important, however, is the results of his jury research leading up to jury selection. Vinson said that in discussions with the prosecution team, Clark made it clear she preferred to have black women over black men on the jury, because culturally it is known that domestic abuse is more prevalent in black households than in white families. Her thinking was that black women were becoming more liberated, were fed up with being beaten, would identify with Nicole, and would be angry with Simpson for having brutalized her. (Of course, partially militating against this is the fact that Nicole had started seeing Simpson when he was still married to Marguerite, Simpson's black first wife, so Nicole had taken Simpson away from a black "sister.") But the problem is that the polls didn't show that. In a four-hundred-person phone survey conducted for the prosecution by DecisionQuest of blacks and whites, while 23 percent of black males thought Simpson was guilty, only 7 percent of black women thought so.

More tellingly, Vinson and his staff also conducted several small (fifteen-person) "focus group" sessions to "put some meat and flesh on the statistics," as he said. In these sessions, the black females, per Vinson, were "more vociferous" in support and defense of Simpson than were the black males. When confronted with the fact that Simpson had beaten Nicole, their basic response, Vinson told me, was that "every relationship has these kinds of problems." It simply was not a big deal to the black females. Ironically, DecisionQuest's research showed that black females who were the victims of domestic violence, or had it in their family, were even more forgiving and accepting of it than those who hadn't.

"My working hypothesis, which I told Marcia and Bill," Dr. Vinson said, "was that black females were the worst conceivable jurors for the prosecution in the Simpson case. The charts and poll results I submitted to Marcia and the DA's office clearly reflected this."

Since Vinson stopped working with the Simpson prosecutors after the second day, it is not known for sure whether Marcia Clark disregarded the advice and data provided for her by Vinson or not. But the evidence certainly suggests she did. Having learned that black females did not like her (see following discussion) and were also markedly more sympathetic to O. J. Simpson than black males, Clark nevertheless settled for a jury with six black females on it! There were only two black males. The jury which ended up returning the not-guilty verdict had eight black females and only one black male.

One possibly unfair criticism which has been leveled against the prosecution in this case is that they exercised only ten of their allotted twenty peremptory challenges (challenges for which you don't have to give a reason). Since a jury with close to 75 percent blacks on it could not be considered a favorable jury, why not use the remaining peremptories to see if you can get a better racial mix, the argument goes. But many times a prosecutor doesn't use all of his peremptories, even when he isn't too pleased with the present composition of the jury, because when he turns around and glances at the remaining prospective jurors seated in the courtroom, they look worse than the ones already in the box. Since I have no way of knowing who these remaining jurors were or what they looked like, I have no opinion on the matter. I do find it curious, however, that with ten remaining peremptories, the prosecutors left on the jury the black male who worked for Hertz Rent A Car, the company Simpson had been employed by as a spokesman for years. (The juror was excused by Judge Ito shortly thereafter when evidence surfaced that during jury selection he had failed to disclose meeting Simpson at a party for Hertz employees years earlier.)

Both sides submitted to Ito proposed questionnaires for the jury. (Ito distilled them into one seventy-eight-page questionnaire containing hundreds of questions.) These questions are the heart of a jury consultant's job, their main area of expertise. Although the defense jury consultant, Jo-Ellan Dimitrius (whom the defense attorneys have credited, in no small way, for their ending up with the jury that heard the case, to the point where Cochran, after the not-guilty verdict, directed his first expression of thanks to her), was highly instrumental in the preparation of the defense's proposed questionnaire, Clark insisted that she and her team prepare the prosecution's proposed questionnaire themselves without any input from Vinson's firm. "Marcia didn't even want us to provide a draft. She gave me a copy of the prosecution's eventual questionnaire on the day she submitted it to Judge Ito," Dr. Vinson told me.

Perhaps most disturbing, Vinson told me that it emerged from the focus groups that black women viewed Marcia Clark "extremely negatively, actually calling her names like 'bitch.' They hated her. They saw her as a pushy, aggressive white woman who was trying to bring down and emasculate a prominent black man." Norma Silverstein, Vinson's assistant, said, "black women displayed a lot of hostility toward Marcia." Clark, Hodgman, and Garcetti knew this, Vinson said. This came out of the first two separate focus group sessions (conducted over a three-hour period, back to back, on the same day in late July 1994). In fact, in two subsequent focus group sessions, Clark, Hodgman, and Garcetti were present, listening in from an adjacent room, and the same harsh sentiments against Clark by black women were expressed.

The focus group members, each of whom was paid $50, were unaware of the presence of the prosecutors listening in the room next to theirs behind a one-way mirror. The focus group members were told, however, that associates of Vinson were watching them, but not who those associates were. In late August 1994, DecisionQuest conducted a single focus group session at a hotel in Phoenix, Arizona, this time with twenty members. Clark and Hodgman (but not Garcetti) attended this session, watching it by closed-circuit TV from an adjacent conference room. The results were the same. For some reason, black women didn't like Marcia Clark. This raises the very serious question, of course, of whether Clark, knowing that black females felt this curious antipathy toward her, should have chosen to remove herself from the case. And since she didn't, shouldn't the DA's office, with knowledge of this fact, and with one thousand prosecutors to choose from, have insisted on going forward with a replacement prosecutor? After all, the purpose of this prosecution was not to advance women's rights and promote their equality in the workplace, but to secure a conviction of someone the district attorney's office believed was responsible for two brutal murders.

An additional item of information furnished to me by Vinson: From their answers to the jury questionnaire before the case started, of the actual jury that ended up deliberating whether Simpson was guilty or not guilty (as indicated, one black male, eight black females; also, two white females, and one Hispanic man), *not one out of the twelve* read the newspaper regularly, and eight did not watch the evening news on television. After the Simpson verdict, Dr. Vinson and his firm went on to assist the prosecution in jury selection and graphics in the second Menendez trial.

Before I get into the virtually continuous incompetence of the pros- ,
ecution during the actual trial of this case, I want to talk about what is by
far the worst part of their performance, something that goes beyond incompetence. The term incompetence implies conduct that is within the
range of known human conduct in a given field. What the DA did in this
case, on the other hand, was unprecedented, unique, unheard of.

In all my years in the criminal law, I have never heard of another case
where the prosecution decided not to introduce such a *great* amount of
very incriminating evidence against the defendant. I mean, that's what
the prosecutor does in a criminal case—present incriminating evidence.

Here, and I still can't believe this, they never presented the suicide
note Simpson wrote when he learned he was going to be charged with
these murders. If he was innocent, why would he want to commit suicide? If he was innocent, it seems he would have been outraged that he
was being accused of murders he did not commit, and desperately want to
prove his innocence and find out who murdered the mother of his two
children. Simpson, instead, became completely passive and wrote a "To
whom it may concern" letter which reads exactly like a suicide note. (The
full text of this letter is in Appendix B.) The language of the letter reeks
with guilt. Show me an innocent person charged with murder who would
write a note like that.

For those who cling tenaciously to Simpson's innocence and argue that
the reason he wanted to commit suicide is that he couldn't live without
Nicole, consider that Simpson has got to be considered one of the most
self-absorbed persons there could ever be, one whose narcissism is of jumbo
proportions, and he gives no indication of being the type of person who
would kill himself over the loss of another human being. Secondly, such an
argument would be diametrically opposed to an integral element of
Simpson's defense to these murders—that he was over Nicole, had started
a life without her, and therefore had no motive to kill her. And if that's not
enough, if the reason he wanted to die was that he couldn't live without
Nicole, what conceivable reason would he have had for not saying this in
his farewell note? Nowhere does he say or even vaguely imply in the note
that Nicole's death is why he wants to end his life. In fact, in the letter he
says that God had brought his current girlfriend, Paula Barbieri, to him,
and he tells her how sorry he is that they will not have their chance.

Yet this note, which points irresistibly in the direction of Simpson's
guilt, was never seen by this jury because the prosecutors chose not to
introduce it into evidence.

But it gets worse. After the slow-speed chase of Simpson and his friend

Al Cowlings in the latter's Bronco, the police found in the Bronco a gun (there were photos of Simpson during the chase holding this gun to his head, and Cowlings, from the vehicle's cellular phone, told the pursuing police that Simpson was threatening suicide), Simpson's passport, and a cheap disguise (a fake goatee and mustache). Additionally, Cowlings, upon being told to empty his pockets, pulled out a wad of currency totaling $8,750. These items, of course, have guilt written all over them. Indeed, they could hardly be more persuasive evidence of guilt, and it would be insulting to your intelligence to explain to you (as I would have to the jury if I had prosecuted Simpson) why this is so. Yet again, the jury never heard all this evidence because, unbelievably, the prosecutors decided not to present it. Thus far, these are the reasons the DA's office has given for not introducing all this evidence, including the slow motion chase that led up to the seizure of the evidence. During the chase, Simpson was talking to friends and also his mother on the Bronco cellular phone, and predictably was proclaiming his innocence, and the prosecution didn't want the jury to hear this. But this is silly beyond imagination. It's a self-serving declaration that is meaningless. *Of course* he's going to say he's innocent. Did they expect him to confess to these murders?

Another argument the prosecutors have floated for their not introducing the slow-speed chase and the evidence subsequently seized is that, as William Hodgman said on television, "it was coming at a point in time when we were also starting to lose jurors. So we felt, on balance, a need to conclude our case, and get into the defense case if they were going to present one." As much as I respect Bill Hodgman, I can't tell you how much total and complete nonsense this is. Number one, there's never a valid reason for not offering powerful, incriminating evidence against the defendant. Even if, in a given case, the jury's fatigue is an issue, on balance, you *always*, 100 percent of the time, offer the strong incriminating evidence. It's not even a close call.

Secondly, that argument doesn't even apply here. The jury in the Simpson case started getting antsy after the first half of the trial. The normal point in the trial to offer the slow-speed chase would have been near the *beginning* of the DA's presentation of evidence. Thirdly, evidence of the chase, and the seizure of the defendant's gun, passport, etc., would have taken very little time to present on direct examination, perhaps one to two hours. (Mind you, these are the prosecutors who took eight *days* of direct examination of the coroner to elicit testimony, the important parts of which could easily have been introduced in two hours.) And, of course, relative to all the extremely technical and boring DNA scientific evidence in the Simpson case that went on for months, the jury could have been counted on to perk up and listen very attentively to the testimony about the chase and the seizure of all the incriminating items in Simpson's possession at the end of it.

These excuses, of course, are merely an effort by the DA's office to explain away an incredible tactical blunder on its part.

During the slow-speed chase, Simpson also supposedly told his mother, "It was all her fault, Ma." Since we know Simpson committed these murders, we can just about know what Simpson meant by this. Poor Nicole had said or done something to him which so enraged him it led to her murder. Of course, the defense could argue that what Simpson meant was that unsavory types Nicole hung around with were responsible for her murder. Let them argue it. They still couldn't come up with any evidence to support it, inasmuch as it never happened.

Also, the police booked the cash under Cowlings', not Simpson's, name and the prosecutors, afraid of their own shadow throughout the trial, thought this could hurt them. "The detectives' decision to book the cash as Cowlings' personal property and not as evidence would be damaging to the prosecution at the trial," an October 27, 1994, DA internal memo said. But how? When Cowlings took the $8,750 in currency out of his pockets, and the police asked him why he had all this money on him, he told them Simpson had given him the money when they were in the Bronco.

All of this, of course, is a nonsensical discussion. When you have exceedingly powerful evidence of guilt, you automatically offer it. You don't stumble on your way to the courtroom over the smallest thread in your path. Of course, the defense will always raise some arguments against your incriminating evidence, even if they are totally spurious. If a defense attorney doesn't do this, he would have pled his client guilty. And sometimes your evidence actually does have a carbuncle or two on it. But you balance the strength of your evidence against its weakness. Here, the passport alone is very strong evidence of guilt, against which there is no *valid* defense argument. Why would Simpson have his passport on him if he wasn't at least thinking of escaping? And why would he *think* of escaping if he was innocent and being framed? He, of all people, would know he would be able to offer, through himself and his attorneys, all types of evidence to prove his innocence and expose the frame-up. It should be noted that Simpson would even be deprived of making the argument that he always kept his passport in his Bronco (which seems highly unlikely in the first place), because this wasn't his Bronco the passport was in. It was Cowlings' Bronco.

One of the unanswered questions which has fascinated Simpson case addicts is whether Simpson decided to kill Nicole on the night of the murders or had contemplated it for some time. Nicole's close friend Faye Resnick, who knew Simpson very well, is convinced Simpson had planned the murder for some time. And there is a solid piece of documentary evidence circumstantially supporting Resnick's view which the DA had, but again chose not to introduce.

Item 146 of the LAPD property report in the Simpson case lists a fake goatee, fake mustache, bottle of spirit gum (to put the disguise on), and bottle of makeup adhesive remover (to remove the disguise). While the goatee and mustache have been widely reported, what hasn't been is Item 147, three receipts found inside the same bag in the Bronco along with Item 146. The receipts for the purchase of the disguise materials are from Cinema Secrets Beauty Supply at 4400 Riverside Drive in Burbank. The date they were purchased is what is so incriminating. It was May 27, 1994, *just over two weeks prior to the murders!*

Again, let Simpson explain, on the witness stand, why he felt the need for a disguise just prior to the murders. Then let's see if there is any evidence that Simpson has ever worn a disguise at any other time in his life. Was this the first time in his life, at age forty-seven, and just before the murders, that he had a need for a disguise? And if he had bought the disguise for some innocent purpose, why was it necessary for him to bring it with him in Cowlings' car?

There's an old observation that celebrities are people who have spent all their time and energy trying to become famous, and when they do, they wear dark eyeglasses so no one will recognize them. This very definitely didn't apply to Simpson. By all accounts, he loved the attention of fans and people who recognized him. And when he didn't get it he would actually become depressed. Faye Resnick, in fact, who was with Nicole and Simpson on many occasions in public, said that whenever Simpson wasn't noticed, "his mood would change and he would become angry." Simpson himself, in his biography O.J., *the Education of a Rich Rookie*, says about his celebrity: "I loved it when people recognized me on the street." So why did Simpson purchase the disguises shortly before the murders? The DA never offered this evidence of guilt to the jury.

What makes the prosecutors' failure to do so all the more astonishing is that they were alleging in their criminal complaint that Simpson had premeditated these murders, and they suggested to the jury that the premeditation commenced long before the night of the murders. For instance, defense witness Jack Mackay, an executive for the American Psychological Association, testified at the trial that he had played golf with Simpson *four days before* the murders at a celebrity golfing event sponsored by Simpson's employer, the Hertz Corporation. Simpson, he said, appeared cordial and happy to sign autographs, shake hands, etc. Clark asked Mackay on cross-examination: "If someone was planning to commit murder would you expect him to come to you if he wanted to get away with it and grumble about the person he wanted to kill?"

But the prosecution presented no evidence at all that Simpson had premeditated the murders that far back. All it had to offer the jury was its speculation. The lone piece of documentary, circumstantial evidence it had to support its contention remained in its files, and the jury never learned of it. Is it possible the prosecutors hadn't read the police property report closely and missed this evidence? Things like this happen in life.

One parenthetical observation about the slow-speed chase. The LAPD had notified Simpson's attorney, Robert Shapiro, at 8:30 in the morning on Friday, June 17, 1994, that they were ready to charge and arrest Simpson for the murders. The LAPD gave Shapiro until 11:00 that morning to have Simpson voluntarily turn himself in at Parker Center, LAPD's downtown headquarters. As we know, Simpson didn't do this, and sometime before noon, he and Cowlings disappeared from the Encino home of his friend Robert Kardashian. At 5:56 p.m. that day, the police, responding to a citizen's tip, pinpointed the location of Cowlings' Ford Bronco on an Orange County (just south of Los Angeles) freeway. It was about sixty miles from Simpson's Rockingham estate. After a two-hour slow-speed chase, Simpson returned to his home, where he was subsequently arrested. The whole incident of Simpson's not turning himself in and the slow-speed chase should definitely have been offered by the prosecution. It could only have helped, and since the jury, like everyone else, already knew about it, it must have looked downright strange to them that the prosecution did not introduce it as an integral part of its case. But contrary to the view of many laypeople, the slow-speed chase itself was not greatly incriminating because it was somewhat ambiguous.

Normally, flight is highly incriminating evidence because it shows a consciousness of guilt. But in a typical flight case, the suspect is found in a place like an attic, or in the mountains, or in Canada, Mexico, or some other distant place. Here, Simpson and Cowlings, after being gone for five hours, were only sixty miles away. And the Bronco was driving in the general direction of, not away from, Simpson's Brentwood residence. What this "flight" (coupled with evidence of the passport, money, etc.) shows is that Simpson only thought about escaping, but hadn't definitely decided to do it. If he had, in the five-hour interlude before his whereabouts were picked up, he'd have been a lot farther than sixty miles down the road. Of course, the very fact that he thought about escaping was itself extremely powerful evidence of his guilt.

When you offer evidence like the suicide note, passport, cash, disguise, etc., you're offering something that even the simplest of laypeople can understand. It's the type of evidence upon which they have formed opinions throughout their lives. For instance, running away from anything, be it adults running from the scene of a liquor store robbery or children running from the apple tree in one's backyard, is automatically associated by all humans with a guilty state of mind, and the passport, cash, and disguise, of course, fall into that category. DNA evidence, on the other hand, is totally foreign and alien to a jury. This is not to suggest that the DNA evidence should not have been presented (although the prosecution piled complex DNA evidence upon more DNA evidence, instead of condensing its presentation and simplifying it). But under no circumstances should it have been presented to the exclusion of so much conventional evidence that was available to the prosecution in this case.

These conventional pieces of evidence have been the basis for hundreds of thousands of criminal convictions throughout the years. In addition to jurors' associating this type of evidence with guilt, it has two other built-in advantages. It's the type for which there rarely is a legitimate answer other than guilt; and if the fleeing party attempts an innocent explanation, those words — usually a fabrication — not only sound silly, but can be shown and demonstrated to be silly in court. Secondly, this type of evidence confirms the scientific evidence (here, mostly DNA), and vice versa — i.e., the two types of evidence have a synergistic effect upon each other.

Most unbelievably, more so than the suicide note and gun, passport, cash, and disguise evidence put together, the prosecutors never presented the extremely incriminating statement Simpson made to the police on the day after the murders. Give me a yellow pad and one hundred hours, and I would have convicted Simpson on that statement alone.

The interview took place at Parker Center from 1:35 to 2:07 p.m. on June 13, 1994. It was tape-recorded by the interviewing officers, Philip Vannatter and Thomas Lange, and I have heard the entire thirty-two-minute audio. (The unedited transcript of the interrogation is in Appendix A.) The detectives were rather inexpert questioners who failed to pin Simpson down as much as they could have on his precise activities throughout the entire previous evening. They also did not ask good follow-up questions, and most unfortunately, it was they who terminated the interview. Since, at the time of the interview, they already strongly suspected he was guilty, why didn't they try to elicit from him as much as they could, continuing until either he said he didn't want to talk anymore or his celebrity lawyer finally deigned to enter the room and instruct Simpson or insist that he not answer any more questions? Isn't this just common sense?

In any event, the detectives *did* succeed in getting enough out of Simpson to convict him out of his own mouth alone. Since Simpson's left middle finger was bandaged, they asked him: "How did you get the injury on your hand?" Simpson responded, "I don't know." He then proceeded to say that the first time he cut his finger was in Chicago, but then immediately added words that suggested he had first cut himself the previous night, saying, "But at the house I was just running around." He was "running around," he told the detectives, the previous night (the night of the murders) while he was getting ready at his Rockingham estate to go *to* Chicago.

Lest there be any confusion in anyone's mind that Simpson admitted cutting himself the night of the murders, i.e., *before* he allegedly cut himself again later in Chicago, the following questions and answers clear this up.

> Vannatter: *We've got some blood on and in your car, we've got some blood at your house,* and it's sort of a problem.
> Simpson: Well, take my blood test.
> Lange: Well, we'd like to do that. We've got, of course, the cut on your finger that you aren't real clear on. Do you recall having that cut on your finger the last time you were at Nicole's house?
> Simpson: A week ago?
> Lange: Yeah.
> Simpson: No. *It was last night.*
> Lange: Okay, so last night you cut it.
> Vannatter: Somewhere after the dance recital?
> Simpson: *Somewhere when I was rushing to get out of my house.*
> Vannatter: *Okay, after the recital?* [The recital was several hours before the murders.]
> Simpson: *Yeah.*
> Vannatter: What do you think happened? Do you have any ideas?
> Simpson: I have no idea, man.

The detectives also tell Simpson that in addition to the blood in his car and home they also found blood in the driveway of his home.

> Lange: Well, there's *blood at your house and in the driveway,* and we've got a

search warrant, and we're going to get the blood. *We found some in your house.*
Is that your blood that's there?
Simpson: If it's dripped, it's what I dripped running around trying to leave.
Lange: *Last night?*
Simpson: *Yeah.*

In another part of the interview, Simpson says, referring to his bleeding at his Rockingham estate while getting ready for his trip to Chicago, "I knew I was bleeding, but it was no big deal. I bleed all the time. I play golf and stuff, so there's always something, nicks and stuff, here and there." Of course, no one, even a hemophiliac, bleeds "all the time." Not only isn't Simpson a hemophiliac, but "nicks" don't cause you to bleed all over your car and home and the driveway of your home. Moreover, the cut to Simpson's left middle finger was not a "nick." It was a deep cut.

To anyone listening to Simpson's voice on the thirty-two-minute audio, he comes across as having a guilty mind. Most noticeably, there's a total absence of outrage and resentment, or even surprise on his part, that he's being considered a suspect in these murders. Also, his rather sluggish inflection certainly suggests no eagerness on his part to participate in the endeavor to find out what happened. If anything, there's a suggestion that he's cooperating only because he senses it would look curious if he didn't. He also seems to be somewhat hesitant, halting, and uneasy in his answers. This lack of spontaneity suggests he was thinking about what was the best answer for him to give. He was also contradictory. For example, when the detectives asked him when was the last time he had driven his Ford Bronco the previous day (June 12, 1994, the day of the murders), he first responded that it was "in the morning," then immediately changed his answer to "in the afternoon," then shortly thereafter changed it again to "eight-something, seven, eight, nine o'clock, I don't know, right in that area." Additionally, there's no indication in his voice or his words that he is grieving over what happened to Nicole, or even shocked by what happened. Simpson's demeanor during the interview is consistent with and fortifies all of the other evidence pointing unerringly to his guilt.

The testimony of the prosecution's many witnesses (including Pablo Fenjves, a neighbor of Nicole's, who heard the "plaintive wail" of Nicole's Akita dog around 10:15 p.m.) places the time of the murders somewhere between 10:15 and 10:20 p.m. The defense witnesses place the murders around 10:30 to 10:40 p.m. So we can conclude the murders occurred somewhere between 10:15 and 10:40 p.m. The last time anyone saw Simpson before the murders was around 9:35 p.m. when Simpson's houseguest friend, Kato Kaelin, says he and Simpson returned to Simpson's home after going to McDonald's for a hamburger. The first time anyone saw Simpson thereafter is around 10:55 p.m., when the limo driver saw a large black figure, who turned out to be Simpson, even by the defense's own admission, enter the front door of his home. At the trial, the defense presented no evidence attesting to the whereabouts of Simpson between 9:35 and 10:55 p.m., and the murders occurred around the same time, between 10:15 and 10:40 p.m.

This is what we have, then, from Simpson's tape-recorded interview with the LAPD detectives. *From Simpson's own lips, he admits dripping blood all over his car and home and on his driveway around the time of the murders!* And when they asked him how he got the cut to his left middle finger that caused all the bleeding, he answered: "I don't know." When they asked him again later in the interview, he replied: "I have no idea, man." That ridiculous statement alone, all by itself, shows an obvious consciousness of guilt. But much, much more important, what is the statistical probability of Simpson's innocently cutting himself very badly on his left middle finger *around the very same time* his former wife and male companion are brutally murdered? One out of ten million? One out of a million? One out of one hundred thousand? And even if we make that extravagant assumption, when you cut yourself, unless you're in a frantic, frenzied state—as Simpson obviously was—you stop the bleeding with your hand or your handkerchief and you put on a bandage. You don't bleed all over the place.

The statement could hardly be more powerful and irresistible circumstantial evidence of guilt, yet unbelievably, the jury never heard the tape because the prosecutors never introduced it into evidence. I hate to embarrass Clark and Darden, who are good people. But a brutal murderer walked out the courtroom door with a smile on his face in large part because of their virtually unprecedented incompetent performance at the trial. As the West Virginia mountaineer said: "No matter how thin I make my pancakes, they always have two sides." But there aren't two sides to this issue. Simpson's statement should have been introduced. Whatever small negative it might have had to the prosecution (and there appear to be absolutely none here, but even if there were, small negatives are not uncommon, sometimes even where a defendant flat-out confesses—e.g., he adds he had been drinking) was greatly overshadowed by its extremely incriminating nature. And whatever reason the prosecutors may come up with to justify not introducing Simpson's tape-recorded statement, it will be pure, unadulterated claptrap, bunkum, tommyrot, rubbish, blather. There is no *valid* explanation. Whatever they come up with can only be a lame excuse.

What reasons have they given thus far? They wanted Simpson to testify at the trial, they have said, so they could cross-examine him, believing he couldn't withstand cross-examination. During cross-examination they would, of course, use the statement he gave the police to impeach him if his trial testimony varied in any way from this previous statement. Introducing the statement on their own during their case-in-chief (when they present their evidence), they argue, would have allowed Simpson to get his version of events before the jury without his having to subject himself to cross-examination.

As can be seen from the transcript of the interview, Simpson accounts, though poorly, for his time on the night of the murders, and a source of mine (on the prosecution team in the Simpson case) down at the district attorney's office told me, "Marcia wanted to be able to argue" — as she did in her summation — "that Simpson couldn't account for his whereabouts during the subject time." If the DA introduced the statement, this line of "reasoning" continues, "she couldn't make this argument because Simpson did account for his time, even though we knew he wasn't telling the truth."

This is astonishing nonsense coming from supposedly experienced prosecutors. Anyone knows that in the criminal law, accounting for one's time means an accounting that can be verified or corroborated by a third party or parties, or at least by documentary evidence, not just the defendant's word. *Of course* Simpson was going to say he was doing something (something else) at the time of the crime. He wasn't going to say he was dead between 9:35 and 10:55 p.m. But his version of events, as we have seen, couldn't have been more incriminating to himself.

There were two fundamental problems with this trial tactic of the prosecutors. Number one, they were taking an enormous risk that Simpson would decide not to testify (which, indeed, is what happened), and at that point it might be too late for the prosecutors to introduce his statement, since during their rebuttal, they would be limited to controverting evidence and testimony offered by the defense during the defense's case. And if Simpson didn't testify, the defense could argue there would be no testimony of his to impeach.

Number two — an even more fundamental problem, one that clearly shows me these prosecutors knew very little about prosecuting a criminal case — is that the jury already knew that Simpson had made the statement. On direct examination of Lange and Vannatter before the jury, the prosecutors elicited the information that the detectives had taken a statement from Simpson, but then the prosecutors went on to other matters. At that point, the jurors naturally wondered two things. One, they wondered what Simpson had told the police, and two, they undoubtedly wondered why the DA wasn't offering the statement into evidence for their

The police pursue the white Bronco, June 17, 1994. *(Los Angeles Times Photo / Robert Lachman)*

RIGHT. Prosecutor
Christopher Darden shows
a portrait of Nicole Brown
Simpson to the jury to
contrast with photos of a
battered Nicole during
closing arguments.
(AP/Wide World Photo)

BELOW. Prosecutor Marcia
Clark shows signs of weari-
ness during the closing
days of the Simpson trial
as fellow prosecutor Hank
Goldberg looks on.
(AP/Wide World Photo)

ABOVE. Defense Attorney Johnnie Cochran puts on a knit ski cap before the jury to disprove the prosecution's theory that Simpson wore a cap to hide his identity the night of the murders. (AP/*Wide World Photo*)

LEFT. O. J. Simpson defense attorney Robert Shapiro emerges from a group of media as he arrives at the Criminal Courts Building. (AP/*Wide World Photo*)

ABOVE. O. J. Simpson and fiancée Nicole Brown are shown here attending the Los Angeles Dodgers vs. Cincinnati Reds baseball game in Los Angeles on August 18, 1980. *(AP/Wide World Photo)*

RIGHT. An undated family photo of Ronald Goldman. *(AP/Wide World Photo)*

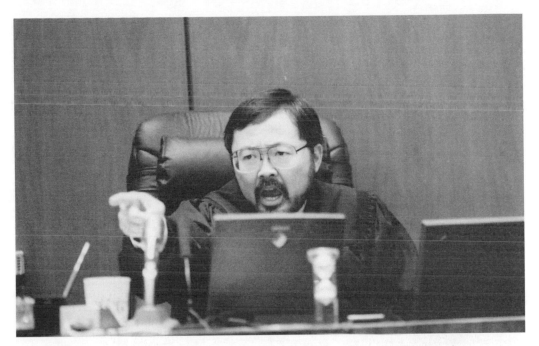

ABOVE. Los Angeles Superior Court Judge Lance Ito yells in court during the trial. *(AP/Wide World Photo)*

BELOW. O. J. Simpson and his defense attorney F. Lee Bailey, left, consult with each other. At right is Simpson defense attorney Carl Douglas. *(AP/Wide World Photo)*

ABOVE. Thomas Johnson, from San Diego, California, autographing one of the many signs in support of O. J. Simpson at the front gate of his house in the Brentwood section of Los Angeles before the trial. *(AP/Wide World Photo)*

RIGHT. A security guard and a dog, believed to be the Akita dog named "Kato" owned by Nicole Brown Simpson, stand by the gate of Simpson's home Saturday, July 2, 1994. Authorities believed the persistent barking of "Kato" alerted neighbors to quickly discover the murder scene. *(AP/Wide World Photo)*

ABOVE. Los Angeles District Attorney Gil Garcetti talks to the media after the verdicts on Tuesday, October 3, 1995. At right is prosecutor Hank Goldberg. Woman at left is not identified. (AP/Wide World Photo)

BELOW. John Hobbs, of Los Angeles, reading one of the many publications featuring stories on O. J. Simpson on sale at a newsstand in Los Angeles. (AP/Wide World Photo)

This photo of a photo of evidence presented July 5, 1994, at Simpson's preliminary hearing, shows a glove described to have been found by Los Angeles police detective Mark Fuhrman at the Simpson home in Los Angeles. The photo indicates where the glove was found. (AP/Wide World Photo)

LEFT. Blood-stained sheets strewn along the entryway of the Los Angeles–area condominium of Nicole Brown Simpson on Monday, June 13, 1994, the day after the murders. (AP/Wide World Photo)

ABOVE. Prosecutor Marcia Clark points to an evidence chart during her closing arguments. (AP/Wide World Photo)

BELOW. O. J. Simpson attempts to put on the bloody glove found at the crime scene, declaring to the jury that it doesn't fit. (AP/Wide World Photo)

ABOVE. Prosecutors Marcia Clark and Christopher Darden listen to defense attorney Johnnie Cochran (not pictured) as he gives closing arguments. (AP/Wide World Photo)

BELOW. Witness "Kato" Kaelin points to an overhead projection while testifying. (AP/Wide World Photo)

RIGHT. Los Angeles police detective Mark Fuhrman testifies at a hearing. (AP/Wide World Photo)

BELOW Attorney Johnnie Cochran holds on to O. J. Simpson as the not-guilty verdict is read on October 3, 1995. Left is F. Lee Bailey and second from left is Robert Kardashian; at right is Robert Shapiro. (Los Angeles Daily News/Myung J. Chun, pool)

RIGHT. Deborrah Hopkins Neely and Ken Mitchell, right, react at Godfather II, a Chicago southside restaurant, as the verdict comes in. Neeley is a waitress at the restaurant and Mitchell is a jewelry sales rep. *(AP/Wide World Photo)*

BELOW. Barbara Sipes, of Humboldt, Tennessee, reacts to the verdict as she and others gathered in the television and electronics department of Sears in Jackson, Tennessee, to watch the announcement. *(AP/Wide World Photo)*

consideration. This couldn't possibly have been good for the prosecution in the jury's eyes. And as if that weren't bad enough, on cross-examination of prosecution witnesses, whenever the defense alluded to the statement in any of its questions, Clark or another prosecutor would stand up in front of the jury and vigorously object to any reference to the statement. That looked absolutely terrible, and has to have hurt the prosecution's credibility in the jury's eyes. The jurors have to have asked themselves why the prosecution wanted to prevent them from hearing what Simpson had said.

Above all—and I know they say there are exceptions to every rule, but this rule has no exceptions, and if there are any budding prosecutors reading this book, they can laminate what I'm about to say in their wallets— the prosecution should *always* convey to the jury that as representatives of the people they *want* to present all relevant evidence on the issue of guilt. They should never be put in a position before the jury of trying to suppress relevant evidence. It's for the defense to try to suppress evidence, not the prosecution. How is it possible the prosecutors in this case apparently did not know this?

So the statement Simpson gave the police—which by itself was enough to convict him—not only wasn't used by the prosecutors to help their case, but it actually hurt them. Cochran, in summation, could have made so much more than he did out of the fact that the prosecution didn't want the jury to hear Simpson's statement. But he did obliquely suggest to the jury what was already very clear to them—that the prosecution didn't want the jurors to hear it. Cochran told the jury: "We know, according to the testimony in this case, that he [Simpson] talks with Vannatter and Lange once he gets down there. [But] *we heard nothing else about this conversation.* After he makes this statement, *which we haven't heard . . .*"

I want to pursue this matter of Simpson's statement a bit further because it is so very important and, as it played out in the courtroom, so very strange. You'll have to pay close attention to follow the convoluted reasoning of the prosecution *and* the defense, and if somewhere along the way you began to wonder if you're hearing about insanity, you are. Keep in mind throughout this discussion that other than the DNA evidence, Simpson's statement to the police was by far the most incriminating piece of evidence against him, extremely helpful to the prosecution and extremely damaging to the defense.

On May 24, 1995, Rockne Harmon, one of the district attorney's two DNA specialists, asked LAPD criminalist Collin Yamauchi—in an effort to show that Yamauchi did not have a belief in Simpson's guilt that could have influenced him in interpreting his initial DNA blood analysis in the

LAPD lab against Simpson—if what Yamauchi had heard in the media caused him to expect what the outcome of his test would be. Yamauchi said he heard in the media that Simpson had been in Chicago at the time of the murders and had an airtight alibi (i.e., that Simpson was innocent). In a sidebar conference requested by Judge Ito, Johnnie Cochran argued, "The people have brought this out, and now we think we have a right to put on Mr. Simpson's entire statement. They've opened the door, Your Honor, with a Mack truck, and we think we can walk through it." Cochran cited a California Evidence Code section (Section 356) providing that if one side introduces a part of a statement, the other side can present the whole of the statement so that the part that was heard will not be taken out of context. (Ostensibly, then, Cochran is saying he wants to introduce Simpson's statement, a statement that can only bury his client.) Quoting the *Los Angeles Times* coverage of the court proceedings: "Marcia Clark, her voice rising to a shout, argued heatedly against the statement's admission"—i.e., Judge, you just can't let this statement in, this statement that will win the case for us. Earlier, when Cochran was cross-examining Lange, and Cochran began to allude to the statement, Clark had objected so many times (right in front of the jury, of course) that Ito called the attorneys to the sidebar to discuss the issue outside the jury's presence.

In fact, Cochran thought that Clark was so strident that he said Clark had "become hysterical" in her opposition to Simpson's statement coming in. Judge Ito ruled that Section 356 of the Evidence Code did not apply here, since what Yamauchi heard was not a part of or included in anything Simpson said to the police on the afternoon after the murders.

Throughout the trial, the defense acted as if it wanted to introduce the statement, this statement which all by itself convicts Simpson. The question is, were they as hopelessly and utterly and completely incompetent as Clark and her colleagues were on this issue? Did they not see how the statement could bury their client? Or, knowing how damaging it was, and knowing also how incompetent the prosecutors were, did they bluff the prosecutors into believing that they truly *wanted* the statement to come in, and the prosecutors reflexively said to themselves, "Well, if the defense wants this, we have to keep it out"? The evidence is clear that it's the latter. Incompetence is very common, but the prosecutors' type of incompetence was so extreme that I doubt it was shared by the defense in this case. Proof that the defense didn't want the jury to hear their client's *entire* statement, as Cochran had originally said, is that when push came to shove and Ito asked for briefs on the issue, the defense asked to have introduced *only* "those portions" of Simpson's statement to the police dealing with what he was doing at his estate around the time of the murders — i.e., the defense did *not* want the jury to hear about all the bleeding its client admitted to, and the fact that he had no idea how he got cut.

Listen to the remarks on this issue (before Ito ruled that the defense could not introduce the statement, or any portion thereof) by the two law professors employed by the *Los Angeles Times* as trial analysts on a day-to-day basis. One said: "What could be better [for the defense] than jurors hearing O.J.'s claims of innocence without subjecting him to cross-examination?" (But what's *in* the statement crucified Simpson, out of his own lips, with virtually nothing in the statement helping him.) The other analyst said: "What a windfall. If the defense can get O.J.'s statement [the one that buries O.J.] before the jury without his taking the stand, then they have overcome a big hurdle. The defense can explain the cut on O.J's finger without O.J.'s having to testify." (But Simpson doesn't explain. He says he doesn't know how he got the cut.) This same analyst, a bitter enemy of common sense, told the media, "The statement that he gave police was not all that damaging. He doesn't go in there and confess."

So the prosecution is desperately trying to keep out evidence that can win the case for them, and the defense (originally) is *ostensibly* trying to get into evidence that which will lose the case for them. How do you make sense of this? You don't. What I have described here is logic turned on its head, a topsy-turvy world, like the one Alice found on the other side of the looking glass, where nonsense makes sense. Or maybe it's like a farce, or a cartoon, where one angry combatant says to the other, "If you don't shut up, I'm going to hit your fist with my nose." I have the type of humor that can laugh at absurdity, but visualizing in my mind's eye what Simpson did to the two victims in this case, this type of insanity over Simpson's statement only induces the most mirthless of smiles in me.

A sobering footnote to the prosecution's not offering Simpson's statement. A few weeks after the verdict I spoke on the phone with one of the main prosecutors in this case, who worked on it behind the scenes full-time. This is someone whom I respect, a salt-of-the-earth type who is one of the most highly regarded prosecutors in the office. When I asked him why he and his people hadn't introduced Simpson's tape-recorded statement, he told me something which sums up the inadequacy of the prosecution in a nutshell. He said to me, and I remember his exact words, "Well, Vince, you know, he never *did* say he did it." If this doesn't stagger you, then you probably wouldn't notice if Mike Tyson punched you in the face. What difference does it make if he didn't confess and say he did it? It means nothing at all. In fact, no one in his right mind expected Simpson to confess. Yet the prosecution treated Simpson's not confessing as evidence which they wanted to keep away, *at all costs*, from the jury. But this is madness. To treat his not confessing as sufficient justification for not admitting the exceedingly incriminating things he *did* say is simply mind-boggling. It's the type of thing that makes you wonder if you heard right.

But sure enough, the same prosecutor, in a subsequent television interview (a two-hour A&E special on the Simpson case on December 20, 1995, that I also participated in), said: "The statement was tantamount to a denial. And as a prosecutor, ah, such statements tend to be very self-serving, and there's a tactical evaluation that goes into whether or not you're going to admit a self-serving statement made by a defendant." In an interview for the same show, another prosecutor who was part of the support prosecution team said: "There was enough in [Simpson's] statement that he was clearly denying the crime. Yes, there were things we could have argued about, but the overriding fact was that what would have come out of this evidence was that he denied doing this." *So what* if it's obvious from Simpson's statement that he's denying guilt? The jury *already knows* he has pled not guilty and is denying guilt. If he hadn't denied guilt, if he had admitted committing the murders, there wouldn't have been a trial. To these prosecutors, Simpson's admitting dripping blood in his car, home, and driveway on the night of the murders and his having no idea how he got the cut were overridden by the fact he denied committing the murders. And these are the people who were representing the state in the case of *People of the State of California v. Orenthal James Simpson, a.k.a. O. J. Simpson,* Los Angeles County Superior Court Case BA#097211.

The first prosecutor I've referred to here did add in the interview for the A&E special something that had at least a small amount of substance to it. He said that one consideration for not introducing the statement is that Simpson's cutting himself on the night of the murders came out anyway through two defense witnesses, Drs. Huizenga and Baden. But this, of course, is not a valid explanation. By the time the doctors testified, the prosecutors had already rested their case, and when they did so, the prosecutors would not have had any way of knowing for sure that there would be any testimony from the doctors about Simpson's cuts. Secondly, Huizenga, who examined Simpson two days after the murders at the request of the defense, said he never asked Simpson, nor was told by him, *how or even when* Simpson had sustained the cuts he saw on Simpson's left hand at the time of the examination.

Baden testified Simpson told him he got a small cut before leaving for

Chicago when he went into his Bronco to retrieve some items and he saw "some blood" (and cut himself again in Chicago on a drinking glass in his hotel room when he learned of Nicole's death). In any event, this testimony was fleeting and tangential to the main testimony of both doctors. There was nothing to indicate to the jury it was a major issue, and what the jury did hear was secondhand. In no way can it even begin to compare with the prosecutors' playing Simpson's thirty-two-minute tape-recorded statement for the jury as the centerpiece of their case (aside from the scientific evidence), and the jury's hearing Simpson's own voice saying that he cut himself on the night of the murders but had no idea how. Merely telling Dr. Baden that he got a small cut and saw "some blood" is light-years away from the jury's hearing Simpson acknowledge he was bleeding in his car, in his home, and on the driveway.

When I spoke to Detective Tom Lange about why the district attorney didn't introduce Simpson's taped statement, he said: "We [referring to himself and his partner, Phil Vannatter] pushed and pushed and pushed the DA to put this statement on because we knew it was devastating, but it was Marcia's decision not to do it." When I asked him why, he responded: "I don't know. I respect Marcia. I think that because of the Fuhrman thing they [the prosecutors] were trying to distance themselves from the LAPD whenever they could."

"But the time during the trial that the DA should have introduced the Simpson statement," I said, "was long, long before the Fuhrman tapes even surfaced. Furthermore, this was Simpson's own voice. What was the defense going to say, that it was you and Phil impersonating him?"

"Vince, I know what you mean. I agree with you," Lange said.

When I asked Lange, a twenty-five-year veteran of the LAPD who has investigated over two hundred homicide cases, "Tommy, have you ever been on another case in your career where the DA decided not to introduce so much incriminating evidence?" he responded, "To be perfectly honest with you, no."

Another very powerful piece of evidence that the prosecution mysteriously did not introduce, at least during its case-in-chief, was photos and videos of Simpson from his days as a TV football commentator wearing highly distinctive Aris Isotoner Light leather gloves identical (right down to the extra-thin leather, stitching pattern, V-shaped vent at the wrist, and cashmere lining) to the gloves found at the Bundy murder scene and on Simpson's Rockingham estate. The photos and videos dated from a Chicago Bears game on December 29, 1990, through games in early 1994. In some photos and videos Simpson wore dark brown gloves (the color of the evidence gloves), and in others black.

A buyer from Bloomingdale's in New York testified at the trial that on December 18, 1990, eleven days before the Bears game, store records showed Nicole had bought Simpson two pairs of these same men's Aris Isotoner Light leather gloves for $77, the color and size unspecified in the charge-card receipt. Only three hundred pairs of these gloves, manufactured in 1990 exclusively for Bloomingdale's, were extra-large (Simpson's glove size) brown gloves, the type found at the murder scene and at Simpson's Rockingham estate. And of these three hundred, Bloomingdale's sold 200 to 240 of them in 1990. Pretty good circumstantial evidence of guilt, right?

It doesn't even take a law degree to understand that the prosecutors should have introduced this evidence during their case-in-chief right after they marked the Bundy and Rockingham gloves as evidence, but they didn't. After the prosecution rested, the defense, which knew from discovery that the prosecutors had this evidence, made every effort to ensure it did nothing during its case-in-chief which would allow the district attorney to introduce the evidence during rebuttal. Predictably, when Clark told the court in rebuttal she wanted to introduce the photos and videos in evidence, Cochran objected: "We've opened no doors on this . . . and we vigorously oppose any attempt on their part to introduce the evidence. Why didn't they put it on in their case-in-chief?" Judge Ito, who was liberal to both sides on the admissibility of evidence, hesitated, but decided to allow the prosecution to present the evidence.

I don't know about the videos, but I do know the prosecutors had a photo, a still frame, from one of the videos way back in 1994 before the trial started. I know because I sent them one I had seen, and I assume other people must have, too. So, inexplicably, the prosecution took an enormous risk, and could easily have been prevented from introducing this strong evidence of Simpson's guilt.

Since the trial, the Simpson jurors, of course, have heard about much of the evidence of guilt that the prosecution, because of its incompetence, did not offer, such as the suicide note, passport, disguise, etc.

The Simpson jurors, naturally, have a vested interest in sticking by their verdict. Nonetheless, Carrie Bess, one of the Simpson jurors and coauthor of *Madam Foreman* with two other Simpson jurors, writes in that book: "Since I've been out, I'm dealing with a lot more things that I had no idea were involved. I was shocked, truly shocked, over a lot of the evidence that was held from us, because I would have thought if [the prosecutors] were truly trying to get to the root of this case, they would have brought everything to us. I don't know how the defense would have handled it but I would have given it a lot more consideration because what we had to deal with was *no comparison* to what they had on the outside."

And on NBC's *Dateline* show on January 16, 1996, host Stone Phillips interviewed Carrie Bess, Armanda Cooley, and Marsha Rubin-Jackson, the three coauthors of *Madam Foreman*. Phillips mentioned Simpson's taking off with Cowlings in the Bronco and having a gun, a passport, a lot of cash, and a disguise. When Phillips then asked why Simpson would be running away, and with all these items, if he wasn't guilty, Rubin-Jackson said, "Right." Phillips then said: "In the [upcoming] civil case, the question is not reasonable doubt, it's preponderance of the evidence. In other words, is he more likely than not to have done it? How would you vote on that based on what you know now?" Whereupon Rubin-Jackson said: "I don't want to get this wrong because I'm standing by my verdict, but based on what I've heard since I've been out, I would have to vote guilty."

As we have seen, a great amount of very incriminating evidence was never presented by the prosecution to the Simpson jury. Despite this, Marcia Clark told the jury at the start of her opening argument: "We have exhaustively tried to give you every piece of information that could possibly be relevant to answer the question we are here to answer." Unbelievable.

When we get away from all the powerful evidence of guilt the prosecutors did not introduce at the trial and into the way they handled the rest of their case, we leave the realm of the unprecedented, the bizarre, and encounter more conventional manifestations of incompetence. I'm not going to nitpick the prosecutors' performance. And if I had covered the trial I'm sure I would have been aware of many blunders in addition to ones I'm going to mention briefly here. But the mistakes and blunders I will mention are more than enough for the purposes of this book.

There was, of course, the typical incompetence that one sees in the great run of prosecutors and trial lawyers in general—inadequate preparation. For instance, the prosecutors in the Simpson case did not prepare some of their witnesses for cross-examination nearly as well as they should have. Take Dennis Fung. Fung admitted to me there was no such preparation of him by the prosecution. "We were just caught off-guard," he said.

Indeed, it was clear that they didn't even put in enough time preparing themselves and their own witnesses for *direct* examination. Just one example: Clark, trying to establish that Officer Robert Riske, the first officer at the Bundy murder scene, had preserved the integrity of the crime scene for the arrival of the police technicians, asked Riske rhetorically about his training in securing crime scenes at the police academy. Riske's answer, which stunned Clark: "They kind of glossed over it. They don't really train you."

The glove demonstration, of course, we all know about. Many feel it was the pivotal point in the trial, from which the prosecution never recovered. This, from the June 26, 1995, edition of *Newsweek*: "It was either one of the greatest acting jobs of all time (by an actor of limited skills), or one of the biggest bungles ever committed by a district attorney's office. Or it may be both. But last week . . . as O.J. Simpson poked and wormed his hands into the infamous bloody gloves . . . he seemed to wiggle his way a bit closer to being a free man."

"Too tight" (some newspapers reported the words were "They don't fit"), Simpson said loudly enough for the jury to hear as he *seemingly* struggled to tug the leather gloves over his broad palms.

In *Madam Foreman*, Simpson juror Carrie Bess writes: "When I saw that demonstration, I thought, why in the hell didn't the prosecution try that glove on somebody else that had the same size hands as O.J. before they allowed him to get out here and do this? I was sick when I saw they didn't fit because I just thought for sure that they were going to fit."

It is, of course, astonishing that the prosecutors would ask Simpson to try on, before the jury, the left-hand glove found at the murder scene and its right-hand mate found on the grounds of Simpson's Rockingham estate without knowing, *for sure*, they would fit. You simply don't take an enormous gamble like that at a trial, particularly when there is no pressing need to. I doubt if a first-year law student would so recklessly roll the dice. Certainly the defense was not putting pressure on the DA to have the demonstration. And it wasn't as if the prosecutors didn't know there could be problems. In fact, in the sidebar conference shortly before the glove demonstration took place in front of the jury, Clark said: "The only problem is, he has to wear latex gloves [worn to prevent contamination of the evidence gloves] underneath . . . and they're going to alter the fit." (The other problem, it turned out, was that because portions of the gloves had been soaked in blood and left to dry, they had shrunk. Also, the gloves, undoubtedly Simpson's, had been worn by him in the rain and snow covering NFL games, and when left to dry, some shrinkage would have been inevitable.)

At that sidebar, Darden only asked the court to permit a glove demonstration with a *new* pair of the subject gloves, not the evidence gloves themselves, and Ito had overruled Cochran's objection, merely making the passing observation that it might be "more appropriate for him [Simpson] to try the other gloves [the evidence gloves] on." When the sidebar ended, there was no indication whatsoever one way or the other what the prosecution was going to do. Court reporter Janet M. Moxham, who was present, told me: "Chris [Darden] didn't want to have O.J. try on the evidence gloves, but a few minutes after the sidebar Marcia whispered something in Chris's ear and Chris almost immediately asked for the demonstration. It took everyone by surprise. It was Marcia's idea, I'm sure."

However, Darden has always been the one whom everyone criticizes for the demonstration since it was he who asked for it. And whether it's because chivalry among men for women (Darden for Clark) isn't dead in America or what, he has always accepted full responsibility for the blunder, never indicating that blame should be placed elsewhere or shared. But not only was Marcia Clark with him while all this was going on, she was the chief prosecutor, and therefore the reasonable assumption is that he acted with her knowledge as well as consent. As indicated, the court reporter goes further and fixes the blame on Clark. But whoever is to blame, it was a disaster, and although the prosecutors put on evidence to mitigate the damage (the evidence gloves had shrunk, though this was disputed by the defense; the new gloves, which were the same as the evidence gloves in style, make, and size, were eventually used in a demonstration, and fit Simpson well, etc.), the vivid memory etched in the jury's mind was that the gloves they knew the killer used did not fit Simpson comfortably—he was not able to extend his fingers fully into the tips of the gloves. "In plain English," Simpson juror Brenda Moran told reporters after the verdict, "the gloves didn't fit."

But should these very same gloves have fit Simpson properly? Perhaps forgetting he was still onstage, Simpson did in fact slip these same gloves *off* his hands quite easily, a fact which Marcia Clark noted to the jury in her final summation. And that gets us into perhaps an even more fundamental error committed by the prosecution team with respect to the glove demonstration. I have seen no mention of this elsewhere, but I was shocked the moment I saw it.

The prosecution took the position that even though the gloves had shrunk and even though Simpson was wearing latex gloves, they still would have fit Simpson if Simpson had not prevented the fit by the way he positioned his hands and fingers. Darden said Simpson faked it. "Could we ask him to straighten his fingers and put them in the gloves as one would normally put them in the glove?" Darden asked sarcastically during the demonstration. And Clark, in her summation, told the jury that the gloves did fit, but Simpson "didn't want to show" that they did.

Well, the gloves were very important pieces of evidence in this case. And you don't turn over any evidence in any case to the defendant, of all

people, and have *him* tell *you* whether there's a fit or match. That's ludicrous. You have a third party put the gloves on him, feeling Simpson's
hand and fingers along the way to ensure he doesn't do anything to inhibit the fit. Say, for example — and this isn't an exact parallel — a gun is
found on the defendant's person or in his home and the police believe it
may be the murder weapon. They test-fire the gun, and with a comparison microscope see if the markings or striations on the test-fire bullets
match up with the evidence bullets. Obviously, they don't turn the gun
over to the defendant and have him conduct the test and report back to
them. It's absolutely remarkable what the prosecutors did with the gloves,
letting Simpson be in complete control and be the one to decide whether
there was a fit.

Going on, I found the number of prosecutors trying the case was not
only completely unjustified, but more importantly, counterproductive.
Apart from DNA, which is so complex that both the prosecution and the
defense teams had to bring in special DNA lawyers to handle this phase
of the case for them, the Simpson case was not a complex case at all. The
prosecution could have easily gotten by with one lawyer to handle the
DNA, and one lawyer (two at the very most) to handle all the other witnesses, such as the lay witnesses, the coroner, LAPD detectives and
criminalists, and so forth. That's what happens in virtually all cases, and
there's no problem at all. And then they needed at least one prosecutor,
possibly even two, to handle the blizzard of written motions filed by the
defense, which required long hours in the library the trial prosecutors
didn't have time for.

But like a wide-eyed neophyte, Garcetti foolishly assigned an unprecedented twenty-five prosecutors to the case, thirteen full-time and twelve
part-time. Instead of Marcia Clark's handling nearly all the non-DNA
witnesses, several different prosecutors handled witnesses before the jury.
This resulted in a disjointed, almost amorphous prosecution, with no one
prosecutor establishing the rapport and credibility with the jury that is so
important at the time of final summation. Remarkably, Clark, the lead
prosecutor, went three entire months (from March 31, 1995, to June 30,
1995) without handling one witness before the jury.

Whenever I prosecuted a murder case, I always at least aspired to a
masterpiece. Whether I achieved it or not is another story. But you cannot have a prosecutorial masterpiece with so many hands in the pot. By
analogy, if you're painting the *Mona Lisa*, you don't assign different sections to different painters.

Another very surprising and harmful error the prosecution made in this case is that they frequently violated a basic, fundamental prosecutorial technique, namely, that when you know the defense is going to present evidence damaging or unfavorable to your side, you present that evidence yourself. Now that's just common sense, right? Well, apparently it's not. I'm absolutely amazed how day in and day out, even with many experienced trial lawyers around the country, this isn't done. The damaging evidence comes out, for the first time, on cross-examination.

Introducing negative evidence yourself achieves two objectives. Number one, it conveys to the jurors your willingness to see that all evidence, unfavorable to your case as well as favorable, comes out—that you are not trying to suppress it in open court or outside their presence. And this helps to establish your credibility with the jury. Secondly, it frequently converts a left hook by your opposition into a left jab. If it doesn't do that, it will almost always shave at least a few decibels off the opposition's trumpets. It indicates to the jury that the evidence can't really be all that bad if it was matter-of-factly and almost cavalierly brought out by you on direct examination of your own witness. What I try to do on direct examination, basically, is conduct my opponent's cross-examination for him, but bringing out the information the way I want it to be brought out. When my opponent stands up for his cross-examination, he has very little to ask. For the most part, almost to his embarrassment, he's going over old ground. Again, this is just common sense, right?

Let me give you a few examples of how the prosecutors in this case didn't do that. Nicole's sister, Denise Brown, and Candace Garvey (baseball Hall-of-Famer Steve Garvey's wife) testified that at the dance recital just hours before the murders, Simpson was acting strange. He wasn't friendly at all, ignored their glance, seemed to be "simmering," and had a faraway, "spooky" look on his face, the inference being that he was in a dark, ugly mood, the type of mood that culminated in the murders later that evening. On cross-examination, the defense presented a video, *which the prosecution had*, showing Simpson right after the recital in a very good mood, laughing, at one time almost doubling over with laughter. That was just terrible for the prosecution. It was very embarrassing. It is unbelievable to me that the prosecution never presented the video itself on direct examination. Denise Brown and Candace Garvey could have testified that yes, that's the way he looked afterward, but that's not the way he was looking and acting before and during the recital. The effect of their damaging testimony against Simpson would probably have been diminished only slightly. As it was, however, their testimony was totally negated by the video.

Here, as with Simpson's statement to the detectives, it looked as if the prosecution was trying to suppress evidence. Although Cochran failed to make this argument in his summation, he easily could have walked over to the prosecution table during his address and told the jury: "These prosecutors here are representing the People of the State of California. They are public prosecutors who are supposed to be dedicated to fairness, justice, bringing out the truth. But if you had to rely on them, you never would have seen that video. They weren't about to show it to you. We had to show it to you." (Cochran, in fact, did make a similar argument with respect to other evidence allegedly suppressed by the prosecution during the trial. This will be discussed later in the book.) What could be worse than to have the jury believe the prosecution is suppressing evidence favorable to the defense, and deliberately deceiving the jury? I mean, if Clark and Darden didn't know that you're supposed to present evidence like this, wasn't there anyone in their humongous supporting staff to advise them of it?

Another example. Cellmark, the lab in Germantown, Maryland, that conducted most of the DNA testing of blood for the prosecution, failed two proficiency tests back in 1988 and 1989. That's the type of thing a prosecutor automatically brings out on direct examination. Yet it came out, for the first time, when the defense conducted its cross-examination.

In Marcia Clark's opening statement, she failed to mention that the first part of a preliminary DNA report said that Nicole Simpson had EAP [erythrocyte acid phosphatase] enzyme type B blood under her fingernails and on her thigh. The problem is that neither Nicole, Goldman, nor Simpson had that EAP type. But the very next sentence read: "Nicole cannot be excluded as a source of the blood if the EAP enzyme type B observed on the items were degraded [by the elements] from enzyme type BA [Nicole's EAP enzyme type] to [EAP enzyme] type B." Since the first part of the report, by itself, is very misleading in that it points to a killer other than Simpson, and since a prosecutor has to assume (unless he knows otherwise) that his opposition is going to have the morals of an alley cat, Clark should have mentioned the entire paragraph in her opening statement. Instead, she never referred to it at all. Cochran in his opening statement only mentioned the first, misleading part of the paragraph. So until this matter was cleared up by the prosecution during its DNA presentation on May 11, 1995 (more sophisticated DNA tests found that the blood *was* Nicole's), the Simpson jurors had been viewing all the evidence in the case through a clouded lens. In their minds, that blood probably belonged to some unknown assailant. All they had heard on the subject up to that point was Cochran's misleading statement to them way back on January 25, 1995. And even after the DA cleared the matter up, there remained the problem of undoing over three months of impressions by the jury about the entire case, which had been influenced by the original erroneous information.

Another instance of the prosecutors' inability to handle negative evidence is found in the testimony relating to Simpson's response to hearing of Nicole's murder allegedly for the first time. Clark tried to establish through LAPD detective Ronald Phillips that when he called Simpson at Simpson's hotel room in Chicago the morning following the murders (6:05 a.m.) to notify him of his former wife's death, Simpson did not respond as an innocent person would. She asked Phillips, "Did he ask you how she was killed?" "No." "Did he ask you when she was killed?" "No." "Did he ask you where it had occurred?" "No." "Did he ask you anything about the circumstances of how his ex-wife had been killed?" "No."

But on cross-examination, the detective said Simpson *had* asked him, when he was first told his wife had been killed, "What do you mean she's been killed?" Although Simpson, by asking only this one question and no more, clearly did not react to the news as one would expect an innocent person to react, that one question did certainly go in the direction of the precise type of curiosity which Clark had tried to suggest that Simpson did *not* have. Either Clark did not realize that she should have brought out on her direct examination what came out on cross, or she didn't know this information herself because she never adequately questioned her witness during trial preparation. In other words, I cannot exonerate her of one charge without thereby convicting her of the other. This type of situation occurred time and again at the trial, making it look to the jury as if the prosecution was deliberately trying to conceal from them relevant information which was helpful to the defense. Nothing can be worse for a prosecutor's credibility with the jury.

The level of prosecutorial sophistication by Clark and Darden in this case was so low that I can't even be sure that they know they were supposed to introduce evidence negative to the prosecution themselves. After all, if they knew, why did they fail to do it so often? My guess was that they were vaguely familiar with the technique, but it wasn't something that they naturally did, that was automatic to them.

There *were* instances during the trial when the prosecutors did put the negative evidence on first. Even there, however, they failed in the most obvious effort they made at preemption.

The deputy medical examiner who conducted the autopsies on Nicole and Ron was Dr. Irwin Golden. According to the August 1, 1994, edition of *Time* magazine, several deputy DAs had urged Clark to get someone else assigned as the autopsy surgeon because of Golden's alleged sloppiness, but she reportedly declined, saying, "It'll be okay." Clark was assigned to the case on June 13, 1994, and the autopsies were conducted on June 14, 1994, so she would have had time to intervene.

Golden had other problems. It was obvious at the preliminary hearing in the Simpson case that he was not a good witness, as many people are not. He couldn't have been less personable, he gave curious looks to his questioners, and he spoke with little authority. Moreover, as opposed to many coroners, whose occupation one would never guess, Golden *looks* like a coroner.

In his autopsies of Nicole and Ron, the prosecution conceded that Golden made many errors. He discarded the contents of Nicole's stomach, which would have helped pinpoint the time of death (Golden did, however, dutifully record the contents and the state of the food's digestion); he did not run a sexual assault test on Nicole's body (he didn't feel the need to, since Nicole's intimate apparel was in place and there was no other evidence suggesting a sexual assault); he, or his assistants, mislabeled a container of Goldman's bile as urine; he didn't ensure that coroner lab technicians X-rayed the bodies; he failed to detect knife cuts in Goldman's shirt and jeans; he failed to take a palm print from Nicole's right hand; he overlooked a contusion on her brain; and so on. Errors of this sort occur in virtually every autopsy. It's just that in this case Golden made more than usual, some thirty of them. And in a previous case, Golden reportedly had confused an entry with an exit gunshot wound, not an uncommon thing.

Feeling that Golden would be a liability and embarrassment on the witness stand, the prosecutors decided not to call him to testify at the trial. Instead they called Golden's superior, the coroner himself, Dr. Lakshamanan Sathyavageswaran (hereafter, Dr. Lak), to testify to the autopsies that Golden had performed. Right off the top, this was a very poor strategy. It looked, once again, as if the prosecutors were trying to hide something from the jury, and this fact was spotlighted by the defense when Dr. Lak conceded on cross-examination that it was the first time in his career he had ever heard of the DA's calling to the stand a doctor other than the one who had conducted the autopsy relevant to the case.

All prosecutors, all lawyers, in fact, have been confronted many times in their careers with very poor witnesses. But if you prepare them adequately, there's no problem at all. There is no question that Dr. Golden could have been prepared to the point where (apart from his autopsy report, which was water over the dam) he would not have been a further liability. After all, he had been with the coroner's office since 1981, had conducted more than five thousand autopsies, and had testified in close to a thousand cases during his career. The fact that he was still around means that he couldn't have been that bad. If he had been, the DA's office, long ago, would have insisted to the coroner that he not be used on any criminal homicide case. Golden's colleagues, in fact, consider him to be competent. The prosecutor could easily have had Golden himself concede the errors he made in the Simpson case, and that would have been it. Even his mistaking an entrance for an exit wound in a previous case is no problem at all. Suppose it had gone as follows:

"Doctor, in the case of so-and-so, you apparently misidentified an entrance wound as an exit wound, is that correct?"

"Yes."

"You do, of course, know the difference between an entrance wound and an exit wound?"

"Of course."

"Would you briefly explain to the jury the differences between the two types of wounds, such as their configuration, the presence or absence of an abrasion collar, and so forth, which a pathologist such as yourself looks to in distinguishing these wounds?"

"Yes." And the witness does so.

"How many autopsies in your career have you had where you had to determine whether a wound was an entrance or exit wound?"

"Probably five hundred or so."

"In any of these other five hundred autopsies did you misidentify an entrance wound as an exit wound?"

"No."

And that would be it.

Even if, because of Golden's incompetence in a particular case, he reached an improper conclusion as to the cause of death, or his incompetence went so far as to affect the outcome of the case, it is not fatal when you concede it and also bring out that these were one or two out of five thousand autopsies. Instead, the DA hid Golden from the jury, and the defense kept reminding the jury of this fact.

But the DA's mishandling of the situation went far beyond not calling Dr. Golden to the stand. Their handling of the coroner, Dr. Lak, was counterproductive. Dr. Lak's testimony on direct examination in this case should have taken no more than two hours, at the very most. In the Manson case, with similar issues as to the time of death, the type of knife used, etc., and with seven victims and two coroners, and with 169 stab wounds, seven gunshot wounds, and many other types of wounds, I probably took about a total of two hours on direct examination. Here, the special prosecutor who handled Dr. Lak, a highly intelligent prosecutor by all accounts who was the head of the DA office's Medical-Legal unit, apparently did not use his fine mind as much as he should have. And if Marcia Clark was the chief prosecutor, and knew herself how to handle the testimony of the coroner, how could she have *permitted* this prosecutor to do what he did?

Dr. Lak was on the stand for eight entire days of *direct* examination, probably a record, going into extraordinary detail and depth on every single point imaginable. The testimony even included a reenactment of the murders themselves, with Dr. Lak playing the villain's role. But none of this was necessary. The coroner only had to be called to testify to key things like the cause of death (which, of course, everyone already knew), the number of stab wounds and which ones were the fatal ones, the approximate time of death, a description of the murder weapon or weapons (single- or double-edged blade, etc.), and whether any of the mistakes made by Dr. Golden were the type which could have affected the ultimate conclusions.

Examining Dr. Lak for eight straight days created problems harmful to the prosecution. Such an extremely detailed and lengthy direct examination could only convey to the jury that the prosecution felt there were many critical issues surrounding the autopsy (which there were not), and furthermore that the prosecution was very worried about these issues. If it wasn't, why would it spend so much time on them? When you have the burden of proving guilt beyond a reasonable doubt, injecting this type of thought into the jury's mind is nothing but a self-inflicted wound.

But the examining prosecutor, Brian Kelberg, was not satisfied with this. He wanted Dr. Lak to tell the jury *exactly how* these murders happened, right down to the order of the stab wounds. If I, being as pro-prosecution as I am, found myself saying, "How in the hell does the doctor know this?" you can imagine what the jury was thinking. It was pure speculation and conjecture. By trying to prove precisely what happened, the DA was setting up a burden for himself which he not only didn't have under the law—the DA only had to prove Simpson committed these murders, not precisely how—but couldn't possibly meet.

And when Dr. Lak was unable to come up with a plausible scenario himself as to any particular point, Kelberg was gracious enough to help him speculate. For instance, at one juncture, Kelberg suggested to Dr. Lak that with a blunt object like a fist or the butt of a knife, the killer inflicted a powerful head blow that knocked Nicole to the ground, then he inflicted four stab wounds to the left side of her neck, and as she lay there bleeding and unconscious, but not dead, the killer left her and entered the adjacent area to attack and kill Ronald Goldman, then returned minutes later to inflict the final and fatal ear-to-ear cut, from left to right, across Nicole's throat. Could this have happened, Kelberg wanted to know from Dr. Lak. The coroner paused, then said: "That's a possibility."

This scenario suggested that the murders took place contemporaneously—as opposed to Simpson's killing Nicole first, and when Ron showed up within seconds, killing him to eliminate a witness. But if that was so, why didn't at least one of the victims run away or at least scream? Apart from that problem with the hypothetical, why would the prosecution be offering these hypothetical scenarios that would induce its witness to answer using the word "possibility"? What could be gained by this? Again, the prosecution only has the burden of proving Simpson's *guilt* beyond a reasonable doubt. It did not have the burden of proving *how* he committed the crime beyond a reasonable doubt. Above all, you do not want to bombard the jury for eight consecutive days with speculation, with conjecture, or with words like "possibility."

Naturally, and predictably, when the defense called its own expert forensic pathologist to the stand, Dr. Michael Baden, he testified that the county coroner's testimony about "possible" ways the murders were committed was somewhat ludicrous. When Kelberg challenged Baden's position on this point, Baden replied: "It's possible [the murders were committed] by a bushy-haired stranger who is right-handed from behind," he said, smiling, "but it's also equally consistent with a bald-headed midget from the front who is left-handed."

Baden, who testified he had billed the Simpson team in excess of $100,000 for his services, challenged Dr. Lak's findings in several areas. Lak, for instance, concluded that Ronald Goldman was killed in one minute; Baden concluded Goldman could have fought for five, ten, or even fifteen minutes after his jugular vein was cut. He also disputed the conclusion of Dr. Lak, who once worked under him at Bellevue Hospital in New York, that Nicole's head injury (believed by both sides to be before the fatal knife slash) would have rendered her unconscious.

What the jury was left with was experts on both sides speculating about what happened, never a healthy situation for the prosecution in a criminal case. Though a certain amount of this is inevitable, Kelberg, with the obvious knowledge and consent of the lead prosecutors, ratcheted the problem up considerably by his eight-day orgy of speculation.

I mentioned earlier how, with the errors committed by Golden in the autopsy, the prosecution finally was determined to preempt the defense. And Kelberg did so, in spades, pushing Dr. Lak to describe, in detail, all of Dr. Golden's errors, and broaching, himself, the estimate that Golden had committed at least thirty errors, an estimate Dr. Lak acknowledged reluctantly. (Dr. Lak testified, however, that all of the errors were minor and insignificant lapses of judgment that in no way fundamentally changed or undermined the findings of Dr. Golden on the "big-ticket items.") But in an eight-day direct examination of the coroner (which, as I've indicated, was seven and a half days too long), out of the hundreds upon hundreds of questions the prosecutor asked to preempt the defense, neither he nor his colleagues had it within themselves to ask the most important preemptive question: "Doctor, I take it you cannot testify to a reasonable medical certainty whether there was one or more than one killer?"

Coroners can many times reach this conclusion when, for instance, it's obvious from the dimensions of the wounds that one or more than one knife was used in the killing. Kelberg did elicit from Dr. Lak that although it was his belief that only one knife with a single-edged blade was used to cause all of the stab wounds, he could not exclude the possibility that some of the wounds were caused by a knife with a double-edged blade. However, he not only failed to preempt the defense on the "reasonable medical certainty" language, but more importantly, after asking his knife question, Kelberg failed to ask the obvious but necessary follow-up question whether Dr. Lak could testify to a reasonable medical certainty that only one killer was involved. (The possibility of more than one killer was from the start a key argument of the defense, since the prosecution's stated position was that Simpson and Simpson alone committed these murders. If the defense could establish that more than one killer was involved, although that wouldn't exonerate Simpson from a theoretical or legal standpoint, it would severely harm the credibility of the prosecution's entire case.) This question should have been an automatic one for Kelberg, particularly since he was so determined to preempt the defense. But it wasn't. On cross-examination, Shapiro almost immediately asked: "Doctor, can you tell us with a reasonable degree of medical certainty how many people are responsible for these homicides?" "No," the coroner replied. Of course, when Shapiro got this concession it had to have sounded important to the jury, whereas if it had been brought out matter-of-factly on direct examination, its impact would have been substantially diminished. Do you know what the headline was here in Los Angeles the following day, after Kelberg spent eight days trying to preempt the defense? "Defense Elicits Key Concession from Coroner."

Shapiro, on cross-examination, spotlighted the fact that eight days of direct examination was far more speculation than substance when he asked this good question: "Isn't it true, doctor, that after eight days of testimony, there's only four facts you can testify to with a reasonable degree of medical certainty: that the deaths were homicides, that the fatal injuries were stab wounds, that the victims bled to death, and that they were killed between 9:00 and shortly after midnight?" Though the doctor gave a long, defensive answer, the essence of it was that this was true.

The real core of the defense case had to be a police frame-up. After all, Simpson's blood had been found at the murder scene, and if it wasn't planted there by the police he had to be guilty. Thano Peratis, the male nurse from the Los Angeles Police Department who withdrew blood from Simpson's right arm at approximately 2:30 p.m. on the afternoon following the murders, testified at the preliminary hearing that he withdrew around "7.9 to 8.1 cc" (cubic centimeters) of blood from Simpson's arm. This is the vial of blood that Detective Philip Vannatter carried to Simpson's Rockingham estate so he could personally deliver it to police criminalist Dennis Fung. (See further discussion in Appendix C.) But at the trial the prosecutors could account for only 6.5 cc of the blood. The defense, throughout the trial, tried to persuade the jury that the missing, unaccounted-for 1.5 cc of blood was what LAPD detectives sprinkled at the murder scene and inside Simpson's Bronco and home in their effort to frame him.

Now, since the prosecutors knew there was no frame-up and there had to be some innocent explanation for the discrepancy, wouldn't common sense (if not on the part of the two lead prosecutors, then on the part of one out of the remaining twenty-three) have told them to go back to Peratis to ask him if he could have been mistaken, or ask Peratis's coworkers if they could shed any light on the matter? I mean, does one have to be especially bright to think of something this obvious?

Here, with twenty-five prosecutors, not one apparently thought to do something that's so basic a teenager would know to do it: *Pick up the phone and talk with Peratis.* Instead, long after his earlier testimony, he had to call them. During the trial, Peratis was recovering from coronary bypass surgery. When he learned that the defense was in effect building most of its case around what he called a "goof" on his part, Peratis told me he ran a test with water at the dispensary with his supervisor and found he had withdrawn a little over 6 cc. So, he said, he contacted the DA's office and stated he was certain he had simply made a mistake in his preliminary hearing testimony, that he had in fact probably withdrawn about 6.5 cc.

What does the DA then do? They send one of their prosecutors, Hank Goldberg, together with a DA investigator and photographer, to Peratis's home to interview him on tape explaining his "goof." Judge Ito permitted the prosecution to play the tape before the jury, which was a blatant error on his part, because you simply can't offer testimony against a criminal defendant without his having an opportunity to confront and cross-examine the declarant on the point of the declarant's testimony. (Ito's ruling was in clear violation of the confrontation clause of the Sixth Amendment to the U.S. Constitution.)

But shouldn't the prosecutors have made the assumption that Ito would not permit them to introduce the tape without there being a defense attorney present to cross-examine Peratis?

And even if they assumed Ito would make a wholly improper ruling and admit the tape, why would they want to do this anyway? With the defense screaming about a law enforcement conspiracy to frame Simpson throughout the trial, why would they want to do something—going out to Peratis's home without having a defense attorney present to cross-examine him—which could only look suspicious to the jury? Cochran, predictably, argued all these points in his final summation and suggested that the prosecution had actually put words in Peratis's mouth and got him to say what he did on the tape. To compound the problem—remember Rosemary Woods's eighteen-minute Nixon tape gap?—the video had a fourteen-minute gap. Defense attorney Peter Neufeld, smelling a rat, accused the DA investigator, on cross, of probably coaching Peratis during the gap, which, of course, the investigator denied.

But what is the even more obvious thing the prosecutors should have done in this case if Peratis had, in fact, goofed in his earlier testimony and he had only withdrawn 6.5 cc from Simpson's arm as he said on the tape? When I saw how the DA was handling this matter it took me one second, and no longer, to think of it. There is no reason why it should take any of you readers any longer.

The obvious thing to do was to ask Peratis how much he *normally* withdrew from people's arms, and if he said 6.5 cc, the next thing you do is go to his office and speak to the other nurses to see if they could confirm that Peratis normally withdrew only around 6.5 cc. If they could, you call these people to court, of course, as witnesses. And again, you also ask the nurses how much blood *they* normally withdraw, and if they too withdraw around 6.5 cc, and it appears to be a pattern, or a policy, you of course put this evidence on. Only in that way could the prosecution even hope to establish Peratis's credibility—to satisfy the jury that Peratis wasn't just trying, as an LAPD employee, to save the prosecution's case, or worse yet, had been coached by the prosecutors.

Does any of this require any intelligence at all? Isn't this just common sense? Yet none of this was done in this case. There's an old proverb that there are forty lunacies, but only one common sense. Voltaire once observed that common sense is not that common. We certainly know it wasn't among the twenty-five prosecutors who represented the state in the

Simpson case, and the lead prosecutors were supposedly among the top trial lawyers in an office of over one thousand prosecutors, the largest DA's office in the nation.

It should be noted that several of the jurors, posttrial, have referred to the missing blood as the blood the LAPD planted to frame Simpson, and they found Peratis's taped statement to be suspicious and not worthy of belief.

When we look at the way the prosecutors handled the Mark Fuhrman issue, once again, it seems they hardly could have done any worse. How is it possible that the prosecutors ignored the allegations of two people— Kathleen Bell and Andrea Terry, both of whom gave every indication of being responsible people, neither of whom had any ostensible ax to grind— that Fuhrman had, in fact, used the word "nigger" in the ten years prior to the trial? Bell, a real estate agent who is white, said she met Fuhrman at a Marine recruiting station in Redondo Beach, California, in 1985 or 1986, and Fuhrman told her that if he had his way, "he would like nothing more than to see all niggers gathered together and burned." Although Bell eventually said publicly she believed Simpson was guilty and did not want to testify because it might help his defense, she nonetheless had written a letter to the defense setting forth her contact with Fuhrman and his racial animus and use of the word "nigger," a letter the prosecution had. In addition, the prosecution knew that Bell's friend Andrea Terry, also white, was present with Bell at a tavern and dinette in Redondo Beach in 1986 when Bell ran into Fuhrman again, and she heard Fuhrman make similar remarks to Bell.

Why would Bell and Terry and, subsequently, people like Natalie Singer, the former girlfriend of Fuhrman's police partner, who said Fuhrman told her that "the only good nigger is a dead nigger"—be willing to commit perjury? Yet Marcia Clark referred to the charges of these people as "nonsensical allegations" and dismissively labeled Fuhrman's accusers "Kathleen Bell and her ilk."

But if Clark didn't believe Fuhrman's accusers, what about Fuhrman himself, her own witness? Didn't she believe what he himself had said in the past? The prosecutors knew that in September 1981 Fuhrman had applied for a stress-related disability pension from the LAPD, and in interviews with psychiatrists, he used racist slurs and spoke of his antipathy for minorities. For example, he told Dr. John Hochman (page eight of Dr. Hochman's December 16, 1981, report to the Workers' Compensation Section of the Los Angeles City Attorney's Office) that in the Marines, he "got tired of having a bunch of Mexicans and niggers, that should be in prison, telling me they weren't going to do something." These interviews and hearings were more than ten years before the trial, but obviously they were illuminating and lent credibility to what others had said about Fuhrman.

True, all of this was completely irrelevant to the murder trial—objectively speaking. But since the defense had desperately sought to inject race into the case and Judge Ito, in a gross judicial error, was going to let them get away with it, isn't it common sense that you sit down with Fuhrman in a room, tell him the facts of life, that there is little doubt in your mind that "nigger" has been one of his favorite words, and make him cough up the fact that he has, in fact, used racial slurs in the past ten years? Don't you tell him that if he admits it, we can put it behind us? But if he denies it and the defense controverts what he said with witnesses the defense said they already had (the defense was claiming at the time there would be many more), it most likely would be blown completely out of proportion, thereby helping the defense case immeasurably, and there would even be calls that he be prosecuted for perjury?

Don't you automatically do basic, fundamental things like this? And isn't it very likely that if this had been done, Fuhrman would have admitted his past use of the word "nigger"? This fact could then have been brought out in the way the prosecutors wanted it to be brought out on direct examination. Fuhrman could have simply admitted using the term, telling the jury how his life on the streets dealing with the criminal element (see discussion later in this chapter) had caused him to use it. If true, he could have added that he no longer used the term. If this had been done, his use of the word "nigger" would have been a dead issue. Some damage would have been sustained, but if the prosecution had preempted the defense, it would have been a molehill compared to what the prosecution ultimately suffered the way the issue played out. The testimony of Kathleen Bell and the others, even the Fuhrman tapes, would have been irrelevant and inadmissable, since they would not be impeaching Fuhrman's testimony. Isn't that the way you prosecute a case?

It was bad enough that the prosecutors did not preempt the defense on the Fuhrman issue, but even failing to do that they still could have perhaps saved the day if they hadn't literally folded their tent on Fuhrman. Winning is often simply getting up off the ground one more time than your opponent. After the Fuhrman tapes surfaced, the prosecution stayed away from Fuhrman the way the devil stays away from holy water. He was a leper, a pariah, to the prosecution. As for the defense, they couldn't get enough of him. They loved him. He was like the manna miraculously supplied to the Israelites in the wilderness. On the one hand, the defense vilified Fuhrman, yet it also embraced him for the lifeline he represented to them.

But did the prosecution have to distance itself from Fuhrman the way it did? I'm not so sure. Since the prosecutors continued to believe firmly that however much of a racist Fuhrman was he did not plant the glove or try to frame Simpson, why didn't they try to rehabilitate Fuhrman with the jury? I know I would have. It had long been reported in the media that many who knew Fuhrman well not only rejected the notion that he would have framed Simpson but said his racism, if any, was limited to the black street criminal element.

The best piece on this was a November 8, 1995, article in the *Los Angeles Times*. The reporter, Greg Krikorian, interviewed partners and coworkers of Fuhrman's in his years at the LAPD. As you read the comments, ask yourself if you agree with my assessment that they could only have helped the prosecution in mitigating the damage done by the Fuhrman tapes, Kathleen Bell, and the other civilian witnesses. Also be aware that even on the Fuhrman tapes, the last time Fuhrman used the word "nigger" was in 1988, seven years before his testimony in the Simpson trial. My excerpts from the article are lengthy, but since Fuhrman was such a central figure at the Simpson trial, a witness around whom the defense built its main contention that the police framed Simpson because of his race, I feel they are necessary. Some have said that Fuhrman has become one of the most hated men in America. But just as God always gets good press, and we never hear the devil's side of the story, I think it's important that Fuhrman, who has become reclusive, be heard from through those who knew him.

"The person that the world knows . . . on the tape . . . is racist, who made terrible remarks, who probably represents all the filth the world has to offer. The Mark Fuhrman I know . . . is not that. He's not a racist," said Sergeant Roberto Alaniz, a Latino whom Fuhrman sought as a partner in 1984.

Sergeant Ed Palmer, an African-American who first met Fuhrman at the West Los Angeles Station last year [1994], said: "I am as shocked as anybody. . . . If Mark were a racist and especially as big a racist as he sounded on the tapes, I would have no trouble telling him he was the scum of the earth. But I really can't." And this from Carlton Brown, a black homicide detective who was Fuhrman's partner for most of 1993: "I really can't say whether Fuhrman was racist or not, but if he harbored those feelings, it was not evident to me. I don't know, maybe I'm naive. But I don't think so."

Recent interviews with more than half a dozen LAPD officers, all but one of them black or Latino, do not prove that the now-infamous former detective did not commit the brutalities he bragged about on a series of taped interviews between 1985 and 1994. Nor do they prove he did not mask racist views while sharing a patrol car, meals, even an apartment, with the officers who worked with him, trained him, and even partnered with him. But the portrait that emerges from these interviews is clearly one at odds with the Mark Fuhrman whose conduct and comments have sparked investigations of the Los Angeles Police Department—including a new probe by the U.S. Justice Department. Instead of the rogue-racist cop whose very presence in the O. J. Simpson case has again put the LAPD on trial, interviews suggest that Fuhrman was aggressive, even arrogant, but if he harbored the vile views expressed to others, he concealed them from many with whom he worked.

Not unlike Clint Eastwood's fictional San Francisco film detective Harry Callahan, several LAPD officers said Fuhrman could be sullen and purposely shocking. But that was just his personality, they added, and it never overruled his logic when it came to arrests. Maybe, some say, he never shared his true feelings with them. Or maybe, they suggest, he changed after he underwent psychological counseling in the mid-1980s. But their view of Fuhrman, the officers insisted, was not based on naiveté. Palmer said: "Being African-American, when you come into contact with someone, you listen to them and pick up on things. There have been times I have worked with people [and] you wonder about them. I never wondered with him. I knew he was aggressive. I knew he was a little arrogant. But I never got racism at all. If he were that way, and as much a racist as the tapes indicated, then it would have come out somewhere, and somebody would have spoken up. That code of silence nonsense," Palmer said, "you get to that point, somebody would have spoken up."

Sergeant Paul Partridge, who has known Fuhrman since the two were rookies 20 years earlier, said about Fuhrman:

"If he were back on the job [today] he would risk his life for anyone on the job or anyone in this city, just like he always had. And he wouldn't care who they were."

Partridge recalled that Fuhrman had one long-term girlfriend who was a Latina—a fact some might find curious for a man many see as an uncontrollable racist. And, he recalled, the woman was not one to tolerate any racial slights. "She was very vocal, very proud of her heritage," Partridge said. And [Fuhrman] had no problem with that."

Partridge and other officers told the *L.A. Times* reporter that in the language of police work, where officers can risk their lives each day confronting the worst society has to offer, a distinction is made between what is said in the moment and how someone really feels. After hearing the Fuhrman tapes, Partridge said that he was angered that someone he knew would say such things, but he was still convinced that in Fuhrman's mind the remarks were directed at criminals, not an entire race. Alaniz agreed. When Fuhrman returned to work in 1982, after being denied a stress-induced early retirement, Alaniz had a talk with Fuhrman.

"I asked him [his feelings about minorities] after he told me about his stress thing," Alaniz said. "He said he never had problems with blacks, that he only had problems with the criminal element. He told me what he said [to the pension board] . . . that having worked his assignments, he couldn't stand the criminal element, that he couldn't stand gang members. He hated them. [He said] that it got to the point that he would probably shoot them rather than give them the benefit of the doubt" in a standoff.

Several months after Fuhrman was back on duty, Alaniz said, he asked Alaniz to be his partner—a move Alaniz and some others say flies in the face of Fuhrman's reputation as an officer who disdained minorities. "I just don't understand how a person that is very racist would choose to work with a minority officer in a two-man car," Alaniz said.

Before they became patrol partners, Alaniz said, LAPD superiors decided that Fuhrman's true feelings about race should be put to the test by making Fuhrman's first partner—after his pension hearings—a black female officer. Fuhrman was paired for two months with Officer Toish Ellerson. Alaniz said Fuhrman told him he enjoyed working with Ellerson. And he recalls Fuhrman saying, "They have this idea that I can't stand working with a black person and a woman. But they are wrong. She is a very pleasant person to work with."

For her part, Ellerson, now a sergeant in the West Los Angeles Station's Community Relations office, also had no unpleasant recollections of her time as Fuhrman's partner.

"To be blunt, I never had any problems with him," she said.

Alaniz says that Fuhrman was known as a solid cop. "His uniform was impeccable. He kept himself in shape. Shoes shiny. His tactics were good. He didn't do anything reckless."

It should be noted that Fuhrman placed second in his class at the police academy when he was receiving training to become an LAPD officer, and a review of his police file revealed that in his nineteen years on the force there were only four citizen complaints filed against him, an average number. Alaniz said the only time he saw Fuhrman lose his temper was during the arrest of a long-haired transient who Fuhrman, a former Marine and a Vietnam veteran, learned had avoided the Vietnam War by fleeing to Canada.

Alaniz said Fuhrman told the transient, "You know what I was doing when you were in Canada?" Alaniz said it was the only time he had ever seen Fuhrman really loud with somebody. "He got pretty hostile."

Detective Carlton Brown, Fuhrman's black partner in 1993, said he got along fine with Fuhrman, adding that race "was never an issue. He treated everyone fairly. I never observed him violate civil liberties."

And as recently as last year [1994], Fuhrman never offered any hint that he harbored racist views, according to officer Palmer, who met Fuhrman at the West Los Angeles station about a month before the murders in Brentwood. As often as several times a week over a period of six months, Palmer said, he and Fuhrman met before the day shift to play basketball, often with other African-Americans. Palmer said, "We would get there at 6:30 in the morning and sometimes it would be just the two of us. I would think this man had to get up at 5:40 in the morning to play basketball with me. Why . . . if you really hate African-Americans, why would you do that? In fact, you know how some guys joke [to African-Americans] and say, 'you guys are all quick' or, 'you guys can all jump'? He never even said anything like that," Palmer said.

"Ask yourself this," Alaniz said. "What do you do with the racist? You just show them a better way . . . so they can learn. Here is a person who told the department that he was having problems dealing with minorities . . . then they put him through the psychological program and they said at some point he was rehabilitated. And later in his career he was hanging out with minority officers."

For those who may say the remarks of Fuhrman's fellow officers in the *L.A. Times* piece merely reflect the officer's code of silence, that code, which does exist to a certain degree, only applies to official inquiries about an officer's misconduct, the type that could get the officer arrested, disciplined, or fired. It doesn't apply to a statement to a reporter about a retired cop like Fuhrman. Moreover, the code of silence means you don't talk. You say you didn't see or hear anything. You don't, as in the *Times* story, say very positive, affirmative things, particularly if you are a black police officer.

And there were others besides police officers who disputed Fuhrman's racism. In an October 1994 CNN report on Fuhrman, two African-American women spoke to correspondent Art Harris. Connie Law, who met Fuhrman when he was one of the investigators on the murder of her uncle, told Harris: "As far as O. J. Simpson goes, I think he's innocent. As far as Mark Fuhrman goes, I think he's a great detective. He was great with us. . . . He didn't show any signs of racism towards me and my family." Fuhrman also investigated a case in which a black woman, Patricia Foy, resisted a purse snatcher and chased him after he fled with the purse. She told Harris that Fuhrman "told me I was incredibly brave, but I was also incredibly foolish and I should not do that again because I could end up dead. He's not a racist. They're just trying to hang something on him so they can cover up for the defense. That's all they're doing."

Another black who is convinced Fuhrman is not now a racist is Danette Meyers, a Los Angeles deputy district attorney. Although Ms. Meyers has refused to talk to the media, her close friendship with Fuhrman is well known. It started when a defendant she was prosecuting (and whom

Fuhrman had investigated) made a death threat to her. Fuhrman took it upon himself to personally guard her on his own time. They became good friends and on several occasions he had her over for dinner with his wife and two children.

Despite the positive remarks made by Fuhrman's former fellow officers and others that he was not a racist, it would seem that you don't, even in jest or to embellish a movie script for effect, say the things Fuhrman did without having some amount of racism coursing through you. And the president of an association of black LAPD officers told the *Los Angeles Times* reporter who wrote the article that several officers had approached him and told him racist stories about Fuhrman, but he never furnished any names to the reporter. In fact, Fuhrman was perceived as a racist even by those who knew him growing up in his small hometown of Eatonville, Washington, at the foot of Mount Rainier. In life there are nuances, shades of gray, and degrees, to virtually everything. But the prosecution in this case permitted the defense to paint Fuhrman before a predominantly black jury as the biggest and most virulent racist ever, someone who would've embarrassed George Wallace in his segregationist days. The jury never heard one sentence, one word, one syllable from the prosecution in defense of Mark Fuhrman. The DA treated him as if he were beyond redemption or rehabilitation. The defense, of course, treated Fuhrman as if he were the devil himself, a soul mate of Attila the Hun, Torquemada, and all the other great villains of history. Cochran, in his summation, called Fuhrman "a genocidal racist, a perjurer, America's worst nightmare, the personification of evil," even compared him to Adolf Hitler — all this without one word of rebuttal from either Darden or Clark, who even joined in the vilification. In speaking to the jury on how she was "disgusted" with Mark Fuhrman, Marcia Clark actually said. "Do we wish there were no such person on this planet? Yes." Darden told the jury: "I'm not even going to call him Detective Fuhrman if I can help it because he doesn't deserve that title." There's no question that Mark Fuhrman was defamed, vilified, maligned, and slandered far, far more at the trial than Simpson, who was accused of a brutal and gruesome double murder.

To be sure, we can be fairly certain that as to at least one matter, Fuhrman was not just "talking trash" on the tapes, that he had "walked the talk." In fact, in the entire fourteen hours of tape, it was the *only* incident that Fuhrman referred to which we know actually happened. Fuhrman told McKinny: "Two of my buddies were shot and ambushed. Policemen. Both down when I arrived. I was first unit at the scene. Four suspects ran into a second-story apartment, and we kicked the door down, grabbed the girl, one of their girlfriends, by the hair, stuck a gun to her head, and used it as a barricade. We basically tortured them. There were four policemen, four guys. We broke 'em. Their faces were just mush . . . there was blood everywhere. All the walls, all the furniture. We had them begging that they would never be gang members again. . . . The bottom line is you don't shoot a policeman. That's all there is to it."

The LAPD found that many of the things Fuhrman said matched the details of a 1978 incident in Boyle Heights, an old, heavily Mexican-American enclave hard by downtown Los Angeles in which two officers were shot (they both survived) and which generated twelve citizen complaints against sixteen officers, including Fuhrman. It was the subject of an LAPD Internal Affairs investigation, but Fuhrman told McKinny that he escaped punishment. (All sixteen officers were cleared.) "Oh, they knew damn well I did it. But there was nothing they could do about it. Most of the guys worked 77th [Street Division] together. We were tight. I mean, we could have murdered people. We all knew what to say."

Several officers who were with Fuhrman at the time say he grossly exaggerated this incident of vigilante justice. But whether he did or not, the important point to know is that all the mileage made by the defense in the Simpson case because of Fuhrman was based on the supposition that he was anti*black*, that Fuhrman and his colleagues framed Simpson because he was black. Yet this incident, the *only* one in which we know for sure he was not spinning some sort of fantasy and making himself look as macho as he could, the victims weren't black but Hispanic. More important, Fuhrman said that "*you* [not black, white, or any other color] don't shoot a policeman. That's all there is to it." There is no reason to believe that if the shooters of the two policemen had been white, Fuhrman and his fellow officers would not have responded exactly as they did.

When I asked Detective Robert Tapia, Fuhrman's supervisor at the West Los Angeles Division of the LAPD between 1989 and 1994, if he sensed Fuhrman was prejudiced against blacks during this period, he replied: "Mark's not prejudiced against blacks, he's only prejudiced against criminals, whatever their color."

One thing, I think, is clear. Clark and Darden should have fought back with every resource at their disposal. They didn't do that. They permitted Fuhrman to be tried and convicted by the defense attorneys through the testimony of complete strangers like Kathleen Bell, without the jury's ever hearing from those who knew Fuhrman best. Certainly, comments like those I presented a few pages back would have reduced the damage to the prosecution's case over the Fuhrman issue. "Up until they brought the [Fuhrman] tapes out, I thought O.J. was gone," Simpson juror Carrie Bess writes in *Madam Foreman*.

What has to rank as one of the most startling utterances to come from the prosecutors in the Simpson case was William Hodgman, the senior member of the prosecution team, telling the *Los Angeles Times* after the verdict that he and his co-prosecutors had information "about how Mark Fuhrman as a detective was a very professional detective, that in a number of instances he worked to clear suspects who happened to be African-American when new evidence [exonerating them] came out." But Bill, if you had evidence like this, don't you think it would have been a good idea to share it with the jury? I was able to confirm one of these instances. On October 6, 1994, in West Los Angeles, Shawn Stewart, a white male, was shot to death out on the street in a drug deal gone sour. Witnesses identified Arrick Harris, a thirty-year-old black male with a criminal history as the killer, and Fuhrman, the lead detective on the case, secured a criminal complaint against Harris for murder. Before the preliminary hearing, Fuhrman received information that someone else was the killer. After going out and investigating further, he formed the opinion Harris was innocent. His partner, Ron Phillips, told me that Fuhrman "worked extremely hard on the case to establish that Harris was not involved. I remember Mark telling me, 'Ron, we've got to prove this guy didn't do it before the prelim or he's going to sit in jail for a murder he didn't do.' He even got the DA to request a continuance of the prelim so he could have more time to work on the case." Fuhrman proved Harris' innocence and the district attorney's office had the case dismissed before the preliminary hearing. Phillips said he furnished the prosecutors in the Simpson case with all of the above information, but they did not introduce it. With the revelations about Fuhrman on the Fuhrman tapes being perceived by everyone as devastating to the prosecution's case, it's almost criminal that the prosecution never introduced evidence like this to the jury.

Let's stop now and ask ourselves what the prosecutors *did* do right in this case. Well, they presented scientific evidence, such as Simpson's blood being found at the murder scene, that proves Simpson's guilt. True, but is this really anything to write home about? I mean, let's grant that all of the prosecutors, as well as the defense attorneys, were intelligent, and most were also experienced trial lawyers. But presenting evidence favorable to your side, such as the prosecution's presenting DNA evidence, or the defense's calling witnesses whose testimony indicated the time of the murders was later in the evening than the prosecutors were alleging, is simply routine; it's not even worth talking about. If a lawyer's incompetence is so pronounced that he doesn't even know how to go about presenting evidence favorable to his side, it's time for him to turn the job over to one of the spectators in the courtroom.

Beyond that, I thought Darden's opening statement was articulate and persuasive, and his cross-examination of the El Salvadoran housemaid, Rosa Lopez, was effective, although clearly she was not the worthiest of opponents. There was prosecutor Brian Kelberg's cross-examination of Dr. Huizenga, in which the prosecutor's considerable medical knowledge and careful preparation converted the doctor into a prosecution witness. In her opening argument to the jury, I liked Marcia Clark's discussion of the hair and fiber evidence and how the murders were committed. I also liked her closing words to the jury in her final summation. But all of this was only getting 10 percent, instead of 110 percent, out of their case.

I should also point out to anyone who might believe that this has been Monday-morning quarterbacking on my part that they are wrong. I talked about most of these things long before the verdict. One example among many, a quote from me in the June 21, 1995, edition of *USA Today* (over three months before the verdict) as the prosecution was nearing the end of their presentation without having introduced certain key pieces of evidence: "'I'm stunned,' Bugliosi said. 'I'm aware of some very incriminating evidence they have and didn't use, and when you prosecute a case you put on everything you have,'" whereupon I mentioned Simpson's tape-recorded statement, suicide note, passport, etc. And when the prosecutors finally rested their case without introducing the evidence, I made the same comments in the July 8, 1995, edition of the *New York Times*. In fact, every time I was on radio and TV *during* the trial, one of the last times being on *This Week with David Brinkley*, I lamented the fact that the prosecutors were making very serious errors and could be doing "a much, much better job."

Before we move on to final summation, let's look at a few more miscellaneous areas of prosecutorial ineptitude in the Simpson case.

The DA's office felt that domestic violence and abuse was so much an integral part of its case that in its December 14, 1994, "Response to Defendant's Motion to Exclude Evidence of Domestic Violence," an eighty-five-page brief, the very first words were these: "This is a domestic violence case involving murder, not a murder case involving domestic violence." And later: "This is a domestic violence case at its core." The brief set forth a considerable number of examples of Simpson's physical and psychological abuse of Nicole. The brief went on to say that there was "a pattern" of abuse by the defendant that started almost immediately after he met Nicole in 1977 and continued, unabated, right up to the night of the murders, not a few "isolated events."

In a January 18, 1995, ruling, Ito said the prosecution would be permitted to tell the jury about more than a dozen incidents where Simpson had allegedly beaten, frightened, and stalked Nicole during their tempestuous relationship. And in Chris Darden's opening statement on January 24, 1995, he told the jury the murders were the final act in an abusive seventeen-year relationship. Darden set forth many instances of physical and psychological abuse, among them the incidents triggered by Nicole's leaving Simpson in February 1992 and filing for a divorce. Simpson began stalking her, following her to restaurants when on dates with other men, staring at her and her date in an intimidating way, even peering through the window of her home and watching her in an act of intimacy with a man.

Yet at the trial Darden and Clark presented only one out of several incidents of stalking Ito had ruled they could, and even to call it stalking is a stretch. A husband and wife who lived next door to Nicole testified to seeing Simpson walking back and forth for two or three minutes on the sidewalk one evening in April of 1992 around eleven o'clock outside Nicole's home on Gretna Green in Brentwood, where she lived before moving to her condo on Bundy. He never stepped off the sidewalk onto Nicole's property but stopped twice to look towards her residence before leaving. They didn't know why he was there and weren't even sure if Nicole was home, since her car wasn't parked in the driveway. Darden, in his summation, grossly misstated the evidence and said the witnesses had testified they saw Simpson step onto Nicole's property and "peer through the window." Cochran, in his summation, pointed out there was no such testimony by the neighbors.

Another incident they did not present was one just a few months before the murders in which Simpson saw Nicole with Ronald Goldman and another man having coffee at Starbucks and he stopped his car and angrily motioned for her to come over to him. In fact, the prosecution only offered about half of the incidents of domestic abuse Ito had ruled they could present, giving the defense a built-in argument that there was no pattern of domestic violence and abuse that inevitably culminated in murder, but just a few isolated incidents. The prosecution, for some mysterious reason, took a very robust case of domestic abuse that led up to murder and, eviscerating it in contravention of its own legal briefs and opening statement, transformed its case into a much weaker one. In his summation, Darden told the jury: "On domestic violence I told you [in opening statement] I was going to call a few other people. I didn't. I think you got the point. And I can't keep you here forever. Apparently this sequestration thing is a real drag, right, and I would like to end this experience."

Even the chronology with which the prosecutors presented their case to the jury was unorthodox and gave the impression of being haphazard and choppy. The facts of a case should be presented in a natural, logical sequence so they can easily be followed and understood by the jury. This was not done in the Simpson case. Bear with me for a moment, and you'll see how important this is.

Right from Cochran's opening statement (before any of the evidence was even presented) to his and Scheck's summation, the defense said the prosecution's blood evidence was "contaminated," and hence their constant "garbage in, garbage out" argument. In other words, once the blood was contaminated (which was just a theory the defense postulated throughout the trial but never once proved to be true), it was garbage, and therefore this garbage submitted for analysis could only yield a garbage result.

I don't know much about DNA, but common sense immediately told me that the defense theory had to be bogus. Even if the blood at the scene was contaminated, why would the lab test on that blood produce the result that it was Simpson's blood if it wasn't? Howard Coleman, president of Genelex, a Seattle DNA laboratory, says: "Everything we get in the lab is contaminated to some degree. What contamination will lead you to is an inconclusive result. It doesn't lead you to a false positive." In other words, contrary to what the defense argued throughout the entire trial, contamination could only decrease, not increase, the likelihood of a DNA match — that is, only decrease the likelihood that the DNA in blood found at the crime scene and at Simpson's estate would match the DNA in blood removed from Simpson's body by the police after the murders.

The problem with the word "contamination" is that it connotes to everyone something negative. But negative to whom? Since contamination can only decrease the likelihood of a DNA match, the defense argument throughout the trial that the DNA test results shouldn't be used against Simpson because the blood submitted to the lab was contaminated (by bacteria, soil, leaves, etc.) was patently absurd and fallacious. If at all, contamination should only be a prosecution argument. For instance, in a case where the prosecution is convinced that the defendant's blood has been found at the murder scene, I can see the prosecution arguing to the jury that the reason there was no DNA match is that there was contamination of the blood, which *prevented* the match.

So "garbage in, garbage out" should definitely have been the prosecution, not the defense mantra at the Simpson trial. There was no "garbage in" in this case, because if there had been, there would have been "garbage out," i.e., *there would not have been a Simpson blood match* — the test would have yielded no results. Instead, unbelievably, it was the defense (playing on the jury's conventional understanding of the word "contamination") which used the concept of contamination and the term "garbage in, garbage out" to its distinct and overwhelming advantage. Because the prosecutors weren't forceful and did not know how to make the above point effectively with the jury, the defense got away with it. With almost any jury, you have to spoon-feed them. That's what I do. I never take a chance on assuming a jury is going to see something important without my help. So many times in life things are only obvious once they are pointed out.

Certainly the prosecution did not spoon-feed the jury in this case. Whenever I caught a snippet of the DNA testimony, with its extremely complex genetic, molecular, and statistical principles and completely unfamiliar and arcane terminology, I wondered how the jury, particularly the seventy-two-year-old black woman on the jury who said during jury selection she never read the newspaper or anything at all except the Racing Form, and had difficulty understanding even it, could have followed what they were talking about.

What does any of this have to do with chronology? For over a month, the jury had to listen to endless cross-examination of the LAPD criminalists like Dennis Fung and Andrea Mazzola by the two New York DNA lawyers on how all the evidence (except, miraculously, that which had been planted by the cops who were framing Simpson) had been contaminated and mishandled. The thrust of the cross-examination was that there was so much contamination of the blood during its collection and preservation, so many errors and slipups, that the jury should disregard all the DNA test results. The reason? Garbage in, garbage out. It was only *after* the long, painful ordeal of the highly misleading cross examination of the LAPD criminalists that the DA called Dr. Robin Cotton, laboratory director at Cellmark and one of the DA's DNA expert witnesses, to explain to the jurors that none of the alleged mishandling of the evidence they had been hearing about for days on end was relevant, since contamination couldn't produce a false DNA positive of Simpson's blood. But by that time, the incorrect contamination theory had been burned into the jurors' brains, where it apparently remained. For instance, two of the jurors, Lionel Cryer and David Aldana, when asked by the media after the trial about the DNA evidence, blurted out like automatons, "Garbage in, garbage out." In *Madam Foreman*, coauthor and Simpson juror Marsha Rubin-Jackson writes: "There was a lot of discussion about how sloppily the evidence had been handled. How it could have gotten contaminated."

Since we know that first impressions are important, and since the prosecutors had already been placed on notice as far back as Cochran's open-

ing statement that the defense was going to try to float the specious contamination argument, wouldn't common sense seem to dictate that you
call Cotton to the stand for a primer on DNA *before*, not after, the LAPD
criminalists?

The DA's chronology of evidence was so, shall we say, eccentric, that
as I've indicated, instead of putting on photos and film of Simpson wearing gloves identical to the evidence gloves right after the testimony about
the discovery of the gloves (in mid-February 1995), the prosecution didn't
offer this evidence at all during its case-in-chief and tried to squeeze it in
during rebuttal on September 12, 1995, *seven months later.*

The prosecutors didn't even know when to call the coroner. The coroner is always called by the prosecution to testify to the autopsy findings
and cause of death right at or near the start of any homicide case. Here,
remarkably, the prosecutors called the coroner on June 2, 1995, over four
months after they called their first witness on January 31, 1995. Unbelievable. Show me a precedent.

There is undoubtedly much more prosecutorial incompetence in the
area of incriminating evidence which was not offered. When I told Detective Lange that I had never seen a case where the prosecution decided
not to introduce such a great amount of evidence damaging to the defendant—the suicide note, the passport, Simpson's statement, etc.—he said:
"Vince, there is so much more evidence you don't know about that the
DA didn't present."

But enough.

One final, important tag before getting into final summation. More
than being a celebrity, the main thing that Simpson had going for him
with the jury in this case was that he was a black celebrity. If the defendant had been Joe Montana, his celebrity wouldn't have gotten him a
first down with this black jury.

One of the very, very first questions the prosecutors in the Simpson
case should have asked themselves is: How can we neutralize this advantage Simpson has? The prosecutors obviously did not do this. How do I
know? Because they made no effort during the trial to chip away and
erode that advantage. In fact, they went to the other extreme. They joined
in with the millions of Simpson idolaters and encouraged the jury in the
glorification of Simpson. Picture Simpson with a sharp knife stabbing
two human beings over and over again. Now, with this thought still in
your mind, listen to Marcia Clark talking to the jurors during jury selection: "He's such a famous guy. He's such a popular guy." And, "We all saw
Naked Gun. He made us laugh." She also referred to him as a "good-

looking man" with a clean-cut image. "This is not a fun place for me to be," she said. Then, softly, "Do you feel a certain loyalty to the defendant? The defendant is such a famous guy, he's such a sympathetic guy." And, "You may not like me for bringing this case. I'm not winning any popularity contests for doing so." Unbelievable. Unbelievable. There is no other word. Again, picture in your mind what Simpson did to the victims when you think of Clark's words to the jury.

Although Clark added that whether or not the jurors personally liked Simpson, the law required them to convict Simpson if his guilt was proved, these highly flattering, sympathetic words for Simpson, particularly coming from the prosecutor's own mouth, could only serve to fortify the good feelings the jury already had for Simpson. Wouldn't a two-year-old know this?

While it was advisable for Clark to meet Simpson's fame and popularity head-on, gushing over him and granting him sympathy was clearly not the way to do it. She could simply have said words to this effect: "The defendant in this case, Mr. Simpson, has obviously been a famous and popular sports figure. You all realize, of course, that in determining whether he is guilty or not guilty of these two terrible murders, the fact of his fame and previous popularity cannot enter, in any way whatsoever, into your deliberations."

In answering the question of how to neutralize Simpson's popularity, the thought that should instantly have come into the prosecutors' minds was that throughout his adult life, Simpson had been black in color only. Many observers have postulated that part of the reason for the not-guilty verdict in this case was the antipathy for whites that some blacks have. But if there is *anyone* such a black person dislikes more than whitey, it's an Uncle Tom. And although Simpson wasn't the classically passive and submissive black memorialized in Harriet Beecher Stowe's novel *Uncle Tom's Cabin*, he easily fell within the more expansive popular definition of the term—a black who has not only forgotten his roots, but virtually turned his back on the black community, striving to become a white man in every possible way.

The prosecutors in this case should have immediately opened up an "Uncle Tom" file for Simpson and had an LAPD detective, or one of their own detectives from the DA's Bureau of Investigation, start working full-time on it to fill it up. And they should have started looking for some opportunity furnished by the defense to present the contents of that file to the jury. If Cochran intended to clothe Simpson with the garments of the oppressed black man, the prosecutors should have been ready to show the jury that those garments (like, supposedly, the gloves) just didn't fit.

More important, by far, they should have been prepared to show the jury that with all of Simpson's wealth and connections, he had never helped the black community, even when requested to do so.

Such a tactic would have been improper if the defense had decided to try the case solely on the evidence, which is the way a case is supposed to be tried. But since it decided to make a racial case out of one that involved no racial issue, the prosecutors should at least have tried to tell the jury the truth about Simpson, something they made no effort to do.

Cochran, because of his consistently loose statements and arguments to the jury in his opening statement and final argument, provided the prosecutors with the legal opportunity to introduce evidence of Simpson's not helping the black community. In opening statement, a lawyer can only refer to evidence he intends to introduce at the trial. As I will point out in the Epilogue, Cochran not only *argued* during his opening statement (which is not allowed), but referred to the expected testimony of many witnesses whom he never ended up calling. In this same vein, he blurted these words out to endear Simpson to the predominantly black jury: "This man gives five thousand dollars a year to the Angel City Links, the inner-city black organization, and the only condition of his gift every year is it has to be anonymous, that he doesn't want them to know he does this."

This was a totally improper remark, since Cochran knew he could not introduce the fact of such a charitable contribution at the trial, it having no relevance to any issue in the case. And since he couldn't, he had no right to mention it in his opening statement. But inasmuch as he did, the prosecutors should have argued (supported by a legal brief) that they had the right to offer contrary evidence. In fact, even without the Angel City Links reference by Cochran, since the defense built most of its case on the contention that Simpson was framed simply because he was a black man, evidence that showed Simpson to be black in color only would arguably be admissible. It would logically decrease the likelihood that the police would treat Simpson in the same way the defense claimed racists like Fuhrman treated a typical black man: evidence such as that Brentwood contains an extremely small percentage of blacks; that Simpson moved exclusively in the white corporate and establishment world; that other than his childhood friend Al Cowlings, virtually all of his close friends were white; that he joined an all-white, stuffed-shirt golf club in New Jersey five years ago, the first black member in the over-one-hundred-year history of the conservative club; *but above all, that he never found time to help those in need in the black community.*

In writing this book, since I had always been under the impression that Simpson had not been that supportive of black causes, if at all, I wondered what in the heck the Angel City Links were, the *only* black organization Cochran mentioned. It was a rather strange name, one I had never heard. There was no listing for such a group in the telephone directory, so I called the Los Angeles chapter of the NAACP. The woman on the switchboard had never heard of the group, nor had the person on the staff to whom she referred me. Same at the Urban League, and at the Community Services Department at Los Angeles City Hall, and at black city councilman Ridley Thomas's office, and at several other offices in the black community.

A week later I found a few free moments from my writing, so I started calling the same organizations and offices again, asking to speak to different people. Finally, I found someone at the NAACP who had heard of the Angel City Links. It was a black sorority, my informant told me, and the reason the group had no listing, he said, was that whoever becomes the sorority president each year operates the group out of her home, not a permanent office. The group, I was told, did on occasion raise money for black causes. Since the Angel City Links was a sorority, I immediately started to think it might be one that Simpson's first wife, Marguerite, or daughter Arnelle was a member of, but I reached dead ends on this inquiry, not being able to locate anyone in the group. I even called Howard University, the black school in Washington, D.C., from which Arnelle graduated, but they had no sorority by that name.

On the issue of Simpson's relationship with the black community, the first prominent black person I thought to call was Jim Brown, the Cleveland Brown's all-time football great. In the 1980s Brown and I played a lot of fairly competitive tennis together. (When he has time, he now plays golf instead, telling me it's "addictive.")

Brown, a brooding, introspective, and very intelligent man who has never been comfortable with the white establishment, has for many years been an involved activist for black causes and economic power. But in 1988, he almost completely forsook his Hollywood lifestyle to work full-time helping black criminals turn their lives around. He formed an organization called Amer-I-Can, shorthand for "In America, if I try, I can make something of myself." The underlying motivational themes of Amer-I-Can are education, a sense of self-worth, and economic empowerment. Brown oversees a sixty-hour self-improvement and life skills training program which is provided to inner-city gang members and to convicts in the major cities and prisons of the land. Amer-I-Can employs close to two hundred former gang members and ex-convicts to administer the course.

Brown has had measurable success with many young street blacks and convicts, who, of course, look up to him. Last year, the Los Angeles chapter of the Urban League honored him for his contributions in helping troubled black youth.

The football legend works closely with the very toughest black cats, none of whom, however, get tough with Big Jim, who at six feet two and just a few pounds over his football playing weight of 230 remains an imposing physical figure. In fact, in 1991, when the first edition of my drug book came out, I had a meeting with Jim at his Hollywood Hills home to try to enlist his support with black congressmen for my proposals, and as I was leaving, who starts walking in the door but the leaders of the Crips and Bloods, two notorious black gangs, for a summit meeting with Brown, which, upon Brown's invitation, I stayed to attend. There were around twenty gang members at the meeting, and although they may be the toughest dudes in the world out on the street, young men with names like Chopper, Wig Out, T, Jawbone, Playmate, Hannibal, and Twilight (now all *former* gang members, Jim told me) acted almost (not quite) like reverential choirboys around Brown.

Brown and Simpson have always maintained a friendly but not close relationship, being rivals for the title of greatest running back ever. But according to what I read, as great as Simpson was, most knowledgeable fans consider Brown to be the greatest running back ever. In yards per carry, probably the most meaningful statistic, only Brown, at 5.2 yards, is at 5 or over. All the other great runners, including Simpson, are in the 4's. Brown told me once that the reason he retired in 1965, when he had a few good years remaining in him, was that he had broken all the records at the time, including total yards gained, and was only "competing against myself."

The professional rivalry between Brown and Simpson dates all the way back to when Simpson was establishing himself as a promising runner at San Francisco's Galileo High School. One Sunday afternoon after attending a pro football game between the 49'ers and the Cleveland Browns, Simpson and his friends went to a nearby ice cream shop. To their surprise, in walked Jim Brown, the NFL's leading rusher. In a biography of Simpson, *The O. J. Simpson Story*, Simpson is quoted as saying: "The other kids were really awed but, you know, I was the leader of the gang and so I had to say something." He told Brown, "Jim Brown, you ain't so great. When I get to play pro ball, I'm gonna break all your records." Brown, who revels in competition, replied: "We'll see what you do when you get there."

Shortly after the murders, Brown, who has always been extremely outspoken and candid, remarked on television that everyone knew Simpson had a cocaine problem. He later explained that he wasn't trying to hurt Simpson, only to comment on the possible availability of an insanity defense.

When I called Brown to talk about Simpson, he was out of town on Amer-I-Can business. I left a message for Jim to call when he returned.

In the meantime, I got in touch with Celes King, the California state chairman of the Congress of Racial Equality (CORE) and for over forty years a well-known black activist. I had spoken to him a few times in the early 1970s. When I asked him if Simpson had ever helped his group, Celes said no.

"Celes, did you ever ask him?"

"You learn not to ask useless questions," Celes said.

"Are you saying Simpson never helped the black community?"

"The only group I'm aware he's ever helped out is a black sorority his daughter, Arnelle, is a member of, the Angel City Links. And she drags O.J. to some of their functions. You know, like when children drag their parents to the park on weekends."

And this is what Cochran had said (and got by with) to convince the black jury Simpson had been generous to black causes. And even with the Angel City Links we can't be sure Simpson had been giving them $5,000 annually, since Cochran told the jury that "the only condition of his gift [to them] every year is it has to be anonymous, that he doesn't want them to know he does this."

Beyond calling Celes King, I just made a few calls to knowledgeable staff members of the major black civil rights and charitable organizations. For the most part, they were reluctant to talk freely. Here's what my limited research disclosed. A staff employee at the Los Angeles chapter of the Urban League, asking that I not use her name, told me that in the seven years she has been with the organization, to her knowledge Simpson had not contributed to it or been involved with it in any way. But the previous week (early December 1995), she said, a representative of Simpson's had called the group and Simpson had then sent a contribution, the amount undisclosed. I got the very distinct impression from an NAACP staff member—who was purposely more vague than his counterpart at the Urban League—that Simpson had not helped the NAACP, at least during this person's tenure, the length of which I never learned. When I called the fund-raiser in Fairfax, Virginia, for the United Negro College Fund and asked her whether the rumor was true that Simpson had refused to participate in the annual Lou Rawls telethon to raise money for the college fund unless he was paid a fee, she answered brusquely: "I don't want to stir up any debate in the black community on an issue like this." When I nonetheless repeated my question, she said it was not true.

In the August 29, 1994, edition of Newsweek, the reporter wrote:

"Simpson often appeared at tony charity events and visited so many sick kids in the hospital he began to refer to himself as 'the Angel of Death.' But he did not give much back to African-American causes. He would promise to appear at community centers or youth programs in South-Central Los Angeles, then bow out at the last moment."

I did learn from a black acquaintance of mine, Michael Zinzun, chairman of the Coalition Against Police Abuse in Los Angeles, that for several years at Thanksgiving time Al Cowlings has delivered a truckload of turkeys from Simpson to his group, so we cannot say that Simpson has completely ignored the black community.

When Jim Brown called upon his return from back east and I asked him if he had ever called Simpson to help him out with his efforts in the black community, Big Jim chuckled and said, "I'm like Celes"—I had earlier repeated to him Celes's remark that you don't ask useless questions. Brown added: "I don't ask people I know aren't going to help." When I asked Brown for an assessment of Simpson, he said: "O.J. is the modern representation of the house Negro," who, he said, dressed well and lived much better than the plantation workers. "O.J. is not unique," he said, explaining that many blacks who have made it are like him. He lives a life, Brown said, "below whites [his white country-club contemporaries] but above blacks."

Brown, who keeps very current on what's going on in the black community, said that throughout the years, *there was no evidence of O.J. in the black community.*" He added that this neglect was "not mean-spirited on O.J.'s part." It was just that Simpson had left the community behind and it was no longer a part of his life. Brown said, "The tragedy of white America is that they find a comfort level in elevating so-called good Negroes, but this is always going to end up in disappointment, because it's false. The blacks that will make a positive difference are the ones who make the whites uncomfortable by telling the truth." He said the Simpson case had "caused confusion among blacks and whites because the African-American community tried to get behind O.J.'s cause, but he doesn't care about that community. And the white community is angry because he let them down."

Jim Brown would, of course, have responded to a subpoena in the Simpson case, and his testifying that Simpson "never had any presence in the black community" (along with all the other evidence of Simpson's exclusively white and affluent lifestyle, and testimony from witnesses in the black community whom the "Uncle Tom" investigation would surely turn up that Simpson had no time to help out poor black youth, even reneging on promises to do so), would probably have gotten the jury and the black community to actually dislike Simpson. Information like this coming from any black leader would be harmful to Simpson, but particularly if it came from someone like Brown, a football player, easily Simpson's equal, who not only did not turn his back on the black community like Simpson but has now devoted his life to it.

The bottom line is that the prosecution, like absolute fools, permitted the defense to depict Simpson to the mostly black jury—without any opposition or even attempted rebuttal on their part—not only as a football hero, but as a hero to *blacks*, which he never had been before the trial, and never deserved to be. Just another example of the terribly and pathetically incompetent prosecution of this case by the Los Angeles County District Attorney's office.

Final Summation

The Weak Voice of the People

This chapter, like the previous one, concerns the DA's incompetence during the trial, but because final summation is such a unique and critical part of the case, I am dealing with it separately.

I've always considered final summation the most important part of the trial for the lawyer. It's the climax of the case, where the lawyer has his last and best opportunity to convince the jury of the rightness of his cause. Consistent with their poor performance throughout the trial, both prosecutors (Clark and Darden) gave exceptionally bad summations, particularly in their rebuttal arguments.

Before I make some observations on the substance of the lawyers' arguments in the Simpson trial, particularly those of the prosecutors, let me tell you how I feel about final summation.

Usually, the very first thing I think about when I get on a case and begin to learn the facts is: *What* am I going to argue, and *how* can I best make the argument to obtain a favorable verdict? In other words, I work backward from my summation, the exact reverse of what is normally recommended. Since final summation has to be based on the evidence at the trial, virtually all of my questions at the trial, and most of my tactics and techniques, are aimed at enabling me to make arguments I've already determined I want to make. In fact, before the first witness at a trial

148

has even been called, I've usually prepared my summation to the jury. As soon as I learn the strengths and weaknesses of my case I begin to work on how I'm going to argue these strengths and what I'm going to say in response to the opposition's attacks on the weaknesses. Getting an early start on my summation, and continuing to expand and modify it during the trial, gives me ample time to develop arguments and articulations.

I realize I have almost an obsession about the preparation of a final summation. For instance, in the Manson case, I put in several hundred hours working on my opening and closing arguments. Of course, I was dealing with 28,354 pages of transcript. Conceding that I probably go to an unnecessary extreme, I still feel it cannot be wise to go to the other extreme and wait until the last second. You've all heard of Melvin Belli, of course. Here's what Mel says about final summation in an interview he gave for a book called *The Trial Masters*. "The night before you give your summation, when you go to bed, think in your mind's eye about what you are going to discuss the next day."

This thinking and disregard for adequate preparation of final summation is very common in the legal profession, and one of the main reasons most lawyers give terrible summations.

Louis Nizer, who passed away in 1994, was a celebrated lawyer who had always been known in the legal profession for the considerable preparation he used to put into all of his cases. His motto was that "preparation is the be-all and end-all in the trial of a lawsuit." Yet even Nizer apparently shortchanged final summation, relegating it to a relatively minor role.

I say that because in his most famous trial, in which he represented newsman Quentin Reynolds in a libel suit against columnist Westbrook Pegler, a case that Nizer was involved in for over a year, taking depositions around the world, he apparently literally waited until one second before midnight to prepare his summation. On pages 153–154 of his book *My Life in Court*, he describes the night of the last day of testimony, the night before final summation. This is what he says: "With my assistants I culled the citations from the record and *organized* a summation that would predigest the enormous amount of testimony without sacrificing emotion or lucidity. A few of my associates found themselves in grotesque postures of slumber on the edge of a sofa or on the carpet before the sun rose."

As great a lawyer as Nizer was, I have to differ with him on this point. I just don't think that's a good practice, if for no other reason than you want to be fresh for the jury when you give your summation. And yet there are so many lawyers who start working on their summation the night before they give it. (In fact, this is apparently what the two prosecutors in this case did for their rebuttal argument. See dicussion later in this chapter.) I was with Nizer about ten years ago in Chicago, and after drawing his attention to this paragraph in his book, I said, "Louie, is that *really* your practice?" When he replied it was, I asked why. Nizer proceeded to tell me something that at least to me was almost as unbelievable as what one of the prosecutors in the Simpson case had told me in explaining why they didn't introduce Simpson's statement to the police at the trial. Nizer said: "Vince, you just never know what's going to happen on the last day of testimony."

I don't think Nizer had been watching too much Perry Mason, but I can tell you that his position makes no sense at all. In the first place, even if something Perry Mason–like does happen on the last day of the trial which turns everything around, unless you decide to fold your tent and give no summation at all, you still have much to argue about in the case you've been putting on for weeks or months. But secondly, when does such a thing ever happen in the real world? Has any lawyer reading this book ever had it happen to him? And even if it has happened, it's so extremely rare that it surely shouldn't govern your way of handling final summation in every case you try.

The closest encounter I've had with something like that was a murder trial I prosecuted years ago against a man named Camden Davidson who murdered a man he learned had been having an affair with his wife while he was away in the service. When he got out, he stalked the man for two weeks and finally waited for him in the backseat of the man's car, directed the man to a deserted lot, and shot and killed him. One thing I remember about the case was the rare beauty of Davidson's wife, who attended every day of the trial, despite constant gawking from courtroom spectators. In any event, I had built up what I felt was a pretty solid case of circumstantial evidence against Davidson. About two or three days before final summation, there was a torrential downpour here in L.A., and the next day a young boy walking along a gully next to the Pasadena freeway found a gun that had been washed down from an adjacent hillside. I forget how the gun reached the LAPD (probably through the boy's father), but the firearm people over at LAPD concluded that it was the murder weapon, and I was able to connect the gun indirectly to Davidson, actually fortifying, obviously, not undermining, my case against him.

One of the main reasons why lawyers spend so little time preparing their summation is that they don't feel it's the most important part of the trial. And I've never understood why. In life, if you want someone to come around to your viewpoint, isn't it all-important *what* you say and *how* you say it? Is a trial any different? Isn't the lawyer trying to convince someone, in this case, the jury, of the rightness of his cause? Therefore, shouldn't most of his preparation and efforts be directed toward this final appeal to the jury? Not so, say many experts. Louis Heller, a former justice of the New York Supreme Court and before that a prominent trial lawyer, writes in his book *Do You Solemnly Swear*, "An address to the jury should be *extemporaneous* and reflect spontaneity."

In my opinion, a summation must either be written out or set down in a comprehensive outline. The problem with even an outline is that although all the points the lawyer wants to make are there, he does *not* have the all important articulations; that is, he does not have his points expressed in the most effective way. And it's simply not possible to powerfully articulate a great number of points, one immediately following another, extemporaneously. There *is* a best way to make a point, and to find it takes time and sweat on the yellow pad. But whether one should write out one's summation or put it into an outline, it has been my experience that the majority of trial lawyers—even many high priced ones in major, nationally publicized criminal trials—do neither, addressing the jury after scandalously little preparation. Far too often this results in their delivering arguments which are disjointed and sterile in articulation, and which, most injurious of all to their clients, omit a number of salient facts and inferences.

In a complex trial involving many witnesses and thousands of pages of transcript, to discuss the highlights and nuances of the case and draw the necessary inferences, in the most telling sequence, always seeking simplicity and clarity of expression, requires an enormous amount of written preparation.

The one advantage in arguing extemporaneously is to be able to talk to the jury eye to eye, with the candor of spontaneity. But if a trial lawyer is willing to put in the hours, he can have such a grasp of his written or outlined argument that, like an actor on a stage whose lines flow naturally, he can deliver it to the jury giving the appearance of spontaneity. (Mark Twain knew whereof he spoke when he said, not just facetiously, that "it takes three weeks to prepare a good ad lib argument.") If I've had adequate time to prepare, I only have to glance at my notes sparingly. I can look at one word on a page, and the whole page is vivid in my mind.

Final argument is nothing more than a speech, and I know of no great speech in history that was not carefully prepared before it was delivered. Lincoln's Gettysburg Address consisted of only ten sentences. Of his 271 words, 202 of them were just one syllable. But these historic words went through five drafts and were the result of two weeks' thought and preparation, handwritten on two pages that were in front of him as he spoke.

The conventional wisdom is that a summation should be succinct, focusing only on the main points in the case. Not only can't a lawyer keep a jury's attention for more than an hour or so, it is said, but discussing the smaller points only clutters and dilutes the thrust of the main arguments. I may be wrong, but my personal opinion is that this couldn't possibly be a more serious mistake—in many cases, perhaps a fatal one. Juries, unaccountably, often base their verdict on (or are heavily influenced by) the most tangential, seemingly insignificant points. Just as in surveying the ocean bed "no rock or prominence can be left unnoted with safety to the mariner," a lawyer should want to be heard on virtually every point in the case.

Moreover, I do not agree that it is difficult to hold a jury's attention for more than an hour or so. In fact, it is not difficult to keep their attention for one, two, or even three days if the lawyer can deliver a powerful, exciting summation that is sprinkled with example, metaphor, and humor; and particularly when he makes it obvious to them that he has a lot of important observations to make about the case and they can only fulfill the oath they took to reach a proper verdict if they listen to him closely— that is, *if he convinces them that they need him.*

My editor suggested that I write out in this book what my summation would have been in the Simpson trial if I had been the prosecutor. I told him, as I now tell the reader, that that is not realistic. If I had been the prosecutor in the case, I would have easily put three to four hundred hours into the preparation of my summation, and it would probably be close to a thousand transcript pages long. Here and there, however, I will set forth a few arguments, in bold type, that I would have made in the case.

For instance, since this was such a long and hotly contested trial, it's possible—not being the prosecutor, and not having a sense of the feeling in the courtroom, this is just a possibility—I would have commenced my opening argument to the jury by making an obvious and rhetorical statement which, right at the start, might have psychologically jarred the jury back into reality:

"I'd like to make this observation, ladies and gentleman, about a matter that could be in your mind, either consciously or subconsciously. You folks have been sitting here now for over nine months, listening to a great number of issues being vigorously contested by each side. You've heard well over one hundred witnesses give thousands of pages of testimony. Because of this, it could be natural for you, as lay people, to think that there must be a real issue here as to guilt. I mean, if there was no issue, why have you been here for nine months? Well, ladies

and gentlemen of the jury, we have been here for nine months not because there is any real issue of guilt. Mr. Simpson's guilt couldn't possibly be any clearer. When your blood is found at the murder scene, and the victims' blood inside your car and home, that's really the end of the ballgame. There's nothing more to say. We've been here simply because he pled not guilty to these murders and came up with a desperate defense—as most people in his shoes would, too, if the only other option they had was to plead guilty and go to prison. In America, no matter how guilty you are, even if there are one hundred eyewitnesses to your crime, our system of justice—and I wouldn't change it for anything—allows you to plead not guilty and have a trial. And that's the *only* reason why we've been here in this courtroom the past nine months. There is no other reason."

There are many elements that go into an effective summation, of course, and one of them is the way it is delivered. One thing I underline in speaking to trial lawyer groups around the country is that a lawyer cannot expect a jury to buy his cause if they detect that he does not believe in it *completely* himself. There is no question in my mind that Clark and Darden completely believed in their case. The problem is they didn't clearly show it to the jury. Both of them were far too laid-back and casual in their presentation. There was no fire, no passion, at all. Cochran and Scheck, the ones who should have had much more difficulty summoning up fire and passion (since their client was guilty and they had to know it), spoke with more flame than the two prosecutors. In fact, throughout the trial, the sad irony was that the defense attorneys seemed to be fighting harder for injustice than the prosecutors were for justice.

Although the soft sell (which both prosecutors embraced as their modus operandi before the jury) might be efficacious in selling a life insurance policy to someone in the privacy of his home, it hardly serves a trial lawyer well in summation, particularly if you're the prosecutor. Not only are you asking a jury to put someone behind bars for life, but you've got the burden of proof, a high one at that. And it's difficult to meet that burden if you're not forceful. My sense is that it simply isn't Darden's nature to be forceful, but I have the sense that it is Marcia Clark's. I have the feeling, and it's only a feeling, that early on, long before final summation, she unfortunately bought into the notion advocated by many of the silly talking heads that in front of the jury she should not be forceful, but rather be sensitive, and soften her image. I don't know if any of you readers noticed, but throughout the trial (particularly at the beginning, before she got beaten down by Judge Ito), Clark performed differently before Judge

Ito outside the jury's presence than she did before the jury. It was as if she had two different personalities. She was considerably more forceful and effective before Judge Ito than before the jury, where she was less dynamic and more timid.

But if the defendant committed the crime, the DA is the one in the courtroom fighting for justice, avenging the murders, as it were. And in doing so, the jury doesn't mind it at all if the DA is forceful and aggressive. Not shrill or abrasive, but forceful. They even expect it. What the jury wants from the prosecutor is that he or she be eminently fair. Not sensitive, but fair.

One other distinct possibility for Clark's schizophrenic performance at the trial is that since she had learned that black females disliked her, viewing her as pushy, she felt she had to change her natural personality in front of them and become much more soft. But if this is, indeed, the reason for her less forceful and dynamic performance in front of the jury, wouldn't it have been the right and proper thing for her to have removed herself from the case before the trial started, rather than to perform in front of the jury in a way that was unnatural for her, and where she was therefore not at her best? Wouldn't that have been in the best interests of justice?

No more than two minutes after Clark gave her opening statement at the beginning of the trial, which was months and months before her final summation, a reporter for the *New York Times* called me to evaluate Clark's performance. The very first words out of her mouth were "Was she sensitive enough?" "*Sensitive* enough," I said, "that was her problem. She was too sensitive. She wasn't nearly forceful or dynamic enough."

The same was true of Clark's and Darden's final summations to the jury, where both were surprisingly weak. Not only weren't they forceful and decisive, they actually went to the other extreme, making statements which psychologically, with this jury, were very damaging to the prosecution. As I said earlier, Darden actually told the jurors in a passive manner, "*Nobody* wants to do anything to this man," which is almost tantamount to telling them that everyone, whites as well as blacks, was hoping for a not-guilty verdict. That wasn't even true, but even if it had been, nothing could be worse than to suggest to a jury that if it lets a defendant go, most people would be relieved, perhaps even happy.

Then he made an even more unbelievable statement. He told the jury that in deciding whether Simpson was guilty or not guilty, "whatever you do, the decision is yours, and *I'm glad that it is not mine*." Now what the hell does that mean? Isn't that the same thing as telling the jury that this is a tough, close case? It's almost telling them it's a reasonable-doubt case.

The prosecutor, of course, should always convey to the jurors just the opposite, that the evidence of guilt is so clear, obvious, and overwhelming that they shouldn't have any trouble at all reaching a guilty verdict.

Also, a trial lawyer *has* to be confident in front of the jury. If he's not, then he has to be a good actor and at least appear to be confident. It's one of the most important ingredients of a successful trial lawyer. If he's not confident, the jury will pick it up just like that—in the way he talks, the way he walks, the expression on his face, the inflection in his voice. And again, a lawyer cannot expect a jury to buy his cause if they detect that he doesn't believe in it completely himself. (A lawyer must be very careful, however, that he doesn't cross over from confidence into the area of arrogance or condescension. That can only hurt him with the jury.)

In this case, in addition to their both speaking softly and without force (at one point, Judge Ito had to tell Darden, "Mr. Darden, if you would keep your voice up just a little bit so I can hear you"), there was the weak body language conveying a lack of confidence. Darden constantly shifted his body from side to side in front of the jury, rarely establishing eye contact with the jurors. In fact, the *New York Times* claimed, I believe erroneously, that Darden "never did look at the jury." And Armanda Cooley, the foreperson of the Simpson jury, writes in her book that although she felt the prosecution believed in their case, "a lot of times Marcia would sigh and make gestures with her hands as though she were throwing in the towel. That didn't help her."

In addition to being weak in their demeanor and far too casual in the delivery of their words to the jury, the two prosecutors didn't fight at all for fairness in the courtroom. Nowhere was this fact exemplified more clearly than in Clark's and Darden's rebuttal, where the defense interrupted the two prosecutors seventy-one times, which is unprecedented in my experience. No one whom I've spoken to has ever heard or read about such an egregious display of gross and improper courtroom behavior during an opponent's summation. It simply isn't done. Summation is the time during the trial when the court gives the lawyers far more latitude than in any other part of the trial. The lawyer's inferences have to be based on the evidence, but they can be as ridiculous and unreasonable as can be; and outside the evidence, the lawyer can give examples, refer to matters of common knowledge, and literally tell stories, real as well as fictional, to illustrate his point. The opposing lawyers, through time-honored tradition in the legal profession, rarely object, interrupting only when the advocate clearly trespasses beyond the already broad perimeters of permissible oratory. And indeed, during the opening arguments of Clark and Darden, the defense objected a total of only three times.

The defense attorneys, of course, were well aware of the fact that objections are supposed to be extremely rare in final summation. Listen to Cochran's statement to Judge Ito when he interrupted Marcia Clark for the first time in her opening argument: "I would like to ask to approach the bench because I don't want to object to Ms. Clark's argument"; then later in the same objection: "I don't want them objecting in my argument"; then later still in the same objection, ". . . that is the reason I ask because I don't want to object to Marcia's argument." Three apologies from Johnnie Cochran for just one interruption. Now listen to Barry Scheck when Clark objected for one of the very few times during his final summation: "I resent this interruption."

But in Darden's *rebuttal* argument (when the defense had completed its final summation, and knew the prosecution couldn't reply in kind), Cochran and Scheck interrupted Darden twenty-one times. In Marcia Clark's final address to the jury, the last address that either prosecutor could make in the case, and the most important address to the jury for the prosecution, Cochran and Scheck objected an incredible fifty times.

Even if Clark had been giving a powerful summation, constant interruptions would have substantially reduced its effectiveness. But because she was already giving a very weak summation, the interruptions made it almost pitiable. An objection destroys the speaker's flow and momentum and the speaker's and listeners' concentration. Even something as minor as someone opening the courtroom door is a distraction, and if the judge doesn't instruct the courtroom bailiffs to keep the door closed during summation, I always remind him to do so. But again, Cochran and Scheck interrupted the two prosecutors an astounding seventy-one times. Yet Judge Ito, knowing that Cochran and Scheck were deliberately making frivolous objections (the proof is that Ito sustained only two out of the seventy-one objections) to destroy the effectiveness of the prosecutors' summations, did not once hold Cochran or Scheck in contempt of court, or even once admonish them to discontinue their outrageous, unprofessional, and yes, dishonorable conduct. This is the same judge who held Darden in contempt of court when Darden spoke over the judge's voice just once to a serious insult by Cochran when they were at sidebar outside the presence of the jury, with absolutely no harm being done by Darden to anyone, much less the opposing side.

What Darden and Clark, particularly Clark, should have done after the third or fourth frivolous objection by Cochran or Scheck, the ill-mannered fighter from the streets of New York, was to ask to approach the bench. She could have said:

"Judge, you know that all of these objections, particularly those by Mr. Scheck, are frivolous and outrageous and designed solely to destroy the effectiveness of the people's final address to the jury. I'm not asking you, I'm demanding that the next time Mr. Scheck interrupts me with a silly objection, you hold him in contempt of court. And if he continues after that, I want Scheck in the lockup. If either Mr. Cochran or Mr. Scheck continues to object and you let him get by with it, my remarks to you, as well as to them, will not be made here at the bench, but in open court before the jury and the millions of people who are watching. I can assure you, I'm not going to tolerate this anymore."

If that would have been too difficult for Marcia Clark to do, after one of Cochran's or Scheck's interruptions calculated to frustrate justice, at an absolute minimum she should have turned away from the jury and toward Cochran (or Scheck, as the case may be) and, giving him a look that could freeze fire, say: "Mr. Cochran, there's *going* to be justice in this courtroom." Instead, Clark did absolutely nothing at all. She registered her disapproval of the two defense attorneys' odious conduct only by rolling her eyes. The prosecutors were far too civilized for the defense attorneys. That would not have happened if I had been in that courtroom.

Let me show you, with just one observation, how the summations of Marcia Clark and Chris Darden, based on this one point alone, could hardly have been any worse. The main core of the defense case was that their client, Simpson, had been framed by racist cops. This was so much the heart of their case that by the time of final summation they were deemphasizing somewhat the second prong of their defense—that contamination caused by the LAPD's incompetence in the gathering and preservation of evidence had rendered all the subsequent scientific test results, mostly DNA, unreliable. With the exception of that portion of his final argument dealing with contamination, all the rest of defense attorney Barry Scheck's argument strongly implied an LAPD conspiracy to frame Simpson. And virtually all of Cochran's argument, the main argument for the defense, suggested, in paragraph after paragraph, rhetorical question after rhetorical question ("Isn't it strange that . . ."; "Why is it that . . ."), that the police had framed Simpson.

These are just a few of the literally hundreds of allegations by Cochran and Scheck, in their summations, of a police conspiracy to frame Simpson and then cover up their foul deed.

Cochran: "It took all four detectives [Lange, Vannatter, Fuhrman, and Phillips] to notify Mr. Simpson of what had happened? They didn't have a criminalist to go over to notify him? Who's fooling who here? They're lying, trying to get over that wall to get in that house. . . . They just want to be inside that house and make her [Arnelle, Simpson's daughter] leave to give Fuhrman a chance to start what he's doing." "Something's wrong here, something's sinister here." "The depths to which they sunk, as part of this cover-up." "From [officers] Riske to Bushey, you've seen this code of silence, this cover-up." "Why would the glove be moist and sticky unless Fuhrman brought it over there and planted it there to try to make this case?" "We talked about socks where evidence was planted on them." "You can't trust him [Detective Vannatter] . . . this man with his big lies. You can't believe anything he says." "He [Fuhrman] put a bloody footprint in that Bronco." "All them police officers, including Lieutenant Spangler, they were all covering for him [Fuhrman]." "How could the socks be there at 4:35 when they're not there at 4:13? They're setting this man up." "They went and took [the socks] out of the hamper and staged [planted] it there." "Was the blood planted at the back gate? Why didn't they see the blood before that?" "[The prosecution's case] has been reduced to a molehill under an avalanche of lies and conspiracy." "Thank heaven [out of all of law enforcement in the case] there is only one person [the black police photgrapher] who wasn't a part of the cover-up."

Scheck: "You cannot convict Mr. Simpson when the core of the prosecution's case is built on perjurious testimony of police officers, unreliable forensic evidence and manufactured evidence." "It's [Thano Peratis's videotaped statement] obviously a convenient recantation and appears to have been prepared to suit the prosecution's purposes when things just didn't fit [i.e., Scheck is accusing the prosecutors of subornation of perjury]." "That Rockingham glove [the one found by Fuhrman] started at Bundy. Somebody took it somewhere else. And you know who that was." "We can't allow dishonest, manufactured evidence to lie at the heart of a case like this."

At least 90 percent of Cochran's five-hour argument and 60 percent of Scheck's two-hour argument dealt, in one way or another, with the suggestion of a conspiracy by the police to frame Simpson for the two murders. Everywhere they looked, they smelled a rat. But who were the real rats in the courtroom?

So it was no secret that the heart and soul of the defense's case was that Simpson was framed. Everyone knew this. In fact, if the prosecutors didn't get the message during Cochran's and Scheck's summations, it had been obvious throughout the previous nine months of trial. Virtually every question the defense attorneys asked of most of the witnesses suggested a police frame-up. It got so bad at the trial that Hank Goldberg, the lead prosecutor on physical evidence, derisively asked all the LAPD criminalists and chemists (even those like young rookie Andrea Mazzola, who had never even heard of Simpson before this case): "Are you a part of any conspiracy to frame Mr. Simpson?"

And the newspapers reported the allegation of frame-up on a regular basis during the trial. Here are just a few examples. June 25, 1995, *Los Angeles Daily News*: "As Johnnie Cochran made clear in his opening statement five months ago, the defense maintains Simpson is the victim of a conspiracy between police investigators and criminalists who have planted or manufactured evidence to frame Simpson." July 21, 1995, *Los Angeles Times*: "From the start of the trial, Simpson's attorneys have suggested that police planted evidence in their quest to build a case against the former football star." September 13, 1995, *New York Times*: "Defense lawyers contend that corrupt LAPD officers sprinkled the missing blood around anything incriminating in their conspiracy to frame Simpson."

Since it had been obvious to everyone for months, then, that a police conspiracy to frame Simpson was the essence of the defense, as the prosecutor don't you automatically sit down with your yellow pad and come up with seven, eight, or nine very powerful arguments why a frame-up in this case was ludicrous, and argue for at least an hour or two on this point alone? Since you know that if the jury buys the police-conspiracy, frame-up argument (which the Simpson jury, we know, did), the verdict will have to be not guilty, don't you instinctively and automatically do this? I mean, this has nothing to do with being a lawyer. In any area of human endeavor, if you know the other side (to a contract, a war, a sporting event, argument at work, or what have you) is placing its primary emphasis in a particular area, and you want to prevail, again, don't you automatically devote a lot of time, energy, and resources in your effort to counter and overcome the main thrust of your opposition?

Yet unbelievably, Clark, in her opening argument, *never uttered one single word to knock down the frame-up, conspiracy allegation*. She treated it like a nonissue. All she told the jury (her only words on the subject) was, "If there was evidence of a conspiracy, it would be my obligation to dismiss [the case], pure and simple, and I can go on to the next case."

In reality, after commencing her opening argument on an affirmative note by arguing that, in looking at the case as a whole, it was clear that the evidence pointed overwhelmingly to Simpson's guilt, she should have dealt with the conspiracy issue in depth in her opening argument. She should have done this *before* she got into the heart of her summation setting forth all the evidence, and the inferences from that evidence, that established Simpson's guilt. The reason, I think, is obvious. If a lawyer doesn't first try to eliminate the negative (here the allegation of a frame-up), then at the very moment he is making his positive arguments, the jury is thinking, "Well, what you say may be true, but what about this and what about that?" and this necessarily dilutes the force and persuasiveness of his argument. By the time the lawyer argues the strong points of his case, he should want the jurors' minds to be completely clear and receptive to the arguments they are hearing. But again, Clark never said *one word* throughout her entire opening argument to knock down the alleged police conspiracy to frame Simpson! Did she feel that if she ignored it, somehow it would go away all by itself?

And in her rebuttal, her last address to the jury, she treated the issue so superficially that she commented on it for less than one minute, and she waited until the end of her argument to do so. After over one year to think about and prepare a strong response to the heart of the defense case, these are the only words she uttered to attempt to rebut the police conspiracy, frame-up allegation in her final address to the jury: "Do you realize how many people would have had to have gotten involved in a conspiracy within an hour? Can you imagine how this could happen? Detective Vannatter and Detective Lange never even knew Mark Fuhrman until they met him that night at Bundy, and yet the allegation by the defense is that they got together that night meeting for the first time, the very first time, and everybody is covering up and conspiring all of a sudden. Impossible. Not only that, but there are other people involved as well, people we don't even know who they are, according to the defense, who are willing to get involved in this. You realize how many people have to be involved? I mean it boggles the mind. We don't even know who they are talking about. But that's the contortion you have to go through to believe in this conspiracy theory."

Just one paragraph, Marcia, to respond to the central thrust of the defense's whole case? Just one paragraph in your entire opening and closing arguments to convince the jury there was no police conspiracy in this case?

And it wasn't as if Clark didn't realize the police conspiracy argument was the defense's main argument. She even told the jury: "They have got to make you believe that the blood was planted. It is the cornerstone of their defense. If you don't buy the planting theory, he's guilty." So in an opening argument and a rebuttal by her that consumed close to four hundred pages of transcript, Clark spent less than one page, *less than one four-hundredth of her argument*, responding to and trying to knock down the main argument of the defense. (Elsewhere in her argument, Clark did deal briefly [see later discussion] *not* with the conspiracy argument (a conspiracy requires *two or more people*, in this case many LAPD officers allegedly plotting to frame Simpson), but with whether Fuhrman, *by himself*, planted the *lone* item of the glove.)

Darden was even worse. Out of his approximately 170 pages of opening argument and rebuttal, he devoted one-sixth of one page, *about one one-thousandth of his argument*, to rebutting the main argument of the defense. I know this sounds impossible, but unfortunately it's true. These were his only words on the subject: "They want to tell you the police conspired against O. J. Simpson. Nicole says they had been out there eight times before and never did anything to him. I don't know." And later, referring to the testimony of black police photographer Willie Ford (who Cochran, in his summation, told the jury was the *only* member of the LAPD who was *not* a part of the conspiracy to frame Simpson), Darden said: "You heard that brother testify. Did he look like a coconspirator to you?"

So neither Clark nor Darden, in their four collective final summations to the jury, even begin to come up with any kind of a response to the heart, the centerpiece, the core of the defense case. They treated the issue that was most responsible for the not-guilty verdict in this case as if it didn't even exist. Yet to my knowledge, not one reporter or talking head covering this trial mentioned this perfectly obvious point. In fact, recall what one of the most prominent talking heads of all, the former prosecutor from back east, said. His answer to the question how he would have performed differently if he had been the prosecutor? "I don't have an answer for that question. . . . I think they did a damn good job."

None of this surprises me, however. Lincoln said, "You can fool all of the people some of the time, and some of the people all of the time, but you can't fool all of the people all of the time." But there should be an addendum to that: "You can fool most of the people most of the time."

The essence of Clark's few words to rebut the conspiracy frame-up argument was the *difficulty* of pulling it off. It would have been "impossible," she said. That is an argument she should have worked on for hours and hours, and in which she should have explained and spelled out in detail and depth to the jury, for at least a half hour or so, what would have been involved in such an enormous endeavor, not merely state the one-word conclusion of how "impossible" it would be. And as I've indicated, the entire counterconspiracy argument should have taken at least an hour or two to deliver, consuming one hundred pages of transcript, at a minimum.

Among the seven, eight, or nine arguments Clark should have made in this area, in addition to telling the jury how difficult or impossible such a frame-up would be—which only suggests how tough it would be to pull it off, not how absolutely repugnant to the officers such an idea would be in the first place—don't you at least also tell the jury how preposterous, on its face, the whole idea of a police frame-up is?

Don't you tell the jury something like this?

"To believe a frame-up, in addition to the many people who would have had to be involved, you'd have to believe that the two teams of LAPD detectives in this case—Lange and Vannatter, Fuhrman and Phillips, who were from different divisions of the LAPD and didn't work with or even know each other—arrive at the murder scene in the middle of the night and all four suddenly agree that whoever killed these two poor people, they didn't care, they were going to let the killer or killers go free. And instead they all decided—there were no dissents—to frame someone they believed to be innocent, O. J. Simpson. And in the process, not only jeopardize their careers, but also risk their very lives, since if you plant evidence and testify falsely in a capital case in California, as we have already pointed out to you folks, under some circumstances you can get the death penalty yourself. Take Detective Vannatter here. Twenty-eight years on the force. Due to retire in just a few months with his wife, Rita, to a farm of theirs in Indiana. And he's going to risk his good name, his pension, and possibly his life to frame O. J. Simpson? That's what the defense in this case wants you folks to believe.

"And why were these officers willing to risk their lives to frame Simpson? What was their motive? What was in it for them? Oh, I guess they were upset that Simpson was born black. Or maybe it was because he married a white woman. Anyone who would believe an incredible fable like that would believe someone who told him he had seen an alligator doing the polka. Is there anyone in this courtroom who doesn't realize how absolutely and utterly and completely insane it is to suggest, as the defense in this case has, that all four of these detectives, or even one, would be willing to risk their lives, risk going to the gas chamber, to frame someone for murders they believe he didn't commit? It's so insane a thought I hate to even utter the words. I wouldn't believe a story like that if you screamed it in my ears for one hundred years.

"Incidentally, it's an enormous, ridiculous leap to suggest that just because Fuhrman is a racist, as we know so many people are, he's going to go around framing innocent people of murder. That doesn't follow at all. And even if we make the crazy assumption, for which there is not one speck of evidence to support it, that Fuhrman tried to frame Simpson because he was black, what's the defense's explanation for Lange, Vannatter, and Phillips doing so? The defense hasn't even suggested they were racist. Why would they be willing to participate in an act that couldn't possibly be more sick, perverse, and evil?

"How dare these defense attorneys accuse these officers of framing an innocent man for murder, the foulest, most reprehensible deed, short of murder itself, that one human being can do to another human being? I mean, where do they get the guts to make a charge like that? Where do you buy guts like that? I haven't seen any on display in storefront windows here in L.A. Are they for sale back east?"

Cochran, in fact, did come up with a motive for the LAPD's framing Simpson. And it was even more laughable than the ones I hypothesized about. And naturally, the prosecution let him get by with it. Either he or one of his many associates must have realized that maybe one, just one member of the jury might be bright enough to ask himself why *all* the police, with no dissents, would get together and decide to frame someone they believed to be an innocent man. So buried within the millions of words the defense had uttered in this case for almost a year, Cochran, after strongly suggesting in his opening statement, throughout the entire nine-and-a-half-month trial, and through his entire summation that the LAPD had framed someone it believed to be innocent, squeezed in just seventeen words (two lines) to cover himself. This is what he said in answer to his own question "Why would all these police officers set up O. J. Simpson?": "They believed he was guilty. They wanted to win. They didn't want to lose another big case." Unbelievable. Johnnie had come up with a new twist. Everyone has heard of framing innocent people. My *Random House Dictionary*, for instance, defines the word "frame" as "incriminating an *innocent* person through the use of false evidence, information, etc." But according to Cochran, the LAPD thought it was framing a guilty person.

Shouldn't the prosecution have come back and told the jury, in rebuttal, that Cochran was speaking out of both sides of his mouth at the same time, being as two-faced as a tower clock? If we're to believe the other 99.9 percent of the defense's case, the LAPD must have believed it was framing an innocent man. How could they possibly have felt he was guilty *if they thought it was necessary* to plant his blood on the rear gate at Bundy and inside his Bronco and home, plant his and Nicole's blood on socks in his bedroom, plant a bloody glove on the grounds of his estate, etc.? By definition, if the LAPD felt they had to plant *all* that evidence against him, they must have felt he was innocent. That's just common sense. There would only be a need to start planting evidence against someone you believe is guilty if the existing evidence doesn't already do the job for you. But here, it did. Yes, the LAPD did believe, did know, that Simpson was guilty, but that was because *all* of the evidence they already had, without exception, pointed to his guilt. What Cochran was trying to do, of course, was to have it both ways, and as I said, the prosecution let him get by with it. The entire thrust of the defense case was that the LAPD was framing someone they thought was innocent.

Shouldn't the prosecution, in rebuttal *to Cochran's seventeen words which he slipped under the door,* have argued:

"So the reason all these officers would risk going to San Quentin's gas chamber was that they didn't want to lose another big case? Has this man Johnnie Cochran no shame? After a whole year to think about it, is this the best he and the other members of Mr. Simpson's million-dollar defense team can come up with as a motive for framing this defendant?

"And if he's going to make such a wild and absurd allegation, don't you think he should at least have the common decency to tell you folks what other big cases the LAPD has been losing recently? Is he talking about the Menendez case? The LAPD didn't handle that case. That was a Beverly Hills Police Department case. It should be noted that every single juror in that case voted to convict the two defendant brothers of some degree of criminal homicide, from first-degree murder down to voluntary manslaughter, but because the jury couldn't agree on the degree, it was a hung jury, and that case is going to be retried, so it's still very much alive. The Damien Williams case? Let Mr. Cochran tell Damien Williams, who's presently behind bars, that the LAPD lost that case. Williams was convicted of mayhem and is presently serving ten years in the state prison. The Rodney King case? You mean all the officers who framed Simpson in this case were *upset* that four other members of the LAPD—two of whom, *as you folks know*, were *in fact* eventually convicted—were found not guilty in Simi Valley? If they were upset, then they were pretty good people, right? Not the kind who are racist. Not the kind who would frame a black man, right? And if he's going all the way back to the McMartin child molestation case in 1990, that wasn't the LAPD either. That was the Manhattan Beach Police Department.

"I want to know. What other big cases was Mr. Cochran talking about? Even though this is my time for argument, I'm going to give Mr. Cochran the opportunity to stand up right now in front of you folks in this courtroom and identify, without a speech, what other big cases he was referring to that the LAPD lost within the past four or five years that caused all the LAPD officers in this case to risk going to the gas chamber for, just so the LAPD wouldn't lose another big case. Mr.

Cochran? I'll give you the amount of time it takes you to name these other cases."

And don't you at least, in your one- or two-hour argument on this issue of a police conspiracy and frame-up, go on and make this follow-up argument to the jury?

"**Even if the police were to frame a black man, Simpson would have been one of the last black men on the face of this earth they would have framed. Here's someone who had always been a friend of the LAPD, someone they had always liked, even pampered.**"

I'd then remind the jury of the many examples of this, e.g., Nicole's anguished cry to the officers when they responded to her 911 call in 1989: "You come out, and you talk to him, but you never do anything to him"; the fact that many officers from the West Los Angeles Division of the LAPD attended parties at Simpson's home, and several used his pool and tennis court; his usually attending their Christmas parties and autographing footballs for them; etc. Isn't this an obvious argument you make? But the prosecutors never made any such argument.

To fortify this argument, as well as weaken the bond of identification the blacks on the jury may have had with Simpson because of his color, I'd also point out to the jury that the police, if they were of the mind to frame a black, would likely not even look upon Simpson as a black man:

"**Stop to think about it, ladies and gentlemen. Here's someone who is a multimillionaire, lives in a very fashionable, virtually all-white neighborhood, divorced his black wife and married a white woman, Nicole, and moved and socialized exclusively in the white corporate and establishment worlds, with powerful connections. Why would they want to mess with someone like this? You jurors, particularly those of you who are black, know better than I do that this defendant is no typical black man. I mean, he'd need a road map to get back to the hood.**"

Now let's take Mark Fuhrman himself, the defense's devil incarnate, who was the primary member of the alleged police conspiracy. Fuhrman went out to Rockingham in 1985 (there was uncontroverted testimony by Fuhrman on this at the trial—the defense never tried to challenge it), pursuant to a call from Nicole, and saw Nicole crying and sitting on the hood of her Mercedes-Benz, with Simpson standing nearby. Simpson, Nicole told Fuhrman, had in a rage smashed the window of her car with a baseball bat. So here we have a situation where Fuhrman (according to the defense such an extreme racist that he framed Simpson for the murders) has knowledge that Simpson had committed a crime, and to exacerbate the situation, this black man, Simpson, was with a white woman. Yet because Simpson was the celebrity he was, Fuhrman does nothing at all.

In fact, he doesn't even fill out a police report. Nothing. *So we have proof that even Fuhrman pampered Simpson*, gave him special treatment. Don't you argue this to the jury if you're the prosecutor?

Along the same line, don't you argue to the jury that if Simpson was, in fact, framed, and was innocent, how did the LAPD conspirators get Simpson, who was innocent, to act like the guiltiest person imaginable? Did they come up to Simpson and say, "O.J., we're going to frame you, but we could use your help, ol' buddy. We need you to act guilty," and Simpson replied, "No sweat. Tell me what you guys need"? The prosecutors should have pointed out to the jury that if Simpson was innocent, how did they get him to tell the monumental lie to the limo driver about having overslept and just gotten out of the shower, when the limo driver had just seen him enter his home thirty seconds earlier? To insist, when he and Kato Kaelin were putting his bags into the limo for the trip to the airport, that Kato not pick up, out of the four traveling bags, the one bag, the small dark one, that has never been seen again? To perspire profusely in the limo on the way to the airport on the night of the murders even though it was a cool night and the air-conditioning was on? To stay up virtually all night staring out the window on the flight he took that departed for Chicago at 11:45 p.m., even though he had been up since 6:00 that morning? To not ask the L.A. detective who called him in Chicago to inform him that Nicole was dead how, when and where it happened, etc.? How did they get him to write a suicide note, to get a gun, his passport, and a cheap disguise, and to flee instead of turning himself in? If there is a police conspiracy to frame Simpson, how did they get Simpson to be such an extremely cooperative framee? Did Simpson, by any chance, decide to join the conspiracy against himself?

Don't you tell the jury:

"We have the incredibly ridiculous situation here where Mr. Simpson's defense attorneys are claiming to you folks that he was framed by the LAPD for these murders, but not even their own client, Mr. Simpson, agrees with them. If you know you're completely innocent of a crime, yet there's a ton of evidence pointing to your guilt, you immediately know, of course, that you've been framed. Yet although Mr. Simpson's defense attorneys have tried to convince you for over nine months that he was framed by the LAPD, Mr. Simpson himself has never told anyone or even vaguely suggested such a thing to anyone.

"If he knew or suspected he had been framed, wouldn't he have said so in the thirty-two-minute interview he gave the police the afternoon after the murders? Wouldn't he have said so in the farewell letter he wrote five days later before he fled in his friend Al Cowling's Bronco?

And during the slow-speed chase, when he was talking on his cellular phone to the police and his friends and family, he said nothing about being framed by the LAPD or anyone else. In fact, at the end of that chase, when the LAPD detectives took him into custody, he told the arresting officers, 'I'm sorry, you guys. I'm sorry.' He kept telling them he was sorry for having led them on the chase. Is that what you say to people you believe are framing you for murder? That you're sorry for putting them out?

"I mean, when you're being framed for murders you didn't commit, don't you shout out you're being framed from the highest rooftops? Yet in all these times I've told you folks about when he had all the opportunity in the world to say he was framed, not one word, not one single word came from this man over here [pointing to Simpson] that he was framed. Mr. Simpson's lawyers want you to believe something, then, that he doesn't believe himself. There oughta be a law against things like this.

"Quite apart from all the scientific evidence in this case that conclusively proves this man's guilt beyond all doubt, other than his getting up in court right now and confessing to you folks, he has already told you, by all his words and all his conduct, that he's *guilty*. Guilty of these two murders."

Christopher Darden's opening *argument* (remember, we are talking about a part of the final summation) to the jury was an attempt to establish the motive for the murders. The essence of his argument, as in his opening *statement* many months earlier, was that Simpson was obsessed with controlling Nicole and when he lost control, he felt he had no choice but to kill her.

A few preliminary observations should be made. One is to distinguish motive from intent, two terms which are sometimes used interchangeably in the criminal law. Motive is the emotional urge which induces a person to say or do something. It is different from intent, for a person may intend to steal property or kill someone, and will be guilty of the theft or homicide irrespective of what his motive was (e.g., need, avarice, revenge, jealousy, etc.). While intent is an element of every serious crime, motive is never an element of the *corpus delicti* of any crime. Therefore, the prosecution *never* has to prove motive. The former Los Angeles DA referred to earlier who was a commentator for one of the networks during the Simpson trial, and who has never prosecuted a felony case, proclaimed in print and on TV that "a jury will almost never convict unless they think they understand why somebody did it." This isn't so at all. I've put people on death row without knowing for sure what their motive was — that is, why they did it. All I knew for sure was that they had put someone in his or her grave and had no right to do it. And if I, the prosecutor, didn't know for sure what their motive was, how in the world could the jury have?

However, even though the prosecution doesn't have any legal burden to prove motive, it is always better if it can, because just as the presence of motive to commit a crime is circumstantial evidence of guilt, the absence of motive is perhaps even stronger circumstantial evidence of innocence. Motive takes on far more importance in cases where the defendant did not physically commit the crime, because if he didn't commit it, number one, and number two, never had any ostensible motive or reason to have someone else commit it for him, it's obviously difficult to secure a conviction under these circumstances. I was faced with this problem in the Manson case, because Manson was not present when the murders took place. And although there were supplementary motives for the Tate–LaBianca murders, the overriding motive Manson used to work his killers up into such an emotional lather that they were willing to commit murder was exceedingly bizarre — so bizarre, in fact, I knew that if the jurors heard the many components of it from the lips of just one or even two witnesses, they might think there was something wrong with me to even offer such a motive for their consideration.

Briefly, Manson convinced his followers that the best way to bring about a new and better social order was to start a race war between blacks and whites, a war he called Helter Skelter. And he said the way to do this was to frame the black man for the murders. This would cause the white community to turn against the black community in an apocalyptic war to end all wars. At the murder scene, the killers printed words from Beatles songs in blood — code words like "rise," "pigs," and "Helter Skelter." Manson preached to his disciples that the Beatles used these words to convey subliminally their own desire for Armageddon. During Helter Skelter, Manson told his followers, he would take them to the bottomless pit in the desert, a place he derived from Revelation 9, a chapter in the last book of the New Testament from which Manson told his followers he found complete support for his philosophies on life. (Manson equated Revelation 9 in the Bible with the Beatles song "Revolution 9.") The bottomless pit, he said, was a land of milk and honey, twelve types of fruit on every tree, and his family (his followers) was going to grow to a size of 144,000 people, which refers to the twelve tribes of Israel mentioned in Revelation 7.

Manson believed that the black man was going to win this war because they had been stepped on for centuries by the white man and it was their karma, their turn to take over. But Manson was a racist, and he believed blacks were subhuman and less evolved than the white man, so he told his followers that even though the blacks would win this war, they'd never know how to handle the reins of power, because "blackie only knows what whitie has told him to do." So the black man would have to turn over the reins of power to those white people who had survived Helter Skelter, i.e., Charles Manson and his family. Then, he said, "we'll pat blackie on his kinky hair, send him on his way to picking cotton," and take over the leadership of the world.

Again, since Manson didn't participate in the murders, it was critical to prove that Manson had the motive to commit them, and that that motive was Helter Skelter. Through various witnesses testifying to different aspects of it (virtually all of whom were afraid to testify, fearing retribution from Manson), I put the whole picture of Helter Skelter before the jury, proving that Helter Skelter was Manson's philosophy, that it was he who introduced it into his family and spoke of it all the time. And when the words "Helter Skelter" (the title of a Beatles song) were found printed in blood at the murder scene, I argued to the jury that this was tantamount to Manson's fingerprints being found at the scene.

But in the Simpson case, although Simpson's motive for the murders was important (and, as I've indicated, the prosecution should have presented more evidence of it than it did, such as the stalking, which showed obsession), it wasn't nearly as critical as it was in the Manson case, because Simpson was the one who committed the murders. Since his blood was found at the murder scene and the victims' blood inside his car and home, it didn't make any difference why he committed these murders. Even if the murders arose out of an argument over basketball tickets, so what?

Darden's argument to the jury on the *known* facts of physical and psychological abuse by Simpson against Nicole throughout their marriage as it related to motive was effective. But when he started to argue, *as fact*, exactly what was on Simpson's mind during the days leading up to the murders, as well as on the day of the murders, including precisely why Simpson murdered Nicole, he was doing nothing but hurting the prosecution's case with his speculation. For example, when Simpson and his girlfriend, Paula Barbieri, had an interior decorator over at Simpson's house on June 6, 1994, six days before the murders, Darden told the jury in no uncertain terms: "The fuse is burning and it is getting short, okay? He is trying to erase her [Nicole's] presence from his home, okay? He has hired an interior decorator to redecorate the bedroom and bathroom. He is going to erase her presence from the house, or at least he is going to try." But isn't one among several other possibilities that it was all Barbieri's idea to redecorate?

Like his co-prosecutor Brian Kelberg with Dr. Lak, Darden was setting up a burden for himself that he not only didn't have under the law, but had no way of meeting. As he was telling the jury everything that was going on in Simpson's mind, I was thinking to myself, "How in the heck does he know for a fact what was going on in Simpson's mind?" And if I, as pro-prosecution as anyone could be, was having these thoughts, one has to wonder what the jurors were thinking. So here, in a criminal case where the prosecution has the burden of proving guilt beyond a reasonable doubt, the prosecution was devoting a large part of its summation to the jury talking about things that could only be speculation on its part. But speculation and proof beyond a reasonable doubt are as incompatible with each other in a criminal case as a mouse and a hungry cat.

Everything Darden said would have been much more effective if he had gone about it differently. After prefacing his argument on motive by reading to the jury (as he did) the instruction that motive does not have to be proved by the prosecution, he could have then told the jury, "Based on the evidence, what probably happened, although we cannot be sure, and I want to remind you once again that we have absolutely no burden at all to prove this . . ." and then proceeded to say essentially what he said, but in a much more condensed form, which would have conveyed to the jury that proving what was on Simpson's mind wasn't so critical an issue in the case. Speculation isn't as bad if you call it speculation. Darden did not do that. He claimed to know *for sure* what Simpson was thinking.

Both prosecutors, particularly Darden, handled the Fuhrman issue, the most explosive single issue at the trial, very poorly. Clark did argue that Fuhrman could not have planted the glove because "all the other officers who were there before him saw only one glove," but to dismiss this highly critical fact with just these few words is exceptionally weak and flabby advocacy. Such a brief reference could easily have gone over the heads of, or been missed by, the jury. Clark should have spoon-fed the jury with the necessary follow-up reality: ". . . *and therefore, there was no second glove at the Bundy murder scene for detective Fuhrman to have picked up and deposited at the defendant's Rockingham estate.*" Because of its importance, this fact should have been repeated, and even referred to once again in Clark's later, final address to the jury. But it was not.

Also, Clark grossly misstated the evidence when she told the jury that "all the other officers who were there [the Bundy crime scene] before Fuhrman saw only one glove." Although the LAPD has said that fourteen uniformed officers arrived at the Bundy murder scene before Fuhrman, and all saw only one glove there, the prosecution, at the trial, very unwisely only called two of the fourteen (Officer Robert Riske and Sergeant

David Rossi) who arrived *before* Fuhrman to testify to this fact. Since these two officers testified they only saw one glove there, Clark should have gone on to make the obvious and critical observation to the jury that for the jury to buy the defense allegation that Fuhrman planted the glove at Rockingham, and hence committed perjury in denying it, they would *necessarily* have to conclude that these two officers who testified they only saw one glove were also committing perjury. Because if they were telling the truth, then Fuhrman also had to have been telling the truth when he said he never picked up a second glove at Bundy and planted it at Rockingham.

Actually, Clark should definitely have had several more of the fourteen uniformed officers testify to seeing only one glove at Bundy, because the more who testified, the less likely all of them were lying. When you have fourteen witnesses to prove a critical point in your case, why only call two? On direct examination of them during the trial, Clark could have elicited information from them — assuming it was the truth — that some of them never even knew Fuhrman, or hardly knew him at all, thus decreasing the likelihood even more that they had committed perjury for him. She could have argued to the jury:

"What did Fuhrman do? Come up to these officers individually or in a group and say, 'Listen, I don't know you guys too well. You're uniform and I've been working detective for quite a few years. But here's the skinny. I've got this thing about blacks, particularly when they're sleeping with white women, as Simpson was. And, you know, I'd like to see this SOB go down, so I need you guys to back me up on the witness stand and say there was only one glove at the Bundy murder scene. Okay? I'll owe you one.' Wouldn't something like this have had to happen, ladies and gentlemen of the jury, in order for there to have actually been *two* gloves at the murder scene and for Fuhrman to have seized one and planted it at Rockingham? Are we really to believe not only that Fuhrman lied on the witness stand, but that several other officers, with nothing to gain, also agreed to jeopardize their careers and risk their lives to help him out?"

Yet this point was never made by the prosecutors.

In negating the argument that Fuhrman planted the glove, Clark pointed out to the jury that he wouldn't have done it because "he didn't know if the defendant had an airtight alibi and maybe left on the 9:00 flight to Chicago," and said Fuhrman, if he lied, would be committing a felony which could have gotten him "in big trouble." But since this was such a key issue at the trial, she should have dwelled much longer than she did on this issue and made these additional arguments: Fuhrman, as previously indicated, would not just be doing something that could get him in trouble, he was doing something that could have resulted in his own execution. Also, how could Fuhrman possibly have had any confidence that the glove he allegedly planted to frame Simpson would even fit Simpson's hand? And the glove Fuhrman testified he found at Rockingham had blood on it. How could Fuhrman possibly know that the blood was going to turn out to be Simpson's (as well as Ron's and Nicole's), as opposed to that of some other party? She could have concluded by pointing out that not only was there no affirmative evidence of any kind that Fuhrman planted the glove, but the evidence, in fact, clearly refuted the defense's theory.

Clark at least made an effort, as weak as it was. We know it was weak and unconvincing because several jurors, posttrial, said they believed Fuhrman planted the glove. If Clark was weak on Fuhrman, Darden was ten times worse. His argument on Fuhrman bordered on the unbelievable. Not once in his very brief reference to Fuhrman did he assert or even vaguely imply that Fuhrman was telling the truth about finding the glove or about anything else he testified to. In fact, he almost seemed to suggest the opposite when he told the jury: "I am asking you to put it [Fuhrman's lying about the use of the word "nigger"] in the proper perspective. You decide what it means. If it helps you in assessing his credibility—and it should, or his lack of credibility, I don't know—then you use it."

With these words, isn't Darden just about saying, by implication, that he agrees that because Fuhrman lied about not using the racial slur, maybe he lied about finding the glove? I mean, when Darden said, "If [Fuhrman's lie about using the racial slur] helps you in assessing his credibility—*and it should*," what does that mean? Particularly when Darden didn't then go on and defend Fuhrman's credibility on the issue of whether he was telling the truth or lying about finding the glove. He simply abruptly left the subject completely and went on to another part of his summation.

Nowhere did Clark or Darden make the argument which I made earlier that just because someone is a racist, as so many people are, doesn't mean they are likely to go around framing innocent people of murder. What they did with Fuhrman after they learned he had lied was in effect to drop him like a hot potato. But since they knew he was telling the truth about what counted, finding the glove, why would they do that? Their reaction to the fact Fuhrman had lied was like that of callow, wet-behind-the-ears prosecutors trying their first case. Surely they must have known that lying is not only common in criminal as well as civil trials, it's routine and expected. The late Francis L. Wellman, a distinguished member of the New York bar, once observed: "Scarcely a trial is conducted in which perjury does not appear in a more or less flagrant form." Perjury is so common that instead of being surprised by it, seasoned prosecutors expect it.

Essentially, there are two basic types of perjury at a criminal trial, the first being when the defendant who has committed a crime denies guilt under oath. This form of self-defense is obviously anticipated and almost invariably overlooked by prosecutors. We expect it. If the defendant was not going to deny having committed the crime, he normally would have pled guilty and there would not have been any trial. In every case where a defendant has denied guilt from the witness stand and is subsequently convicted, the finding of guilt by the jury, by definition, is a concomitant finding that the jury believes the defendant committed perjury when he denied guilt under oath. Yet for the hundreds of thousands of defendants convicted every year throughout the land for various crimes, it is almost unheard of for there to follow, after their conviction, a prosecution against them for perjury. (This holds true even for members of their family who may have lied under oath on their behalf.)

The second type of perjury at a criminal trial is the kind that is not self-protective in nature, one example of which would be a witness knowingly and falsely accusing an innocent party of a crime. This kind of perjury, if it can be proved, usually does result in a criminal prosecution.

Fuhrman's lie, on a private matter that had no relevance to the facts of this case, is a third category that hardly even merits attention.

The prosecutors should have met the issue of Fuhrman's lie head on in their summation, explaining that it was not relevant to any issue in the case, and that although Fuhrman should have told the truth, he simply was too embarrassed to do so before the jury and a national television audience. Yet Fuhrman's lie, a third category of lying under oath which is so common and legally irrelevant it doesn't even rise to the dignity of being a separate important category of perjury, was treated as an extremely serious matter not only by the defense, the media, and millions of people, but by the prosecutors themselves, who uttered not one syllable in defense or explanation of it.

Let's briefly look at the way I handled not just a third-rate lie such as Fuhrman told but a blatant, serious perjury by my client in a desert island murder case that was the subject of my 1991 book *And the Sea Will Tell*. It was a lie she told in an earlier theft trial that was directly related to an important issue in the murder case. The following is an excerpt from the book quoting a part of my argument to the jury on my client's perjury:

> "With respect to Jennifer's lying under oath at her theft trial about the *Iola* going aground while being towed out of the channel, and being left behind,

Mr. Enoki [the prosecutor] argued that this shows Jennifer cannot be trusted to tell the truth now. In other words, once a liar, always a liar. The only problem with that type of reasoning is that I don't believe any human being *always* tells the truth. I'll wager every penny I have on that proposition. *No human being always tells the truth,*" I repeated very loudly in the packed but quiet courtroom. My intonation made it very clear that I was referring to every single person in the courtroom, including judge and jury, and I was openly challenging the jury to take conscious recognition, for Jennifer's benefit, of this incontrovertible fact. "They may *say* they always tell the truth, but they don't. And if we were to accept the notion that once a liar, always a liar, then we could never believe anyone.

"But I guess the position of the prosecution is that since Jennifer lied once *under oath*, before another jury, she should never be believed again on that witness stand, as long as she lives. Charge her with the assassination of President John F. Kennedy," I roared. "If she denies it, don't believe her. Of course she did it. She and Oswald were just like this," I said, thrusting my crossed fingers into the air.

In reminding the jury that Jennifer had lied about the *Iola*'s going aground because one of her lawyers had advised her that if she contradicted the statement she had already given the FBI, the theft trial would go badly for her, I noted: "You know, the prosecution didn't call, on rebuttal, this former lawyer to deny this. In any event, when a human being is faced with the dilemma of being innocent of the crime they are charged with committing, but if they tell the truth as to a particular matter, chances are they will be wrongfully convicted, so they lie, is that the type of situation where they should never, ever be believed again under oath? Obviously not, ladies and gentleman."

The prosecution treated Fuhrman like a leper after the tapes surfaced primarily because of the racism revealed there, but almost as much because Fuhrman had been caught in a clear lie about the racism. The prosecutors' reaction was one of horror and contempt. Not only had they forgotten their own experience in criminal trials, but they were bowing to another deeply entrenched myth in our society, which is that one should never lie. The myth is so powerful, and the word "lie" is so ridiculously stigmatized in our society, that being aware of this enabled me to utilize it to my advantage in the Manson case.

During the guilt trial, Manson and his three female co-defendants professed their innocence. But after they had already been convicted of first-degree murder and we were in the penalty phase of the trial, where the jury had to decide on a sentence of life imprisonment or the death penalty for the four defendants, the three female defendants and several other members of Manson's family made an effort to exonerate Manson and save his life. The three female defendants now confessed to the murders from the witness stand to give themselves credibility for their main contention that Manson was not involved in the murders, the idea for the murders being hatched by the girls themselves and Charles "Tex" Watson, the main killer. The myth about how terrible it is to lie under any circumstance led to this absurd testimony during my cross-examination of a Manson family member who was seeking to save Manson's life:

Question by Mr. Bugliosi: Would you give up your life for Charles Manson if he asked you to?
Answer: Many times he has given you his life.
Q. Just answer the question, Brenda.
A. Yes, I would.
Q. Would you lie on the stand for Charles Manson?
A. No, I would tell the truth on the stand.
Q. So you would die for him but not lie for him?
A. That's right.

The reality, of course, is that we all lie from time to time. I'm always amused by people who say they never lie, and in the very next breath, without being aware they are acknowledging a lie on their part, relate how they made a few extra dollars from an insurance company, or Uncle Sam, by putting in for something they are not entitled to, or not declaring something they should have. The irony is that those who say they never lie usually (not always) lie more than those who are at least truthful enough to admit they lie. And they lie in the very worst way possible, to further their own interests at the expense of others. One is reminded of Ralph Waldo Emerson's remark that "the louder he talked of his honor, the faster we counted our spoons."

There are several reasons why virtually all human beings lie, one of the most important of which is that we all do things at one time or another that we are not proud of. And if we are immoral enough to do that which we are not proud of, surely we are capable of the lesser immorality of denying that we did it. (For example, "Yes, it's true, I did steal that coat, but if they ever ask me about it, I'd never ever lie and deny it" is an obvious absurdity.) So for someone to make the assertion that he never lies is almost the equivalent of saying he never does anything wrong.

And yet even a supposedly profound intellectual like the famous German philosopher Immanuel Kant insisted that all lies were immoral and never permissible, even in situations of imminent peril. Lying is absolutely essential in a civilized society (if we all said to people's faces what we say behind their backs, society would be impossible), and absolutely necessary in many circumstances. During wartime, Churchill said, "the truth has to be protected by a battalion of lies." Lying is also sometimes the only moral thing to do. Imagine German SS agents knocking on the door of a residence in Berlin in the late 1930s and inquiring of a young Jew as to the whereabouts of his parents, who are in hiding. Kant would apparently insist that the lad tell the SS the truth. And why would any decent human being, upon being asked by a particularly unattractive girl or boy how he or she looks in a new outfit, not say "Good," or "Fine," even if the young person looked awful?

Lying is so common that virtually every runner in a football game and catcher in a baseball game thinks nothing of lying, almost every single time, in front of thousands and, if the game is televised, millions of people. Show me a high school, college, or professional runner who, when tackled, doesn't try to place the ball a tad farther down the field than it should be. The referee has to move the ball back a couple of inches to the proper place all the time. Show me a catcher in a baseball game who doesn't automatically pull a ball that just missed the plate back into the strike zone for the benefit of the umpire. Would anyone be silly enough to suggest that if you deceive by your conduct it is okay, but never by your words? That is, it's okay for the catcher to try to deceive the umpire by moving the gloved ball closer to the plate, but if he were to take it a step further, turn around and tell the umpire the ball was a strike, it would be understandable for the umpire to bark at him: "You lowlife liar, you're outta this ballgame"? That would be elevating words over conduct in importance, something at odds with what our society has always believed. One of my favorite expressions is "Your conduct speaks so loudly I can't hear a word you are saying." All deception in life, whether in words or conduct, is the same.

So although not lying, as a basic proposition, is something to aspire to, we all lie, from presidents and cardinals on down. When President Carter, certainly one of the most principled and moral men ever to occupy the Oval Office, told the American people at the start of his presidency, "I will never lie to you," I said to myself, "Carter just told his first lie."

Lying, then, is a common, everyday part of life. "Mom, tell him I'm not home." Yet the myth that a lie is an intrinsically immoral thing persists unchallenged, and because of it, and because the prosecution in the Simpson case took such a naive and sophomoric approach with respect to Fuhrman's lie, that lie, inherently insignificant, became a major liability to the prosecution's case, assuming enormous importance.

In every case, but particularly one like the Simpson case, where guilt is so obvious, and the defense's only defense is smoke, mirrors, and hubris, prosecutors should use their opening argument to paint the defense attorney into so many corners that he is afraid, or at least embarrassed, to stand up. (And in final argument, the words and argument should be so piercing and powerful they should cause defense counsel to slink beneath their table.) I routinely did this in my cases. Why should this case have been any different when there were so many opportunities for the prosecution?

Let me give you one or two examples. The defense in the Simpson case never once flat-out accused the LAPD of "framing" Simpson. As we have seen, it was the core of the defense's entire case, and the defense attorneys certainly very strongly suggested and implied it with virtually every question they asked and every argument they made. The reason they never explicitly said so, of course, was they knew the mere uttering of the words would make them look ridiculous. Somehow, though it is the same thing, saying the police "planted" this or that does not make one sound as absurd as saying the police "framed" Simpson. Can you imagine how the defense would have sounded if they had said: "The evidence shows, and we believe, that Vannatter, Lange, Phillips, and Fuhrman got together and framed Mr. Simpson for these murders"? They would have sounded absurd.

But the defense didn't have to "sound" absurd. It achieved the very same objective simply by making the accusation by innuendo. What the defense did in this case was not quite the same but nonetheless reminded me somewhat of what defense attorney Gerry Spence did when he defended Lee Harvey Oswald in the twenty-one-hour television docu-trial in London. In his cross-examination of my witnesses and in his summation, he strongly implied to the jury, without expressly charging, that either the CIA, the FBI, or some other group was behind the assassination of President Kennedy, and had framed his client—"Lee," as Spence called him. And ever since the assassination and frame-up in 1963, he claimed, there had been a massive cover-up. This is a brief excerpt from my summation in London on this point:

"Why doesn't Mr. Spence come right out and say it? Why doesn't he accuse the CIA and FBI of murdering the president and framing his client for these murders? One thing you can say about Mr. Spence, he's not a shy man. If he thinks something, he comes right out and says it. I'll tell you folks why he didn't say it. Because if he said the CIA murdered the president, or the FBI murdered the president, it would sound downright silly," I thundered. "You'd laugh at him. Maybe to yourself, but he knows you'd laugh at him. So he doesn't utter those words. He tries to get the same benefit by implying these things."

Walking over to Spence's counsel table, I said: "He implied to you that there was some nebulous, mysterious, powerful group that murdered the president and framed Lee Harvey Oswald, but he never put this hat here [Spence's Stetson] on anyone's head. He kept his hat on this table.

"If, perchance, Mr. Spence isn't suggesting that the CIA, FBI, Secret Service, or KGB did it, then who is he suggesting *did* do it? Who is he suggesting that the CIA and FBI have been covering up *for*? The Department of Agriculture? What is Mr. Spence saying? I really don't know.

"When you stop to analyze it, what Mr. Spence is really saying in his down-home, front-porch way is that 'I don't know this, and I don't know that, but one thing I do know. I know I need help in this case. And I also know that only you people can help me out, you folks. Why should you help me? Well, you know, I'd really appreciate it.' Isn't that really the substance of what he said on the issue of conspiracy when he got up in front of you?"

The Simpson prosecutors, in their opening argument, should have said words to this effect to the jury:

"**The defense in this case has never flat-out accused Fuhrman and the three other detectives in this case of framing Simpson, because they know if they did, they'd sound ridiculous. Although they've strongly suggested that evidence was planted and tampered with, not once have they used the word 'frame.'** *They've never explicitly told you folks these detectives framed Simpson for these murders.* **But that's precisely, of course, what they want you to believe. And if I'm wrong, if that's not what they want you to believe, then I want Mr. Cochran, when he stands up here to address you after me, to tell you this. In other words, we're going to flush this man out. If he doesn't want you to believe this, this means Mr. Simpson is guilty, because with his blood at the murder scene along with an atticful of other evidence, the only way he can be innocent is if he was framed. And if Mr. Cochran, when we flush him out, says he doesn't want you to actually believe this, then let's end the trial right now with a guilty verdict. If Mr. Cochran gets up and refuses to be flushed out, saying things like 'maybe this' or 'maybe that' happened, I say maybe,** *shmaybe.* **If I had wings, maybe I could fly.**

"**On the other hand, if he does want you folks to believe there was a frame-up here, and he's not going to waffle, then I want Mr. Cochran,** who's been accusing, by strong innuendo, the four detectives in this case and several other employees of the LAPD, like the criminalists, of framing his client for murder, I want him to step forward like a man, come out of the shadows, stop playing word games, and directly and explicitly and unequivocally say what he and his colleagues have only been implying to you for nine months. Detectives Lange and Vannatter are here right now in this courtroom. And I want Mr. Cochran to say, right in front of them, that he believes they and their colleagues framed Mr. Simpson for these murders. I'm going to be waiting to see what Mr. Cochran does when he addresses you, and I'm sure you folks and everyone else in this courtroom will be, too. And of course, when I talk to you again after Mr. Cochran addresses you, I'll comment, in no uncertain terms, on what Mr. Cochran has said."

If Cochran felt he had no choice but to flat-out accuse the LAPD of framing his client, I believe he'd necessarily look and sound foolish. In addition, I'd ask, in my rebuttal, that if he truly felt there was a frame-up, why had it taken him over nine months to finally say it, and then only after I forced him to? Of course, if he did not make the flat-out accusation, the damage to the defense's case would be severe.

The prosecutors, in their opening argument, should have also given Cochran a list of questions, prepared for the jury on exhibits they could refer to, that he could not answer.

"For instance, Mr. Cochran, these folks on the jury and I want you to reconcile three contradictory statements. In your opening statement, you told the jury that Mr. Simpson was practicing his golf at the time of the murders. But Mr. Simpson told the limo driver he was sleeping, and in his statement to the police, which we have all heard in this courtroom, when they asked him everything he had done that evening, all he said was that he was very busy packing and getting ready for his trip to Chicago. He said nothing about playing golf or sleeping. Again, we want you to reconcile these three contradictory statements, and we want you to do so confining yourself to the evidence that came from that witness stand at this trial. When I later address the jury, I'll of course respond to what you have to say, or comment on the fact that you refused to answer the question."

Finally, in their opening arguments, since they had almost a whole year to learn (from Cochran's opening statement, from the defense's cross-examination of the prosecution's witnesses, and from the witnesses they, the defense, called) what Cochran's and Scheck's arguments had to be, Clark and Darden should have told the jury, in summary form, of course, what the defense was going to argue. (They did very, very little of this.)

When you do this it lessens the psychological impact of the defense arguments. To use a trite expression, it takes the wind out of their sails. Defense counsel sound almost silly saying exactly what you said they were going to say.

Incidentally, near the end of my opening argument, I might have left a Bible and a copy of the U.S. Constitution on the lectern, telling the jury: "Mr. Cochran talks about the Bible and the Constitution in all of his cases, and if he decides to do so in this case as well, I just want to help my colleague out." If, when Cochran got up, he started quoting from the Bible and Constitution, he'd look a little foolish, and if he didn't, he'd have to do without a lot of the emotional underpinnings of his argument.

I've already indicated how Simpson's statement to the police about bleeding on the night of the murders was, alone, enough to convict him. The prosecutors, not introducing that statement, focused mainly in summation on Dr. Baden's testimony concerning Simpson's cutting himself on the night of the murders, and because of it, they were terribly restricted. On tape, Simpson said he had no idea how he cut himself. Because this is highly improbable, it shows a consciousness of guilt on his part. Simpson told Baden, on the other hand, that he received a small cut when he went out to his Bronco, according to Baden's testimony, "to retrieve his phone or some material from the Bronco . . . He had gone to the Bronco to get something and may have somehow cut himself while getting stuff, stuff from the Bronco to bring with him to Chicago." Note that what Simpson told Baden does not indicate a consciousness of guilt.

The second big weakness of the prosecution's relying on Baden's testimony for Simpson's cut is that Simpson only told Baden he cut himself and he saw "some blood," not that he was dripping blood anywhere, whereas in the statement he gave the police, he *admits* to dripping blood in his car, at home, and on the driveway. Without Simpson's admission on the tape-recorded statement, the prosecution could only argue to the jury that the police said they saw Simpson's blood in his car and home and on the driveway before he returned from Chicago. So the jury had the LAPD's word for this, *not Simpson's*.

Marcia Clark, then, because of the prosecution's self-inflicted wound, was substantially handicapped in arguing the single most incriminating piece of evidence against Simpson in the entire case. (Normally, the statement would have been the second most important piece of evidence, behind the DNA evidence putting Simpson's blood at the murder scene, which is absolutely conclusive evidence of guilt. But since we know the jury bought into the frame-up theory and the contamination-of-blood theory, Simpson's own very incriminating words to the police would have stood head and shoulders above all the other evidence of guilt.)

Being handicapped was bad enough, even if Clark had made the most out of what she had. But she proceeded to make the most garbled, God-awful argument imaginable concerning Simpson's cut on the night of the murders. Talking about the fact that Simpson had blood on the outside door handle of the Bronco, she told the jury that Simpson had told Baden he cut himself while going out to the Bronco to get his cellular phone. She then proceeded to tell the jury in garbled language: "Now, although we don't know for a fact that he certainly did not receive that cut on some razor-sharp cell phone, it certainly does not make sense that when he went out to get the phone [Clark is actually embracing what Simpson told Baden as true] he opened the door to the Bronco and his knuckle grazed the wall of the door handle reopening the cut [he had received during the murder]." If you are a little confused at this point, you can imagine the jurors' confusion.

When she got to the key inference to be made about the cut and bleeding, again, she was so inarticulate she actually took a coincidence of astronomical odds down to something that sounded almost plausible. Listen to this: "So now we have the defendant getting his hand cut on the night of his wife's stabbing, cut on his left hand, *which just happens to be the hand that the murderer cut that same night.* That's an alarming coincidence." From the literal context of what she said, Clark seemed to be arguing to the jury that the coincidence was not that Simpson innocently cut himself around the time of the murders, but that he cut himself on "his left hand, which *just happens* to be the hand that the murderer cut that same night." Remarkably, she succeeded in reducing a coincidence in the millions down to one out of two hands.

On a roll, she became even more off-base in her argument. Referring to Dr. Huizenga, the defense doctor who examined Simpson two days after the murders and saw four cuts and seven abrasions on Simpson's left hand, but didn't ask him how or even when he got the cuts, Clark made this incredible statement to the jury: "You know, *I can see getting one cut, maybe two on your hand* [What? Marcia, please!], but four cuts and seven abrasions? And we're supposed to believe that that's unrelated to a murder in which the killer's left hand was cut and bleeding as he left the scene?"

In view of this statement, maybe Clark hadn't misspoken after all when she seemed to say earlier that the *main* coincidence was that Simpson had cut himself on the same hand as the murderer had. Maybe Clark really didn't believe that innocently cutting yourself around the very same time your former wife was murdered is much of a coincidence at all. It was only the *number* of cuts that was suspicious to her. Unbelievable.

Continuing on her bad roll, she asked the jury: "What does a person do when we cut ourselves and we drip blood? What do we do?" I was sure she was going to say the obvious, that we stop the bleeding, not bleed all over the place. But she said: "We clean it up." Again, what? If we're to believe Clark, the first thing one normally does when bleeding is to clean up the floor, not stop the bleeding. Doesn't everyone know that stopping the bleeding is a much more immediate and automatic response than cleaning it up? In fact, even though we know Simpson is guilty, since he had to catch a plane to Chicago, his postponing cleaning up until he returned from Chicago isn't incriminating at all. But whether you're going to Chicago or not, if you're dripping blood all over your car and home you instinctively try to stop the flow of blood. As if her drawing the far weaker of the two inferences were not bad enough, after saying that if she and the jury had dripped blood they'd have cleaned it up, but Simpson didn't, Clark just left it at that, not bothering to go on and tell the jury what, in her mind, the failure to clean up meant in terms of guilt. The reason may have been that there was nothing for her to say, since under the circumstances, Simpson's failure to clean up before he left for Chicago meant very little, if anything at all.

I have to believe that if Clark had bothered to look over, just once, her prepared remarks on this all-important issue of Simpson's bleeding on the night of the murders, this intelligent and experienced criminal prosecutor would have vastly improved her argument and articulation on this issue. If she in fact did look over her prepared remarks and still did not see how weak her argument was and how poor and garbled were the logic and language she used, then Garcetti had no business assigning a prosecutor of this level of ability to this case. But if she didn't look over the remarks she prepared for her opening argument, then I say to her that she owed it to her client, the People of the State of California, to have done a hell of a lot more preparation than she did before she stood up and argued on their behalf.

And don't let anyone tell you about a lack of time to prepare. No prosecutors, perhaps in any case in criminal history, had more help than Clark and Darden did on the Simpson case. And the trial dragged on for almost a year. So they had all the time in the world. Going over a five- or six-hour argument only takes five or six hours. (Of course, it should have been gone over ten times.) Whatever personal problems Clark had in her custody fight with her husband, she had time (as Darden did) to be seen here and there on weekends and in the evening throughout the trial, and at least one time, in March 1995, with Darden throughout the evening and into the early-morning hours at the House of Blues on Sunset Boulevard in West Los Angeles.

When a prosecutor is on a big case like this, there shouldn't be any "sightings" of the prosecutor by the paparazzi. He or she should be in one of only three places (except for necessary time Clark had to spend with her two children outdoors)—court, office, and home. Even to and from work is valuable work time, and a driver should be found to free up the prosecutor. (In the Manson case, my driver was a bodyguard from the DA's Bureau of Investigation.) Routinely, I put in one hundred hours a week on all complex murder cases. This was not done here. No way. It couldn't have been. The terrible performances prove that.

The argument to the jury on the subject of Simpson's bleeding on the night of the murders should have gone something like what follows. (Had I been the prosecutor on the case, I would have put in many, many more hours than I have here to prepare such an argument, and all the items of evidence I am "throwing out the window" here would obviously have been separately argued to the jury in much more depth elsewhere in my summation.)

"Ladies and gentlemen of the jury, the evidence of Mr. Simpson's guilt is so overwhelming in this case that you could throw 80 percent of it out the window and there still would be no question of his guilt. For instance, as we've previously discussed, we know that Simpson beat poor Nicole savagely, and she was in fear of her life at his hands. You recall she told officer Edwards, 'He's going to kill me, he's going to kill me.' I mean, who else would have had any reason to murder these two young people, who apparently were both very well liked and popular, and particularly in such a brutal, savage way? But let's throw this evidence out the window. Let's assume Mr. Simpson and Nicole got along well, just swimmingly, that he never laid a hand on her.

"When he was charged with these murders, if he were innocent, he would have been outraged, blazing mad, at being charged with murders he did not commit, and would desperately want to prove his innocence and find out who murdered the mother of his two children. Instead, he writes this suicide note that absolutely reeks with guilt. Show me an innocent person on the face of this globe charged with murder who would write a note like that. But let's assume there was no such suicide note, let's throw it out the window. After that slow-speed freeway chase, as you recall, the police found a gun, a passport, and a cheap disguise in Mr. Simpson's possession. And his closest friend, Al

Cowlings, just happens to have $8,750 in currency stuffed in his pockets, which he told the police Mr. Simpson gave him in the Bronco. We all know what all of this means. We've already discussed it. Throw this evidence out the window. It doesn't exist.

On the night of the murders, the limo driver, Alan Park, arrived at the Simpson estate at 10:22 p.m., and he was scheduled to pick Mr. Simpson up at 10:45 p.m. for the trip to L.A. International Airport. Incidentally, we can rely on all of the times Mr. Park testified to, since knowing the exact time is a limousine driver's stock in trade. As you know, Park testified that at 10:22 p.m., which the evidence has shown is around the very time of the murders, he didn't see Mr. Simpson's Bronco at the estate. It wasn't parked on Ashford or Rockingham. He then parked his limo on Ashford, and at 10:39 p.m., when he drove over to the Rockingham side of the estate, the Bronco, which was found parked there in the morning, *still* wasn't there. Park further testified that from 10:40 to 10:50, he rang the intercom on the gate several times, and there was no answer from inside Simpson's residence.

At about 10:55 p.m. he sees a black person around six feet tall, two hundred pounds, and wearing all dark clothing walking briskly toward the front door of Mr. Simpson's home. After this person enters the residence, the light in the entryway is immediately turned on, and within seconds Mr. Park goes back to the gate and rings the buzzer again, and this time Simpson immediately answers the intercom. So we know it was the defendant who had just entered the front door. Simpson tells the limo driver, 'I overslept, I just got out of the shower, and I'll be down in a minute.' It's pretty obvious what Mr. Simpson was trying to do here. Only he knew exactly when these murders took place, and he was trying to establish an alibi for himself. What other reason under the moon would he have had to tell this blatant lie to the limo driver if he hadn't just committed these murders? Throw all of this evidence out the window. It doesn't exist.

"In fact, throw out the bloody glove found on his estate with Mr. Simpson's and Ron's and Nicole's blood on it, the glove that matches the glove found at the murder scene. We don't have the glove anymore. In fact, let's throw out all the DNA evidence that puts Mr. Simpson's blood at the murder scene, and that conclusively proves his guilt beyond all doubt. Let's also throw out the DNA evidence that Ron's and Nicole's blood was found inside Mr. Simpson's Bronco, and Nicole's blood was found on the socks inside the bedroom of his home. Throw out all of that evidence. It doesn't exist. There's *still* no question of this man's guilt. Why do I say that? Because the defendant, from his own lips, told us he committed these two murders. How did he tell us? Let's take this step by step.

"You heard his statement to the police on the day after the murders. We played it for you folks here in this courtroom. As you know, the detectives told Mr. Simpson that they found blood in his car, in his home, and on the driveway, and when they asked him why that was so, he answered that he had cut himself the previous night, and was dripping blood while he was getting ready to leave for Chicago, which we know was somewhere between 10:00 and 11:00 p.m. on the night of the murders. And we know from the testimony of several witnesses that the murders occurred somewhere between 10:15 and 10:40 that night. Mr. Simpson admits, then, that around the very time of the murders — which was around sixteen hours *before* the police removed blood from his arm and would have had any opportunity to sprinkle or plant it, which we know is pure moonshine — he was dripping blood in his car and home and on his driveway. So even if we bought the absurd defense allegation that the police in this case tried to frame Simpson by planting his blood in various places, including his car and home — which never happened, and there isn't a speck of evidence that it did — it still couldn't be more obvious he's guilty. Because whatever blood that would have been planted had to be *in addition* to blood of Mr. Simpson's that was *already* in his car and home and on his driveway on the night of the murders. We know that because the defendant, from his own lips, told us so.

"And as we heard on the tape, when the detectives asked him how he had cut himself on the night of the murders, his exact words were: 'I don't know.' When they asked him again, a little later in the interview, how he had cut himself, you'll recall he answered: 'I have no idea, man.' I have no idea, man. Can you imagine that?

"Now let's just stop to think about this for a moment. We're not talking about a little nick or scratch here. We're talking about a deep cut to his left middle finger. You've seen photos of it, and Detectives Lange and Vannater told you that it was bandaged on the day after the murders. And yet Mr. Simpson claims he has no idea how he got that cut. This ridiculous statement alone shows an obvious consciousness of guilt on his part. You folks ask yourself back in the jury room how many times, if at all, in your life that you've cut yourself badly enough to bleed all over your car and home, and yet you had absolutely no idea how you cut yourself. It's absurd on its face, and all by itself tells us that this man is guilty of murdering these two poor people.

"But there's an even more powerful reason why Mr. Simpson's own statement shows that it was he who, on the evening of June 12, 1994, viciously murdered the two victims in this case. What is the likelihood, I ask you, what is the likelihood that Mr. Simpson innocently cut himself very badly on his left middle finger around the very same time that his former wife and Ron Goldman were brutally murdered? I mean, come on. What is the statistical improbability against such a thing happening? One out of ten million? One out of a million, one out of a hundred thousand? We're talking DNA numbers here, aren't we?

"I want you folks to think back, not to when you were children, but to your adult life. It hasn't been too often, has it, that you've cut yourself badly? The last time I remember cutting myself badly was almost thirty years ago when I was working with a small electric saw in the garage of my home and I cut my wrist. But it's not common, is it, that adults cut themselves badly? Here, Mr. Simpson just didn't cut himself badly within the same *decade* his former wife was murdered, not just within the same *year* she was murdered, not just within the same *month*, or even within the same *week* she was murdered. In fact, not just within the same *day* she was murdered. No. The defense wants us to believe that around *the very precise time* she was murdered, he innocently cut himself very badly. And to top it off, he tells us he has absolutely no idea how. Is there one reasonable person in this entire courtroom who would believe a cockamamie story like that? People who would believe a story like that would believe someone who told them they once saw a man jump away from his own shadow. Remember, the prosecution only has the burden of proving guilt beyond a reasonable doubt, not beyond all doubt. But here, of course, we have proved this man's guilt beyond all doubt. His guilt is so obvious I'm almost embarrassed having to stand up in front of you folks telling you these things. But he's pled not guilty, which is his right, so I have no choice.

"One very important footnote to this man's dripping blood in his car and home and on his driveway on the night of these murders. Even if we made the extremely absurd and extravagant assumption that the coincidence of his cutting himself badly around the very same time Ron and Nicole were murdered is not far-fetched—which we know it is—has it ever happened to you, or to any adult you know or have heard of, that you cut your finger and the blood got all over your car and home? Don't you see how silly it sounds to even make this argument? When you cut yourself, unless you're in a frantic and frenzied state—which Mr. Simpson obviously was in—you stop the bleeding with your hand or your handkerchief and you put on a bandage. You don't bleed all over the place.

"Ladies and gentlemen of the jury, there is *no explanation* for what happened in this case other than Mr. Simpson's guilt. None at all. Sometimes in life there is more than one possible explanation for an event. But not with what we've been talking about. If there were, obviously the defense would have presented that explanation to you. But not even a Houdini can pull a rabbit out of a hat when there is no rabbit in the hat. I repeat, even if there were no other evidence in this case, Mr. Simpson, in so many words, and from his own lips, admitted murdering these two victims. *Within minutes of these murders, there is blood all over his car, home, and estate.* And he says he has absolutely no idea how he got cut. Under these circumstances, it isn't possible for him to be innocent—that is, not in the world in which we live. You know, I'm talking to you folks and you can hear me, there will be a dawn tomorrow, that type of world. Only in a fantasy world could this man be innocent. As sure as I'm standing here, as sure as night follows day, this man is guilty."

Marcia Clark's clumsy and inept way of arguing the most important piece of evidence in the case against Simpson extended to her discussion of reasonable doubt, the most important *legal* issue in the case. We will see in the Epilogue that Cochran also did not have a solid grasp of the doctrine. We know this from his having told the jury, during his opening statement, that it had to determine "the guilt or innocence" of his client, which is not the issue at a criminal trial. It's whether the prosecution has proved guilt beyond a reasonable doubt. During his final summation, Cochran continued to betray his lack of knowledge of the doctrine of reasonable doubt by this new (at least I've never heard it before) and clearly incorrect statement: "This case is about whether these facts establish guilt *or innocence* beyond a reasonable doubt." Accomplished criminal lawyers just don't talk that way.

Clark articulated the doctrine of reasonable doubt in a way that could only hurt the prosecution. It was bad enough that she didn't state the strength of the prosecution's case strongly enough ("We have more than met our burden of proof in this case" and "The defendant has been proven guilty easily beyond a reasonable doubt" is fine for many cases, but when the evidence is as strong and unequivocal as this case, the prosecutor should argue to the jury that although the prosecution only has the burden of proving guilt beyond a reasonable doubt, in this case it proved his guilt beyond *all* doubt), but she also misstated the doctrine, telling the jury that reasonable doubt "is a doubt founded in reason." One would think that would be correct—a reasonable doubt is a doubt founded in reason. But the courts in California and elsewhere have held that a judge instructing the jury that "reasonable doubt means just what it says, a doubt based upon reason" is an incorrect statement of the law (*People v. Garcia*, 54 CA 3d 61 [1975]).

I actually was quite surprised when I heard Clark, a supposedly experienced prosecutor, define reasonable doubt the way defense attorneys, not prosecutors, do. In fact, later in his summation, Cochran told the jury: "What [reasonable doubt] really is is a doubt based upon reason." Chris Darden knew that Cochran's defense articulation of reasonable doubt was incorrect. In his closing argument to the jury, he correctly told the jury (thereby contradicting Clark, his co-prosecutor): "Mr. Cochran said to you, 'Reasonable doubt is doubt with a reason.' That is not reasonable doubt."

So the lead prosecutor and lead defense attorney in the most publicized murder case of our time were both defining reasonable doubt incorrectly to the jury, and unfortunately the incorrect definition they were using favored the defense.

Since virtually all people (including jurors) believe they are reasonable, any doubt they have must, by definition, also be reasonable. But we all know this isn't true. In fact, the jury instruction obliquely alludes to this when it says that reasonable doubt "is not a mere possible doubt, because everything relating to human affairs is open to some possible or imaginary doubt." Clark did go on to tell the jury: "I have a possible doubt that the sun will come up tomorrow. Do I have a reasonable doubt about it? No. I have no doubt founded in reason that that is going to happen." Nonetheless, to these jurors, an extreme example like the one Clark gave to them is not going to eradicate the basic thought in their minds that since they are reasonable people, *any* doubt that's not knowingly far-fetched must be reasonable.

What *is* a reasonable doubt? As I point out in the Epilogue, it does not lend itself to a definition, and the attempt to define it only confuses further, but I always told juries, without objection from the judge or opposing defense counsel, that a reasonable doubt was "a sound, sensible, logical doubt based on the evidence in the case."

The most damaging word by far in the term "beyond a reasonable doubt" is "beyond." When I first started out as a prosecutor, I was always troubled by defense counsel's arguing to the jury that the prosecution had the burden of proving guilt "beyond" a reasonable doubt. They emphasized the word "beyond" as if the prosecution had to go beyond the horizon and to the ends of the earth to prove guilt, which is consistent with laypeople's erroneous impression that guilt has to be proved "beyond a *shadow* of a doubt." I sensed something was wrong, but I didn't know what it was. So I sat down with my yellow pad (my security blanket) one day and started to analyze the word "beyond" as it related to the doctrine of reasonable doubt. Finally, it dawned on me that the word "beyond" was not only a needless appendage, but much more important, in the term "beyond a reasonable doubt," it is misleading to the jury because it is not used in its principal sense of "further" or "more than." If it were, the prosecution would have to prove there is *more* than a reasonable doubt of a defendant's guilt, when obviously, they have to prove just the opposite—that there is *less* than a reasonable doubt. Instead, "beyond" is used in its secondary sense of "to the exclusion of."

In my cases thereafter, after explaining to the jury the true sense in which the word "beyond" is used, I would say this to the jury: "The prosecution, then, has the burden of proving the guilt of this defendant *to the exclusion* of all reasonable doubt. With this in mind, we can completely eliminate the word 'beyond' from the term 'beyond a reasonable doubt' and come up with this [which I'd also write on the blackboard]: 'If you do not have a reasonable doubt of the guilt of this defendant, convict. If you do have a reasonable doubt, acquit.' We have eliminated the word 'beyond' from the term 'beyond a reasonable doubt' and we still have a very accurate definition and statement of the doctrine of reasonable doubt."

When I was a prosecutor, I never had any judge or defense counsel object to the verbal surgery I had performed on the term "beyond a reasonable doubt," and as a prosecutor I found this surgery to be an important point.

Johnnie Cochran's final summation to the jury was his best performance at the trial. Contrasted to the uninspiring and flat delivery of the two prosecutors, Cochran spoke with more style, flair, and, though the facts were against him and he was attempting to thwart rather than bring about justice, more passion. One quality Johnnie Cochran has which most trial lawyers don't have, one that is essential to being a successful trial lawyer, is that he's a fighter. Not a superb one at all, but an adequate one. He clearly demonstrated that he was more of a courtroom battler than either of the two lead prosecutors in the Simpson case.

But although Cochran spoke with more passion, he definitely did not, as the media proclaimed, give a stirring, fire-and-brimstone speech remindful of a Southern revivalist preacher. If that is the simile, Cochran was a rather pale imitation of such a religious orator, as just a few minutes of TV-watching on any Sunday morning will show. In fact, Cochran's few transparent attempts at such evangelical tent-preaching for the obvious benefit of the black jurors rang hollow, since his cadence and intonation were obviously changed for effect.

Cochran, surprisingly, was more specific in his summation than either Darden or Clark. He quoted the actual trial testimony much more than they, and wasn't saying "I think" the way the prosecutors so often did. He came across as being more confident and knowledgeable about the facts of the case then the prosecutors. This is inexcusable. A prosecutor should have an unexcelled command of the facts, which gives the argument he makes force and credibility.

And Cochran proved to be better than the prosecutors at the art of argumentation. Although his argument was very poorly structured and he rambled discursively from one issue to another, with the help of the many lawyers on the defense team (and even lawyers not involved in the case sending in suggestions), at one point or another in his summation he managed to point out to the jury all the small problems with the prosecution's case. Though he could have gotten appreciably more out of many of his articulations on these points, he was nonetheless effective since he *did* make the points, and his tone and delivery throughout suggested these were actually *big* problems with the prosecution's case. And although it should have been the prosecution expressing outrage at the conduct of the defendant and his lawyers, it was Cochran, and later Scheck, who acted as if they were on the side of truth and justice and had been wronged by the LAPD and DA's office.

For instance, though they interviewed him, the prosecutors failed to call Robert Heidstra, a defense "time-line" witness who testified he heard Nicole's Akita dog start barking crazily at around 10:35 p.m. (several prosecution witnesses said the time was around 10:15 to 10:20 p.m.), narrowing the time for Simpson to have committed the murders and do what the prosecution alleged he did before being seen back at his estate at 10:55 p.m. Though this was an obvious argument, Cochran argued: "It came out that Robert Heidstra had been talking to the prosecution. But they don't call him because [his testimony] doesn't fit in their time-line. What about this search for truth? Can they handle the truth? You see, their job is not just to try to convict. Their job as prosecutors is to make sure the innocent go free also."

Yet another instance where the prosecutors in the Simpson case gave the impression to the jury that it was they who were trying to suppress evidence, even though *outside* the presence of the jury it was the defense, of course, in motion after motion, who tried to keep out almost all the physical evidence in the case, such as all the blood, hair, and fiber evidence found at Simpson's Rockingham estate. As Denise Brown, Nicole's sister, so aptly put it: "If he's innocent, why are they trying to keep out all the evidence?" But in front of the jury, where it counted, time and time again, by their abject incompetence, the prosecutors conveyed to the jury that they were trying to keep the jury from hearing relevant evidence.

Witnesses like Heidstra should have been called by the prosecution to preempt the defense, since the prosecutors knew that, despite some testimony from Heidstra that might hurt the defense (see discussion in next chapter), there was at least a fifty-fifty chance that the defense would call Heidstra if the prosecution didn't. And there is really no huge problem with such a witness. Witnesses give conflicting testimony all the time. Five people see an auto accident and each one gives a slightly (sometimes substantially) different version. You call a Heidstra and later argue and point out to the jury that although there's a diversity of opinion as to when the murders occurred, the decided weight of the testimony, as well as all of the surrounding circumstantial evidence, indicates the murders happened around 10:15 to 10:20 p.m. And you don't lock yourself unnecessarily into this precise time, as the prosecutors did at the beginning of the trial, forcing them to retreat, before the jury's eyes, as the defense called witnesses like Heidstra. Calling Heidstra as a prosecution witness would hardly have hurt the prosecution at all. But as a witness for the defense, his testimony was damaging to the prosecution.

In the same vein, with respect to the prosecution's very imprudent decision not to call to the witness stand the deputy coroner who conducted the autopsies, Cochran argued: "Nobody around here can remember any time that the coroner who did the autopsy, the actual autopsy on a body, wasn't called by the prosecutor. Why do you think they didn't call the coroner? They spent eight days trashing their own coroner and they didn't call him. Why is that in this search for truth? [I'll tell you the answer to your question, Johnnie. It's not the sinister motive you're implying to this jury. The answer is pure and simple prosecutorial incompetence, the shocking kind.] They call somebody else who's not even there at the autopsies. . . . It's basic that you've got to call the coroner. But they did a number of things in this case, ladies and gentlemen, that had never been seen before."

Since Cochran was facing two prosecutors who, by and large, were very weak at the art of argumentation, he was able to make loose and ill-advised remarks that left him vulnerable, and still get by with it. Take Simpson's refusal to testify in his own defense. Prosecutors used to comment routinely to the jury during their argument that a defendant's silence was evidence of his guilt. But in 1964, the United States Supreme Court (*Malloy v. Hogan* 378 U.S. 1) ruled that if a defendant exercised his right against self-incrimination under the Fifth Amendment to the United States Constitution and refused to testify, he was "to suffer no penalty . . . for such silence." The following year, the Court, in *Griffin v. California* (380 U.S. 609), held that the Fifth Amendment "forbids either comment by the prosecution on the accused's silence or instructions by the court that such silence is evidence of guilt." The rationale? To comment on the defendant's silence "cuts down on the [Fifth Amendment] privilege [against self incrimination] by making its assertion costly," i.e., if, indeed, the defendant has such a privilege, he should not be penalized for exercising it.

In trials where the defendant does not testify, the defense makes every effort to make sure this fact is not spotlighted for the jury. And the prosecution doesn't even indirectly comment on it at all before the jury, because in the event of a conviction, the comment could constitute reversible error.

Yet in this case, Cochran boldly and brazenly suggested to the jury, as oblique as the implication was, *that Simpson didn't even have the right* to testify in his defense. He said: "Let me ask each of you a question. Have you ever in your life been falsely accused of something? Ever had to sit there and take it and watch the proceedings and wait and wait and wait all the while knowing that you didn't do it? *All you could do* during such a process is to really maintain your dignity; isn't that correct? Knowing that you were innocent, but maintaining your dignity and remembering always that all you're left with after a crisis is your conduct."

When Cochran said that "all you could do" is maintain your dignity, wasn't he suggesting that Simpson didn't have the right to do anything else? If that's all Simpson could do in defending himself from the charges, doesn't that suggest he didn't have the right to take the stand and respond to the charges? Is it possible that these jurors may have had that thought enter their minds after Cochran's remark? Later, Cochran alluded once again, in my opinion, to the fact that perhaps Simpson didn't have a right to testify in his own defense. He said to the jury: "There is one place you can't take away somebody's voice, and that is in the courtroom. If you want to tell the truth, for sixteen [sic] months this man sat over here and heard people talk about him day in and day out, judged him and prejudged him against the American way. What right, how dare they do that?

And he has one day or two days to have somebody stand up for him." Again, isn't Cochran thereby implying that all Simpson could do was have some-one stand up for him? That he couldn't stand up for himself in his own defense?

In any event, all Cochran did by these remarks was leave himself and his client open to an argument by the prosecution (which the prosecution, in its incompetence, did not make) that "Mr. Cochran suggested to you folks that all Mr. Simpson could do to fight the charges against him was maintain his dignity, and have someone else stand up for him in his defense. That, of course, is 100 percent untrue, as the court will tell you. He also had the right to testify in his defense, and he chose not to." Note that this comment by the prosecutor would not be asking the jury to draw an inference of guilt from Simpson's failure to testify. It would simply be clarifying two very misleading statements by Cochran. Normally, even that remark from a prosecutor would not be permitted, since he cannot even make any reference to the defendant's failure to testify. But here, Cochran very clearly opened the door by making two improper, mislead-ing remarks to the jury which the prosecution could have properly ex-ploited to draw attention to the fact that Simpson, as guilty as sin, was remaining as quiet as a statue to the charges against him.

There were examples after examples of the prosecution's showing not the slightest instinct for argumentation. When Cochran argued to the jury (concerning the failed glove demonstration), "If it doesn't fit, you must acquit," a singsong, childlike rhyme suggested to him in this case by co-counsel Gerald Uelman, don't you automatically (in addition to all the arguments why the glove didn't fit) say: "If it doesn't fit, you must acquit? *Nothing* fits better than DNA. DNA fits a person to the exclusion of all other people on the face of the earth, better than any glove or any other item of clothing could possibly fit. And Mr. Cochran, with DNA tests putting his client's blood at the murder scene, has the audacity to argue, "If it doesn't fit, you must acquit"?

Quite apart from this easy, off-the-top-of-your head response to Cochran's rhyme, there's virtually no question in my mind that if the prosecution had requested it of Judge Ito, Ito would have told the jury that Cochran's words were improper and misleading. Although Cochran obviously didn't mean to suggest that if the gloves didn't fit, the jury, *as a matter of law*, was required to acquit, this, indeed, is precisely what he told them, and it is hardly a defense to say, "Well, I didn't really mean what I said." "If it doesn't fit, you *must* acquit" is no less an improper argument than if the prosecution had argued to the jury, "If the DNA matches, you *must* convict." With Ito telling the jury that Cochran's words were improper, as he really would have had no choice but to do if the prosecution had requested it (in fact, Ito, on his own, should have clarified this matter for the jury), Cochran's rhyme would probably have ended up hurting the defense more than helping it, since the judge, in effect, would be telling the jurors that the fact the gloves didn't fit didn't mean as much as the defense wanted them to believe it did. But like docile lambs, the prosecutors neither responded verbally to Cochran's rhyme nor requested Ito to clarify the matter with the jury. And like trained mynah birds, two jurors after the trial informed the media, "If it doesn't fit, you must acquit."

Cochran referred to Detectives Vannatter and Fuhrman as "the twins of deception," and argued in his summation that the Book of Luke in the Bible says that if a man tells a lie, you can't trust him on anything else he says. If you have even the slightest ability at the art of argumentation, don't you, as the prosecutor—since you know Simpson had lied in this case many times—at a minimum argue during your rebuttal:

"**Whether or not Detective Fuhrman used a racial slur within the past ten years obviously has no connection at all to the facts of this murder case. So his lie on this personal matter is irrelevant. But Mr. Simpson, Mr. Cochran's own client, *on the night of the murders in this case*, tells an enormous, blatant lie to the limo driver that he had overslept, just gotten out of the shower, and would be right down, when the limo driver had just seen him enter his home thirty seconds earlier, a lie Mr. Simpson wouldn't have had any reason to tell if he hadn't just committed these murders. And Johnnie Cochran has the guts to argue the Book of Luke to you folks?**"

When Cochran and Scheck pointed out to the jury that this was a case of circumstantial evidence, that is, no eyewitnesses, and Cochran added smugly, "The prosecution has no shoes, no weapon, no clothes," I kept waiting for one of the prosecutors to forcefully respond with words to this effect:

"**Common sense is going to tell you folks that there rarely are going to be eyewitnesses to a premeditated murder, as these murders clearly were. Someone who premeditates a murder doesn't go down to Pershing Square here in Los Angeles, get on an orange crate, and with a megaphone announce his plans to the world. In a premeditated murder, as opposed to one committed on the spur of the moment, the killer obviously takes steps to help ensure that no one sees him commit the murder. That is why most premeditated murders are committed, like these ones were, in the dark of night. If, as Mr. Cochran suggests, the pros-**

ecution needed eyewitnesses, the murder weapon, and the killer's shoes and clothing to get a conviction, in effect we'd be telling prospective killers — make sure no one is watching and dispose of the murder weapon and all of your clothing and you're home free. But it's not quite that easy, ladies and gentlemen of the jury, and when you folks come back into this courtroom with your verdict of guilty, you're going to be telling this defendant, *It's not quite that easy*."

I mentioned earlier how Dr. Henry Lee's credibility had been severely damaged by the testimony of FBI agent William Bodziak, yet the jury felt Lee was the most impressive witness at the trial, and although his "something is wrong" testimony was a conclusion of Lee's about a small piece of evidence in the case, the defense and the jury treated it as if it were a description of the prosecution's entire case. "In the words of Dr. Lee, something is wrong. Something is terribly wrong with the evidence in this case," Barry Scheck told the jury in his summation. In fact, "something is wrong" became the anthem and theme of the defense's final summation, Scheck using the term no less than sixteen times, and Cochran several more. Having knowledge of all this, wouldn't you think that Clark, in her final, rebuttal argument to the jury, would have forcefully and mockingly pointed out to the jury how worthless the testimony of Dr. Lee was? Particularly when she had all the ammunition she needed to do so?

But she did virtually nothing with Lee in either her opening or her closing arguments. She did not even remind the jury that one of Lee's "imprints" (that was supposed to be the shoe print of a second assailant) had proved to be from one of the workmen who had laid the cement years ago, and that a second "imprint" was actually "tool marks" made from the laying of the cement. She never uttered one word about these matters. Her entire statement on the shoe print and tool marks left by the workmen, and Lee's destroyed credibility, was: "Now, Dr. Lee tried to tell us about a second set of shoe prints but I think Mr. Bodziak made it very clear what this was all about." That's all, Marcia? Nothing more? Just these couple of words? If you're not going to recall, summarize, and emphasize Bodziak's testimony on these points for the jury, and then draw inferences from it, why bother to give a final argument? This is just incredible. A clerk at a department store would have done a better job of handling this issue than Marcia Clark did.

On Lee, don't you tell the jury something like this?

"**How can this man come before you folks posing as the leading forensic scientist in the country and suggest to you, without expressly** saying, that a shoe print made in concrete years ago, which he personally saw and photographed, could have been a shoe print belonging to a killer other than the defendant in this case? How dare this man not tell you that this 'imprint' he said he saw and photographed was a permanent indentation in the concrete whose ridges and grooves you can feel with your fingers? How dare this man, who should have been ridden out of town on a rail, try to do this to you folks?

"If we hadn't had agent Bodziak go back to that walkway and look at, physically touch, and photograph for you that permanent shoe print, we would have never known that Lee's testimony was one hundred percent wrong. Pardon the pun, but we have 'concrete' evidence that something is wrong, terribly wrong, with Dr. Lee to give testimony like this."

Don't you make an argument at least similar to this when you have indisputable evidence to support you, and it's obvious that Dr. Lee is a witness for the defense who can damage your case in a substantial way?

From Johnnie Cochran's opening statement through his closing argument, he kept telling the jury that in the LAPD's "obsession to win" it had "rushed to judgment" against Simpson, ignoring any and all evidence that may have pointed away from him in a different direction. The "rush to judgment" argument was another big theme of the defense's case. I kept waiting for either Marcia Clark or Chris Darden, in their rebuttal arguments, to respond to this, but they didn't. Not one word. Only in Darden's opening argument did he even mention the issue, and then very briefly and inadequately. Here's what he said: "If this is a rush to judgment, why did the police stand out in front of 875 South Bundy that night for a couple of hours doing nothing, as the defense has asserted, doing nothing but waiting for Vannatter and Lange? That is a rush to judgment? This is no rush to judgment. Unfortunately, this is just how things go. Those cops got out there to conduct a murder investigation and that investigation led them to Rockingham. They followed the blood trail."

Couldn't one or the other of the prosecutors, in their final, rebuttal arguments, have said something like this?

"As you folks know from your everyday experiences, the evidence—I guess in your private lives you would call it the situation or circumstances—is what leads you in a certain direction. You don't go to the door to open it for someone unless you hear the doorbell ring or there's a knock at the door. If you wake up in the morning after an all-night rain and you find a puddle of water on the *kitchen* floor, when you call the roof man you don't tell him to check for a leak above the *living room*. These things are so obvious it's silly to even talk about them. But it's just as obvious in a criminal investigation. You follow the trail of evidence, in this case the trail of blood that leads from the murder scene to Mr. Simpson's car right up to and inside his home.

"*All* of the evidence in this case led to one person, and one person only, O. J. Simpson. There was no piece of evidence that led to anyone else. Under those circumstances, what were the police supposed to do? Pretend that evidence existed pointing in a different direction toward someone else? When Detective Lange was asked during the trial by Mr. Cochran if the LAPD had pursued the possibility that someone else may have killed the victims, as you recall he responded: 'I had absolutely no other evidence that would point me in any other direction. There was nothing to pursue.'

"If Mr. Cochran is going to make the charge he has, don't you think with all the police reports he has been provided on this case, and all the reports he undoubtedly has been given by his own defense team's private investigators, who have been working on this case for over a year, full-time, that he should have told you, "Now, take this,' and then given you some fact or circumstance? 'Why didn't the LAPD check this out?' But he couldn't refer you to even one such fact or circumstance, not one, that pointed in the direction of anyone other than his client being responsible for the brutal murders of Nicole Brown Simpson and Ronald Goldman."

There was one part of Cochran's argument that may have received more attention than it deserved from the media, his supposedly suggesting "jury nullification" to the Simpson jury; that is, asking the jurors to disregard the evidence and the law in favor of their own view of justice. As the *Wall Street Journal* pointed out (October 4, 1995), this practice of jury nullification "has played an important role at key times in U.S. history. . . . During colonial times, for instance, jurors used the power to acquit colonial defendants of political crimes against the Crown. In the mid-nineteenth century, Northern jurors kept the tradition alive by acquitting people who harbored runaway slaves, even though the law explicitly made this a crime." The *Journal* cited some current cases where black juries in big cities may have acquitted black defendants, despite obvious guilt, as evidence that the practice is still alive.

One point should be made off the top. Despite some language in the

Journal article (and in other newspapers at the time of Cochran's summation) arguing that jury nullification is a practice "which the U.S. Supreme Court explicitly affirmed one hundred years ago," no court in this country has ever suggested that a jury has any *right* to disregard the law. Courts have only recognized that the jury does, indeed, have the *power* to do so, which is quite another thing. By analogy, Simpson had the power to murder Nicole and Ron, not the right. And this power of the jury is, as one federal court noted, "an unreviewable and unreversible power to acquit in disregard of the instructions on the law given by the trial judge" because of the Fifth Amendment prohibition against double jeopardy, which forbids trying a person twice for the same crime. Bills introduced in various state legislatures (most recently, in New York by state senator Joseph Galiber in 1991) to give juries the right, not just the power, to disregard the law have invariably been rejected.

At one time, juries did not even have the power, much less the right, to vote the way they wished. In *Wall Street Journal* reporter Steven J. Adler's well-received book *The Jury* (Times Books–Random House, 1994), he cites the case that gave the jury independence from the government:

> The trial of William Penn and William Mead at the Old Bailey courthouse in London in 1670 marked a turning point in the development of the jury as an independent popular voice. With the jury in the case deadlocked over charges that the defendants had illegally preached in the streets, court officials invaded the jury room to determine which jurors favored acquittal. Finding four, the officials locked them up without food or water. When they refused to convict, they were fined and then imprisoned, as was the custom. But in this case, one of the dissenters, a man named Bushell, took the matter back to court and won a ruling that jurors could no longer be punished for their verdicts. If the judge could compel a jury to find one way or another, wrote Chief Justice Vaughn, 'then the jury is but a troublesome delay, . . . and of no use.'

The language Cochran used which the media said constituted a request for jury nullification was when, referring to Fuhrman, he said: "This man could've been off the force long ago if they had done their job, but they didn't . . . they didn't have the courage. . . . That is what I am asking you to do. Stop this cover-up. . . . If you don't stop it, then who? Do you think the police department is going to stop it? Do you think the DA's office is going to stop it. . . . [I]t has to be stopped by you." Then later, referring to Fuhrman's use of racial slurs: "And when you go back in the jury room, some of you may want to say, well, gee, you know, boys will be boys. . . . That is not acceptable as the conscience of this community if you adopt that attitude. . . . You are empowered to say we are not going to take that anymore. I'm sure you will do the right thing about that." And later: "Who then police the police? You police the police. You police them by your verdict. You are the ones to send a message. Nobody else is going to do it in our society . . . nobody has the courage. . . . Maybe you are the right people at the right time at the right place to say no more. We are not going to have this." This is a pitch of Cochran's to juries which he has fine-tuned during three decades of police brutality lawsuits against law enforcement agencies here in Los Angeles.

Looked at by itself, Cochran's language does seem to be flirting rather heavily with jury nullification. But it couldn't have been clearer from the context in which he made the remarks, as well as his entire argument, that he was telling the jury that *the facts and evidence in the Simpson case, and the law applicable thereto, required a not-guilty verdict.* In other words, he coupled traditional jury nullification language with a much heavier dose of, and reliance on, the evidence and law of the case he was trying.

Nevertheless, I think Cochran's argument was improper, and the prosecutors should immediately have asked Ito (who again, on his own, should have acted) to instruct the jury that any suggestion by Cochran that in reaching their verdict they should be thinking about anything other than the evidence and law in this case (stopping racism, sending a message, etc.) was wrong, and their doing so would be a violation of their oath. Instead, the prosecutors made no objection to Cochran's argument. All Clark did was tell Ito (during a hearing much later on a defense objection to Clark's arguing to the jury the ethical obligations of a prosecutor only to prosecute someone he believes is guilty) that "I have never seen a defense attorney get up and ask for jury nullification in this way." *If she felt he was doing this, why didn't she object?* And Darden, in his summation, actually lent legitimacy to the jury nullification argument: "You can't send a message to Fuhrman, you can't send a message to the LAPD, you can't eradicate racism within the LAPD or within the Los Angeles community or within the nation as a whole by delivering a verdict of not guilty in this case," he argued. In other words, Darden wasn't telling the jury that it would be wrong for them to try to send a message, just that it would be ineffective, which could have had the same effect as waving a red flag in front of a bull. Darden, of course, made it clear to the jury in other parts of his argument that the jury had a duty to base its verdict on the evidence, and the evidence proved Simpson's guilt.

Of the four lawyers who argued for the prosecution and defense, Barry Scheck's argument was the most structured and organized. It was also the most ridiculous. If one were to believe the Bronx lawyer, all the blood, hair, and fiber evidence in the case against Simpson was either planted by LAPD detectives or contaminated by the incompetent police department criminalists who sloppily collected and preserved it. Since Scheck (and Cochran in his argument) at times also suggested that the criminalists themselves may have been a part of the planting or at least the cover-up, and since both he and Cochran also argued that the LAPD detectives were incompetent in many ways, they were arguing simultaneously that the same sophisticated conspirators who framed Simpson were also incredible bumblers; he was picking and choosing, trying to have it both ways.

The core of Scheck's contamination argument was that the LAPD's Scientific Investigation Division (SID) was a cesspool of contamination, a "black hole." The New York lawyer said that any laboratory has to have the following things: rules and training; quality assurance (proper documentation of how, when, and where the evidence was collected); chain of custody (documentation of what is picked up and who turns it over to whom); and security (preservation of the evidence and protection from tampering). The LAPD, per Scheck, was lacking in all of these things to a great degree. So much so, if we are to believe Scheck, that all convictions of criminal defendants in Los Angeles for at least the past ten or fifteen years based on evidence like fingerprints, blood, hair, etc. should automatically be reversed and the defendants set free. To Scheck, just collecting blood from the murder scene was a science mastered by few, and if the slightest thing went wrong, such as temporarily mislabeling a vial, all tests thereafter were invalid. But the defense's own top forensic scientist, Dr. Henry Lee, testified on cross-examination at the trial that one could even pick up blood on one's shoe at a crime scene, and if the bloody shoe was given to a criminalist to test for DNA, he could easily do it, and the results would be valid.

Scheck argued that once the blood evidence was contaminated in the evidence processing room at SID (or before it got there through bacteria, soil, etc.), it didn't make any difference how many times it was thereafter tested for DNA—at the prosecution's Cellmark Diagnostics lab in Germantown, Maryland, or the California Department of Justice lab in Berkeley, California—because "garbage in, garbage out," i.e., the evidence was already contaminated, so all tests thereafter showing it was Simpson's blood at the murder scene (or Ron's or Nicole's blood in the Bronco, etc.) were invalid.

Clark, amazingly, did not respond to Scheck's allegations in her *rebuttal* argument by pointing out that all the contamination or degradation of blood in the world could not convert someone else's blood into Simpson's blood. Neither did Darden in his rebuttal argument. All Clark said on this critical issue was the following: "If you have contamination, what you should expect to find are results that are out of sync, willy-nilly if you will." This, of course, in no way tells anyone, particularly this jury, that contamination can't change someone else's blood into Simpson's. In fact, by failing to tell the jury explicitly that contamination can't do this, it still leaves that possibility open.

What makes their failure to argue this absolutely critical, all-important point in their final argument to the jury all the more astonishing and unbelievable is that Clark's and Darden's own prosecution witness, Cellmark lab director Robin Cotton, on direct examination by co-prosecutor George "Woody" Clarke, testified during the prosecution's case-in-chief that contamination *cannot* change someone's DNA into someone else's. If you don't argue this point to the jury, *over and over again*, why in the hell are you even bothering to stand up in front of the jury?

In paragraph after paragraph of his argument, Scheck, as suspicious as a cat in a new home, smelled contamination and degradation everywhere.

The outrageous Scheck had another theory up his snake-oil salesman's sleeve for the jury. In those cases where contamination or degradation didn't invalidate the results—listen to this, folks—there was *cross*-contamination; that is, he hypothesized that some of the evidence blood had become so degraded because of bacteria, sunlight, moisture, etc. that it had lost all its DNA. Thereafter, because of negligence and inadvertence (these were the moments when the LAPD personnel were taking a breather from their planting of evidence), the blood that had been removed from Simpson's arm for comparison purposes and was in a vial was accidentally spilled onto all of the degraded evidence blood, thus being an additional reason why some of the evidence blood came back from the DNA laboratories identified as Simpson's. What evidence did Scheck have that this actually happened? None. Because the LAPD crime lab was a "cesspool of contamination," it *could* have happened, Scheck argued, and that was good enough. He told the jury that "*if* there was cross-contamination," the results would be invalid.

Clark, in her rebuttal, spent all her time arguing to the jury that nothing happened in the case that would have caused cross-contamination to occur. That was all right, but she failed to go on in her rebuttal (she touched on it in her opening argument, *before* Scheck's argument) and point out:

"Under the law a jury verdict must be based on the evidence, not possibilities and speculation. But in Mr. Scheck's world, the mere pos-

sibility of cross-contamination, even though there's not a *speck* of evidence to support it, is the equivalent of proof that it happened. But if *Scheck* doesn't have a *speck*, ladies and gentlemen, under the law you must reject his argument on cross-contamination. Remember, as Judge Ito will instruct you, we don't have to prove guilt beyond all *possible* doubt, only beyond a reasonable doubt. His exact words to you on this matter will be: 'A reasonable doubt is not a mere possible doubt, because everything relating to human affairs is open to some possible or imaginary doubt.'"

There were two very powerful arguments Clark failed to make with respect to Scheck's ludicrous theory of cross-contamination. It's particularly astonishing she never made these arguments in view of how big an issue DNA (as well as EDTA) was throughout the whole trial, and the further fact that the prosecution had two DNA experts (Harmon and Clarke) working on the case.

A rather remarkable thing happened during the defense summations in this case. Although Cochran and Scheck argued that the Rockingham glove was planted, that Simpson's blood was planted on the rear gate at Bundy, that Simpson's and Nicole's blood was planted on the sock in Simpson's bedroom, and that the police also planted Simpson's, Nicole's, and Ron Goldman's blood in the Bronco, neither of them argued that the five blood drops at the murder scene, the most incriminating evidence against Simpson in the entire case, were planted. Cochran never even dealt with the issue, only saying, once, that "we have already covered the Bundy blood drops, that Mr. Scheck did such a great job on." And Scheck didn't say they were planted, claiming only they had been cross-contaminated with Simpson's reference blood by negligent and sloppy chemists at the LAPD laboratory. Shouldn't this argument have been made?

"Apparently Mr. Cochran and Mr. Scheck, in their frantic scurrying around during their final summations to plug up all the holes through which Mr. Simpson's guilt has been gushing, arguing contamination here, planting here, cover-up here, forgot to claim in their summation that the five blood drops of Mr. Simpson's found at the murder scene, the most incriminating evidence against Mr. Simpson in this case, were planted.

"As you know, with one of the blood drops, there is only a one out of 170 million chance that it belongs to someone other than Mr. Simpson, and with each of three others, only a one out of 240,000 chance. With the fifth, one out of 5,200. So we know, we don't just believe, that Mr. Simpson left his blood at the murder scene. Yet Mr. Cochran, in his summation, never even dealt with the issue, and as you recall, Mr.

Scheck merely said that those blood drops had been cross-contaminated. But maybe they didn't forget to claim the blood drops were planted. Maybe even they realized it would be too preposterous for anyone to believe that the police planted drops of Simpson's blood just to the left of bloody shoe prints walking away from the murder scene.

"Let's talk about Mr. Scheck's cross-contamination argument. He claims the five Bundy blood drops had been cross-contaminated with blood drawn from Mr. Simpson's arm, and claims further that the blood drops had become so degraded by the elements that no DNA was left in them. So therefore, he says, when the cross-contamination took place at the police laboratory, only Simpson's blood from his vial showed up on the DNA tests of those blood drops.

"But quite apart from the fact that the defense presented not a speck of evidence that any of the Bundy blood drops had been cross-contaminated—they only talked about possibilities—there are two realities that conclusively disprove Mr. Scheck's argument.

"Number one, if, in fact, the reference blood from Mr. Simpson's vial, because of mishandling by the technicians and chemists at the LAPD lab, had somehow gotten on the five blood drops which were removed from the crime scene by cotton swatches, those blood drops would then have had the preservative EDTA in them, since EDTA, we learned at this trial, is added to all blood drawn from the arms of suspects. And although the defense has claimed there was EDTA present on the blood found on the back gate and on the socks, they've never even alleged that any EDTA at all was found on the Bundy blood drops. So we know that there was no cross-contamination here for that reason alone.

"Secondly, although the Bundy blood drops had been exposed to the elements and therefore were degraded, if they had been cross-contaminated with Mr. Simpson's reference blood, which had not been exposed to the elements, a much higher concentration of DNA would have shown up on the drops. But we know that's not the case. We know that on four out of the five drops, the DNA had been degraded to the point where only small amounts of DNA remained, and this is why only a PCR test could be conducted on them. Even the fifth blood drop, which was sufficiently rich in DNA for an RFLP test, had been degraded by the elements. So this is the second reason we absolutely know there could not have been cross-contamination here."

The prosecutors did not make either of these two obvious arguments. After making them, they could have told the jury that since the defense never even claimed the Bundy blood drops had been planted, and since we know that no cross-contamination took place because the blood drops had no EDTA in them, and the level of the DNA was very low, that only left one catch-all argument for the defense to make—its pet argument that all the blood which wasn't planted had been contaminated by bacteria, dirt, leaves, etc., making all the DNA test results on them "unreliable."

But after pointing out to the jury once again that the statistical improbability, per the testimony of the forensic scientists at the trial, of one out of the five blood drops at the Bundy murder scene not belonging to Simpson was 1 out of 5,200, of three others 1 out of 240,000, and of the fifth, the only one on which an RFLP test was conducted, 1 out of 170 million, and that the statistical improbability of *all five* blood drops belonging to someone other than Simpson would produce numbers that would run off the edge of any paper, don't you automatically go on and point out to the jury that the whole issue of contamination only has relevance if the blood at the murder scene belonged to some other party, some third party?

If it belonged to Simpson, what difference does it make if it became contaminated? That is, if it was Simpson's at the beginning, and the tests showed it was still Simpson's even after the contamination, what difference does it make if there was contamination? So don't you argue to the jury, as Clark and Darden never did, something like the following?

"To believe this ridiculous contamination theory that the defense has worked so hard to get you folks to buy during this trial, we'd have to believe that this blood at the murder scene which has been identified as Mr. Simpson's actually belongs to X, the true killer. During the trial, X, the true killer, has been somewhere else, maybe in some motel room in San Antonio, or Topeka, or maybe Boise, Idaho, watching these proceedings on television. And because of contamination caused by dirt, bacteria, or what-have-you, out of the five and a half billion people on this globe, X's blood was miraculously transformed into Simpson's blood. And not just once. Because of contamination, apparently all five separate blood drops of X's at the murder scene were each magically transformed into Simpson's blood. That's insane, of course, on its face, ladies and gentlemen, too ridiculous to even contemplate or talk about. And yet when you separate the wheat from the chaff, that's precisely what the defense in this case is trying to get you folks to believe. Aren't you folks insulted by this? I mean, how much respect for your intelligence can these defense attorneys possibly have to ask you to believe something like this?"

Don't you make this kind of an argument to expose the absurdity of the defense's contention with respect to contamination? But neither Marcia Clark nor Christopher Darden, in either of their two arguments to the jury, made any such obvious argument or even one remotely similar to it.

The opening arguments of both prosecutors, though far from first-rate, were in fact much better than their closing arguments, or rebuttal, the most important address to the jury a prosecutor makes during a trial. The prosecutor's rebuttal, like his opening argument, should be prepared before the first witness has been called at the trial. Yet it was very clear that not only didn't Clark and Darden do this, they did what the overwhelming majority of prosecutors do—they started thinking about *most* of what they were going to say while defense counsel were making their arguments.

I'm always perplexed when I see prosecutors writing furiously as defense counsel is making his summation. A prosecutor shouldn't have to do that. It's *his* case. He knows the weaknesses in his case better than anyone else, so he should anticipate what the defense attorney is going to say before he even says it, and have already prepared his response. Not just what he's going to say, but the sequence, and how he's going to say it. In other words, the prosecutor has to make the assumption that defense counsel, as incompetent as he may be, is at least going to see and argue, however poorly, the main weaknesses in the prosecution's case. The dilemma arises when defense counsel doesn't see one or more of these weaknesses in the prosecution's case, particularly the more subtle ones. As a general but not ironclad rule I find a way in rebuttal to raise and discuss these issues myself. Why? Because a jury consists of people with hundreds of years of collective human experience, and even though defense counsel never spotted a particular weakness, chances are at least one of the jurors will have. And if just one juror sees it, all twelve learn about it as soon as he brings it up during deliberations. And if the jury is talking about a weakness in my case back in the jury room, I want to have been heard on that issue.

Obviously, the prosecutor's final address to the jury will have to be amended (by additions, deletions, etc.) as the trial proceeds, since you cannot have a 100 percent handle on the case before the opening bell. But you can have a draft which you work on, amend, and fine-tune nearly every day of the trial.

It's hard to believe that Clark and Darden, two of the top prosecutors in the largest prosecutor's office in the land, and trying the most publicized murder case in U.S. history, would be so incredibly incompetent as to wait until the last second to prepare their rebuttal, but that's precisely what it appears they did. I didn't need *Time* magazine to tell me, but in its October 16, 1995, edition, it reported that Darden was up till 4:30 a.m. on the night before he gave his rebuttal argument, preparing it. (In all fairness to Darden, there were unconfirmed rumors that whoever was calling the shots for the DA's case asked Darden, at the last second, to argue in rebuttal.) When I told a source of mine on the prosecution team that after watching Clark give her rebuttal argument, I had little doubt that she did not put more than fifteen to twenty hours, if that, into preparing it, he replied, "She didn't."

This is not boasting, but if I had been on the Simpson case, since I would've had well over a year to work on my rebuttal, I would have put literally hundreds of hours into it, and gone over it a minimum of eight or nine times.

How do I know, even without asking anyone, that Darden and Clark put hardly any time at all into the preparation of their arguments? For one thing, both of their arguments were rambling and disjointed, clearly reflecting a lack of preparation. Also, Darden's argument was very weak and short, and Clark's summation was not only weak and relatively short, but there was an unmistakable telltale sign. She was continually admitting to the jury she didn't know or wasn't sure of something, or didn't have something she needed.

One of the two out-of-town DNA prosecutors on the Simpson case told me something that made me angry. He confirmed what I had already inferred. Incredibly, he and his colleague, he said, worked with Marcia Clark on the DNA part of her rebuttal for close to four hours down at the district attorney's office on the evening before she gave her final argument, and the session didn't end until 2:30 in the morning, just a few hours before Clark had to stand up and address the jury. Driving back to his hotel room after the session, the prosecutor, who likes and respects Clark, said he nevertheless wondered "why Marcia had waited all this time to have this session with us, the first in-depth meeting she had ever had with us. We went over things she could have discussed with us months earlier."

With the weight of the prosecution on this final address of yours to the jury urging a guilty verdict, how could you possibly, Ms. Clark, show so little dedication to your job—which was representing the People of the State of California in a brutal double murder case—that you put off the preparation of your rebuttal until the last moment, cramming like a high school kid before an exam? And if, in fact, you were aware of the tremendous responsibility you have as a lawyer for the people to bring about justice, and you didn't prepare most of your rebuttal much earlier simply because you had no idea that it should be prepared way in advance and gone over again and again, then shame on the district attorney's office for not having any prosecutors who know how to prosecute a big case effectively and successfully. And if there are such prosecutors in the office, then shame on the DA for being so incompetent he had no idea who they are.

Marcia Clark's inexcusable lack of preparation for her closing argument, something a prosecutor shouldn't be guilty of even in his first or second jury trial, was reflected in many ways, including statements like the following, which are sprinkled throughout her closing argument (rebuttal): "Vannatter and Lange came out to Bundy, *and I guess* they showed up around 4:00, 4:30, *I think it was.*" (You *guess*? You *think*? You've been on the Simpson case for over a year and you don't *know*? And if you didn't know, you didn't even bother to check the transcript?) "They still didn't run out to Rockingham, okay? *I can't remember, I think* he said it was around the time . . ." "Even then they didn't go immediately. It wasn't— *I think* about 5 o'clock when they finally went to Rockingham." "And that instruction is 2?—2.80? *Do you have it on the bench, Your Honor? Wait. I have it. Thank you.*" After a break, "*I forget where I left off,* so I'm just going to pick up with something else." "*I can't remember exactly.* You can have it read back because *I think* what he said was 10:23." "There was some testimony, *I think,* from Dr. Baden that . . ." Turning away from the jury, "It's in evidence, *isn't it,* Your Honor, the blood search sheet, work sheet? Yes, it is. Good. Good. You'll [jury] be able to see it." "At the end of the trial, or the end of the people's case, or maybe it was the end of the whole trial . . ." "The testimony from Mr. MacDonell *and from Dr. Lee— I believe—but certainly from Mr. MacDonell* . . ." And so on.

I can't tell you how bad this is. This is all proof that Clark never went over her summation *even once.* If she had, how was it possible she could have said even one, much less all, of these things to the jury? Unless we want to believe something equally bad, that she was aware she didn't have certain information nailed down and made no effort to get it herself or have one of her colleagues get it for her.

It was obvious that the defense attorneys, particularly Scheck, had put more effort and preparation into their summations than the two prosecutors had. And, of course, if the prosecutors didn't even spend enough time to bother confirming what they were saying to the jury, they didn't even begin to spend enough time preparing a powerful argument to the jury with irresistible inferences of guilt. Is it right that the lawyers representing a killer who deserves to be punished are working harder than those representing the victims?

Although both Clark and Darden gave embarrassingly bad rebuttal arguments, most of the talking heads and legal experts were very impressed. Remarkably, one of the former DAs who was a network commentator opined that Clark had given a "brilliant rebuttal." It was. To him. And a law school professor gave Clark's rebuttal an A+ for presentation, B+ for strategy, and B+ for impact. The professor gave Darden an A for presentation, an A- for strategy, and an A- for impact. In other words, both Clark and Darden were about as good as you can get.

The reality is that the two prosecutors could have hardly been any worse. *New York Times* reporter David Margolick was one of the very few who sensibly reported what had occurred. Clark, he said, was "largely listless, and clearly exhausted." (Margolick probably had no way of knowing that Clark had been up nearly all night.) He goes on to say that "at times Clark seemed like a student with too little time in which to answer too many test questions, who opted for the short true or false rather than the more important essays. At other times she had the very air she attributed to Mr. Simpson following the killings, pressed and frantic. Her task was complicated because of her obvious exhaustion. Ms. Clark sighed frequently, occasionally rubbed her eyes, forgot facts, reached for words and tripped over phrases."

And Margolick was for the most part just talking about Clark's terrible delivery. Substantively speaking, she was appreciably worse.

A big error both prosecutors made in their rebuttal arguments — one that the overwhelming majority of prosecutors make — is that for the most part they confined their closing argument to merely answering (rebutting) the defense arguments. But if you do that, your argument is almost necessarily *defensive* in nature, and the golden opportunity the law gives the prosecution to end its case on a powerful, affirmative note is almost converted into a negative, a liability. In rebuttal, the prosecutor can only discuss evidence which the defense has spoken about, or evidence which rebuts what the defense has spoken about. But neither Clark nor Darden apparently know that rebuttal does not have to be a restrictive summation at all. After the prosecutor has responded to and rebutted all the defense allegations, he has the opportunity to argue his entire case all over again. All he has to do is quote the defense attorney's inevitable assertion that the prosecution did not offer sufficient evidence to prove guilt beyond a reasonable doubt. This legally enables the prosecutor, in rebutting this contention, the right to cite all the evidence of guilt again. (However, in rebuttal, although the evidence itself is set forth more briefly, the prosecutor should draw new or expanded inferences of guilt from the evidence.)

Here, both Darden and Clark, like inexperienced prosecutors, spent 90 to 95 percent of their closing arguments responding to the defense allegations, thereby coming across as defensive and permitting the defense to determine the prosecutors' agenda in their final appeal to the jury. Clark was at her best when she finally, in the very closing moments of her final address, briefly went over with the jury what she called "unrefuted evidence" of Simpson's guilt. Though she did not draw inferences of guilt from these items, they were the kind that bespeak guilt by themselves, e.g., "between 9:36 and 10:53 [on the night of the murders], the defendant's whereabouts are unaccounted for"; "Alan Park buzzed the intercom at Rockingham at 10:40, at 10:43, and at 10:49. There was no response"; "The [bloody] shoe prints at Bundy were from a size-12 Bruno Magli shoe . . . the defendant wears a size-12 shoe," etc.

And I felt Clark ended her summation effectively by playing for the jury a compilation of Nicole's 1989 and 1993 911 calls where she is heard being in terror of Simpson, and crying out for help. While the tapes were being played, the prosecution flashed slides of a bruised and battered Nicole on the courtroom screen. Clark argued: "I think the thing that perhaps was so chilling about her voice [on the tapes] is that sound of resignation, inevitability. She knew she was going to die. And Ron, he speaks to you by his struggling so valiantly. He forced his murderer to leave evidence behind that you might not ordinarily have. They both are telling you who did it with their hair, their clothes, their bodies, their blood. He did it. Mr. Simpson. Orenthal Simpson. He did it."

It was moving and eloquent. But it was far too little and far too late.

It was difficult for Darden to be effective. Because he spent so little time preparing his rebuttal, his summation consumed only forty-seven pages of transcript. I've already pointed out that in his opening argument a few days earlier, Darden had very unwisely told the jury that on the issue of whether Simpson was guilty or not guilty, "the decision is yours, and I'm glad that it is not mine," thereby implying that it's a close, tough case, the very opposite of what a prosecutor should be conveying to the jury. But apparently not one of his twenty-four colleagues on the case brought this fact to his attention, nor did he apparently realize how inadvisable such a remark was himself, because in his closing argument two days later, he made it even worse, expressly telling the jury: "You've got a tough job, a very tough job. I don't envy you in that regard." You don't even have to be a lawyer to realize what a mistake this is.

Darden's strength in summation was the obvious sincerity with which he spoke. And he is someone who, like Hemingway, can elicit a lot of meaning and a certain amount of power from the simplest of words. But that only takes one so far in summation. There's got to be substance, a tremendous amount of it, to prevail. And one also has to have common sense. Darden displayed neither in either of his summations.

Take the issue of domestic abuse, which was Darden's major assigned bailiwick at the trial. Although his remarks in his opening argument about the "shortening fuse" of Simpson leading up to a murderous rage were very interesting and probably right, as I have previously indicated, he was setting up an unnecessary burden for himself and compounding the problem by engaging in obvious speculation to meet it. The moment the words were leaving Darden's lips, I knew Cochran, in his summation, would have a field day with Darden's speculations. "When people theorize about short fuses," Cochran told the jury, "it's just speculation." Other references: "Darden's speculative theories"; "Then he [Darden] goes into this kind of make-believe fantasy world"; and "Dr. Darden" for Darden's suggesting that like a psychiatrist, he knew what was on Simpson's mind.

Darden's stating *as fact* his speculation that Simpson had a fuse that got shorter and shorter until it exploded was bad enough. But what made his "shortening fuse" argument even less credible to the jury was the following: the dance recital video showing Simpson in a very good mood just hours before the murders (Cochran told the jury: "Mr. Darden could speak a thousand words, and I could show you that video. It puts the lie to this theory about some murderous rage"); and the fact that, around 9:00 p.m., just an hour and fifteen or twenty minutes before the murders, Simpson had a telephone conversation with Dr. Christian Reichart, a chiropractor friend of his, and Reichart testified that Simpson "seemed very jovial." Darden really got into the wildest of speculations when he told the jury that the reason Simpson was jovial is that he had already made the decision to kill Nicole, and therefore was at peace with himself and happy. Cochran's response? "Instead of Chris Darden standing here and saying, well, that [Reichart's testimony] is pretty tough evidence for us to overcome, he says O. J. Simpson was happy because he was going to kill his wife. I don't think any of you believe that. It flies in the face of everything that is reasonable"; and around 9:15 p.m., an hour before the murders, Simpson and Kato Kaelin went to McDonald's to get a hamburger, something that Cochran again argued flew in the face of Darden's "shortening fuse" argument. "I suppose if you're in this jealous rage," Cochran argued, "if the fuse is running so short, it's interesting, isn't it, to stop and go get a hamburger at McDonald's."

So Darden's handling of the domestic abuse issue in his opening argument was ill-advised and fraught with vulnerability. In his rebuttal, however, if it's possible, he was even worse. Throughout the trial and even before it, many people said, in conversation and on call-in talk shows, that just because Simpson beat Nicole didn't mean he murdered her They'd point out that the overwhelming majority of men who do beat their wives do not, in fact, go on to kill them. Knowing this type of remark is out there and hence likely to be in the minds of one or more jurors, don't you automatically work up an argument to answer this, whether or not Cochran makes this same argument, which you can assume he will?

Cochran, in his summation, surely and predictably downplayed the significance of the domestic violence in the Simpson case, suggesting to the jury that any physical abuse Simpson may have inflicted upon Nicole had no relevance to the murder case, yet this was Darden's entire response to Cochran on the domestic abuse issue: "The defense sloughed off the testimony and evidence about domestic violence like it didn't mean anything. That is because they can't touch it and they can't deal with it." That's all? Just one line, in your final address to the jury, to respond to defense attacks on the relevance of the domestic abuse evidence? Try to imagine it. You've been on a case for almost a year, and you're the prosecution's domestic abuse guy, it's the main area for you to argue, and you *know* the defense has no choice but to argue that Simpson's domestic violence doesn't mean anything. Don't you think that with a *whole year* to mull it over, you could come up with more to knock down the defense's position than just these thirteen words: "That is because they can't touch it and they can't deal with it"?

In responding to Cochran's argument that the domestic violence by Simpson against Nicole was not relevant to the murder charges, and just because he hit her doesn't mean he would murder her, don't you argue to the jury that although most men who beat their wives may indeed not go on to murder them, that that is looking at the statistics the wrong way? That even without statistics, common sense will tell you that in those cases where husbands have, in fact, murdered their wives, the overwhelming majority have previously physically abused and battered their wives. So certainly, though it is not conclusive, Simpson's history of physical abuse against Nicole makes it "more likely" that he murdered her. At no time in his opening or closing addresses to the jury did Darden use the "more likely" (or similar language) argument. Instead, though he opted to present a skeletal case of domestic violence and abuse (see earlier discussion), the whole thrust and essence of Darden's argument to the jury was that what limited evidence he did offer proved that Simpson killed his former wife. In post-trial interviews with the jurors, no part of the prosecution's case was viewed as weaker by them than the domestic abuse evidence.

To expose the absurdity of Cochran's argument that Simpson's prior domestic violence and abuse against Nicole didn't have any relevance to the murder case, instead of his pitiable thirteen words, couldn't Darden at least have said something like this?

"Let me give you folks absolute proof that Mr. Simpson's history of physical and psychological abuse against his wife is very relevant to these murder charges against him. If the evidence had showed that Mr. Simpson and his wife, Nicole, had gotten along wonderfully, that he never once touched her in an offensive way or even yelled at her, does anyone really believe that Mr. Cochran would not have argued to you words to this effect? 'It's ridiculous for the prosecution to suggest that Mr. Simpson murdered Nicole Brown. In all their years of marriage, they got along beautifully. Not once did he hit her, slap her, or even push her. He never even raised his voice to her. And suddenly, out of a clear blue sky, he is going to take a knife and stab her viciously to death? That's crazy, and the prosecution knows it. It doesn't make any sense.' Surely, none of you doubt that he would have made that precise argument to you if his client and Nicole had gotten along well during their marriage. There's the proof, ladies and gentlemen of the jury, that the presence or absence of physical and psychological abuse by Mr. Simpson against Nicole is very relevant to the issue of his guilt for these murders. Since you know Mr. Cochran would have made this argument to you if there had been no physical abuse, and it would have been a valid argument, this is proof of the relevance of the evidence where there *has* been physical abuse."

But the prosecutors apparently didn't have it in them to make simple, obvious arguments like this.

I said earlier that it's possible Darden wasn't told until a few days before he gave his rebuttal argument that he was going to give it. If that, in fact, is true, is that any excuse for his failure to make the arguments I've suggested to rebut what Cochran said? None whatsoever. Firstly, these are automatic arguments that don't take more than a few moments to think of. Secondly, in Darden's opening argument he told the jury he knew Cochran was going to make these arguments. After telling them this, he could have gone on and made the above points, as well as many others he should have come up with during the preceding year.

With respect to circumstantial evidence, the prosecutors let the defense attorneys get away with highway robbery. In addition to arguing, of course, that the prosecution hadn't proved Simpson's guilt beyond a reasonable doubt, both Cochran and particularly Scheck argued to the jury on several occasions that there was a reasonable doubt as to whether a *certain fact* was true, and hence this entitled them to a not-guilty verdict. There were, Cochran argued, "many, many, many reasonable doubts" in the case.

Scheck argued that the LAPD crime lab was a "cesspool of contamination" and therefore its conclusions gave rise to "a reasonable doubt." He even went so far as to argue that the prosecution "had to prove the blood evidence wasn't tampered with beyond a reasonable doubt," i.e., the prosecution had to prove a negative beyond a reasonable doubt, for which there is no legal authority. Apparently all the other evidence of guilt was irrelevant if the blood evidence had been tampered with. I kept waiting for the prosecutors, in their rebuttal, to point out that "the *only* thing we have to prove beyond a reasonable doubt *is Mr. Simpson's guilt*." But they never did. Not once.

The circumstantial evidence instruction says that "each fact which is *essential* (obviously, not every fact in a case) to complete a set of circumstances *necessary* to establish the defendant's guilt must be proven beyond a reasonable doubt." Using this instruction, Scheck argued to the jury that there was a reasonable doubt as to whether the police had planted blood on the socks in Simpson's bedroom, and, he said, the socks were "an essential fact" in the prosecution's case. Therefore, he concluded, this was another "reasonable doubt." But of course the socks were not *essential* to proving Simpson's guilt. Even if they had never existed, or even if blood had been planted on them, if there was sufficient *other* evidence in the case to prove Simpson's guilt beyond a reasonable doubt, as there was, the prosecution would still be entitled to a guilty verdict. Likewise, Scheck somehow had it figured out that if Mr. Simpson had in fact been wearing the bloody glove found at his Rockingham estate, and had cut his finger the way the prosecution claimed he did during the murders, then blood of Mr. Simpson's would be expected to be found on "the top fingers of the glove," and because it wasn't, he told the jury "that has to give you a reasonable doubt."

Just as the defense attorneys never told the jury that contamination would change someone else's blood into Simpson's (knowing they would sound ridiculous if they said this), only that contamination made the results "unreliable," Scheck and Cochran never said that each one of these individual alleged problems with the prosecution's case created a reasonable doubt "of guilt." As I've indicated, they simply said there were "many reasonble doubts," i.e., a reasonable doubt here and a reasonable doubt there.

And the Simpson jurors swallowed this hook, line, and sinker. Discussing the fact that Simpson's blood was at the murder scene, jury foreperson Armanda Cooley says in her book, "We [the jury] can't explain it away. Me, personally, I have not tried to explain it away at all. That was not one of the issues [Simpson's blood at the murder scene was not one of the issues?] and that was definitely not *the* reasonable doubt we based our decision on"—i.e., Armanda and her friends had more important things to concern themselves with than Simpson's blood being at the murder scene. The game, apparently, was not about whether or not *Simpson's guilt* had been proved beyond a reasonable doubt, but whether a reasonable doubt could be found anywhere at all in the case. And if it could, it was a "reasonable doubt" case and Simpson was entitled to a not-guilty verdict. For instance, Cooley said that if Fuhrman was a liar, "you've got reasonable doubt right there."

The bottom line, of course, is that even if the LAPD laboratory was a cesspool of contamination, or even if a certain item of evidence was planted or tampered with, or even if Fuhrman was a liar, this did not preclude the jury, *as a matter of law*, from concluding that the prosecution, by the weight of all the *other* evidence, had proved Simpson's *guilt* beyond a reasonable doubt. Yet the jury was led to believe that if there was a reasonable doubt as to *any* contested fact, Simpson was entitled to a not-guilty verdict. But in their rebuttal arguments, not one word was uttered by either prosecutor to clarify this point, which could not possibly have been more important, nor did they ask the judge to clarify this point in his instructions to the jury.

With the circumstantial evidence instruction on reasonable doubt, Scheck committed armed robbery in broad daylight and all the prosecutors did was stand by and watch. Scheck must have felt as if he were taking candy from a baby.

What was *totally* lacking from both prosecutors' arguments, opening as well as closing, was drawing powerful inferences of guilt from the evidence, one after another, that no one else in the courtroom had thought of—the type that causes one to say, "Hey, I never thought of that." When this happens you know you're listening to a first-class summation, one that is elevated above the pedestrian, prosaic summations that are virtually all one hears in American courtrooms. In the Simpson case, the two prosecutors didn't even make many of the most obvious arguments, much less those no one else had thought of.

And what was *almost totally lacking* from both prosecutors' arguments was any imagination, or eloquence, or oratorical style. Nothing is more effective in driving home an important point than a colorful and well-chosen example, metaphor, or even a humorous story. The virtual absence of soaring oratory by the prosecutors—their very few attempts at a colorful example or parable, with the lone exception of Darden's talking about the jury's rescuing a baby ("baby justice") from a burning building, were banal and dull—showed that both had the mentality of journeyman lawyers, ill equipped to have been thrust on center stage in what the media called "the trial of the century."

For example, this type of argument would have been ideal for the Simpson jury at the very beginning of closing argument, even though none of the jurors may ever have read Victor Hugo:

"I wonder if any of you folks have read Victor Hugo's account of the octopus. He tells us of how it doesn't have any beak to defend itself like a bird, no claws like a lion, nor teeth like an alligator. But it does have what could be called an ink bag, and to protect itself when it is attacked it lets out a dark fluid from this bag, thus making all of the surrounding water dark and murky, enabling the octopus to escape into the darkness.

"Now I ask you folks, is there any similarity between that description of the ink bag of the octopus and the defense in this case? Has the defense shown you any real, valid, legitimate defense reasonably based on the evidence, or has it sought to employ the ink bag of the octopus, and by making everything dark around Mr. Simpson, tried to let him escape into the darkness?

"I intend to clear up the water which defense counsel have sought to muddy, so that you folks can clearly see the evidence, the facts, the issues in this case, so that you can behold the form of the retreating octopus and bring this defendant back to face justice."

With respect to the use of colorful examples to make a point, this is an argument I gave in a double-murder case based on circumstantial evidence. The prosecutors should have used some variation of this:

"I think that counsels' problem is that they misconceive what circumstantial evidence is all about. Circumstantial evidence is not, as they claim, like a chain. You could have a chain spanning the Atlantic Ocean from Nova Scotia to Bordeaux, France, consisting of millions of links, and with one weak link that chain is broken.

"Circumstantial evidence, to the contrary, is like a rope. And each fact is a strand of that rope. And as the prosecution piles one fact upon another we add strands and we add strength to that rope. If one strand breaks—and I'm not conceding for a moment that any strand has broken in this case—but if one strand does break, the rope is not broken. The strength of the rope is barely diminished. Why? Because there are so many *other* strands of almost steel-like strength that the rope is still more than strong enough to bind these two defendants to justice. That's what circumstantial evidence is all about."

There were all types of opportunities in this case for the prosecutors to use humor in their summation to point out the changing and in-

consistent positions the defense took—for instance, the three different stories they floated as to what Simpson was doing at the time of the
murders. This type of argument, from one of my murder cases, is illus-
trative: "Jack Dodd's flip-flops on the witness stand in this case remind
me of a story people tell about a civil case years ago. The plaintiff," I
recalled to the jury, "sued his neighbor alleging that while he was
walking along the sidewalk in front of his neighbor's home, the
neighbor's dog had run out and bitten him, causing injuries. The neighbor filed an answer to the complaint in which he set forth three contentions: Number one, he said, 'my dog was chained to the house, and
the chain doesn't extend out to the sidewalk, so there was no way for
my dog to bite the plaintiff'; number two, 'my dog is an old dog, he
doesn't have any teeth, so even if he did bite the plaintiff, he couldn't
possibly have hurt the plaintiff'; and number three," I shouted out," 'I
don't even *own* a dog.' This is Jack Dodd," I told the jury, whose laughter
cleared some of the tension that had been building up in the final
hours of the trial.

I was also waiting for the prosecution to point out to the jury that the
prosecution doesn't have the burden to prove every little point in a case
and answer every single, conceivable question the defense might raise or
the jury might have, and that the prosecution's failure to prove every single
point doesn't negate all that *has* been proved. I kept waiting for the prosecutors to point out that the heart of the defense case for over nine months,
both as to the frame-up and the contamination theories, was to treat every
question asked as the equivalent of proof, to split hairs, to focus in on one
penny-ante mistake, discrepancy, or inconsistency after another, and try
to blow their significance totally out of proportion. Yet the prosecutors
never once made an argument such as this to the jury:

**"If you put virtually *any* criminal case under a high-powered micro-
scope, you're going to find a few discrepancies here and there, inconsistencies, slip-ups, unanswered questions, incompetence, etc. That's
true because of the nature of life. But they don't add up to anything.
Things don't happen in life with mathematical precision and in apple-
pie order. And the law takes cognizance of this. That's why the prosecution only has to prove guilt beyond a reasonable doubt, not beyond
all doubt. If the prosecution had to cross every *t* and dot every *i* to get
a conviction, we'd rarely get one."**

This could have been followed by a current example of human fallibil-
ity which the jury could relate to, such as this, from my summation in the
murder case upon which *Till Death Us Do Part* was based:

Mr. Goldin devoted almost fifty percent of his closing argument to attacking Michael Brockington and accusing him of murder, mind you. He also said that Brockington made many inconsistent statements on the witness stand, and hence he is not a believable witness. Well, I don't think any normal human being could take that witness stand and answer several hundred questions pertaining to fifty or more events taking place over a period of two years without there being some minor discrepancies in his or her testimony.

Goldin's theory is that if the prosecution doesn't call robots and computers to that witness stand, if we only call human beings, somehow or other Alan Palliko didn't pull that trigger on Henry Stockton. If Dave Goldin wants to play a game like that, ladies and gentlemen, let him play it by himself.

Recall Frank Borman—Colonel Frank Borman? He was the commander of the Apollo 8 flight that just recently circumnavigated the moon. On the first day of that flight, when Borman was sending transmissions back to Cape Kennedy, he referred to the Apollo 8 flight as the Gemini 8 flight, a flight he had participated in back in 1965.

Now, just consider the monumental preparation that Frank Borman must have put into that Apollo 8 flight, and yet Frank Borman is sending back messages from Gemini 8. Can't you just hear Mr. Goldin in the control center down at Cape Kennedy when Borman sent any messages thereafter? "We can't believe that man. His credibility has been destroyed. He is unreliable, and these photographs he's sending of the moon—how do we know they are not fake?"

I was particularly amazed that the prosecutors never argued to the jury the ridiculous improbability of all the things pointing to Simpson's guilt in this case being just a coincidence. Both prosecutors acted as if they hadn't the faintest idea how to prosecute a circumstantial evidence case. I've put people on death row—and this is not an exaggeration—where the circumstantial evidence was one hundred times less powerful than in this case. Although Clark and Darden did, a surprisingly few times, say "Is it just a coincidence that . . ." and although the prosecutors, in their arguments to the jury, *did* cite most of the pieces of evidence they presented at the trial which pointed to Simpson's guilt, they never, remarkably, put all of the evidence and circumstances *together* and pointed out that as the number of circumstances pointing to guilt increases, the likelihood of *any* of them being a mere coincidence dramatically decreases. That is, they never made the obvious argument that the *combination* of all these coincidences made the conclusion of Simpson's guilt mandatory.

In other words, argue to the jury:

"The five drops of blood at the murder scene as well as the blood on the rear gate *just happen* ["Is it just a coincidence that . . ." phrasing could also be used in the following litany] to be Mr. Simpson's; the killer's size-12 shoes *just happen* to be the defendant's shoe size; only 299 pairs of these size-12 rare Italian-made Bruno Magli shoes were ever distributed in the United States in 1991 and 1992, and were sold in only forty stores in the entire country, one of which is Bloomingdale's in New York, and we know that Mr. Simpson *just happens* to have been a regular customer at Bloomingdale's during this same period, buying size-12 dress and casual shoes there; the glove left at the murder scene *just happens* to be the same, identical type Nicole bought for Mr. Simpson at Bloomingdale's in December of 1990, one of only two hundred pairs like them sold throughout the whole country that year; in photos and videos of Simpson broadcasting NFL games from January of 1991 through 1994, he *just happens* to be wearing these same, highly distinctive gloves; shortly after hearing two men arguing at the crime scene, Robert Heidstra, a defense witness no less, *just happens* to have seen a white utility vehicle—which he said could very well have been a Ford Bronco—rapidly leaving the area where the murders were committed; these murders *just happen* to have occurred on the same day Nicole rejected Mr. Simpson's company at the dance recital, and he was unable to reach his girlfriend, Paula Barbieri, all day, suggesting a rejection by her, also; Mr. Simpson *just happens* to have beaten Nicole severely in the past, to the point where she was in fear of her life and told people he was going to kill her; Mr. Simpson *just happens* to have cut himself very badly around the very same time of the murders; he *just happens* to have cut himself on his left hand, and we know the killer most likely got cut on his left hand, because his left glove was found at the murder scene and four out of the five blood drops were just to the left of his bloody shoe prints; dark-blue cotton fibers, the same color and material as the sweatsuit Simpson was wearing on the night of the murders, *just happen* to have been found on Ron Goldman's shirt; nine hairs with the same microscopic characteristics as Mr. Simpson's *just happen* to have been found inside the dark knit cap found at the feet of Ron Goldman; another of these same hairs *just happens* to have been found on Ron Goldman's shirt; a fiber with the same microscopic characteristics and rose-beige color as those from the carpet of Mr. Simpson's Bronco also *just happens* to have been found on the knit cap discovered at the murder scene; Nicole's and Ron's blood *just happens* to have been found inside Mr. Simpson's Bronco; Nicole's blood *just happens* to have been found on socks of

Mr. Simpson's found on the floor in his bedroom, and Mr. Simpson's blood *just happens* to have been found on one of the socks; a bloody glove matching the glove found at the murder scene *just happens* to have been found on the defendant's property within hours of the murders; Ron's, Nicole's, and Mr. Simpson's blood, as well as a hair with the same microscopic characteristics as Ron's and Nicole's, and a fiber matching those from the carpet of Mr. Simpson's Bronco, *just happen* to have been found on this glove; it *just so happens* that at the same time Kato Kaelin walked outside his guest house with a flashlight to investigate the source of the three thumps on his wall, the limo driver, who saw Kaelin searching the grounds, also saw Mr. Simpson coming from the same general direction of where the thumps were heard, and saw him enter the front door of his home; of the 392 exhibits the defense introduced at this trial, it *just so happens* that the gloves Nicole bought Mr. Simpson, which we know are identical to the evidence gloves in this case, the dark-blue or black cotton sweatsuit that Kato Kaelin saw him wearing less than an hour before the murders, and the little black bag which Mr. Simpson insisted Kato Kaelin not pick up to put in the limo about to depart for the airport, were not among the exhibits; even though the temperature around 11:00 to 11:30 p.m. on the evening of June 12, 1994, in the area between Brentwood and LAX was in the high fifties or low sixties, a cool evening, and even though the air conditioner was on in the limo, Mr. Simpson *just happens* to have been sweating and very hot, complaining two or three times to the limo driver about the heat; two plastic bags *just happen* to have been missing from the hotel room in Chicago where Mr. Simpson stayed for a few hours on the morning after the murders; of the twenty-four hours of the day on June 12, the only one of those twenty-four hours that the defendant, Mr. Simpson, couldn't provide an alibi for *just happens* to have been the hour in which these murders occurred. [And so on with at least ten or fifteen other items of circumstantial evidence pointing to Simpson's guilt that obviously were not coincidences.]

"At what point do these things stop being a coincidence, ladies and gentlemen of the jury? When you folks, as intelligent human beings using your common sense, say to yourself: 'Aw, c'mon, you've got to be kidding. It's ridiculous to suggest all of these things are just an incredible coincidence. That's not life as we know it.' *That's* when all this circumstantial evidence stops being a coincidence. When you people, as intelligent, sensible human beings—and that's why we selected you folks for this jury—say to the defense attorneys in this case, 'Let's stop living in a fantasy world and come back to earth.'

"When a person is innocent of a crime, ladies and gentlemen of the jury, chances are there isn't going to be anything whatsoever pointing toward his guilt. Chances are there will be nothing. But now and then, because of the very nature of life and the unaccountability of certain things, maybe one thing, in rare situations maybe even two things, will peculiarly point toward his guilt even though he is innocent. And in highly unusual and virtually unheard-of situations, maybe even three things will point to his guilt, even though he is innocent. But ladies and gentleman of the jury, in this case, everything, everything, points to this man's guilt. Not only does the physical, scientific evidence in this case conclusively prove this defendant's guilt, but virtually everything he said and did points irresistibly to his guilt. We've set forth for you a staggering number of pieces of evidence that point to this man, and this man alone, as the murderer of these two precious human beings. Under these circumstances, it is not humanly possible for him to be innocent. If O. J. Simpson didn't commit these murders, ladies and gentlemen of the jury, then the two victims in this case are still alive."

If anyone reading this book is saying to himself or herself, "How could it be possible for the performance of the prosecutors in this case to have been as poor and defective as Mr. Bugliosi says it was?" don't make the mistake of then concluding that it must not have been, because that would be an assumption on your part without any evidence to support it. The point is, very unfortunately for justice in this case, that it was this bad, and if there is any doubt that I am telling you the truth, order a copy of the transcript of their arguments from the court reporter, or get a copy of the video of their arguments, and you'll see. I mean, when the prosecution spends more time in their summation to the jury talking about Ronald Shipp than the defense's claim of a police conspiracy, does anything else have to be said?

Going on, the prosecutors did make the argument that the brutality of the murders showed they were personal, the killer having a rage and passion against Nicole, as the evidence showed Simpson did, and that the killings were not, therefore, committed by a professional hit man or some stranger. And Darden argued: "Who in the past has ever raised a hand to this woman? Who during the days and the hours leading to her death was upset with her? Who had a score to settle with Nicole?" But these few words were far, far too brief a statement on such a major point. And Marcia Clark's very short argument to the jury—"Who else would know when the children were going to be in bed? Who else would know the perfect time to attack and get Nicole without the children being in the way?"— fails to address the issue of who else would have had any *reason* to commit these murders. It is also a poor question since in its language it excludes far too little of the rest of the world as possible killers.

On the critical issue of excluding all other possible killers, I believe the prosecutors should have argued that point in much more depth and much more powerfully. The following is an abbreviated version of an argument that could have been made on this issue.

"I'm sure you folks recall that in Mr. Cochran's summation to you, when he said that Mark Fuhrman should have been booted off the police force a long time ago, he said that you, the jury, by your verdict, should stop the Mark Fuhrmans of the world and the cover-up for him by others. Then he said, 'If you don't stop it, *then who?*' But there's no evidence at all that Mark Fuhrman did anything wrong in this case for anyone to cover up for. And even if there were, the only job you folks have to do in this case—and you of course know this—is to determine whether we've proved Mr. Simpson's guilt beyond a reasonable doubt. Your job is not to try to change the police or society by your verdict. No jury, in any case, has such a duty. Not only don't you have such a duty, and not only would it be a violation of your oath to try to take on such a duty, but any verdict by you in this case would be incapable of materially changing society as we know it.

"So rather than the wholly improper question by Mr. Cochran, 'If you don't stop it, *then who?*' let's ask a much more proper question, one that you, as jurors, should definitely be thinking about. To paraphrase Mr. Cochran, 'If Mr. Simpson didn't commit these murders, *then who?*' *Who else* would have had any reason to commit these murders? We know Mr. Simpson beat his wife severely, to the point of the photos you saw where poor Nicole's face is swollen and black and blue. To the point where she had to call the police *nine* times during their marriage. To the point where she was in fear of her life at his hands. Recall her crying out to Officer Edwards, 'He's going to kill me, he's going to kill me, he's going to kill me.' People, even those who are getting a beating, don't normally use words like that. You only use those words when you sense it's going to really happen. I ask again, *who else* would have had the motive to kill these two young people? We know from the evidence that both Ron and Nicole were apparently well-liked and fun-loving young people in the prime of their lives— Nicole was only thirty-five, Ron just twenty-five. What is the likelihood that someone they knew would have had a reason to kill either one of them, much less both of them, and particularly in such a savage and brutal way?

"And we know it wasn't a burglar or robber, because there was no burglary or robbery. These aren't the type of murders that burglars or robbers commit anyway. And it's clear the murders weren't done by a professional hit man. Who in the lives of these young people would have had any reason to hire someone to kill either one of them? And contract killings almost always are with a gun—they are quick and not messy. These murders, ladies and gentlemen of the jury, bear the unmistakable signature of a killer who was intimately involved with at least one of the victims. The vicious knife thrusts were born out of angry and wild passion, not just an intent to get a job done for some third party. I ask you once again to ask yourself this question back in the jury room—*who else* had any reason at all to kill Ron and Nicole, particularly in this way? There is simply no one except O. J. Simpson, the defendant in this case.

"And you know, one thing we know about the defense team in this case. We know they had all the money they needed to defend this man. There was testimony that one of their witnesses, Dr. Baden, who was on the stand for only a few days, was paid in excess of one hundred thousand dollars by the defense in this case. I don't know about any of you folks, but I don't even make that much money in a whole year. So we know that money was no object in their defense of Mr. Simpson. A large staff of lawyers and assistants, private investigators, you name it, they had it. And they had to know that the very best defense to these murders was to prove that someone else committed them. And you know, you just know they've been scouring every nook and cranny of this city and elsewhere to see if they could put the hat on someone else for these murders. They even set up an 800 number begging for any scrap of evidence they could find pointing to someone else. We also know the defense has the power of subpoena, and we've seen they weren't hesitant about calling witnesses to that stand when they wanted to prove a point. Yet consider this. After all these months and all the money expended on Mr. Simpson's defense, they never offered one witness, one speck of evidence that anyone, anyone other than their client, committed these murders. And the reason they didn't is that no such witness, no such evidence, existed.

"*No one on the face of this earth other than this man right here had any reason to kill these people.* Or even physically hurt them in any way whatsoever. And ladies and gentleman of the jury, I know you're not going to fall for the argument Mr. Cochran and Mr. Scheck made to you with respect to other matters that the reason they never did this or that is that the defense has no burden of proof, the prosecution does. If they're really operating under that assumption, why did they call fifty-eight witnesses to the witness stand? Why did they put on any evidence at all? Yes, the prosecution does have the burden of proof, but I've never heard of a defense attorney watching his client get convicted and going to prison and saying, 'Well, I know a lot of witnesses and a lot of evidence that could clear my client, but the prosecution has the burden of proof, so I'm not going to say boo.' Surely, you have to know, that if the defense attorneys had *any evidence at all* in this case pointing to some other specific person or persons, they would have presented this evidence to you. We know that.

"In fact, Mr. Cochran was so desperate to have you believe someone else committed these murders that you'll recall he even suggested during cross-examination—he didn't have any evidence, of course, to support this wild speculuation—that maybe Colombian drug lords were responsible for Nicole's murder. Can you imagine that, folks? Colombian drug lords. You know, lawyers do give wings to their imagination, but when Johnnie came up with that Colombian drug lord talk, I was glad there were no windows in this courtroom, because if there had been, Johnnie would have flown right out of here. As you know, even Mr. Cochran eventually realized how deranged and preposterous that suggestion was, and in his final summation to you folks he decided to come up with a new theory. But it turned out to be just as absurd and irrational as the first one—that maybe the killer or killers were really after Ronald Goldman because of what Ron had in the envelope he took with him to Bundy. But that argument is so ridiculous no one would buy it. For one thing, if the killer or killers were after the contents of the envelope, why didn't they take the envelope? In fact, as you know, the envelope, which we know contained Nicole's mother's eyeglasses, wasn't even opened. I have to say I'm disappointed in Johnnie. He is a bright fellow, but he's been on this case for well over a year, and this is the best he and his associates can come up with? Colombian drug lords, or killers out to get the contents of an envelope they don't take or even bother to open? I mean, these arguments are simply embarrassing.

"Only one person, O. J. Simpson, committted these murders, and only one person, O. J. Simpson, had any motive or reason to. The defense attorneys know this, so in desperation they have come up with speculations and arguments so light in substance they are not only floating lazily up in the clouds, unconnected to any evidence in this case, but worse yet, are unconnected to any previously recognized form of logic."

The prosecutors in the Simpson case, inexcusably, elected not to present a great amount of highly incriminating evidence during the trial. And in their summations, they were clearly outargued by the defense team, particularly Cochran. The prosecutors failed to make one powerful argument after another, and even those they did make were not made well. In summation, the force and power of the prosecutor's remarks have to be so compelling that the jury feels it has no choice *but* to convict. I got no sense of that at all from Clark's or Darden's summations.

As I said at the start of this book, this long conversation with you, the prosecutors were dealing, number one, with a jury that was difficult, but no worse than a great number of other juries that routinely convict criminal defendants charged with serious crimes. So the jury wasn't sharp. With any jury, particularly one like the Simpson jury, the prosecutor, as I indicated earlier, has to put a bib on the jury and spoon-feed it. These prosecutors, by failing to make a number of obvious arguments, and arguing others very poorly, did not do that.

They were also dealing with a jury many of whose members were probably biased in favor of Simpson, one that wanted to find some way to acquit him. That is, the jurors were predisposed to search for enough evidence to raise a reasonable doubt in their minds. (No juror just decided, "The evidence is immaterial and the trial is a waste of time. I'm going to find O.J. not guilty even if he committed these murders." I don't believe that for one moment.) And the prosecutors accommodated the jury, with the glove demonstration, with the way they handled Fuhrman, and in many, many other ways. In other words, the prosecutors *allowed* the jury to acquit Simpson. They gave the jurors a choice, as opposed to clearly eliminating, by evidence and argument, any verdict other than guilty. Even though they easily could have, the prosecutors didn't even began to foreclose, in the jury's mind, all possibilities of their finding Simpson not guilty.

Simpson juror Carrie Bass said on NBC's *Dateline* on January 16, 1996: "I'm sorry, O.J. would have had to go if the prosecution had presented that case different, without the doubt. As a black woman, it would have hurt me. But as a human being, I would have to do what I had to do." It bears repeating that as bad and incompetent as the prosecution was in this case, in the first vote taken by the jury, two jurors, one black and one white, voted guilty. There is no question in my mind that if there had been a powerful prosecution in this case, the strong probability is that Simpson would have been convicted. At an absolute minimum it would have been a hung jury.

Black people are often religious (Cochran, of course, knows this, and it's the reason he sprinkled his argument liberally with references to God and the Bible), and having it on their conscience that they knowingly let a murderer go free is something that anyone, particularly a religious person, would want to avoid. Evidence, for instance, like the suicide note, Simpson's having a gun, passport, and a cheap disguise at the time of his arrest, and particularly his admission he was dripping with blood in his car and home around the very same time of the murders and had no idea how he got cut, is the type of evidence, in fact, that causes any juror, who knows he has to live with his decision for the rest of his life, to feel he has no choice. If he doesn't give this evidence the weight which he immediately recognizes it's entitled to, he knows it's going to bother him always, and humans instinctively recoil from the thought of so burdening themselves.

Religious people know that in the Bible, murder is the ultimate crime, and they believe it should be severely punished. The prosecutors in the Simpson case, by their extremely poor performance, permitted the jurors to live with their consciences. After I had already written these words in the first draft of this book, I read *Madam Foreman*. On page 154 of the book, Armanda Cooley, the foreperson of the jury, describes her state of mind before reaching the verdict: "My whole thing was I wanted to be able to live with myself." I, for one, already knew this. It's just common sense. On Oprah Winfrey's show, juror Gina Rosborough said the jury went through the deliberation process "to clear everybody's conscience." The jurors told each other, she said, they would "be able to wake up in the morning and look at yourself in the mirror and be proud of what you did. The prosecution, they did a good job. But . . . everybody had questions."

Interestingly enough, the prosecutors, by the language they used in arguing reasonable doubt, even suggested to the jury that perhaps there was some doubt about Simpson's guilt. Not once did they ever tell the jury that they had proved Simpson's guilt beyond *all* doubt, which they of course had, and which, I'm sure, they strongly believed. When Simpson's blood was found at the murder scene, that fact alone proved his guilt beyond all doubt. Yet the prosecutors insisted on implying to the jury that although there was no *reasonable* doubt of Simpson's guilt, there was some small doubt. In fact, Darden, in response to the defense's chart and argument that "beyond a reasonable doubt" meant the prosecution had to eliminate almost all doubt, told the jury: "That isn't reasonable doubt. *That is not what I'm required to prove to you. There is always some degree of doubt, no matter how small.*" Not in this case, Chris. Not in this case.

Even Clark, in her very final words to the jury, said, "We have proven beyond a reasonable doubt, far beyond a reasonable doubt, that the defendant committed these murders." By her obvious failure and refusal to say the prosecution had proved Simpson's guilt beyond *all* doubt, isn't she necessarily saying that maybe they hadn't? While it is always wise and proper to point out to the jury more than once, as Darden did, that the prosecution, under the law, does not have to prove the defendant's guilt beyond *all* possible doubt, only beyond a *reasonable* doubt, shouldn't you automatically then go on—particularly when you have, in fact, proved guilt beyond all doubt, and you're dealing with a jury which has probably believed for years that "beyond a reasonable doubt" means the colloquial "beyond a *shadow* of a doubt"—to tell the jury: "But here, even though we don't have the burden, we have, in fact, proved this man's guilt beyond all possible doubt." To repeat, not once, at any time during the trial, did either prosecutor tell the jury that the prosecution had proved Simpson's guilt beyond all doubt. Their articulation to the jury on the matter of reasonable doubt, in fact, contained the implication they had not done so.

Although I'm not satisfied beyond all doubt, I'm satisfied beyond a reasonable doubt that it was because of the prosecution's terribly inferior performance from the beginning of the trial to the very end that the Simpson jury had a clear conscience giving Simpson his ticket to freedom. And instead of our now reading about how he's adjusting to life at San Quentin, we see him smiling and bathing in the warmth of the California and Florida sun.

Epilogue

Book Ends

The Simpson case raised a number of fascinating and important issues that do not fit neatly into the organization of this book. I could, of course, just stop now and leave well enough alone; but the various questions and considerations that make up this epilogue have come up in countless conversations I've had, and also on television or radio call-in shows focusing on the Simpson case. It is my hope that any reader who has stuck with me this far will find what follows both interesting and provocative.

Q. J. Simpson was acquitted—so have the defense lawyers earned the right to be called the Dream Team?

Nothing could be further from the truth. In fact, it was only the *greater* incompetence of the prosecution that saved Cochran, Shapiro, Bailey, Scheck, et al. from defeat.

Though the trial went on for nearly a year, I defy anyone to come up with one example of brilliant lawyering by the defense team, the type of thing that would cause an *intelligent* person to say to himself, "That was really something." Indeed, the only hint of *skill* I saw on the entire defense team, including the two DNA lawyers, throughout the whole trial was Bailey's cross-examination. Bailey wasn't particularly effective on cross because of his style and a lack of adequate preparation, but it was obvious that Lee (whom I had seen cross-examine one previous time in Rochester, New York) at least has a sense of what cross-examination is all about, and was able to craft a skillful question on cross.

The cross-examination of all the other lawyers was limited to the garden variety: the routine eliciting of testimony from the prosecution witnesses favorable to the defense (as the prosecutors did with the defense witnesses); impeaching the credibility of defense witnesses by the simple technique of confronting the witness with evidence of prior inconsistent or contradictory statements; showing the witness's bias or vested interest, his poor character for truth, etc. This can clearly be very *effective*, but there is no *skill* involved. It's the most basic, rudimentary type of cross-examination, and most defense lawyers never rise above it. Cross-examination is a lost art, and I doubt you could find more than a handful of superb cross-examiners in the entire country.

One example of skillful cross-examination would be where, by the nature and composition of the questions, and their juxtaposition to one another, an otherwise truthful-appearing and able witness is forced into saying something that sounds patently implausible and ridiculous. Another example is when, by blocking off all possible escape hatches before springing the key question, the witness has nowhere to go and is precluded from having any reasonable explanation for his conduct or the statement he made. In the first draft of this book, my editor put this note opposite what I have just written: "Can you give an example to the reader of one of these?"

It is hard to give an example of what I'm talking about in a paragraph or two, but I'll try to keep it brief. Before I do, however, a discussion of the use of the "why" question, perhaps my main technique on cross-examination, is called for. Virtually all human beings, from childhood on, regularly cross-examine those with whom they interact. And the main technique they employ is to ask "Why?" or "How come?" Wife to husband: "If your meeting ended at 8:00, *why* did you get home at 10:30?" Girl to boy: "You say you like me so much. *How come* you didn't ask me to the dance?" Yet ironically, this most natural, instinctive, and practiced of all cross-examination techniques is frowned upon by the very people who need it most, trial lawyers. Books on the art of cross-examination, from Francis Wellman's 1903 classic *The Art of Cross-Examination* on down, all advocate *never* asking an adverse witness why he did or did not do something the lawyer feels is implausible. Louis Nizer, in his book *My Life in Court*, says: "One can quickly spot a bad cross-examiner if he asks 'why.'" The reason given is that the "why" question gives the witness free rein to explain away his conduct, and in so doing he also frequently incorporates within his explanation to the open-ended question a statement extremely damaging to the questioner's case.

Admittedly, real witnesses, unlike their fictional counterparts in novels and on the screen who crumple under the pressure of the first or second good question, are as elusive as all hell. When cornered on the stand and on the brink of public humiliation, they seem to secrete a type of mental adrenaline that gets their minds working as fast as Houdini's hands worked in a trunk at the bottom of the Hudson River. Textbooks on the art of the cross-examination, wherein classic courtroom cross-examinations compiled throughout the years are presented, reveal that contrary to popular belief, even the most piercing cross-examination rarely, if ever, completely destroys a witness. At best, the witness is only hurt, not demolished. So the witness a lawyer is facing on the stand, for some curious reason, is almost inherently formidable. But just as no one, not even a Houdini, can pull a rabbit out of the hat when there isn't any rabbit in the hat, a witness can't escape when he has nowhere to go.

If I feel a witness is lying, I just about know, in advance, that he would not have acted, in a given circumstance, the way a person telling the truth would have acted. Frequently, I already have evidence that he did not. To expose the fact that he is an untruthful witness, I usually employ the following technique to block off the exits. First I elicit answers from the witness on preliminary matters, answers which, when totaled up, show he would be expected to take a certain course of action, or act in a certain way. The witness having committed himself by his answers, I then ask him what course he in fact took, and follow this up with the "why" question. If a witness is unable to justify or explain conduct of his which is incompatible with the behavior of a normal person under the same circumstances, the jury will usually conclude that his testimony is suspect. Note that there is at least one common denominator between the "why" question technique I have just mentioned and other approaches—you first have to get the witness to commit himself. In his best-selling book *The Defense Never Rests*, F. Lee Bailey (who does not use the "why" question technique) makes this excellent observation. He says: "The most common error lawyers make on cross-examination is that of immediately attacking a witness who has not been sufficiently pinioned. The result is that the witness escapes."

In the case I prosecuted and wrote about in *Till Death Us Do Part*, there were two murders, and they were for the most reprehensible motive there can be, money. As Damon Runyon once said, these were murders "in the worst degree." Both murders, completely circumstantial evidence cases, bore a startling similarity to the James Cain novel *Double Indemnity*, although the *New York Daily News* opined, "but this real-life plot makes Cain's melodrama read like a wholesome, old-fashioned strive and succeed story." In the second murder I was alleging that the male defendant, Alan (a former Los Angeles police officer), was responsible for the murder of his wife, Judy. But the defense presented evidence that on the night before Judy's murder, two friends of Alan and Judy's, Mr. and Mrs. Daryl Lott, had stopped by Alan and Judy's apartment, and that Judy was alone and armed with a gun because she was in deathly fear of some other man, a former boyfriend from New York City, the implication being that this other man was the true murderer. Using the approach of first eliciting answers from the witness on preliminary matters, which, when totaled, show he would be expected to take a certain course of action, then asking what course he in fact took, and then asking why, I started in on the issue of whether Mr. and Mrs. Lott had ever even stopped by the victim's apartment on the night in question, as they claimed they did. What you will see is not complex or esoteric at all. But no matter how bright the lawyer is, if he doesn't sit down with his yellow pad (during his preparation for cross-examination) and block off all possible escape hatches, the witness (if he is a typical witness) will find one.

Q. How did you happen to stop by Alan's and Judy's apartment, as you claim you did, around 11:00 p.m. Friday night, April 19, Mr. Lott?
A. I don't know. I do a lot of things on the spur of the moment. Just decided to stop in, say hello.
Q. I understand you were a closer friend of Alan's than you were of Judy's, is that true?
A. Well, I knew Alan longer. Let's put it that way.
Q. Is there any question in your mind that you were much closer to Alan than Judy?
A. No. I was.
Q. You had been to Alan's Grand Duke Bar on previous Friday nights, had you not?
A. Yes.
Q. About what time did Alan normally close the bar on these Friday nights?
A. 2:00 in the morning.
Q. Did you think that this particular Friday night Alan would be home instead of at the Grand Duke?
A. I had no idea.
Q. The Grand Duke is pretty close to their apartment, isn't it?
A. Sure is.
Q. Would it have been out of your way to *first* stop at the Grand Duke?
A. No.

Q. *Did* you first stop at the Grand Duke to see if Alan was there before you went to Judy's apartment?
A. No, I don't believe we did.
Q. Any particular reason *why* you didn't, Mr. Lott?
A. Uh . . . no reason at all.

Since the witness's conduct was implausible, and he had no satisfactory explanation for his conduct, the cross-examination raised the inference that he and his wife had not, as they claimed, stopped by the victim's apartment at all.

Getting back to the defense's cross-examination in the Simpson case, DNA blood testing is one of the most complex sciences, where molecular biology, genetics, and statistics converge, often in confusing ways. It's a relatively new field, with very few lawyers in the entire country specializing in it. Among them are Barry Scheck and Peter Neufeld, pioneers in the field. Shapiro, when he was putting the defense team together, earned his fee by the hiring of Scheck and Neufeld alone. The proof of the complexity of DNA is that both the prosecution and the defense felt it was necessary to bring in lawyers who specialized in DNA to handle that part of the case for them. Scheck and Neufeld clearly proved to be competent in their specialty. They not only demonstrated they were very knowledgeable about the subject, but they did more preparation than the average lawyer, and that enabled them to conduct *effective* cross-examination. But being effective and being skillful are two different things, and the media covering criminal trials almost invariably confuse them.

Let me give you an example. At the grand jury in the Simpson case, LAPD criminalist Dennis Fung testified that he, not his rookie associate, Andrea Mazzola, had collected most of the blood evidence at the Bundy murder scene and Simpson's Rockingham estate. On cross-examination at the trial, however, Scheck confronted Fung with a videotape of Mazzola (provided to the defense by the prosecution as part of mandatory discovery) collecting most of the blood evidence. Likewise, Fung testified on cross-examination by Scheck that at Simpson's Rockingham estate on the afternoon of June 13, 1995 (the day after the murders), LAPD detective Philip Vannatter handed him an envelope containing a vial of blood drawn from Simpson's arm at LAPD's Parker Center earlier in the day and that he had carried the envelope back to his crime scene truck; whereupon Scheck confronted Fung with a videotape showing Fung walking back to the truck without anything in his hands. (Fung had forgotten that Mazzola had taken the envelope to the truck.) At another point, after Fung had testified that he and Mazzola hadn't collected evidence until *after* the coroner's technicians had left the Bundy murder scene, Scheck confronted Fung with yet another videotape of the crime scene.

> Scheck: Now this is Ms. Mazzola putting the hat in the bag, correct?
> Fung: Yes.
> Scheck: Now, you remember Mr. Jacobo from the coroner's office. He was the gentleman in the blue garment?
> Fung: Yes.
> Scheck: Do you see those blue pants?
> Fung: Yes.
> Scheck: That's Mr. Jacobo, isn't it?
> Fung: Appears to be, yes.
> Scheck: So you did begin evidence collection before the coroner's technicians left.
> Fung: Yes.
> Scheck: So what you said before wasn't true?
> Fung: It was to the best of my recollection at the time.

Now, Scheck contradicting Fung at every turn with videos, certainly was effective cross-examination, but absolutely no skill was involved. I mean, your local cabby could do this. If you have a film controverting the testimony of a witness, you present it, right? Is any superb lawyering involved here? If you can't impeach a witness when you are armed with a film that supports your position, it's time for you to take down your shingle. Yet the media couldn't rhapsodize enough about this kind of cross-examination by Scheck of Fung. This was brilliant Perry Mason stuff, they assured their readers. And the talking heads were opining that this was the best, or among the best, cross-examination they had ever seen. It was. For them. When Marlon Brando weighed in (rather heavily, I might add) with how impressed he was with Scheck, it was now official. Barry Scheck was simply a great cross-examiner.

Perhaps nothing illustrates the incompetence of the main lawyers (not the DNA lawyers) for the defense more than the fact that although they went through millions of dollars of Simpson's money, and had all the time in the world, unbelievably they never even bothered to interview most of the prosecution witnesses, relying, instead, on statements of the witnesses they were given by the prosecution by way of discovery. This doesn't just border on incompetence. This *is* incompetence, astonishing incompetence. I had sensed they hadn't interviewed most of the prosecution witnesses because during their cross-examination of them they frequently were receiving answers they didn't like, and if they had interviewed the witnesses they never would have asked those questions. Also,

during their efforts at impeachment by way of prior inconsistent or contradictory statements, they were almost always referring to statements furnished to them by the prosecution, as opposed to saying, "Didn't you tell
me that . . ." or "Didn't you tell our investigator that . . ."

Just to see if my suspicions were correct, I called attorney Robert
Tourtelot, Mark Fuhrman's lawyer. Now, as you know, almost from the
beginning of the case, even long before the discovery of the Fuhrman
tapes, Fuhrman was by far the main witness the defense team had talked
about for months, suggesting he had planted the glove and boasting how
they intended to destroy him on cross-examination. I asked Tourtelot if
Bailey, who had cross-examined Fuhrman, had interviewed Fuhrman.
Answer: No. Did Bailey make any effort to? No. Did any member of the
defense team, including investigators, interview Fuhrman or make any
effort to do so? No. Can you imagine that? Bailey only handled a few
witnesses during the long trial, and had all the time in the world to prepare for them, and yet he never even bothered to interview these witnesses before he was scheduled to cross-examine them, even, unbelievably, Mark Fuhrman.

I learned subsequently from Detective Lange that he wasn't interviewed
by Johnnie Cochran, the defense attorney who cross-examined him, and
Vannatter wasn't interviewed by Shapiro, his cross-examiner (nor did
Cochran or Shapiro even request an interview), before these two defense
attorneys conducted their cross-examination of the detectives at the trial.
This was true not just of the investigating officers, but of many of the lay
witnesses. When I checked with Wendy Putnam Park, the mother of the
limousine driver, Alan Park (Ms. Park is a lawyer herself and represented
her son throughout the proceedings), she informed me that Cochran had
not interviewed her son before conducting his cross-examination of him
on the witness stand. She said Cochran had talked to her son only once
very briefly during a break from the trial in the courthouse hallway.

Interviewing the opposition witnesses is absolutely essential to effective cross-examination. It gives you one additional statement to impeach
them with if their trial testimony differs from the statement in any way,
and even though they are adverse witnesses, if you interview them enough
times you can elicit from them at least some information helpful to your
side.

When I first pointed out, during one of my few television appearances,
that the defense hadn't even bothered to interview most of the prosecution witnesses, a few criminal defense attorneys in town called me to say
that although they didn't know about the lay witnesses for the prosecution, the LAPD detectives probably wouldn't have even agreed to be in-

terviewed by the defense team. These lawyers, of course, were just confirming their own incompetence. Number one, almost assuredly the detectives would have agreed to be interviewed. But even more important, since the defense in the Simpson case didn't have one shred of evidence to support its preposterous claim that the LAPD detectives framed Simpson, if the defense attorneys had tried to interview the detectives, I would think they would have been hoping and praying the detectives would refuse to talk to them. Because on cross-examination, this refusal to be interviewed could be brought out in front of the jury to show the bias of the detectives against Simpson. It would have been the only tiny speck of circumstantial evidence they would have to support their outrageous claim of a police frame-up. As it turned out, with the Simpson jury and Simpson prosecutors, they didn't need it, but they certainly had no way of knowing this at the time.

Not one of the many talking heads, who watched this entire case intently, mentioned this failure of the defense attorneys to interview most of the prosecution witnesses. And the obvious reason they didn't is that they almost undoubtedly don't do it themselves in their own cases, and therefore the thought that Simpson's lawyers weren't doing it never even occurred to them. Even a lawyer of the stature of Gerry Spence apparently doesn't always interview the prosecution witnesses. At least in the docu-trial of Lee Harvey Oswald in London he and I worked on for five months, and in which he had two members of his law firm helping him, neither he nor any member of his team interviewed any of my witnesses, not even once, whereas I interviewed all of his, some three or four times. In the double murder case upon which my last true crime book, *And the Sea Will Tell*, was based, the chief prosecutor, who was the head trial attorney in the Honolulu office of the U.S. attorney, never interviewed one of my witnesses, whereas I interviewed, or sought to interview, all of his witnesses.

The evidence of mediocrity and incompetence among the main members of the Dream Team (again, not the DNA lawyers) was ample. Another example: Kato Kaelin testified that around 11:00 p.m. on the night of the murders when he was loading Simpson's five bags into the limousine for Simpson's trip to the airport, the smallest of the five bags was at the edge of the driveway. When he walked toward the small black bag to pick it up, Simpson told Kaelin not to, that he would. The limo driver, Alan Park, testified he recalled hearing Simpson tell Kaelin: "No, no. That's okay. I'll get it. I'll get it." It was the only bag Simpson directed Kaelin to stay away from, and the prosecution naturally believed that this was the bag into which Simpson had placed his bloody clothing and the murder knife.

If they were correct in their assumption, which they almost certainly were, it was bad enough for the defense that this small black bag was never seen again. But the defense attorneys, supposedly the best lawyers that money could buy, all by themselves and with no pressure on them to do so, made their problem much worse, spotlighting the missing bag for the jury. With Cochran in charge, they brought five pieces of luggage into court to show to the limo driver and one James Williams, the skycap who had seen Simpson standing by a trash can shortly after the limo arrived at Los Angeles International Airport. They had a golf bag, a Louis Vuitton garment bag, two dark-colored duffel bags, and, yes, a small black bag. But, unbelievably, the small black bag was brand spanking new, and the plastic line to which the price tag had been fastened and the keys were still attached. Cochran and his Dream Team colleagues hadn't even bothered to remove them in their obvious attempt to trick the limo driver and sky-cap into identifying it as the mysterious missing bag about which Simpson had been so possessive and solicitous on the night of the murders. Because it was such a transparent and amateurish ruse, Judge Ito wouldn't even allow the defense to show this bag to the witnesses. (They were shown the other four, and although no positive identification was made, the witnesses thought the bags looked similar to those they had seen in Simpson's possession on the night of the murders. The limo driver had seen five bags, but when the limo arrived at the airport, the skycap only saw three, the prosecution inferring that en route, Simpson had stuffed the small dark bag and one of the duffel bags into the larger bags.)

Marcia Clark brought out before the jury, in her redirect examination of Park, the limo driver, that the one bag Simpson wouldn't let Kaelin pick up on the night of the murders was definitely not among the four bags shown to him by Cochran. The small black bag had previously been mentioned only briefly by Kaelin and Park in their testimony, so the reference to it could easily have been largely forgotten in the raft of testimony and evidence in the case, and there was nothing visual to help underline its importance in the jurors' minds. But by bringing in the four bags, Cochran had now shown the jurors, in front of their very eyes, that the defense had considered this a very important issue. The defense had tried to account for all of Simpson's bags, but had failed to produce for the jury the only bag that counted. Let me tell you. This was brilliant lawyering by Cochran and his Dream Team colleagues, the kind that can only be bought with a million dollars. Someone like a lowly deputy public defender would never have the experience and legal smarts to pull off something like this.

Looking at the performance of the individual defense lawyers, I have to say I was disappointed in Johnnie Cochran, at least up until his final summation. Cochran is an intelligent and seasoned courtroom performer. I expected more of him.

Let's start with his opening statement. Other than the evidence, nothing is more important to a trial lawyer than his credibility with the jury, because once a lawyer gains the trust of the jury, it is more likely to see the case his or her way. Here, Cochran did something at the start of the case that could only hurt his credibility in the minds of any *normal* jury. The fact that it may not have hurt him with this jury is no defense against the charge of incompetence. What kind of trial lawyer makes an opening statement that caused judge Ito to tell the jury that he, Cochran, was not playing by the rules, that he violated the law? (Cochran referred in his opening statement to the anticipated testimony of fourteen witnesses whose names and statements he hadn't furnished to the prosecution as required by California's Reciprocal Discovery Law.)

What kind of trial lawyer makes all kinds of promises to the jury in his opening statement that he has to know, or at least should know, he might not be able to keep? It's a cardinal rule of opening statements that you don't bite off more than you can chew, that you don't promise the jury you will prove something that you might be unable to prove. You must be careful, therefore, in your opening statement so that you don't have to contradict yourself or retract something by trial's end. It's very effective for opposing counsel to point out to the jury in summation at the end of the case that in your opening statement you promised to prove something and you failed to do so. (Darden did this to Cochran reasonably well, and the fact it had no effect with *this* jury doesn't transform Cochran's incompetence into competence.) It hurts your credibility with the jury and can adversely affect its perception of your entire case.

Cochran mentioned several witnesses in his opening statement and then chose not to call them at the trial. He said that one Mary Anne Gerchas would testify she saw four men, two Hispanics and two Caucasians, in knit caps leaving the murder scene and speeding away in their car. He said that another witness, Lenore Walker, a Denver psychologist who is a recognized authority on battered woman syndrome, would testify that Simpson did not fit the profile of a batterer. Another, Rosa Lopez (the El Salvadoran maid of a neighbor of Simpson's), had seen Simpson's white Ford Bronco, Cochran told the jury in his opening statement, parked in front of his home at the time of the murders, and later heard men's voices talking at the Simpson estate between midnight and 2:30 to 3:00 a.m. (both sides conceded at the trial that Simpson left his home for Chicago shortly after 11:00 p.m.). Cochran and his colleagues called none of these witnesses during the trial. If, indeed, Cochran ever did intend to call these and other witnesses, what kind of lawyer vouches in his opening statement for the credibility of witnesses who *have* no credibility? What does that say about his *own* credibility?

For instance, quoting the January 27, 1995, edition of USA *Today*:

Rosa Lopez, the maid who lives next door to Simpson, is supposed to be able to give the ex-football star an alibi on the night of the murders. But she has a problem. She wasn't trustworthy enough for the *National Enquirer*. "She didn't meet our traditional standards of credibility," said *Enquirer* celebrity editor Steve Cos. "Information she gave us was patently ridiculous." Defense lawyers say Lopez said she saw Simpson's Ford Bronco parked outside his house at 10:15 p.m.—when prosecutor's say the murders happened—and told that to Detective Mark Fuhrman, who kept the information secret. That's not what she told the *Enquirer* in repeated interviews, said David Perel, the *Enquirer*'s "O.J. editor." Perel said Lopez was insistent about two things: She had seen and heard nothing on the night of the murders, and there had been a big party "with a bunch of little boys, friends of Jason (Simpson's twenty-five-year-old son)" on the night before the murder. "The party story turned out to be false," Perel said. "She was a very confused lady."

And Mary Ann Gerchas, it turns out, had had thirty-four lawsuits against her, many alleging fraud and the nonpayment of bills.

Actually, Cochran wasn't more than ten or fifteen minutes into his opening statement when it was very evident to me that he was a very mediocre criminal defense attorney. I had to chuckle to myself when Cochran told the jurors that they had to base their verdict on the facts and evidence, not speculation and conjecture. Cochran was just talking and couldn't have thought out what he said, because what he said was a prosecution argument, and in a case like this where there was no evidence pointing toward Simpson's innocence, it was the worst thing to tell a jury. The only hope and chance the defense had at the time Cochran made his remarkable statement was that the jury *would* base its verdict, not on the facts and evidence, but on speculation and conjecture. I mean, the box containing evidence favorable to the defense in this case was as empty as a bird's nest in winter.

Also, unbelievably, Cochran told the jury in his opening statement that Simpson's arthritis was so acute on the day of the murders he couldn't even deal a hand of cards a few hours before the murders at the Riviera Country Club. But then he went on to tell the jury that Simpson was practicing golf, with those same hands, on the grounds of his estate at the time of the murders. Apart from that inconsistency, didn't Cochran even know that Simpson had told the limousine driver he was sleeping during this period? And that when the LAPD detectives interviewed Simpson on the day after the murders and asked him all the things he did on the night of the murders, he made no reference to either sleeping or playing golf?

Then Cochran told the jury they had to "determine the guilt or innocence of Mr. Simpson," which is not true: they had to determine whether the prosecution had proved guilt beyond a reasonable doubt. Furthermore, such an articulation is always harmful to the defense, since it's easier for the prosecution to prove guilt, when the alternative for the jury is innocence, than it is for them to have to prove not just guilt, but guilt beyond a reasonable doubt. The moment Cochran uttered those words I immediately knew he did not even have a firm grasp of the most fundamental rule at a criminal trial: that to convict, a defendant's guilt has to be proved beyond a reasonable doubt. He obviously understands it, but not well, because if he did, it wouldn't have been possible for him to utter those words. You can talk about guilt and you can talk about innocence, but never in the context of "guilt or innocence" being the issue for the jury to resolve.

In 1981, I wrote an article titled "Not Guilty and Innocent — The Problem Children of Reasonable Doubt." The article dealt with the critical distinction between the terms "not guilty" and "innocent." (It is nothing short of remarkable that with legal treatises having been written on virtually every point of law imaginable, apparently none had ever been previously published on the subject in America. At least, none is listed in the *Index to Legal Periodicals*, or the *Criminal Justice Periodical Index*.) The genesis of the distinction is in the requirement that guilt must be proved "beyond a reasonable doubt." But what does that hallowed phrase actually mean?

The doctrine of reasonable doubt is, as Sir Winston Churchill once said of Soviet Russia, "a riddle wrapped in a mystery inside an enigma." "This elusive and *undefinable* state of mind," said J. Wigmore, the foremost authority on the law of evidence, in reference to reasonable doubt. "It is coming to be recognized that all attempts to define reasonable doubt tend to obfuscate rather than to clarify the concept," said E. Morgan, another authority. However, one all-important principle is implicit in the term — namely, that a jury does not have to believe in a defendant's innocence in order to return a verdict of not guilty. *Even the jury's belief in his guilt*, if only a moderately held one, should result in a not-guilty verdict. To convict, their belief in his guilt must be *beyond a reasonable doubt*. In federal courts throughout the country, the judge properly instructs the jury that to convict, guilt must be proved beyond a reasonable doubt. Inconsistently, however, in the very same instruction (No. 11.06 of *Fed-*

eral Criminal Jury Instructions by Devitt and Blackmar), the judge tells the jury: "You are here to *determine the guilt or innocence of the accused.*" Under existing law, this added instruction should not be given, since it is not the central purpose of a criminal trial to decide the factual question of the defendant's guilt or innocence. Yet even the U.S. Supreme Court, in case after case, uses this language, continuing to define loosely and erroneously the jury's function in a criminal trial. Needless to say, far less insightful state, county, and municipal courts throughout the land, as well as authorities on the criminal law, make the same mistake.

In ordinary lay usage, the term "not guilty" is often considered to be synonymous with "innocent." In American criminal jurisprudence, however, the terms are not synonymous. "Not guilty" is simply a legal finding by the jury that the prosecution has not met its burden of proof, not that the defendant is innocent. While a defendant's guilt or innocence obviously is the most important *moral* issue at every criminal trial, the ultimate legal issue for the jury to determine is whether or not the prosecution has met its legal burden of proving guilt beyond a reasonable doubt. If the jury does not fully understand this critical distinction, its ability to fulfill its function as the trier of fact will almost necessarily be impaired.

Instead of the correct term "guilty or not guilty," the incorrect "guilty or innocent" has insidiously crept into the American language and consciousness. Although the precise date and locus of its misconceived birth are not known, it has led a very robust life, shows no signs of aging, and, as I have said, has received the imprimatur of the highest court in the land.

When jurors are deliberating, the media report that they are deciding "the guilt or innocence" of the accused. So, too, in novels, theater, movies, and television. With this constant bombardment, many jurors start out believing that their principal duty is to determine "Did he do it, or did he not do it?" as opposed to "Did the prosecution meet its burden of proof or did it not?" This is not the forum to debate whether guilt or innocence should be the issue at a criminal trial. Many philosophical and societal considerations are involved. But since it is not the issue, as long as juries are told (along with the correct instruction) that it is, thousands of defendants throughout the nation will continue to be tried before juries who are misinstructed on the most fundamental issue at a criminal trial.

Instead of clearly and unequivocally disabusing jurors of their misconception, courts throughout the land repeat the incorrect notion. Along with judges, the great bulk of prosecutors use the phrase "guilt or innocence." Chris Darden did so in this case. And defense lawyers everywhere, like Cochran, can be heard arguing to juries that the prosecution has not proved guilt beyond a reasonable doubt, and in the next breath stating, "Now, in determining the guilt or innocence of my client, take into consideration . . ." In fact, the textbook of the Association of Trial Lawyers of America states that "the determination of guilt or innocence is the sole province of the jury, and is the essence of our system."

So here we had the highest-profile murder case in this nation's history, and remarkably, the chief lawyer for the defense didn't even have a solid grasp of the most basic and fundamental issue at a criminal trial—the doctrine of reasonable doubt. He understands it, but not well, because if he did, those words would have never come out of his mouth. His grasp of reasonable doubt, like that of so many lawyers, exists in what Dutch Protestant theologian Willem Visser't Hooft has described, in a different context, as "a twilight between knowing and not knowing."

In opening statement, a lawyer can only tell the jury what he expects the evidence will show. He cannot argue, i.e., draw inferences from that evidence. Yet Cochran improperly argued throughout his opening statement. His arguing was so constant, and such a flagrant violation of the rules, and he referred to so many matters that he knew he couldn't possibly introduce at the trial, that co-prosecutor William Hodgman was forced to object several times. The unfailingly civil and gentlemanly Hodgman told Ito at the bench that "the prosecution has been severely prejudiced. This conduct [by Cochran] is outrageous and unbelievable." In fact, Hodgman was so upset he was hospitalized with chest pains at the end of the day, and never returned as a trial prosecutor in the case, although continuing to work full-time behind the scenes as a member of the prosecution team.

And Marcia Clark told Ito that Cochran, in his opening statement, had "carefully and cynically weighed the risks and benefits of his misconduct. It is outrageous. It's disgusting, and it's appalling to me as an officer of this court." She said Cochran's conduct was "egregious and a willful desire to flout the law." The prosecutors actually asked Ito for a thirty-day delay in the trial because of Cochran's improper opening statement in referring to the many witnesses whose identity and statements the defense had not provided them. Ito did not grant the request, but, because Cochran's conduct was so improper, Ito did allow Clark the highly unusual right to reopen her opening statement for five minutes to respond to Cochran's remarks.

With respect to Cochran's cross-examination at the trial, it was the most rudimentary type imaginable. He could hardly have been more mediocre. Watching him I asked myself how it was possible he could have been a trial lawyer for thirty-two years and not have picked up even the slightest degree of skill at cross-examination. Not only did he appear virtually weaponless as a cross-examiner, but he magnified his lack of expertise by obviously minimal preparation and fumbling, inarticulate questions. He basically limited himself to seeking to elicit from the prosecution witnesses he cross-examined information he had learned was helpful to his side, i.e., cross-examination in an important but very unsophisticated form.

Before getting into Johnnie Cochran's direct examination, let me digress for a moment to discuss briefly two adjectives that the media used to describe Cochran at this trial, silver-tongued and smooth. There is nothing silver-tongued about Johnnie Cochran, even remotely so. These are just featherbrains in the media who have no respect for the English language, and have been thoughtlessly using this flattering adjective to describe criminal defense attorneys since time immemorial. The first simple metaphor (they don't really even require this) or colorful word a criminal defense attorney uses qualifies him for this appellation in their minds. They could listen to C-Span and hear much more colorful and powerful oratory and wouldn't think of using the word "silver-tongued" to describe it. That's mostly reserved for criminal defense attorneys. I understand.

The other adjective to describe Cochran is "smooth." Reporters who use this word use it in a complimentary way. What they don't realize is that in the context of a trial lawyer before a jury, the word "smooth" is pejorative. I say that because "smooth," though not an exact antonym, suggests the opposite of honest, sincere, the very qualities a trial lawyer seeks to convey to a jury in his quest to garner their trust, his quest for credibility. "Smooth" might be a complimentary term for a riverboat gambler, or even a Bourbon Street hawker, but not for a trial lawyer. I don't know how the black jurors in front of whom Cochran performed in the Simpson case viewed him, but to me (and this is subjective and I could obviously be wrong), he came across more like a hired gun than a sincere and dedicated advocate. In fact, of all the lawyers for the defense, he came across as the least sincere to me.

As far as Cochran's direct examination of his own witnesses, Cochran descended below mediocrity into outright incompetence when he actually called several witnesses to the stand whose testimony was more favorable to the prosecution than to the defense.

For example, it was Cochran, not the prosecutors, who put on the only witness (Robert Heidstra) who testified to seeing a *white* utility vehicle, which he said could have been a *Ford Bronco*, rapidly leaving the crime scene area. Cochran did get in return the witness's testimony that he heard

Nicole's Akita dog barking twenty minutes later than a host of prosecution witnesses did, but he admitted he wasn't sure of the time.

Also, Simpson did an exercise video for Playboy Enterprises Inc. just one month before the murders. It was introduced by the prosecution during cross-examination of a defense witness. Since it was *already* clear to the jury from the video that Simpson's mobility was not 100 percent, Cochran (who was trying to show that Simpson was too infirm to have committed the murders) had very little to gain by calling Richard Walsh, the fitness instructor for the video, to testify to this lack of complete mobility and the fact that Simpson was given a chair and ice packs during the breaks. But on cross-examination by the prosecution, Walsh said the shooting for the video went on for close to fifteen hours, being completed in one day, and Simpson showed remarkable stamina and determination, being able to exert himself vigorously for minutes at a time without letup. He also testified that Simpson was a lot more physically fit than he thought he'd be. As if that weren't bad enough, he added that while Simpson was shadow-boxing on the tape, he twice made unscripted remarks which many feel implied that he hit his wife. "You just gotta get your space," Simpson said once, "if you're working out with the wife, if you know what I mean. You could always blame it on working out."

The question is, how could any lawyer, even an inexperienced one, call such a witness to the stand? And yet Cochran did exactly that.

Wherever one looked with Cochran, one found an obvious lack of preparation, and preparation is the single most important ingredient of a successful trial lawyer. A key piece of evidence the defense claimed was planted by the LAPD to frame Simpson was the bloody socks which were found at the foot of Simpson's bed by the police on June 13, 1994, the day after the murders. Since the socks, with Nicole's and Simpson's blood on them, were black, the LAPD criminalists at first did not see the blood. LAPD criminalist Dennis Fung had testified that he picked the socks up around 4:30 p.m. on June 13. But LAPD photgrapher Willie Ford testified later for the defense that when he videotaped the defendant's bedroom at 4:12 p.m. (routinely done to protect the city from claims the police stole or damaged anything inside a searched home), he did not see the socks, the defense therefore suggesting that the police must have planted the socks at some time thereafter.

Although Ford acknowledged on cross-examination that Fung instructed him to video the room *after* Fung had completed his search and picked up items of evidence (and hence, either Ford or Fung had been innocently wrong on the time), the defense still trumpeted Ford as one of its star witnesses for the police conspiracy, frame-up argument, contending that since the socks weren't there at 4:12 p.m., they had to have been planted there later by the LAPD.

So what does Cochran do? He subpoenas LAPD detective Adelberto Luper to testify to the search for evidence at Simpson's home, and on direct examination by Cochran of his own witness, mind you, Luper testified that he saw the socks there earlier in the day, at 12:30 p.m., confirming that the socks were there all the time, not planted there after Ford's video. When I called Luper on December 26, 1995, to ask him if Cochran had even bothered to interview him, he said he had not. "He just came up to me in the hallway a few minutes before calling me to the stand and told me the three areas he was going to be asking me questions about."

Cochran's not bothering to interview most, maybe all, of the prosecution witnesses was bad enough. But not even interviewing his *own* witnesses? I'm confident that if I checked more I'd find that Detective Luper wasn't the only one. Even in simple drunk-driving or petty-theft cases, in fact in all cases, in preparing for trial you have to interview your witnesses by going over their projected testimony with them, because you obviously have to know what their testimony is going to be, and what they're capable of testifying to. Here, the lead defense attorney for the "Dream Team" in the "Trial of the Century" is calling his witnesses cold to the stand.

Although both sides in the Simpson case received the witness lists of the opposing side, and therefore the prosecutors knew Luper was scheduled to be a defense witness, he said no one from the DA's office had interviewed him either. So here you have a moderately important witness in the "Trial of the Century," and neither side had the vaguest idea what he was going to say. Luper told me he hadn't even prepared a police report, which would have at least given the lawyers something to go on.

Briefly touching on the two other main lawyers (other than the two New York DNA lawyers) for the defense, Shapiro and Bailey, I have to say I was pleasantly surprised by Shapiro. He was better than I expected him to be. He certainly is no legal heavyweight by any stretch of the imagination, but he demonstrated that he knows his way around the courtroom, and he has good courtroom presence. Although he handled only a few witnesses on cross-examination, with those he did, he knew what he wanted to elicit from them, asked intelligent questions, and sat down.

But on witnesses *he* called to the stand, he was, if possible, even worse than Cochran. Shapiro called Dr. Robert Huizenga to the stand to establish that Simpson's arthritic condition would have prevented him from committing these murders. Huizenga, at one time the team physician for the Los Angeles Raiders, examined Simpson, at Shapiro's request, two days after the murders. He testified that his examination revealed that Simpson had severe arthritis, and that although Simpson "*looked* like Tarzan," in reality he was "like Tarzan's grandfather." But apparently Tarzan's grandfather was in pretty good shape. The exercise video, shown to Huizenga on cross-examination, reflected that. And the witness Shapiro called to the stand for the express purpose of testifying to Simpson's infirmities and physical inability to have committed the murders testified to just the opposite. On cross-examination by the prosecution, he conceded that Simpson definitely was physically capable of committing the murders of Ron and Nicole!

But even worse, because the LAPD detectives negligently failed to closely examine and photograph every injury to Simpson's hands (the LAPD had this opportunity the day after the murders, which was before Huizenga examined him), during the prosecution's case-in-chief they only told the jury that Simpson had two cuts, both to his left middle finger, the main one being a deep, fishhook-shaped cut about three-quarters of an inch long. Moreover, the police detectives had only taken a photograph of one of the two cuts, the main one. But not to worry. Shapiro, on direct examination of his *own* witness, Huizenga, brought out, for the first time in court, that Simpson had two additional cuts that law enforcement and the DA missed: a serious, jagged cut to Simpson's left ring finger, and a tiny cut to the fourth finger of Simpson's *right* hand. In addition, Shapiro, moonlighting for the prosecution, brought out that Simpson had *seven scrapes and bruises on his left hand*. And to make sure that he wasn't fired by the DA's office his first day on the job, Shapiro introduced excellent photos of all four cuts and seven abrasions. I realize that for laypeople reading this, it has to be shocking. But for years I have been referring to criminal defense attorneys, even many high-priced ones in major, nationally publicized criminal cases, as "professional undertakers," who come into court with their well-oiled and polished spades and literally bury their clients. I am not being facetious when I tell you that in many cases their clients would have been better off if they had just sat there at the counsel table and never opened their mouths. The chronicling of legal disasters and misadventures far worse than Shapiro's handling of Huizenga can be found in the many books written about criminal cases.

F. Lee Bailey, of course, has for years, along with San Francisco lawyer Melvin Belli, been the most famous of America's trial lawyers, and he and Edward Bennet Williams (now deceased) were considered by many to be the preeminent criminal defense attorneys in the land. Since his loss in the Hearst case, however, he hasn't maintained the stature he once enjoyed, and the cowboy lawyer from Wyoming, Gerry Spence, is now considered the premier criminal defense attorney in the country. Incidentally, I don't use the word "cowboy" in denigration. Spence *thinks* he's a cowboy, coming into court with his Stetson hat and cowboy boots.

Bailey is highly intelligent and has enormous trial experience. He has also distinguished himself in several murder cases throughout the years. His forte, for certain, is cross-examination. As the saying goes, in a world of blind men, a one-eyed man is a king. And since the great bulk of trial lawyers have no instinct for cross-examination and have developed no skills in that area, Bailey is among the top cross-examiners among trial lawyers in the nation. My personal view is that if he didn't shy away, as almost all experienced lawyers do, from the "why" question, he'd score more on cross. But I'm sure Bailey would have suggestions on how to improve my cross, also. The other problem I have with his cross is that he is often relentlessly sarcastic in tone and demeanor. I have no problem with being tough on cross-examination, but I feel it should be selective, intermittent—for instance, when you catch a witness in a lie or a discrepancy. But if you are continuously sarcastic, without letup, as Bailey is with too many witnesses, always implying by his tone of voice that the witness is lying or concealing information, I think it wears thin after a while with the jury.

If there is one thing that has hindered Lee's courtroom performance throughout the years, it's the very same weakness that the overwhelming majority of trial lawyers are guilty of — inadequate preparation. For one thing, by his own admission he hardly ever takes a note. But I've always subscribed to an old Chinese proverb that the palest ink is better than the best memory. I watched about a half hour of Bailey's cross-examination of Sergeant David Rossi, the LAPD officer who was in charge of securing the murder scene, and in that short time it was obvious to me that he hadn't interviewed Rossi (for which there is no excuse), he kept referring to the California Health and Safety Code as the California Penal Code, and, most embarrassing of all, he tried to establish that Rossi had violated police procedure by not calling for the coroner. When Rossi said that it wasn't his job, that he was the watch commander, not the investigating officer, Bailey marched up to the witness stand with an LAPD manual which was supposed to prove it was Rossi's job. But instead, the manual confirmed it wasn't. It was the job of the investigating officer. Hadn't Bailey even bothered to read that part of the manual?

A good example of the inaccuracy of the puffed-up reputation of lawyers is Bailey's cross-examination of Fuhrman. As I've indicated, Bailey is often referred to as one of the very best cross-examiners in the legal profession, which consists of 840,000 lawyers in the United States. Fuhrman, on the other hand, was depicted by the defense as a terrible liar. Since the main purpose of cross-examination is to expose untruthfulness and destroy credibility, it appeared to be a match made in heaven. In fact, Bailey was dry-washing his hands waiting to cross-examine Fuhrman, and unwisely created high expectations for himself by predicting to the media that he would destroy Fuhrman. But it was the consensus of virtually everyone that he never laid a glove on Fuhrman, if you'll pardon the expression. (And, as I pointed out earlier, Bailey didn't even do the most fundamental and important thing to prepare for effective cross-examination—interview the witness, in this case, Fuhrman.) If the supposedly best cross-examiner in town couldn't touch a terrible liar, what does that tell you about the nonsense that never ceases to come from the media? Yet, we can count on those who cover criminal trials and write about lawyers to continue to write in the future about witnesses who are expected to face "withering" cross-examination from some lawyer who has no ability at all to cross-examine. Why is the cross-examination described as "rigorous" or "withering"? Because cross-examination is *supposed* to be rigorous and withering.

In all fairness to Bailey, one of the main reasons he was unable to hurt Fuhrman is that Fuhrman was not, in fact, a liar. Other than his denial of using a racial slur, he was telling the truth. But a superb cross-examiner can usually make even a truthful person appear to be lying.

In Bailey's cross-examination of Fuhrman, Bailey did lay the foundation for impeaching Fuhrman's credibility by asking him if he had used the word "nigger" in the past ten years. At the time of his cross-examination, the Fuhrman tapes hadn't yet surfaced, but the defense already had statements from two witnesses (each furnished to the prosecution by way of discovery) who were prepared to testify that Fuhrman had in fact used the word "nigger" in the past ten years. Armed with this information, a two-year-old would ask Fuhrman, as Bailey did, if he had ever used the word, so that his expected denial could be impeached when the defense presented its case. Yet when the Fuhrman tapes later surfaced (tapes whose existence Bailey could not have imagined existed at the time of his cross-examination of Fuhrman), furnishing incontrovertible evidence of Fuhrman's lie, suddenly, Bailey's earlier cross-examination of Fuhrman became superb. Legal analysts and experts covering the trial gushed that Bailey's earlier, simple cross-examination on Fuhrman's use of the word "nigger" was "brilliant" and "was the cap" to a great career in the law.

As with Cochran, I'm very disappointed in Bailey, whom I have known, though not well, for years. I felt embarrassed *for* him, and outraged *at* him for eagerly embracing and becoming an outspoken propagator of the police frame-up theory, which he took to new and absurd heights. I actually heard him say on television during the trial that if the LAPD and DA's office found the true killer of Ron and Nicole, they wouldn't even tell the defense and would continue to prosecute Simpson. That remark was worse than inexcusable; it was beneath contempt.

Throughout all the demonstrated mediocrity and often incompetence of the main lawyers for the defense, they were still invariably referred to as the Dream Team by the media. Not only didn't their prior records and backgrounds as criminal defense attorneys (which were sorry at best except for Bailey's) prevent the media from saying they were the best that money could buy, but their mediocre performance at the trial didn't affect the media's view of them one iota. But if one's prior record and one's current performance aren't the basis for evaluating someone, what is? What they *might* do in the future? None of this mattered to the media. Being a criminal defense attorney on a big publicity case was enough for them. They knew a Dream Team when they saw one.

"God, where are you?"

When tragedies like the murders of Nicole and Ron occur, they get one to thinking about the notion of God. Nicole was only thirty-five, Ron just twenty-five, both outgoing, friendly, well-liked young people who had a zest for life. Their lives were brutally extinguished by a cold-blooded murderer. How does God, if there is a God, permit such a horrendous and terrible act to occur, along with the countless other unspeakable atrocities committed by man against his fellow man throughout history? And how could God—all-good and all-just, according to Christian theology— permit the person who murdered Ron and Nicole to go free, holding up a Bible in his hand at that? When Judge Ito's clerk, Deidre Robertson, read the jury's not-guilty verdict, Nicole's mother whispered, "God, where are you?"

I said earlier "if there is a God" because although there are good arguments for the existence of God (e.g., the cosmological one, that is, the first-cause theory; or the teleological, which takes as its starting point the observed order in the universe), in my own little mind, I, for one, can't be sure at all there's a God.

The previously mentioned *Playboy* magazine interview ended with the question of whether I believed in God. I answered: "If we were in court I'd object on the ground that the question assumes a fact not in evidence." When the interviewer then asked, "So you don't believe in God," I responded, "I'm not in a position to believe or disbelieve in him. You know, the athiests, who not only believe but know there is no God, are just as silly as those who seem to have no doubt that there is. Over the centuries, thousands of tomes and trillions of words have been written on the subject, yet neither side can come up with one single fact to support its position. But in this realm, where people's minds have been on permanent sabbatical, that fact is apparently immaterial."

"So what's your bottom line?" the interviewer asked.

"I like Clarence Darrow's observation about the existence vis-à-vis nonexistence of God: I do not pretend to know what ignorant men are sure of."

I was surprised by the number of letters I received from people expressing surprise I didn't believe in God, apparently missing the point I thought I had clearly made that I don't disbelieve in him either. I'm an agnostic, and have been since the day in my early twenties when I said to myself that if there was a heaven and if I ever went there, I wanted to take my reason with me; that there was no earthly justification to *unthinkingly* buy into the myth of a God and of heaven and hell. In other words, although I'm actually from a little town in northern Minnesota, Hibbing, I'm from Missouri on the God issue.

Not only is there a question in my mind about whether there's a God, but perhaps more important, what type of fellow is he? We certainly know he's shy, keeping his whereabouts and form, if he has one, known only to himself. I realize that there are many people who claim to have actual conversations with God, but the question I've always had for these people (which I've never asked them) is what voices are talking to them when the Lord isn't on the line?

I grew up a Catholic, attending Assumption Hall, a Catholic school with nuns of the Benedictine order as teachers, through the eighth grade. And of course it was inculcated into me that God was all-good, all-powerful, and all-knowing. The conundrum which most of us have heard, that either God can prevent evil but chooses not to, which means he is not all-good, or he wishes to prevent evil but cannot, which means he is not all-powerful, was not something I, as a believer, concerned myself with in those early years. But something similar was troubling to me.

The head of the Blessed Sacrament Church, which was associated with the school I attended, was a gray-haired eminence named Monsignor Limmer. The monsignor appeared ancient to us kids, and with his deep, baritone voice and dour expression, someone not only to look up to, but fear. Though he lived in the back of the church, we sensed that he really came from some other place, some place where ordinary humans did not go. The good monsignor would visit our classroom for ten minutes or so once every week or two, and we listened in awed silence to his wisdom about God and Christ. One day when I was in the third or fourth grade, he was explaining that God was all-good, all-powerful, and all-knowing, and I asked him why (I had a yen for the why question even back then), if God was all-good, he would put people on this earth who he knew were going to end up in hell, burning throughout eternity. The monsignor proceeded to tell me it was a good question for someone my age, but he had the answer. God gives all of us free will, the monsignor assured us, and when we come to the fork in the road where one path will lead us to heaven and one to hell, we have a choice, and God is not responsible for what choice we make. Yes, I said, but if God is also all-knowing, he knows what path we're going to take before we take it. So, I said, I still didn't understand how God would put people on this earth who he already knew were going to end up in hell. The monsignor coughed nervously, noted it was the end of the hour, and said we'd talk about it some other time, a time that never came. No one in Christianity, to my knowledge, can answer that question. And the reason is that it is anchored upon the unproved and contradictory premise of an all-good, all-knowing and all-powerful God, and a heaven and hell.

Since that early age of nine or ten, I have come to see one patent absurdity after another in the whole notion, so numerous they could be the subject of hundreds of pages.

I even have trouble with the whole concept of prayer, in which literally billions of people throughout history have begged God for mercy. But since God is supposed to be all-good and merciful, why would we have to beg him to be what he supposedly already is? Most of those who believe in God also believe in the devil. I'm going to sound laughable here, and it's nothing I'm recommending, since I don't believe in the devil, but logically speaking, shouldn't people be praying to the devil? One doesn't have to beg a good being to be good, one only has to ask a bad being to be good. No? Since the devil is the bad guy, isn't he the one we should be begging for mercy? Isn't that correct? Yet the Jesus prayer (and informal personal ones) says: "Lord Jesus Christ, have mercy on me."

We of course always hear people saying, "God answered my prayers." But I know that those who say this do not realize the import of what they are saying, because if they did, they wouldn't think very much of God, which they do. Saying that "God answered my prayers" necessarily means two things: that God has the power to answer prayers, and more important, for the 99 percent of the other humans who pray and beg for God's merciful intervention in time of desperate need, God told them to take a walk, get lost, he couldn't care less. He said no. "God answered my prayers," necessarily and inevitably means he chose to disregard the prayers of others who were begging for mercy or compassion in their lives; in fact, the vast majority of others. We have proof throughout history that if God is sitting up there deciding who gets mercy, he rejects the plea 99 percent of the time. Don't you think people pray to be spared when they have terminal cancer? Or AIDS? Don't you think the Jews at Auschwitz prayed to God to be spared? Maybe we have been praying to the wrong entity all along. People who believe in prayers could hardly do worse praying to the devil.

About the devil, in Christianity he is a fallen angel (Lucifer), and hence a creation of God, since God, we are told, created Lucifer and all things. Why does it seem that the devil is more powerful than God? Since there seems to be more evil, immorality, and greed in the world than good, how can God be losing the battle to Satan, someone he created?

I've heard that at Nicole's funeral, one of the speakers told Nicole's grieving survivors and friends that we can't "question God's will." *So it was God's will* that Simpson slaughtered Nicole? Really? When a Puerto Rican mother of three young children in New York City whom she supported all by herself, holding down three jobs to do so, was murdered out on the street by an addict to get a few dollars for a fix, leaving the three youngsters without any parent, the pastor at her funeral said, "It was God's will." When an eighteen-year-old black youth from San Diego who was an honor student, student body president, and champion wrestler, who dreamed of becoming a doctor, who "did all the right things and said no to all the wrong things," was gunned down in a drive-by shooting as he left a graduation party, again, a pastor said: "It was God's will." When a leukemia patient whose mother in El Salvador had finally won permission from federal authorities, after a long struggle, to visit him one last time died just hours before her plane landed, the young man's cousin said: "He tried to wait for her, but I guess it was God's will that he didn't want him to wait." When a young woman who had gone to Russia to devote her life to helping some of the most desperate people of an increasingly troubled nation, the orphaned children of Russia, was found slain in her apartment in Moscow, her mother said: "God had always taken care of her. What happened was God's will. I guess he decided he wanted her back." But why would he want her back? To keep him company? She's doing good things for young people in need, and the mother is satisfied that God had better things for her to do in heaven?

When, in fact, six million Jews were murdered during the Holocaust in perhaps the darkest chapter in human history, we again were told by many members of the cloth that it was God's will. When President

Kennedy was blasted into eternity by Lee Harvey Oswald on November 22, 1963, again, preachers everywhere said, "It was God's will." The evangelist John R. Rice wrote: "The assassin's bullet which cut down President Kennedy did the will of God."

My question, of course, is that if it was God's will that Ron and Nicole be butchered (in other words, this is what he wanted, or this is what he had no desire to prevent), why would anyone feel he is all-good or want to spend eternity with this type of being?

But, we are told, "God has his reasons" for permitting these atrocities. As the Reverend Rice wrote: "It was a matter of his choice. He had reasons for permitting the assassination of President Kennedy." And, of course, the unquestioned assumption is that whatever the reasons, they are good ones, reasons that justify what he did or permitted to happen. So even though he wanted these horrors to occur, he is still all-good. No matter what happens (murder, famine, genocide, deadly plagues, etc.), don't question God. He has his reasons and they're all good.

On April 19, 1995, a bomb exploded inside the Federal Building in Oklahoma City, and 168 people, including fifteen children, were killed. The consensus in highly religious Oklahoma City was that there had to be a reason God chose one of the most religious areas in the nation (where nearly 75 percent of the population are regular churchgoers) for the blast. The answer was that God had put the city to the test, and it passed. "It's like it had to happen in Oklahoma, in the Bible Belt, where people are neighbors and we do give," a parishioner said. But though the tragedy was "God's will," said a minister, God still got credit. "It was one of God's miracles that so many people survived," he said.

But my question is: If a good and powerful God doesn't prevent evil, why should we automatically assume that there is a good reason *for* the evil? Who tells us that when it comes to God, we must reject all conventional notions of logic and common sense and assume there is a valid and satisfactory reason for all the horrors and tragedies and misery in the world? It would seem that the only justification we would ever have for taking that position would be if God, appearing in the sky, told us that although what has happened doesn't make sense to us mortals, it is part of a grand scheme he has for life in the universe. Wouldn't that be the only possible sufficient cause for our belief that despite his willing or permitting the horrors of life, he is still all-good? Apart from God's apparition in the sky telling us this, what human being can possibly convince us of this absurdity?

The myth in Christianity that God is all-good, all-knowing, and all-powerful is so ingrained in our history, civilization, and culture that it may persist no matter how much our civilization progresses. Imprinted on all of our coins and all of our currency are the words "In God We Trust." But why? What has God done to earn this trust? Won't someone please tell me? I know it is said that there are always 10 percent who "don't get the word." Maybe I'm in that 10 percent. No one, but no one, even the tyrants of history, ever bad-mouths God, even though he supposedly permits all the evil in the world to exist. I mean, if people can believe it's "God's will" that a building is blown up killing 168 people, and still praise him for sparing the lives of others in the building, I have a question: What's God's secret? Who's his PR agent?

In the Simpson case, God (if there is a God) not only permitted the butchery of Ron and Nicole, but seemed to be working overtime to ensure that the killer, Simpson, would get off, that justice would be thwarted. If anyone was ever in the corner of a murderer, it was God with Simpson. He didn't just permit an atrocity to be committed. Like a perverse force at play, he seemed to be conspiring to see that Simpson walked out of court a free man, and with a smile on his face. And apparently Simpson knew. As I wrote earlier, on the night of the not-guilty verdict, Simpson, at his victory party, smiled broadly and held up a Bible in his outstretched right hand. This, from the October 4, 1995, edition of the *Los Angeles Times*: "O.J. is free and God deserves the thanks. That was the message—delivered with unbridled cheer and relief—that came pouring forth from the Simpson family Tuesday as his celebrated trial came to a climactic close. 'God is good, see?' said Tracy Baker, O.J.'s niece. 'I know that praying to God is the answer,' Simpson's mother Eunice said. 'Me and my famly want to thank God, without whom, I don't know where we'd be,' said Simpson's son, Jason."

Simpson's daughter, Arnelle, said to her brother in the courtroom when the jury returned its verdict, "We did it, Jason. God got us through." And the very first words Johnnie Cochran used in his postverdict news conference were: "I want to thank God."

When it comes to theology, I am too confused to be anything but an agnostic. But if there is a God, as there may very well be, the deist philosophy, which holds that after creating the universe, God bailed out, indifferent to that which he created, would seem to do less violence to the accepted principles of logic and common sense. At least the deist philosophy is free of inherent contradictions.

The root cause of the Simpson verdict

Perhaps the most important and all-encompassing question to be asked about the Simpson case is: What was the main reason the mostly black

Simpson jury bought the defense argument that the LAPD had conspired to frame Simpson? I'm confident I know the answer. How confident am I? Well, I'm not positive. I'm not as sure as I am that a crooked tree will leave a crooked shadow, but I'm certain enough to give ten-to-one odds, even though I'm not a gambling man. I'm even more sure that what I'm about to tell you, though it takes no intelligence at all to reach the conclusion I have, has not yet been mentioned by anyone commentating on the case, despite the fact that millions upon millions of words have been written and uttered about the Simpson case since the verdict. There's one other person who I think knows, and that's Johnnie Cochran, although it's just possible that he himself was not aware of the misleading nature of what he was arguing. I'm confident he did know, however, and that it was his duplicity on this point, which went over the heads of the prosecutors without their even feeling the breeze, that contributed mightily to the verdict in this case.

In a few, shorthand words (which I will elaborate on), Cochran argued a police frame-up to the black jurors from their experience of police brutality, two completely different types of police misconduct, and the prosecution failed to point out and illuminate for the jury this extremely important and critical distinction, one that was instantly obvious to me. Though the jury never thought about the distinction (I'll show you later that even the black prosecutor, Darden, did not), the latter type of police misconduct, police brutality, is common, and the former, police frame- . ups, exceedingly rare.

Virtually every black person living in the ghetto, and perhaps even most of those living outside the ghetto, has either had a bad, dehumanizing experience with a white police officer at some time in his or her life or is aware of some member of his or her family or a relative who has. It's been a part of the black experience in this country for centuries. In the article I wrote on police brutality a few years ago, I said, "In the minority communities, I sense a fire in the systems of the masses, a fire that can only be extinguished by justice." What I was talking about, of course, was the small but virulent strain of Los Angeles police who not only manhandle and mistreat members of the minority communities (Mexican-American as well as black), but in many instances go far beyond that. There is absolutely no doubt in my mind that many minority citizens of Los Angeles and other large cities have been murdered by this element.

How do I know they have been murdered? Number one, there have been a significant number of cases in Los Angeles and elsewhere where the victim was not only unarmed but shot several times in the back. And if that wasn't enough, in several of those cases there were independent witnesses to confirm that the shooting was unjustified. The further proof is that when the DA is almost criminally derelict and refuses to prosecute (see later discussion), the survivors of the murdered victims hire lawyers like Johnnie Cochran to sue the LAPD (or other police agencies) for wrongful death. And far more often than not, they win, receiving large awards from juries.

Suits brought against the police for excessive force resulting in injuries short of death are even more common, of course, and it seems as if every few weeks or so here in L.A. the newspapers are reporting a jury verdict or a large settlement for the plaintiff against the police. As I am writing this book, the January 6, 1996, edition of the *Los Angeles Times* reported that Los Angeles County had agreed to pay eighty black and Mexican-American plaintiffs $7.5 million to settle three lawsuits involving forty incidents in which members of the Los Angeles County Sheriff's Department were accused of "systematic acts of shooting, killing, brutality, terrorism, house-trashing and other acts of lawlessness and wanton abuse."

At the time of my writing the article in 1992, I learned that from 1986 through 1990, the city of Los Angeles paid in excess of $20 million in judgments, settlements, and jury verdicts in more than three hundred lawsuits against LAPD officers alleging excessive use of force. And in 1991 alone, $14.7 million was paid. These figures don't even include settlements and verdicts against the Los Angeles Sheriff's Department ($15.5 million between January 1989 and May 1992) and the many other local police agencies in the county.

Although the standard of proof in a civil case is lower than in a criminal case (beyond a reasonable doubt), the plaintiff's lawyer in a civil suit still must prove that the victim's charges *are true* by a "preponderance of the evidence," which in itself is a substantial burden. Civil lawyers in these cases routinely prove to juries that an officer caused unjustifiable injury or death (frequently with clear evidence of malicious intent, which qualifies for criminal responsibility). As indicated, many times, the evidence of guilt is so obvious that the city or county settles out of court, as in a relatively recent $1 million settlement described by one Long Beach police officer as a "sheriff's execution." Does anyone think the city or county would voluntarily pay amounts like this if it thought the officer or officers were innocent?

A month after the March 3, 1991, beating of Rodney King, Los Angeles mayor Tom Bradley appointed a seven-member commission (later augmented by three members appointed by LAPD chief Daryl Gates) to conduct a comprehensive review of the excessive-force problem in the LAPD. The so-called Christopher Commission found "a significant number of LAPD officers who repetitively used excessive force" against the public, mostly members of the minority communities.

The commission reviewed eighty-three civil lawsuits against the police and concluded that "a majority of cases involved clear and often egregious officer misconduct resulting in serious injury or death to the victim. The LAPD's investigation of these eighty-three cases was deficient in many respects, and discipline against the officers involved was frequently light and often nonexistent."

In a survey conducted by the commission of 650 LAPD officers, 24.5 percent agreed that "racial bias on the part of officers toward minority citizens currently exists." And 27.6 percent agreed that prejudice sometimes leads to the use of excessive force.

Among the Christopher Commission's more shocking findings were computer messages sent between patrol cars over the LAPD's mobile digital terminals. Although they were obviously far from the norm, there were such transmissions as the following: "I would love to drive down Slausen [a street that runs through South-Central Los Angeles, a heavily black area] with a flamethrower. We would have a barbecue." "I almost got me a Mexican last night but he dropped the damn gun too quick." "Capture him, beat him, and treat him like dirt." "If I find it, it will be [officer-involved shooting] time. God, I wanna kill something oh so bad." "Wanna go over to Delano later and hand out some street justice." "It was fun, but no chance to bust heads." Only after a few of these messages were made public by the commission did the LAPD start auditing the system. The LAPD then found, per the commission, "260 patently offensive comments over a one-month period."

The black community knows that in these many cases of police brutality, the offending officer rarely, if ever, tells the truth; he lies, not just out of court, but on the witness stand. And in a very small number of these cases, particularly where they have unlawfully taken the life of a victim, they have planted a deadly weapon, such as a knife or gun, at the victim's side.

"African-American jurors who live in communities where cops are the enemy don't have to be educated that police lie," says Peter Kirscheimer, a onetime Bronx Legal Aid attorney who is now a federal defender in Brooklyn, in an October 4, 1995, *Wall Street Journal* article.

Because of police brutality, and the police lies to cover it up, members of the black community naturally are distrustful of law enforcement. But when the officers lie and plant evidence in these cases, *it's to protect themselves* when they have violated the law, i.e., it's self-defensive in nature.

This is the police misconduct that the black community has experienced throughout the years. Police framing blacks, on the other hand, for robberies, rapes, burglaries, murders, etc., is almost unheard of. In no way has it been a part of the black experience. If it happens at all, *almost invariably* it's in the area of drug cases—for example, when the police know someone is complicit but he wasn't in close proximity to the drugs found in the house, and they say he was. This is a very simple and easy frame-up to pull off, and the framing officers justify it in their minds because they feel the person is guilty anyway. Percentage-wise, this type of behavior is very, very uncommon, but it does happen.

What is more common is police perjury to justify probable cause to conduct a search of a person or vehicle—again, usually for drugs. Like Customs and INS agents at our nation's borders who become adept at spotting someone who is "dirty" among the vast majority of cars they almost routinely wave through, experienced narcotic officers sense when someone is in possession of illicit drugs. However, they know that what they see often is not enough to justify a search under the Fourth Amendment to the United States Constitution, so from time to time they fabricate a "furtive" move on the part of a suspect, such as throwing something out the window or reaching underneath the seat of the car, to justify the search, which turns up drugs, of course. The great majority of officers do not do this. However, prosecutors know that a certain percentage of drug cases they prosecute are most likely predicated on fabricated probable cause. But there's virtually no way for the prosecutors to know whether the drug case they're handling is one of them.

It should be added that even in the Deep South in the twenties and thirties, where many innocent blacks were prosecuted and convicted by white juries of serious crimes, according to the books on the subject it was never as a result of an elaborate and complex conspiracy, as would have had to occur even to attempt to frame Simpson for these murders. The convictions were usually in situations where the actual evidence against the black defendant was extremely weak, but aided by lies told on the witness stand by the local sheriff, it was enough for the white jury to convict.

When the Christopher Commission was formed in 1991 to investigate the LAPD, it was solely to investigate police brutality and excessive force, not police frame-ups. Why? Because police frame-ups, as I've indicated, are almost unheard of. When the black community erupted in violence after the not-guilty verdicts in the first Rodney King trial, Vernon Leggins, a black resident of South-Central Los Angeles, where the riots occurred, said at the height of the riots: "I knew this would happen. A lot of anger has been building up during the years. The way we have been beaten and talked to, this should have happened long ago." He didn't say "The way we have been beaten, talked to, *and framed*." He wouldn't say this because it is not part of the black experience.

If any of you readers don't believe me, call Johnnie Cochran's office in Los Angeles. For over thirty years in Los Angeles, Cochran has been representing black plaintiffs in lawsuits against the LAPD, the L.A. Sheriff's Department, and other law enforcement agencies. Ask him or his secretary if he can furnish you with the name of just one case in those thirty years where the basis of his lawsuit was not excessive force or some other type of police misconduct, but that his client had been framed by the police on a burglary, robbery, rape, arson, murder, or any other felony.

Without thinking, blacks everywhere were confusing what the defense was alleging in the Simpson case with their own experience of police brutality. "The only thing O.J.'s case has done is it made the majority see what we've been saying for years about *police brutality*. They've wanted to put their heads in the sand and ignore it," said Frank Holoman, the black owner of the Boulevard Café in South-Central Los Angeles. And before and after the verdict in the Simpson case, one heard blacks saying it was "payback time." But payback time *for what*? Being framed? That's absurd. If this had been a prosecution of a young black man for the killing of a white police officer, one would know what they meant by payback time. But that's not what this case was.

"What happened to O.J. has been going on for years in our country to black people," Bonnie Beasley, a fifty-five-year-old black woman in San Francisco told a reporter for the *New York Times*. But *what* has been going on for years? Police brutality, but certainly not frame-ups. Yet, throughout the land, to support their belief that Simpson was framed, blacks could be heard saying things like "If they [the police] did it to me, they probably did it to O.J." They wouldn't say "If the police framed me," just "If the police did *it* to me." "We always reach out to another black person we perceive as being mistreated by [white police officers] because it has happened to so many of us," says Darlene Powell Hopson, a black clinical psychologist. But what is *it* that has happened to so many blacks? These blacks and the black Simpson jurors *didn't bother to stop and think or realize* that the police misconduct being alleged by the defense in the Simpson case, planting evidence and a frame-up, is not what they and their families have been experiencing throughout the years. It was all "police misconduct" in their minds, and the prosecutors never distinguished for them these two very different types of police misbehavior.

How could the prosecutors? As I indicated earlier, the issue completely escaped them, even Darden, who of course is black himself. Not only didn't Darden see the issue, and therefore was incapable of knocking it down, he made it worse by telling the jury in so many words that what the black community had experienced in the past was no different from what the defense was alleging in this case. Remarkably, he told the jury in his summation: "If you mistrust the police, I understand why you mistrust the police. Perhaps you ought to, but I think we have to take every case on a case-to-case basis" — i.e., just because the police have been framing blacks throughout the years doesn't mean they framed Simpson in this case. Unbelievable.

And in an October 28, 1995, speech at the University of Miami Law School he said the reason for the not-guilty verdict was "the black community's *bad experiences* with the LAPD." But Chris, what have these bad experiences been? If you think it's been the LAPD framing black people, you're dead wrong. But of course you don't think that. The problem, Chris, is that you just weren't thinking, period, when you said what you did in Miami, and more important, when you let Cochran get by with his exquisite deception at the trial. If the obviously intelligent black prosecutor (and the equally intelligent Marcia Clark) didn't see this deception at the trial, how could anyone expect the Simpson jurors to have?

The prosecutors in the Simpson case, during their rebuttal, should have pointed out the obvious distinction between the two types of police misconduct and simply told the jurors to look back into their own lives and experiences to see if they or anyone else close to them had ever been framed by the police for a serious crime like rape or murder. It would have been a moment of inevitable enlightenment for the jury. So often in life things are only obvious once they are pointed out.

Just to test my instincts on what happened in this case, I have purposefully engaged several blacks in a conversation about the Simpson case. Whenever they have said that they agreed with the verdict because of all of the trouble they or those close to them have had with the police, or that they didn't trust the police, or what have you, I have asked them, "*What* trouble?" and "*Why* don't you trust the police?" The word "frame-up" not once has come from their mouths. What they invariably refer to is police brutality, excessive force, being pushed around, cursed at, and spoken down to. When I then remind them that what the police were supposed to have done in the Simpson case was to frame Simpson, there's always an uneasy silence. One black man I spoke to at the public tennis courts where I play has a master's degree in communication from Howard University, perhaps the leading black university in the country. This particular black *does* believe Simpson is guilty, but when I asked him why he believed the predominantly black jury had bought the defense argument that the LAPD had framed Simpson, his exact words were: "Sure, they know the police do this type of thing. Look at the beating they gave Rodney King." When I reminded him that the defense didn't claim the LAPD beat Simpson, they claimed the LAPD had framed him, and he wasn't drawing any distinction between the two types of police misconduct, there was a thoughtful silence.

Time magazine, in its December 25, 1995, edition, likewise failed to make the distinction. It said: "Jurors did not require too much coaching from Cochran to believe that Simpson may have been a victim of the Los Angeles Police Department; all they had to do was replay in their minds the videotape of the savage beating administered four years earlier to an unemployed black construction worker named Rodney King."

In other words, according to *Time*, beating Rodney King and framing O. J. Simpson were no different. Again, if *Time* and *Darden* didn't see the difference, how could the Simpson jurors, who needed help crossing the street on a green light, see it without any help from the prosecution?

It's my view that because the Simpson jury could easily relate to police misconduct in the form of brutality, and lying to cover it up, they went on, without thinking and with no help from the prosecution, to buy the frame-up theory. As I indicated earlier, I cannot be positive that this is why they were so receptive to the police frame-up argument, but I am very confident it is the reason. One thing I *am* sure of. The framing of blacks by the police for crimes like robbery, burglary, rape, arson, and murder is not a part of the black experience in Los Angeles. There is no evidence to support that proposition. All the evidence is to the contrary. Talk to black people. *They* will tell you that being framed is not a part of their experience. So instead of the jury in the Simpson case thinking that it would be exceedingly rare, virtually unheard of, for the LAPD to have framed Simpson, their state of mind most probably was "This is the LAPD, and we all know they can't be trusted." There may be things about the LAPD that can't be trusted by some in the black community, but this definitely was not one of them. Yet the prosecution, not seeing the issue, never made this obvious point to the jury.

Had I been the prosecutor in the case I would have told the jury the following to increase whatever rapport I had already established with them:

"You black folks on the jury know about police brutality. You've lived it, either personally or through those you know. But although I haven't experienced it, I know it, too. In fact, just three years ago I wrote an article about how a certain strain of law enforcement officers here and around the country have been manhandling, brutalizing, and

in general mistreating members of your community for years and getting by with it. And I publicly took a position calling for the prosecution and conviction of these officers to put an end to it."

After then pointing out that being framed by the police is not a part of the black experience, the prosecutors should have made this type of remark (in abbreviated form) to the jury in the Simpson case:

"Let me give you ladies and gentlemen of the jury virtual proof that the police frame-up theory in this case is pure, unadulterated nonsense, the type that should be very insulting to your intelligence. The defense in this case, at one time or another, has suggested to you folks that just about everyone involved in the investigation of this case was a part of the conspiracy to frame Mr. Simpson. Not just the four detectives, but many of their colleagues, from officers Riske and Spangler to Commander Bushey, even the two police criminalists, Dennis Fung and his young rookie assistant, Andrea Mazzola, who told you that prior to this case she had never even heard of O. J. Simpson. Even, in fact, Thano Peratis, the male nurse who withdrew Simpson's blood and is now at home recovering from major bypass surgery. Remember, they suggested that he changed his testimony to account for the supposedly missing 1.5 cc of Mr. Simpson's blood. I mean, everyone was involved. I can just picture Phil Vannatter on the phone calling some of his colleagues on the force on the night of the murders: 'Hey, Sam, we got a great conspiracy going on down here. We're framing that black dude, O. J. Simpson.' 'For Christ's sake, Phil, do you know what time it is? It's three in the morning!' 'I know, I know. But how many times do you get an opportunity to nail someone like Simpson?' 'Yeah, I guess you're right, ol' buddy. Let me take a quick shower and I'll be right down.' 'Well, you better get your rear end down here right quick. We're not going to wait all night.' 'Okay, Phil, okay.'

"You know, it reminds me of the film *JFK* a few years back about the assassination of President John F. Kennedy. I don't know if any of you saw it, but at one time or another in the film, the director, Oliver Stone, unbelievably had the CIA, FBI, KGB, organized crime, Secret Service, Vice-President Lyndon Johnson, Dallas Police Department, Castro, anti-Castro Cuban Exiles, and the military-industrial complex all involved in the conspiracy. Where did all these people get together to hatch their elaborate conspiracy? Madison Square Garden? And was Lee Harvey Oswald's wife, Marina, the hostess when they broke bread? I walked out of that ridiculous movie thinking that I was one of the few people not involved in the conspiracy. Apparently no one wanted poor President Kennedy to live. Even bitter enemies like the CIA and KGB got together on this plot.

"Anyway, getting back to this case, although everyone and his grand-mother was apparently out to frame Mr. Simpson, according to the defense, the main conspirator, the head guy, the maharajah of this dirty, rotten plot to frame this defendant, was Mark Fuhrman, the supreme racist, the devil incarnate. You'll recall that Kathleen Bell testified that when she met Fuhrman sometime between 1985 and 1986 at a Marine recruiting office he told her that when he sees a black man with a white woman driving in a car he pulls them over, and when she asked him, 'Well, what if they didn't do anything wrong?' he told her that 'he'd find something.' And so Mr. Cochran argued to you: 'This man will lie to set you up. That is what he is saying there. He would do anything to set you up because of the hatred he has in his heart.'

"Number one, Ms. Bell did not say in the letter she wrote to Mr. Cochran about the incident, nor did she testify at this trial, that Fuhrman said he'd frame the black man and his woman friend, did she? Only that he'd come up with some reason, valid or invalid, to pull them over. But since Mr. Cochran is alleging that Fuhrman and his colleagues framed Mr. Simpson for these murders because of their racism, let's stop to think about this terrible, vile charge for a moment. Mark Fuhrman has been a Los Angeles police officer for close to twenty years. During that time he has undoubtedly arrested hundreds upon hundreds of black people. In fact, for several years, he even worked South-Central. Now, I think most of you will agree that if there's one thing that's even worse than excessive force by the police, it's being framed for a serious crime you didn't commit. A bloody nose, even a broken arm, can heal, but going to prison for five or ten years and being classified as a felon for the rest of your life is a lot worse, wouldn't you agree?

"Now, don't you think that if this fellow Fuhrman were the type who liked to frame black people for crimes they didn't commit, there would have been a considerable number of black people framed by him through the years? And that all or at least most of these people would have immediately gotten on the phone and called Mr. Cochran or some other member of the defense team, and you would have heard them testify from that witness stand at this trial? There certainly can-not be even one of you who doubts this. You have to absolutely know this would've happened. Particularly in a big case like this where coming forward would make them a hero to many in the black com-munity, and they'd be able to sell their stories for a lot of money. If

Fuhrman had been the framing cop the defense wants you to believe, there would have been a virtual parade of black people he had framed throughout the years taking that witness stand at this trial. *Yet not one, not even one such black person came forward.*

"After all his years on the force, the only black person the defense called to the witness stand to testify against Fuhrman was Roderick Hodge. He said Fuhrman had mistreated him and told him after his arrest, 'I told you we'd get you, nigger.' But he didn't say anything about Fuhrman framing him. Not one word. As far as testimony coming from this witness stand that any black person has ever been framed by Mark Fuhrman or, for that matter, any of the other three detectives in this case, that witness stand was silent. As quiet as a small-town cemetery on a rainy Sunday afternoon. As quiet as a church mouse. As quiet as a painting on a wall. Why? Because it never happened. No framed black people came forward because they don't exist. You folks should not only feel insulted that the defense attorneys have tried to deceive you like this, you should be angry at them. How dare they think so little of your intelligence that they try to sell you a preposterous argument like that?"

With a case that was in existence almost sixteen months before the final summations were given, couldn't at least one of the two lead prosecutors have found enough time to work up an argument at least something like this?

Yes, I told you I'm angry about this case. I'm *outraged* every time I think of what happened, every time I see Simpson smiling and playing golf at some country club, or capitalizing on the murders from some book or video he is hawking.

A modest proposal on police brutality

Inasmuch as it is my firm belief that the not-guilty verdict in the Simpson case has historical origins, conscious or otherwise, in the maltreatment, mostly physical, of blacks by white police officers throughout the years, a brief discussion on how to ameliorate the situation follows.

In our society, we try to deter criminal conduct by the threat of punishment. This system is hardly peculiar to modern society. From the ancient Egyptians and Babylonians to the present, it has been the secular way to control the dark impulses of humankind. For the police, however, there is little threat of punishment, and hence no real deterrent. Police are human beings. If police were prosecuted, most would also be deterred by the threat of punishment. But this hasn't happened. For years, the black community has been saying there is no equal justice. In the cruel poetry of their lives, the police can violate the law and get by with it, but they sure as hell can't.

This is an excerpt from the article I wrote on police brutality in 1992 following the beating of Rodney King and the ensuing riot.

With approximately twenty thousand police officers in Los Angeles County, there are around two thousand complaints registered annually against police officers in the county. But the Special Investigations Division (SID) of the Los Angeles County DA's Office prosecutes an average of just two of these cases per year, and then usually against police agencies in the county other than the LAPD or Los Angeles Sheriff's Department (LASD). In fact, to find a significant excessive-force prosecution against the LAPD prior to the King case, one has to go all the way back to the Bloody Christmas beating of seven prisoners on December 25, 1951. (Eight police officers were indicted for felonious assault and five were convicted.)

In officer-involved *shooting* cases, by agreement with the LAPD, LASD, and more than half of the eighty-seven incorporated cities in Los Angeles County, the DA's office is immediately notified. At least one deputy DA and DA investigator "roll out" to the scene of the shooting, where they conduct an independent probe to determine if a crime was committed by the officer or officers involved. Each year the Special Investigations Division rolls out on approximately 150 such cases throughout the county.

The *Los Angeles Daily News* [in an impressive series of articles by reporters David Parrish and Beth Barrett in 1990 and 1991] found 387 officer-involved shooting cases—including 153 fatalities—at the LAPD between 1985 and mid-1991. In many cases the victims or their survivors received large civil judgments from juries. In none of them, however, did the DA file criminal charges.

Over at the sheriff's department, the *Daily News* reviewed 202 officer-involved shootings between January 1, 1985, and August 27, 1990. It found fifty-six cases where people were shot under "seriously questionable circumstances"—victim unarmed, shot in the back, etc. In *none* of the 202 shootings did the DA's office file criminal charges.

The situation gets scarier. When I spoke with one present and two past SID deputy DAs as well as with other people long connected with Los Angeles law enforcement (including a former prosecutor in the DA's office with decades of experience), they could recall only one instance, in 1973, when an LAPD officer was tried for murder or even manslaughter in an on-duty shooting of a private citizen. And manslaughter can be committed where there's only criminal negligence.

In fact, for at least the last decade, though there have been hundreds of officer-involved shootings by the LAPD, no one can remember a single case in which an LAPD officer was prosecuted for even an on-duty *nonfatal* shooting of a private citizen.

If we're to believe the Los Angeles DA's Office, there has been only one case, then, in several decades where an LAPD officer has unlawfully shot someone to death. And for at least the past ten years, no officer has even committed an unlawful *act* with his gun. To believe this gives logic a bad name. Even the LAPD doesn't believe this. Between 1985 and mid-1991, Chief Daryl Gates himself found thirty-five cases in which he ruled that officers wounded or killed persons in avoidable or unnecessary circumstances.

It's estimated that during the past half century, on-duty police officers in L.A. County shot and killed well in excess of one thousand people. [This sounds bad, of course, but 99 percent of the killings were justified. The problem is that some were not.] According to the California Department of Justice's Bureau of Criminal Statistics, between 1988 and 1991 alone, there were 223 homicides by police officers in L.A. County. Yet, the indictment in 1992 of a Compton police officer for voluntary manslaughter in the killings of two Samoan brothers is believed to be the first homicide prosecution of any law-enforcement officer in the county for the on-duty killing of a private citizen since the LAPD prosecution almost two decades earlier in 1973. (An LASD deputy sheriff was prosecuted and convicted of second-degree murder in the 1982 shooting death of a pregnant woman's fetus.) The only homicide prosecution anyone can remember before 1973 was of a Los Angeles deputy sheriff in 1969.

Perhaps the most alarming statistic of all is that in the ten years between 1982 and the Compton police officer prosecution, Special Investigations rolled out to the scene of more than a thousand officer-involved shooting cases. *Yet not once* did they find criminality on the part of any officer in the entire county, not even criminal negligence.

It couldn't be clearer, then, that the Los Angeles DA's Office looks the other way at police brutality. Johnnie Cochran, a former L.A. assistant district attorney and now a plaintiff's lawyer in many successful civil suits against L.A. County police agencies, says, "There have been a number of police brutality cases throughout the years where the DA should definitely have filed charges, but he didn't." A current L.A. County Superior Court judge said a few years ago, "I have a distinct feeling that the district attorney, either intentionally or unintentionally, has a double standard when it comes to filing criminal complaints against the police."

Would prosecuting the police ultimately hurt society by forcing officers to act tentatively in situations that call for aggressive conduct? I doubt it. Although prosecutions would heighten awareness among all officers in the proper use of force, 95 percent of the police wouldn't feel handcuffed on the job because they simply don't harbor the impulse to mistreat or brutalize those whom they detain or arrest. Knowing that officers on the street are compelled to act spontaneously in highly dangerous, life-threatening situations, the DA should continue to give officers considerable latitude and discretion in their use of force, with the benefit of the doubt always going to the officer. But carte blanche authority—essentially the current situation—must cease. When the officer's conduct clearly trespasses beyond permissible margins into blatant, egregious, and unnecessary use of force, the officer has to be criminally accountable for his conduct. To hold otherwise is to hold that in the process of enforcing the law, an officer is legally entitled to violate the law himself.

During the Rodney King beating there were several civilian witnesses. Ask yourself this question: If the officers who beat King knew that there was a district attorney downtown who would prosecute them for police brutality, would they have been as likely to rain fifty-six blows with their batons to the head, torso, and legs of a defenseless person in front of independent civilian witnesses? What I'm saying is that if the district attorney and his predecessors had done their job throughout the years there is a reasonable probability that the Rodney King beating would not have taken place.

Likewise, if the district attorney had been prosecuting police brutality cases through the years, with a fair share of convictions, the likelihood of a riot following the Simi Valley verdict would have been substantially diminished. The black community would most likely have viewed the stunning verdict—as most nonblacks have—as being mostly attributable to the conservative venue in which the case was tried: nearly all-white Ventura County. Instead, they viewed it as confirmation of their indictment of the criminal justice system in America.

I spoke earlier in the book about the staggering incompetence in our society. Warren Christopher, by all accounts an honorable and conscientious public servant, headed up the 1991–92 Commission named after him to investigate excessive force and police brutality in the LAPD and come up with proposals to end it. Of the 129 recommendations made by the commission to stop excessive force, unbelievably, *not one* is a recommendation for increased prosecution by the district attorney of police brutality, the *only* recommendation which, if carried out, would substantially reduce it. In fact, there isn't *one word* in the entire 228-page report of the Christopher Commission that refers to the lack of DA prosecutions of police brutality. Nor is there one word about how the DA, whose job it is to prosecute police brutality cases, can play a part in reducing police brutality.

Instead, after months of highly publicized inquiry and investigation, the celebrated Christopher Commission concluded that the key to reducing excessive force was to implement a "major overhaul of the disciplinary system" within the LAPD. The same, identical recommendation—even to the extent of using an independent inspector general to monitor the discipline—had been urged twenty-seven years earlier by the McCone Commission, which followed the Watts Riot and on which Christopher served as vice-chairman. Not only hadn't Warren Christopher learned anything at all about the problem in twenty-seven years, but even with a staff of 130, 101 of whom were lawyers, helping him, he exhibited not the smallest grain of common sense. In Christopher's view, internal discipline by the LAPD was the best way to deal with police brutality. In other words, the police (as opposed to everyone else in our society) should be relied on to continue to police themselves. *And Warren Christopher is our present secretary of state.*

It's not as if Christopher and his commission were unaware of the law. The commission report points out that LAPD policy *and the penal code*, which the DA prosecutes under, require that force be *reasonable*. It's just that the Christopher Commission apparently believed that the DA's job is to prosecute all members of the community except the police.

If one had confronted members of the commission with their colossal incompetence and lack of insight, they would have been forced to invoke the anemic argument that they were commissioned only to investigate the LAPD, not the DA's office. However, the commission itself stated that it "ought to examine *all* aspects of the law-enforcement structure in Los Angeles that might cause or contribute to the problem of excessive force." The DA's office, of course, is an integral part of the law enforcement structure of Los Angeles, being the agency responsible for prosecuting all felonies in the county. Moreover, the Christopher Commission did make recommendations concerning an entity *outside* the LAPD: "Community councils are to be created composed of local residents and community and business leaders to work with the police . . . in matters that affect their neighborhoods," the commission said.

There are few tyrants like blind custom, and I believe that the Christopher Commission never recommended more aggressive DA action against police brutality cases simply because the absence of such prosecutions has been institutionalized in Los Angeles and around the country. And their abject incompetence prevented them from lifting their vision beyond the custom.

At present, the only thing a rogue cop really has to fear is internal discipline by his own department. But only a small percentage of police brutality allegations result in internal discipline. For instance, the Christopher Commission found that of 2,152 citizen allegations of excessive force from 1986 through 1990, only forty-two (2 percent) were sustained by LAPD's Internal Affairs Division. Former assistant chief Jesse Brewer, now deceased, estimated at the time that for every complaint, there were three or four incidents that citizens did not report. And even when Internal Affairs did sustain the complaint, the typical punishment was suspension without pay for a week or, in unusual cases, dismissal from the force. As a deterrent, none of this begins to compare with a criminal prosecution and possible incarceration in the state prison.

Was the LAPD incompetent?

The defense in the Simpson case, by its two-pronged attack—the LAPD framed Simpson, and were also butterfingered incompetents in their collection and preservation of evidence—put the LAPD on trial during the Simpson case, and the defense succeeded in convincing the jury of both of these charges. But because the jury bought the defense allegations doesn't, perforce, make them true.

Obviously, the LAPD did not frame Simpson, and as far as I can determine, they were no more incompetent or competent in this case than in the other major cases they investigate. It would be impossible to find any murder case having the amount of physical, scientific evidence that existed in this case in which there weren't some slip-ups and unexplained discrepancies here and there in the investigation of the case and the collection and preservation of the evidence. It's normal and to be expected, particularly when so many people are involved.

For instance, in the Manson case, the LAPD criminalists neglected to take blood samples from several pools of blood at the murder scene. Horn-rimmed glasses (whose owner was never identified) were seen by the first officer arriving at the murder scene near two trunks in the living room. Though the crime scene was supposed to be preserved for the criminalists, the glasses somehow ended up on top of a desk. Two pieces of a gun grip, first seen near the entryway, ended up under a chair in the living room. As stated in an LAPD report, "They were apparently kicked under the chair by one of the original officers on the scene. However, no one is copping out." An officer accidentally wiped off a bloody fingerprint on the gate of the Tate residence when he departed. The police sent out flyers all over the country and Canada looking for a gun they already had in their own Van Nuys division. A detective and his partner crossing a busy street near the courthouse dropped a vial of dog hairs I was going to introduce, losing all but one. (I did not introduce the hair, since it wasn't absolutely key evidence and presenting one hair would have looked too desperate and speculative.) And so it went.

Discrepancies in times and everything else are extremely common. Again, in the Manson case, the LAPD report on the Tate-LaBianca murders says: "At 0914 hours, West Los Angeles Units 8L5 and 8L62 were given a radio call, 'Code 2, possible homicide, 10051 Cielo Drive.'" There were one-man patrol cars in those days, and the first officer to arrive at the scene of the five Tate murders was Jerry Joe De Rosa, who wrote in his report that he arrived at 9:05 a.m., which was nine minutes *before* he received the Code 2. The second officer who arrived, William Whisenhunt, set the time of his arrival at between 9:15 and 9:25, while officer Robert Burbridge, who arrived *after* DeRosa and Whisenhunt, said he arrived at 8:40 a.m.

But you see, all of these things, when viewed in the context of the entire case, don't add up to a hill of beans.

Make no mistake about it. The DA lost this case, not the LAPD. In no way, as so many talking heads have said, did the LAPD lose the case for the DA. The DA's office lost this case all by itself.

In summary form, in my opinion the LAPD did an adequate job in this case, though it definitely could have been more competent, but the Los Angeles DA's Office could hardly have been more incompetent. And yet, because they do not know whereof they speak, many in the media have decided that the LAPD lost the case. "By acclamation: LAPD blew an open and shut case" read the caption of an October 5, 1995, *Los Angeles Daily News* article.

Even in the areas where LAPD officers or employees did not perform well, their poor performance was usually on the witness stand, not in the work they did on the case. Examples are Dennis Fung, Mark Fuhrman, and Phil Vannatter. If the prosecutors had adequately prepared Fung for cross-examination, which they failed to do, Barry Scheck wouldn't have had anything like the success he had with Fung. And the prosecutors should have known how to deal, *beforehand*, with police officer witnesses who didn't want to admit something on the witness stand: Fuhrman did not want to admit he had used the word "nigger" in the past ten years; Vannatter did not want to admit that he had said to two witnesses and within earshot of an FBI agent, that Simpson was "a" suspect in the case at the time he and three fellow detectives went to Simpson's Rockingham estate in the early-morning hours of June 13, 1994. With proper preparation by the prosecution, neither Fuhrman nor Vannatter would have had his credibility undermined with the jury.

Even Phil Vannatter's bringing the vial of Simpson's blood over to Rockingham to deliver it personally to the criminalist, Fung, though clearly ill-advised, was not what I would call "incompetent," and if Vannatter had been adequately prepared by Chris Darden, and a much fuller explanation had been given as to why Vannatter didn't immediately book the vial (see later discussion under blood evidence), it probably would have only been a blip on the radar screen, particularly if there hadn't been so many other errors by the DA in the presentation of their case.

Let me put it this way. There have been countless examples through the years where murder cases have been successfully prosecuted, yet the investigations of the cases by law enforcement were substantially more incompetent than the LAPD's performance in the Simpson case.

Unreasonable doubts

Simpson supporters may say that this book did not discuss *all* of the defense evidence, arguments, and contentions. For example, when the LAPD detectives covered Nicole's body with a blanket from inside her home, hair and fibers that *may* have been left by Simpson on the blanket when he visited Nicole at an earlier time *may* have gotten on Nicole and *may* have somehow contaminated the entire murder scene; if Simpson were wearing the blood-stained socks found at the foot of his bed, why wouldn't his ankle have prevented blood on one of the socks from soaking through from the exterior of the left side to the interior of the left side and through to the interior of the right side?; when Fuhrman found the Rockingham glove around 6 a.m. on June 13, 1994, he said it appeared to be sticky and moist. Although there is dew on California mornings, and Fung told me that even at 7 a.m., when he arrived at Rockingham, the grass was still wet from the dew, the defense argued (without a word of response from the prosecution) that if the glove had been out there all night as the LAPD claimed, as opposed to Fuhrman's removing it from a bag of his or his pocket and planting it, why hadn't it dried? and so on. But the reader knows this book is not an analysis of every single issue in the Simpson case. It is an analysis and exploration of why the case was lost by the prosecution. In the process, of course, all of the important issues were discussed, several in considerable depth. But more importantly, discussing every one of the defense points and arguments was not necessary in order to make this book's essential conclusion about Simpson's guilt correct.

Here's the reason. Since we know Simpson is guilty, any defense points or arguments which have not been dealt with in this book, regardless of what they are, by definition could not change that reality. (And any reader who, at this point in the book, isn't convinced beyond all doubt of Simpson's guilt, certainly would not become so if I addressed myself to some additional ancillary issues.) Let me give you an example of what I mean. Say that we know X committed a bank robbery in Detroit, Michigan, on October 25, 1993, at 10:00 a.m. We know this because there are ten eyewitnesses who have positively identified him; his fingerprints are found at the teller's window even though he lives in El Paso, Texas, and there is no evidence he had ever been in Detroit (much less at this bank) to have left the fingerprints on some prior occasion; and at the time of his arrest, all of the bank's marked money is found in his possession.

Now let's say that a witness comes forward and says X was actually in his presence in El Paso at 10:00 a.m. on October 25, 1993. Since we know X is guilty, we also thereby know that the witness is either honestly mistaken or is lying. Say the bank robbery was a very famous one because of a record amount stolen, and Y steps forward and actually proclaims it was he who committed the robbery (in sensational murder cases, it's not uncommon, for instance, for innocent people called "chronic confessors" to confess to a murder just to be in the limelight). Again, we know Y is either a kook trying to get into the news, or he's clinically psychotic. Why? Because we already know who committed the Detroit robbery.

Likewise with Simpson in this case. Since we know that in view of the evidence it's not even possible for him to be innocent, we know that whatever evidence the defense offered on his behalf, there's an explanation for it, even in those cases where we might not know what that explanation is. Whatever argument the defense makes, we know it is invalid. On the other hand, if we didn't *know* Simpson was guilty, then in the absence of an examination of every single defense argument, we could not feel sanguine about any conclusion of guilt.

The media circus

From the very beginning, the O. J. Simpson case received a vastly disproportionate amount of publicity. Although this was a highly sensational murder, this was so for one reason and one reason only, O. J. Simpson. When you remove him from the equation, there is simply no way that this case could be considered an unusual or exceptional murder case. Simpson killed Nicole (and Ron Goldman since he needed to eliminate a witness to his murdering Nicole) out of some passion and rage induced by jealousy, frustration, taunting, or what have you. But that couldn't possibly be more common. Every year, approximately 30 percent of all female homicide victims in America are killed by their husbands or boyfriends.

And yet from the very beginning the media treated this case as if it had everything, everything that anyone would ever want in a murder case. A typical remark from the media that was uttered ad nauseam was "This case has everything: Sex, violence, mystery, celebrity, affluent lifestyle, etc." But let's examine this statement. *Sex* did not play any part at all in this case, and if I'm not mistaken it was not even mentioned once in the trial The media must have been confusing what they read in the tabloids about Simpson's and Nicole's sex life as being a part of this case, which it wasn't. *Violence.* I have to hand it to the media there. That's a point I can't rebut. A murder case with violence. Highly unusual. *Mystery.* To anyone who thinks this case was a mystery, my only response is that it was only a mystery to them. Some members of the media were a little bit more specific, and they spoke "of all the mysteries in this case. For instance, if O.J. did it, how did he dispose of the knife and his bloody clothing?" But I always thought a murder mystery was one where you didn't know, until the end, who the murderer was. Of the thousands upon thousands of movie, television, and book murder mysteries, how many were cases where it was obvious, right from the beginning, who the murderer was, but the two-hour movie, one-hour television production, or 300-page book concerned themselves with the "mystery" of how the known killer disposed of the murder weapon and other indicia of guilt? *Celebrity.* That's all this case had. O. J. Simpson. *Affluent lifestyle.* Number one, Simpson and Nicole's lifestyle wasn't that affluent, and more importantly, their easy lifestyle did not come into play as a factor in this case, nor was there even testimony about it.

Actually, this case was lacking in two ingredients that have traditionally been necessary to attract the interest of people: a love triangle, or, at least, a suggestion of a mistress or lover (e.g. the Sam Sheppard murder case in Cleveland, the Claus von Bülow case in Newport, Rhode Island, the Dr. Bernard Finch case in Los Angeles, and many, many more) where the third party is either the reason for, or somehow involved in, the murder; and mystery. Here, there was no triangle and no mystery, since we know Simpson committed these murders. How interesting can such a case be?

As the case went on, a very few interesting things happened, such as the Fuhrman tapes. But long, long before that, the media had officially anointed this case as "having everything," and whatever happened during the trial that was even the most insignificant of surprises (e.g., allegation that there had been some friction between Mark Fuhrman and Judge Ito's wife, Captain Margaret York, the highest ranking woman in the LAPD) was treated by the media as confirmation that there had never been such a case, as if surprises and unusual allegations simply didn't occur in other cases. But this, of course, is pure drivel. Startling and unusual turns of events happen fairly regularly in major trials. For instance, in the recent trial of the woman charged with the murder of the Latin-American singing star, Selena, the defendant alleged that Selena's father had recently raped her and she had purchased a gun to protect herself from him. This is why, she said, she was armed at the time Selena visited her on the night of the murder.

But the media would have no dissent from the orthodoxy they were preaching. Even when a July 7–8, 1994, *Newsweek* poll showed that 85 percent of Americans thought the media was giving far too much coverage to the Simpson case (only 12 percent said it was about the right amount), and just one percent said the media coverage wasn't enough, the media would have none of it. They were hell-bent on seeing that the one percent got their way. The other 85 percent just didn't understand. And by telling the public over and over that there had never been a case like it, and by inundating the airwaves with coverage on the case, the public eventually came to agree with the media, whereupon the media said, without blushing, "See? We only blanket the news with the case because this is what the people want." In law school, they call this picking yourself up by your own bootstraps.

Does anyone really believe that if the trial had not been televised, and if the media had treated this case in a responsible way, that at the time of the reading of the verdict "the entire nation" (from coffee shops, bars, and offices to Wall Street and the White House, President Clinton interrupting a meeting in the Oval Office) would be holding its breath, as was so frequently reported? Of course not. It would simply have been another sensational murder case and it would not have become anywhere near the cultural and epochal event it became.

Newsweek, which did seven cover stories on the case, devoted almost its entire October 16, 1995, edition to the Simpson trial verdict. On the week of the Simpson verdict, Hurrican Opal tore through Florida and contiguous states. More than 100,000 people were left homeless, thousands lost their homes and businesses, much of a 140-mile stretch of coastline between Mobile, Alabama, and Panama City, Florida, was demolished, and eighteen people died. Yet Opal's devastation only warranted one paragraph in *Newsweek*'s Periscope section, and even then, not one single word on the damage the hurricane had wrought. The paragraph dealt exclusively with Dan Rather's reporting on the hurricane, and a photograph showed him clinging to a pole in the wind. *Newsweek* wryly added that "Rather nabbed what some would argue was the real story [of the week]."

The electronic media was even more excessive in its coverage, if possible, than the print media. Even though the trial was already being covered in its entirety by Court TV and other cable outlets, CNN also carried gavel-to-gavel coverage, thereby telling its audience day in and day out that this was the most important news story in the world. And *Larry King Live*, the principal talk show on CNN in the evening, and the leading interview show on television, dealt far, far more with the Simpson case than with any other news event. King told his viewers, "If we had God booked, and O.J. was available, we'd move God."

The television networks weren't too much better. From the time of the murders to the end of the trial, CBS, NBC, and ABC, in addition to doing a great number of specials, had thirty-eight hours and fifty-four minutes of news coverage on the case. During that same period, only four hours and fourteen minutes were devoted to the entire debate over national health care, including Medicare.

Not only was O. J. Simpson the *only* reason for this case being special, but he himself, though the most famous murder defendant in American history, was really not that big at the time of the murders. O. J. Simpson was a football star years ago. Since then he has had only modest success in television sportscasting and movies. Before these murders he was not someone who was being talked or written about, and even the value of his football cards was in decline. When Nicole was introduced to him she had never heard of him. Neither had her mother. Neither, in fact, had Marcia Clark. When Detective Vannatter called her at her home in the early morning of June 13, 1994, for help in the preparation of a search warrant, he told her the house to be searched was that of O. J. Simpson. "Who's that?" he recalls her asking. "O. J. Simpson, the football player." "Phil, I'm sorry. I don't know him."

Here's the proof that the treatment of the case was totally disproportionate: If Magic Johnson or Michael Jordan, each of whom is bigger, and much more of a current celebrity than O. J. Simpson was before the murders, had been accused of this type of crime, the media coverage wouldn't have been any more intense. I daresay that if President Clinton had been accused, the media coverage wouldn't have been more pervasive. How could it be? All three major networks, for instance, carried the preliminary hearing live. There is nothing you can do beyond that. It's already at the max. It reflects the increasingly superficial nature of our society. We have gone from the Lincoln-Douglas debates to campaigns for the presidency—where the destiny of the nation is at stake—being conducted by sound bites. Yet the Simpson case, which originally (before the bogus issue of race was injected into the case) affected no one outside the immediate families, was covered live, all day, on the three major networks. The nation should be proud of itself. To compound the idiocy of it, the greater portion of the trial was tedious and boring because of all the scientific testimony.

If there is one person I would have liked to have resurrected from his grave for the Simpson case it would have been the Baltimore sage and iconoclast, H. L. Mencken. Only Mencken, who did not suffer fools gladly and had little patience with his intellectual inferiors, of whom there were many, could have pointed out, with his pungent wit and searing social commentary, the absurdity, silliness, and folly surrounding the Simpson case.

Would I have defended O. J. Simpson?

During my radio and television appearances on the Simpson case, I was frequently asked if I would have represented Simpson. Since I knew he was guilty, I always responded I would not have.

Some have been disturbed by my not wanting to represent anyone charged with murder or any violent crime unless I believe him or her to be innocent or unless there are substantially mitigating circumstances. Isn't everyone entitled to be represented by an attorney, guilty or innocent? In fact, that's the idealistic chant often recited by defense attorneys as justification for representing even the most vicious criminals in our society. The concept is unassailable, but idealism is rarely what motivates lawyers who represent guilty defendants. They take the work because trying cases is their livelihood, and they are ambitious to advance their careers. These motivations, while perfectly proper, are clearly not idealistic.

True idealism would be demonstrated in a hypothetical situation such as the following. Suppose a family is brutally murdered in a small town, and none of the five lawyers in town is willing to represent the suspect because the enraged citizens are all convinced of the suspect's guilt and no lawyer wants to be ostracized in the community for attempting to get the suspect off. Finally, one attorney steps forward and says, "I don't care what my friends at the Rotary Club and the First Baptist Church say. This is America, and everyone is entitled under the Sixth Amendment to our Constitution to be represented by an attorney."

That would be idealism. I, too, would represent a defendant—even one I believed to be guilty of murder—if I were the only lawyer available, because the right to counsel is a sacred right in our society and much more important than any personal predilection I might have. But this type of situation simply does not exist in a city like Los Angeles, where 35,000 lawyers stumble over each other's feet for cases. (For instance, when Charles Manson was charged with the Tate-LaBianca murders, over two hundred lawyers signed in to see him at the county jail, obviously for the purpose of seeking to represent him.) So I am free to follow my inclination.

Since nothing in the canons of ethics of the American Bar Association says a lawyer has to represent everyone who comes to his door, I choose not to defend anyone charged with a violent crime unless I believe he or she is innocent or unless there are substantially mitigating circumstances. (By the latter, I don't mean the question said to be asked about the victim by hard-bitten sheriffs in rural Texas at the start of any homicide investigation: "Did he *need* killing?") I investigate my own cases, and if I become satisfied in my own mind that the person is guilty, with no substantial mitigation, I routinely refer the case to other lawyers.

My position is not a matter of high ethics. It's more a matter of motivation. Let's take some vicious SOB who picks up young girls, sexually abuses and brutalizes them, then murders them and dumps them on the side of the road. What conceivable motivation could I possibly have to knock myself out working a hundred hours a week trying to figure out a way to get this type of person off?

I am also not unmindful of the fact that were I to secure a not-guilty verdict for one of these defendants I represented and he went out and did it again, I could rationalize all I wanted, but I would be partially responsible. If I had not deceived the jury the first time around, there would not have been a second murder.

In a nutshell, although I have never been a law-and-order fanatic — in fact, I'm suspicious of those who are — I do believe that those who have committed serious crimes should be severely punished, and I do not want to be in a position of actively seeking to thwart this natural justice.

One illustration of my dilemma in legal defense work was the case of Dr. Jeffrey MacDonald, the Princeton-educated former U.S. Army Green Beret who was accused of savagely stabbing to death his pregnant wife and two young daughters in their Fort Bragg, North Carolina, home one rainy night in March 1970. He was first charged with the murders that year, but the case against him was dropped because the evidence was insufficient. It was sometime in late 1973 or early 1974 that a close woman friend of MacDonald's came to my office in Beverly Hills and told me that the doctor, who was then working as an emergency room physician in nearby Long Beach, had learned he was about to be reindicted. She said the doctor wanted to know if I would be interested in representing him. We could talk about it, I said, if the doctor was innocent. I told her, "Tell him, though, that for starters I want him to take and pass a polygraph test." While waiting to hear from him, I telephoned the federal prosecutor handling the case in North Carolina and asked what he had against MacDonald. The prosecutor would not say very much, but did mention a few pieces of evidence to me, one of which was that fibers from MacDonald's blue pajamas had been found embedded beneath the fingernails of his two-and-a-half-year-old daughter. That evoked in my mind the horrifying scene of a little girl crying out, "Daddy, Daddy, no," as she reached out and struggled against her father while he stabbed her to death. That was enough for me. I wanted nothing to do with the case. MacDonald's lady friend called a week later anyway to say that he did not think it was necessary to take a polygraph as a precondition to my representing him. Convicted of the triple murder in 1979, he was sentenced to three consecutive life terms in prison.

My disinclination to defend a murderer also resulted in my electing not to represent former San Francisco supervisor Dan White for the 1978 assassination murders of Mayor George Moscone and Supervisor Harvey Milk when friends of White's from the San Francisco Police Department—White was a former officer—asked me to.

Those are the only two really big murder defendants who have ever come to me. Since my image is still that of a prosecutor, when people get in trouble with the law, I'm usually one of the very last people they think of.

Just because I could never have defended O. J. Simpson for these murders since I know he committed them does not mean I'm critical of the lawyers who did defend him for having done so. What I *am* very critical about is in *the way* several of them went about doing it. It's one thing to defend someone you know is guilty, even defend him vigorously. Who can validly criticize such a lawyer? Our system of justice and jurisprudence not only allows but encourages this.

But inasmuch as the defense lawyers had to know Simpson was guilty of these two terribly brutal murders, I personally wonder how they could possibly have found it within themselves to go far beyond a vigorous representation, defending him with the same passion and fervor with which one would defend his own parents, wife, or children who were being charged with a serious crime.

Moreover, although it's perfectly proper to defend a guilty person by trying to poke holes in the people's case, you don't, for instance, deliberately violate the rules, as Cochran did when he argued throughout his opening statement (which is not allowed), and you don't, in your opening statement, refer to witnesses whose identity and statements have not been turned over to the prosecution (in violation of the law). More important, you don't (Cochran, Bailey, Scheck) accuse innocent police officers of framing your client for murder. You don't (Cochran, Bailey) inject the transparently fraudulent issue of race into the trial, particularly when it's to the detriment, as it was with Cochran, of your own race. You don't (Cochran and Scheck) object time and again during the prosecutors' final summations, in a concerted, unprofessional, and unethical effort to interrupt the flow of their arguments, therefore denying the people their right to a fair trial.

The reason I am omitting any reference to Robert Shapiro here in this legal rogues' gallery is that I am unclear as to his state of mind and intentions with respect to some of these matters. Although he is on record as saying before the trial started that race was not going to be an issue at the trial, and immediately after the verdict he distanced himself from Cochran and condemned him for playing the race card, and from the bottom of the deck at that, there is the troubling July 25, 1994, article in *The New Yorker* magazine titled "An Incendiary Defense," which was written well in advance of July 22, 1994, the date Cochran joined the defense team. The author, respected journalist Jeffrey Toobin, said that "leading members of Simpson's defense team" had told him the defense intended to present evidence and argue that Mark Fuhrman framed Simpson, and "the defense will assert that Mark Fuhrman's motivation for framing O. J. Simpson is racism."

Shapiro was the lead defense lawyer at the time of this article, and a large photo of him (by photographer Richard Avedon, taken for the article on July 11, 1994, confirming the article was in the works weeks *before* Cochran came aboard) appeared in the piece, with the caption "Robert Shapiro, Simpson's top defender, in Los Angeles."

So at least based on what I know thus far, in my mind the jury's still out on Shapiro.

A note about Barry Scheck. Scheck has a reputation as a lawyer for the poor and dispossessed, having worked for three years as a Legal Aid lawyer in the Bronx. He and his colleague Peter Neufeld later created the Innocence Project, which has reportedly used DNA testing to free a dozen innocent people previously convicted of crimes. But in the Simpson case, where we know Simpson was guilty, Scheck showed just how conceptually pristine and intellectually honest his *Innocence* Project really is—pristine and honest all the way up to the point of a big publicity case beckoning him to oppose justice for a man he had to know was guilty of murder.

To borrow a phrase from Henry Roth's recent novel, *From Bondage*, in the ensuing years each of the aforementioned defense attorneys in the Simpson case will have to "reconcile himself with himself." Unless, that is, as another novelist, Gertrude Stein, once said about Oakland, California, "there's no there, there."

Black support for O. J. Simpson and its consequences

As if African-Americans haven't suffered enough throughout this nation's history because of the calcified minds of squint-eyed bigots, because of their fiercely partisan and ultimately unjustified support of someone most know to be a savage killer, they may start suffering, though more indirectly, at the hands of those who have been traditionally supportive of them.

As *Newsweek* magazine said in its October 16, 1995, edition: "What was different—and disturbing—about the racial talk last week was that so many white liberals sounded fed up. Many middle-class professionals who have always supported integration, maintained office and social friendships with African-Americans, and resisted the backlash against affirmative action were appalled by what black novelist Dennis Williams called the "end-zone dance" [by blacks] over the Simpson acquittal. It made them wonder aloud whether they really knew African-Americans as well as they thought they did, and whether the racial gap wasn't much wider than they had believed."

I find it curious and ironic that although Johnnie Cochran used the black community to its own long-term detriment when he manufactured a racial issue in the Simpson case out of whole cloth, he is now being perceived as a hero among African-Americans. "He is a national hero, especially among African-Americans," says former Los Angeles mayor Tom Bradley. The October 4, 1995, edition of the *Los Angeles Times* said: "When the Congressional Black Caucus held a Washington conference last month, it was not President Clinton or retired General Colin L. Powell who received several ovations or were besieged for autographs. It was Cochran. 'Johnnie was well received,' said Kim Hunter, a Los Angeles advertising and public relations executive. 'The audience of five thousand embraced him. They were very proud.'"

The black community's apotheosis of Johnnie Cochran makes it obvious that many of them don't understand what has happened, or at least it hasn't sunk in yet with them.

But if it hasn't sunk in with the black community, it's rather obvious to just about everyone else. Since the trial and verdict, I personally (and this is an observation I've heard many others make) have never heard so much antiblack sentiment in all my years, even from people I know have never been racist and whom I have never heard utter an antiblack word before.

The verbal assaults on blacks are threefold. One is that blacks must be awfully stupid to believe Simpson is innocent. But blacks are no more stupid than whites or anyone else. I think those assailing blacks would be more accurate to call the millions of blacks who passionately supported Simpson ignorant of the facts.

The second criticism I now hear of blacks—partly because of the burst of jubilation with which they responded to the not guilty verdict—is that they simply are not nice people, and couldn't care less that two white people were butchered to death. This is a very unfortunate and, I feel, erroneous charge. At least my association with blacks through the years (I'm not referring to the criminal element) has shown them to be people with a compassionate heart and rich sense of humor. Callousness, greed, and meanness of spirit are not at all the norm for the blacks I've known.

The third charge, which is somewhat related to the second, is that the blind support of Simpson by fellow blacks, and the seemingly *personal* pleasure they derived from the verdict, which conveyed a sense that they had somehow gotten even with whitey, reveals them to be more racist than whites. This may be true, and may even be understandable, since if a race has been discriminated against by another race for centuries because of racism, the victim race has good cause to develop even deeper racism than the perpetrating race.

Black racism is a social phenomenon which apparently has been close to the surface but largely unfocused upon by the white majority. For many years the social engineers and reformists among the white majority have viewed the obliteration of white racism against blacks as a moral imperative, and diverse groups and movements have consecrated their existence to this end. Has there ever been one such counterpart group or movement in the black community? Of course, it's a lot easier to be magnanimous when you are on top.

In any event, the experts have weighed in with their views on the injurious impact upon blacks of the Simpson verdict. Here's a random sampling. David Horowitz, president of the Center for the Study of Popular Culture, said that the verdict may have set race relations in this country back thirty years. Though most experts do not predict consequences quite this dire, they are no less certain that the black community will suffer. "A lot of [black] people will pay the price for O.J.'s freedom, because there's no question there will be a backlash," says Susan Estrich, USC law professor and *USA Today* columnist.

Columnist Ronald Brownstein asserts that "the apparent responsiveness of the predominantly black jury to the defense claim that Simpson was the victim of a vast, racially motivated police conspiracy . . . has widened the separation" of the races. Will Marshall, president of the Progressive Policy Institute, a centrist think tank in Washington, D.C., adds that "what this episode does is deepen the polarization." Andrew Hacker, author of the book *Two Nations: Black and White, Separate, Hostile, Unequal*, predicts that the acquittal *and the black response to it* will translate, because of white anger, into a lowering of support for affirmative action, welfare, and other social programs that are important to blacks. "A lot of white people were very upset to see black people on television looking that happy," Hacker says. Earl Ofari Hutchinson, a black sociologist who is writing a book about the Simpson trial, expects the acquittal and the black response to it to result in immeasurable harm to the black community. And Roger Boesche, professor of politics at Occidental College in Los Angeles, also predicts that as blacks rioted after the first Rodney King trial, whites will riot against blacks at the ballot box.

There can be little question that the racial tensions fanned by the defense attorneys in this case, mostly Johnnie Cochran, have increased (and with many people, *created*) white antagonism against blacks, and therefore, with only 12 percent of the nation's population anyway, it is not improbable that blacks are going to get hurt by it, at least to some degree, in the policies and votes of the white majority in the years ahead. So Johnnie Cochran, instead of being viewed in his community as a hero, should be judged by them for what he did—cynically and blatantly use and exploit them, to their very serious detriment, just to promote the interests of himself and his client.

Again, what makes all of this so painfully ironic and sad is that O. J. Simpson, who used the black community, has not been a member of that community for years and years. George Curry, black editor in chief of the black news magazine *Emerge*, observes: "O. J. Simpson is not a person who has cast his lot with African-Americans. In fact, you could say just the opposite. He's gone out of his way to not align himself with blacks." William Safire, *New York Times* syndicated columnist, sums it up this way: "The wealthy celebrity who lived white, spoke white, and married white, wrapped himself in the rags of social injustice." And blacks, who have suffered enough because of the color of their skin, unfortunately bought into it, and in the process may have contributed to their continuing misfortune.

The American jury system, in light of the Rodney King and O. J. Simpson verdicts

Even before the Simpson verdict, there was a rising chorus among many in America that something should be done about the jury system, that there was a tremendous need for "jury reform." Some have gone so far as to recommend abolishing the jury system as we know it. People could not accept the results in cases where it seemed that guilt was certain—the Menendez brothers, Lorena Bobbitt, Damien Williams—yet the defendants walked or the juries hung. Have jurors taken leave of their senses, Americans wanted to know. To them, it seemed as if today in America, anything, even murder, can be excused if you just claim you were abused. Juries will buy it, just as they did in the Bobbitt and Menendez cases, they said.

People are alluding here to the so-called "abuse is an excuse" defense. Obviously, there is no such defense. However, abuse can be of such a severe nature that it gives rise to a recognized legal defense, such as irresistible impulse, which was the defense in the Bobbitt case. Irresistible impulse, at least in some states, is a species of insanity. Under the basic law of insanity, you are deemed to be insane only if, because of a defect of reason caused by a diseased mind, you did not know that what you did was wrong. In irresistible impulse, the person *does* know the wrongfulness of his act, but is unable to control the impulse to commit it. Most states don't have this defense, but in Virginia, where the Bobbitt case was tried, it's a legitimate defense. As far as the first Menendez trial was concerned, the jurors were hung up on whether it was first- or second-degree murder or voluntary manslaughter, not on whether the defendants should go free.

How did this "abuse is an excuse" concept come into play? It's just a new, catchy phrase for an old concept that has been around for years. But it's been given increased prominence because of the supposed Oprahization of the jury syndrome. Through watching shows like Oprah, Donahue, and Geraldo, Americans are exposed to endless numbers of people who are the victims of abuse from dysfunctional families and relationships. A subliminal empathy develops for these purported victims when they thereafter engage in antisocial behavior against their alleged abusers. That's the theory. But, as it is said in the Book of Ecclesiastes, there is nothing new under the sun. Juries have always given a break, where they legally can, to victims of abuse as well as to people suffering from mental disorders. Any trial lawyer will tell you this. There's nothing different about or wrong with today's juries. Way back in 1835, when Americans were supposedly as hard as nails, a jury found Richard Lawrence, a housepainter, not guilty by reason of insanity for attempting to assassinate President Andrew Jackson. Likewise with the attempt on President Reagan's life by John Hinckley in 1981.

So I don't think juries are softer on criminal defendants today at all. Why would they be? Americans are more concerned and conservative about crime today than they have been in many years. It makes absolutely no sense that when they walk into that courtroom they leave their concern and their conservatism at the courtroom door. I just think it's been a quirky coincidence that a few recent high-visibility cases have resulted in seemingly unsatisfactory verdicts. The reality is that some of these cases have turned on subtle legal issues that laypeople don't understand.

For instance, in the case of Damien Williams, who was charged with attempted murder and other crimes during the Los Angeles riots, when the jury found him not guilty of attempted murder, people were angry. The erroneous impression was that he had "gotten off." Even several syndicated columnists, who should have known better, made this assertion. But Williams did not get off. He was convicted of mayhem and sentenced to ten years in prison, a not insubstantial term. The reason he wasn't convicted of attempted murder is that the law of attempted murder requires a specific intent to kill. Firing a bullet at someone's head clearly shows such intent. But throwing a brick at someone's head, as Williams did, does not necessarily show, beyond a reasonable doubt, that you specifically intended to kill that person. The argument could be made that if Williams had intended to kill Reginald Denny—as opposed to merely intending to cause great bodily harm, or not caring whether he killed him or not, neither of which states of mind would satisfy the specific intent-to-kill requirement of attempted murder—instead of dancing around after throwing the brick, he would have followed it up to make sure he got the job done. The crimes actually committed in the Williams case were mayhem, assault with a deadly weapon, and assault by means of force likely to produce great bodily harm. If Williams had the requisite intent to kill, there may indeed have also been an attempted murder, but it isn't clear from the evidence and circumstances that he did. The attempted-murder charge was a typical overfiling by the DA in the hope of inducing a plea of guilty to a lesser charge. The defense called the DA's bluff and got a not-guilty verdict. But there was a proper verdict of guilty (for mayhem) in that case, despite the popular perception there was not.

Some verdicts, of course, have been clearly improper, bringing about gross miscarriages of justice. Two of the worst ever, both inflicting very black marks on our jury system, were those in the Simpson case and in the first Rodney King trial in Simi Valley, where a nearly all-white jury acquitted the white LAPD police officers despite the fact their crime was captured on film. The verdict threatened, overnight, to convert the aphorism "One picture is worth a thousand words" into an anachronism.

We have seen how the Simpson case was improvidently transferred by District Attorney Garcetti to a venue unfavorable to the prosecution, and a judge did the exact same thing in the King case. In the latter case, the original judge assigned to the case denied a defense motion for a change of venue out of Los Angeles, but on a writ of mandate-prohibition taken by the defense to the Second District Court of Appeal, the court granted the writ and ordered the respondent Los Angeles Superior Court to grant the venue motion. The eventual trial judge was given three counties outside of Los Angeles to choose from by the State Judicial Council: Ventura, Riverside, and Alameda. Both Ventura and Riverside are conservative, Ventura even more so than Riverside, and the defense predictably asked the judge for one of them, preferably Ventura. The DA's office asked for Alameda County (Oakland), which has a racial mix resembling that of Los Angeles.

Inexplicably, the judge selected the most conservative county of all, Ventura. He rejected Alameda because of the added cost and inconvenience necessitated by the transfer to the Bay Area. But as I said earlier, you can't place a price tag on justice. Moreover, this was an important case of considerable sociological implications, and cases a hundredfold less important have been transferred even greater distances on changes of venue. The murder case upon which my book *And the Sea Will Tell* was based was transferred to San Francisco all the way from Honolulu.

In my opinion, no one is as responsible for the shocking verdict in the King case as much as the trial judge. Yet, remarkably, all one hears in this regard is that the case was probably lost for the prosecution when he transferred it to Ventura County, not that he himself therefore committed the gravest of judicial errors, and hence was the proximate cause of the verdict. But like a magician, he somehow managed to separate himself from his act. At a minimum, he should have transferred the case to Riverside County, which is very close to Los Angeles. Yet the judge, the bench's Teflon man, has heretofore miraculously escaped criticism. In fact, after the Rodney King verdict and subsequent riot it induced, the judge was rewarded by being assigned to preside over the Menendez trial.

As most know by now, the jury that heard the King case had no blacks on it. In fact, only one black was called to the jury box for questioning during the entire jury selection process. Predictably, the defense immediately excused her, using a peremptory challenge. If four or five blacks had been on the jury—if even two or three, perhaps even one, had been—and the verdict had been the same, not guilty, there is a much greater likelihood the black community would have accepted the verdict, and the biggest and most costly race riot in American history might have been averted. Not only were there no blacks on the jury (ten whites, one Latina, and one Asian-American), but it was decidedly conservative. Although only two of the jurors ultimately came from the city of Simi Valley (1.5 percent black), a conservative bedroom community of Los Angeles which is home to the Reagan presidential library, the remaining ten came from the equally white, conservative surrounding area of Ventura County (2.2 percent black). Three of the twelve jurors were members of the right-wing NRA, one's brother was a retired LAPD sergeant, one was a former security guard, and two others had been police officers in the military. Just as the Simpson jury, with nine blacks out of twelve jurors, was not a representative jury, neither was the jury in the King case a representative cross-section of American society. In fact, the all-white King jury con-sisted of people who, in moving to Ventura County from Los Angeles, had run away from the Rodney Kings of the world.

In light of the dynamics at play and the probable stereotypical percep-tions by the conservative Simi Valley jury, the roles of the trial partici-pants were reversed. To the Simi Valley jury, the man on trial was Rodney King, and the main lawyer arguing on his behalf, the prosecutor, was another black man. Assisting the black man was his co-prosecutor, who is Jewish. To many hidebound white conservatives, Jews are liberal, left-leaning ACLU types who deep down are really on the side of the crimi-nal. The four white defendants, on the other hand, had four white, Chris-tian, God-fearing lawyers defending them.

Although many law-enforcement-minded people were supportive of the not-guilty verdicts, even the officers' own chief, Daryl Gates, was ap-palled by the beating. Inasmuch as Gates has always made it a practice to review personally each case of alleged excessive force, if anyone should recognize it, it is he. And Gates, who said he looked at the film of the beating twenty-five times, says that the beating was "a very, very extreme use of force—extreme for any police department in America." He de-scribed the incident as "revolting and unconscionable. This was some-thing that never should have happened. We have in place procedures to keep it from happening."

And Gates's predecessor, the deep-dyed conservative Ed Davis, had this to say: "If that kind of police conduct is lawful, as the jury said it was . . . then I don't want to live here. If this wasn't excessive force, what is?"

The not-guilty verdicts called up memories of Mississippi and Alabama justice in the first half of this century, where white defendants were al-most invariably acquitted by all-white juries when charged with crimes against blacks, no matter how strong the evidence of guilt was. The ver-dict of the jury in the King case clearly appears to have been wrong, occasioning a miscarriage of justice which produced momentous conse-quences.

So the jury system is not infallible. No system, in any field of human endeavor, is. But because there are a few aberrational cases like the Simpson and King cases doesn't mean that it's time to overhaul an institution which has served this nation well in literally millions of cases over the past two centuries. That's just the voice of the unenlightened being manipulated by patently demagogic arguments. This is not to say that some small improvements could not be made. Jury instructions, for one thing, are in many instances poorly drafted and confusing, in some cases (e.g., "guilt or innocence") actually wrong. A concerted effort should be made to formulate instructions that are a lot clearer and easier to understand for jurors.

Another possibility would be to mandate a minimum educational requirement for jurors who are to sit on highly complex and technical cases. This would be establishing a potentially dangerous precedent, however. If we start making changes in the jury system to meet some perceived need in a particular type of case, the changes may start to be applied to cases that were never intended to be covered by the change. Moreover, at what point, and under what criteria, would a case be considered highly complex and technical? It would be like trying to measure the immeasurable with a rubber ruler. Another proposal, removing highly complex and technical criminal cases from juries completely and placing them solely in the hands of a judge, would of course require a constitutional amendment. I personally would oppose it, having a lot more faith in twelve citizens chosen from the community than in one individual, a politician at that.

I think state laws requiring employers to pay employees when they are serving on juries might be advisable, since this would free up a lot of otherwise qualified people who are being excused at the present time because of hardship reasons. This should be a part of a movement to make jury service more mandatory than it presently is, which will result in a higher quality of juror.

Juries of experts, of course, make no sense at all. But for every foolish idea there will always be some fool to champion it, and this idea has been mentioned a great many times, even by some lawyers and judges. Hundreds of thousands of jury cases are heard every year in the United States. With twelve jurors to every jury, are we supposed to employ (and pay!) millions of experts to hear these cases? When an idea isn't feasible on its face, why waste a breath talking about it?

One suggestion for change in our jury system which is rarely heard but which, in my opinion, has merit and should at least be given serious consideration is to eliminate all peremptory challenges, challenges for which no reason has to be given. (Only challenges for cause could be made.) This would undoubtedly serve to expedite the trial of a case, and I'm not too sure either side would suffer from it. I say that because many experienced trial lawyers will tell you that after weeks and sometimes months of voir dire, the jury you end up with is more often than not no better than the first twelve in the box. The reason for this phenomenon is that the juror one side wants is nearly always the one the other side does not. As each side excuses jurors who look good for the opposition, little progress is made and neither side benefits much.

Eliminating peremptory challenges would have the additional meaningful benefit of promoting the principal purpose of voir dire — to get a fair and impartial jury. Although each side publicly attests that that is what it is seeking during the voir dire process, what each side is really looking for is jurors who will be biased in their favor.

The change in our jury system which has been broached the most, and one for which I feel there is at least some arguable merit, is to eliminate unanimous jury verdicts in criminal trials, i.e., instead of needing all twelve jurors to convict, ten or eleven out of the twelve would suffice. This, the proponents say, would *substantially* reduce the number of hung juries. But would it? One has to realize that approximately 95 percent of all felony cases in the major metropolitan areas of our country never go to trial. They are disposed of by way of a plea bargain. And of the remaining 5 percent which are tried, only about 10 percent result in a hung jury. (In Los Angeles County it's usually higher, around 12 or 13 percent.) This is about one-half of 1 percent, a minuscule number. Also, statistics clearly show that most hung juries are not 11–1 or 10–2 anyway. They usually range from 9–3 to 6–6, with most of them 8–4, 7–5 and 6–6. So in the majority of cases, a 11–1 or 10–2 requirement would still produce a hung jury.

In fact, the only two states in the union which have majority verdicts, Oregon and Louisiana, 10–2 and 9–3 respectively, *also* have hung juries, although they are always slightly below the national average. Granted, 11–1, 10–2, or 9–3 would eliminate some hung juries. The question is whether the change is worth it.

My personal view is that it's not. In a criminal case, a defendant's liberty, sometimes his life, is on the line, and to deprive an American citizen or any defendant in an American courtroom of his liberty or life should require not only a very high burden of proof for the state, but that all twelve jurors agree. It shouldn't be forgotten that having a hung jury doesn't mean the defendant walks out of court. You simply retry the case, and the majority of times a conviction is secured the second time around.

A unanimous verdict gives a legitimacy and finality to a verdict that a majority verdict, by definition, could never have. And I find no problem with securing convictions where a unanimous verdict is required. In those cases where the defendant did, in fact, commit the crime, if the police do their job and the DA does his, there is normally no difficulty at all persuading all twelve jurors to vote guilty. Making it easier to get a guilty verdict, it seems to me, increases the likelihood that law enforcement, instead of being more diligent and more competent in putting their case together, as we want them to be, will become less diligent and competent, feeling they don't have to work quite as hard to secure a conviction.

Also, human nature being what it is, it would seem that under the majority system, those jurors in the majority wouldn't have as much of a motivation to listen carefully, if at all, to the views of the minority jurors, because they would know the vote of these jurors wasn't necessary for a verdict, and this is not a healthy circumstance. A majority verdict would eliminate the type of situation portrayed in the movie *Twelve Angry Men* — a hold-out juror (Henry Fonda) finally convinces the other eleven of his point of view. Surprisingly, this isn't an uncommon phenomenon. Although one juror turning around eleven is very rare, two or three turning around a majority is not. A University of Chicago study a few years back found that in roughly 10 percent of all cases, which would translate into thousands of cases, the minority jurors eventually succeeded in persuading the original majority to come over to their side.

Despite some recent bad experiences, I still have confidence in the jury system. And I view it as perhaps the most fundamental safeguard against tyranny we have. When you stop to think about it, in America only a jury can cause a fellow human being to end up behind prison bars. For instance, unless a defendant in a criminal case gives up his constitutional right to a jury trial, no judge can find him guilty and place him behind bars. Even the president of the United States cannot put someone behind bars. Law enforcement — the police, the FBI, etc. — can put you in the pokey, but if you are not convicted in a court of law, they can't keep you there. Only a jury made up of everyday American citizens can cause someone to end up behind prison bars. So in a very real sense, the American jury is all that stands between the accused and his loss of liberty. And this realization is at once awe-inspiring and supremely reassuring. I think that one can see at a glance the very high and delicate ground the American jury occupies. It should be tampered with very little, if at all, and always with caution.

Louis Nizer once said: "I would rather trust twelve jurors with all their prejudices and biases than I would a judge. I think the reason democracy works is because as you multiply judgments you reduce the incidence of errors." Richard Lempert, a professor of law and sociology at the University of Michigan, adds that "the jury benefits from diverse perspectives. The janitor may know something about pipes, and somebody else might know something about how the police work."

I have found that like Truman rising to the presidency, jurors usually rise to the occasion. They normally put aside their petty biases and differences because they know they have a tremendous responsibility to do the right thing—they're judging a fellow human being, and it's something they're going to have to live with for the rest of their lives. By and large, they are very conscientious and honorable, and base their verdict exclusively on the evidence that comes from the witness stand.

The jury system, throughout the years, has been subject to many attacks, but no one has yet come with a better system, in my opinion, to determine the fate of one's fellow man.

One thing is clear, however. The Simpson verdict, being a terrible miscarriage of justice, and one of the darkest days ever *for* American justice, has had an injurious effect on Americans' faith in the jury system. The majority of Americans believe O. J. Simpson is guilty, and they saw the issue of his guilt being subverted by the fabricated and extraneous issue of racism. Justice, of course, was the victim. What happened in the Simpson case takes one back to what Supreme Court Justice Oliver Wendell Holmes, Jr., said to a young whippersnapper lawyer who injected the word "justice" one too many times into his oral argument before the Court: "I must remind you, young man, this is a court of law, not a court of justice."

The fate of O. J. Simpson

It will be interesting to see if, with the passage of time, O. J. Simpson is accepted back into the good graces of the majority of American people. So far, he has not been. In fact, he isn't even welcome in his own community of Brentwood, the board of directors of the Riviera Country Club expelling him from club membership. And many of his neighbors, by signs such as "Welcome to Brentwood, home of the Brentwood Butcher," have let him know he is *persona non grata*. Also, the Hertz Corporation did not renew his contract, and his agents, International Creative Management, dropped him. My guess is that Simpson will eventually be able to ease his way *partially* back into normal society. However, because there was such a massive torrent of publicity in this case, and over such a protracted period of time, the beliefs of those who feel he is guilty have hardened and become more immutable than they would normally be. And therefore his road to rehabilitation will reach a point beyond which he will never proceed.

It should be noted that crowds of tourists, mostly white, still congregate daily outside the gates of Simpson's Rockingham estate, hoping for a glimpse of him. When, on occasion, he decides to grace them with his presence, they swarm about him, hugging him, seeking his autograph, and, if especially fortunate, even securing a photo of themselves smiling with Simpson. There's less to these people, of course, than meets the eye.

The other possibility is that Simpson will become an even greater national pariah than he already is, and like another person acquitted of a double murder just over a century ago, be forced to live an even more ostracized life. In 1892, Lizzie Borden, like Simpson, was acquitted of a highly publicized double murder—that of her stepmother and father, in her parents' home in Fall River, Massachusetts. Also like Simpson, Lizzie Borden did not testify in her defense, and like the Simpson jury, the Borden jury deliberated only briefly, a little over one hour. The trial, however, lasted but thirteen days.

Despite her acquittal, Lizzie Borden was shunned and scorned by the people of Fall River, who believed her to be guilty, and she led a reclusive existence until her death in 1927 at the age of sixty-six. Her presumed guilt became immortalized not just in a spate of books and plays on the case, but in this well-known ditty:

Lizzie Borden took an ax
And gave her mother forty whacks
When she saw what she had done
She gave her father forty-one.

As we all know, O. J. Simpson was very popular before these murders. I've been told that if a popularity poll had been taken among employees when he was working in the sportscasting department at NBC, he would have won hands down. He is a charming, friendly, personable, and likable human being in many ways. He is also a cold-blooded killer, as well as the most audacious one I have ever known.

There's an old Turkish proverb that whoever tells the truth is chased out of nine villages. Because this book has been so hard-hitting, I hope I'll still be allowed to sit on a park bench in the town square, feed a resident pigeon or two, and contemplate the real complexities of life.

I can tell you, the reader, that I have enjoyed this personal conversation with you that my editor suggested just a few months back. I hope that, despite the subject matter, you have also enjoyed it, and more important, that it shed some light for you on the most publicized murder trial of our time, and why it ended the way it did, with someone who we know committed two particularly terrible and savage murders walking free among us.

VINCENT BUGLIOSI
March 1996
Los Angeles, California

Appendix A

Complete LAPD Interrogation of O. J. Simpson on Day After Murders

(transcribed from tape)

Note: P.V. is Detective Philip Vannatter; T.L. is Detective Thomas Lange; O.J.S. is O. J. Simpson.

P.V.: My partner, Detective Lange, and we're in an interview room in Parker Center. The date is June 13, 1994, and the time is 13:35 hours [1:35 p.m.], and we're here with O. J. Simpson. Is that Orenthal James Simpson?
O.J.S.: Orenthal James Simpson.
P.V.: And what is your birthdate, Mr. Simpson?
O.J.S.: July 9, 1947.
P.V.: Okay, prior to us talking to you, as we agreed with your attorney, I'm going to give you your constitutional rights. And I would like you to listen carefully. If you don't understand anything, tell me, okay?
O.J.S.: All right.
P.V.: Okay, Mr. Simpson, you have the right to remain silent. If you give up the right to remain silent, anything you say can and will be used in a court of law. You have the right to speak to an attorney and to have an attorney present during the questioning. If you so desire and cannot afford one, an attorney will be appointed for you without charge before questioning. Do you understand your rights?
O.J.S.: Yes, I do.

P.V.: Are there any questions about that?

O.J.S.: (Unintelligible.)

P.V.: Okay, you've got to speak louder than that.

O.J.S.: Okay, no.

P.V.: Okay, do you wish to give up your right to remain silent and talk to us?

O.J.S.: Ah, yes.

P.V.: Okay, and you give up your right to have an attorney present while we talk?

O.J.S.: Mmm hmm. Yes.

P.V.: Okay. All right, what we're gonna do is, we want to . . . We're investigating, obviously, the death of your ex-wife and another man.

T.L.: Someone told us that.

P.V.: Yeah, and we're going to need to talk to you about that. Are you divorced from her now?

O.J.S.: Yes.

P.V.: How long have you been divorced?

O.J.S.: Officially? Probably close to two years, but we've been apart for a little over two years.

P.V.: Have you?

O.J.S.: Yeah.

P.V.: What was your relationship with her? What was the . . .

O.J.S.: Well, we tried to get back together, and it just didn't work. It wasn't working, and so we were going our separate ways.

P.V.: Recently, you tried to get back together?

O.J.S.: We tried to get back together for about a year, you know, where we started dating each other and seeing each other. She came back and wanted us to get back together, and . . .

P.V.: Within the last year, you're talking about?

O.J.S.: She came back about a year and four months ago about us trying to get back together, and we gave it a shot. We gave it a shot the better part of a year. And I think we both knew it wasn't working, and probably three weeks ago or so we said it just wasn't working and we went our separate ways.

P.V.: Okay, the two children are yours?

O.J.S.: Yes.

T.L.: She have custody?

O.J.S.: We have joint custody.

T.L.: Through the courts?

O.J.S.: We went through the courts and everything. Everything is done. We have no problems with the kids, we do everything together, you know, with the kids.

P.V.: How was your separation? Was that a . . . ?

O.J.S.: The first separation?

P.V.: Yeah, was there problems with that?

O.J.S.: For me, it was big problems. I loved her, I didn't want us to separate.

P.V.: Uh huh. I understand that she had made a couple of crime . . . crime reports or something?

O.J.S.: Ah, we had a big fight about six years ago on New Year's, you know, she made a report. I didn't make a report. And then we had an altercation about a year ago maybe. It wasn't a physical argument. I kicked her door or something.

P.V.: And she made a police report on those two occasions?

O.J.S.: Mmm hmm. And I stayed right there until the police came, talked to them.

T.L.: Were you arrested at one time for something?

O.J.S.: No. I mean, five years ago we had a big fight, six years ago, I don't know. I know I ended up doing community service.

P.V.: So you weren't arrested?

O.J.S.: No, I was never really arrested.

T.L.: They never booked or . . . ?

O.J.S.: No.

P.V.: Can I ask you, when's the last time you've slept?

O.J.S.: I got a couple of hours' sleep last night. I mean, you know, I slept a little on the plane, not much, and when I got to the hotel I was asleep a few hours when the phone call came.

T.L.: Did Nicole have a housemaid that lived there?

O.J.S.: I believe so, yes.

T.L.: Do you know her name at all?

O.J.S.: Evia, Elvia, something like that.

P.V.: We didn't see her there. Did she have the day off perhaps?

O.J.S.: I don't know. I don't know what schedule she's on.

T.L.: Phil, what do you think? We can maybe just recount last night.

P.V.: Yeah. When was the last time you saw Nicole?

O.J.S.: We were leaving a dance recital. She took off and I was talking to her parents.

P.V.: Where was the dance recital?

O.J.S.: Paul Revere High School.

P.V.: And was that for one of your children?

O.J.S.: For my daughter Sydney.

P.V.: And what time was that yesterday?

O.J.S.: It ended about six-thirty, quarter to seven, something like that, you know in the ballpark, right in that area. And they took off.

P.V.: They?

O.J.S.: Her and her family, her mother and father, sisters, my kids, you know.

P.V.: And then you went your own separate way?

O.J.S.: Yeah, actually she left, and then they came back and her mother got in a car with her, and the kids all piled into her sister's car, and they . . .

P.V.: Was Nicole driving?

O.J.S.: Yeah.

P.V.: What kind of car was she driving?

O.J.S.: Her black car, a Cherokee, a Jeep Cherokee.

P.V.: What were you driving?

O.J.S.: My Rolls-Royce, my Bentley.

P.V.: Do you own that Ford Bronco that sits outside?

O.J.S.: Hertz owns it and Hertz lets me use it.

P.V.: So that's your vehicle, the one that was parked there on the street?

O.J.S.: Mmm hmm.

P.V.: And it's actually owned by Hertz?

O.J.S.: Hertz, yeah.

P.V.: Who's the primary driver on that? You?

O.J.S.: I drive it, the housekeeper drives it, you know, it's kind of a . . .

P.V.: All-purpose type vehicle?

O.J.S.: All-purpose, yeah. It's the only one that my insurance will allow me to let anyone else drive.

P.V.: Okay.

T.L.: When you drive it, where do you park it at home? Where it is now, it was in the street or something?

O.J.S.: I always park it on the street.

T.L.: You never take it in the . . . ?

O.J.S.: Oh, rarely. I mean, I'll bring it in and switch the stuff, you know, and stuff like that. I did that yesterday, you know.

T.L.: When did you last drive it?

O.J.S.: Yesterday.

P.V.: What time yesterday?

O.J.S.: In the morning, in the afternoon.

P.V.: Okay, you left her, you're saying, about six-thirty or seven, or she left the recital?

O.J.S.: Yeah.

P.V.: And you spoke with her parents?

O.J.S.: Yeah, we were just sitting there talking.

P.V.: What time did you leave the recital?

O.J.S.: Right about that time. We were all leaving. We were all leaving then. Her mother said something about me joining them for dinner and I said no thanks.

P.V.: Where did you go from there, O.J.?

O.J.S.: Ah, home, home for awhile, got my car for awhile, tried to find my girlfriend for awhile, came back to the house.

P.V.: Who was home when you got home?

O.J.S.: Kato.

P.V.: Kato? Anybody else? Was your daughter there, Arnelle?

O.J.S.: No.

P.V.: Isn't that her name, Arnelle?

O.J.S.: Arnelle, yeah.

P.V.: So what time do you think you got back home, actually physically got home?

O.J.S.: Seven-something.

P.V.: Seven-something? And then you left, and . . .

O.J.S.: Yeah, I'm trying to think, did I leave? You know I'm always . . . I had to run and get my daughter some flowers. I was actually doing the recital, so I rushed and got her some flowers, and I came home, and then I called Paula as I was going to her house, and Paula wasn't home.

P.V.: Paula is your girlfriend?

O.J.S.: Girlfriend, yeah.

P.V.: Paula who?

O.J.S.: Barbieri.

P.V.: Could you spell that for me?

O.J.S.: B-A-R-B-I-E-R-I.

P.V.: Do you know an address on her?

O.J.S.: No, she lives on Wilshire, but I think she's out of town.

P.V.: You got a phone number?

O.J.S.: Yeah, of course, [310] 470-3468. [The number is no longer in service.]

P.V.: So you didn't see her last night?

O.J.S.: No, we'd been to a big affair the night before, and then I came back home. I was basically at home. I mean, anytime I was . . . whatever time it took me to get to the recital and back, to get to the flower shop and back, I mean, that's the time I was out of the house.

P.V.: Were you scheduled to play golf this morning, some place?

O.J.S.: In Chicago.

P.V.: What kind of a tournament was it?

O.J.S.: Ah, it was Hertz, with special clients.

P.V.: Oh, okay. What time did you leave last night, leave the house?

O.J.S.: To go to the airport?

P.V.: Mmm hmm.

O.J.S.: About . . . the limo was supposed to be there at ten forty-five. Normally, they get there a little earlier. I was rushing around, somewhere between there and eleven.

P.V.: So approximately ten forty-five to eleven?

O.J.S.: Eleven o'clock, yeah, somewhere in that area.

P.V.: And you went by limo?

O.J.S.: Yeah.

P.V.: Who's the limo service?

O.J.S.: Ah, you have to ask my office.

T.L.: Did you converse with the driver at all? Did you talk to him?

O.J.S.: No, he was a new driver. Normally, I have a regular driver I drive with and converse. No, just about rushing to the airport, about how I live my live on airplanes, and hotels, that type of thing.

T.L.: What time did your plane leave?

O.J.S.: Ah, eleven forty-five the flight took off.

P.V.: What airline was it?

O.J.S.: American.

P.V.: American? And it was eleven forty-five to Chicago?

O.J.S.: Chicago.

T.L.: So yesterday you did drive the white Bronco?

O.J.S.: Mmm hmm.

T.L.: And where did you park it when you brought it home?

O.J.S.: Ah, the first time probably by the mailbox. I'm trying to think, or did I bring it in the driveway? Normally, I will park it by the mailbox, sometimes . . .

T.L.: On Ashford, or Ashland?

O.J.S.: On Ashford, yeah.

T.L.: Where did you park yesterday for the last time, do you remember?

O.J.S.: Right where it is.

T.L.: Where it is now?

O.J.S.: Yeah.

T.L.: Where, on . . . ?

O.J.S.: Right on the street there.

T.L.: On Ashford?

O.J.S.: No, on Rockingham.

T.L.: You parked it there?

O.J.S.: Yes.

T.L.: About what time was that?

O.J.S.: Eight-something, seven . . . eight, nine o'clock, I don't know, right in that area.

T.L.: Did you take it to the recital?

O.J.S.: No.

T.L.: What time was the recital?

O.J.S.: Over at about six-thirty. Like I said, I came home, I got my car, I was going to see my girlfriend. I was calling her, and she wasn't around.

T.L.: So you drove the, you came home in the Rolls, and then you got in the Bronco?

O.J.S.: In the Bronco 'cause my phone was in the Bronco. And because it's a Bronco. It's a Bronco, it's what I drive, you know. I'd rather drive it than any other car. And, you know, as I was going over there I called her a couple of times, and she wasn't there, and I left a message, and then I checked my messages, and there were no messages. She wasn't there, and she may have to leave town. Then I came back and ended up sittin with Kato.

T.L.: Okay. What time was this again that you parked the Bronco?

O.J.S.: Eight-something, maybe. He hadn't done a Jacuzzi, we had . . . went and got a burger, and I'd come home and kind of leisurely got ready to go. I mean we'd done a few things.

T.L.: You weren't in a hurry when you came back with the Bronco?

O.J.S.: No.

T.L.: The reason I ask you, the car was parked kind of at a funny angle, stuck out in the street.

O.J.S.: Well, it's parked because . . . I don't know if it's a funny angle or what. It's parked because when I was hustling at the end of the day to get all my stuff, and I was getting my phone and everything off it, when I just pulled it out of the gate there, it's like, it's a tight turn.

T.L.: So you had it inside the compound, then?

O.J.S.: Yeah.

T.L.: Oh, okay.

O.J.S.: I brought it inside the compound to get my stuff out of it, and then I put it out, and I'd run back inside the gate before the gate closes.

P.V.: O.J., what's your office phone number?

O.J.S.: 820-5702 [This is not the current number.]

P.V.: And is that area code 310?

O.J.S.: Yes.

P.V.: *How did you get the injury on your hand?*

O.J.S.: *I don't know.* The first time, when I was in Chicago and all, but at the house I was just running around.

P.V.: How did you do it in Chicago?

O.J.S.: I broke a glass. One of you guys had just called me, and I was in the bathroom, and I just went bonkers for a little bit.

T.L.: Is that how you cut it?

O.J.S.: Mmm, it was cut before, but I think I just opened it again, I'm not sure.

T.L.: Do you recall bleeding at all in your truck, in the Bronco?

O.J.S.: *I recall bleeding at my house, and then I went to the Bronco.* The last thing I did before I left, when I was rushing, was went and got my phone out of the Bronco.

T.L.: Mmm hmm. Where's the phone now?

O.J.S.: In my bag.

T.L.: You have it?

O.J.S.: In that black bag.

T.L.: You brought a bag with you here?

O.J.S.: Yeah, it's . . .

T.L.: So do you recall bleeding at all?

O.J.S.: Yeah, I mean, I knew I was bleeding, but it was no big deal. I bleed all the time. I play golf and stuff, so there's always something, nicks and stuff, here and there.

T.L.: So did you do anything? When did you put the Band-Aid on it?

O.J.S.: Actually, I asked the girl this morning for it.

T.L.: And she got it?

O.J.S.: Yeah, 'cause last night with Kato, when I was leaving, he was saying something to me, and I was rushing to get my phone, and I put a little thing on it, and it stopped.

P.V.: Do you have the keys to that Bronco?

O.J.S.: Yeah.

P.V.: Okay. We've impounded the Bronco. I don't know if you know that or not.

O.J.S.: No.

P.V.: Take a look at it. Other than you, who's the last person to drive it?

O.J.S.: Probably Gigi. When I'm out of town, I don't know who drives the car, maybe my daughter, maybe Kato.

P.V.: The keys are available?

O.J.S.: I leave the keys there, you know, when Gigi's there, because sometimes she needs it, or Gigi was off and wasn't coming back until today, and I was coming back tonight.

P.V.: So you don't mind if she uses it, or . . . ?

O.J.S.: This is the only one I can let her use. When she doesn't have her car, 'cause sometimes her husband takes her car, I let her use the car.

T.L.: When was the last time you were at Nicole's house?

O.J.S.: I don't go in, I won't go in her house. I haven't been in her house in a week, maybe five days. I go to her house a lot. I mean, I'm always dropping the kids off, picking the kids up, fooling around with the dog, you know.

P.V.: How does that usually work? Do you drop them at the porch, or do you go in with them?

O.J.S.: No, I don't go in the house.

P.V.: Is there a kind of gate out front?

O.J.S.: Yeah.

P.V.: But you never go inside the house?

O.J.S.: Up until five days, six days ago, I haven't been in the house. Once I started seeing Paula again, I kind of avoid Nicole.

P.V.: Is Nicole seeing anybody else that you . . . ?

O.J.S.: I have no idea. I really have absolutely no idea. I don't ask her, I don't know. Her and her girlfriends, they go out, you know, they've got some things going on right now with her girlfriends, so I'm assuming something's happening because one of the girlfriends is having a big problem with her husband, because she's always saying she's with Nicole until three or four in the morning. She's not. You know, Nicole tells me she leaves her at one-thirty or two or two-thirty, and the girl doesn't get home until five, and she only lives a few blocks away.

P.V.: Something's going on, huh?

T.L.: Do you know where they went, the family, for dinner last night?

O.J.S.: No. Well, no, I didn't ask.

T.L.: I just thought maybe there's a regular place that they go.

O.J.S.: No. If I was with them, we'd go to Toscano. I mean, not Toscano, Poponi's.

P.V.: You haven't had any problems with her lately, have you, O.J.?

O.J.S.: I always have problems with her, you know. Our relationship has been a problem relationship. Probably lately for me, and I say this only because I said it to Ron yesterday at the — Ron Fishman, whose wife is Cora — at the dance recital, when he came up to me and went "Oooh, boy, what's going on?" And everybody was beefing with everybody. And I said, "Well, I'm just glad I'm out of the mix." You know, because I was like dealing with him and his problems with his wife and Nicole and evidently some new problems that a guy named Christian was having with his girl and he was staying at Nicole's house, and something was going on, but I don't think it's pertinent to this.

P.V.: Did Nicole have words with you last night?

O.J.S.: Pardon me?

P.V.: Did Nicole have words with you last night?

O.J.S.: No, not at all.

P.V.: Did you talk to her last night?

O.J.S.: To ask to speak to my daughter, to congratulate my daughter, and everything.

P.V.: But you didn't have a conversation with her?

O.J.S.: No, no.

P.V.: What were you wearing last night, O.J.?

O.J.S.: What I wore, I wore on the golf course yesterday, some of these kind of pants, some of these kind of pants, I mean I changed different for the whatever it was. I just had on some . . .

P.V.: Just these black pants.

O.J.S.: Just these . . . they're called Bugle Boy

P.V.: These aren't the pants?

O.J.S.: No.

P.V.: Where are the pants that you wore?

O.J.S.: They're hanging in my closet.

P.V.: These are washable, right? You just throw them in the laundry?

O.J.S.: Yeah, I got a hundred pair. They give them to me free, Bugle Boy, so I've got a bunch of them.

P.V.: Do you recall coming home and hanging them up, or . . . ?

O.J.S.: I always hang up my clothes. I mean it's rare that I don't hang up my clothes unless I'm laying them in my bathroom for her to do something with them. But those are the only things I don't hang up. But when you play golf, you don't necessarily dirty pants.

T.L.: What kind of shoes were you wearing?

O.J.S.: Tennis shoes.

T.L.: Tennis shoes? Do you know what kind?

O.J.S.: Probably Reebok, that's all I wear.

T.L.: Are they at home, too?

O.J.S.: Yeah.

T.L.: Was this supposed to be a short trip to Chicago, so you didn't take a whole lot?

O.J.S.: Yeah, I was coming back today.

T.L.: Just overnight?

O.J.S.: Yeah.

P.V.: That's a hectic schedule, drive back here to play golf and come back.

O.J.S.: Yeah, but I do it all the time.

P.V.: Do you?

O.J.S.: Yeah. That's what I was complaining with the driver about, you know, about my whole life is on and off airplanes.

P.V.: O.J., we've got sort of a problem.

O.J.S.: Mmm hmm.

P.V.: *We've got some blood on and in your car, we've got some blood at your house, and it's sort of a problem.*

O.J.S.: Well, take my blood test.

T.L.: Well, we'd like to do that. *We've got, of course, the cut on your finger that you aren't real clear on. Do you recall having that cut on your finger the last time you were at Nicole's house?*

O.J.S.: *A week ago?*

T.L.: *Yeah.*

O.J.S.: *No. It was last night.*

T.L.: *Okay, so last night you cut it?*

P.V.: *Somewhere after the dance recital?*

O.J.S.: *Somewhere when I was rushing to get out of my house.*

P.V.: *Okay, after the recital?*

O.J.S.: *Yeah.*

P.V.: *What do you think happened? Do you have any idea?*

O.J.S.: *I have no idea, man.* You guys haven't told me anything. I have no idea. When you said to me that my daughter had said something to me today that somebody might have been involved, I have absolutely no idea what happened. I don't know how, why or what. But you guys haven't told me anything. Every time I ask you guys, you say you're going to tell me in a bit.

P.V.: Well, we don't know a lot of the answers to these questions yet ourselves, O.J., okay?

O.J.S.: I've got a bunch of guns, guns all over the place. You can take them, they're all there, I mean, you can see them. I keep them in my car for an incident that happened a month ago that my in-laws, my wife and everybody knows about that.

P.V.: What was that?

O.J.S.: Going down to . . . and cops down there know about it because I've told two marshals about it. At a mall, I was going down for a christening, and I had just left and it was like three-thirty in the morning and I'm in a lane, and also the car in front of me is going real slow, and I'm slowing down 'cause I figure he sees a cop, 'cause we were all going pretty fast and I'm going to change lanes, but there's a car next to me, and I can't change lanes. Then that goes for awhile, and I'm going to slow down and go around him, but the car butts up to me, and I'm like caught between three cars. They were Oriental guys, and they were not letting me go anywhere. And finally I went on the shoulder, and I sped up, and then I held my phone up so they could see the light part of it, you know, 'cause I have tinted windows, and they kind of scattered, and I chased one of them for awhile to make him think I was chasing him before I took off.

T.L.: Were you in the Bronco?

O.J.S.: No.

T.L.: What were you driving?

O.J.S.: My Bentley. It has tinted windows and all, so I figured they thought they had a nice little touch.

T.L.: Did you think they were trying to rip you off?

O.J.S.: Definitely, they were. And then the next thing, you know, Nicole and I went home. At four in the morning I got there to Laguna, and when we woke up, I told her about it, and told her parents about it, told everybody about it, you know? And when I saw two marshals at a mall I walked up and told them about it.

P.V.: What did they do, make a report on it?

O.J.S.: They didn't know nothing. I mean, they'll remember me and remember I told them.

P.V.: Did Nicole mention that she'd been getting any threats lately to you? Anything she was concerned about or the kids' safety?

O.J.S.: To her?

P.V.: Yes.

O.J.S.: From?

P.V.: From anybody?

O.J.S.: No, not at all.

P.V.: Was she very security-conscious? Did she keep that house locked up?

O.J.S.: Very.

P.V.: The intercom didn't work apparently, right?

O.J.S.: I thought it worked.

P.V.: Oh, okay. Does the electronic buzzer work?

O.J.S.: The electronic buzzer works to let people in.

P.V.: Did you ever park in the rear when you go over there?

O.J.S.: Most of the time.

P.V.: You do park in the rear?

O.J.S.: Most times when I'm taking the kids there, I come right into the driveway, blow the horn, and she, or a lot of times the housekeeper, either the housekeeper opens or they'll keep a garage door open up on the top of the thing, you know, but that's when I'm dropping the kids off, and I'm not going in, and some times I go to the front because the kids have to hit the buzzer and stuff.

P.V.: Did you say before that up until about three weeks ago you guys were going out again and trying to . . . ?

O.J.S.: No, we'd been going out for about a year, and then the last five months it hadn't been working so we tried various things to see if we can make it work. We started trying to date and that wasn't working, and so, you know, we just said the hell with it, you know, we just said the hell with it, you know.

P.V.: And that was about three weeks ago?

O.J.S.: Yeah, about three weeks ago.

P.V.: So you were seeing her up to that point?

O.J.S.: It's, to say I was seeing her, yeah, I mean yeah, yeah it was a done deal, it just wasn't happening. I mean, I was gone. I mean, I was in San Juan doing a film, and I don't think we had sex since I've been back from San Juan, and that was like two months ago. So it's been like . . . for the kids we tried to do things together. We didn't go out together, you know, we didn't really date each other. Then we decided let's try to date each other. We went out one night, and it just didn't work.

P.V.: When you say it didn't work, what do you mean?

O.J.S.: Ah, the night we went out it was fun. Then the next night we went out it was actually when I was down in Laguna, and she didn't want to go out. And I said, "well, let's go out 'cause I came all the way down here to go out," and we kind of had a beef. And it just didn't work after that, you know? We were only trying to date to see if we could bring romance back into our relationship. We just said, let's treat each other like boyfriend and girlfriend instead of, you know, like seventeen-year-old married people. I mean, seventeen years together, whatever that is.

P.V.: How long were you together?

O.J.S.: Seventeen years.

P.V.: Seventeen years. Did you ever hit her, O.J.?

O.J.S.: Ah, one night we had a fight. We had a fight and she hit me. And they never took my statement, they never wanted to hear my side and they never wanted to hear the housekeeper's side. Nicole was drunk. She did her thing, she started tearing up my house, you know? And I didn't punch her or anything, but I . . .

P.V.: Slapped her a couple of times?

O.J.S.: No, no, I wrestled her, is what I did. I didn't slap her at all. I mean, Nicole's a strong girl. She's a . . . one of the most conditioned women. Since that period of time, she's hit me a few times, but I've never touched her after that and I'm telling you, it's five, six years ago.

P.V.: What's her birthdate?

O.J.S.: May 19th.

P.V.: Did you get together with her on her birthday?

O.J.S.: Yeah, her and I and the kids, I believe.

P.V.: Did you give her a gift?

O.J.S.: I gave her a gift.

P.V.: What'd you give her?

O.J.S.: I gave her either a bracelet or the earrings.

P.V.: Did she keep them or . . . ?

O.J.S.: Oh, no, when we split she gave me both the earrings and the bracelet back. I bought her a very nice bracelet, I don't know if it was Mother's Day or her birthday, and I bought her the earrings for the other thing, and when we split, and it's a credit to her, she felt that it wasn't right that she had it, and I said good, because I want them back.

P.V.: Was that the very day of her birthday, May 19th, or was it a few days later.

O.J.S.: What do you mean?

P.V.: You gave it to her on the 19th of May, her birthday, right, this bracelet?

O.J.S.: I may have given her the earrings. No, the bracelet. May 19th. When was Mother's Day?

P.V.: Mother's Day was around that . . .

O.J.S.: No, it was probably her birthday, yes.

P.V.: And did she return it the same day?

O.J.S.: Oh, no, she . . . I'm in a funny place here on this, all right? She returned it—both of them—three weeks ago or so, because when I say I'm in a funny place on this it was because I gave it to my girlfriend and told her it was for her and that was three weeks ago. I told her I bought it for her. You know? What am I going to do with it?

T.L.: Did Mr. Weitzman, your attorney, talk to you anything about this polygraph we brought up before? What are your thoughts on that?

O.J.S.: Should I talk about my thoughts on that? I'm sure eventually I'll do it, but it's like I've got some weird thoughts now. I've had weird thoughts . . . you know when you've been with a person for seventeen years, you think everything. I've got to understand what this thing is. If it's true blue, I don't mind doing it.

T.L.: Well, you're not compelled at all to take this, number one, and number two, I don't know if Mr. Weitzman explained it to you—this goes to the exclusion of someone as much as to the inclusion so we can eliminate people. And just to get things straight . . .

O.J.S.: But does it work for elimination?

T.L.: Oh, yes. We use it for elimination more than anything.

O.J.S.: Well, I'll talk to him about it.

T.L.: Understand, the reason we're talking to you is because you're the ex-husband.

O.J.S.: I know I'm the number one target, and now you tell me I've got blood all over the place.

T.L.: *Well, there's blood in your house and in the driveway, and we've got a search warrant, and we're going to go get the blood. We found some in your house. Is that your blood that's there?*

O.J.S.: *If it's dripped, it's what I dripped running around trying to leave.*

T.L.: *Last night?*

O.J.S.: *Yeah*, and I wasn't aware that it was . . . I was aware that I . . . you know I was trying to get out of the house, I didn't even pay any attention to it. I saw it when I was in the kitchen, and I grabbed a napkin or something, and that was it. I didn't think about it after that.

P.V.: That was last night after you got home from the recital, when you were rushing?

O.J.S.: That was last night when I was . . . I don't know what I was, I was in the car getting my junk out of the car. I was in the house throwing hangers and stuff in my suitcase. I was doing my little crazy what I do, I mean, I do it everywhere. Anybody who has ever picked me up says that O.J.'s a whirlwind. He's running, he's grabbing things, and that's what I was doing.

P.V.: Well, I'm going to step out and I'm going to get a photographer to come down and photograph your hand there. And then here pretty soon we're going to take you downstairs and get some blood from you. Okay? I'll be right back.

T.L.: So it was about five days ago you last saw Nicole? Was it at the house?

O.J.S.: Okay, the last time I saw Nicole, physically saw Nicole, I saw her obviously last night. The time before, I'm trying to think. I went to Washington, D.C., so I didn't see her, so I'm trying to think. I haven't seen her since I went to Washington. I went to Washington—what's the day today?

T.L.: Today's Monday, the 13th of June.

O.J.S.: Okay, I went to Washington on maybe Wednesday. Thursday I think I was in . . . Thursday I was in Connecticut, then Long Island Thursday afternoon and all of Friday. I got home Friday night, Friday afternoon, I played, you know . . . Paula picked me up at the airport. I played golf Saturday, and when I came home I think my son was there. So I did something with my son. I don't think I saw Nicole at all then. And then I went to a big affair with Paula Saturday night, and I got up and played golf Sunday, which pissed Paula off, and I saw Nicole at . . . it was about a week before, I saw her at the . . .

T.L.: Okay, the last time you saw Nicole, was that at her house?

O.J.S.: I don't remember. I wasn't in her house, so it couldn't have been at her house, so it was, you know, I don't physically remember the last time I saw her. I may have seen her even jogging one day.

T.L.: Let me get this straight. You've never physically been inside the house?

O.J.S.: Not in the last week.

T.L.: Ever. I mean, how long has she lived there? About six months?

O.J.S.: Oh, Christ, I've slept at the house many, many, many times, you know? I've done everything at the house, you know? I'm just saying . . . you're talking in the last week or so.

T.L.: Well, whatever. Six months she's lived there?

O.J.S.: I don't know. Roughly. I was at her house maybe two weeks ago, ten days ago. One night her and I had a long talk, you know, about how can we make it better for the kids, and I told her we'd do things better. And, okay, I can almost say when that was. That was when I, I don't know, it was about ten days ago. And then we . . . the next day I had her have her dog do a flea bath or something with me. Oh, I'll tell you, I did see her one day. One day I went . . . I don't know if this was the early part of last week, I went 'cause my son had to go and get something, and he ran in, and she came to the gate, and the dog ran out, and her friend Faye and I went looking for the dog. That may have been a week ago, I don't know.

T.L.: (To Vannatter) Got a photographer coming?

P.V.: No, we're going to take him up there.

T.L.: We're ready to terminate this at 14:07.

Appendix B

Farewell Letter of O. J. Simpson

On June 17, 1994, Simpson was staying at the home of his friend Robert Kardashian, located in the upper-middle-class San Fernando Valley community of Encino. That day, Robert Shapiro, Simpson's attorney, had arranged with the Los Angeles Police Department to have Simpson voluntarily turn himself in at 11:00 a.m. at Parker Center, LAPD headquarters, on charges of first-degree murder which had been filed against him by the Los Angeles County District Attorney's Office. When Simpson did not show up by 11:00 a.m., the LAPD called Shapiro and informed him that officers would come out and take Simpson into custody. But when they arrived after noon, Simpson and his friend Al Cowlings had already departed in Cowlings's Ford Bronco (the same kind of vehicle, even in year and color, as Simpson's Bronco), leading eventually to the famous slow-speed chase. It has been reported many times that the following letter, printed in ink by Simpson, was written by him at Kardashian's home that morning just before he and Cowlings departed. However, it should be noted that it is dated June 15, 1994, two days earlier. This is relevant, since if Simpson was planning to escape on June 17, 1994, he wasn't at the same time contemplating suicide. Although Simpson wrote the "O" in "O.J." with a happy face, even his lawyer, Shapiro, said he had little doubt it was a suicide note.

To Whom It May Concern: 6/15/94

First, everyone understand I had nothing to do with Nicole's murder. I
loved her, always have and always will. If we had a problem, it's because I
loved her so much.

Recently we came to the understanding that for now we were not right
for each other, at least not for now. Despite our love, we were different
and that's why we mutually agreed to go our separate ways.

It was tough splitting for a second time but we both knew it was for the
best. Inside I had no doubt that in the future we would be close friends or
more. Unlike what has been written in the press, Nicole and I had a great
relationship for most of our lives together. Like all long-term relationships, we had a few downs and ups.

I took the heat New Year's 1989 because that was what I was supposed
to do. I did not plead no contest for any other reason but to protect our
privacy and was advised it would end the press hype.

I don't want to belabor knocking the press, but I can't believe what is
being said. Most of it is totally made up. I know you have a job to do, but
as a last wish, please, please leave my children in peace. Their lives will
be tough enough.

I want to send my love and thanks to all my friends. I'm sorry I can't
name every one of you, especially A. C. Man, thanks for being in my life.
The support and friendship I received from so many: Wayne Hughes,
Lewis Markes, Frank Olson, Mark Packer, Bobby Kardashian. I wish we
had spent more time together in recent years. My golfing buddies: Hoss,
Alan Austin, Mike Craig, Bender, Wyler, Sandy, Jay, and Donnie. Thanks
for the fun.

All my teammates over the years—Reggie, you were the soul of my pro
career. Ahmad, I never stopped being proud of you. Marcus, you've got a
great lady in Catherine. Don't mess it up. Bobby Chandler, thanks for
always being there. Skip, and Kathy, I love you guys. Without you I never
would have made it through this far.

Marguerite, thanks for the early years. We had some fun. Paula, what
can I say? You are special. I'm sorry I'm not going to have—we're not
going to have—our chance. God brought you to me, I now see. As I leave,
you'll be in my thoughts.

I think of my life and feel I've done most of the right things. So why did
I end up like this? I can't go on. No matter what the outcome, people will
look and point. I can't take that. I can't subject my children to that. This
way, they can move on and go on with their lives.

Please, if I've done anything worthwhile in my life, let my kids live in peace from you, the press.

I've had a good life. I'm proud of how I lived. My mama taught me to do unto others. I treated people the way I wanted to be treated. I've always tried to be up and helpful, so why is this happening.

I'm sorry for the Goldman family. I know how much it hurts.

Nicole and I had a good life together. All this press talk about a rocky relationship was no more than what every long-term relationship experiences. All her friends will confirm that I have been totally loving and understanding of what she's been going through.

At times I have felt like a battered husband or boyfriend, but I loved her. Make that clear to everyone. And I would take whatever it took to make it work.

Don't feel sorry for me. I've had a great life, great friends. Please think of the real O.J. and not this lost person. Thanks for making my life special. I hope I helped yours.

Peace and love.

O.J.

Appendix C

Blood Evidence

One of the myths the defense has sought to propagate in the Simpson case, even after the trial, is that there was very little of Simpson's blood found in his car and on his Rockingham estate. But the record proves the falsity of this allegation. Even excluding the inevitable blood drops that were not discovered, and the blood found on the glove and socks, as well as the fact that the LAPD criminalists did not collect blood from all of the blood drops and stains (collecting "representative samples" is typical), forty-one blood drops and stains were collected.

Dennis Fung told me that thirty were collected from the Bronco (Fung said there were "easily another twenty lighter blood stains we did not collect inside the Bronco"), most of which were Simpson's blood, some that of the two victims. All the other blood was Simpson's. There was one blood drop behind the Bronco on the street (Rockingham), one on the driveway just inside the Rockingham gate, three more on the driveway leading to the front door of Simpson's residence (there were three other blood drops on the driveway which were not collected), five on the floor of the foyer (the LAPD criminalists found and collected three, and Dr. Lee saw three others, one of which was believed to be a splatter from one of the three the LAPD had collected), and one on the bathroom floor.

Not all of these samples of blood were subjected to DNA tests. A total of forty-five samples of blood from all places and sources (including Bundy) were tested for DNA.

Another myth the defense has tried to sell is that the killer would have been, as Cochran argued to the jury, "covered with blood," and therefore there should have been much more blood in the Bronco, etc., if Simpson were the killer. But this argument doesn't hold up. The killer's bloody shoe prints had already faded out by the time he reached the alleyway at Bundy. And when a person is stabbed or cut in the front of his or her body, the blood of the victim is only likely to get on the assailant if the assailant is in front of the victim, an artery as opposed to a vein is severed or punctured (veins, such as the jugular vein of Ron Goldman which was severed, do not spurt blood; only arteries do), and there is no clothing covering the body in the vicinity of the wound. None of the stabbings of the two victims in this case met all three of these requirements. Both of Nicole's carotid arteries were, indeed, severed, and since there was no clothing covering her neck there may have been spurting of blood. But the slash wound to Nicole's neck that severed the arteries was from left to right, and it was the consensus of Dr. Lak, which Dr. Baden did not dispute, that the killer was behind Nicole when he slashed her throat. There *were* "two perforating, one-half inch wounds" to Goldman's aorta, but the aorta is an artery that doesn't spurt its blood because it is sealed off within the body. Moreover, because of the paucity of blood in the aorta region of Goldman's body, Dr. Lak concluded that the two stab wounds to the aorta were among the last to Goldman, when little blood would have remained. And, of course, even if there had been spurting of blood from these two wounds to the aorta, clothing covers this area of the body. Most stab wounds to the body merely cause internal bleeding and bleeding on the surface of the skin. Although in killing the two victims, the killer would likely have gotten some blood on him, particularly since it is believed there was a brief struggle with Ron Goldman, it is equally unlikely he was "covered with blood."

Additionally, as Marcia Clark pointed out in her summation, under no circumstances would the killer be likely to "get any blood on his back, which is where he is going to be in contact with the seat [of the Bronco, leaving blood]." Finally, let's not forget that besides the two blood spots on the exterior of the driver's door to the Bronco, 28 other blood spots and stains were collected from inside the Bronco (including from the steering wheel, instrument panel, center console, right front edge of the driver's seat, interior of driver's door, interior of driver's side wall, carpet on passenger side, etc.), not just one or two.

*   *   *

Barry Scheck's main theory, the crown jewel in his tiara of nonsense upon which he based most of his cross-contamination argument, was that Collin Yamauchi, the LAPD criminalist who conducted initial DNA tests at the LAPD crime lab on the evidence blood, testified on cross-examination that in opening up the vial of Simpson's reference blood, a small amount of the blood got on the latex glove on his left hand. But Yamauchi testified that he immediately discarded both his left and right gloves in a nearby receptacle and put on a new pair. Moreover, at the time this happened, all of the swatches of evidence blood were on top of a table ten to fifteen feet away, and the swatches of blood were inside paper bindles (wrappers) which were themselves enclosed within coin envelopes. So, as Marcia Clark argued, unless there is such a thing as "flying DNA," which even the defense didn't contend, cross-contamination could not have taken place.

Yamauchi explained to me that "when you take the rubber cap off the vial — it's like a cork in a bottle — nine times out of ten you get a little blood on the paper Kimwipe that's surrounding the cap, and sometimes it soaks through to your glove." He said that's what happened in this case. When I asked Yamauchi to estimate the size of the blood deposit on his glove, he said it was just "a tiny dot of blood, about one-eighth of an inch in diameter." Now listen to Scheck's argument on this point in his summation to the jury: "We now know there was a *spillage* of blood there. Now, that is extraordinarily significant. Because there's plenty of high molecular weight DNA in the smallest drop if you get it on your gloves or if you don't change the gloves. *And frankly, I think there's no reason to believe he did* [note that there would have been no way for Scheck to even know about the blood getting on Yamauchi's glove if Yamauchi had not been honest enough to tell him, yet Scheck distrusts Yamauchi when Yamauchi told him he changed his gloves, which is automatic, routine behavior for criminalists in such situations], and the evidence samples *could* have then become contaminated."

The question is, why wasn't the fact that Yamauchi got blood on his left glove brought out by the prosecution? Instead, it came out on cross-examination. And other than Yamauchi's testimony that he got "a little blood" on his glove, the prosecutor never asked Yamauchi just how little. "Little" can mean a lot of things. "One-eighth of an inch in diameter" would have been a lot better for the prosecution in the jury's eyes. If the prosecution had matter-of-factly brought out all of this on *direct examination*, I doubt very much that Scheck would have been able to make this completely insignificant incident the centerpiece of his cross-contamination argument.

*   *   *

The degradation of the LAPD blood samples from the five blood drops at the Bundy murder scene is believed to have occurred when the cotton swatches which soaked up the blood were placed inside sealed plastic bags and left to sit for hours (at Bundy and later at Simpson's Rockingham estate) on a hot summer day (June 13, 1994) inside the stifling interior of the LAPD crime scene truck. The truck's refrigeration unit was continually breaking down, and was therefore not used to store the blood. Heat and moisture (the swatches absorb distilled water before they are used) within the sealed plastic bags, alone, cause DNA degradation, and also produce a fertile environment for the growth of bacteria, which is a further, main cause of degradation.

The defense argued that the *lack* of degradation of the three stains of blood on the back gate, and the fact that they weren't collected on June 13, 1994 (the day after the murders) meant they must have been planted by the LAPD conspirators closer to the time they were collected on July 3, 1994. But unlike the five blood drops, when the three stains were collected by LAPD criminalist Dennis Fung on July 3, they were immediately brought downtown and refrigerated.

Another reason for the lack of degradation of the back gate blood is that DNA would break down much faster on the terra cotta walkway at Bundy where the blood drops were found than on the far less absorbent paint of the rear gate. Although blood of the victims on the front gate, also on top of paint, *had* degraded, the probable explanation is that that blood *was* collected on June 13, and together with the swatches from the five blood drops, was stored for hours in the hot interior of the crime truck.

As far as the defense argument that the fact that Fung collected the blood on July 3 proves it was not there at the time of the murders on June 12, several LAPD officers, including Lange, Phillips, Vannatter, Riske, and Riske's partner, Officer Terrazas, saw the blood on the gate when they arrived at the murder scene in the early-morning hours of the 13th, and Lange testified he even told Fung to collect it. But the crime scene was awash in blood, Fung was very busy, and he himself never saw the blood there, nor can he recall Lange's directing his attention to it. A perfectly normal and common slipup. Moreover, an LAPD photograph taken on June 13, 1994, of the inside of the gate *does* show one of the three stains which turned out to be Simpson's blood. The photo did not pick up the second stain on the inside of the gate, and no photo of the outside of the gate, where the third stain was, was taken. It should be additionally noted that by the evening of June 16, which was over two weeks *before* samples from the three bloodstains on the gate were collected on July 3 by Fung, Collin Yamauchi's preliminary DNA testing of the Bundy blood drops leading away from the victims' bodies showed them to be consistent with Simpson's blood. So there was no need for the LAPD to plant any of Simpson's blood on the gate.

*   *   *

Many have wondered why only one drop of blood was found in Simpson's bathroom (on the floor between the sink and the shower), and why no blood was found in the area of Simpson's estate where the bloody glove was found. A phenolphthalein test, called a "presumptive" test for blood, was conducted on three locations at Simpson's Rockingham estate. In this test, distilled water is applied to a cotton swab and the swab is then applied to the area of interest. A drop of phenolphthalein, a reactive chemical, is then put on the swab. If the swab turns pink, it's called a "false positive" and no further tests are conducted. However, if it doesn't, then a drop of hydrogen peroxide is put on the swab to interact with the phenolphthalein. If the swab then turns pink immediately, this is positive for blood, although it doesn't distinguish between human and animal blood.

The LAPD criminalist who was in charge of collecting evidence at the crime scene and at Rockingham, Dennis Fung, conducted a phenolphthalein test on the drain area of the shower in Simpson's bathroom, as well as on the lip of the drain circle in the washbasin, because these are, of course, areas blood would flow through if one was washing blood off. *In both Simpson's shower and washbasin, there was a positive reaction for blood.* Unless Simpson gave an animal of his (I've been told he had a dog, a chow) a shower, and also bathed the animal in the washbasin a day before the murders or just after the murders before he left for Chicago, and unless the animal was also bleeding at the time, the phenolphthalein test was evidence that Simpson washed the blood off himself right after the murders (which common sense already told us).

Andrea Mazzola, Fung's assistant LAPD criminalist, also conducted a phenolphthalein test on a long, thick wire hanging over the narrow walkway or path running alongside the rear of the guest rooms at the Simpson estate between the air conditioner (jutting out from the outside wall of Kato Kaelin's room, the area from which Kaelin heard three loud thumps on the night of the murders) and where the bloody glove was found. She applied the swab to that area of the wire one would have to move aside with one's hands to proceed, and it too came up positive for blood. In none of the above three areas was there any visual amount of blood to collect for further conventional serology and/or DNA tests.

It should also be noted that defense forensic expert Henry Lee saw a red stain on the air conditioner itself during his examination of the area. He ran a presumptive test using ortholotuidine, another reactive chemical agent like phenolphthalein, and the report he prepared, a copy of which was provided to the prosecution, showed that the stain produced a positive for blood.

The jury never heard about the results of any of these presumptive tests, because Judge Ito had ruled that the results of all such tests in the case would be inadmissible at the trial. *Another* bad ruling by Ito. Although no one would quarrel with the position that the jury should not hear the results of presumptive tests from a place frequented by animals, it would seem that blood found, for instance, in the washbasin area of one's bathroom should have been evidence the jury was definitely entitled to hear, letting them give it whatever weight they thought it was entitled to.

As for the supposed absence of blood on the narrow walkway behind Kato Kaelin's guest house where the bloody glove was found, Fung told me, "The area is heavily foliaged with a large mass of leaves on the ground [see photo section]. We didn't even bother to check the leaves." (When Fuhrman found the glove, he did not touch or move it. Fung is the person who eventually picked it up, and he told me he didn't even bother to look for blood on the ground or leaves upon which the glove had been lying.) Andrea Mazzola told me the same thing. The "whole area," she said, "including the pathway, was covered with dry and discolored brownish and reddish leaves and twigs. It looked like no one had been back there for ages. We didn't get down on our hands and knees checking leaves." With blood already visible in Simpson's car, on the driveway, and in his house, it's understandable, knowing what Fung and Mazzola knew at the time, that they didn't start checking every leaf.

But at the trial, the jury received a totally different and incorrect message. On cross-examination of Fung, Barry Scheck asked him, "Along the walkway, you found no red [blood] stains?" Fung answered, "That's correct," and it was left at that. On redirect, instead of the prosecution clarifying the matter for the jury by establishing that the reason Fung never found any red stains is that he never really searched, the prosecutor never asked Fung any questions about the matter. (On redirect examination of Vannatter at the trial, after Shapiro, on cross, had asked Vannatter how much blood was found in the area behind the guest house and Vannatter replied, "None, none that I'm aware of," Darden asked

Vannatter if he, Vannatter, had checked the leaves for blood, and he said he had not. Vannatter, of course, is not the person whom the prosecutors should have asked that question. In the morning his main job was to prepare the affidavit to secure the search warrant, and he was at Parker Center with Lange almost all afternoon. Fung and Mazzola were the main LAPD representatives searching for, and collecting, blood evidence.) If the prosecution had elicited testimony from Fung and Mazzola that they did not examine the leaves for blood, it would have precluded a big argument of Cochran's.

Cochran told the jury in his summation that there was no blood found on the leaves (which implies there had been a search) in the subject area, and this, he argued, was strong evidence that it wasn't Simpson or anyone else who dropped the bloody glove on the pathway. Fuhrman had planted it there. And several jurors bought this argument. In *Madam Foreman*, Simpson jury foreperson Armanda Cooley writes, "Another [problem we had with the prosecution's case] was the glove found at Rockingham. Supposedly someone had come down the pathway along the side of the house, hit the side of the air conditioner, and made this noise that Kato heard, and dropped the glove. The question was, if the person—Mr. Simpson is about six feet—if he dropped the glove and it was so bloody, why wasn't there blood on anything else? If the glove hits the ground, surely some blood would stick to the leaves. We checked our notes and went over that." Juror Sheila Woods, on the *Today* Show, told Katie Couric that the most questionable piece of evidence in the case was "the Rockingham glove," because although the glove was moist and sticky when it was found, "There was no evidence of blood in that area."

"So if you believe the prosecution's theory [that Simpson ran into the air conditioner jutting into the dark pathway behind Kato Kaelin's guest house, causing the loud thumping sounds on the wall]," Cochran argued in his summation, "where's the blood back there, ladies and gentlemen? There's not one drop of blood. Where's the blood back there?" And later: "Where's the blood on the leaves around there? Their theory doesn't hold water. It doesn't make sense."

So the LAPD criminalists' not even searching for blood on the leaves was transformed, without any solid evidence to support it, into their looking for blood and not finding any. Near the end of Cochran's final summation, one of the questions he asked Clark to answer was: "Why was there no blood on the narrow walkway?"

Yet Clark and Darden, in their rebuttal, didn't address themselves to the question, and at no time in their opening and closing arguments did either one of them even say one word about the defense allegation that no blood had been found on the pathway behind Kato Kaelin's guest house. The prosecutorial incompetence was endless in the Simpson case.

*   *   *

Many references have been made by the Simpson prosecution, the media, even a book already in publication on the case, to a supposed partial bloody Bruno Magli shoe print in Nicole's blood on the carpet of the driver's side in Simpson's Bronco. If true, since we know the killer wore Bruno Magli shoes, this fact, all by itself, would prove the killer had been in Simpson's Bronco car on the night of the murders.

Marcia Clark argued to the jury: "On the driver's side of the floor mat of the Bronco there was a bloody imprint that [FBI agent William] Bodziak told you had characteristics consistent with the Bruno Magli shoe of that pattern." But Bodziak's actual testimony wasn't nearly as strong as Clark suggested. He testified that although there was an area of the bloody imprint "which could *possibly* have been a border of the [Bruno Magli] shoe, and there also is some little, what I call, squiggles or little "S" shapes which *might* represent the curved areas between the design elements [of the Bruno Magli Silga sole], they weren't clear enough or reliable enough to make *any* kind of a positive determination."

Bodziak told me, in fact, that not only couldn't he identify the bloody imprint on the driver's carpet as coming from the sole or heel of a Bruno Magli shoe, he couldn't even identify it as an imprint from a shoe sole or heel.

*   *   *

Everyone who followed the Simpson case knows that in addition to the defense's allegation that Fuhrman planted the glove, the other main contention of the defense in its conspiracy argument was that when Detective Vannatter (who didn't book Simpson's vial of reference blood when he received it from Thano Peratis at 2:30 p.m. on June 13, 1994) took the vial back to Rockingham that afternoon, it was for the purpose of sprinkling some of it (the allegedly missing 1.5 cc) in various incriminating places.

Vannatter testified that the reason he never booked the vial is that he knew Fung had all the evidence collected from Bundy and Rockingham (each piece of evidence being assigned a property item number) and he didn't know what item numbers Fung had already assigned to each item of evidence. Also, he didn't yet have a DR (Divisional Record) number to book the reference blood under, so he brought the vial directly to Fung to be booked at the same time as all the other evidence in the Property Division of the LAPD. Fung explained to me, "If Vannatter had booked the vial of blood it would have screwed up all my numbers. The vial would have been Item 1, but I had already assigned Item 1 to the bloodstain on the outside passenger door handle of the Bronco."

Lange told me that when he and Vannatter got the vial of Simpson's reference blood, although it would technically have been possible for them to get a DR number and book it, it would have been very unusual under the circumstances. He said they had only been on the case for a matter of hours at the time they withdrew Simpson's blood, they had to "deal with the media, brief LAPD brass, and so forth. Getting a DR number was the furthest thing from our mind. The DR number is nearly always gotten after the evidence is collected by the criminalists pursuant to the search warrant. So we decided to bring the vial directly to Fung. Phil and I left for Rockingham in separate vehicles."

Vannatter personally handed the vial, inside an eight-and-a-half-by-eleven-inch gray envelope (a blood collection envelope marked "LAPD refrigerated storage"), to Fung at Rockingham in the late afternoon of June 13. Fung looked inside the envelope and saw the vial, then wrote on the envelope, "Received from Vannatter on 6-13-94, at 1720 hours (5:20 p.m.)." Fung in turn put the envelope in a plastic bag and gave it to Mazzola to put inside the LAPD's crime scene processing truck. Fung said he never told Mazzola what was inside the bag and she just assumed it was another item of evidence, which of course it was. Not only does television color film show Vannatter arriving at Rockingham at 5:16 p.m. and carrying the gray envelope into Simpson's home, but a police video a minute or so later shows Fung, in the foyer of the home, holding the envelope. Television film then shows Mazzola carrying a plastic bag to the evidence van minutes later. Fung testified that at the time Vannatter showed up with the vial, he and Mazzola had *already* collected all the blood evidence at the Rockingham estate and were getting ready to leave. "Here, I got some more evidence for you," Fung told me he recalls Vannatter saying. Shortly thereafter, Fung and Mazzola left Rockingham, bringing the vial, along with all the other evidence, down to the lab at the Scientific Investigation Division (SID) of the LAPD, and after the detectives got a DR number the following day, Fung booked all the evidence with the Evidence Control Unit of SID at Piper Tech, about a mile from LAPD headquarters.

Much of the defense's cross-examination of Vannatter, Fung, and Mazzola dealt with the chain of custody of the vial of blood, the implication from all of the questions being that something amiss, sinister, and conspiratorial was going on, most probably that Vannatter had not given the vial to Fung, and instead he and his colleagues had used it to plant blood *that evening*.

And in Cochran's and Scheck's final arguments to the jury, although they never directly accused Vannatter of planting this blood, they both strongly suggested that's precisely what happened. For instance, Scheck argued to the jury: "I think there is something really wrong here. . . . Detective Vannatter is walking around with [the vial of blood] he should have sealed and he should have booked for three hours at least, unaccounted for. . . . Something is terribly wrong at the heart of this case. . . . If you can't trust the man who carried the blood, if you can't trust where this blood went, something is terribly wrong."

And Cochran asked rhetorically in his summation: "Vannatter could have booked that blood at Parker Center. Why is Vannatter carrying Mr. Simpson's blood out there to Rockingham? Why is he doing that? . . . Vannatter, the man who carries the blood, starts lying in this case from the very, very beginning. Remember these two phrases. Vannatter, the man who carries the blood. Fuhrman, the man who found the glove." And one of Cochran's questions at the conclusion of his summation which he asked Marcia Clark to answer in her rebuttal was: "For what purpose was Vannatter carrying Mr. Simpson's blood in his pocket for three hours and a distance of twenty-five miles instead of booking it down the hall at Parker Center?"

In posttrial interviews with the Simpson jurors as well as in the book by the three jurors, it is obvious that the prosecution failed to have Vannatter explain adequately to the jury why he brought the vial of blood back to Rockingham. The jurors made it very clear they found Vannatter's conduct with respect to the blood highly suspicious. Interviewing several jurors shortly after the verdict, the *Los Angeles Times* wrote: "They questioned why Detective Philip Vannatter would carry a vial of blood taken from Simpson at Parker Center back to Brentwood." Carrie Bess writes in *Madam Foreman*: "Vannatter said the reason he had the blood vial and brought it to Rockingham was due to the fact that he did not have a booking number. . . . Well, let me ask you this. Who would be the better person to get the booking number than the head investigator or the detective?"

Wouldn't you thereby think that Clark and Darden, in their arguments to the jury, would each (like their counterparts Cochran and Scheck) have a lot to say to counter this charge that went to the very heart of the defense's conspiracy allegation? That in the months since the defense leveled the charge, at least one of them would have thought about (and written down) what he was going to say to the jury about this defense charge? You know, things like Vannatter testified he handed the vial of Simpson's blood to Fung on the afternoon of June 13 as soon as he arrived on the premises, and Fung testified he received it from Vannatter. So to believe the sprinkling and planting argument we'd have to accept the completely unrealistic theory that Dennis Fung, the obviously decent young man who looks like the guy who walks onstage when the magician asks for volunteers, was one of *the* main conspirators who framed Simpson for the murders. That either he planted the blood himself, or he never got the vial from Vannatter and committed perjury when he testified Vannatter gave it to him. Arguments such as why would Vannatter take a vial of Simpson's blood back to Rockingham with the intent of planting the blood when he knew that an enormous swarm of media and reporters had already congregated at Rockingham, their cameras blanketing the premises, and even picking up, for the evening news, the movements of everyone walking around the estate? And that the blood could not have been planted in the evening either (as the defense was alleging), because a sizable contingent of the media remained at Bundy and Rockingham throughout the evening and night—that is, around the clock. Arguments such as if Vannatter were going to bring the vial of Simpson's blood back to Rockingham to plant some of it, why not conceal it inside his suit coat or pants? Why advertise to everyone that you're bringing something to the premises by carrying it there in a large envelope? Arguments such as reminding the jury that by the time Vannatter arrived at Rockingham, the Bronco, which was found to have Simpson's blood all over it, had *already* been removed from the premises, and all of the other blood evidence from Bundy and Rockingham had *already* been collected, so what was it that Vannatter and his co-conspirators had planted? And four or five other reasons why the defense argument makes no sense. For instance, if the prosecutors had introduced Simpson's statement to the jury, which they should have, why would Vannatter even feel there was any need to plant any of Simpson's blood at Rockingham? By the time he brought the vial to Rockingham, Simpson had already admitted to him and Lange several hours earlier (the tape-recorded statement being between 1:35 and 2:07 p.m.) that he had bled all over his Rockingham estate—in his Bronco and home, and on his driveway.

Unbelievably, in Clark's and Darden's opening and closing arguments, they never said one word, not one word between them, to knock down this core defense argument about Vannatter's bringing the vial of Simpson's blood back to Rockingham. They never once even touched on the issue. Once again, the lawyers for the people just took it on the chin without offering any defense or fighting back at all, seemingly telling the defense attorneys, "This courtroom is too small for the two of us, so we're leaving." Either they thought that by not mentioning the Vannatter vial problem it would somehow evaporate by itself into thin air, or their lack of preparation was so abysmally and shamefully poor (this is undoubtedly what happened) they never even bothered to jot down, at any time during the trial, that in their summations they obviously had to respond to this charge, and in a powerful way. You only have huge gaps in your argument like this when you've devoted virtually no time to its preparation. In any murder case, but particularly one where the prosecutors knew millions of people were going to be watching, this is astonishing.

I would find it hard to believe that any prosecutors, in any previous important and publicized case in America, ever gave arguments (particularly in rebuttal) any worse than those of the prosecutors in this case. I mean, when you get to the point where you don't even open up your mouth and utter one word on a terribly important subject, how can it get any worse? Neither Clark nor Darden seemed to have any sense or feel at all for what matters they were supposed to address themselves to in their final summations. It was painful to watch.

Notes

INTRODUCTION

p. 19: Some of the occupations of the Simpson jurors: The foreperson of the jury, a contracts administrator, was the 1990 Los Angeles County employee of the year. Two of the twelve were retired, the other ten being gainfully employed, with diverse jobs ranging from mail carrier and truck driver to computer repair, environmental health specialist, and handling insurance claims.

p. 21: DNA tests put Simpson's blood at the crime scene: It should be noted that for the preliminary hearing prior to the trial, one of the blood drops at the crime scene which was later identified by DNA tests as Simpson's was also subjected to conventional serological (blood serum) tests, and it had Simpson's blood type (A, the same as Nicole's; Goldman's was type O) and, more specifically, enzyme breakdown, characteristics shared by fewer than one-half of 1 percent of the population—0.43 percent, around one out of 233 people. That is, 99.57 percent of the population was excluded.

p. 23: "That's what 999 out of 1,000 guilty defendants say": When I say "guilty defendants" in reference to defendants who haven't yet been convicted, theoretical purists might say I am prejudging the accused, and that a person cannot be considered guilty of a crime unless brought to trial and found so by a judge or jury. But under that argument, Adolf Hitler never committed any crimes, Jack the Ripper never committed any crimes, and the only crime Al Capone ever committed was income tax evasion. Obviously, if a person, for instance, robs a bank, he is guilty of having robbed a bank, irrespective of whether or not the prosecution can prove this fact to the satisfaction of the jury. A legal verdict of "not guilty" doesn't change the reality of what he did.

p. 24: Simpson is paid $3 million for video declaring his innocence: In the video, he asserts that he has lost more than the families of the victims. He says to the Brown and Goldman families: "I lost more than you did. I lost a person that I loved. . . . And I've lost my ability . . . to provide for the people around me."

p. 25: If Simpson were innocent, he would have testified: An instance where it would be difficult for an innocent defendant to testify would be if he has been previously convicted, several times, of the very same offense, such as robbery or rape, for which he is presently on trial. Even if his own lawyer never elicited this fact, under the law it could properly be brought out on cross-examination.

1. IN THE AIR

p. 28: The "in the air" phenomenon was even present in the courtroom: For example, Richard Rubin, an important prosecution witness who testified that the bloody gloves were identical to those manufactured by his company (another witness said Nicole had bought the gloves, obviously as a Christmas gift for Simpson), walked over to Simpson's table after he left the stand and proceeded to shake his hand and wish him good luck—right in front of the jury.

p. 31: "[Simpson] was being given special treatment at the Los Angeles County Jail": As reported by *Los Angeles Times* reporter Ralph Frammolino in a December 1994 article, Simpson, unlike any other inmate, was allowed unlimited noncontact visits with his girlfriend Paula Barbieri and others. "The deference shown to Simpson," Frammolino writes, "even extends to the attitude of the guards, who, according to a defense attorney who asked not to be identified, are normally aggressive with other inmates but are 'very solicitous of O.J., almost to the point of toadying.'"

p. 33: There's a myth in our society that criminal defense attorneys on big cases are brilliant, great, etc.: The myth does not hold for prosecutors, however, who normally aren't even referred to as attorneys. The lawyer representing the defendant is called the defense *attorney*. The lawyer representing the people normally is simply referred to as the prosecutor. In fact, for far too many years the stereotype of the prosecutor has been either that of a right-wing, law-and-order type intent on winning convictions at any cost, or a stumbling, fumbling Hamilton Burger, forever trying innocent people who are saved at the last minute by the foxy maneuvering of a Perry Mason fighting for justice. Not only is this pure bunk, but ninety-five times out of a hundred the defendant is not innocent, and the prosecutor is the one on the white horse fighting for justice.

p. 35: A civil jury returned an award against Kim Basinger for $8.1 million: Without Weitzman handling the appeal, the judgment was later overturned on a legal technicality, not a substantive matter, and was set to be retried when it was settled for $3.8 million.

p. 37: Simpson's lawyer, Howard Weitzman, claims police told him if he were present there would be no interview of Simpson: Detective Tom Lange told me, "Here's what happened. When we got down to Parker Center, Weitzman and Skip Taft [Simpson's business lawyer] went into a room alone with Simpson for around half an hour. When they came out of the room, Weitzman said, 'He's ready, go ahead and talk to him. Just tape-record everything. We're going to get a bite to eat. We'll be back.'" Lange said he actually invited Weitzman to be present during the interrogation, but Weitzman declined. "Howie is now trying to cover his ass," Lange said.

p. 38: Media covering Simpson case did not know this was Shapiro's first murder trial: A reporter for the *Los Angeles Daily Journal,* a legal publication, told me she had made an effort to find any murder case Shapiro had tried, and was unsuccessful. This reporter did not cover the Simpson trial.

p. 38: Johnnie Cochran joins defense team in July of 1994: Prior to the Simpson case, neither Shapiro nor Cochran was known outside of Los Angeles, and even in Los Angeles, other than in legal circles (and Cochran in the black community), you'd be hard pressed to find anyone who had ever heard of either of them. Cochran got some brief media exposure on the Michael Jackson civil case, but not nearly enough to make a lasting impression on the general population. Bonnie Erbe, legal reporter for the Mutual Radio Network, said on the Jesse Jackson television show on March 25, 1995: "Three, six months ago, nobody knew who Cochran was, basically. I'm a lawyer. I cover legal issues, and I'd never heard of him. Now he's a celebrity."

p. 38: Reporters don't ask Cochran for proof he had ever won a murder case before a jury: However, a researcher for a writer doing a piece on lawyers for *Playboy* magazine did ask Cochran. He told me he has made no less than five written requests to Cochran for the name of just one murder case prior to the Simpson case that Cochran had won before a jury. Although Cochran has provided all types of background information on himself for the article, he has not yet provided the requested information.

p. 40: Media was dead serious about Simpson's lawyers being the "Dream Team": Although I am very harsh on the media in this book, I am obviously speaking in generalities. Actually, most reporters are quite intelligent, but if there's one thing you can count on with the media, it's their doing a minimum of thinking. Their philosophy seems to be "I came, I saw, I concurred." There are certainly some perceptive and reflective members of the media, but they are the small exception to the rule, and I wish there were more of them.

p. 42: The opinion-makers "rarely know their posteriors from a hole in the ground": From the tone of my remarks in this book, I'm sure it's very obvious to the reader by now how upset I am with incompetence and the lack of common sense in life. If I can sum up the reason in a few words it's that these characteristics are not benign. They are responsible for much, if not most, of the great problems, misery, and injustice in the world. The example we're dealing with in this book is the not-guilty verdict in the Simpson case.

p. 43: "... Shapiro's apparent disapproval": As those who followed the case know, there was a severe schism between Shapiro and the other defense attorneys after the verdict. Shapiro, alluding to Cochran, said: "Not only did we play the race card, we dealt it from the bottom of the deck." Stung, Cochran responded that "we did not realize the damage it would do to his [Shapiro's] ego not to be lead attorney."

p. 47: Defense suggests LAPD conspirators "planted and tampered with the blood evidence": The principal suspicious thing which caused Lee to say, in broken English, "something wrong," to wit, the transfer stains, wasn't suspicious at all. Contemporaneous with these transfer stains from the blood drop swatches (Item 47), some of the swatches of Nicole's blood (Item 42) taken from the pool of blood around her body also leaked, on the very same day at the LAPD lab, onto the paper of the separate bindle enclosing them. Since no one would be crazy enough to believe that the LAPD, for no reason whatsoever, would be planting Nicole's blood in the crime lab, we know there was a perfectly innocent explanation for the transfer stains on the other bindle, too.

p. 48: "... Bodziak felt [permanent indentation in the concrete] with his own hands": The third imprint which Lee had testified was a bloody shoe print was, in fact, a shoe print, but the prosecution proved it was not left at the time of the murders. LAPD photographs on June 13 of the same area Lee photographed on June 25 do not show the shoe print, proving it was the shoe print of someone (police, criminalists, perhaps even the postman, etc.) who left it there after the 13th, but before all the blood was washed away several days later.

p. 49: *New York Times* reporter David Margolick said Dr. Henry Lee was "largely unassailable": Margolick, a lawyer himself, made few miscues during the trial, normally covering its events in a stylish, professional, and sensible way. One small lapse was when he fell momentarily into the myth about defense attorneys, saying that the "usually silver-tongued" Cochran had not been so during Cochran's cross-examination of a particular witness. Cochran, even during argument, is not silver-tongued, but when asking questions it would be impossible for even Shakespeare or Churchill to be silver-tongued, since questions simply don't lend themselves to this. Actually, it would sound odd and hence be ineffective to even make an attempt.

In fact, Cochran's questions during the trial were clearly less articulate and less well phrased than those of any of the other lawyers. He put them together seemingly off the top of his head with a fractured syntax that would rival President Eisenhower's.

p. 52: "... but how would a lay listener ever know?": For whatever it's worth, I felt that Geraldo Rivera (who has taken some cheap shots from the media in his career) and the surprising Charles Grodin (on the one night a week he devoted to the case) were the best and most provocative talk show *hosts* during the trial.

p. 52: Intelligence is not the key ingredient of being a great trial lawyer: What goes into making a great trial lawyer? Actually, I've done very little thinking about this, and with more thought what I'm going to say could undoubtedly be improved upon. I'd say that number one, you have to have a born instinct for how to try a case before a jury. It's almost a feral instinct not only to survive, but to destroy (in an ethical fashion) whatever obstacle stands in your way. It's nothing that can be taught. You either have it or you don't, and there are few who possess it. The instinct, like someone who has a natural instinct for the violin, a particular sport, or what-have-you, enables the possessor to see and handle, very easily, matters that are difficult or even impossible for others. It enables the possessor to take the facts of a case and play with them in such a way that the point you want to make becomes irresistible. If I can compare the facts of a case to the black and white keys on a piano, a mediocre pianist just hacks out a tune, but working with the very same keys a Horowitz can play soaring music. You also have to have the personality and style—with all that these terms imply—to sell your case to the jury. This too, obviously, is something you're born with.

The problem is that most of those few lawyers who do have the instinct and personality to be highly effective trial lawyers aren't willing to invest the hundreds upon hundreds of hours of preparation necessary to put everything together as well as to maximize the potential of their instinct and personality.

2. THE CHANGE OF VENUE

p. 56: Jury only deliberates for three and a half hours: Judge Ito, like all judges, instructed this jury no fewer than three or four times a day not to discuss the case among themselves until it was submitted to them for their deliberations on the verdict. So either the jurors had violated Ito's instructions all along and had been talking to one another throughout the trial, or when the case was finally submitted to them for their deliberations they in no way even began to adequately discuss and evaluate the immense amount of evidence in the case. *Newsweek*'s Jonathan Alter said it well: "Unless they're lying, the jurors talked about the case with each other for a far shorter time than 100 million other Americans talked about it with each other."

p. 60: DA's office keeps offering new reasons for transferring case downtown: One reason which has gained currency among some is that Garcetti feared that if Simpson was convicted by a mostly white jury in Santa Monica, it might have caused a riot in the black community. But at the time the case was transferred downtown there wasn't the slightest hint in the black community of a possible riot over the case. (There was, right from the beginning, in the Rodney King case.) Even at the end, when the defense had succeeded in inventing a racial issue in the Simpson case, LAPD intelligence reported there was absolutely no indication of a possible riot in the event of a conviction. Garcetti himself has never suggested that the fear of a riot was even one of the reasons for transferring the case downtown.

p. 62: Santa Monica courtrooms were just as large as Department 103: Because of the smallness of Department 103, the *New York Times*, for instance, had to share its seat on an alternating basis with *La Opinion*, a local Spanish-language newspaper.

p. 63: Defendants are entitled to be tried by a jury which is a representative cross section of the community: One often hears that defendants are entitled to be tried "by a jury of their peers." No one has yet defined precisely what this term means. Certainly it does not mean that serial killers are entitled to have their cases heard by other serial killers, or someone like Simpson tried by professional football players.

But the lack of a definition is unnecessary, since "a jury of one's peers" is simply a term that has become a part of the American vernacular but has no foundation in American law. (The term did appear, actually, in the Magna Carta, the thirteenth-century charter granted by King John, which is regarded as the foundation for English constitutional liberty and a predecessor to this nation's constitution.) Under the Sixth Amendment to the U.S. Constitution, an accused is entitled to be tried by "an impartial jury." American case law has engrafted upon this constitutional mandate the requirement that the impartial jury be chosen from a "representative cross section of the community."

3. A JUDICIAL ERROR

p. 65: "... Simpson is now a free man": It is nothing short of remarkable to me that thus far Cochran and the defense team have received virtually all the criticism for injecting race into the case, and Ito, the man who let it all happen, has gotten a free ride from everyone on this matter.

p. 67: Ito relies on *In Re Anthony P.*, 167 CA 3rd 502 (1985), to let defense inquire into Fuhrman's racial bias: There was much more reason to allow inquiring into racial bias in the *Anthony* case Judge Ito relied on than in the Simpson case, where Mark Fuhrman's finding of the glove was only one among many pieces of evidence in the prosecution's case, and Fuhrman was not accusing Simpson of anything. In *Anthony*, a fifteen-year-old white girl accused a seventeen-year-old black boy of sexually molesting her near her locker at school after she turned down his request for a date. His lawyer was not permitted, on cross-examination, to ask her if she was offended by a black person asking her for a date, and the appellate court held that constituted reversible error. The fifteen-year-old girl's racial bias, if any, went to the core of the case, and there was no evidence against the defendant other than her word. Yet Ito ruled that the *Anthony* case was "controlling" on the issue of whether Fuhrman could be cross-examined on his past use of the N-word.

p. 68: It's a non-sequitur to conclude that just because Fuhrman is a racist he framed Simpson: The principal contention of the defense with respect to Fuhrman is that he planted a bloody left-hand glove (which they claim he had seized from the Bundy crime scene, and which matched a right-hand glove found there) on the grounds of Simpson's Rockingham estate, and then said he found it there. They also alleged, among other things, that Fuhrman brushed the glove (which had Simpson's and the two victims' blood on it) across the console of Simpson's Ford Bronco, leaving blood from all three of them there.

p. 69: "... the massive publicity surrounding ... the Fuhrman tapes": Anyone interested enough in the Simpson case to be reading this book already knows about the Fuhrman tapes and the tremendously harmful impact they had on this case. Between April 1985 and July 1994, Laura Hart McKinny, an aspiring North Carolina screenwriter who was writing a movie script about policewomen, had a series of tape-recorded conversations with Fuhrman for the purpose of Fuhrman providing her with realistic dialogue, police procedures, and insights into a police officer's thought process. McKinny agreed to pay Fuhrman $10,000 if the script was picked up. Since the script was fictional, the argument was made by some that nothing Fuhrman said should be taken seriously. But the consensus was that the statements Fuhrman made on the close to fourteen hours of tape, though almost assuredly part bluster to increase the marketability of the script so he could collect his $10,000, essentially reflected Fuhrman's state of mind with respect to blacks. On the tapes, Fuhrman uses the word "nigger" forty-one times, and comes across as being so racist, and so extreme, as to be almost cartoonish, a caricature of a bigot, and hence his words don't sound as real as their literal meaning. Did even members of the Ku Klux Klan in the thirties in the Deep South sound this bad?

p. 70: A small percentage of racist police hurt the reputations of the LAPD and L.A. Sheriff's Department: Police brutality, obviously, is not confined to Los Angeles. As Hubert Williams, president of the Police Foundation in Washington, D.C., and former chief of police in Newark, New Jersey, says: "Police use of excessive force is a significant problem in this country, particularly in our inner cities." Steven Hawkins, assistant counsel at the NAACP Legal Defense Fund headquarters in New York, adds that "from rural America to America's big cities, police brutality has been and continues to be pervasive in the black and Latino communities."

p. 72: Ito kept out statements on tapes from which defense could infer Fuhrman framed people: The only allegation (not referred to on the Fuhrman tapes) of Fuhrman or his partners planting anything on a black man arose out of a April 7, 1987, incident in West Los Angeles. One Joseph Britton and a confederate were fleeing the scene of an ATM robbery when Fuhrman and three other officers pursued Britton, who claims he discarded a knife he was carrying before he was found hiding behind a concrete fence. Britton says one of the officers said, "You stupid nigger, why did you run?" and proceeded to shoot him six times. He sued Fuhrman and his partners for police brutality, and claimed they planted the knife at his feet to justify the shooting. The first trial resulted in a hung jury, and before the retrial set for late 1994, the City of Los Angeles settled with Britton. Ito did not allow the defense to introduce this evidence because in a February 19, 1993, deposition, Britton said he did not know which of the four officers planted the knife at his feet, and the officer who shot him "was a white male with red hair and a red mustache," clearly not Fuhrman.

p. 74: Simpson tells Ronald Shipp he had dreams of killing Nicole: In offering this testimony against his close friend Simpson, Shipp knew he was permanently ending this relationship. But in dramatic courtroom testimony he said, "I'm doing this for my conscience. . . . I will not have the blood of Nicole on Ron Shipp. I can sleep at night, unlike a lot of others." If the jury didn't know Simpson was guilty, Shipp was telling them the obvious in so many words. At Nicole's urging, Shipp, an expert on domestic violence who taught a course on it at the LAPD, counseled Simpson after Simpson's battery of Nicole in 1989. Feeling a sense of guilt over Nicole's death, he told the jury that "perhaps I didn't do as much as I could have." At one point while Shipp was on the witness stand and the attorneys were at sidebar, Shipp mouthed the words "Tell the truth" to Simpson.

p. 74: There was a "Himalayan mountain of other very solid evidence against Simpson": Putting on highly speculative evidence normally bespeaks desperation and weakness on the part of the side offering the evidence.

p. 79: Ito made "another bad ruling, this one of pivotal and momentous consequences": One legal issue Judge Ito did rule properly on concerned a matter where the law, unfortunately, was against the prosecution. On the morning of June 7, 1994, just five days before she was murdered, a crying Nicole had telephoned Sojourn, a shelter for battered women and their children in Santa Monica, expressing fear of Simpson, saying he couldn't accept that their marriage was finally over. However, she declined an offer from Sojourn to move into the shelter. Although the law in California used to be different, current law treats as inadmissible hearsay a victim's out-of-court declaration of fear of the defendant. Ito, saying on the record that "the relevance and probative value of [Nicole's statement to the Sojourn hot-line operator] is both obvious and compelling," said he nonetheless had no choice under the law but to exclude it.

p. 79: Faye Resnick, Nicole's friend, writes book on Nicole and Simpson: *Nicole Simpson: The Private Diary of a Life Interrupted*, written with Mike Walker, general editor at the *National Enquirer*, and published by Dove Books.

p. 85: Ito gives lawyers latitude in all cases, not just the Simpson case: Long before the trial, on July 22, 1994, Los Angeles deputy district attorney Norman Montrose, who had been assigned to Ito's court the previous one and a half years, told a reporter that "Judge Ito has a tremendous amount of patience" with both sides in a trial.

p. 87: A "judge is normally both a politician and a lawyer . . .": Judges, with the ironic exception of justices of the U.S. Supreme Court, must be lawyers. No nonlawyer has ever sat on the U.S. Supreme Court, although Lyndon Johnson did try to get nonlawyer Dean Rusk, his secretary of state, to accept a nomination.

p. 87: Most judges are appointed as part of political patronage system: If not appointed (the usual situation), to become a judge one has to run, like any other politician, for the office.

p. 88: There's almost always a political connection when one is appointed a judge: In the DA's office, Judge Ito was a close friend of the district attorney, who in turn was a close personal friend of the governor, George Deukmejian, and I've been told by several people that's how Judge Ito was appointed to the Los Angeles County Municipal and eventually Superior Court bench.

p. 88: Many judges have little or no trial experience: Ito, as a former prosecutor, did have good trial experience.

p. 89: "Ito was democratic about his surliness . . .": Ito spoke rudely to everyone in his courtroom, including the media. When Cynthia McFadden, a class act who did a thoroughly professional job covering the trial for ABC News, stood up and asked to be heard when Ito decided to terminate live television coverage of Marcia Clark's opening argument, she immediately got a sharp "Sit down" from Ito.

4. THE TRIAL

p. 93: "As far as the selection of a jury . . .": Jury selection is an area of the trial I have never felt that confident about, having never been a particularly good judge of people early on. Moreover, at least in my opinion, even under the best of circumstances it is only one-third art and skill and two-thirds guesswork. Back in the seventies I was on *The Merv Griffin Show* with Mel Belli and F. Lee Bailey, and either Belli or Bailey (or perhaps both) told Griffin he had a lot of confidence in his ability to choose a favorable jury, using psychiatrists, sitting in the courtroom and passing notes to him, to help decide whom to chose. When Griffin asked me for my views, I responded that not only couldn't psychiatrists agree on the time of day, but you can live with someone for thirty years and not really know them. How can you have a real sense of someone after the relatively superficial voir dire process? (Voir dire, French for "to speak the truth," is the jury selection process.)

p. 94: Dr. Vinson and his staff conducted "focus group" sessions: Around three-fourths of the participants in these sessions were black. The reason, Norma Silverstein, said, was that "we already knew how whites felt about the case. We were much more interested in the views of blacks."

p. 102: Simpson thinking about escaping is powerful evidence of his guilt: Lest there be any doubt in anyone's mind about whether Simpson thought about escaping, after the slow-speed chase the police found a bag in the Bronco containing clean and folded socks (four pairs), t-shirts (four), and underwear (two pairs).

p. 102: People associate flight with a guilty state of mind: Marcia Clark, the prosecutor who elected not to offer this evidence, knows this. When, on October 19, 1994, the defense asked Judge Ito to permit Simpson to be released on bail, arguing he wasn't a flight risk, Clark countered that the proof he was a risk was his "attempt to escape" on the day he was supposed to turn himself in. She alleged Simpson only changed his mind when he realized that because of his celebrity, he'd be recognized and hence be unsuccessful. "A man in possession of a gun, passport, and $7,000 or $8,000 and a disguise reasonably leads a logical person to conclude that a flight was attempted but unsuccessful," Clark argued, adding: "The people are asking that the defendant not be given the opportunity to succeed where previously he had failed." Since you apparently knew this evidence was incriminating, Marcia, it certainly would have been nice if you had introduced it at the trial.

p. 102: Attempted innocent explanations for flight sound silly: For example, way back in January 1995, before opening statements in the case, when the defense was making the assumption that one hundred out of one hundred people would make—that the prosecutors were going to offer the evidence of Simpson's having his passport with him at the time of his arrest—the defense told reporters that "the passport was identification he [Simpson] had gathered to use in connection with his surrender." Perhaps the LAPD did not know what Simpson looked like? Perhaps prior to the trial they intended to incarcerate him in Albania?

p. 103: Simpson convicted himself out of his own mouth: The detectives also elicited from Simpson the important admission that he had *not* cut himself the last time (a week earlier) he was at his former wife's residence, thereby largely eliminating any defense argument that any of Simpson's blood found at the murder scene had been left by Simpson on a previous occasion.

p. 106: "[Simpson] wasn't going to say he was dead between 9:35 and 10:55 p.m.": This reminds me of the fellow who returns unexpectedly to his home in the middle of the day and finds his wife in a negligee and a man hiding in his closet. When the fellow asks the man in the closet what he is doing there, the man responds, "Everybody has to be somewhere." That's right, everybody does have to be somewhere.

p. 108: "[What] Simpson said to the police on the afternoon after the murders": A note on Simpson's statement and the hearsay rule. The prosecution had the right to introduce Simpson's statement, because it was incriminating, and was therefore an exception to the hearsay rule, which otherwise excludes out-of-court statements. But the defense cannot normally (unless Section 356 applies) introduce an out-of-court statement by a defendant, since if the defense wants to introduce it there is a presumption it's self-serving, and self-serving declarations are not an exception to the hearsay rule.

p. 109: "... where nonsense makes sense": The theater of the absurd continued later in the trial when Cochran, having full knowledge that his own client had admitted to the police he had cut himself on his left middle finger on the night of the murders and was bleeding at his Rockingham estate, all *before* he left for Chicago, actually called a string of witnesses (including the American Airlines pilot on Simpson's flight to Chicago, who got Simpson's autograph, and Muhammad Ali's photographer, Howard Bingham, a passenger on the flight) who testified they never saw any cut on Simpson's left hand (as if they would have been looking, and he would have been displaying it). Maybe Johnnie Cochran is a better lawyer than I give him credit for being. Maybe he was shrewd enough to realize that with these prosecutors he could get by with virtually anything, with all the outrageous things he said and did. After all, he knows them better than I do. In fact, before this trial I had never heard of Clark and Darden. In addition to all the other reasons why Simpson's tape-recorded statement should have been introduced, wouldn't it have been effective for the prosecutors, after this deception by Cochran on the timing of the cut, to try to get the statement in during their rebuttal, and then point out to the mostly black jury in summation how Cochran (a fellow black) had deliberately attempted to deceive them?

p. 110: "Simpson's admitting dripping blood ... [was] overridden by the fact he denied committing the murders": To everyone but the Simpson prosecutors, denial is an automatic and expected response from virtually every person, guilty or innocent, charged with wrongdoing, and hence is an almost meaningless term. The word "denied," in fact, is the most common front-page verb in the nation's daily newspapers, whether it be in response to an allegation of conventional crime or any other form of misconduct, such as corruption, sexual harassment, misrepresentation, etc. What makes the Simpson prosecutors' reaction (in not introducing Simpson's statement) to Simpson's denial all the more astonishing is that the jury already knew Simpson had denied committing the murders.

p. 114: **"They don't really train you"**: With respect to this, it is always said that a lawyer should never ask a witness a question unless he knows what the answer is going to be. Time and again the talking heads would say this, having heard it in law school. I reject this venerable maxim as a blanket rule. Although there never is an excuse for asking questions of your *own* witness, as Marcia Clark did, to which you do not know the answer, the rule does not apply to cross-examination. Although the ideal situation obviously would be to know, in advance, what the adverse witness's answers are going to be to all of your questions, the reality is that inasmuch as you frequently have not had, or taken (which applies to the vast majority of lawyers in criminal cases, prosecutors as well as defense attorneys—see discussion in Epilogue) the opportunity to interview the adverse witness, of necessity, cross-examination often is a trek through new terrain, and experience, caution, and instinct sometimes are one's only guide. I can assure you that if the lawyers on both sides had adhered to this utopian law school rule that even trial lawyers continue to echo, but violate, there would have been precious little cross-examination in the Simpson case.

p. 116: **Because DNA is complex, both sides bring in specialists**: DNA is always complex, whether it's in a paternity, rape, or murder case.

p. 116: **Garcetti assigns twenty-five prosecutors to the case**: It was alleged by many during the trial that Garcetti himself was micromanaging the case. If he did, this would be very bad and unwise, since the trial lawyers handling the case in front of the jury should make all the tactical and strategic decisions, not the DA, who is removed from the trenches. Garcetti consistently denied quarterbacking the prosecution effort, adding he was spending no more than 5 percent of his time, if that, on the case. And Bill Hodgman, who worked on the case full-time, has publicly stated that this was true.

p. 119: **The prosecution frequently led jury to believe they were trying to suppress relevant evidence**: Simpson jury foreperson Armanda Cooley, in *Madam Foreman*, showed her disturbance with Clark when she said, regarding Detective Phillips' testimony: "Why did we have to go through all that testimony on direct examination [by the prosecution] and wait until he was cross-examined to say, well, you know, there were differences here about what [Simpson] said and what his reaction was?"

The prosecutors made this error so often one almost expected it of them. When Chris Darden called the Bloomingdale buyer to the stand to testify that the charge-card records showed Nicole had bought Simpson gloves exactly like the evidence gloves, it was no surprise at all that, on cross-examination, Cochran brought out that the records didn't reflect the color or size of the gloves, making it look once again to the jury as if the DA had been hoping the jury wouldn't learn this.

p. 122: **"... the approximate time of death ..."**: This was estimated by Dr. Golden at the preliminary hearing and Dr. Lak at the trial as between 9:00 p.m. and midnight, which sounds extremely inexact but is actually typical. Narrowing the time of death, by reference to body temperature, degree of rigor mortis, lividity (discoloration in lower surfaces of body), and decomposition, etc., down to even one and one-half to two hours is considered very good.

p. 122: "... were the type which could have affected the ultimate conclusions": Although the mistakes made by the coroner's office in the Manson case weren't as numerous as in the Simpson case, they were much more substantive, and hence, far more potentially harmful to the prosecution. For instance, Dr. Golden made no mistake which, if left uncorrected, would change the complexion of the case. But in the Manson case, the autopsy surgeon for Leno and Rosemary LaBianca, deputy medical examiner Dr. David Katsuyama, failed to measure the dimensions of most of the stab wounds. Coupled with the LAPD's initial investigative report which erroneously stated that "the bread knife [from the LaBiancas' kitchen] recovered from Leno LaBianca's throat appeared to be the weapon in both homicides," the medical examiner's oversight presented a very serious problem. Even if I were successful in convincing the jury that Manson had sent his minions into the LaBianca residence, had he sent them in unarmed? (He hadn't.) If so, was it then probable that Manson, the main defendant, had no intent to have them commit murder? Only robbery? Much worse, Katsuyama's initial autopsy report estimated the time of death for the LaBiancas to be Sunday afternoon (3:00 p.m.), more than twelve hours after the murders actually happened. This gave all the killers, who could prove they were elsewhere at 3:00 p.m., an airtight alibi.

Several of the autopsies on the five Tate victims were also flawed, though not nearly as seriously—e.g., the coroner for one of the autopsies concluded the victim had one more gunshot wound than he did, and the same coroner actually overlooked one gunshot wound on a second victim. And Dr. Thomas Noguchi, who was the coroner of Los Angeles County at the time and a competent pathologist, had failed to say in his autopsy report on Sharon Tate that abrasions on Sharon's left cheek were in fact rope burns, suggesting she had also been hung for less than a minute.

p. 123: "... from left to right, across Nicole's throat": The prosecution contended—and the defense did not challenge the contention—that at the time of Nicole's fatal slash wound she was most likely face down, and that her killer, from behind, had pulled her head back by the hair, and with her neck thereby "hyperextended" had slashed her throat from left to right.

p. 123: "... with speculation, with conjecture, or with words like 'possibility' ": When Kelberg asked Dr. Lak how a certain injury to Nicole's left hand could have been inflicted, Dr. Lak proceeded to give two possible ways, then added that there were "many other possibilities."

p. 123: The defense calls Dr. Michael Baden to the stand: Dr. Baden is a prominent New York doctor who was the chief pathologist for the House Select Committee on Assassinations when it reinvestigated the assassination of John F. Kennedy, 1977–79.

p. 126: "... in clear violation of the confrontation clause of the Sixth Amendment of the U.S. Constitution": The theory the prosecution used to introduce the Peratis tape was a specious one. The defense had introduced the transcript of Peratis's testimony at the preliminary hearing, in which he said he had withdrawn about 8 cc of blood from Simpson's arm. Peratis was legally "unavailable" as a witness under Section 1291 of the California Evidence Code, and the prosecution offered his out-of-court taped statement, it said, only to "impeach" his prior testimony, not to establish the truth of his taped statement, and hence cross-examination wasn't required. This, of course, is a sophistic argument, one a blind man could see through. Obviously, the prosecution had no reason to introduce the taped statement other than to convince the jury that Peratis had, in fact, only withdrawn around 6.5 cc of Simpson's blood. And therefore, permitting the statement of Peratis to be introduced into evidence with no opportunity for cross-examination was just another one of the many highly improper rulings Judge Ito made during the Simpson trial.

p. 126: "Yet none of this was done in this case": Peratis told me he has no knowledge that any of his coworkers were contacted by the prosecutors in this case. He said he normally withdraws between 6 and 8 cc. "It's very imprecise, and none of us ever measure or check, because this is the first time in over thirty years working at the dispensary that anyone had made an issue of how much blood I had withdrawn. It just never came up before." I also spoke to Donald Baker, a coworker of Peratis's. He said he normally withdraws around "5, 6, or 7 cc" of blood. He said no one from the DA's office spoke to him on this case.

p. 128: ". . . had caused him to use it": Armanda Cooley, the black foreperson of the Simpson jury, says in her book, Madam Foreman: "He [Fuhrman] should have come right out and said 'Of course I've said the n-word, tell me who doesn't use the n-word out there dealing with these people [criminal element]?' He would have been a lot better off."

p. 128: "Isn't that the way you prosecute a case?": Incidentally, I reject the view of many that knowing Fuhrman was a racist (the prosecutors claim they didn't, that they were surprised by the Fuhrman tapes), the prosecution shouldn't have even called Furhman as a witness or, some go further, even introduced the glove into evidence (since it wasn't absolutely needed), and the whole Fuhrman issue would have been avoided. But, that would have been even worse. The defense needed Fuhrman the way fish need water. He was easily their most potent weapon. And since they knew that Fuhrman had found the glove, and long before the trial had evidence of his racism, they unquestionably would have called him to the witness stand themselves (making it look as if the DA was hiding Fuhrman from the jury). Furthermore, the defense would easily have gotten permission from Judge Ito to treat him as a hostile witness, and cross-examined him in the same way they ended up actually doing at the trial. Since Fuhrman had found the glove, he was a material witness, and the defense would have had every right to call him to the stand to elicit his testimony with respect to it. Make no mistake about it. Fuhrman was the defense's salvation, and one way or another they would have gotten him up on the witness stand, even if they had to carry him up there on a stretcher to do so.

p. 130: "[Fuhrman] underwent psychological counseling in the mid-1980s": In 1981, Fuhrman applied for a permanent disability stress-related pension, among other things claiming he could no longer deal with minorities and gang members and had "this urge to kill people." From 1981 to mid-1983, he was on paid leave and the city

Pension board denied his claim in mid-1983 by a 6–0 vote. Basically, they didn't believe Fuhrman. One member of the board pointed out that despite Fuhrman's boasts of continually beating suspects, other than a 1978 incident (discussed later), there were "no complaints [from citizens] of excessive force." A psychiatrist who examined Fuhrman for the board, wrote: "There is some suggestion here that the patient was trying to feign the presence of severe psychopathology. This suggests a conscious attempt to look bad and an exaggeration of problems." Also, a standard psychological test indicated he was faking. He even told the board psychiatrist of his "fond memories" of being a "trained killer" in Vietnam, but *New York Times* reporter Fox Butterfield learned from Marine Corps records that "the nearest Mr. Fuhrman got to Vietnam was aboard the USS *New Orleans*, an amphibious transport ship stationed offshore."

This all lends support, of course, to the belief of many that the contents of the Fuhrman tapes are 90 percent fabrication. If so, why the need for this on Fuhrman's part? His second wife (he is presently married to his third wife), told Butterfield, "Looking back on it, I think he joined the Marines and the police as if he was trying to prove himself. On the outside Mark is very poised, but inside he had the lowest self-esteem you can imagine."

p. 134: There was only one incident on the Fuhrman tapes where we know he wasn't spinning a fantasy: In one of the supreme ironies and coincidences in the Simpson case, civil rights leader Antonio H. Rodriguez sent a letter on December 5, 1978, to the district attorney's office demanding a prosecution of Fuhrman and his colleagues for the Boyle Heights incident. DA records show that the letter was eventually routed to the person who (along with the DA himself) was responsible for making the decision whether there should be a criminal prosecution. This person had oversight of the Special Investigations Division of the office, the division which handled prosecution of police misconduct cases. That person did not recommend a prosecution against Fuhrman and his colleagues. I could give you a hundred guesses and you still wouldn't guess who that person was. It was Johnnie Cochran. As I mentioned earlier, District Attorney John Van De Kamp had appointed Cochran to be assistant district attorney, the number three man in the office. (He left the office in 1980, returning to private practice.) So the only case we know of for sure in which Mark Fuhrman engaged in serious police misconduct reached the desk of the man who was most responsible for making Mark Fuhrman and alleged police misconduct the very heart of the Simpson defense, and he passed. As a further irony, the person who routed the letter to Cochran was Gil Garcetti, who headed the Special Investigations Division at the time.

p. 137: Prosecution doesn't offer all the evidence of Simpson's abuse of Nicole Ito had ruled they could: The prosecution *did* present the beating incident that led to Simpson pleading *nolo contendere* (the legal equivalent of a plea of guilty, although the defendant is merely saying "I will not contest" the charges against me) in 1989 to misdemeanor spousal battery in which he was given probation. Los Angeles police officer John Edwards testified at the trial that at 3:58 a.m. on January 1, 1989, he and his partner responded to Nicole's 911 call at the Rockingham address. He said Nicole, wet and shivering, and with mud and blood caking on her right pant leg, came running out of the bushes when they arrived at the estate and collapsed into Edwards' arms, crying and yelling, "He's going to kill me. He's going to kill me. He's going to kill me." Nicole said Simpson had punched, slapped, and kicked her. Edwards observed her to have a one-inch cut on her upper left lip, a bruised forehead, swelling around her left eye and right cheek, and a hand imprint on her throat. Simpson told the officers he had not struck Nicole, only pushed her out of the bedroom. Nicole told the officers the fight arose out of Simpson's having sex with another woman staying overnight at the estate and then later wanting to have sex with her. Nicole told Edwards the police had been out to Rockingham eight previous times she had called, but they never did anything to her husband.

p. 140: Defense put prosecution on notice as far back as opening statement they intended to argue blood evidence was contaminated: In his opening statement at the start of the case, Cochran told the jury: "If the evidence was contaminated at the scene or mishandled by the Los Angeles Police Department, it doesn't matter what DNA tests are done afterwards . . . the results will not be reliable . . . if you have garbage in, you get garbage out." He also referred to the LAPD's laboratory as a "cesspool of contamination." It should be noted that throughout the trial the defense only argued that because of contamination the results were "unreliable," another negative word that could only redound to Simpson's benefit. But the *only* type of unreliability that would be relevant to this case would have been if the results were incorrectly Simpson's. However, the defense never argued that because of contamination, the DNA tests incorrectly showed it was Simpson's blood, because to say that would be explicitly drawing attention to the absurdity of their allegation. And they didn't need to. Simply saying the results were "unreliable" achieved the very same effect with the jury, without exposing the absurdity of their argument. It was up to the prosecution to expose this, which they never did, even in final summation (see next chapter).

p. 141: Simpson wanted to be white "in every possible way": Simpson took speech lessons to Anglicize his diction, and one should note that the very thick lower lip of Simpson's early years no longer exists.

p. 143: Jim Brown has for years been an activist for black causes: In the 1960s, Brown headed up a group of famous black athletes (including Muhammad Ali, Bill Russell, Kareem Abdul-Jabbar, etc.) called the Negro Industrial and Economic Union, which raised money for and (with the help of black MBAs from Ivy League schools) gave economic guidance to blacks in starting over four hundred businesses, mostly in the Deep South.

5. FINAL SUMMATION

p. 148: Final summation is "the most important part of the trial for the lawyer": In recent years, the opening *statement*, which is at the beginning of the case, has taken on, in my opinion, inordinate importance in the eyes of trial lawyers, some claiming it's the most important part of the trial. To me, opening statement is one-tenth, if that, as important as final summation, at least in a criminal trial. There is no comparison. They should hardly be discussed in the same breath. Among other things, in opening statement you are not even allowed to argue, i.e., draw inferences from the evidence and urge the jury to accept them. The rationale for the belief that opening statement is so very important is that first impressions are frequently lasting impressions. Indeed, at least one survey has shown that 70 percent of jurors who formed an opinion in favor of one side at the end of the opening statements voted for that side at the end of the trial. However, no one apparently bothered to consider that maybe the reason was that that side simply had the better case, as was apparent even during opening statements.

Implicit in the notion that an opening statement is enormously important is the false assumption that juries, without having yet heard one single word of testimony, are going to be permanently (or at least substantially) influenced in their view of the case. On grounds of pure logic, this appears very unlikely. Even when jurors *do* form an opinion during the opening statement, it certainly is not etched in marble, and can be overcome by actual evidence and testimony from the witness stand. Lawyers making opening statements are like two opposing coaches talking on television before a Super Bowl game about what their teams hope to accomplish on the field of play. Jurors, I've long thought, are in the position of TV viewers who tire of prelims and want the game to begin.

p. 149: ". . . most lawyers give terrible summations": An important element in the preparation of final summation is to secure and read the transcripts of one or two summations given by your opponent in the past—to see the logic he is accustomed to employing, look for holes in his methodology, and learn his favorite examples and analogies.

p. 153: It isn't Darden's nature to be forceful: However lacking in fire, Darden spoke with a certain amount of fervor and emotion, more so than Clark. He conveyed sincerity, clearly spoke from the heart, and, though misguided, was a reasonably effective communicator of his views. Darden's opening argument, as seriously flawed as it was, was far superior to his closing address. For whatever it's worth, I feel Darden has talent, and the potential to be appreciably better than the average trial lawyer.

p. 154: Clark performed differently before Judge Ito than before the jury, where she was more timid: Her statement to the jury during voir dire—"You may not like me for bringing this case. I'm not winning any popularity contests for doing so"—was not only one of the most ill-advised statements that any prosecutor has ever made to a jury, but it was of course the antithesis of a forceful statement. Ms. Clark didn't have to apologize for prosecuting O. J. Simpson. In fact, for what he did, he should have thanked God every day that the DA didn't seek the death penalty against him, and that he wasn't convicted and sent to death row. When Ms. Clark told the jurors she wasn't winning any popularity contests for prosecuting Simpson, in effect she was telling them that the majority of people outside that courtroom didn't even want Simpson to be prosecuted. And, by extension, if they brought back a verdict of guilty they would be going against the majority of people. What other reasonable interpretation of her words is there? Psychologically, I can't think of anything worse a prosecutor could suggest to a jury. What a prosecutor wants to convey to the jurors from the very beginning of the case to the end is that based on the evidence they have *no choice but to convict*, that the evidence is so overwhelming that the People of the State of California (or New York or Texas, as the case may be), the people outside that courtroom, not only want but *expect* a verdict of guilty. That the victims, from their graves, are crying out for justice, and based on the evidence it is the jury's sacred duty to return a verdict of guilty. Telling the jury "You may not like me for bringing this case. I'm not winning any popularity contests for doing so," is definitely not the way to go.

p. 155: ". . . Clark's and Darden's rebuttal": The first argument the prosecutors give at the *end* of the case is called their opening argument, not "closing" argument as most of the media would say. (The opening *argument* should not be confused with the opening *statement*, which is at the *beginning* of the case.) Then the defense gives its one and only argument. Then the prosecution gives its second argument (the prosecution is given two arguments to the defense's one because the prosecution has the burden of proof), called rebuttal, or closing or final argument, or final summation. Generically, all the arguments for the prosecution and defense can be called final summation.

p. 157: The Simpson prosecutors let defense attorneys get by with continually interrupting their summation: After forty-three objections, Clark was called to the bench by the court (i.e., *not* because Clark asked to approach the bench to complain) to discuss the merits of a defense objection. Ito said, "I'm not optimistic we're going to finish today," and only then did Clark say: "Well, if you don't tell them—you know, Judge, this is such an obvious ploy. Every other thing they're objecting to." Ito's only response was to brush Clark off with "All right, you say [page] 25,962?" returning to the discussion in progress before Clark's statement—i.e., there was no response one way or the other from Ito, and he said nothing to Cochran or Scheck. At no time during her entire rebuttal argument did Clark specifically ask Ito to admonish or sanction the defense attorneys for objecting (nor did Darden say one word at all), and as indicated, at no time during the two prosecutors' summations did Ito, on his own, tell either one of the defense attorneys to stop making frivolous objections.

p. 158: The four detectives wanted to "give Fuhrman a chance to start what he's doing": Of all the LAPD detectives, Cochran had the kindest words for Lange, at times suggesting in his argument that he wasn't one of the bad cops in this case. But this statement by him clearly accuses Lange of being part of the conspiracy to frame Simpson. And when Cochran alleged that Simpson's blood had been planted on the back gate at Bundy after June 13, 1994, even though Lange had testified he saw blood there on the night of the murders, he was necessarily accusing Lange of perjury and hence being a part of the conspiracy. Likewise, when he told the jury that black LAPD photographer Willie Ford was "*the one* person [among all the LAPD officers and personnel involved in the case] who wasn't part of the cover-up," he was again accusing Lange of being a part of the conspiracy to frame Simpson. Lange, in his demeanor, reminds me of a legendary LAPD detective I worked with years ago, "Jigsaw" John St. John, who was liked even by those he relentlessly pursued and ultimately arrested.

p. 158: Cochran and Scheck, in their summations, suggest a conspiracy by the police to frame Simpson: Isn't that nice? Police officers, particularly during the early years of their careers, risk their lives almost every day, not even knowing when they give a traffic ticket to a speeding motorist if he's going to be some zany or an escaping criminal who might blow their brains out. Because of this daily risk of life, police officers are the most underpaid people in our society, hardly earning a living wage. They're sued, they're called pigs, and then, after detectives like Lange and Vannatter have put in twenty-five long and hard, gritty years serving the public and are about to retire and enjoy a few years with their families, criminal defense lawyers like Cochran and Scheck come along and falsely accuse them in front of millions of people of the foulest, most despicable and ignominious act imaginable: framing an innocent man for two murders. That's really nice, isn't it?

p. 158: **The defense attorneys, in their questions of the prosecution witnesses, suggested a police frame-up:** Many of the questions went beyond mere suggestion. For instance, Barry Scheck, to convey to the jury his belief that Dennis Fung had planted blood from Simpson's vial of blood in the Bronco, asked Fung: "And at some point that morning, before you left to search the Bronco at the print shed, you poured off some blood from Mr. Simpson's blood vial?" Fung: "No."

p. 160: **Marcia Clark devotes but one paragraph to respond to central thrust of defense's whole case:** The defense drenched the jury throughout the trial and in final arguments with the concept of a police conspiracy, and the DA did virtually nothing at all to disabuse the jury of the notion. The jury took that notion, virtually intact, back to the jury room with them, and concluded, by their verdict, either that Simpson had indeed been framed by the police or at least that this issue fell under the rubric of reasonable doubt. Many of the jurors have come right out and said that evidence was planted against Simpson, e.g. — "Somebody planted the glove," Brenda Moran said; Gina Rosborough said she believed Fuhrman had "planted evidence"; "the blood [on the back gate and in the Bronco] was planted," juror Marsha Rubin-Jackson says in *Madam Foreman*, etc. Jurors Yolanda Crawford and Lionel Cryer said they weren't sure, however, that all of the LAPD officers were in on the conspiracy to frame Simpson. Crawford said she felt the civilian criminalists at the LAPD were a part of the conspiracy.

p. 161: **". . . been involved in such an enormous endeavor . . .":** For instance, since the dark cotton sweatsuit Kato Kaelin saw Simpson wearing less than an hour before the murders never surfaced, for dark cotton fibers to end up on Ron Goldman's shirt, the detectives would have had to go out and buy a dark cotton sweatsuit, remove fibers from it, check Goldman's shirt out of the Property Division of the LAPD, and then embed these fibers into Goldman's shirt. They'd have to remove fibers from the Bronco carpet, check the glove found on Simpson's estate out of the LAPD's Property Division, and embed them into the glove. A specified number of hairs (one hundred) were removed, by court order, from Simpson's head for comparison purposes, so without the defense catching it, the detectives would have had to purloin several hairs from the tissue containing Simpson's hair, and embed nine of these hairs into the black knit cap found near the slain bodies of the victims and one into Ron Goldman's shirt. And so on as to twenty or twenty-five other things to illustrate to the jury how silly and absurd the defense's allegation of conspiracy is, that a person would have to have a brain smaller than the point of a fine needle to believe a story like that.

p. 162: In California, testifying falsely in a capital case in some circumstances can result in the death penalty: A capital case, strictly speaking, is one in which the DA is seeking the death penalty. Although on September 9, 1994, nearly three months after the murders, the DA decided against seeking the death penalty against Simpson, certainly, on the night of the murders, with not one but two persons having been brutally murdered, any detective would have to assume there was a substantial likelihood the DA would seek the death penalty. Since I always, as indicated, work backward from my final summation, and since this is a very powerful argument which I would immediately know I would want to make, I would have had each of the four detectives, during my direct examination of them, testify to their knowledge and awareness of Section 128 of the California Penal Code. Section 128 provides that any person whose perjury helps procure the conviction and execution of an innocent person *shall* be sentenced to death or life imprisonment without possibility of parole. Prior to 1977, the death penalty was mandatory.

p. 163: "They didn't want to lose another big case": Juror Lionel (Lon) Cryer bought Cochran's argument 100 percent. Right after the verdict, he told reporters he believed that because "the LAPD had such a bad track record with their high profile cases in the past, they pounced on this case to try to not blow it at all costs. 'No matter what, we're going to make this case.' "

p. 165: ". . . but you never do anything to him": In this regard, couldn't the prosecution at least have said to the jury: "Why would the same police department which sheltered Mr. Simpson all these years against domestic abuse charges suddenly want to frame him for murder?"

p. 165: "I mean, he'd need a road map to get back to the hood": If I had been successful in getting in evidence of Simpson's having turned his back on the black community years ago, and not helping the community even when requested to do so, I obviously would have made an argument on this, too.

p. 166: Even Fuhrman pampered Simpson on prior occasion: Since malicious mischief (smashing the window of Nicole's car) is a misdemeanor, as opposed to a felony, Fuhrman did not have the authority to place Simpson under arrest, since absent an arrest warrant, a police officer cannot arrest someone for a misdemeanor unless it was committed in his presence. Here, it wasn't. However, Fuhrman could have patted Simpson down, asked him for his identification, interrogated Simpson about the incident, and attempted to persuade Nicole to sign a crime report (which could have possibly led to a criminal complaint and an arrest warrant based thereon), things Fuhrman might very well have done if he hadn't given Simpson special treatment. But he did nothing, not even filling out a police report of the incident. The prosecution knew all these things, eliciting testimony from Fuhrman on them during the trial, yet they failed to craft and deliver one word of argument on this point in their summation.

Some legal commentators have said the Mercedes belonged to Simpson, and hence it was no crime for him to damage his own property. But the Mercedes was owned by Nicole. Even the defense, in a January 23, 1995, written motion (page 2) filed with the court, concedes this fact.

The defense argued at the trial that in a January 18, 1989, letter Fuhrman was asked to write about the car incident at the time of Simpson's no-contest plea to spousal battery against Nicole, Fuhrman said the incident was "indelibly impressed" in his memory—evidence, the defense contended, that Fuhrman had harbored a hatred for Simpson all the years leading up to his opportunity to frame him in June of 1994. But in his 1989 letter, Fuhrman explains why the incident remained so firmly in his memory. "It is not every day that you respond to a celebrity's home for a family dispute," he wrote.

p. 167: Motive is never a part of the *corpus delicti* of a crime: The *corpus delicti* of a crime, contrary to what is believed by many laypeople, does not refer to the dead body in a homicide. It means the body (or elements) of a crime, which (in addition to the identity of the perpetrator) has to be shown by the prosecutor in order to secure a criminal conviction.

p. 168: ". . . a war he called Helter Skelter": Early in the summer of 1969, Manson told those close to him that "the spades" (blacks) were about to come out of Watts (the Watts riots were just four years earlier) and go into the homes of Bel Air and Beverly Hills, up in the "rich piggy district," and commit some terrible murders, cutting bodies up and writing things on the wall in blood that would "really make whitey mad," and that would start the war. But as the summer wore on and nothing happened, he said, "We're going to have to show blackie how to do it."

p. 169: In Manson's bizarre motive of Helter Skelter he envisioned himself as taking over the leadership of the world: Truman Capote, commissioned by the *New York Times Magazine* to do a feature story on the Manson case, thought he would come to L.A., sit in on the trial for a few days, and get a handle on the case for his article. But after three days, he gave up on writing the piece, telling me in the hallway outside the courtroom, "This case is just too bizarre. I'm going to Palm Springs for a few days to relax."

p. 169: Helter Skelter is the title of a Beatles' song: There were several other words I found in the lyrics of Beatles' songs which I connected to Manson, tying him in further to the murder scene. The Beatles' *White Album* came out in December of 1968, and Manson considered it prophetic, playing it over and over, believing the Beatles were sending messages to him and other tuned-in people beneath the lyrics of their songs. Two examples: In the song "Piggies," the Beatles say the piggies need a "damn good whacking." Manson interpreted this to mean that the piggies, the white establishment, should be murdered. The word "pig" was printed in blood on the front door of the Sharon Tate residence, and the words "Death to Pigs" on the living-room wall of the residence of Leno and Rosemary LaBianca. In the song "Blackbird," there is the lyric: "All your life you were only waiting for this moment to *arise*." Manson interpreted "blackbird" to mean the black man, and the black man was supposed to rise up against the white man. The word "Rise" was printed in blood on the living-room wall of the LaBianca residence.

p. 170: It may have been Paula Barbieri's idea to redecorate Simpson's home: In a December 14, 1995, pretrial deposition in the wrongful death civil action against Simpson, Barbieri testified that at 7:00 a.m. on June 12, 1994, the day of the murders, she left a "Dear John" message for Simpson on his answering machine, saying she no longer wanted to see him, that their relationship was over. Since Nicole was also through with him, Barbieri's rejecting him just fifteen hours before the murders would certainly have been relevant evidence for the prosecution to use against Simpson showing his state of mind on the day of the murders. Detective Tom Lange told me the police and the DA were unaware of Barbieri's call to Simpson on June 12, 1994. He said that a week or so after the murders, he conducted two brief telephone interviews with Barbieri (she was at her Florida home), but she was "afraid and uncooperative." When he persisted in his efforts to interview her, the defense got a court order from Judge Ito requiring that any further attempts to talk to her be cleared through her attorney. The attorney, Michael Nasiter, informed Lange that Barbieri did not wish to be interviewed. In a criminal (as opposed to civil) case in California, the prosecution cannot subpoena a witness and take his or her deposition before trial. The only way the prosecution can achieve the same end in some situations is through the grand jury. Barbieri, in fact, testified at the grand jury before the Simpson trial, but the proceedings and inquiry were limited to the investigation by the DA to determine whether he would seek an indictment against Simpson's friend Al Cowlings for being an accessory after the fact to the murders. The DA decided not to. Parenthetically, Simpson, in his pretrial deposition in the civil case, denied having knowledge on the night of the murders that Barbieri had called off their relationship earlier that day, saying he hadn't checked his phone messages that day. He apparently forgot what he told Lange and Vannatter the afternoon after the murders. Following the dance recital on the day of the murders, he said, "I called her [Barbieri] a couple of times, and she wasn't there, and I left a message, *and then I checked my messages.*"

p. 172: ". . . could have resulted in his own execution": The defense was claiming that virtually all of the LAPD officers and employees involved in the investigation of the Simpson case were either part of the conspiracy to frame him or participated in the conspiracy to cover up. But Fuhrman was the *only* officer who Clark pointed out to the jury would be taking a risk by violating the law if the defense charges were true, and even then she did so very weakly, not mentioning the possible penalty of death.

p. 173: Members of defendants' families lying under oath to help them: In fact, some European nations, by statute, go further and specifically exclude family members from prosecution for harboring their loved ones to help them evade apprehension by the law. For instance, the family of Dr. Joseph Mengele, the notorious Nazi "Angel of Death" who was responsible for the extermination of about 400,000 people, mostly Jews, in Poland during the Second World War, helped him avoid apprehension from the law for thirty years, and the authorities knew this. The family even later admitted it. But West German law protected them from being prosecuted.

If any readers are surprised by this, perhaps you shouldn't be. As a sign of their intellectual maturity, these European nations have simply enacted into law what we are doing over here without laws governing the situation. These statutes recognize that just as you cannot legislate morality, all the laws in the world cannot tear asunder the bond of blood and love that unites human beings to one another. These relationships, of course, are the protoplasm, as it were, of all human existence, without which there would be no laws, without which there would be no civilized society as we know it today. In other words, there are laws other than those written in our lawbooks: laws, emotions, and feelings as indestructible and imperishable as human nature itself, and which no system of jurisprudence has ever yet been able to ignore.

p. 173: Fuhrman's type of lie on the witness stand is a relatively unimportant one: It's this very fact of irrelevance that makes his lie almost assuredly not perjury. Laypeople are under the erroneous impression that lying under oath is automatically perjury. But it's not. Lying is only one element (albeit the most important one) of the *corpus delicti* of perjury. The second element is that the lie has to concern some "material matter," meaning that it must be relevant to an issue in the case which could influence the outcome of the trial. For instance, unless one's age or weight is somehow relevant to an issue in a case, a witness lying under oath about his age or weight or about where he lives is not committing perjury. Likewise, Fuhrman's lie about not using a racial slur in the past ten years was not material, since it had nothing to do with anything he said or did in his investigation of the Simpson case.

p. 174: ". . . thrusting my crossed fingers into the air": Little could I possibly know (or even wildly imagine) that just six months later in London, England, in an exact replica of a Dallas federal courtroom, and after nearly five months of preparation as intense as I've ever done for any murder case in my career, I would be "prosecuting" Lee Harvey Oswald for the assassination of President John F. Kennedy. The twenty-one-hour British television "docu-trial" had no script, no actors, a real United States federal judge and Dallas jury, the actual lay and expert witnesses in the case, and a prominent defense attorney (Gerry Spence) representing Oswald.

p. 174: Manson jury had to decide on life or death for Manson and his co-defendants: Manson and his three co-defendants (as well as Charles "Tex" Watson, whom I prosecuted in a separate trial) were all sentenced to death in 1971. But in 1972, the United States Supreme Court, in *Furman v. Georgia*, ruled that the death penalty was unconstitutional as it was then being implemented by the states. They made their ruling retroactive, and the sentences of everyone on death row throughout the country (over 600 at the time) were irreversibly reduced from death down to life imprisonment.

p. 175: People admit lying without realizing it: A February 1996 poll by the Josephson Institute of Ethics found 47 percent of adults who admitted they would accept an auto body repairman's offer to include unrelated damages in an insurance claim, and 65 percent of high schoolers who cheated on an exam in the past year. The pollster said the real numbers are probably higher. And it's been estimated that over 90 percent of Americans cheat (lie) on their income tax.

p. 180: Prosecutors, in summation, focus mainly on Dr. Baden's testimony that Simpson cut himself on night of murders: Clark, at one point in her argument, also very briefly mentioned that "Kato Kaelin saw some blood drops in the foyer" of Simpson's residence on the morning (7:00 a.m.) after the murders.

p. 182: ". . . and we drip blood?": Recall that Baden had only testified that Simpson got a slight cut on one of his fingers, not that he had dripped blood in his car, home, and on the driveway.

p. 190: **A prosecutor should have a complete command of the facts of the case:** The Simpson prosecutors' sloppiness, imprecision, and poor grasp of the facts can only be categorized as shocking, and the defense nearly always pointed out their misstatements of the evidence, which some on the jury undoubtedly had already noticed. A few representative examples of Clark's misstatements of the evidence: Clark told the jury in summation that both of Nicole's jugular veins had been severed, but the coroner had testified that the left one was "almost transected" (severed) and the right one had only been nicked. Clark argued that when Alan Park, the limo driver, left with Simpson from the Rockingham gate just after 11:00 p.m. for the airport on the night of the murders, he saw Simpson's Bronco parked near the gate on Rockingham, but Park had testified that he didn't pay any attention to whether or not Simpson's Bronco was parked near the gate when he left and he couldn't be sure if the Bronco was there. With respect to Simpson's cutting himself on the night of the murders, as we've seen, Dr. Michael Baden, the defense pathologist, testified: "He said he recalled seeing some blood after trying to retrieve his phone *or* some material from the Bronco. . . . He had gone to the Bronco to get something and may have somehow cut himself while getting stuff from the Bronco to bring with him to Chicago." With this testimony, Clark argued to the jury: "So he [Simpson] comes up with a story that he gives to Dr. Baden, which is 'I went into the Bronco and cut myself on that razor-sharp cell phone.'" (Of course, Clark wouldn't have had to mockingly misstate the evidence if she had introduced Simpson's statement to the LAPD on the afternoon after the murders where he said he had no idea how he cut himself.) She told the jury that all of the officers who arrived at the murder scene before Fuhrman (fourteen) saw only one glove, but only two of these officers (the only ones she called) had so testified. Arguing about the physical advantage Simpson had over the victims which would have enabled him to overpower them, Clark said Ron Goldman was "only five feet five," but the coroner's report clearly states that he was five feet nine inches tall.

p. 190: **Cochran receives help from many sources for his summation:** A local Los Angeles criminal defense attorney, per the September 30, 1995, edition of the *Los Angeles Times*, prepared the first draft of Cochran's final argument, Cochran giving the lawyer, who was not a member of the defense team, an outline to work from.

p. 192: ". . . he should not be penalized for exercising it": Last year, after a heated debate in Parliament, Britain enacted legislation allowing the prosecutors for the Crown to draw adverse inferences from an accused's failure to testify in his own defense.

p. 194: **There are rarely eyewitnesses to a premeditated murder:** Clark argued premeditation well, pointing out, among other things, that the killer arrived at the murder scene wearing gloves and a dark watch cap, and armed with a knife.

p. 195: **Marcia Clark makes inadequate comment on Dr. Henry Lee's testi-**

mony: With respect to Lee's third shoe print, a real one, Clark added in her summation: "The only shoe print that did not match the Bruno Magli shoes was the one shoe print [Lee] found on June 25th after police officers had walked through the crime scene." Even on this third shoe print, Clark failed to remind the jury of the photographs taken of the spot on June 13 that did not show the print, proving that the shoe print was not left there at the time of the murders.

p. 196: ". . . doing nothing but waiting for Vannatter and Lange": Darden's example made no sense. The defense wasn't even claiming that the uniformed officers who arrived at the murder scene were the ones who "rushed to judgment." They were claiming that Vanatter and Lange, along with fellow detectives Phillips and Fuhrman, all of whom arrived hours later, were the ones who "rushed to judgment."

p. 200: ". . . who sloppily collected and preserved it": But it surfaced at the trial that when Dr. Henry Lee, the defense's leading forensic scientist, visited the LAPD crime lab, he did not wear a hair net or change his gloves while handling various articles of evidence in the lab.

p. 201: Neither Clark nor Darden point out in their summations that contamination can't convert one person's blood to another: There was also no clear reference in either Clark's or Darden's *opening* argument to this critical and all-important point with respect to *contamination*. The only oblique, wholly unsatisfactory reference was this brief statement by Clark: "They [defense experts] could have come here . . . and shown you why the blood drops only got contaminated in a way that showed the defendant's DNA type, not that they possibly could have." Only in Clark's opening argument (before Scheck argued) was there any reference to this fact with respect to *degradation*, and then only, the way she phrased it, as a relatively unimportant afterthought. Remarkably, these are the only words she said on this highly important point: "And by the way [by the way?], when DNA degrades, it doesn't turn into someone else's type. You get no result." Just eighteen words on the entire subject, and then as an apparently parenthetical observation, an aside?

p. 203: ". . . on the back gate and on the socks . . .": EDTA, a preservative put into the test tubes of reference blood to prevent it from coagulating, is also present in many types of food, and FBI agent Fred Martz, chief of the FBI's Chemistry and Toxicology Department, testified that when he conducted tests of his own unpreserved blood, he found about the same level of EDTA present as was found in the back-gate blood and the blood on the socks. He said that if the blood on the gate and socks had been sprinkled, as the defense claimed, with blood from Simpson's reference vial, the level of EDTA in this blood would have been much, much higher.

p. 203: ". . . on the Bundy blood drops": Rockne Harmon, a Vietnam veteran and the lead DNA prosecutor in the Simpson trial on loan from the Oakland DA's office, told me that the defense was furnished with swatches from two of the five Bundy blood drops (Items 47 and 50) to test for the presence of EDTA. He said Dr. Kevin Ballard of Baylor University in Waco, Texas, conducted the tests. "Since the defense never presented evidence that EDTA was found in Items 47 and 50, one can only conclude that Ballard found no EDTA," Harmon said. Harmon added that Ballard was in court throughout all of the testimony on EDTA, although the defense never called him to the witness stand. Harmon and his associate, George "Woody" Clarke (on loan from the San Diego DA's office), were very helpful to me in answering my questions about parts of the blood evidence in this case.

p. 204: The need to point out to jury that issue of contamination only has relevance if blood belongs to someone other than Simpson: I say "point out" this obvious fact because although the entire defense was implicitly predicated on the contention that it was some third party's blood at the murder scene, the defense attorneys never expressly spoke about this, probably because they didn't want to focus the jury's attention on the question of who this third party could possibly be. Since no one had any motive to kill Nicole other than their client, they only wanted to focus on the allegation that it wasn't Simpson's blood, not the necessary corollary that it therefore had to belong to some other human being. And the prosecution, helping the defense, was virtually silent on the matter, too.

p. 206: There were unconfirmed rumors that Darden was asked at last second to give a rebuttal argument: The record itself is ambiguous on this point. In Darden's opening argument, he said these cryptic words to the jury: "I'm not going to have *much* of an opportunity later [in rebuttal] I think to talk to you."

p. 206: Clark was continually admitting to jury she wasn't sure of her facts: This was even true, in fact, in both of their *opening* arguments. Clark: "I'm trying to remember the date of, I think it was '92, in which . . . " (if you've gone over your prepared remarks even once, and you see you don't have a date or anything else, if you don't get it yourself, don't you automatically have one of the twenty-four other prosecutors helping you on the case get it for you?); "First of all, premeditation. Let me see. I think we have a jury instruction here for this. I don't think we have it right now. That's okay. I'll just tell you"; "You may recall we heard the testimony of the—I think it was Luellen Robertson of Airtouch." Darden: "As we search for the motive jury instruction, let me say to you . . ."; "And the next month, I think it's February—I don't know"; "Look back at Eva Stein. I believe her time was 10:20. Was it 10:30?"; "If my memory fails me, then, you know, rely on the testimony in case I'm incorrect" (What, Chris? In preparing your summation you didn't look at the transcript yourself? The one you get at the end of each day? You're just winging it in front of the jury?).

p. 207: Rebuttal argument should be prepared way in advance, and then gone over many times: Celebrated defense attorney Gerry Spence, in his best-selling book *How to Argue and Win Every Time*, says: "Now that we have written out the argument, let us go over it again, not once, but many times."

p. 209: Clark plays a compilation of Nicole's 1989 and 1993 911 calls to jury: I was reminded of some of my closing words to the jury in the Manson trial, which the media came to call "the roll call of the dead." After each name I paused, so the jurors could recall the person, once a living human being. "Ladies and gentlemen of the jury," I quietly began, "Sharon Tate . . . Abigail Folger . . . Voytek Frykowski . . . Jay Sebring . . . Steven Parent . . . Leno LaBianca . . . Rosemary LaBianca . . . are not here with us now in this courtroom, *but from their graves they cry out for justice. Justice can only be served by coming back to this courtroom with a verdict of guilty.*"

p. 210: "... opening argument about the 'shortening fuse'...": The "shortening fuse" was perhaps the main part of Darden's opening argument to the jury. He said the fuse was lit way back in 1985 when Simpson "took that baseball bat to Nicole's car," and it continued to burn and get shorter until he finally killed her.

p. 210: Cochran argues that Simpson's conduct on night of murder isn't reflective of someone planning to commit murder: It's just speculation on my part and of no moment, but I've always had the sense that in the early-evening hours on the night of the murders and at the time Simpson went to get a hamburger with his houseguest, Kato Kaelin, he was not planning to kill Nicole. My guess is that he had probably thought about killing her many times in the past, and with the purchase of the disguises on May 27, 1994, the thought had gone at least a step beyond mere contemplation but had not been finalized yet. My further guess is that he spoke to Nicole over the telephone a half hour or so before the murders (for which there would be no records, since his home was less than two miles away and not a toll call), during which they had an argument and she said something to him that ignited the murderous rage we know he had.

It should be noted that after the murders, when the police were driving Simpson's and Nicole's two children (Sydney Brooke, age nine, and Justin Ryan, age six) to the police station in the early-morning hours of June 13, 1995, Sydney told one of the police officers that from her and Justin's upstairs bedroom, she heard her mother arguing loudly with someone on the phone. The precise time is not known, but it most likely was after 9:00 p.m., since Nicole and her children didn't leave the Mezzaluna restaurant until just after 8:30 p.m., and Nicole then took the children to a Ben and Jerry's ice cream shop before heading home. The children were believed to be asleep at the time of the murders.

p. 211: "... looking at the statistics the wrong way?": Surprisingly, there seem to be no national statistics on this matter. Calling the Police Foundation in Washington, D.C., the FBI, the International Association of Chiefs of Police in Alexandria, Virginia, prominent researchers on national crime statistics like Carolyn Block of Chicago, even the National Center for Violence Prevention and Control in Atlanta, Georgia, I found that among their volumes of statistics none had any on this precise point. The only statistics I was referred to arose out of a 1973 grant from the Police Foundation to a team of researchers to explore the relationship between domestic disturbances and the violent crimes of homicide and aggravated assault in 1970 and 1971 in Kansas City, Missouri. Their report showed that the Kansas City Police Department "had responded to at least one such disturbance call at the addresses of approximately 90 percent (94.5 percent in 1970 and 84.1 percent in 1971) of the homicide victims or suspects." (The aggravated assault statistics were 86.9 percent in 1970 and 81.2 percent in 1971.) To remind the reader, when the police responded to the 911 radio call at Simpson's Rockingham estate on January 1, 1989, there had been eight previous 911 or disturbance calls from that address since the Simpsons married on February 2, 1985.

p. 213: The circumstantial evidence instruction with respect to reasonable doubt: This mildewed and very ambiguous instruction should be discarded. The jurors are the triers of fact and only they decide what facts are enough, in their mind, to prove guilt. But if facts are "essential" and "necessary" for a conviction, doesn't this necessarily imply they are essential and necessary as a *matter of law*? (After all, the instruction doesn't tell the jury, "essential and necessary *in your mind*.") But if so, why doesn't the judge tell the jurors what these facts are? There are certain elements of a crime that have to be proven before there can be a conviction, but not certain facts. This extremely poorly drafted instruction is tailor-made for defense attorneys to misuse, as Barry Scheck did in this case.

p. 214: ". . . I have not tried to explain it away at all": Cooley's coauthor and Simpson juror Marsha Rubin-Jackson *did* try to explain away Simpson's blood at the murder scene, and her explanation was a beaut. "I had no doubt in my mind that that wasn't O.J.'s blood, the blood drops," says Rubin-Jackson, "but by them being so degraded they could have been there before. Prior to the murders. He [Simpson] visited that place often." Right. And later, I suppose, on the night of the murders, the killer just happened to leave his bloody shoe prints to the right of four of those blood drops. Apart from the absurdity of this juror's speculation, and the fact that Fung had testified that all the blood drops "appeared to be fresh," this was yet another reason to have introduced Simpson's tape-recorded statement in which he says he did not bleed the last time, about a week earlier, that he was at the Bundy address. If you're a killer, it must be nice to be able to do what Simpson did—not answer the evidence against you by testifying, and have jurors offer innocent explanations for you. And also to have a prosecutor who doesn't offer evidence against you which would refute the jurors' explanations. That's leading a charmed existence.

p. 216: ". . . doesn't negate all that *has* been proved": In *Madam Foreman*, Simpson juror Marsha Rubin-Jackson says there were a lot of "questions we had that never got answered," as if it were the prosecutor's burden to answer all of the jury's questions. And jury foreperson Armanda Cooley, to support the not-guilty verdict, says in the book, "There were many questions that were not answered."

p. 216: Inconsistencies, slip-ups, incompetence, etc., are normal occurrences in life: Everyone knows this, but if you don't specifically and expressly draw jurors' attention to this reality and fact of life, some people just don't think of it. In the A&E television special on the Simpson case on December 20, 1995, Simpson juror Yolanda Crawford said, "The police said they came back to Bundy a couple weeks later and find blood on the rear gate they didn't see earlier. [Not so, Ms. Crawford. Where were you when several officers, including Lange, Phillips, and Riske, testified they saw the blood on the gate on the night of the murders? Only Dennis Fung testified he didn't see the blood there.] *But not seeing something like this just doesn't happen.*"

p. 219: It was cool on the night of the murders: A meteorologist for the National Weather Service in Oxnard, California, told me that the temperature at the civic center in downtown Los Angeles at that time was sixty-four degrees, and he estimated the temperature in West Los Angeles, closer to the ocean, to be "in the high fifties or low sixties."

p. 222: Who else would have had any reason to kill the victims in this case?: Another big reason why the tape of the LAPD's interrogation of Simpson should have been introduced at the trial is that when Vannatter asked Simpson, "Did Nicole mention that she'd been getting any threats lately to you? Anything she was concerned about, or the kids' safety? . . . From anybody?" Simpson replied, "No, not at all."

p. 222: The defense set up an 800 number before the trial to get tips on who the killer or killers might be: The prosecution should have presented evidence of all this during its case-in-chief.

p. 222: The defense offered no evidence that anyone other than their client committed these murders: The defense presented evidence that there were eight sets of unidentified fingerprints at the Bundy address. This fact didn't come from the defense's efforts, however. It came from the LAPD fingerprint expert. But not even the defense suggested there were eight killers, we know there was only one set of bloody shoe prints, and the killer wore gloves, which would not, of course, leave any fingerprints. This issue was mentioned but not dwelled on by the defense attorneys during their final summations, since the inference was that these were random fingerprints which had been left by some of the considerable number of people and law enforcement personnel who came to the crime scene after the murders, or had been left there earlier by friends of Nicole's or people like mailmen, salesmen, etc.

p. 223: ". . . responsible for Nicole's murder": The defense theory was that the drug lords were really out to kill Nicole's close friend Faye Resnick, and mistook Nicole for Faye, who bears no resemblance to Nicole, even in the color of her hair. Ms. Resnick, who lived with Nicole for a short while before the murders, checked herself into a drug rehabilitation center just days before the killings, a fact that the defense elicited from Detective Lange on cross-examination. The defense theorized, without any evidence to support the theory, that maybe Ms. Resnick owed her drug dealer money, and that this prompted the murders. Since it was just rank speculation, Judge Ito would not permit the defense to inquire any further into the Resnick matter before the jury. And since the jury heard no evidence of any drug use by either of the two victims, the Colombian drug lord talk must have sounded curious to them.

Incidentally, this was not a typical drug killing at all. Drug killings are usually shootings. When there is brutality such as this (thirty-seven stab wounds, in some of which the killer actually was cutting), there is normally an abduction and torture at a place removed from the abduction, and the victim is someone important, such as an informant or a competing drug trafficker, not some private user.

p. 225: Religious people would not want it on their conscience that they may have let a murderer go free: In *Madam Foreman*, Carrie Bess writes: "I often asked the Lord to help me because there was a time when I thought about that place in the Bible where it says 'Judge ye not.' It really came to a point where I was wondering, Carrie, are you really doing the right thing? Should you be the one here to say whether or not this person did that or this person did not do this? But I prayed and the Lord answered my prayer because I feel my decision was fair."

EPILOGUE

p. 228: Legal experts strongly recommend against the use of the "why" question: The principal book on cross-examination currently out there is *Cross-Exami-*

nation: Science and Techniques by Larry S. Pozner and Roger J. Dodd, a 763-page tome that is being widely read and is in all the law libraries. On page 302, the authors advise their readers: "The adept cross-examiner *never* uses questions that begin with 'how' or 'why.' "

p. 231: Trial lawyers frown on use of "why" question: When I said the why question is almost universally frowned upon by trial lawyers, I should refine that to say "by experienced trial lawyers who are students of cross-examination." Inexperienced ones, or those who haven't studied the art of cross-examination, *do* use the why question, and not knowing how to use it, get hurt by it. Darden's cross-examination of Laura McKinny was a perfect example, and the harm was considerable. Judge Ito's basis for excluding all statements by Detective Fuhrman on the Fuhrman tapes wherein Fuhrman referred to acts of misconduct (including police officers covering up for one another) was that there was no factual support that the conduct referred to by Fuhrman had ever taken place. But Darden came to the defense's rescue on something that went to the very heart of the defense—that certain members of the LAPD in the Simpson case had framed Simpson, and their colleagues had covered up for them. After McKinny testified she was offended by Fuhrman's use of the word "nigger," Darden asked her (obviously without having any idea what her answer was going to be, his first big mistake) *why* then hadn't she asked him to stop? Her response caught Darden by surprise: "For the same reason I didn't tell him to stop when he told me of police procedures, *cover-up* and other information I felt was important to me." It was the first (and ultimately only) testimony the jury heard at the trial about police-officer cover-ups, presumably of the misconduct of their colleagues. Darden having opened the door, Ito allowed a jubilant Cochran, on redirect, to have McKinny explain what she meant: "Sexism [on the force] is inextricably related to certain *cover-ups* that some men in the police department are doing, and some women are not able to agree with that or follow along those lines, and it was a huge schism."

p. 235: ". . . a Louis Vuitton garment bag . . .": Throughout the day after the murders, June 13, 1994, members of Simpson's family and various friends of his visited Simpson at his Rockingham estate. Among them was Simpson's friend, Robert Kardashian. A videotape shows Kardashian leaving the premises with the Louis Vuitton bag, and it appears to be full. When this bag was later seen in Simpson's bedroom closet, and when it was brought to court and marked as a defense exhibit, it was empty. The prosecution sought to call Kardashian (an attorney who around the time of the murders was on inactive status with the State Bar) to the witness stand to testify to his knowledge concerning the contents of the bag as well as that of Simpson's golf club bag which he and Simpson retrieved from LAX on June 14, 1994.

The defense vigorously resisted on the ground of the attorney-client privilege, even though Kardashian, who had since reactivated his status with the bar, was not Simpson's lawyer on June 13 and 14, nor did he participate on the record at the trial in any of the trial proceedings. Because of the sensitivity of the issue, Ito asked the prosecution to submit written questions (for Kardashian) in advance for a hearing outside the presence of the jury to decide whether Kardashian would be required to testify. Because the prosecution felt they could not get to the truth of what happened that way, they dropped the matter.

Immediately after the trial, F. Lee Bailey accused co-counsel Robert Shapiro of trying to negotiate a plea bargain with the DA's office wherein Simpson would plead guilty to voluntary manslaughter, and Kardashian to being an accessory after the fact to manslaughter, but Shapiro denied the charge.

p. 236: Cochran violates the law in his opening statement: A portion of Judge Ito's statement to the jury: "Defense counsel [Cochran] mentioned witnesses who had not previously been disclosed to the prosecution, or whose written statements were not given to the prosecution before trial as required by the law. This was a violation of the law."

p. 237: *National Enquirer* **concludes that Rosa Lopez is not a credible witness:** The *National Enquirer*, with an enormous staff working around the clock on the Simpson case, did a superb job of investigative journalism, time and again uncovering and verifying important pieces of information that the mainstream media missed. The *New York Times* took cognizance of this, noting that the *Enquirer* had become must-reading for all reporters covering the trial. *Star* magazine also scored some journalistic coups during the trial.

p. 238: Simpson told limousine driver he was sleeping (around time of murders): If Cochran, before he gave his opening statement, hadn't even bothered to read the preliminary examination testimony of Alan Park, the limousine driver, didn't he even know that his own co-counsel, Robert Shapiro, had given this alibi (of Simpson's sleeping at the time of the murders) to the media shortly after Simpson's arrest?

p. 238: Cochran doesn't have firm grasp of doctrine of reasonable doubt: Fortunately for Cochran, in his final summation his co-counsel Robert Blasier furnished him with a decent chart of his on reasonable doubt that most likely helped to educate him on the doctrine.

p. 238: Article titled "Not Guilty and Innocent—The Problem Children of Reasonable Doubt": Published in *Mississippi College Law Review*, Jackson, Mississippi, and *Criminal Justice Journal*, Western State University School of Law in San Diego, California.

p. 239: U.S. Supreme Court misstates main issue at criminal trial: E.g., Chief Justice William H. Rehnquist, in *Arizona v. Fulminante*, 111 S. Ct. 1246 (1991): "The central purpose of the criminal trial is to decide the factual question of the defendant's *guilt or innocence.*" *Jackson v. Denno*, 378 U.S. 368 (1964): "There must be a new trial on *guilt or innocence.*"

p. 239: State courts misstate main issue at criminal trial: E.g., Texas Criminal Pattern Jury Charges, Section 0.05: "Your sole duty is to *determine the guilt or innocence of the defendant.*"

If the prosecution had introduced the slow-speed chase of Simpson, Judge Ito would have given the jury this instruction: "The flight of a person immediately after the commission of a crime, or after he is accused of a crime, is not sufficient in itself to establish his guilt, but is a fact which, if proved, may be considered by you in the light of all other proved facts in deciding the question of his *guilt or innocence.*" Both the Texas and the California jury instructions, of course, are wrong.

p. 239: Legal authorities misstate main issue at criminal trial: See *Perkins on Criminal Law*: "Criminal procedure is the formal machinery established to enforce the criminal law. It includes (1) accusation of a crime; (2) *determination of guilt or innocence*; and (3) disposition of those convicted."

p. 240: ". . . and is the essence of our system": When a long piece about my article appeared in *the National Law Journal* of March 1, 1982, a staffer from the *Journal* contacted Judge Edward J. Devitt (Chief Judge, United States District Court for the District of Columbia), the horse's mouth, for his comment on my article. After reading it, Devitt surprisingly told the *Journal* he didn't use the phrase "guilt or innocence" in his own courtroom. (The judge uses the phrase in no fewer than 10 instructions in his own book, which is cheerfully parroted by federal judges throughout the country.)

p. 240: "This conduct [by Cochran] is outrageous and unbelievable": Although Cochran's opening statement could not have been more improper, and the prosecutors were 100% in the right in their objections, a Harvard Law School professor (not Dershowitz) serving as a trial analyst for the *Los Angeles Times* said that Cochran had presented an "honest" defense of Simpson, and the prosecution, in its objections, came off as "whiny, disruptive, and petty." And this professor isn't just any professor at Harvard, which would be bad enough. He's the director of the Criminal Justice Institute at Harvard Law School, the nation's leading law school.

p. 242: Because socks were black, LAPD criminalists did not see blood on them at first: Even defense expert Herbert MacDonnell acknowledged the difficulty of seeing blood on the socks. When Marcia Clark asked him, on cross-examination, "And you will agree, will you not, that the observation of blood on those socks was a difficult one in view of the dark color of the fabric?" he replied, "Not when you've got good high-intensity illumination. It would be difficult in this room, yes."

It wasn't until August 4, 1994, when they conducted their first chemical examination of the socks, that the LAPD criminalists noticed the blood. The reactive agent phenolphthalein was applied to the socks, and the presence of blood was determined. Subsequent DNA tests showed that Nicole's and Simpson's blood was on one sock, and only Nicole's on the other. There were many small bloodstains on the socks. The likelihood of one of the stains coming from any person other than Nicole was found to be one out of 6.8 billion. The likelihood of one of the stains of Simpson's blood coming from any person other than Simpson was found to be one out of 57 billion.

p. 244: ". . . photos of all four cuts and seven abrasions": It should be noted that for all the prosecution evidence Shapiro elicited from Huizenga just to get out the morsel that Simpson had severe arthritis, essentially the same fact could have been introduced to the jury through the testimony of some doctor who might have examined Simpson a few weeks or months before the murders, or by having Simpson examined at a time after the murders when most of his cuts and bruises had healed.

p. 246: ". . . a great career in the law": Bailey's biggest contribution, and it was major, to the defense victory in this case was obviously not his cross-examination of Fuhrman, which achieved nothing that most other lawyers could not have. Rather, it was his successful argument to Judge Ito (at a time when Ito was wavering) to allow the defense to cross-examine Fuhrman on the racial issue. Bailey's argument, though legally flawed and misleading (as opposed to prosecutor Cheri Lewis', which was legally sound) was nonetheless persuasively delivered. It was Bailey's finest, and ultimately most important moment at the trial.

p. 251: "... what human being can possibly convince us of this absurdity?": Now I realize the Reverend Billy Graham, who has spoken to more people about God, Jesus, and Christianity than any other human in history, has said he even knows the precise dimensions of heaven ("sixteen hundred square miles," the Reverend Billy has said). But though Billy Graham, as opposed to so many other preachers, has led an honorable life, and has probably helped millions through his ministry, can any logical person take his preaching seriously? When a fellow revivalist asked him to come to Princeton Theological Seminary to lay a deeper academic foundation for his preaching, Graham balked. "I don't have the time, the inclination, or the set of mind to pursue [these deeper questions]" Graham told *Newsweek* in November of 1993. "I found that if I say 'the Bible says' and 'God says,' I get results." I'm kind of like you, Billy—result-oriented.

p. 256: Police frame-ups are very rare, and almost invariably in drug cases: One of the most publicized cases ever was in Philadelphia. In 1994 and 1995, six white Philadelphia police officers pled guilty to framing fifty-six black people in 1988 and 1989 on drug-trafficking charges. Nearly all the framed victims were active drug dealers who also had past histories and convictions for drug dealing. The illicit conduct involved in many of the frame-ups included stealing drug money, tampering with evidence, falsifying records, perjury, and obstruction of justice.

p. 259: Police framing blacks is not a part of the black experience: I called Michael Zinzun, whom I had spoken to on my police brutality article. Zinzun, who is black, is the chairman of the Coalition Against Police Abuse in Los Angeles. He and his group have been monitoring and fighting against police brutality and other types of police misconduct against the minority communities since 1975. His coalition serves as a clearinghouse for these types of cases, documenting on the average of 2,000 per year in the county, for a total of well over 35,000 cases since Zinzun formed the coalition. When I asked Zinzun to break down the allegations of police misconduct for me he said: "It's about seventy percent excessive force, thirty percent other types of police misconduct, like not advising of rights, verbal abuse, intimidation, not giving (as they're required to do when asked) their name, badge number, division, and supervisor."

When I asked him about allegations of the police framing blacks and other members of the minority community, there was a lengthy pause. He then started citing some cases where the police had, for instance, beaten up a black person, then falsified a report accusing the victim of being the aggressor. More than once I explained to him: "Michael, I'm not talking about a situation where the police had done something wrong and were trying to cover it up by lying and accusing the victim. I'm talking about a situation where the police, for whatever reason—such as just not liking the person because he's black—frame someone they knew was innocent." Finally he focused in on precisely what I wanted. The only case he could come up with was one over twenty years ago. I already knew about the case, since it had received a good amount of publicity here in Los Angeles. In 1975, two black men were convicted of the murder of a Los Angeles deputy sheriff and sentenced to life imprisonment. In 1992, after many appeals and an investigation by a private detective firm, the Los Angeles County District Attorney's office (which felt there had been gross misconduct on the part of the investigating officers but did not go so far as to say the defendants were innocent) joined in with the defense counsel for the two defendants, Barry Tarlow, in asking the appellate court to grant a writ of habeas corpus and release the two. The court, in granting the writ, said, "The conduct of the officers in the case was reprehensible." There was solid evidence they had coerced perjured testimony from witnesses and withheld exculpatory evidence (evidence favorable to the defendants). Each defendant received large settlements from the city. One is back in prison after being convicted of several sexual assaults.

p. 262: Roderick Hodge, a black, testified against Fuhrman: It was not elicited on direct examination or cross-examination that Hodge was arrested by Fuhrman and his partner on a drug charge, and was subsequently acquitted.

p. 263: District Attorneys "Roll Out" program: To Johnnie Cochran's credit, in his brief tenure at the DA's office, 1978–80, he was one of the moving forces behind the creation of the roll-out program. (It has since been discontinued, in 1995, for budgetary reasons.)

p. 264: DA's Special Investigations Division rolls out to scene of crime, but never finds criminality by police: Because I know the Special Investigations Division of the DA's office, for all intents and purposes, never prosecutes police brutality cases, I was surprised when Darden, in his summation to the jury, said, "I spent seven years prosecuting bad policemen." Just on the possibility that I was wrong and Darden had been prosecuting police without me or anyone else knowing about it (perhaps in the middle of the night, with only the goblins as witnesses), I called two current deputy DAs who worked alongside Darden between 1987 and 1994, when Darden was in SID. They both told me Darden only prosecuted one case in seven years, and it wasn't a police brutality case. It was the "39th and Dalton Street" case, a 1990 misdemeanor prosecution (unsuccessful) of several LAPD officers for physically trashing a duplex apartment house searching for drugs. And yet the *Los Angeles Times* said Darden "has long experience in *prosecuting* police officers." *Newsweek* called Darden a "cop-busting DA." Why? Because he was in a section that was "supposed" to prosecute bad cops. Whether he actually did or not was an irrelevant question to these reporters. Chris, you're a good man, and for all I know you wanted your office to prosecute more bad cops then they would. And you were, I'm told, instrumental in getting your office to file murder charges in 1993 against an LAPD officer, one of the few such prosecutions in Los Angeles history. But you yourself only *investigated* bad cops for seven years, not *prosecuted* them. As you know, Chris, it was almost unheard of for your office to do the latter.

p. 268: Vannatter doesn't want to admit on stand he viewed Simpson as "a" suspect: It would have been perfectly normal for Vannatter and his colleagues to have viewed Simpson as "a" not "the" suspect at the time they went to Simpson's Rockingham estate in the early-morning hours of June 13, 1994, since the husband is almost always a suspect when a wife (or here, a recently divorced wife) is murdered. Vannatter should have said that, and then added that Simpson wasn't "the" suspect when they went over the wall at Simpson's estate. (The detectives testified they went over the wall because of a combination of reasons: what they had just seen a short distance away at Bundy; they saw a spot of blood above the driver's door handle of the Bronco; the vehicle appeared to be hastily parked outside Simpson's residence; no one answered the intercom buzzer or regular phone inside the residence even though the detectives saw lights on upstairs and downstairs, there were two cars parked on the driveway inside the gate, and Westec, Simpson's private security firm, had told them there was a live-in maid who should be inside. In their minds these were "exigent circumstances" causing them to go over the wall without first securing a search warrant, since they didn't know if there was anyone inside dead or seriously hurt.) But Vannatter, instead, told Shapiro on cross-examination that in his mind that night, Simpson was no more of a suspect than he, Robert Shapiro, was. Although that is possible, it's not too believable, and the jury has said they did not believe Vannatter.

Both the judge at the preliminary hearing (Kathleen Kennedy Powell, who impressed me) and Judge Ito ruled that the four detectives' conduct that night did not violate Simpson's rights under the Fourth Amendment to the United States Constitution, which prohibits "unreasonable searches and seizures." Ito did say, however, that Vannatter had been "reckless" with some of the facts in the affidavit he prepared seeking a search warrant later in the day.

p. 270: Simpson case "received a vastly disproportionate amount of publicity": The case received more available media coverage than any other case since the Lindbergh kidnapping-murder case in New Jersey in 1935. Perhaps third in terms of media coverage was the Manson murder case in 1970–71.

p. 272: The "entire nation" was tuned in to verdict: National figures released by the A. C. Nielson Company reflected that an incredible 91 percent share of the viewing audience was tuned in. And a survey commissioned by CNN found 142 million Americans listened on TV and radio to the verdict.

p. 273: Media generates interest in case by blanketing the news with case: There are, of course, plenty of precedents for such a firestorm of interest created by media coverage, which doesn't make the phenomenon one bit less depressing or scary. A good recent example would be the war in the Persian Gulf. In the course of just four months the Bush administration, with the help of the media, managed to transform the country of Kuwait, a place many Americans had never heard of, with a nasty, repressive government that had no particular history of friendship towards the United States, into a sentimental favorite of popular imagination, and we were caught up in a seductive riptide of patriotic support for intervention that resembled nothing so much as the fervor surrounding a World Series or a Superbowl.

p. 273: **Simpson is the most famous murder defendant in American history:** In 1921, Fatty Arbuckle, the silent screen star second only to Charlie Chaplin in comedic fame at the time, was charged with and, after two hung juries, acquitted of manslaughter, not murder.

p. 274: **". . . substantially mitigating circumstances":** E.g., mental illness, heat of passion. For instance, in a heat-of-passion killing, you don't deceive the jury by arguing that your client never committed the homicide when you know he did. You concede guilt, but argue it's voluntary manslaughter as opposed to first-degree murder.

p. 277: **Shapiro says before trial that race was not going to be an issue:** Also, during the trial, when F. Lee Bailey cross-examined Fuhrman on his use of the word "nigger," Shapiro told reporters, "My preference was that race was not an issue in this case and should not be an issue, and I'm sorry from my own personal view that it has become an issue in the case." However, the *Los Angeles Times* said that "a source on the defense team dismissed Shapiro's contention, saying that Shapiro had not raised any objections during strategy sessions."

p. 279: **Are blacks more racist than whites?:** After all, polls showed that 88 percent of the white population disapproved of the not-guilty verdict in the first Rodney King trial, where the victim was black and the acquitted defendants were white.

p. 279: **". . . the verdict may have set race relations in this country back thirty years":** A *USA Today*-CNN national poll on October 3, 1995, the day of the verdict, found 57 percent believing that the verdict would hurt race relations.

p. 280: **Johnnie Cochran exploited black community:** An additional irony here is that Cochran, unlike Simpson, has not forgotten his roots, and has an admirable history with the black community, among other things being a generous financial supporter of black causes.

p. 284: **Many in law enforcement supported the not-guilty verdict in the Rodney King case:** I thought the verdict was wrong, but I also feel that the subsequent federal prosecution of the four officers, in which two were convicted, constituted double jeopardy in all but the narrowest and most technical definition, and so it should not have taken place.

p. 285: **Jury service should be more mandatory:** Virtually everyone is called for jury duty, but relatively few ever serve. Here are some of the funny reasons culled from the files of the Los Angeles County office of the jury commissioner: "I cannot serve. My heart stopped." "I have the dizzy flu and I fell on my head. Now hopefully I will be better soon." "Glad to serve if I could get a ride to Los Angeles County from Folsom State Prison." "I am one who has lost all my hair and I need a full wig. I cannot be in an enclosed room for any length of time because of the extreme heat." "I cannot serve. I am under my doctor's car [sic]." "I watch hummingbirds for a living, and the hummingbirds are hatching at this time of the year." "I cannot serve. My poodle is in heat. The dog downstairs is a mongrel and I am afraid he will get to my poodle."

p. 286: **Some suggest eliminating the need for unanimous jury verdicts in criminal trials:** In 1972, the United States Supreme Court ruled that the U.S. Constitution does not require a unanimous verdict in a criminal jury trial. Earlier, in 1970, the Court ruled that the Constitution does not require that a jury in a criminal trial even be made up of twelve people. Today, Arizona allows an eight-member jury, Florida a six-member jury in noncapital cases. In a 1978 Georgia case, however, the United States Supreme Court disallowed a five-member jury as violating the Sixth Amendment right to a jury trial.

p. 289: ". . . this well-known ditty": In fact, the evidence in the case was that Lizzie's stepmother had been struck twenty-one times and her father ten.

HELL AND HIGH WATER

HELL AND HIGH WATER

GLOBAL WARMING—
THE SOLUTION AND THE POLITICS—
AND WHAT WE SHOULD DO

Joseph J. Romm

WILLIAM MORROW

An Imprint of HarperCollinsPublishers

HarperCollins books may be purchased for educational, business, or sales promotional use. For information please write: Special Markets Department, HarperCollins Publishers, 10 East 53rd Street, New York, NY 10022.

FIRST EDITION

Designed by Daniel Lagin

Library of Congress Cataloging-in-Publication Data has been applied for.

ISBN: 978-0-06-117212-0
ISBN-10: 0-06-117212-X

07   08   09   10   11   DIX/RRD   10   9   8   7   6   5   4   3   2   1

To Patricia and the hope she brings

The rarest attribute in any society and culture when things are going generally well . . . is to notice certain cracks in the edifice, some defects and problems, which if not attended to could in time undermine the happy ambience and bring on distress and terror.

—Norman F. Cantor, *In the Wake of the Plague,* 2001

History does not forgive us our national mistakes because they are explicable in terms of our domestic politics.

—George Kennan, 1950

CONTENTS

HELL AND HIGH WATER

INTRODUCTION

We are on the precipice of climate system tipping points beyond which there is no redemption.
> —James Hansen, director, Goddard Institute for
> Space Studies (NASA), December 2005

The ice sheets seem to be shrinking 100 years ahead of schedule.
> —Richard Alley, Penn State climate scientist,
> May 2006

Imagine if inland United States were 10°F hotter, with many states ravaged by mega-droughts and the widespread wildfires that result. At the same time, our coasts were drowning from a 5- to 10-foot increase in sea levels, which were relentlessly climbing 5 to 10 inches a decade or more toward an ultimate sea-level rise of *80 feet.*

This "Hell and High Water" scenario is not our certain future, but it is as likely as the bird flu pandemic we are feverishly fighting to fend off. And it could come as soon as the second half of this century, given the many early warning signs of accelerated climate change that scientists have spotted.

Long before then, the temperature of the inland United States will be rising nearly 1°F *per decade,* enough to cause continual heat waves and searing droughts. At the same time, sea levels will be rising a few inches every decade, with much of our Atlantic and Gulf coasts battered year after year after year by super-hurricanes with savage storm surges.

Let's call this phase Planetary Purgatory, when the world comes to know that 20-foot sea-level rise is all but inevitable, and we must endure a desperate multidecade ordeal to correct the mistakes of the past, to keep sea-level rise as low and slow as possible—to avoid the full fury of Hell and High Water. If the politics of inaction and delay that have triumphed in this country continues for another decade, then Planetary Purgatory is *the likely future facing our country before midcentury—probably in your own lifetime.*

According to a March 2006 Gallup Poll, only about a third of Americans understand that global warming will "pose a serious threat to you or your way of life in your lifetime." And if you think that global warming will mainly affect other, poorer countries, or that we can delay acting until we have new technologies, you come by your opinions honestly. Many of the most sophisticated policy makers and journalists also just don't get it—they don't understand how global warming will ruin America for the next fifty generations if we don't act quickly.

The widespread confusion about our climate crisis is no accident. For more than a decade, those who deny that climate change is an urgent problem have sought to delay action on global warming by running a brilliant rhetorical campaign and spreading multiple myths that misinform debate. As a result, many people still believe global warming is nothing more than a natural climate cycle that humans cannot influence, or that it might even have positive benefits for this nation. Neither is true. The science is crystal clear: We humans are the primary cause of global warming, and we face a bleak future if we fail to act quickly.

We must reverse the growth in U.S. greenhouse gas emissions and assert leadership to bring every country, especially China, along with us. We created this problem, and we can solve it.

I have spent nearly two decades working to achieve this clean-energy future. The cost is far lower and the benefits far higher than the opponents of action argue, yet the winning solution is not well understood by policy makers, the media, or the public. As I will spell out, a very few states, most notably California, have embraced critical clean-energy strategies; we need to adopt these nationwide. These strategies would also deliver vast benefits—a sharp drop in foreign-oil imports and in our massive trade deficit, a large gain in air quality and health, and a big boost in high-wage, high-tech jobs. This win-win-win future, however, requires a rapid change in both domestic and foreign policy. Congress and the president would have to join together to embrace the aggressive government-led regulatory and technological strategy that they have repeatedly failed to adopt.

Time is short. *We have at most a decade to sharply reverse course.*

If we fail to act in time, global warming will profoundly and irreversibly remake every aspect of American life—where we live, how we live, how we grow food and how much we grow, what and how we drive, how we relate to other countries, and so on.

As catastrophic sea-level rise becomes inevitable, we will become consumed by urban triage—how to decide which major seaside cities can be saved and which cannot. Every seaside city will be threatened: Seattle, San Francisco, Los Angeles, San Diego, Houston, New Orleans, Mobile, St. Petersburg, Miami, Jacksonville, Savannah, Norfolk, Baltimore, Jersey City, New York City, New Haven, Providence, Boston, and Portland, Maine—along with hundreds of smaller cities. No other nation has as much wealth along its shores.

The most devastating flooding probably won't occur until after 2100, but long before then, painful choices will be forced upon the nation over and over again by record-breaking hurricane seasons with ever more devastating storm surges. *Protecting* dozens of major coastal cities from flooding will be challenging enough; *rebuilding* major coastal cities destroyed by super-hurricanes will be an overwhelming task, especially if we allow rapid sea-level rise to become unstoppable in the second half of the century. We do not appear to be willing to spend the money now to protect New Orleans from another hurricane like Katrina—let alone the combination of such a hurricane plus the coming sea-level rise—and that suggests that the city will not survive the next super-hurricane, which is likely to come within the next few decades.

In the political realm, global warming is poised to become the Achilles' heel of the American conservative movement. Its fatal mistake: turning global warming into a partisan ideological issue. Conservative politicians, pundits, and think tanks are staking their movement's future on denying the science and delaying the solution. But while they can stop the nation from acting to prevent the worst of global warming, they cannot stop the searing reality of their perverse blunders from becoming painfully clear to all.

The chair of the Senate Environment and Public Works Committee, Senator James Inhofe, calls global warming "the greatest hoax ever perpetrated on the American people" and holds hearings where he and witnesses such as novelist Michael Crichton belittle the work of the entire scientific community. President George W. Bush has blocked all national efforts to limit greenhouse gas emissions and has thwarted international efforts to develop stronger emissions controls. If they continue on this course, Bush and Inhofe will go down in history with other leaders such as Herbert Hoover and Neville Chamberlain who were blind to their nation's gravest threats.

Imagine the impact catastrophic climate change will have internationally. For decades, the United States has been the moral, economic, and military leader of the free world. What will happen when we end up in Planetary Purgatory, facing 20 or more feet of sea-level rise, and the rest of the world blames our inaction and obstructionism, blames the wealthiest nation on earth for refusing to embrace even cost-effective solutions that could spare the planet from millennia of misery? The indispensable nation will become a global pariah.

Predicting the unpredictable and imagining the unimaginable consequences of this climate crisis are among my major goals here. Anyone who wants to understand the disastrous but largely avoidable fate to which we are committing America and the rest of the world—as well as the only sensible way to avoid catastrophe—must understand the three driving forces: climate science, energy trends and technology, and global-warming politics. This book is a primer on all three.

I first became interested in global warming in the mid-1980s, studying for my physics Ph.D. at the Massachusetts Institute of Technology and researching my thesis on oceanography at the Scripps Institution of Oceanography in California. I was privileged to work with Walter Munk, one of the world's top ocean scientists, on advanced acoustic techniques for monitoring temperature changes in the Greenland Sea.

A few years later, as special assistant for international security to Peter Goldmark, president of the Rockefeller Foundation, I found myself listening to some of the nation's top experts on these issues. Even a generation ago, they knew the gravest threats that would face us today. They convinced me that global warming was the most serious long-term, *preventable* threat to the health and well-being of this nation and the world. In the mid-1990s I served for five years in the U.S. Department of Energy. As an acting assistant secretary, I helped develop a climate-technology strategy for the nation. More

recently, I have worked with some of the nation's leading corporations, helping them to make greenhouse gas reductions and commitment plans that also handsomely boost their profits.

But the awesome nature of the tragedy we face did not hit home
for me until Hurricane Katrina struck my brother and his family. A
30-foot wall of water with waves up to 55 feet high crashed into Pass
Christian, Mississippi, where my brother lived with his wife and
son. The ferocious storm surge destroyed their house, one mile inland, while they stayed in a Biloxi shelter. This book began as a research effort I started so I could advise my brother on the tough
question of whether or not he should rebuild his home.

What I learned is that global warming has already begun making Atlantic hurricanes far more destructive. Energy and moisture
picked up from warmer Gulf waters produce more intense winds
and rain. And in the case of Katrina, that extra punch may be what
destroyed the levees protecting New Orleans—the "straw that
breaks the camel's back," in the words of Dr. Kevin Trenberth, head
of Climate Analysis at the National Center for Atmospheric Research.

Katrina reveals what is to come for this country. On our current
path, all our great Gulf and Atlantic coast cities are at risk of meeting the same fate as New Orleans.

If the situation is so dire, why aren't more people running
around with their "hair on fire," as CIA director George Tenet was
in the summer of 2001, trying to get someone, anyone, to hear his
warnings about an impending terrorist attack? In fact, much of the
scientific community has been astonished that their increasingly
strong and detailed warnings have been either ignored or attacked.
I was astounded to learn the full extent of the Bush administration's
methods for muzzling government climate scientists and censoring their work, which has prevented their urgent message from
reaching the American public. The highest ranks of the National

Hurricane Center and the National Oceanic and Atmospheric Administration have misinformed the public about the likely danger of—and increased number of—future super-hurricanes.

One reason I wrote this book is to give voice to those scientists whose warnings have gone unheard or unheeded.

Three full decades have passed since the National Academy of Sciences, the nation's most prestigious scientific body, first warned that uncontrolled greenhouse gas emissions might raise global temperatures a staggering 10°F and raise sea levels 20 feet—and yet the nation has still not taken any serious action. In stunning contrast, less than five years after climate scientists warned us in 1974 that chlorofluorocarbons were destroying the earth's ozone layer, America voluntarily banned their use in spray cans, and a decade later President Reagan and Vice President Bush led the way to creating an international treaty banning them.

One key goal of this book is to provide a fuller answer to the puzzle of why this country has failed to act on global warming. As we will see, the failure stems from weaknesses inherent in the scientific community, strategic and messaging mistakes made by environmentalists and progressive politicians, flaws in the media's coverage of science, and an insidious effort to exploit those weaknesses, mistakes, and flaws by conservative political leaders such as President Bush as well as a small group of scientists and conservative think tanks with funding from fossil fuel companies.

Global warming has also proved intractable because this country has refused to adopt a sensible energy strategy. Our political leaders won't even require Detroit to build fuel-efficient vehicles—which would not only reduce greenhouse gas emissions but also save consumers money and cut oil imports during a time of war in the Persian Gulf and record-high gasoline prices at home. Instead, we have squandered many years and hundreds of millions of dollars on a misguided—and, as we will see, largely cynical—technology strategy focused on hydrogen-fuel-cell cars that offers no hope of cutting overall greenhouse gas emissions (or oil imports) until mid-century, if ever.

Energy is a subject with as many myths as climate science. The most destructive one is that we cannot tackle global warming until we develop new breakthrough technologies. In fact, the reverse is true. We have cost-effective technologies today that can sharply reduce global-warming pollution. If we don't start reducing greenhouse gas emissions very soon with the technology we have, it will be too late for something new to do us any good. Interestingly, while the climate scientists I talk to invariably warn about crossing thresholds of greenhouse gas pollution that could bring catastrophe, few know enough about energy issues to fully understand just how little time we have to act. This book attempts to bridge the gap between climate science and energy policy.

The first half focuses on our country's future if we don't reverse course immediately. Front and center are the climate system's deadly feedback loops—the vicious cycles whereby an initial warming causes changes that lead to more and more warming—all of which reduce the time we have available to act.

The second half of this book focuses on the politics and the solution. I examine the brilliant disinformation campaign created to sow doubt about climate science and the equally clever campaign to create confusion about the crucial climate solutions. Then I lay out how we can achieve deep reductions in greenhouse gas emissions in the electricity and transportation sectors without raising the nation's overall energy bill. We'll see what the car and the fuel of the future will be, since it isn't going to be fuel-cell vehicles running on hydrogen. Finally, I explore the role of China and the role of the media.

The main goal of this book is to lay out the climate-change warning clearly and persuasively. My hair *is* on fire. And yours should be, too.

PART I

THE SCIENCE AND THE FUTURE

CHAPTER ONE

THE CLIMATE BEAST

*The paleoclimate record shouts out to us that, far
from being self-stabilizing, the Earth's climate system
is an ornery beast which overreacts even to small
nudges.*

—Wallace Broecker, climate scientist, 1995

*The ongoing Arctic warming corresponds to the pre-
dictions of the more pessimistic climate models. By
extension, the pessimistic scenarios of climate change
can be expected to unfold in the rest of the Northern
Hemisphere.*

—Louis Fortier, climate scientist, June 2006

We are on the brink of taking the biggest gamble in human
history, one that, if we lose, will transform the lives of the
next fifty generations. I will not focus here on the history of how we
came to our current understanding of global warming or on the
thousands of brilliant scientists whose work brings us this knowledge. That story has been well told already, particularly by Spencer
Weart, a physicist and historian, who has put on the web his extensive "hypertext history of how scientists came to (partly) understand what people are doing to cause climate change."

Similarly, I will not lay out more than briefly the scientific underpinnings for our understanding of global warming or of the extensive and conclusive evidence that climate change is occurring. The case has been made again and again by hundreds of top scientists who have done research and analysis for prestigious bodies such as the U.N.'s Intergovernmental Panel on Climate Change (IPCC), the National Academy of Sciences, and the Arctic Council, the nations that border the Arctic Circle, including ours, in its December 2004 *Arctic Climate Impact Assessment.*

How strong is the scientific consensus? Back in 2001, President George W. Bush asked the National Academy of Sciences for a report on climate change and on the conclusions of the IPCC assessments on climate change. The eleven-member blue-ribbon panel, which included experts previously skeptical about global warming, concluded: Temperatures are rising because of human activities; the scientific community agrees that most of the rise in the last half-century is likely due to increased greenhouse gas concentrations in the atmosphere; and "the stated degree of confidence in the IPCC assessment is higher today than it was 10, or even 5 years ago."

Back in 2001, Donald Kennedy, *Science* editor in chief and president emeritus of Stanford University, commented on the steady stream of peer-reviewed reports and articles documenting global climate change appearing in his and other journals: *"Consensus as strong as the one that has developed around this topic is rare in science."* And in December 2004, *Science* published the results of an analysis of nearly a thousand scientific studies appearing in refereed scientific journals between 1993 and 2003. The conclusion:

This analysis shows that scientists publishing in the peer-reviewed literature agree with IPCC, the National Academy of Sciences, and the public statements of other professional societies, Politicians, economists, journalists, and others may have the impression of confusion, disagreement, or discord among climate scientists, but that impression is incorrect.

The strong consensus has grown even stronger because the case has grown even stronger. "Evidence of global warming became so overwhelming in 2004 that now the question is: What can we do about it?" That was *Discover* magazine in its January 2005 issue, which called the ever-strengthening case for climate change the top science story of the year.

"There can no longer be genuine doubt that human-made gases are the dominant cause of observed warming," explained James Hansen, director of NASA's Goddard Institute for Space Studies, in April 2005. Hansen led a team of scientists that made "precise measurements of increasing ocean heat content over the past 10 years," which revealed that the earth is absorbing far more heat than it is emitting into space, confirming what earlier computer models had shown about warming. Hansen called this energy imbalance the "smoking gun" of climate change.

In June 2005 the national science academies of the United States, Brazil, Canada, China, France, Germany, India, Italy, Japan, Russia, and the United Kingdom issued a joint statement on climate change urging the nations of the world to take prompt action to reduce greenhouse gas emissions. So far, the world has not listened. Worse, in December 2005, the U.S. government shamelessly blocked the world from acting at an international conference in Montreal that was aimed at developing the next steps for action on climate change.

If you are interested in understanding the detailed evidence for global warming and climate science, if you want to know the answer to key questions such as "How do we know that recent carbon dioxide increases are due to human activities?" or "How do we know that an increase in solar activity is *not* the cause of recent planetary warming?" bookmark the website www.realclimate.org. This site, run by climate experts, answers these and other questions and discusses the latest findings.

My focus instead is the question of the century: *Do we humans have the political will to stop the great ice sheets of Greenland and West Antarctica from melting . . . to stop Hell and High Water?*

PUNCHING THE CLIMATE BEAST

Whether human activity will trigger catastrophic climate change depends on two factors: how much heat-trapping, climate-altering greenhouse gases we pour into the atmosphere, and how the climate system responds to those gases. Recent evidence indicates the climate is more sensitive than had been widely thought. Louis Fortier, Canada Research chair on the Response of Arctic Marine Ecosystems to Climate Change at Université Laval, echoed the thinking of many climate scientists when he said at a June 15, 2006, transatlantic conference that we should now expect the more "pessimistic scenarios" of climate change. Let's try to understand why.

The greenhouse effect has made the life we know possible. The basic physics is straightforward. Our sun pours out intense amounts of visible light, along with radiation, across the electromagnetic spectrum, including ultraviolet and infrared. The sun's peak intensity is in visible light. Of the solar energy hitting the top of the atmosphere, about 30 percent is reflected back into space—by the atmosphere itself (including clouds) and by the earth's surface (land, ocean, and ice). The rest is absorbed, mostly into the earth but some by the atmosphere. This process heats up the planet. The earth reradiates the energy it has absorbed mostly as heat, infrared radiation.

Some naturally occurring atmospheric gases let visible light escape through into space while trapping certain types of infrared radiation. Because these greenhouse gases, including water and carbon dioxide (CO_2), trap some of the reradiated heat, they act as a partial blanket that helps keep the planet about 60°F warmer than it otherwise would be, and that is ideal for us humans.

Since the dawn of the industrial revolution 250 years ago, humankind has been spewing vast quantities of extra greenhouse gases into the atmosphere, causing more and more heat to be trapped. Carbon dioxide released from burning fossil fuels—coal, oil, and natural gas—makes up 85 percent of U.S. greenhouse gas emissions. For most of the past two centuries, few worried about the consequences. But thanks to the work of thousands of scientists, the risks are now clear: We are engaging in a dangerous, planetwide, uncontrolled experiment as these emissions push our climate system into a different state, a far less hospitable state, than human civilization has ever known.

The first remarkable, and ominous, fact about our climate system is that it is not steady, not self-stabilizing. It is an "ornery beast," as climatologist Wallace Broecker calls it. That beast is shaped like a spiked monster. Consider figure 1, the temperature record for the past 400,000 years, derived primarily from Antarctic ice-core data. The mile-long ice cores, drilled by hardy scientists in the harshest of climates, are a record of annual snowfall. The trace gases trapped in the ice layers reveal the temperature and atmospheric composition year by year.

The sawtooth temperature pattern reveals that long ice ages (the valleys in the figure) have been followed by relatively brief, warm interglacial periods (the peaks), such as the one we're in now that began with the end of the last ice age some 10,000 years ago. These ten millennia of mild weather have made possible human civilization as we know it today. And yet, as the figure shows, the interglacial period we now live in is only a very few degrees centigrade warmer than the average temperature of the last ice age, which lasted about 100,000 years.

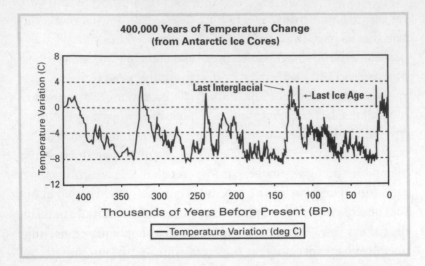

Figure 1. The temperature record for the past 400,000 years from Antarctic ice cores. The "0" for temperature on the *y* axis is the average temperature from 1880 to 1899. The last interglacial (warm period) began 131,000 years ago and lasted 15,000 years. The most recent ice age started about 110,000 years ago and ended about 10,000 years ago. We have warmed about 0.8°C since the industrial revolution (not shown on this chart).

The second ominous fact: Warming can happen fast. As a 2002 study by the National Academy of Sciences explained:

Recent scientific evidence shows that major and widespread climate changes have occurred with startling speed. For example, *roughly half the north Atlantic warming since the last ice age was achieved in only a decade,* and it was accompanied by significant climatic changes across most of the globe. Similar events, including local warming as large as 16°C, occurred repeatedly during the slide into and climb out of the last ice age. [Emphasis added.]

Take a look at figure 1 again. Notice that the warming line at the start of every brief mild interglacial age typically rises very sharply.

You might expect that the temperature would go up gradually. But instead, it all happens very quickly.

Before the 1990s, most scientists saw climate change as a slow, gradual process, linked to variations in Earth's orbit that changed on the timescale of tens of thousands of years, and to changes driven by continental drift over the course of tens of millions of years. But scientific advances, such as those that have allowed us to unlock the evidence found in ancient ice, reveal that huge temperature swings and a doubling of precipitation have occurred "in periods as short as decades to years."

The final ominous fact: The climate has changed most quickly when it has been "forced" to change, such as by increased heating from the sun or from greenhouse gases. We are now forcing the climate to change much, much faster than nature has in the past. The NAS study noted, "Abrupt climate changes were especially common when the climate system was being forced to change most rapidly." The risk, then, is that the rapid greenhouse warming we ourselves are causing today increases the chances for "large, abrupt, and unwelcome regional or global climatic events."

THE FAST FATAL FEEDBACKS

The climate system's ability to warm so rapidly suggests it has strong feedbacks or vicious cycles whereby a small initial warming leads to a disproportionately huge heating. It works like this: Something triggers an initial warming, a forcing event, such as a change in the path Earth takes to orbit the sun, and that brings more intense sunshine (solar insolation) to the planet. Then feedbacks reinforce warming and our planet heats up faster. What kind of vicious cycles? Three in particular are well known.

First, warming causes sea ice to melt and glaciers to retreat. Highly reflective white ice is replaced by the blue sea or dark land, both of which absorb far more solar energy. So the blue oceans and the dark earth heat up more, causing even more ice melting, which results in a larger decrease in Earth's reflectivity (albedo), and that leads to more heating, and so up and up the temperature spiral. We can witness this classic feedback today at the North Pole, where the white summer ice cap has shrunk more than 20 percent from 1978 to 2005, a loss of 200,000 square miles of ice, an area twice the size of Texas, in a single generation.

Second, warming increases evaporation and the amount of water vapor in the air. Water vapor is a greenhouse gas. More water vapor means more warming, which means more water vapor, and so on and on. A 2005 study found that upper-atmospheric moistening from 1982 to 2004 was being accurately modeled by climate scientists. As we will see, more water vapor also leads to more intense hurricanes and rainstorms.

Third, warming can cause the soil or tundra or oceans to release carbon dioxide and methane, both potent greenhouse gases. This set of feedbacks, which will ultimately shape much of our fate, is discussed in detail in chapter 3.

Given all these vicious cycles, you would expect to see the temperature record of the past several hundred thousand years march in lockstep with the level of greenhouse gases such as carbon dioxide (CO_2) and methane (CH_4). And as figure 2 illustrates, this is precisely what has happened. Here is the historical record of carbon dioxide alongside temperature for the last 400,000 years. The rise in carbon dioxide at the start of every interglacial warming period trails the temperature rise by a few hundred years. The warming appears to be initiated by changes in Earth's orbit around the sun, which in turn leads to increases in carbon dioxide (and methane), which then accelerate the warming, which increases the emissions, which increases the warming. . . .

This is one of the most revealing as well as astonishing graphs ever compiled.

The high confidence that scientists have in these records in-

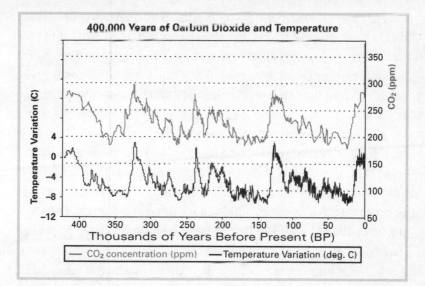

Figure 2. The record of atmospheric concentrations of carbon dioxide, CO_2, in parts per million or ppm (upper curve), together with the temperature record (lower curve), for the past 400,000 years.

The sharp increase in CO_2 concentrations since 1900 is so unprecedented in the historical record, it appears simply as a vertical line extending from 280 to 380 ppm at the far upper-right of the chart. The level of CO_2 is now far outside the bounds humans have ever experienced.

The close coupling between CO_2 and temperature over the past several hundred thousand years is one of many reasons scientists are confident that global temperatures this century will keep rising faster and faster as concentrations of CO_2 rise faster and faster. We have warmed about 0.8°C since the industrial revolution (not shown on this chart).

creased further in 2005 when researchers examined a 2-mile-long Antarctic ice core that extended the records—and extended the tight correlation between temperature and greenhouse gas concentrations—back even farther in time. As NASA's Gavin Schmidt wrote of that research, "That a number of different labs, looking at ice from different locations, extracted with different methods, all give very similar answers is a powerful indication that what they are measuring is real."

The past is prologue. This paleoclimate record is an eye-opener and a heart-stopper. It reveals the enormous risks we are taking with our planetwide, damn-the-consequences climate experiment. Because of human activity, mostly the combustion of fossil fuels, Earth's carbon dioxide levels are literally off the chart. So are methane levels.

Carbon dioxide levels in particular are higher than they have been for millions of years. The rate of increase is even more worrisome than the levels. Levels are rising 200 times faster than at any time in the last 650,000 years. If "Earth's climate system is an ornery beast which overreacts to even small nudges," as Dr. Broecker put it, what will happen to people foolish enough to keep punching it in the face?

On our current emissions path, Earth's average temperature will probably rise 1.5°C by midcentury. By century's end we will be more than 3°C warmer than today. *The last time Earth was 1°C warmer than today, sea levels were 20 feet higher.* That occurred during the Eemian interglacial period about 125,000 years ago, when Greenland appears to have had far less ice.

How fast can the sea level rise? Following the last ice age, the world saw sustained melting that *raised sea levels more than a foot a decade.* Many scientists believe we could see such a melting rate—a catastrophic melting rate of more than 12 inches every ten years—within this century. Sea levels ultimately could rise much more than 20 feet because Antarctica contains far more landlocked ice than Greenland.

The last time Earth was 2° to 3°C warmer than it is now, some 3 million years ago, sea levels were more than 80 feet higher.

THE ANSWER TO THE QUESTION OF THE CENTURY

Carbon dioxide, CO_2, is the principal greenhouse gas forcing the climate to change. In the past 250 years, industrial processes, mainly burning fossil fuels, have released some 1,100 billion tons of CO_2 into the atmosphere cumulatively. Fully half these emissions have occurred only since the mid-1970s, which is why the climate has begun to change so dramatically in recent decades. In 2005, emissions of CO_2 generated by fossil fuel combustion amounted to more than 26 billion tons.

While *emissions* might be thought of as the rate of water flowing into a bathtub, atmospheric *concentrations* are the water level in the bathtub. Concentrations are what affect the climate. Global concentrations of carbon dioxide in the atmosphere had risen slowly from a preindustrial average of about 280 parts per million (ppm) to about 315 ppm by 1960. In 2005, concentrations have soared to 380 ppm, which is not surprising, since emissions have been soaring. Concentrations are now climbing by more than 2 ppm a year.

We have been adding carbon dioxide and other greenhouse gases to the atmosphere at such a fast clip that the planet's warming has not yet caught up to the full forcing of all those heat-trapping gases. So, if we stopped increasing the concentration of greenhouse gases in the atmosphere right now, Earth would still warm up another 0.6°C. Yet, as we've seen, if we warm more than another 1°C, then a 20-plus-foot sea-level rise becomes the likely scenario.

How much do carbon dioxide emissions have to drop to stop increasing concentrations? For the last few decades nearly 60 percent of the carbon dioxide that we have been adding to the atmosphere has stayed there. The other 40 percent is being taken up by the ocean, vegetation, and soils. To stop concentrations from rising, we have to reduce emissions by more than 60 percent (probably closer to 80 percent) from recent levels. Yet far from dropping, carbon dioxide emissions have instead been rising 2 percent per year for the past decade, thanks to steady population and economic growth combined with an absence of collective action to achieve that growth in an environmentally sustainable manner.

Worse still, China, the world's second-largest (and fastest-growing) emitter, is building coal plants and increasing oil use at an accelerating rate. Worst of all, the world's largest emitter, the United States, has not only refused to reduce its emissions, the Bush administration is actually committed to increasing our emissions and blocking other countries from taking action to reduce theirs (see chapter 5). The U.S. Energy Information Administration projects global emissions will rise more than 50 percent between 2000 and 2030.

By about 2015, the planet will be fully committed to another 1°C warming, even if we could cut emissions 80 percent in the span of a few years after 2015. But of course emissions can't drop that quickly in the real world. Replacing the economy's fossil fuel–based industry entirely might take a century. Rather than focusing on impractical impossibilities, let me focus on political improbabilities, since occasionally political realities can change fast.

Instead of replacing the world's existing fossil fuel–based industry, let's ask what it would take just to replace the projected *growth* in emissions for the next fifty years—growth that is now expected to come primarily from more than a thousand *new* large coal plants and more than a billion *new* cars. How that might be done was spelled out in a 2004 *Science* magazine article by Princeton University researchers Stephen Pacala and Robert Socolow, which I here update and modify.

Imagine if the next president, in concert with the U.S. Congress and all the major nations of the world, developed and developing, embarked on an aggressive *five-decade-long* effort to deploy the best existing and emerging energy technology. Imagine that from 2010 through 2060 the world achieves the following astonishing changes:

1. We replicate, nationally and globally, California's performance-based efficiency programs and codes for homes and

commercial buildings. From 1976 to 2005, electricity consumption per capita stayed flat in California, while it grew 60 percent in the rest of the nation.

2. We greatly increase the efficiency of industry and power generation—and more than double the use of cogeneration (combined heat and power). The energy now lost as waste heat from U.S. power generation exceeds the energy used by Japan for all purposes.

3. We build 1 million large wind turbines (fifty times the current capacity) or the equivalent in other renewables, such as solar power.

4. We capture the carbon dioxide associated with 800 proposed large coal plants (four-fifths of all coal plants in the year 2000) and permanently store that CO_2 underground. This is a flow of CO_2 *into* the ground equal to the current flow of oil *out* of the ground.

5. We build 700 large nuclear power plants (double the current capacity) while maintaining the use of all existing nuclear plants.

6. As the number of cars and light trucks on the road more than triples to 2 billion, we increase their average fuel economy to 60 miles per gallon (triple the current U.S. average) with no increase in miles traveled per car.

7. We give these 2 billion cars advanced hybrid vehicle technology capable of running on electricity for short distances before they revert to running on biofuels. We take one-twelfth of the world's cropland and use it to grow high-yield energy crops for biofuels. We build another half-million large wind turbines dedicated to providing the electricity for these advanced hybrids.

8. We stop all tropical deforestation, while doubling the rate of new tree planting.

Other strategies exist, but I consider them more challenging and improbable than any of these.

If we succeeded in every single one of these eight monumental efforts, keeping global CO_2 emissions frozen at 2010 levels for fifty years, and then we somehow were able to sharply *decrease* global emissions starting in 2061, we would stabilize concentrations at about 550 ppm. In this scenario, temperatures would still rise steadily over the course of the century by an additional 1.5°C or more, with further warming after 2100. The Greenland Ice Sheet would likely still melt, with the resulting 20 feet of sea-level rise— but we would have slowed the process significantly and perhaps avoided the worst of the sea-level rise, 40 to 80 feet or more (assuming that we have also adopted strong policies to constrain the emissions of methane and all other greenhouse gases).

This strategy saves the world from misspending trillions of dollars in polluting, inefficient capital over the next quarter-century (in traditional coal plants, gas-guzzling vehicles, and the like). Most important, *it buys the world time to achieve an even stronger consensus for action,* which in turn could lead to a far more accelerated rate of technology deployment after, say, 2030. And that could potentially keep concentrations below 500 ppm and save most of the Greenland Ice Sheet.

Obviously, and tragically, the chances are slim that we will start pursuing these eight changes in 2010. Right now, we don't have the political consensus in this country to begin pursuing even one of them. You may think some of them are implausible, yet none is technically impossible right now. This strategy is the best way to avoid Hell and High Water while expanding living standards at home and around the world—and, as we will see, it is far easier than the alternative strategy we face if we delay much longer.

Pacala and Socolow published their study to show that "humanity already possesses the fundamental scientific, technical, and industrial know-how to solve the carbon and climate problem for the next half-century." The tragedy, then, as historians of the future will most certainly recount, is that we ruined their world not because we lacked the knowledge or the technology to save it but *simply because we chose not to make the effort.*

This scenario might be called "Two Political Miracles" because it would require a radical conversion of American conservative leaders—first, to completely accept climate science, and second, to strongly embrace a variety of climate solutions, most of which they currently view as anathema. To repeat, we lack not the technology but the political will.

The answer to the question of the century—Do we humans have the political will to stop the great ice sheets from melting?—is, at best, "Not yet."

A NOTE ON TEMPERATURES

Reported temperature changes from global warming can be a source of some confusion. Americans use the Fahrenheit scale of temperature and have the most intuitive familiarity with it. I will also use the Centigrade scale because most scientific research uses it. Anyone who wants to become knowledgeable about global-warming research needs to become familiar with thinking in Centigrade terms.

Since I'm focusing on temperature change, here is the key conversion: A 1°C change equals a 1.8°F change. Thus a 5°C change equals a 9°F change—not quite double.

Different parts of the globe are expected to warm up at faster or slower rates than the global average. The land typically warms up faster than the oceans, and higher latitudes warm up faster than the tropics. Most of the inland continental United States is expected to warm up roughly 50 percent faster than the global average. So an additional average global warming of

2°C (3.6°F) means much of this country would be expected to warm 3°C (4.8°F).

Confusion can arise when scientists report how much warming will result from a rise in greenhouse gas concentrations. Some report how much the temperature will rise *from preindustrial temperature levels,* while others talk about how much additional or further warming will occur *from present-day levels.* We have already warmed 0.8°C through 2005, so the difference is significant. I will state which measure I am using each time.

Most analyses suggest that a doubling of greenhouse gas concentrations from preindustrial levels will increase global temperatures about 3°C from preindustrial levels, which is 2.2°C warming from current levels (although many studies suggest the climate could be even more sensitive to a doubling of CO_2 concentrations, as we will see).

A related confusion: Some scientists report how much the temperature will rise ultimately (due to a given rise in greenhouse gas concentrations), while others report only how much the temperature will rise by 2100. Because of the lags in the climate system, those figures can be quite different. I will usually describe how much temperature will rise by 2100.

CHAPTER TWO

2000–2025: REAP THE WHIRLWIND

I don't see any reason why the power of hurricanes wouldn't continue to increase over the next 100 to 200 years.

— Kerry Emanuel, MIT atmospheric
scientist, 2006

On our current warming trend, four super-hurricanes—category 4 or stronger—a year in the North Atlantic is likely to become the norm 20 years from now.

— Judith Curry, Georgia Tech atmospheric
scientist, 2006

On August 23, 2005, a tropical depression formed 175 miles southeast of Nassau. By the next day, it had grown into Tropical Storm Katrina and was intensifying rapidly. Early in the evening on August 25, Hurricane Katrina made landfall near North Miami Beach. Even though it was only a category 1 storm, with sustained wind speeds of about 80 mph, it caused significant damage and flooding and took fourteen lives.

The hurricane's quick nighttime trip across Florida barely fazed the storm. Entering the Gulf of Mexico's warm waters quickly kicked Katrina into overdrive, like a supercharged engine on high-octane fuel. Hurricanes fuel themselves by continually sucking in and spinning up warm, moist air.

On August 28, Katrina reached category 5 status, with sustained wind speeds of 160 mph and a pressure of 908 millibars. A few hours later, wind speeds hit 175 mph, which they maintained until the afternoon.

At 4 P.M. the National Hurricane Center warned that local storm surges could hit 28 feet, and "some levees in the Greater New Orleans Area could be overtopped," a warning that was tragically ignored by federal, state, and local emergency officials. Over the next fourteen hours, Katrina's strength dropped steadily. When the hurricane's center made landfall Monday morning, it was a strong category 3, battering coastal Louisiana with wind speeds of about 127 mph. The central pressure of 920 millibars was the third-lowest pressure ever recorded for a storm hitting the U.S. mainland.

The devastation to the Gulf region was biblical. The death toll exceeded 1,300. The damage exceeded $100 billion. A half-million people were forced to leave their homes, *more than were displaced during the 1930s dust bowl migration.* One of the nation's great cities was devastated.

About 20 miles to the east of the second Gulf landfall is the small town named Pass Christian, Mississippi, where my brother lived with his wife and son. Tropical cyclones in the Northern Hemisphere rotate counterclockwise, and so the most intense storm surge is just to the east of the eye, because the surge represents the intense winds pushing the sea against the shore. A 30-foot wall of water with waves up to 55 feet high crashed over the town. Although my brother and his family lived a mile inland, their house was ravaged by water up to 22 feet high, leaving its contents looking like they had been churned "inside of a washing machine," in my brother's words. While they lost virtually all their possessions, they were safe in a Biloxi shelter.

Thanks to the generosity of many people, my brother's family was able to find a temporary home in Atlanta. But like many families whose lives were ripped apart by the storm, they had difficult choices in the ensuing months. Perhaps the toughest decision was whether to rebuild their home or to uproot themselves and try to create a new life somewhere else.

I very much wanted to give my brother an expert opinion on what was likely to come in the future. After all, climate change was my field, and while my focus has been on climate solutions, I had done my Ph.D. thesis on physical oceanography.

As I listened and talked to many of the top climate experts, it quickly became clear that the climate situation was far more dire than most people—and even many scientists, myself included—realized. Almost every major climate impact was occurring faster than the computer models had suggested. Arctic sea ice was shrinking far faster than every single model had projected. And the great ice sheets of Greenland and West Antarctica were shedding ice decades earlier than the models said. Ecosystems appeared to be losing their ability to take up carbon dioxide faster than expected. At the same time, global carbon dioxide emissions and concentrations were rising faster than most had expected.

As for hurricanes, global warming had been widely projected to make them more intense and destructive, but again the recent increase in intensity was coming sooner than the computer models had suggested. Why is that a concern? Since 1970, the temperature of the Atlantic Ocean's hurricane-forming region has risen 0.5°C (0.9°F). Over the path of a typical hurricane, this recent ocean warming added the energy equivalent of a few hundred thousand Hiroshima nuclear bombs. On our current emissions path, the Atlantic will warm *twice as much*, another 1°C, by midcentury, and perhaps another 2°C beyond that by century's end. Who can even imagine the hurricane seasons such warming might bring?

This is what I ultimately told my brother, the same advice I would give anyone contemplating living near the Gulf Coast:

Only a quarter of Atlantic hurricanes make U.S. landfall, and while there is no question that the frequency of intense Atlantic hurricanes is rising, where they will actually go any given year is somewhat random.

That said, the Gulf of Mexico is going to get warmer and warmer, as is the Atlantic Ocean, and so hurricanes that enter the Gulf are likely to start out and end up far more destructive than usual. I would not bet that the Mississippi Gulf Coast will get hit by a super-hurricane in any particular year, but I would certainly plan on it being hit again sometime over the next ten years; I wouldn't be surprised if it were hit by more than one.

Coastal dwellers from Houston to Miami are now playing Russian roulette with maybe two bullets in the gun chamber each year. In a couple of decades, it may be three bullets.

Some argue that the recent jump in severe hurricanes was caused by a rise in sea-surface temperatures that is just part of a natural cycle. That position is scientifically untenable, which is why most of the people who advance it are not global-warming researchers. We'll see why the natural-cycles argument will no doubt prove to be "largely false," as MIT's Kerry Emanuel said in 2006. Hurricane seasons with four or more super-hurricanes—those with sustained wind speeds of 131 mph or more—will soon become the norm.

THE ERA OF EXTREME WEATHER

Scientists have long known that global warming increases the chances for extreme weather events. Here's how: As it gets hotter, summer heat waves become longer, hotter, and more widespread. Dry areas tend to dry out faster and to stay that way for longer periods. The extra heat puts more water into the atmosphere, and that causes wet areas to become wetter and annual rainfall to become more intense, which, coupled with earlier snowmelt, leads to more flooding. And hurricanes, which feed on warm seas and atmospheric moisture, become more intense.

This well-accepted scientific theory of how global warming should change the weather has begun shifting to grim reality—our weather is changing, and not for the better. In July 2003 the World Meteorological Organization (WMO) cataloged a number of extreme events: Switzerland had experienced the hottest June in "at least the past 250 years," and the United States had suffered 562 tornadoes in May, exceeding the previous record of 399 in June 1992. The WMO linked them to global climate change. As *The Independent* newspaper of London put it, the WMO "signalled last night that the world's weather is going haywire." The WMO, an "organisation that is not given to hyperbole," noted, "New record extreme events occur every year somewhere on the globe, but in recent years the number of such extremes have been increasing." Since that WMO report, Europe has experienced even more extreme events, including an extended heat wave that caused more than 35,000 deaths in August 2003.

In 2005 the weather became even more hellish. The year was the hottest in recorded history, according to NASA's Goddard Institute of Space Studies. In September the Arctic had the smallest amount of sea-ice cover ever recorded by satellites. Mumbai, India, saw that country's most intense recorded instance of rainfall—3 feet of rain in twenty-four hours.

The extremes of wet and dry are astounding. While southern Louisiana was deluged with rain in the summer of 2005, a record-smashing U.S. hurricane season, "the eight months since October 1, 2005," were its driest "in 111 years of record-keeping," the National Climatic Data Center reported in July 2006. While in 2005 much of the Northeast drowned in the wettest October in recorded history, the United States as a whole had its worst wildfire season.

You may reasonably ask, Don't extreme conditions happen somewhere on the planet all the time? How do we know this weather is truly out of the ordinary?

As far back as 1995, analysis by the National Climatic Data Center showed that over the course of the twentieth century, the United States had suffered a statistically significant increase in a variety of extreme weather events, the very ones you would expect from global warming, such as more—and more intense—precipitation. That analysis also concluded that the chances were only "5 to 10 percent" that this increase was due to factors *other* than global warming, such as "natural climate variability." And since 1995 the climate has gotten *much* more extreme.

A 2004 analysis by the center found an increase during the twentieth century of "precipitation, temperature, streamflow, heavy and very heavy precipitation and high streamflow in the East." It found a 14 percent increase in "heavy rain events" of more than 2 inches in one day, and a 20 percent increase in "very heavy rain events"—best described as deluges—more than 4 inches in one day. These extreme downpours are precisely what is predicted by global-warming scientists and models. The deluge that socked the Mid-Atlantic states and the Northeast the last week of June 2006 fits the picture of this global-warming-type rainstorm. Washington, D.C., for instance, was drenched by more than 7 inches of rain in one twenty-four-hour period. And this deluge happened at the same time that 45 percent of the continental United States was experiencing moderate to extreme drought, which is far above the historical norm.

The center, a division of the National Oceanic and Atmospheric Administration (NOAA), which is part of the U.S. Department of Commerce, has developed the U.S. Climate Extremes Index to quantify these climate changes. The index measures the percentage of the country that is subject to a variety of extreme conditions, including:

- much higher (and lower) than normal maximum temperatures
- much higher (and lower) than normal minimum temperatures
- severe drought and severe excess moisture
- an extreme proportion of total rain from intense one-day rainstorms
- much greater than normal number of days of the year with precipitation or without precipitation

It averages each of these five factors with a sixth one—the frequency and intensity of tropical storms making U.S. landfall. The index uses a scale from 0 to 100; 100 means the whole country has extreme conditions throughout the year *for each of the indicators,* "a virtually impossible scenario," the center notes.

The index extends from 1910 to today, during which time the average has been 20. The most extreme year was 1998, with an index of nearly 44, more than double the average. The second-most extreme year was 2005, with an index of about 41. The seventeen least-extreme years of the past century all came before 1980.

The index almost certainly *underestimates* how much the country is suffering the impact of global warming—for two reasons. First, it averages in some extreme conditions that are occurring *less* often because of warming, such as the "percentage of the United States with minimum temperatures much *below* normal." Second, the index excludes Alaska—the largest state and the one suffering the most extreme climate change. For instance, a 2003 report by the General Accounting Office found that "flooding and erosion affects 184 out of 213, or 86 percent, of Alaska Native villages . . . due in part to rising temperatures." *Half or more of the villages may need to be relocated.* In January 2005 the city of Valdez, Alaska, hit 54°F, beating the city's previously warmest January day by 8°.

If the weather is becoming more extreme, what is happening to the most extreme weather events, like hurricanes? The scientists and studies I find most credible conclude that "greenhouse warming is causing an increase in global hurricane intensity." To explain why this is almost certainly true, I will rely on the recent work of scientists at MIT, the Georgia Institute of Technology, the National Center for Atmospheric Research, and NASA's Goddard Institute of Space Studies, and my conversations with many of those scientists. The framework of this explanation comes from a 2006 paper written by Judith Curry and others. The central hypothesis is best explained by dividing it into a causal chain of three sub-hypotheses.

1. GLOBAL TROPICAL SEA-SURFACE TEMPERATURE IS INCREASING AS A RESULT OF HUMAN-CAUSED GREENHOUSE WARMING

A January 2006 report on Katrina by the National Climatic Data Center noted, "There has been an overall increasing trend in July–September Atlantic and Gulf of Mexico sea surface temperatures during the past 100 years. . . . This pattern is similar to that observed across global land and ocean surfaces."

The planet is warming—especially the oceans. Since 1955 the oceans have absorbed roughly *twenty times* more heat than the atmosphere. A team of scientists led by NASA's James Hansen have actually measured the increasing ocean heat content over the past decade. They reported in 2005 that it matches the predicted warming from greenhouse gases.

Another 2005 study, this one led by the Scripps Institution of Oceanography, compared actual ocean-temperature data from the surface down to hundreds of meters (in the Atlantic, Pacific, and Indian Oceans) with climate models and concluded:

A warming signal has penetrated into the world's oceans over the past 40 years. The signal is complex, with a vertical structure that varies widely by ocean; it cannot be explained by natural internal climate variability or solar and volcanic forcing, but is well simulated by two anthropogenically forced climate models. We conclude that it is of human origin, a conclusion robust to observational sampling and model differences.

Anthropogenic is science-speak for "caused by humans." Greenhouse gases, such as carbon dioxide from fossil fuel combustion, are forcing the earth's climate to warm. Even at a depth of 600 feet, the North Atlantic has warmed 0.2°C thanks to human emissions.

The science gets stronger every year. A comprehensive 2006 analysis using the climate model of the Goddard Institute for Space Studies found that greenhouse gas forcings explain nearly four-fifths of the warming in the main region where Atlantic tropical storms start, and human-generated emissions also account for all the warming in the Gulf of Mexico. Other recent scientific analyses come to similar conclusions.

This gives us very solid science for concluding that *global tropical sea-surface temperature is increasing as a result of human-caused greenhouse warming.*

To disprove this statement, a scientist must not merely come up with an alternative explanation for the remarkable recent warming but be able to identify some as yet unknown and unmeasured effect that is simultaneously negating the well-understood warming from greenhouse gases. Nobody has yet done either.

2. AVERAGE HURRICANE INTENSITY INCREASES WITH INCREASING TROPICAL SEA-SURFACE TEMPERATURE

Of the three, this statement is the most scientifically straightforward. As Kerry Emanuel wrote in his 2005 book, *Divine Wind: The History and Science of Hurricanes:* "By trapping heat energy in the ocean, the greenhouse effect sets the stage for the meteorological explosion that is the hurricane." Many factors must coexist to create hurricanes, which are like sophisticated race cars, but a hurricane's engine can't start without warm water to give it a steady supply of fuel.

More than fifty years ago, scientists established that tropical cyclones form only if sea-surface temperatures (SST) exceed 80°F. Absent the natural greenhouse effect, which keeps the planet 60°F warmer than it otherwise would be, we would not have hurricanes. Both theory and observation, including several recent studies, support the relationship between sea-surface temperature and hurricane intensity.

How did Katrina turn into a powerful category 5 hurricane? The National Climatic Data Center 2006 report on Katrina begins its explanation by noting that SSTs in the Gulf of Mexico during the last week in August 2005 "were one to two degrees Celsius above normal, and the warm temperatures extended to a considerable depth through the upper ocean layer." The report continues, "Also, Katrina crossed the 'loop current' (belt of even warmer water), during which time explosive intensification occurred. The temperature of the ocean surface is a critical element in the formation and strength of hurricanes."

An important factor was that the ocean warming had penetrated to a considerable depth. One of the ways that hurricanes are weakened is the upwelling of colder, deeper water due to the hurricane's own violent action. But if the deeper water is also warm, it doesn't weaken the hurricane. In fact, it may continue to intensify. Global warming heats both the sea surface and the deep water, thus creating ideal conditions for a hurricane to survive and thrive in its long journey from tropical depression to category 4 or 5 superstorm.

After Katrina, Georgia Tech scientists reexamined the historical hurricane and SST data using "a methodology based on information theory, isolating the trend from the shorter term natural modes of variability." They looked at four factors that can affect hurricane intensity: atmospheric humidity, wind shear (which can rip storms apart), rising SSTs, and large-scale air-circulation patterns. "Results show that the increasing trend in the number of category 4 and 5 hurricanes for the period 1970–2004 is directly linked to the trend in SSTs; other aspects of the tropical environment, while influencing shorter term variations in hurricane intensity, do not contribute substantially to the observed global trend."

The evidence gives us a high level of confidence that statement number 2 is true: Average hurricane intensity increases with increasing tropical sea-surface temperature.

3. THE FREQUENCY OF THE MOST INTENSE HURRICANES IS INCREASING GLOBALLY

Three major articles published in mid-2005 pointed out that intense hurricanes had become more common in recent decades. These analyses spawned a whirlwind of media attention because the authors were highly credible and because the articles happened to come out in the weeks before and just after Katrina.

Dr. Kevin Trenberth, head of the Climate Analysis Section of the National Center for Atmospheric Research (NCAR), published the first, in *Science*, two months before Katrina. He began by noting that in 2004 "an unprecedented four hurricanes hit Florida; during the same season in the Pacific, 10 tropical cyclones or typhoons hit Japan (the previous record was six)." What we call hurricanes in America are called cyclones or typhoons in other parts of the world. They all have maximum sustained surface winds of at least 74 mph. Trenberth explained that theory suggests global warming will increase the intensity of hurricanes and the rainfall they bring. He noted that from 1995 to 2004, Atlantic hurricane seasons were abnormally active, as measured by the Accumulated Cyclone Energy Index, which tracks "the collective intensity and duration of tropical storms and hurricanes" during each season.

Kerry Emanuel, a professor of atmospheric sciences at MIT, published next, in *Nature*, a few weeks before Katrina hit. Emanuel, one of the world's leading hurricane experts, created a measure of hurricane destructiveness, which he called the *power dissipation index*. This is essentially the maximum sustained wind speed cubed (raised to the third power)—a measure of hurricane intensity that correlates well with the "actual monetary loss in windstorms"— integrated over the storm's life. He then used the best available data from all sources for hurricanes and sea-surface temperature in both the North Atlantic and the western North Pacific.

Emanuel found a sharp increase in the index in the last thirty years and a close correlation between the power dissipation index and SST in both oceans. Tropical cyclones in both oceans have increased both their peak wind speed and their duration substantially since 1949.

Finally, in September, scientists from Georgia Tech (Peter Webster, Hai-Ru Chang, and Judith Curry) and NCAR (Greg Holland) published in *Science* a detailed analysis of hurricanes in six different ocean regions, including the North Atlantic. They examined the record for the past thirty-five years, the period when high-quality satellite data became available. During this time, SSTs increased about 0.5°C. They found a large increase in the number of super-hurricanes (categories 4 and 5) in every region. Comparing the

1975–1989 period with the 1990–2004 period, they found a more than 50 percent increase in super-hurricanes overall and in the North Atlantic. They concluded that "global data indicate a 30-year trend toward more frequent and intense hurricanes, corroborated by the results of the recent regional assessment [Emanuel's 2005 study]."

THE FUTURE IS NOW

The terms *hypothesis* and *theory* are often used interchangeably, but for scientists, a theory is "a hypothesis that has been confirmed or established by observation or experiment, and is propounded or accepted as accounting for the known facts; a statement of the general laws, principles, or causes of something known or observed," as the *Oxford English Dictionary* defines it. Theories have heft. They have credibility. The germ-theory of disease and human-caused global warming are well-established scientific theories.

For a hypothesis like "Greenhouse warming is causing an increase in global hurricane intensity" to be elevated to theory status, it must pass three additional tests, beyond accounting for the observed data. A theory must make accurate predictions, survive scrutiny by critics, and beat out competing theories, as Judith Curry has written. Let's consider the theory's predictive value.

The three papers described above, arguing that an increase in SST was causing an increase in intense hurricanes, were all based on data through 2004. Since 2005 turned out to be the warmest year on record, with high June–November SSTs in the Atlantic and Gulf of Mexico, it is valuable to examine some of the remarkable records set that year, courtesy of the National Oceanic and Atmospheric Administration:

- Twenty-seven named tropical storms—from Arlene to Wilma, Alpha to Zeta—formed during the 2005 season. This is the *most* named storms in a single season, breaking the old record of 21 set in 1933.

- Fifteen hurricanes formed during the 2005 season (a post-storm analysis in 2006 upgraded Cindy from a tropical storm to a hurricane). This is the *most* hurricanes in a single season, breaking the old record of 12 set in 1969.
- Seven category 3 or higher hurricanes formed during the 2005 season. This *ties* the season record for such hurricanes, first set in 1950.
- Four category 5 hurricanes formed during the 2005 season (Emily, Katrina, Rita, and Wilma). This is the *most* category 5 hurricanes recorded in a single season, breaking the old record of 2 set in 1960 and 1961.
- Seven named storms made United States landfall during 2005. This puts the 2005 season in a *tie* for second place for landfalling storms, behind the 1916 and 2004 seasons where eight named storms made landfall. An eighth storm brushed the coast of North Carolina in 2005 but did not make an official landfall.
- The 2005 season was the *most* destructive for United States landfalling storms, largely due to Katrina. Damage estimates for the 2005 season are over $100 billion.
- Dennis became the *most* intense hurricane on record before August when a central pressure of 930 mb was recorded.
- Emily *eclipsed* Dennis's record for lowest pressure recorded for a hurricane before August when its central pressure dropped to 929 mb. Emily's strength was revised in 2006, so it became "*the earliest-forming Category 5 hurricane on record* in the Atlantic basin and the only known hurricane of that strength to occur during the month of July."
- Vince was the *first* tropical cyclone in recorded history to strike the Iberian Peninsula. Vince was the farthest north and east a storm has ever developed in the Atlantic basin.

In the end, 2005 was not just the warmest year on record, it had the most intense and long lasting hurricane season, as measured by the Accumulated Cyclone Energy Index. One hurricane season cannot, however, confirm or disprove this hypothesis (or competing hypotheses). Hurricane seasons are subject to enormous year-to-year variability because of factors such as the El Niño weather pattern, which tends to weaken Atlantic hurricane seasons. But we should expect a general upward trend in the intensity and length of Atlantic hurricane seasons, and we should expect more and more records to be smashed.

A strong hypothesis is hard to criticize effectively and objectively; a weak one is not. Let's see how this one fares. The critique offered by meteorologists in particular is worth exploring in detail because it sheds light on the national global-warming debate and on how the nation is likely to respond to the growing evidence of climate change over the next decade or two.

The first major critique of the theory and the 2005 studies supporting it was "Hurricanes and Global Warming," published in the November 2005 issue of the *Bulletin of the American Meteorological Society.* Among its coauthors were three leading public critics of the warming-hurricane connection—Max Mayfield, director of NOAA's National Hurricane Center, Christopher W. Landsea of NOAA's Hurricane Research Division, and Roger Pielke Jr. of the University of Colorado at Boulder—together with two other NOAA hurricane experts. A subhead that begins the article, "An interdisciplinary team of researchers survey the peer-reviewed literature to assess the relationships between global warming, hurricanes, and hurricane impacts," is followed by:

Debate over climate change frequently conflates issues of science and politics. Because of their significant and visceral impacts, discussion of extreme events is a frequent locus of such

conflation. Linda Mearns, of the National Center for Atmospheric Research (NCAR), aptly characterizes this context:
"There's a push on climatologists to say something about extremes, because they are so important. But that can be very
dangerous if we really don't know the answer."

Wow! I have read hundreds of literature-survey articles by scientists over the years, and not a single one began like that. You don't
have to be a scientist to realize that objective surveys don't start by
questioning the character of those they disagree with—their motives and their scientific method. These authors suggest that Emanuel and the others have a political agenda, and rather than presenting
sound analysis, they have been pushed to say things they can't support.

You would never know from this article (four of whose authors
work at NOAA) that a division of NOAA, the National Climatic
Data Center, had been repeatedly publishing articles and an index
showing that extreme events are in fact becoming more frequent.
You would also never know from this article that there is a strong
consensus among climate scientists that global warming leads to
more extreme weather events. The authors never report that information or even discuss the subject. They just imply that those who
make such arguments are not practicing pure science.

While claiming to be an up-to-date survey, the article bases
most of its critique on old studies that largely predate the recent
surge in SSTs and hurricane intensity examined in the new studies.
When it does examine the new studies, it focuses primarily on Atlantic hurricanes, even though the second *Science* paper found that
"the largest increase [in category 4 and 5 hurricanes] occurred in
the North Pacific, Indian, and Southwest Pacific Oceans." There is
no explanation for this omission. For the specific matter of the
North Atlantic, the authors assert that "much of the recent upward
trend in Atlantic storm frequency and intensity can be attributed to

large multidecadal fluctuations," although the authors never define "much."

This brings us to the competing hypothesis: Atlantic SSTs and hurricanes come in natural multidecadal cycles. This hypothesis deserves attention because the natural-cycles argument is repeated widely in the media, with arguments such as "We had some big hurricanes in the 1940s" used to imply that what we are seeing today is not evidence of human-caused climate change.

NATURAL CYCLES VERSUS GLOBAL WARMING

We have two battling hypotheses. In one corner is the global-warming theory, which says that forcings (natural and human-made) explain most of the changes in our climate and temperature. The natural forcings include fluctuations in the intensity of sunlight (which can increase or decrease warming) and major volcanoes that inject huge volumes of gases and aerosol particles into the stratosphere (which tend to block sunlight and cause cooling). The biggest forcings caused by humans are the greenhouse gases we generate, particularly carbon dioxide from burning coal, oil, and natural gas. But we humans also put significant sulfate aerosols into the atmosphere from burning coal and diesel fuel without advanced emissions controls.

Global warming explains the vast majority of the recent warming in North Atlantic SSTs and most, if not all, of the rise in hurricane intensity in all oceans. A 2006 article in the *Bulletin of the American Meteorological Society* by six leading climatologists noted that recent research "specifically shows an increase [in hurricane intensity] in all ocean basins and an overall global increase, which is the type of signature that would be expected from global warming changes."

In the other corner, we have the natural-cycles hypothesis. This hypothesis offers little or no explanation for the rising hurricane activity in the North Pacific, Indian, and southwestern Pacific Oceans. Nor can it account for most of the rise in North Atlantic SSTs over the past three decades. Its advocates claim it can explain much of the high level of Atlantic hurricane activity in the 1940s, 1950s, and early 1960s and now again in the past decade.

The natural cycle in the Atlantic is called the Atlantic multi-decadal oscillation. Consider figure 3, which is a plot of average sea-surface temperatures for June–November in the North Atlantic's hurricane-forming region. You can just make out what looks like a 60- to 70-year cycle with positive peaks around the 1880s and 1950 (and possibly 2005) and negative peaks around the early 1910s and the mid-1970s. As you can see, however, the dip around the early 1910s is much deeper than the little dip centered in the mid-1970s. Similarly, the peak of each cycle keeps getting higher. Not surprisingly, the 1995–2005 period has had considerably more total tropical storms, hurricanes, and category 4 and 5 hurricanes—the city destroyers—than the peak years from the last cycle of Atlantic hurricane activity (1945–1955).

When I first began researching hurricanes, I believed, like many scientists, that global warming made hurricanes more intense *and* that hurricanes followed a natural oscillation six to seven decades long. I knew that climate scientists had an excellent understanding of the shape of the entire temperature record, including the temperature peak in midcentury, as detailed in several recent modeling studies of the various natural and human-made forcings. But I never connected the dots.

Then, at an October 2005 seminar of the American Meteorological Society, MIT's Kerry Emanuel pointed out that the downswing in temperature and hurricane activity in the 1960s and 1970s may not have been "a natural fluctuation," adding that "a lot of what I thought was natural I now think was forced." Also, Judith Curry from Georgia Tech presented slides showing a stunning parallel be-

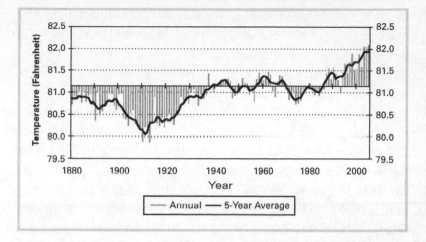

Figure 3. The average sea-surface temperature in °F for June–November in the North Atlantic's hurricane-forming region, since 1880. A 5-year mean is also provided to smooth out annual fluctuations. The data is from NOAA.

tween SSTs and hurricane intensity in the Atlantic over the last century.

As I talked with more climate experts and reviewed the literature, I saw that the dots—the multiple forcings of the past hundred years together with the temperature and hurricane trends—formed a clear picture. Why the temperature dip centered in the early 1910s? A series of six major volcanoes erupted from 1875 to 1912 all around the globe: in Iceland in 1875, Indonesia (Krakatoa) in 1883 (the largest explosion ever recorded), New Zealand in 1886, Guatemala in 1902, Kamchatka in 1907, and Alaska in 1912. The aerosols emitted by these awesome volcanoes kept the planet cooler than it would have been during this time.

The subsequent rise in global temperatures and Atlantic sea-surface temperatures is also well explained by forcings—a slow but steady increase in human-generated greenhouse gases, a slight increase in solar intensity, and the absence of any major volcano eruptions that might otherwise have blocked these trends. The rise in number and intensity of hurricanes in midcentury occurred at the same time as this rise in Atlantic SSTs.

But what explains the drop in SSTs and hurricanes from the mid-1960s through the early 1990s that some critics (mistakenly) believe undercuts the global-warming theory? Not coincidentally, that drop began just around the time of the 1963 eruption of Mount Agung in Indonesia, which "produced the largest stratospheric dust veil in the Northern Hemisphere in more than 50 years." Not coincidentally, the drop also came during a three-decade stretch when humans were emitting unprecedented amounts of industrial aerosol and sulfate. Not coincidentally, the drop continued through the 1982 El Chichon eruption in Mexico and the 1991 Mount Pinatubo eruption in the Philippines, which "produced very large stratospheric aerosol clouds and large climatic effects." Multiple major sun-blocking events all worked together to give us a false sense of security, to shield us from the full impact of the rapid growth in atmospheric carbon dioxide concentrations. And they cooled the air and the seas, resulting in fewer intense hurricanes.

Not coincidentally, temperatures (and hurricanes) rebounded strongly after the major volcanic eruptions ended and the human-made aerosol emissions by the industrial nations dropped sharply thanks to clean-air regulations, even as human emissions of greenhouse gases continued to soar and utterly overwhelmed the aerosol cooling effect.

With all these variables, no wonder this picture took climate scientists so long to bring into focus. This complexity helps explain why many meteorologists, most of whom have little training in global-warming science, keep standing by their flawed natural-cycles hypothesis.

The view that this is not all a grand coincidence gains credence from a 2006 study by American and British climatologists and meteorologists led by the Lawrence Livermore National Laboratory.

They concluded: "Volcanically induced cooling of the ocean surface penetrated into deeper layers, where it persisted for decades after the event." The research makes clear that the combination of natural and human-made forcings, correctly modeled, can explain the key trends in both SSTs and subsurface ocean temperatures for the past 120 years. Subsurface temperatures can be as important to hurricane intensity as sea-surface temperatures.

When I posed all this to MIT's Kerry Emanuel in February 2006, he replied, "It would appear that Atlantic hurricanes are a kind of global thermometer, following closely the trend in global (and especially Northern Hemispheric) temperatures produced by volcanic activity, solar variations, sulfate aerosols, and greenhouse gases. *I think the 'natural cycles' argument will prove to be largely false.*"

In 2006, Emanuel coauthored a study that concluded that the Atlantic multidecadal oscillation (AMO) trend has been overestimated and that "there is no evidence that natural climate oscillations such as the AMO contributed to long-term tropical North Atlantic SST variations." Global warming is now clearly the dominant force behind SSTs in the Atlantic's hurricane-forming region and will become more and more dominant in the future.

Higher SSTs have helped cause the rapid intensification of hurricanes like Katrina, as the post-Katrina report by the National Climatic Data Center explained. And the day before Katrina struck, the *New Orleans Times-Picayune* reported, "The northern Gulf of Mexico is unusually warm," likely "the result of *relentless high temperatures in recent weeks* along Louisiana's Gulf Coast," according to National Hurricane Center meteorologist Eric Blake.

Global warming also increases the incidence of such heat waves and makes them more intense and long-lasting. And it puts into the atmosphere more warm, moist air—the stuff hurricanes are made of. Shortly before Katrina, NOAA's Christopher Landsea said, "The warmer the sea-surface temperature and the more warm, moist air that is available, the stronger a hurricane can become." After Katrina, Max Mayfield, then director of the Tropical Prediction Center at the National Hurricane Center, told CBS's Bob Schieffer, "We think the best correlation [with hurricane activity] we have here is with the sea-surface temperatures." Yet Mayfield testified to Congress in September 2005, "The increased activity since 1995 is due to natural fluctuations/cycles of hurricane activity, driven by the Atlantic Ocean itself along with the atmosphere above it and not enhanced substantially by global warming."

This conclusion is "untenable," said a major 2006 study by climate scientists from NASA, Columbia University, Yale University, MIT, Lawrence Berkeley National Laboratory, and Argonne National Laboratory. They concluded that "to the degree that hurricane intensification of the past decade is a product of increasing SSTs in the Atlantic Ocean and the Gulf of Mexico, human-made greenhouse gases probably are a substantial contributor."

Yet untenable critiques from meteorologists can seem very credible to the public, as can critiques from those with little training in or knowledge of global-warming research. So it is no wonder we do not seem close to achieving the consensus needed to avert catastrophic climate change. Many major media outlets, including CNN, *USA Today,* and the *Chicago Tribune,* bought this story line—proving you can spin hurricanes backward—and the combined mantras of "It's a natural cycle" and "Those who say otherwise have a political agenda" may keep the public, the media, and policy makers confused for years to come.

Even though only a small fraction of hurricanes make landfall, the global-warming signal is starting to show up. Emanuel notes that "a trend in landfalling intensity is already apparent" when one looks at hurricanes worldwide. Significantly, the National Climatic Data Center developed a measure for the "strength and frequency" of tropical storms and hurricanes striking this country for its Climate Extremes Index. That index had an average value of 20 over the past ninety-five years. The two highest values this measure has seen were in 2004 and 2005, at 80 and 92 respectively. No year before 1985 exceeded 65.

"More than half the total hurricane damage in the U.S. (normalized for inflation and populations trends) was caused by just five events," explains Emanuel. Storms that are category 4 and 5 at landfall (or just before) are what destroy major cities like New Orleans and Galveston with devastating winds, rains, and storm surges. We have seen a more than 50 percent increase in category 4 and 5 storms both globally and in the Atlantic. Where precisely such storms make landfall is random on a year-to-year basis, but over time, more and more will inevitably strike this country, especially as the Gulf gets warmer. And that is without considering the combined impact of more intense hurricanes and sea-level rise.

Tropical cyclones are threshold events—if SSTs are below 80°F, they do not form. Some analysis even suggests there is an SST "threshold [close to 83°F] necessary for the development of major hurricanes." Global warming may actually cause some hurricanes to develop or intensify that otherwise would not have (by raising SSTs above the threshold at the right place or time).

For now, we can't know with confidence whether global warming has caused a specific hurricane to develop or intensify. But we can know with very high confidence that global warming has increased the intensity and rainfall of recent hurricane seasons.

The destruction of New Orleans by Katrina, particularly the breaching of the levees, might have been avoided if the storm had been a little less severe and generated a little less wind and rain. In the case of Katrina, the added intensity from global warming may have been the straw that broke the camel's back, as NCAR's Kevin Trenberth put it in October 2005, the extra push that brought the poorly built levees down.

2000–2025: REAP THE WHIRLWIND

*For they have sown the wind, and they shall reap the
whirlwind.*

—Hosea

How will the rest of this era play out? Why did I advise my brother
not to rebuild on the Gulf Coast? Why should New Orleans not be
rebuilt unless the levees protecting it are built to withstand a category 5 hurricane?

"I don't see any reason why the power of hurricanes wouldn't
continue to increase over the next 100 to 200 years," said MIT's
Emanuel. Hurricanes can get much, much bigger than we have so
far seen in the Atlantic. The most intense Pacific storm on record
was Super Typhoon Tip in 1979, which reached maximum sustained winds of 190 mph near the center. On its wide rim, gale-force
winds (39 mph) extended over a diameter of an astonishing 1,350
miles. It would have covered nearly half the continental United
States.

No wonder ABC News reported in 2006 that hurricane scientists are considering adding a category 6 for hurricanes above 175
miles per hour. Ultimately, they may become common.

If we don't reverse our emissions paths quickly, global temperatures will rise faster and faster through 2100 and beyond. This will
translate into warmer oceans in all three dimensions: Warmth will
spread over wider swaths of the ocean as well as deeper below the
surface—we've already seen that in the first known tropical cyclone
in the South Atlantic (2004) and the first known tropical cyclone to
strike Spain (2005). That means we will probably see stronger hurricanes farther north along the U.S. Atlantic coast in the coming
decades.

More intense storms will be seen earlier and later in the season. The 2005 hurricane season was the most striking example of that trend, with Emily, "the earliest-forming Category 5 hurricane on record in the Atlantic" in July, and Zeta, the longest-lived tropical cyclone to form in December and cross over into the next year, where it became the longest-lived January tropical cyclone. We have already seen a statistically significant increase in the length of the average hurricane season over the last several decades, according to a 2006 analysis. The data from the past century indicate that a 1°F increase in SSTs leads to an extra five tropical storms a year in the Atlantic—an ominous statistic in a world taking no actions to stop a projected 2°F increase in sea-surface temperatures by midcentury, and more than double that by century's end.

At the same time, the inland United States will heat up at an even faster rate, so the Mississippi River will not be such a cool stream of water pouring into the Gulf. As the sea level rises, the protective outer delta of the Mississippi will continue to disappear and storm surges will penetrate deeper inland. Hurricanes weaken rapidly over land. Even a foot of shallow delta water can dramatically reduce this weakening effect, allowing hurricanes to reach deeper inland with their destructive force.

So not only will we see increased category 4 and category 5 hurricanes, but sooner or later—probably sooner—one of the hurricanes that enters the Gulf will ride a wide and deep mass of warm water straight to the shore, and rather than weakening as it approaches the shore, like Katrina did, it will maintain its strength. Then a category 5 super-hurricane will bring havoc back to New Orleans and the Gulf Coast.

Americans should plan on the 2004 hurricane season—with its four super-hurricanes (category 4 or stronger)—becoming the norm over the next few decades. But if 2004 is the norm, we should not be surprised if as many as a quarter of the hurricane seasons in this era are as severe as those of 2005 with its five super-hurricanes. After all, the ocean and the entire planet are just going to get warmer.

As of the end of 2005, *this decade has already had five of the six hottest years on record* (the other being an El Niño–boosted 1998), so it will no doubt be the hottest decade in thousands of years. As will the next decade. And the decade after that. And on and on and on. Such is the nature of global warming on a planet that refuses to take serious action.

CHAPTER THREE

2025–2050: PLANETARY PURGATORY

Obviously, if you get drought indices like these, there's no adaptation that's possible.
—David Rind, NASA climate scientist, 2005

We're showing warming and earlier springs tying in with large forest fire frequencies. Lots of people think climate change and the ecological responses are 50 to 100 years away. But it's not 50 to 100 years away— it's happening now in forest ecosystems through fire.
—Thomas Swetnam, University of Arizona climate scientist, 2006

Imagine if the climate changed and extreme weather became so constant that it was no longer considered extreme. Mammoth heat waves like the one that killed 35,000 Europeans in 2003 would occur every other year. Mega-droughts and widespread wildfires, like those of the record-breaking 2005 wildfire season, which ravaged 8.5 million acres, would be the norm. This new climate would wipe out whole forests, including virtually every pine tree in British Columbia. The Arctic would have little or no summer ice, and the Greenland ice cap would melt, eventually raising sea levels by 20 feet.

If we permit this Planetary Purgatory to occur, the nation and the world would be forced to begin a desperate race against time—a race against the vicious cycles in which an initial warming causes changes to the climate system that lead to more warming, which makes adapting to climate change a never-ending, ever-changing, expensive, exhausting struggle for our children, and their children, and on and on for generations.

This chapter will focus on (1) the impacts of accelerated warming, especially drought and wildfires, and (2) the fatal feedbacks that will probably start to kick into overdrive during this era and complicate any effort to stop the Greenland Ice Sheet from melting.

HELL AND NO WATER

By the end of the Planetary Purgatory era, 2050, Earth will probably be hotter than it has been in 125,000 years. By then, the planet is likely to be warming 0.6°F (0.33°C) *per decade* or more, even if global-emissions growth slows somewhat from its current pace. Every three decades, the earth will warm more than it has in the past century. The temperature over much of the inland continental United States will likely rise nearly 1°F per decade (and in Alaska even faster). This unprecedented rate of temperature change could continue for decades.

The first brutal impacts will be marathon heat waves that last for weeks over many states. Americans have not experienced this type of extreme extended heat wave, but Europe did in August 2003. The oppressive heat brought temperatures in the upper 90s or higher across much of the continent for three weeks, and killed 15,000 people in France, 7,000 in Germany, 4,200 in Italy, and more than 2,000 in Great Britain, which on August 10 recorded its first-ever temperature over 100°F.

Scientists have studied this torrid heat wave extensively. A 2004 study in *Nature*, by British scientists from Oxford University and the Hadley Centre for Climate Prediction and Research, examined the role of greenhouse gas emissions. It concluded that human influence more than doubled the risk of such a deadly heat wave. If we stay on our current emissions trajectory, more than half of European summers will be hotter than 2003 within the next four decades. By the end of the century, "2003 would be classed as an anomalously *cold* summer relative to the new climate," the study notes.

Particularly worrisome will be shortages of water, which is essential to human life and agriculture. And large parts of the world already suffer water shortages. Moreover, many proposed solutions to our energy needs, including biofuels and hydrogen production, require huge quantities of water.

THE PRESENT IS PROLOGUE

To see what is likely to happen during Planetary Purgatory, let's look at what has happened already. Since the 1970s, the number of "very dry areas" on the planet, as defined by the widely used Palmer Drought Severity Index, has more than doubled, to about 30 percent of the global land. As a major study by the National Center for Atmospheric Research concluded, "These results provide observational evidence for the increasing risk of droughts as anthropogenic [human caused] global warming progresses and produces both increased temperatures and increased drying."

Not surprisingly, but rarely reported in context, wildfires have been on the rise worldwide for half a century. Every decade since the 1950s has seen an increase in major wildfires in the United States and around the world.

Large parts of the country have been getting hotter and drier, and suffering extended droughts. "The period since 1999 is now officially the driest in the 98 years of recorded history of the Colorado

River, according to the United States Geological Survey," noted a 2004 *New York Times* article. In March 2006, Phoenix set a record with more than 140 consecutive rainless days. "The average temperature for the continental United States from January through June 2006 was the warmest first half of any year since records began in 1895," reported NOAA's National Climatic Data Center. In June, 45 percent of the contiguous United States was in a moderate-to-extreme state of drought. By July, the figure was 51 percent.

Although the 2005 wildfire season, which ravaged 8.5 million acres, was record-breaking, the record it broke was from 2000, when wildfires consumed 8.25 million acres. From 2000 through 2005, wildfires destroyed nearly 30 million acres, some 47,000 square miles—an area *the equivalent of Pennsylvania*. Stunningly, 2006 has already broken the record set in 2005, with 8.7 million acres burned by mid-September.

Not only do drought and high temperatures increase the number of wildfires, they also lead to a greater range of pests that feast on trees whose defenses have been weakened by heat and lack of water. Trees from the Southwest up to Alaska are dying by the millions.

A 2005 study led by the University of Arizona, with the Los Alamos National Laboratory and the U.S. Geological Survey, examined a huge 3-million-acre die-off of vegetation in 2002–2003 "in response to drought and associated bark beetle infestations" in the Four Corners area (Arizona, New Mexico, Colorado, and Utah). This drought was not quite as severe as the one that region experienced in the 1950s, but it was much warmer, hence it fit the global-warming model. The recent drought had "nearly complete tree mortality across many size and age classes," whereas "most of the patchy mortality in the 1950s was associated with trees [more than] 100 years old."

Most of this tree death was caused by bark beetle infestation, and "such outbreaks are tightly tied to drought-induced water stress." Healthy trees defend themselves by drowning the tiny pine beetles in resin. Without water, weakened, parched trees are easy meals for bugs.

"We're seeing changes in [mountain pine beetle] activity from Canada to Mexico," said Forest Service researcher Jesse Logan in July 2004, "and the common thing is warming temperatures." According to the Department of Forest Resource Management at the University of British Columbia, the beetle infestation has spread to higher and more northern regions thanks in large part to climate change. And milder winters since 1994 have reduced the winter death rate of beetle larvae in Wyoming from 80 percent per year to under 10 percent.

In a February 2006 speech on climate change, Senator Lisa Murkowski of Alaska pointed out that the tremendous recent warming had opened the door to the "voracious spruce bark beetle," which devastated more than 3 million acres in Alaska, "providing dry fuel for outbreaks of enormous wild fires." Half of the wildfires in the record-breaking 2005 season were in Alaska.

I have been focusing on U.S. impacts, but the grim reality in British Columbia is too stunning to ignore. The Canadian and British Columbia Forest Service have reported that as of 2004, the mountain pine beetle infestation had killed 280 million cubic meters (10 billion cubic feet) of stately British Columbia pine trees, of which 170 million cubic meters would have been harvestable. By 2014, they project the beetle will have killed 80 percent of the harvestable pine trees—more than 800 million cubic meters. By 2025, virtually all may be gone over a region the size of North Dakota or Washington State. That is especially likely now that "it has become apparent that B.C. is facing the 'worse-case scenario,'" according to the University of British Columbia. So Canada will now log the pines as fast as possible: "Harvest levels in the region will be increased significantly over the next decade." Even so, the infestation may well spread, and then "forests across Canada may be at risk."

The authors of the 2005 study on vegetation die-off warn that the recent drought in the Four Corners "may be a harbinger of future global-change-type drought throughout much of North America and elsewhere, in which increased temperatures in concert with multidecadal drought patterns" cause unprecedented changes in ecosystems. In 2005 climatologist Jonathan Overpeck noted that this study, together with the recent evidence that temperature and annual precipitation are headed in opposite directions, raises the question of whether we are at the "dawn of the *super-interglacial drought.*"

The increased risk of severe drought we are seeing today was predicted back in 1990 by scientists at NASA's Goddard Institute of Space Studies. Their model also suggested that, in the second half of this century, severe drought, which was already occurring with about 5 percent frequency by 1990, will occur *every other year*—and more frequently in the West. The huge population growth in the western United States during the twentieth century happened to coincide with relatively wet weather in the region, weather that will likely prove to be an anomaly. One 2004 newspaper article noted, "The development of the modern urbanized West—one of the biggest growth spurts in the nation's history—may have been based on a colossal miscalculation."

Global warming also reduces the snowpack, and "snow is our water storage in the West," notes Philip Mote, climatologist for the state of Washington. States such as Montana see only 18 inches of precipitation a year. Portland gets 36 inches a year, but only one-tenth of that is during the summer. Snowmelt comprises 75 percent of all water in western streams. The warming of the last few decades has already reduced snowpacks at five out of six western snow-measurement sites. Many have suffered a 15 to 30 percent decline. And warming has moved up the peak of the annual spring runoff. In California's Sierra Nevada, streams peak as much as three weeks earlier than they did only a few decades ago.

By midcentury, warming is likely to reduce western snowpacks *by up to 60 percent* in regions such as the Cascade Range of Oregon and Washington. Summertime stream flows are projected to drop 20 to 50 percent. By century's end, the Cascades might be snow-free by April 1, and western streams might peak two months earlier than they once did. This will inevitably lead to more wildfires. A 2006 study led by the Scripps Institution of Oceanography found that the greatest increases in wildfires since 1970 were associated with warmer temperatures and earlier snowmelts, which reduce humidity and expose forests to the full effect of arid summers.

What will wildfires be like during the Planetary Purgatory era and beyond? The 2006 Scripps study compared the period 1987–2003 with the period 1970–1986. The researchers found that the active wildfire season in the West has increased 78 days and that major fires now burn 37 days—nearly five times as long as they did in the first period. And yet the average spring and summer western temperatures rose only 0.87°C (1.6°F) from the earlier period to the recent one. With current emissions trends, the West is likely to see June–August temperatures rise between 2°C and 5°C over the next half-century—suggesting we can expect a dramatic increase in fires.

Researchers at the U.S. Forest Services Pacific Wildland Fire Sciences Lab looked at past fires in the West to create a statistical model of how future climate change may affect wildfires. Their work suggests that "the area burned by wildfires in 11 Western states could double . . . if summer climate warms by slightly more than a degree and a half" centigrade. On our current emissions path, this is likely to happen by midcentury. By century's end, states such as Montana, New Mexico, Washington, Utah, and Wyoming could see burn areas increase *five times.*

If we don't change course soon, the West faces a scorching climate—Hell and No Water—with summers that are far hotter and drier, longer wildfire seasons with more ferocious fires, and, at the same time, far less water for agriculture and hydropower.

THE NEED FOR SYSTEMS THINKING

Global warming is so challenging and so potentially devastating because it is a systems problem. Although the basic definition of a system is simple—"any set of interconnected elements"—many systems, such as our climate, are exceedingly complicated.

The word *environment* comes from Old French, *viron,* meaning "circle." Since the word *cycle* also derives from *circle,* let's call the environment the cycle of life. I have not centered this book on the environment per se—on the destruction of the coral reefs or the threat to the polar bears—because so many good books have already done so and because my focus here is on the risk to the health and well-being of current and future generations of Americans.

I am a physicist who has studied and written about systems. Systems are dominated by unexpected and nonintuitive behavior because they have feedbacks, thresholds, delays, and nonlinearities. To understand the climate system, it is critical to recognize the distinction between atmospheric *concentrations* of CO_2 (the total stock of CO_2 already in the air) and annual *emissions* of CO_2 (the yearly new flow into the air). A 2002 study led by John Sterman, director of the System Dynamics Group at the MIT Sloan School of Management, found that even "highly educated graduate students" held many myths about the climate system.

> Many believe temperature responds immediately to changes in CO_2 emissions or concentrations. Still more believe that stabilizing emissions near current rates would stabilize the climate, when in fact emissions would continue to exceed removal, increasing GHG [greenhouse gas] concentrations and [planetary heating]. Such beliefs support "wait and see" policies, but violate basic laws of physics.

In fact, until annual carbon dioxide *emissions* drop to about one-fifth of current levels, *concentrations* of heat-trapping carbon dioxide will continue to rise, and with rising *concentrations,* the pace of climate change will continue to accelerate.

During the Planetary Purgatory era, the painful reality of global warming will touch the lives of all Americans. We will be forced to begin a desperate scramble, together with other nations, to stop the planet's temperature rise before the Greenland Ice Sheet melts. All Americans will become expert on both annual CO_2 emissions and total atmospheric CO_2 concentrations—two quantities that will ultimately determine the fate of the next fifty generations of Americans. I predict they will eventually be reported with as much fanfare as the gross domestic product.

As an important aside, scientists and government agencies often use carbon, C, rather than carbon dioxide, CO_2, as a metric. Carbon dioxide is the greenhouse gas. Carbon is found in fossil fuels and soils and trees. The global carbon cycle is what many scientists study. You need familiarity with both quantities to follow the scientific and political debates about climate science and climate solutions. The key relationship to remember is:

1 ton carbon, C, equals 3.67 tons carbon dioxide, CO_2

Thus 11 tons of carbon dioxide equals 3 tons of carbon, and a price of $30 per ton of carbon dioxide equals a price of $110 per ton of carbon.

In 2005, fossil fuel combustion released into the air more than 26 billion tons of CO_2 (more than 7 billion tons of carbon). This is five times the annual rate of emissions from the 1940s. For the past decade, annual emissions have been rising about 2 percent per year, in large part driven by China and the United States. This rate of growth seems likely to continue through 2015 and possibly through

2025, barring a sudden reversal of U.S. (and Chinese) climate and energy policy. In 2005, the U.S. Department of Energy forecast that global annual emissions would exceed 30 billion tons of CO_2 in 2010 and, in 2025, 38 billion tons of CO_2 (more than 10 billion tons of carbon). Such rapid *emissions* growth by 2025 would make *concentrations* soar and take the nation and the world to the very edge of catastrophe.

While emissions might be thought of as the water flowing into a bathtub, atmospheric concentrations are the water level in the bathtub. Emissions are analogous to the federal budget deficit we incur each year, and concentrations are analogous to the total national debt that has been accumulated.

In 2005, atmospheric concentrations of carbon dioxide were 380 parts per million, about a third higher than the preindustrial average of about 280 ppm. In recent years, the rate of growth of concentrations has doubled. Concentrations are now climbing more than 2.5 ppm a year. By 2025, concentrations are projected to be 420–430 ppm. During Planetary Purgatory, concentrations are projected to rise an average of 3 ppm a year. In this scenario, by 2050, atmospheric concentrations would hit 500 ppm. Yet once we get much past 500 ppm, the complete melting of the Greenland ice sheet and the resulting 20-foot sea-level rise become all but inevitable.

Now it begins to be clear how desperate we will be in Planetary Purgatory. Suppose that America takes no serious action on climate while George W. Bush is president, and we successfully block any serious efforts by other nations. Suppose that then, starting about 2010, we take some wishy-washy actions to slow our emissions growth, while China and other developing nations continue their booming growth largely unchecked (thanks to growing populations, industrialization, and a rapidly expanding middle class). Suppose we continue making modest investments in developing new technology. Near 2020, America starts to get more serious, and we organize international commitments that slow global emissions growth *by half.*

Finally, in 2025, the entire world wakes up to the full gravity of global warming. Now we adopt the aggressive five-decade effort to deploy the best existing energy technology described in chapter 1 (modified from the analysis by Princeton's Stephen Pacala and Robert Socolow). From 2025 through 2075, the world achieves eight remarkable changes:

1. We launch a massive performance-based efficiency program for homes, commercial buildings, and new construction.
2. We launch a massive effort to boost the efficiency of heavy industry and expand the use of cogeneration (combined heat and power).
3. We capture the CO_2 from 800 new large coal plants and store it underground.
4. We build 1 million large wind turbines (or the equivalent in renewables like solar power).
5. We build 700 new large nuclear-power plants while shutting down no old ones.
6. We require every car to have an average fuel economy of 60 mpg.
7. We enable every car to run on electricity for short distances (requiring another half-million large wind turbines) before reverting to biofuels (requiring one-twelfth the world's cropland).
8. We stop all tropical deforestation, while doubling the rate of new tree planting.

Pacala and Socolow call these "wedges," since each starts slowly but then rises in impact over the 50 years and ultimately avoids the emission of 1 billion tons of carbon per year.

Had we started these eight wedges in 2010, global carbon emissions would have remained frozen at 8 billion metric tons per year. But because we delayed, because we started in 2025, they will merely *slow* emissions growth, so that global carbon emission will rise from 10 billion metric tons per year in 2025 to 12 billion metric tons per year in 2075. Finally, suppose that, starting in 2075, we adopt even more aggressive use of advanced energy technologies, and global emissions actually start *dropping* 1.5 percent per year.

In this scenario, carbon dioxide concentrations would exceed 600 ppm in 2100—and perhaps exceed 750 ppm, given the likely effect of the climate system's vicious cycles, as we will see shortly—and continue to rise. The temperature rise from current levels to 2100 would be a whopping 2.5°C or more. The outcome: We caused an eventual 20-foot sea-level rise, and we probably caused an eventual 80-foot rise. We didn't prevent a century or more of super-hurricanes and mega-droughts. We were insufficiently desperate and poorly led. We waited for new technology to show up in 2025 instead of deploying existing technology at once.

And if we do wait until 2025, the relatively painless technology-driven solutions that are available in 2007 or 2010 will no longer be sufficient to avoid climate catastrophe. Our actions will have to be far more desperate and aggressive. Just how desperate and aggressive critically depends on the myriad feedback loops in the climate system that will almost certainly punish any unwise delay in taking global warming seriously.

CLIMATE REALITY VERSUS CLIMATE MODELS

The earth's climate system is "far from being self-stabilizing," in the words of climatologist Wallace Broecker, but is "an ornery beast which overreacts even to small nudges." Push it too hard in one direction, you get an ice age, in another direction, you get 80-foot-higher sea levels. This suggests that the climate system has one or more vicious cycles, in which a little warming causes a change that speeds up warming, as when warming melts highly reflective Arctic ice, replacing it with the blue sea, which absorbs far more sunlight and hence far more solar energy, causing the Arctic Ocean to heat up more, melting more ice, and so on. Vicious cycles are often called "positive feedbacks" in the scientific literature, because these feedbacks add to and increase the effect. It is not a term I will use much here because it has a positive connotation in general usage—everybody wants to get positive feedback—whereas everybody should want to avoid the vicious cycles of the climate system.

The models that tell us how much warming we will get from a certain level of carbon dioxide emissions do not fully account for all of the vicious cycles. Thus, these models almost certainly significantly *underestimate* the climate's likely response to our emissions of greenhouse gases, a view shared by a number of recent studies and most of the climate scientists I talked to, such as Harvard's Dan Schrag. Let's look briefly at three studies from 2006.

Scientists analyzed data from a major expedition to retrieve deep marine sediments beneath the Arctic to understand the Paleocene-Eocene Thermal Maximum, a brief period some 55 million years ago of "widespread, extreme climatic warming that was associated with massive atmospheric greenhouse gas input." This study, published in *Nature*, found Artic temperatures almost beyond imagination—above 23°C (74°F)—temperatures far warmer than current climate models had predicted when applied to this period. The three dozen authors conclude that existing climate models are missing crucial factors that can significantly amplify polar warming.

A second study looked at temperature and atmospheric changes during the Middle Ages. The study found that the effect of vicious cycles in the climate system—where global warming boosts atmospheric CO_2 levels—"will promote warming by an extra 15 percent to 78 percent" compared with typical estimates by the U.N.'s Intergovernmental Panel on Climate Change. The study notes that these results may even be conservative because they ignore other green-house gases such as methane, whose levels will likely be boosted as temperatures warm.

The third study looked at temperature and atmospheric changes during the past 400,000 years. It found evidence for significant increases in both CO_2 and methane (CH_4) levels as temperatures rise. The conclusion: If our current climate models correctly accounted for such vicious cycles, "we would be predicting a significantly greater increase in global warming than is currently forecast over the next century and beyond"—as much as 1.5°C warmer this century alone.

Let's look at some key vicious cycles that climate modelers are missing or underestimating.

THE FOUR (POTENTIAL) SOURCES OF THE APOCALYPSE

For the last few decades, nearly 60 percent of the carbon dioxide that we have been adding to the atmosphere has stayed there. Where did the rest go? The other 40 percent has been absorbed by several "sinks"—the ocean, soils (including permafrost), and vegetation. They are called sinks because they absorb carbon and remove it from the ecosystem. Returning to the bathtub analogy, a carbon sink is just like the drain in your bathtub. The sources, including cars, factories, and power plants, are like faucets. As long as the sources generate more carbon dioxide than the sinks can drain, atmospheric concentrations (the water level in the bathtub) will continue to rise.

This is called the *global carbon cycle*. At some threshold of carbon dioxide concentrations and temperature rise, most scientists believe that one or all of these sinks will saturate—like clogged-up drains, they will not be able to absorb any more. Some carbon sinks may actually turn into *sources* of greenhouse gases. Preliminary evidence suggests that may be starting to happen already. I think we will know for certain by the 2025–2050 era. Let's look at four key sinks that could drive vicious cycles: oceans, soils, permafrost, and vegetation.

First, the oceans. According to a 2005 report by the United Kingdom's Royal Society, ocean warming leads to a "decreased mixing between the different levels in the oceans." That, in turn, "would reduce CO_2 uptake, in effect, reducing the oceanic volume available to CO_2 absorption from the atmosphere." In other words, if surface water that has absorbed CO_2 does not switch places with deeper water, the ocean will absorb less and less CO_2 over time and more will stay in the atmosphere. The increased ocean stratification would also tend to separate some phytoplankton from their nutrients, "leading to a decline in oceanic primary production," which would also reduce the ocean's ability to take up carbon, which means more CO_2 would stay in the air, and on and on. Finally, on our current CO_2 emissions trend, the ocean will become so acidic that coral reefs and other sea life will be devastated, further reducing the ocean's ability to absorb carbon.

Second, the soils. Warming can cause soils to stop taking up CO_2 and, ultimately, to start releasing it. A 2002 study of Texas grasslands found that as CO_2 concentrations increase, the ability of the soil to take up carbon slowed more rapidly than expected, "indicating that we are currently at an important threshold." The study notes that "the ability of soils to continue as sinks is limited." British soil experts have been monitoring their soil at several thousand sites in England and Wales since 1978. In 2005, they reported that the soils are releasing their carbon. The net carbon content has been dropping 0.6 percent per year—a huge amount considering that the

CO_2 released from British soils would be enough to erase the industrial-emissions reductions the country has achieved so far with its enlightened energy policies.

Third, the tundra, Arctic permafrost, and frozen peat. The permafrost is soil that stays below freezing (0°C or 32°F) for at least two years. Peat is basically mulch, or organic matter that is partially decomposed. It is found around the globe, but it is frozen near the poles. Normally, plants capture carbon dioxide from the atmosphere during photosynthesis and slowly release that carbon back into the atmosphere after they die. But the Arctic acts like a freezer, and the decomposition rate is very low. So frozen peat is "a locker of carbon," as UCLA scientist Laurence Smith explained at an American Meteorological Society seminar in February 2006.

How much? According to a June 2006 *Science* article by Russian and American scientists, nearly 1,000 billion metric tons of carbon (some 3,600 billion metric tons of carbon dioxide) are locked up in the Arctic's permafrost. That exceeds all the carbon dioxide currently in the atmosphere. The permafrost may contain more than a third of all carbon stored in soils globally, much of it in the form of methane. The problem: Global warming is melting the top layer of permafrost, creating the possibility of large releases of soil carbon, and that is a potentially devastating vicious cycle. We are defrosting the tundra freezer—and at an unprecedented rate.

A 2006 study by Alaska researchers finds rapid degradation to key elements of the permafrost "that previously had been stable for 1000s of years." The study, titled "Abrupt Increase in Permafrost Degradation in Arctic Alaska," concludes that this recent degradation exceeds changes seen earlier in the twentieth century by a factor of ten to a hundred.

New Scientist magazine reported in August 2005 that in western Siberia a frozen peat bog the size of France and Germany combined is turning into "a mass of shallow lakes," some almost a mile wide. In the past 40 years, the region has warmed by 3°C, greater warming than almost anywhere else in the world, in part because of the vicious cycle described earlier: Warming melts highly reflective ice and replaces it with dark soils, which absorb more sunlight and warm up, melting more ice, and on and on.

Russian botanist Sergei Kirpotin describes an "ecological landslide that is probably irreversible and is undoubtedly connected to climatic warming." The entire western Siberian sub-Arctic region is melting, and it "has all happened in the last three or four years," according to Kirpotin, who believes we are crossing a critical threshold. The peat bogs formed near the end of the last ice age some 11,000 years ago. They generate methane, which, up until now, has mostly been trapped within the permafrost, and in even deeper ice-like structures called clathrates. The Siberian frozen bog is estimated to contain 70 billion tons of methane (CH_4). If the bogs become drier as they warm, the methane will oxidize and the emissions will be primarily CO_2. But if the bogs stay wet, as they have been recently, the methane will escape directly into the atmosphere.

Either way we have a dangerous vicious cycle, but the wet bogs are worse because methane has twenty times the heat-trapping power of carbon dioxide. Some 600 *million* metric tons of methane are emitted each year from natural and human sources, so if even a small fraction of the 70 *billion* tons of methane in the Siberian bogs escapes, it will swamp those emissions and dramatically accelerate global warming. Researchers monitoring a single Swedish bog, or mire, found it had experienced a 20 to 60 percent increase in methane emissions between 1970 and 2000. In some methane hot spots in eastern Siberia, "the gas was bubbling from thawing permafrost so fast it was preventing the surface from freezing, even in the midst of winter."

Even if the tundra carbon is all emitted as carbon dioxide instead of methane, the consequences would be disastrous. Carbon emissions from human activity already exceed 7 billion tons a year, and we are on track to be at 10 billion tons a year by 2025. But as we have already seen, if we exceed annual emissions levels of 10 billion tons for any significant length of time, we will have no chance of avoiding catastrophic warming.

A major 2005 study led by NCAR climate researcher David Lawrence found that virtually the entire top 11 feet of permafrost around the globe could disappear by the end of this century. Using the first "fully interactive climate system model" applied to study permafrost, the researchers found that if we somehow stabilize carbon dioxide concentrations in the air at 550 ppm, permafrost would plummet from more than 4 million square miles today to 1.5 million. If concentrations hit 690 ppm, permafrost would shrink to just 800,000 square miles.

While these projections were done with one of the most sophisticated climate-system models in the world, the calculations *do not yet include the feedback effect of the released carbon from the permafrost.* That is to say, the CO_2 concentrations in the model rise only as a result of direct emissions from humans, with no extra emissions counted from soils or tundra. Thus they are conservative numbers—or *overestimates*—of how much CO_2 concentrations have to rise to trigger *irreversible* melting.

David Lawrence told me that NCAR's climate model will not incorporate these feedbacks for many years. And most major climate models do not include these crucial feedbacks (one exception is below). Thus, the *Fourth Assessment Report* by the Intergovernmental Panel on Climate Change, coming out this year (2007), almost certainly *underestimates* greenhouse gas forcings and climate change this century. In short, we have a much tougher task than the U.N.'s consensus-based process has been telling us.

By the end of Planetary Purgatory, most of the tundra may be unsavable.

Fourth, the tropical forests. Tropical forests store carbon, and destroying them releases that carbon. Intact tropical forests serve as a carbon sink for slightly more than 1 billion metric tons of carbon a year. A 2006 article by British scientists reviewing the current state of knowledge on tropical forests and carbon dioxide estimated that tropical deforestation released emissions "at the higher end" of the reported range of 1 to 3 billion metric tons of carbon a year.

Unfortunately, we do not appear prepared to stop current deforestation trends, while the carbon sink is likely to shrink because of increased drought, wildfires, and temperatures. The mechanisms are deadly enough individually, but when they interact synergistically the effects are multiplied and create a classic vicious cycle.

We've already seen how high temperatures and drought have combined to create record wildfires in the United States, but the situation is far worse in other parts of the world. The global fires of 1997–1998 "may have released carbon equivalent to 41 percent of worldwide fossil fuel use," according to a 2003 *Nature* article. Over Southeast Asia and Latin America alone, acreage equal to half of California burned out of control. While Indonesia lost more than double the acreage the United States lost in its record-breaking 2005 wildfire season, that developing country spends only about 2 percent of what we do on fire suppression. The article concluded grimly, "Pan-tropical forest fires will increase as more damaged, less fire-resistant, forests cover the landscape."

In Indonesia, both rain forests and peat lands burned. Carbon-rich tropical peat deposits can be more than 60 feet deep. A 2002 *Nature* article reported, "The extensive fire damage caused in 1997 has accelerated changes already being caused in tropical peatlands by forest clearance and drainage." Using satellite images to compare logging activity for the years 1997 and 2000, the authors found that "logging had increased by 44 percent," which made the remaining forests "more susceptible to fire in the future." Absent a major effort to address the problem, "tropical peatlands will make a significant contribution to global carbon emissions for some time to come."

In 2005, the Amazon was suffering a brutal drought—in many regions the harshest since records began a hundred years ago. By October, the governor of Amazonas State had declared a "state of public calamity." The threat to the Amazon forest is grave. The Woods Hole Research Center in Santarém on the Amazon River reported in 2006 that the "forest cannot withstand more than two consecutive years of drought without breaking down." Dr. Dan Nepstad of Woods Hole expects "mega-fires" to sweep across the jungle if it gets too dry.

Today, about 20 percent of the rain forest has been chopped down, and another 22 percent has been hurt enough by logging that sufficient sunlight can reach the forest floor to dry it out. Models suggest that when 50 percent of the forest is destroyed—which some models project for 2050—it will have crossed a "tipping point" beyond which its destruction cannot be stopped. In the coming decades, drought and heat will combine to devastate the rain forest and its canopy, reducing local rainfall and further accelerating the drought and local temperature rise, ultimately causing the release into the atmosphere of huge amounts of carbon currently locked in Amazon soils and vegetation, another fearsome feedback loop at work.

CROSSING THE POINT OF NO RETURN

Global warming is on the verge of dramatically transforming the global carbon cycle, causing the release of carbon from some soils, tundra, and forests, while slowing the uptake of carbon by the ocean and other carbon sinks.

The United Kingdom's Hadley Centre for Climate Prediction and Research has one of the few climate models that incorporates a significant number of carbon-cycle feedbacks, particularly in soils and tropical forests. In a 2003 study, they found that a typical fossil fuel emissions scenario for this century, which would have led to carbon dioxide concentrations in 2100 of about 700 ppm *without* feedbacks, led instead to concentrations of 980 ppm *with* feedbacks, a huge increase. Even ignoring feedbacks, keeping concentrations below 700 ppm requires the United States and the world to start slowing carbon dioxide emissions from coal, oil, and natural gas significantly by 2015 and to stop the growth almost entirely after 2025.

In 2006 the Hadley Centre, working with other British researchers, published an important study, "Impact of Climate-Carbon Cycle Feedbacks on Emissions Scenarios to Achieve Stabilisation," which included both ocean and terrestrial carbon-cycle feedbacks (though they do not specifically model carbon emissions from defrosting tundra). The study found that such feedbacks reduce the amount of fossil fuel emissions we can release by 21 percent to 33 percent.

We have no room for error. The Hadley study finds that just to stabilize at 650 ppm, annual emissions this century will have to *average* under 9 billion tons of carbon, a level that emissions will probably achieve by 2015. Absent the feedbacks, annual emissions this century could have averaged nearly a third more.

There appears to be a threshold beyond which it becomes more and more difficult for us to fight the feedbacks of the carbon cycle with strong energy policies that reduce fossil fuel emissions into the air. While the threshold is not known precisely today, it appears to be somewhere between 450 ppm and 650 ppm, based on my review of the literature and conversations with climate scientists. By 2025, we'll know much better where it is. Unfortunately, on our current path, the world's emissions and concentrations will be so high by 2025 that the "easy" technology-based strategy will not be able to stop us from crossing the very high end of the threshold range.

That's why I am calling the second quarter of this century Planetary Purgatory. Barring a major reversal in U.S. policies in the very next decade, come the 2020s, most everyone will know the grim fate that awaits the next fifty generations. But the only plausible way to avoid it will be a desperate effort to cut global emissions by 75 percent in less than three decades—a massive, sustained government intervention into every aspect of our lives on a scale that far surpasses what this country did during World War II. That would indeed be punishment for our sins of inaction.

Failing that desperate effort, we would end up at midcentury with carbon emissions far above current levels, and concentrations at 500 ppm, rising 3 to 4 ppm a year—or even faster if the vicious cycles of the climate system have kicked in.

We have passed the point of no return.

CHAPTER FOUR

2050–2100: HELL AND HIGH WATER

We could get a meter [of sea-level rise] easy in 50 years.
    —Bob Corell, chair, Arctic Climate Impact
        Assessment, 2006

The peak rate of deglaciation following the last Ice Age was . . . about one meter [39 inches] of sea-level rise every 20 years, which was maintained for several centuries.
    —James Hansen, director, Goddard Institute for
        Space Studies (NASA), 2004

Sea-level rise of 20 to 80 feet will be all but unstoppable by mid-century if current emissions trends continue. The first few feet of sea-level rise alone will displace more than 100 million people worldwide and turn all of our major Gulf and Atlantic coast cities into pre-Katrina New Orleans—below sea level and facing super-hurricanes.

How fast can seas rise? For the past decade, sea levels have been rising about 1 inch a decade, double the rate of a few decades ago. The *Third Assessment Report* of the U.N. Intergovernmental Panel on Climate Change (IPCC), released back in 2001, projected that sea levels would rise 12 to 36 inches by 2100, with little of that rise coming from either Greenland or Antarctica. Seas rise mainly because ocean water expands as it gets warmer, and inland glaciers melt, releasing their water to the oceans.

Sea-level rise is a lagging indicator of climate change, in part because global warming also increases atmospheric moisture, as we've seen. More atmospheric moisture probably means more snowfall over both the Greenland and Antarctica ice sheets, which would cause them to gain mass in their centers even as they lose mass at the edges. Until recently, most scientists thought that the primary mechanism by which these enormous ice sheets would lose mass was through simple melting. The planet warms and ice melts—a straightforward physics calculation and a very slow process, with Greenland taking perhaps a thousand years or more to melt this way, according to some models.

Since 2001, however, a great many studies using direct observation and satellite monitoring have revealed that both of the two great ice sheets are losing mass at the edges much faster than the models had predicted. We now know a number of physical processes can cause the major ice sheets to disintegrate faster than by simple melting alone. The whole idea of "glacial change" as a metaphor for change too slow to see will vanish in a world where glaciers are shrinking so fast that you can actually watch them retreat.

The disintegration of the Greenland and Antarctic ice sheets is a multistage process that starts with the accelerated warming of the Arctic.

THE END OF THE ARCTIC AS WE KNOW IT

Global warming tends to occur faster at high latitudes, especially in the Arctic. That is called polar amplification. Arctic warming is amplified for several synergistic reasons, as explained in the most comprehensive scientific survey completed to date, the December 2004

Arctic Climate Impact Assessment, by leading scientists from the eight Arctic nations—Canada, Denmark/Greenland, Finland, Iceland, Norway, Russia, Sweden, and the United States:

1. Warming melts highly reflective white ice and snow, which is replaced by the dark blue sea or dark land, both of which absorb far more sunlight and hence far more solar energy.
2. In the Arctic, compared with lower latitudes, "more of the extra trapped energy goes into warming rather than evaporation."
3. In the Arctic, "the atmospheric layer that has to warm in order to warm the surface is shallower."
4. So, when the sea ice retreats, the "solar heat absorbed by the oceans in summer is more easily transferred to the atmosphere in winter."

And this leads to more snow and ice melting, further decreasing Earth's reflectivity (albedo), causing more heating, which the thinner Arctic atmosphere spreads more quickly over the entire polar region, and so on and so on.

We can witness this classic feedback loop today at the North Pole, where the summer ice cap has shrunk more than 25 percent from 1978 to 2005, a loss of 500,000 square miles of ice, an area twice the size of Texas. The Arctic winters were so warm in both 2005 and 2006 that sea ice did not refreeze enough to make up for the unprecedented amount of melting during recent summers. A synthesis report in August 2005 by twenty-one leading climate scientists, supported by the U.S. National Science Foundation's Arctic Systems Science Program, described the future in terms that were unusually stark for a group of scientists:

At the present rate of change, a summer ice-free Arctic Ocean within a century is a real possibility, *a state not witnessed for at least a million years.* The change appears to be driven largely

by *feedback-enhanced global climate warming,* and there seem
to be few, if any, processes or feedbacks within the Arctic system that are capable of altering the trajectory toward this
"super interglacial" state. [Emphasis added.]

We appear to be crossing a threshold in the Arctic, one that existing models did not predict would happen so fast. "The recent sea-
ice retreat is larger than in any of the (19) IPCC [climate] models,"
Tore Furevik pointed out in a November 2005 talk on climate-system
feedbacks. He is deputy director of Norway's Bjerknes Centre for
Climate Research. Once again, the models on which the IPCC bases
its conclusions appear to be "too conservative," either underestimating or missing entirely relevant climate feedbacks. Most models suggest that the Arctic Ocean will see ice-free summers by 2080 to 2100.
At our current pace, this will happen long before then.

According to a 2005 *Science* article, key Arctic landmasses have
warmed "0.3° to 0.4°C per decade since the 1990s," double the rate
of the previous two decades. A 2005 study led by the Institute of Arctic Biology at the University of Alaska at Fairbanks and the U.S.
Geological Survey, estimated that the reduced snow cover and albedo in the summertime Arctic landscape, caused by global warming, added local atmospheric heating comparable to what a doubling
of CO_2 levels (to 550 ppm) would do over many decades to the global
atmosphere. In short, the dramatic climatic changes in the Arctic
today are a warning to us of both the pace and degree of change
America will experience early in the second half of this century.

The study also noted that "the continuation of current trends
in shrub and tree expansion could further amplify this atmospheric
heating by two to seven times." As the permafrost thaws, creating a
moist, nutrient-rich environment for vegetation, polar amplification will accelerate. We have very few climate models that incorporate the impact of such changes in vegetation, which again indicates
how likely it is that we are underestimating the future warming of

the Arctic. The scientific evidence is simply accumulating too fast to model adequately.

New research suggests that the summer Arctic could be ice-free far sooner than anyone ever imagined. Simply looking at the shrinking *area* of the Arctic ice misses an even more alarming decline in its thickness and hence its *volume*. At a May 2006 seminar sponsored by the American Meteorological Society, Dr. Wieslaw Maslowski of the Oceanography Department at the Naval Postgraduate School reported that models suggest that the Arctic lost one-third of its ice volume from 1997 to 2002. He made an alarming forecast: "If this trend persists *for another 10 years*—and it has through 2005—we could be ice-free in the summer" (emphasis added).

The loss of Arctic ice has little effect on sea levels because the ice is floating on the Arctic Ocean. Like a floating ice cube in a glass of water, when it melts, it doesn't change the water level. Why, then, should we be worried? Because in the Arctic, the accelerating warming of the land, air, and ocean sets the stage for one of the severest impacts of climate change facing our country—extreme sea-level rise from the disintegration of the Greenland Ice Sheet.

THE END OF GREENLAND—AND COASTAL LIFE— AS WE KNOW IT

> *Models indicate that warming over Greenland is likely to be of a magnitude that would eventually lead to a virtually complete melting of the Greenland ice sheet, with a resulting sea-level rise of about seven meters (23 feet).*
>
> —*Arctic Climate Impact Assessment,* 2004

The Greenland Ice Sheet extends over some 1.7 million square kilometers (more than 650,000 square miles). It is as large as the entire state of Alaska and almost as big as Mexico. It is 3 kilometers (nearly 2 miles) at its thickest. It contains nearly 3 million cubic kilometers (750,000 cubic miles) of ice. Unlike the Arctic ice cap, Greenland's landlocked ice, when it returns to the ocean, causes sea levels to rise.

Current climate models project that the entire ice sheet will melt if Greenland warms only about 4.5°C (8.1°F). Since Greenland is currently warming much faster than the planet as a whole, that is likely to occur when the planet warms more than 3°C compared with levels of the late 1800s. Exceeding such warming by 2100 is a near certainty if greenhouse gas concentrations significantly exceed 550 parts per million, a doubling from preindustrial levels. On our current path, we may hit 550 by midcentury.

Once the warming passes this threshold, the melting may become almost unstoppable. As climatologist Jonathan Gregory has pointed out, melting lowers the altitude of the ice-cap surface, which leads to more warming and reduced snowfall, another vicious cycle. Until recently, the conventional wisdom was that Greenland would take a thousand years or more to lose its ice sheet. But that assumed that the loss in mass would come exclusively from simple melting. We now know, however, that melting is anything but simple.

A team led by NASA and MIT scientists reported in 2002 that the ice was flowing in parts of Greenland much faster during the summer melting season than the winter. They concluded that some of the water flows to the ice-bedrock interface at the bottom of the glacier and acts as a lubricant for the entire glacier to slide and glide on. This "provides a mechanism for rapid response of the ice sheets to climate change," a factor that has been given "little or no consideration in estimates of ice-sheet response to climate change."

Scientists have observed another crucial change to Greenland's glaciers in recent years—the outlet glaciers have been speeding up, thinning, and disintegrating. The Greenland Ice Sheet drains into the sea through dozens of large glaciers, although roughly half the discharge "is through 12 fast flowing outlet glaciers, most no more than 10 to 20 kilometers across at their seaward margin, and each fed from a large interior basin of about 50,000 to 100,000 square kilometers," reported a 2006 review article in *Science*. The outlet glaciers have ice shelves or floating tongues of ice that can extend tens of kilometers past the point where the glaciers are supported by the ground. The front face of the ice shelves are hundreds of meters thick and calve or break off icebergs into the ocean.

For many years, scientists have been studying Jakobshavn Isbrae, Greenland's largest outlet glacier, which drains some 6.5 percent of the entire ice sheet's area. From 1950 to 1996, the glacier's terminal point, or calving front, was stable, fluctuating about 2.5 kilometers back and forth around its seasonal average. This multidecadal stability may have been due to "resistance from the fjord walls and pinning points" that helped secure the outlet glacier.

The outlet glacier is like a cork in a champagne bottle—and humanity, with our ever-increasing emissions of heat-trapping gases, has been frantically shaking this bottle. So it should not be a total surprise that a study of the Jakobshavn Isbrae glacier using satellite images found that "in October 2000, this pattern [of stability] changed when a progressive retreat began that resulted in *nearly complete disintegration of the ice shelf* by May 2003." The cork popped. Freed from this barrier that had been holding it back, the glacier's speed increased dramatically to 12.6 kilometers (7.8 miles) a year. Ice discharge nearly doubled. The authors concluded that "fast-flowing glaciers can significantly alter ice-sheet discharge at sub-decadal timescales and that their response to climate change has at least the potential to be rapid."

Jakobshavn Isbrae's sudden behavior change is no random event. A 2006 study found a similar change in two East Greenland outlet glaciers—Kangerdlugssuaq and Helheim, which are about 200 miles apart. In both glaciers, "acceleration and retreat has been sudden, despite the progressive nature of warming and thinning over some years." The top surface height of Helheim dropped more than 150 feet in two years. The surface of Kangerdlugssuaq dropped more than 250 feet. The two glaciers together drain about 8 percent of Greenland's ice sheet. They have nearly doubled the ice transport to the sea from this area of Greenland, to 100 cubic kilometers a year, up from about 50. The authors conclude that "the most plausible sequence of events is that the thinning eventually reached a *threshold,* ungrounded the glacier tongues and subsequently allowed acceleration, retreat and further thinning." This represents a step change in ice dynamics "not included in current models." The authors warn that given such behavior in three disparate outlet glaciers, "we should expect further Greenland outlet glaciers to follow suit."

How fast do Greenland glaciers move these days? Using Global Positioning System equipment, researchers have clocked Helheim at speeds exceeding 14 kilometers per year, nearly triple its 2001 speed. That flow rate equals an inch a minute. In 2005, Jakobshavn Isbrae was clocked at a similar speed. You can watch these glaciers move. That isn't "glacial change"—Greenland's glaciers are moving far faster than America's climate policy.

While 2002 had been the record for surface-area melting in Greenland since 1979 (the year systematic satellite monitoring began), 2005 topped that easily. A major 2006 study led by NASA's Jet Propulsion Laboratory found that "accelerated ice discharge in the west and particularly in the east doubled the ice sheet mass deficit in the last decade from 90 to 220 cubic kilometers per year." (Los Angeles uses about 4 cubic kilometers of fresh water a year.) The study's lead author, Eric Rignot, said in 2006, "In the next 10 years, it wouldn't surprise me if the rate doubled again."

Whereas glacier acceleration was widely found below 66° north latitude between 1996 and 2000, that line had shifted to 70° north by 2005. The authors conclude, "As more glaciers accelerate farther north, the contribution of Greenland to sea-level rise will continue to increase." In short, global warming is rapidly speeding up the disintegration of the entire Greenland Ice Sheet, and if we stay on our current emissions path until the 2050–2100 era, the loss of the Greenland Ice Sheet could become irreversible, according to NASA's Jay Zwally.

The IPCC's *Third Assessment Report* in 2001, which is used as the standard by most nations for impact assessment, projected a half-meter (20-inch) sea-level rise by 2100, with a worst case of 1 meter. But that assessment assumed Greenland would contribute little to sea-level rise by 2100. The startling changes now observed in Greenland alone would suggest 20 inches is a best-case scenario for 2100—and we should plan on much worse. If glacier acceleration continues, then by itself Greenland could easily generate sea-level rise of 5 inches or more *per decade* during Hell and High Water—and for centuries to come.

Greenland is not, however, the only major ice sheet showing signs of unexpected disintegration. So is Antarctica.

THE END OF ANTARCTICA—AND CIVILIZATION— AS WE KNOW IT

> *The last IPCC report characterized Antarctica as a slumbering giant in terms of climate change. I would say it is now an awakened giant.*
>
> —Chris Rapley, head of the British Antarctic Survey, 2006

Antarctica is bigger than the United States, and its ice sheet has locked away more than *eight times* as much ice as Greenland's. It holds 90 percent of Earth's ice. As recently as the *Third Assessment Report* in 2001, many scientists were not very worried about an Antarctic contribution to sea-level rise in this century. Antarctica is 99 percent covered by ice that is on average about 2 kilometers (1.2 miles) thick. It is one huge freezer. Until recently, scientists believed that warming-induced increases in snowfall over central Antarctica would just about counterbalance whatever melting occurred along the edges.

But as with Greenland, "in the last decade, our picture of a slowly changing Antarctic ice sheet has radically altered," explained a 2005 report by the Ice Sheet Mass Balance and Sea Level committee, a group of leading climate scientists and glaciologists. As with Greenland, global warming is causing outlet glaciers to thin and disintegrate while ice flow accelerates.

The Antarctic Peninsula, which juts out in the direction of South America, is warming the fastest—about 2.0°C in the past half-century, a rate unprecedented for at least two millennia. In 2002, much of the peninsula's Larsen B Ice Shelf disintegrated in spectacular fashion. The shelf, which had probably been in existence since the end of the last ice age, lost an area larger than the state of Rhode Island in a matter of weeks. After the collapse, glaciers flowing into it sped up two- to eightfold. One glacier's surface dropped 38 meters (125 feet) in six months, leading to an additional mass loss of 27 cubic kilometers per year, just from this small part of Antarctica.

In 2005, the British Antarctic Survey and U.S. Geological Survey reported the results of a comprehensive analysis of the glaciers that drain the peninsula's ice sheet. Of 244 glaciers, 212 have retreated since the earliest positions recorded five decades ago, and they have retreated far greater distances than the few advancing glaciers have expanded. Moreover, the line of retreating glaciers has moved steadily southward during this time, toward the South Pole, suggesting the influence of global warming. The authors conclude that "the cumulative loss of ice at the fronts of these glaciers may be leading to an increased drainage of the Antarctic Peninsula that is more widespread than previously thought."

The peninsula is not the only area of Antarctica with glaciers that are warming up—and speeding up. A 2004 study in *Geophysical Research Letters* noted that over the previous decade, the grounded Amundsen Sea portion of the West Antarctic Ice Sheet has been losing 50 cubic kilometers of volume each year "due to an imbalance between snow accumulation and ice discharge." Satellite measurements reveal that the ice shelves in one major outlet glacier, Pine Island Bay, have been thinning by up to 5.5 meters per year during this time. The reason appears to be ocean currents averaging 0.5°C warmer than freezing. The Pine Island and Thwaites glaciers enter the Amundsen Sea at Pine Island Bay. They are discharging ice three times faster than they were just ten years earlier. The study concludes that "the drawdown of grounded ice shows that Antarctica is more sensitive to changing climates than was previously considered."

A major 2004 study led by NASA researchers using satellite and aircraft laser altimeter surveys found that glaciers in this sector of the ice sheet are "discharging about 250 cubic kilometers of ice per year to the ocean," much more ice than is accumulating in the areas that feed these glaciers. The glaciers are thinning far faster than they were even a decade ago. As noted, that mass loss is partly counterbalanced by increased snowfall over the rest of Antarctica, and in 2001 the IPCC projected that Antarctica would *gain* mass this century. Only three years later, the data showed otherwise.

In a surprising finding, University of Colorado at Boulder researchers reported in 2006 that Antarctica as a whole was *losing* up to 150 cubic kilometers of ice annually. They used twin satellites to measure the mass of the entire Antarctic ice sheet as part of the Gravity Recovery and Climate Experiment (GRACE). That Antarctica is rapidly losing ice was confirmed by another 2006 study, the most comprehensive survey ever undertaken of the ice sheets, led by NASA's Zwally.

Perhaps the most important, and worrisome, fact about the

West Antarctic Ice Sheet (WAIS) is that *it is fundamentally far less stable than the Greenland Ice Sheet* because most of it is grounded far below sea level. The WAIS rests on bedrock as deep as 2 kilometers underwater. The 2004 NASA-led study found that most of the glaciers they were studying "flow into floating ice shelves over bedrock up to hundreds of meters deeper than previous estimates, providing exit routes for ice from further inland if ice-sheet collapse is under way." A 2002 study in *Science* examined the underwater grounding lines—the points where the ice starts floating. Using satellites, the researchers determined that "bottom melt rates experienced by large outlet glaciers near their grounding lines are far higher than generally assumed." And that melt rate is positively correlated with ocean temperature.

The warmer it gets, the more unstable WAIS outlet glaciers will become. Since so much of the ice sheet is grounded underwater, rising sea levels may have the effect of lifting the sheet, allowing more—and increasingly warmer—water underneath it, leading to further bottom melting, more ice-shelf disintegration, accelerated glacial flow, further sea-level rise, and so on and on, another vicious cycle. The combination of global warming and accelerating sea-level rise from Greenland could be the trigger for catastrophic collapse in the WAIS.

Were the Antarctic Peninsula to disintegrate, sea levels would rise globally by half a meter (20 inches). The Pine Island and Thwaites Glaciers could add another 1-meter rise. A collapse of the entire WAIS would raise sea levels 5 to 6 meters, perhaps over the course of a century. Combined with the disintegration of Greenland's ice sheet, that could raise the oceans more than 12 meters (40 feet).

If the planet warms enough, it could experience an even greater sea-level rise, since the East Antarctic Ice Sheet is about eight times larger in volume than the WAIS. Some 3 million years ago, when the earth was a little more than 3°C warmer than preindustrial levels (about 2.2°C warmer than today), Antarctica had far less ice and sea levels were a stunning 25 meters (80 feet) higher than today. If we stay on our current emissions path, the planet will almost certainly be that warm by century's end.

"A warming of this magnitude would risk 'the end of civilisation as we know it by the end of this century,'" said Peter Barrett, director of Victoria University's Antarctic Research Centre in Wellington, at the Royal Society of New Zealand's awards dinner in 2004, where he won the New Zealand Association of Scientists' Marsden Medal for lifetime achievement.

2050–2100: THE TRIPLE THREAT

How much the seas rise—and how fast—depends on how hot the planet gets. If we could avoid doubling carbon dioxide concentrations from preindustrial levels, we would have a very good chance of avoiding the worst of sea-level rise and might even avoid melting most of Greenland and Antarctica.

The scenario I put forward in the last chapter assumes that emissions will continue at current growth rates for another decade, then the growth rate slows by half for a decade, and then we aggressively adopt the seven low-carbon technological wedges for five decades (and stop tropical deforestation), and finally emissions start dropping in 2075. Because vicious cycles kick in, this scenario leaves concentrations at more than 800 ppm in 2100 (nearly a tripling of preindustrial levels), with average global temperatures more than 3°C higher than today *and still rising*.

What precisely happens to our coastal cities in a tripled-CO_2 world? You will not find many detailed studies on the subject, for two main reasons. First, most scientists have based their efforts to model climate impacts on a doubling of CO_2 concentrations because they (and their funders) have expected the world to wake up and take action. Second, most climate scientists did not expect the kind of accelerated flow and disintegration of the ice sheets we are now witnessing.

But in a tripled-CO_2 world, the United States should plan on the melting of Greenland and the West Antarctic Ice Sheet (ultimately augmented by ice loss from East Antarctica) to begin fueling a significant sea-level rise this century and beyond. We should plan for a 0.5- to 1.0-meter (20- to 40-inch) sea-level rise by 2050 and a 1.5- to 2.0-meter (60- to 80-inch) sea-level rise by 2100. How likely is this to happen? My interviews with leading climate scientists indicate that these numbers are emerging as the top of the likely range, even for a world of just 700 ppm. You can cut these numbers in half if you are of the cross-your-fingers-and-hope-for-the-best school of disaster planning.

We also need to plan for the probability that, by 2050, the hurricane season we experienced in 2005 will have become fairly typical. Also, the *rate* of sea-level rise by the end of the century is likely to be several inches a decade, and it could be more than a foot a decade. Thus, we are not trying to adapt to a static situation where sea level jumps 3 feet and stops, as so many analysts seem to have assumed. This amount of static sea-level rise has been well studied, but the impact of a constantly rising sea level has not, nor has the synergistic effect of increasing hurricane intensity.

A 1991 study led by the U.S. Environmental Protection Agency (EPA) noted that any significant sea-level rise "would inundate wetlands and lowlands, accelerate coastal erosion, exacerbate coastal flooding, threaten coastal structures, raise water tables, and increase the salinity of rivers, bays, and aquifers." The first 1 meter of sea-level rise inundates about 35,000 square kilometers (13,000 to 14,000 square miles) of U.S. land, roughly half wetlands and half dry land. Many shores would retreat rapidly, with beaches likely to "erode 50–100 meters from the Northeast to Maryland; 200 meters along the Carolinas; 100–1,000 meters along the Florida coast; and 200–400 meters along the California coast."

As sea level rise increases, the impacts multiply. One 2001 analysis reported that 22,000 square miles of land just on the Atlantic and Gulf coasts are at less than 1.5 meters elevation. While some of that might be salvageable if sea levels rose that high and stopped, in the post-2050 world, steadily rising sea levels would quickly lead to the abandonment of far more area.

Abandonment is particularly likely because the states that have the most area in jeopardy are, in order, Louisiana, Florida, North Carolina, and Texas—Hurricane Alley. By 2100, Louisiana could lose an area the size of Vermont to the sea. Florida could lose a Connecticut. North Carolina and Texas could each lose a Delaware. These numbers are conservative in that they don't consider the impact of tides, storm surges, coastal erosion, or land subsidence. Today, the part of our coast that hasn't been eroded by storm and tide has generally been toughened up by them. Sea-level rise exposes parts of the shore to storms and tides that are not so strengthened.

Now imagine that sea levels keep rising 5 inches a decade or more at the same time that the Gulf of Mexico, Florida, and the South Atlantic coasts are battered year after year by hurricane seasons similar to, or even worse than, what they experienced in 2004 and 2005. There's no chance New Orleans could survive the century. Indeed, the city seems unlikely to survive the next category 4 or 5 hurricane whenever it comes, because so far the U.S. government appears unwilling to foot the bill for designing levees to protect it from such storms—let alone from such storms in a world where sea levels are considerably higher.

If our government won't spend the money to protect New Orleans sufficiently today, what are the chances we will spend the money to protect dozens of coastal cities post-2050, once everyone knows that sea levels will keep rising and intense hurricanes will occur relentlessly? Consider also that by then, we will be devoting huge resources to desperately cutting our greenhouse gas emissions, to figuring out how to reverse catastrophic warming, and to dealing with the devastating consequences of drought, wildfires, and massive relocations. *Protecting* dozens of major coastal cities from future flooding will be challenging enough—*rebuilding* major coastal cities destroyed by super-hurricanes will be an almost impossible task.

This will be the beginning of the era of urban triage. New Orleans, the Outer Banks of North Carolina, the Florida Keys and South Florida, Galveston, and other low-lying Texas cities, Biloxi and other low-lying Gulf Coast cities, will be the first to go. Some will be abandoned before being hit by a category 4 or 5 hurricane. Others, afterward.

In this scenario, most of our coasts, especially along the Gulf and South Atlantic, will be designated permanent (or, more accurately, semipermanent) wetlands and will no doubt be uninsurable for building. Some major ports and cities, such as Houston and Miami, would likely be the subject of major preservation efforts. But I have not seen one estimate of the cost of designing levees and other protections for such large cities against rapidly rising sea levels and a category 5 hurricane.

And this is not the worst case.

The authors of a 2005 study, "Global Estimates of the Impact of a Collapse of the West Antarctic Ice Sheet," led by the University of Southampton in England, point out that theirs is the first paper to consider the global impacts of a 5- to 6-meter (16- to 20-foot) sea-level rise. A 1980 paper by the National Center for Atmospheric Research that considered a similar sea-level rise focused only on the United States. Both these studies are "optimistic" in that they assume that after the ice sheet collapses, the sea-level rise will return to a very slow rate. They also didn't consider how hurricanes will change the cost of any protection measures in Hurricane Alley, or how governments and individuals would perceive the viability of building in those regions.

The 2005 paper's worst-case scenario has some 6 meters of sea-level rise from 2030 to 2130, based on a collapse of the West Antarctic Ice Sheet, with little or no contribution from Greenland. Given recent scientific studies, I believe a more plausible version of the same events might be a steadily accelerating loss of mass from Greenland coupled with periodic collapses of parts of the West Antarctic Ice Sheet, creating much uncertainty and fear.

In their scenario, by 2100, some 400 million people worldwide will be exposed to the rising seas. A total land area of more than 4 million square kilometers will be flooded (absent any protective measures), roughly one-half the area of the continental United States. Low-lying countries such as Bangladesh would be utterly inundated. Trillions of dollars of assets would be at risk. In scenarios where the sea level rises and then stops or slows dramatically (and there is no significant increase in coastal storms), adaptation is straightforward if expensive, and a large fraction of the most populated and valuable coastal lands might well be protected. But if people believed that sea levels would simply continue rising more than a foot a decade, any significant defense of coastal cities would seem untenable, especially in hurricane-prone regions.

In this country, one-quarter of Florida would be submerged—and one-third would be underwater when sea-level rise hit 7.6 meters (25 feet). If one or more category 4 or 5 hurricanes struck what was left of the state on a regular basis, perhaps every other year, how could any significant portion of the state be protected for human population and commerce?

Louisiana would be in the same capsized boat, flooded up to Baton Rouge. In Texas, Galveston, Corpus Christi, Beaumont, and Port Arthur would be submerged. Houston would be seriously at risk and difficult to protect from the combination of rising sea levels and super-hurricanes. Savannah, Georgia, Charleston, South Carolina, Virginia's major coastal cities, one-fourth of Delaware, most land along the Chesapeake Bay, and huge sections of such cities as Washington, D.C., New York, and Boston would be flooded. Large parts of the San Francisco Bay and Puget Sound would also be, although in general the West Coast would be better off since it has fewer low-lying coastal areas and no hurricane risk.

If Americans in 2100 came to see 12 meters (40 feet) sea-level rise as inevitable by 2200, who can even begin to fathom how the nation would respond?

I have focused in this chapter on the "high water" part of the scenario, but let's not overlook the hellish heat we would experience. A November 2005 study in the *Proceedings of the National Academy of Sciences* is one of the few to look at the extreme temperatures that a near tripling of carbon dioxide concentrations would have on United States weather in the last quarter of this century (from 2071 to 2095).

A vast swath of the country would see the average summer temperature rise by a blistering 9°F. Houston and Washington, D.C., would experience temperatures exceeding 98°F for some 60 days a year. Oklahoma would see temperatures above 110°F some 60 to 80 days a year. Much of Arizona would be subjected to temperatures of 105°F or more for 98 days out of the year—14 full weeks. We won't call these heat waves anymore. As the lead author, Noah Diffenbaugh of Purdue University, said to me, "We will call them normal summers." They will be accompanied by extreme droughts on a recurring basis, some in the West lasting for many years at a time, with two to five times the wildfire devastation, as discussed in chapter 3. And temperatures would continue to rise relentlessly into the next century, accompanied by declines in soil moisture over much of this country. Much of the Southwest would be at risk of desertification.

Hell and High Water is not our certain future, but it is the future we should expect and plan for if we do not sharply reverse our energy and environmental policy in the next two decades. As with the avian bird flu, doing nothing would make disaster inevitable.

Scientists once hoped that some as yet unidentified mechanism in the climate system might avert catastrophe, but if climate models have any gaps today, they are gaps that *underestimate* the speed and severity of future impacts.

In any case, even if the worst case of several meters' sea-level rise by 2100 doesn't come to pass, our likely future on a tripled-CO_2 planet Earth is still almost unimaginably grim.

I have left out details of the other impacts scientists see as possible or likely. For example, in a tripled-CO_2 world, the oceans become so warm and acidic that virtually all coral reefs die. In fact, much of the world's oceans, especially in the Southern Hemisphere, become inhospitable to many forms of marine life. Globally, more than a quarter of all species may die, since they are far less capable of adapting than we humans are, especially to such a rapid climate change. In a tripled-CO_2 world, tropical diseases find fertile ground over much larger portions of the planet.

I have focused on impacts in the United States, largely because so many people I talk to mistakenly believe we Americans will not be severely affected by climate change, or at least not anytime soon. But not only will this rich country suffer, poor countries will suffer greatly. Imagine what will happen in Africa, a continent already afflicted with persistent, widespread drought and a shortage of safe drinking water. One 2006 study reported in *Science* found that by 2100, climate change could dry up lakes and streams in one-quarter of the African continent.

Much attention has been given to the possibility that the ocean-circulation patterns could change dramatically, especially by the melting of the Greenland Ice Sheet injecting fresh water into the North Atlantic, which in turn might shut down the so-called thermohaline current that helps warm Europe. This scenario, carried to an absurd extreme in the movie *The Day After Tomorrow,* supposedly plunges the planet into an ice age. This is, as James Hansen put it to me, "the implausible worst-case scenario." While the current may be weakening, a complete collapse is considered very unlikely this century and in any case would be unlikely to put much of a dent in the extreme warming most of the planet is going to experience on our current emissions path.

Some, including James Lovelock, have raised the prospect of a runaway greenhouse effect with ever-accelerating increases in greenhouse gas emissions, which might kill hundreds of millions of people by the end of this century. That view does not find much support in the scientific literature, and I regard it about as implausible as *The Day After Tomorrow*.

The possibility, however, that the thawing tundra might release a large fraction of its carbon in the form of methane is quite genuine, and so we could end up in a quadrupled-CO_2 world (carbon dioxide concentrations of 1,100 ppm) by 2100 or soon thereafter. Such a world is vastly grimmer than anything I have described here.

In a quadrupled-CO_2 world, average temperatures over much of the inland United States would be a scorching 20°F hotter. Soil moisture would drop 50 percent or more over much of the country. Prolonged drought would ravage much of our cropland, turning breadbaskets into dust bowls. Sea-level rise of 80 feet or more would be inevitable. We would exceed global temperatures before the Antarctic ice sheet formed, when sea levels were 70 meters (230 feet) higher on our planet. Humanity would be faced with centuries of suffering from a continuously worsening climate.

Scientists have given us more than enough serious and credible warnings of the consequences of our current path. The IPCC's *Fourth Assessment Report* this year (2007) will present a much stronger consensus and a much clearer and darker picture of our likely future than the *Third Assessment*—but it will almost certainly still underestimate the likely impacts. The *Fifth Assessment*, due around 2013, should include many of the omitted feedbacks, like that of the defrosting tundra, and validate the scenarios described on these pages, especially if we haven't yet sharply reversed our current energy policies. At that point, exceeding a doubling of carbon dioxide concentrations in our air will be a near certainty, and a tripling will be quite likely.

The IPCC process tends to produce an underestimation of worst-case scenarios for two reasons—because it is consensus-based and because it encompasses many greenhouse gas scenarios that assume far stronger action on emissions reduction than the United States or the world seems prepared to embrace.

PART II

THE POLITICS AND
THE SOLUTION

CHAPTER FIVE

HOW CLIMATE RHETORIC
TRUMPS CLIMATE REALITY

*The scientific debate is closing (against us) but not
yet closed.*
　　—Frank Luntz, conservative strategist, 2002

*Global warming is real (conservatives secretly know
this).*
　　—David Brooks, *New York Times* columnist, 2005

The global-warming problem is no longer primarily a scientific
matter. Science has told us what we need to know about how
life on this planet will be ruined if we stay on our current greenhouse gas emissions path. Global warming is also not a technological problem. We have the technologies to avoid the disasters that
await us if we keep doing nothing.

Today, global warming is a problem of politics and political
will. We lack the will to take the necessary actions—and many of
the actions we are poised to take are either inadequate or ill con-
ceived. The great political tragedy of our time is that conservative
leaders in America have chosen to use their superior messaging and
political skills to thwart serious action on global warming, thereby

increasing the chances that catastrophic climate change will become a reality.

Global warming should not be a partisan issue—not when the health, well-being, and security of the next fifty generations of Americans are at stake. But it has become partisan, at least in this country. In order to determine how to create the politics of action in the next decade, we must understand what the politics of inaction has caused in the past decade. That's what this chapter is about.

AMERICA VERSUS THE WORLD

The United States is almost alone in opposing mandatory action to reduce greenhouse gas emissions. The rest of the developed world (other than Australia) believes that the threat posed by warming is so great that they ratified the 1997 Kyoto Protocol, an international climate treaty that requires strong action—reducing emissions to about 5 percent below 1990 levels by 2008–2012. It was a politically difficult move for many of those countries to make given their knowledge that the United States, the world's biggest emitter, would probably not join.

Moreover, the rest of the industrialized world embraced the Kyoto Protocol even though it did not restrict the emissions from developing countries such as China and India, which many in our country see as a fatal flaw in the agreement and a major reason not to vote for it. Yet that flawed agreement is viewed instead in most other countries as a critical first step to solving the climate problem.

British prime minister Tony Blair said in February 2003, "It is clear Kyoto is not radical enough," given the scale of the climate problem. That same year Blair announced that "for Britain, we will agree to the Royal Commission [on Environmental Pollution] target of a 60 percent reduction in emissions by 2050. And I am committed now to putting us on a path over the next few years towards that target," despite the fact that this would force a dramatic change in how England uses energy in transportation, industry, and buildings. In September 2004, Blair gave a speech in which he reiterated Britain's commitment to deep emissions reductions, saying that the accelerating rate of global warming has become "simply unsustainable in the long-term." He went on to explain:

> And by long-term I do not mean centuries ahead. I mean within the lifetime of my children certainly; and possibly within my own. And by unsustainable, I do not mean a phenomenon causing problems of adjustment. I mean a challenge so far-reaching in its impact and irreversible in its destructive power, that it alters radically human existence. . . .
>
> There is no doubt that the time to act is now.

British environmental politics is far, far removed from ours: After the speech, Conservative Party leader Michael Howard accused Blair (the Labor Party leader) of not taking strong enough action and of "squandering the chance to lead efforts against climate change."

The United States has been headed in exactly the opposite direction. President George W. Bush not only rejected the Kyoto Protocol, he has worked feverishly to block other countries from taking any further action to reduce emissions, and he opposes any mandatory action by this country. A major Senate bill from John McCain (Republican) and Joe Lieberman (Democrat) that would put an absolute cap on U.S. greenhouse gas emissions received just 38 votes in the summer of 2005—5 fewer than it received the first time it was offered in 2003—even though its restrictions had been weakened to try to attract support.

"The United States is not going to ratify this process because the U.S. Congress is not going to allow them to do so, even if the

Administration would sign up to it," said John Shanahan, senior counsel to Senate Committee on Environment and Public Works chair James Inhofe (Republican), in February 2006. Shanahan also predicted, "You need 60 votes in the U.S. Senate to pass anything. They have got 38 right now. And they may go for something 'super light' to win a few more symbolic votes. *But they will never get 60*" (emphasis added).

In 2005, Tony Blair convened a climate conference with dozens of the world's top climate scientists. In 2006 he released a major scientific report, *Avoiding Dangerous Climate Change,* which included more than forty peer-reviewed papers. In his foreword, Blair stated, "It is clear from the [scientific] work presented that the risks of climate change may well be greater than we thought," but he noted, "action now can help avert the worst effects of climate change."

In the United States, climate science is not treated seriously. As many newspaper stories have related, and as a number of scientists confirmed, the U.S. government routinely undermines the ability of government scientists to communicate their ideas to the American public. The administration edits their work and blocks their access to the media. I will return to this point shortly.

In 2006, Fred Barnes, executive editor of *The Weekly Standard,* wrote of Bush's opposition to the Kyoto global-warming treaty:

> Though he didn't say so publicly, Bush is a dissenter on the theory of global warming. . . . He avidly read Michael Crichton's 2004 novel *State of Fear,* whose villain falsifies scientific studies to justify draconian steps to curb global warming. Crichton himself has studied the issue extensively and concluded that global warming is an unproven theory and that the threat is vastly overstated. Early in 2005, political adviser Karl Rove arranged for Crichton to meet with Bush at the White House. They talked for an hour and were in near-total agreement.

Bush ignores every major study by the world's leading climate scientists, ignores his strong ally Tony Blair, yet instead reads Crichton's fiction thriller and spends an hour chatting with him. Apparently, science fiction trumps science fact.

Senator Inhofe praised Crichton for "a compelling presentation of the scientific facts of climate change" and actually invited him to be a witness at a 2005 Senate hearing on the role of science in environmental policy. Crichton took that opportunity to accuse the entire scientific community of fudging the science of climate change, a charge he also makes in his book, and one that meteorologist William Gray made at the same hearing.

THE CONSERVATIVE CONSENSUS ON CLIMATE

Those who deny that global warming is an urgent problem and those who seek to delay strong action to reduce greenhouse gas emissions have been more persuasive than climate scientists. I call these people the Denyers and Delayers, and they have been particularly persuasive among conservatives, who currently hold much of the political power in this country. Let's explore a few examples from the conservative media, blogs, pundits, think tanks, and politicians. I've chosen them to show that the misinformed skepticism about climate science among conservative political and intellectual leaders runs deep and wide.

In February 2006, *New York Times* columnist John Tierney wrote: "Scientists agree that the planet seems to be warming, but their models are so crude that they're unsure about how much it will heat up or how much damage will be done. There's a chance the warming could be mild enough to produce net benefits."

Tierney has packed a great deal of misinformation into two sentences.

The overwhelming majority of scientists agree the planet *is* warming—not "seems to be"—the data itself is beyond dispute.

The models are not crude. On the contrary, the models have become very sophisticated and even predictive. If there is an appearance of uncertainty about how much the planet will heat up or how much damage will be done, it's because of the uncertainty of how much greenhouse gases we humans are going to release into the atmosphere. Scientists spend a great deal of time analyzing and publicly discussing scenarios that include both very low growth and very high growth in human-caused emissions and concentrations. That means scientists talk about a wide range of potential impacts, which may look to some like uncertainty. Tragically, however, the low-emission scenarios have become more unlikely with each passing year of political inaction—inaction driven in large part by influential but misinformed people such as Tierney.

Similarly, it is a dangerous myth that global warming could be mild enough to provide net benefits. This possibility has died because we did not seize the moment, thanks in part to those such as Tierney who have successfully argued for inaction based on the myth itself. For warming to be mild and even beneficial requires first that the climate's sensitivity to forcing by greenhouse gases be on the very low side—a possibility that has been all but eliminated by a stream of studies in recent years. It requires the United States and the world to stabilize atmospheric carbon dioxide *concentrations* at levels low enough to avoid starting the vicious cycles of the carbon system, well below 550 parts per million (ppm). Unfortunately, we are headed to well over 700 ppm. As we saw in the last chapter, exceeding 700 ppm would probably mean another sizzling 3°C or more of warming *this century,* widespread droughts, and an eventual sea-level rise of 40 to 80 feet or more, an outcome neither mild nor beneficial.

Those stark facts mean we must start reducing the amount of U.S. greenhouse gas *emissions* immediately. Yet Tierney opposes "spending large sums to avert biblical punishments that may never come." On Tierney's path of inaction, the only real scientific question becomes, How bad will the impact of global warming be—very serious or irreversibly apocalyptic?

Second, consider the late commentator Jude Wanniski. In May 2005 he wrote an open letter to *The New Yorker,* expressing his disapproval of Elizabeth Kolbert's three-part series "The Climate of Man," which he labeled "Un-Journalism." The only scientific critique he offered was that the series begins by "announcing that the scientific community has now concluded that mankind in a significant way is producing the carbon dioxide that is cooking the atmosphere" and then shows pictures of melting glaciers, "although the reader cannot tell from looking that the glacier is melting because too many of us are driving SUVs or because solar activity in the last part of the 19th century heated up the earth by a degree or two, and the icecaps are still melting as a result."

In fact, scientists have studied solar activity for decades and have concluded that its contribution to recent warming is at most very small. Even stranger, the planet *cooled* slightly in the last part of the nineteenth century, primarily due to multiple volcanic eruptions, including that of Krakatoa, whose particulates helped block out the sun. It's surprising that a smart man like Wanniski would trot out an old and discredited argument—and that he would so easily believe that the entire scientific community had missed this important contribution to the earth's climate. This is just one example of the Denyers ignoring the thousands of studies disputing their position and instead grasping onto notions that have been widely refuted by scientists.

Third and fourth, consider columnists Charles Krauthammer and George Will on the subject of hurricanes and climate change. Krauthammer proclaimed on September 9, 2005, "There is no relationship between global warming and the frequency and intensity of Atlantic hurricanes. Period." He provided no evidence in support of this statement.

On the September 25, 2005, broadcast of ABC's *This Week,*

George Stephanopoulos and David Gergen discussed the recent scientific evidence linking hurricane intensity to global warming. Then Gergen, who is so well known for his political moderation that he has served both Democratic and Republican presidents, said, "It does seem to me under these circumstances this is a wake-up call to take global warming and climate change more seriously." George Will was ready with a sarcastic reply:

I have an alternative theory. I think these two hurricanes were caused by the prescription drug entitlement. You will say, "How can you say that? The entitlement hasn't even started." There's no conclusive evidence that global warming, that is to say, an unprecedented, irreversible, and radical change has started. You will say, "There's no scientific proof." Same answer. You will say, "Aren't you embarrassed, Mr. Will, to be attaching your political agenda to a national disaster?" Yeah, I'm embarrassed, but everyone else is doing it.

This may well be the most antiscientific statement Will has ever uttered, if not the silliest, equating a serious cause-and-effect relationship put forward by leading scientists using a widely accepted scientific theory with a causation that is sheer nonsense. Once again comes the accusation that anyone who raises this issue has a "political agenda," when clearly those who dismiss it have the agenda.

Strangely, neither Krauthammer nor Will comes from the wing of the conservative movement that reflexively dismisses key scientific theories, such as evolution. Quite the reverse. Within weeks of their global-warming comments, both wrote strong op-eds against those who embrace the "phony theory," as Krauthammer put it, of intelligent design over evolution. Will's reply to school board members who endorsed a proclamation that "evolution is not a fact" was "But it is."

How can such ardent defenders of the science of evolution be such ardent rejecters of the science of global warming? How can people, even those who question the science underlying evolution, embrace the warnings of scientists that avian bird flu could evolve into a powerful human pandemic but reject warnings from climate scientists? How can so many conservatives dismiss the consensus of thousands of the world's top climate scientists?

The answer is that ideology trumps rationality. Most conservatives cannot abide the *solution* to global warming—strong government regulations and a government-led effort to accelerate clean-energy technologies into the market. According to Jude Wanniski, Elizabeth Kolbert's *New Yorker* articles did nothing more "than write a long editorial on behalf of government intervention to stamp out carbon dioxide." His villain is not global warming; it is the threat to Americans from government itself.

George Will's review of Michael Crichton's *State of Fear* says:

> Crichton's subject is today's fear that global warming will cause catastrophic climate change, a belief now so conventional that it seems to require no supporting data. . . .
>
> Various factions have interests—monetary, political, even emotional—in cultivating fears. The fears invariably seem to require *more government subservience to environmentalists* and *more government supervision of our lives.* [Emphasis added.]

Conservatives such as Will are so opposed to government regulations that they are skeptical of anyone who identifies a problem that requires regulatory solutions—and they are inherently accepting of those who downplay such problems.

George Will believes that advocates for action on climate want more government supervision of our lives. But if we hold off on modest government action today, we will almost guarantee the need for much more extreme government action in the post-2025 era. Only Big Government—which conservatives don't want—can relocate millions of citizens, build massive levees, ration crucial re-sources such as water and arable land, mandate harsh and rapid reductions in certain kinds of energy—all of which will be inevita-ble necessities if we don't act now.

THE ART OF POLITICAL PERSUASION

> *Of all the talents bestowed upon men, none is so pre-cious as the gift of oratory. He who enjoys it wields a power more durable than that of a great king.*
> —Winston Churchill

Anyone who wants to understand the politics of global warming, and anyone who wants to change the politics of global warming, must understand why the Denyers are so persuasive in the public debate and why scientists are not. Science and logic are powerful systematic tools for understanding the world, but they are no match in the public realm for the twenty-five-century-old art of verbal persuasion: rhetoric.

While logic might be described as the art of influencing minds with the facts, rhetoric is the art of influencing both the hearts and minds of listeners with the figures of speech. The figures are the catalog of the different, effective ways that we talk, including alliteration and other forms of repetition, metaphor, irony, and the like. The goal is to sound believable. As Aristotle wrote in *Rhetoric*, "Aptness of language is one thing that makes people believe in the truth of your story."

The figures of speech have been widely studied by marketers and social scientists. They turn out to "constitute basic schemes by which people conceptualize their experience and the external world," as one psychologist put it. We think in figures, and so the figures can be used to change the way we think. That's why political speechwriters use them. To help level the rhetorical playing field in the global warming debate, I will highlight the three rhetorical elements that are essential to modern political persuasion.

First, simple language. Contrary to popular misconception, rhetoric is not big words; it's small words. "The unreflecting often imagine that the effects of oratory are produced by the use of long words," a precocious twenty-three-year-old Winston Churchill wrote in an unpublished essay on rhetoric. "All the speeches of great English rhetoricians . . . display a uniform preference for short, homely words of common usage." We hear the truth of his advice in the words that linger with us from all of the great speeches: "Judge not that ye be not judged," "To be or not to be," "Lend me your ears," "Four score and seven years ago," "blood, toil, tears and sweat," "I have a dream."

In short, simple words and simple slogans work.

Second, repetition, repetition, repetition. Repetition makes words and phrases stick in the mind. Repetition is so important to rhetoric that there are four dozen figures of speech describing different kinds of repetition. The most elemental figure of repetition is *alliteration* (from the Latin for "repeating the same letter"), as in "compassionate conservative." Repetition, or "staying on message," in modern political parlance, remains the essential rhetorical strategy. As Frank Luntz, a leading conservative-message guru and political strategist, has said, "There's a simple rule: You say it again, and you say it again, and you say it again, and you say it again, and you say it again, and then again and again and again and again, and about the time that you're absolutely sick of saying it is about the time that your target audience has heard it for the first time."

Third, the skillful use of tropes (from the Greek for "turn"), figures that change or turn the meaning of a word away from its literal meaning. The two most important tropes, I believe, are metaphor and irony. "To be a master of metaphor," Aristotle writes in *Poetics,* is "a sign of genius, since a good metaphor implies intuitive perception of the similarity in dissimilars." When Bush said in 2006 that the nation was "addicted to oil," he was speaking metaphorically. Curing an addiction, however, requires far stronger medicine than the president proposed: America could become energy-independent, but only through a series of government-led policies identical to the ones needed to avoid catastrophic climate change.

SCIENCE, CLIMATE, AND RHETORIC

Rhetoric works, and it works because it is systematic. As Churchill wrote, "The subtle art of combining the various elements that separately mean nothing and collectively mean so much in an harmonious proportion is known to very few." Unfortunately, the major player in the climate debate, the scientific community, is not good at persuasive speech. Scientists might even be described as antirhetoricians, since they avoid all of its key elements.

Few scientists are known for simple language. As the physicist Mark Bowen writes in *Thin Ice,* his book about glaciologist Lonnie Thompson: "Scientists have an annoying habit of backing off when they're asked to make a plain statement, and climatologists tend to be worse than most."

Most scientists do not like to repeat themselves because it implies that they aren't sure of what they're saying. Scientists like to focus on the things they *don't* know, since that is the cutting edge of scientific research. So they don't keep repeating the things they *do* know, which is one reason the public and the media often don't hear from scientists about the strong areas of consensus on global warming.

Scientific training, at least as I experienced it, emphasizes sticking to facts and speaking literally, as opposed to figuratively or metaphorically. Scientific debates are won by those whose theory best explains the facts, not by those who are the most gifted speakers. This view of science is perhaps best summed up in the motto of the Royal Society of London, one of the world's oldest scientific academies (founded in 1660), *Nullius in verba:* take nobody's word. Words alone are not science.

Scientists who are great public communicators, such as Carl Sagan and Richard Feynman, have grown scarcer as science has become increasingly specialized. Moreover, the media likes the glib and the dramatic, which is the style most scientists deliberately avoid. As Jared Diamond, author of *Collapse,* has written, "Scientists who do communicate effectively with the public often find their colleagues responding with scorn, and even punishing them in ways that affect their careers." After Carl Sagan became famous, he was rejected for membership in the National Academy of Sciences in a special vote. This became widely known, and, Diamond writes, "Every scientist is capable of recognizing the obvious implications for his or her self-interest."

Scientists who have been outspoken about global warming have been repeatedly attacked as having a "political agenda." As one 2006 article explained, "For a scientist whose reputation is largely invested in peer-reviewed publications and the citations thereof, there is little professional payoff for getting involved in debates that mix science and politics."

Not surprisingly, many climate scientists shy away from the public debate. At the same time, the Bush administration has muzzled many climate scientists working for the U.S. government, as we will see. As a result, science journalists, not practicing scientists, are almost always the ones explaining global warming to the public. Unfortunately, the media is cutting back on science reporting in general and finds reporting climate science particularly problematic.

It is not surprising, then, that the American public is so uninformed about global warming, so vulnerable to what might be called the conservative crusade against climate. I say conservative, rather than Republican, because many moderate Republicans have been as strong on climate as Tony Blair, most notably California governor Arnold Schwarzenegger, who said in 2005, "I say the debate is over. We know the science, we see the threat, and the time for action is now." He then committed the state to reduce greenhouse gas emissions to 80 percent below 1990 levels by 2050—precisely the reductions needed to ensure that the Greenland Ice Sheet does not melt. And in 2006, he signed a law crafted with the help of Democratic state legislators that requires a 25 percent reduction in California's carbon dioxide emissions by 2020.

A NOTE ON SKEPTICISM

The people I call global-warming Delayers and Denyers are also called "climate skeptics" or "contrarians." I think those terms are misused here. All scientists are skeptics. Hence the motto "Take nobody's word." Skeptics can be convinced by the facts; Denyers cannot. Skeptics do not continue repeating arguments that have been discredited. Denyers do.

A contrarian is "one who takes a contrary view or action, especially an investor who makes decisions that contradict prevailing wisdom." Contrarians may have a good strategy for making money in the stock market, but how many have a hidden agenda to undermine faith in the stock market itself? Moreover, if the scientific consensus somehow reversed itself, the Denyers wouldn't suddenly reverse themselves. They aren't contrarians.

The Denyers and Delayers, as I use the terms, are those who aggressively embrace one or both parts of a twofold strategy. First, they deny the strong scientific consensus that the climate change we are witnessing is primarily human-caused and likely to have serious negative impacts if we don't reverse our greenhouse gas emissions trends. Second, they work to delay this country from taking any serious action beyond perhaps investing in new technology.

Their beliefs were well articulated by Michael Crichton in a 2006 interview: "If you just look at the science, I, at least, am underwhelmed. This may or may not be a problem, but it is far from the most serious problem. If you want to do something, [limiting emissions] is not what to do. We don't at this moment have good technology to do this, if, in fact, it's necessary to do it."

Such is the road to ruin. Those who advance such a view, including President Bush, deserve a strong label. No doubt many Denyers and Delayers are sincere in their beliefs, but the quotes of Luntz and Brooks suggest that some are not. Sincere or insincere, they spread misinformation or disinformation that threatens the well-being of the next fifty generations of Americans. Denyers and Delayers are also not content merely to dispute the work of climate scientists—they are actively engaged in smearing those scientists' reputations.

THE CONSERVATIVE BATTLE PLAN

The Denyers and Delayers do not just have messaging skills superior to scientists (and environmentalists and most progressive politicians), they also have a brilliant strategy, a poll-tested plan of attack. A 2002 memo from the Luntz Research Companies explains precisely how politicians can sound as if they care about global warming without actually doing anything about it. It focuses in particular on casting doubts about the science. The memo can be found on the web, and anyone who cares about the future of America should read it.

Luntz's team has "spent the last seven years examining how best to communicate complicated ideas and controversial subjects." A big fan of rhetorical devices, Luntz specifically urges conservatives to "use rhetorical questions" whenever discussing the environment.

Like any good rhetorician, Luntz says that "it can be helpful to think of environmental (and other) issues in terms of a 'story.'" His next line is stunning: "A compelling story, even if factually inaccurate, can be more emotionally compelling than the dry recitation of the truth."

Luntz explains, *"The three words Americans are looking for in an environmental policy . . . are 'safer,' 'cleaner' and 'healthier,'"* (emphasis in original throughout). So people who want to seem to care about the environment should use those very words often. He also notes:

> *"Climate change" is less frightening than global warming.* As one focus group participant noted, climate change "sounds like you're going from Pittsburgh to Fort Lauderdale." While global warming has catastrophic connotations attached to it, climate change suggests a more controllable and less emotional challenge.

Focus groups are nothing new in politics, nor is coming up with the best spin for your ideas. But rarely has it been done with such callous disregard for the gravity of a scientific matter.

Luntz's lessons have been taken to heart in more places than you might imagine. An e-mail message sent in July 2005 from NASA headquarters to the Jet Propulsion Laboratory in Pasadena, California, criticized a web presentation that used the phrase "global warming," stating that it is "standard practice" in the agency to use the phrase "climate change." At the insistence of political appointees, the NASA press office had "a general understanding that when something in this field was written about that it was to be described as climate change and not global warming," as one retired press officer put it in 2006.

Interestingly, "climate change" has become for some conservatives, such as Senator Lisa Murkowski, a phrase to describe the obvious changes in climate we are observing in places like Alaska that (in their thinking) may or may not be caused by human activity, whereas "global warming" is reserved for change that is caused by human emissions of greenhouse gases. Like most scientists, I use the terms interchangeably.

Luntz writes, *"The most important principle in any discussion of global warming is your commitment to sound science. Americans unanimously believe all environmental rules and regulations should be based on sound science and common sense."* Luntz did not invent the phrase "sound science"—a good history can be found in Chris Mooney's book, *The Republican War on Science.* Luntz's strong suit is identifying what phrases work and then convincing conservatives to repeat those phrases over and over. "Sound science" works not only because of its alliteration but because it makes the speaker seem to care about science, even when he or she is actually peddling unsound science.

In theory, "sound science" means genuine peer-reviewed and widely corroborated science, as opposed to speculative Soviet-style "politicized science." In the case of global warming, virtually every single piece of peer-reviewed science supports humans as the primary cause, and as we've seen repeatedly the recent literature strongly suggests the impacts will be somewhere between serious and catastrophic if we don't change course soon.

Luntz's central point is the height of cynicism: *"You need to continue to make lack of scientific certainty a primary issue in the debate. . . . The scientific debate is closing (against us) but not yet closed. There is still a window of opportunity to challenge the science."*

This is one of the great tragedies of our times: For Luntz and a large number of conservatives, global warming is strictly a partisan political issue. He acknowledges that the science is moving against his position, but this does not persuade him. He suggests that conservatives muddy the waters, by providing people with information that supports an erroneous view, so that serious action on global warming can be delayed for as long as possible.

Do conservative political and intellectual leaders truly understand that they are on the wrong side of the scientific debate? *New York Times* columnist David Brooks wrote these astonishing words in 2005: "Global warming is real (conservatives secretly know this)." Delay, delay, delay. That is the goal. But we know that with just one more decade of delay, the only way to be sure the Greenland Ice Sheet doesn't melt would be onerous government action.

The Luntz strategy isn't new. One 1969 tobacco-industry memo famously states, "Doubt is our product since it is the best means of competing with the 'body of fact' that exists in the mind of the general public. It is also the means of establishing a controversy." Other, less famous lines are eerily prescient about global warming: "Doubt is also the limit of our 'product.' Unfortunately, we cannot take a position directly opposing the anti-cigarette forces and say that cigarettes are a contributor to good health. No information that we have supports such a claim."

The Denyers and the Delayers are luckier than the cigarette makers because they feel free to tout the "fact" that global warming might have benefits, as John Tierney did in the quote above, or as George Will does when he wrote in December 2004 that the climate models don't tell us "how much warming is dangerous—or perhaps beneficial." This sales pitch—combining doubt with the false hope of potential benefit—is one the tobacco companies could only dream of.

DENY, DENY, DELAY, DELAY

In a box labeled "Language That Works," Luntz recommends lines for Republican speeches that have been repeated endlessly in various forms by the Delayers:

> "We must not rush to judgment before all the facts are in. We need to ask more questions. We deserve more answers. Until we learn more, we should not commit America to any international document that handcuffs us either now or into the future."

In science, the facts are never completely in, making this a highly effective rhetorical strategy in any scientific debate. And this line of attack can be used equally well in ten or twenty years, or forever, because "*all* the facts" are never in. If we must wait until the painful reality of mega-droughts and rapid sea-level rise are upon us, the point of no return will have long passed.

Paula Dobriansky, the Bush administration's under secretary of state for global affairs, justified U.S. efforts to block further action on climate change at a December 2004 international conference with these words: "Science tells us that we cannot say with any certainty what constitutes a dangerous level of warming, and therefore what level must be avoided."

Apply this "certainty" test to all public policy, and we would never take any action to avoid any future problem. The Pentagon cannot say with any certainty what constitutes a dangerous level of opposing forces. Epidemiologists cannot say with any certainty what constitutes a dangerous number of birds infected with avian flu. Doctors cannot say with certainty what constitutes a dangerous weight. Does that mean we have no army? No avian flu policy? That a 300-pound patient with health problems shouldn't be put on a weight-loss regimen?

A core element of the White House's climate strategy has been to call for more research into climate change, but here we clearly see the administration saying one thing and doing the opposite. The Government Accountability Office reviewed the administration's research effort and in April 2005 came to the stunning conclusion that the effort was missing a major piece required by law—a plan to assess the impact of global warming on "human health and welfare," agriculture, the environment, energy, and water.

The White House's constant call for more research is nothing but a smokescreen. The Bush team has systematically worked to hold back the results of such research, to censor the information about the real dangers of global warming that its own agencies are supposed to provide to the public. For instance, since the 1990s, the U.S. Global Change Research Program had been working on a "U.S. National Assessment of the Potential Consequences of Climate Variability and Change." The Competitive Enterprise Institute (CEI), a conservative think tank funded in part by ExxonMobil, sued the Bush White House, under the little-known Federal Data Quality Act, to remove this comprehensive peer-reviewed study from circulation, labeling the report "junk science." A Freedom of Information Request revealed in 2003 that the White House had secretly asked CEI to sue it to get the nation's premier climate assessment withdrawn.

In short, the White House conspired with an oil-company-funded think tank to block a major government scientific report that sought to spell out the dangers of climate change to Americans. The failure of our government to warn us of the dangers, to provide our people with a national assessment of the potential consequences of climate change, denies Americans the information they need to make decisions.

The White House heavily edited a 2003 report from the U.S. Environmental Protection Agency, removing several paragraphs that described the dangers posed by rising temperatures, as the *New York Times*, CBS News, and other media outlets reported. It actually removed a reference to key findings of the National Academy of Sciences, a study that the president himself had commissioned. Ultimately every substantial conclusion in the EPA report was gutted. Even the sentence "Climate change has global consequences for human health and the environment" was considered too strong to be left in and it was removed.

The White House actually hired Philip Cooney, a former lobbyist for the American Petroleum Institute, to do its scientific censoring.

Much of what we have learned about the censoring comes from a whistleblower, Rick Piltz, a senior associate from the government office that coordinates federal climate-change programs, who resigned in March 2005. His documents showed that the White House had systematically edited reports by government scientists to make the otherwise strong scientific conclusions and consensus seem doubtful. Two days after Piltz's story broke, Cooney resigned from the White House. Within days, he was hired by ExxonMobil, which has devoted millions of dollars to supporting groups that advance the Denyer and Delayer agenda.

More recently, we have learned the shocking extent of the administration's censorship efforts, thanks to reports in the *New York Times, The New Republic,* and *60 Minutes.* The Bush administration has been engaged for a number of years in muzzling government scientists, according to a number of scientists inside and outside the government. I myself have spoken to many scientists—some of whom are afraid of speaking out publicly—and they confirm this. Rick Piltz has launched a website, www.climatesciencewatch.org, that regularly reports on government censorship of climate research.

Political appointees at NASA put in place a policy to limit media access to James Hansen—director of NASA's Goddard Institute for Space Studies—and all NASA climate scientists. After Hansen reported the NASA data showing that 2005 was the warmest year on record, and after he began giving lectures warning that we have at most a decade to sharply reverse our greenhouse gas emissions trends, NASA's public-affairs staff was ordered to review his forthcoming lectures, journal articles, web postings, and media contacts. Hansen was told he would face "dire consequences" if he continued to speak out about climate change.

After Hansen went public with his charges in early 2006, NASA seems to have changed its public-affairs policy, but the muzzling has continued at other government agencies. Interview requests from the media have been routinely rejected. And at agencies such as the National Oceanic and Atmospheric Administration, those media interviews that are granted can occur only if public-affairs staff monitors the conversation. As Hansen said in February 2006, "On climate, the public has been misinformed and not informed."

As we saw in chapter 2, some NOAA meteorologists have been publicly advocating an untenable scientific position—that recent increases in hurricane intensity have been well correlated with recent increases in sea-surface temperatures, but that the temperature increases have nothing to do with global warming. The NOAA meteorologists who take this position seem to have unfettered access to the press, even though few of them are experts on global warming. On the other hand, we rarely hear from the numerous global-warming experts at NOAA, many of whom disagree with the agency's official position. "Scientists who don't toe the party line are being intimidated from talking to the press," says MIT climatologist Kerry Emanuel. "I think it is a very sad situation. I know quite a few people who are frightened, but they beg me not to use their name."

The man in charge of NOAA is Vice Admiral Conrad Lautenbacher, a Bush appointee with a Ph.D. in applied mathematics and forty years of Navy service. At a December 2003 conference in Milan, for instance, he repeated the standard rhetoric: "I do believe we need more scientific info before we commit to a process like Kyoto." But it isn't clear what "scientific info" would impress him. In

2005 remarks shortly after Katrina hit New Orleans, he said of the connection between hurricane intensity and global warming: "People have hunches, certainly everybody can have a hunch, but the information is not there at this point that would allow you to make that connection. We have no direct link between the number of storms and intensity versus global temperature rise."

Lautenbacher describes the scientific studies that disagree with his view as merely "hunches." He then repeats the argument that the increase in hurricane intensity is just part of a natural cycle, completely unaware that the natural-cycle explanation is itself closer to a hunch than a proven theory, as we've seen. In February 2006, Lautenbacher wrote a letter to NOAA staff stating that "a few recent media reports have (incorrectly) asserted that some NOAA scientists have been discouraged from commenting on the question of whether human-caused global warming may be influencing the number or intensity of hurricanes." In reply, Jerry Mahlman, former director for sixteen years of NOAA's Geophysical Fluid Dynamics Laboratory, wrote:

> Contrary to Dr. Lautenbacher's assertions, I state emphatically that climate scientists within NOAA have indeed recently been systematically prevented from speaking freely. A number of NOAA scientists have directly and openly disagreed with Lautenbacher's statements that deny his direct connection with censorship of climate science.

Mahlman further notes that "the ideologically driven distortion of the truth about the relationship between hurricane intensity increases and warming ocean temperatures has been thoroughly refuted" in the scientific literature.

A great many people and businesses are making major investments and plans based on their understanding of the risk that the Gulf region could get hit by another powerful hurricane. Everyone, from those rebuilding the Gulf Coast and the levees to insurance companies to home owners like my brother, are trying to make plans—plans that involve the lives, the life savings, and the livelihoods of millions of people. They must have good information. They all rely on NOAA for the most objective scientific analysis and projections. Repeating over and over again the scientifically untenable claim that the recent spate of intense hurricanes is just a "natural cycle" with no link to global warming is dangerously misleading. Mahlman noted to me: "What value is there in obscuring the truth or flat-out lying about it?"

The global-warming Denyers and Delayers wish to do far more than just stop the public from learning the truth; they attack the credibility of those who try to tell the facts. The most virulent of them is Senator James Inhofe. In July 2003 he said, "With all of the hysteria, all of the fear, all the phony science, could it be that man-made global warming is the greatest hoax ever perpetrated on the American people? It sure sounds like it." Why would climate scientists pull such a horrible hoax? At his 2005 Senate hearing with Michael Crichton and meteorologist Bill Gray, Inhofe and his witnesses repeated the smear that climate scientists fudge their results in order to satisfy their funders and convince them to hand over more money.

Some of these attacks are very sophisticated and use the best rhetorical tricks. In his 2002 strategy memo, Frank Luntz recommends this attack:

> Scientists can extrapolate all kinds of things from today's data, but that doesn't say anything about tomorrow's world. You can't look back one million years and say that proves that we're heating the globe now hotter than it's ever been. After all, just 20 years ago scientists were worried about the new Ice Age.

Let's look at the worries of scientists 20 years ago. A 1977 report by the National Academy warned that uncontrolled greenhouse gas emissions might raise global temperatures 10°F and sea levels 20 feet. A 1979 academy report warned that "a wait and see policy may mean waiting until it is too late." A 1983 report from the Environmental Protection Agency warned that "substantial increases in global warming may occur sooner than most of us would like to believe," and the result of inaction might be "catastrophic." Twenty years ago, the leading American scientists were worried about global warming.

Michael Crichton repeats this attack in his novel *State of Fear*, in which he has one of his fictional environmentalists say, "In the 1970s all the climate scientists believed an ice age was coming." Snookered, columnist George Will picked this up in his glowing review and then repeated it on the March 26, 2006, edition of ABC TV's *This Week* with George Stephanopoulos. This clever and popular attack tries to make present global-warming fears seem faddish, saying current climate science is nothing more than finger-in-the-wind guessing.

The Denyers insist that climate scientists used to believe in cooling and now they believe in warming. Like all good attacks, this one is built around a partial truth, in this case, a milli-truth, one part in a thousand of the truth. Global warming leveled off between 1940 and 1975. As explained in chapter 2, this was largely a result of dust and aerosols sent by humans (and volcanoes) into the atmosphere, which temporarily overwhelmed the already well-understood warming effect from greenhouse gases. In the 1970s, a few scientists wondered whether the cooling effect from aerosols would be greater than the heating produced from greenhouse gases, and some popular publications ran articles about a new ice age. Most climate scientists were far more worried about the long-term greenhouse gas trends, even in the midst of short-term cooling— and they proved to be right.

The aerosol effect was fully explained in the 1980s and became part of scientific modeling "that is in remarkable agreement with the observations," as Tom Wigley, a leading climatologist with the National Center for Atmospheric Research, wrote in a 2003 letter to the U.S. Senate. Ignoring the science, the Denyers keep repeating the fiction as if it were the latest argument, sounding a bit like flat-earthers but much more dangerous. Senator Inhofe used this smear in his 2005 Senate hearing with Crichton, and George Will wrote, "Thirty years ago the fashionable panic was about global *cooling*," and then he cited a number of quotes that seem to support him. In January 2005 the website realclimate.org debunked the whole notion in a post titled "The Global Cooling Myth." They showed that Will's quotes from scientific magazines are misattributed or taken out of context in a way that nearly reverses their meanings.

Since Inhofe, Crichton, and Will are not scientists, they won't get drummed out of their community for repeating what is factually untrue.

A spring 2003 workshop of top atmospheric scientists in Berlin concluded that the shielding effect of aerosols may be far greater than previously estimated. Nobel laureate Paul Crutzen said, "It looks like the warming today may be only about a quarter of what we would have got without aerosols." This conclusion would suggest the planet may be far more susceptible to warming than previously thought. Crutzen noted that aerosols "are giving us a false sense of security right now." A 2005 study led by researchers at the National Oceanic and Atmospheric Administration concluded, "Natural and anthropogenic aerosols have substantially delayed and lessened the total amount of global ocean warming—and therefore of sea level rise—that would have arisen purely in response to increasing greenhouse gases."

The real irony here is that the aerosol-shielding issue, fully explained, gives the public *greater* reason to act preemptively on climate, not less. The entire record of climate science, rather than being a narrative based on fickle fads, is one of relentless, hard-used, continual progression of knowledge, which is characteristic of science, as opposed to politics or propaganda.

TRUTHINESS OR CONSEQUENCES

I believe the most effective piece of propaganda on global warming is Michael Crichton's 2004 novel, *State of Fear*. Everywhere I speak, I am asked questions based on unsubstantiated assertions in his book. More than any other single document published on global warming, the book captures the essence of Frank Luntz's vision: "A compelling story, even if factually inaccurate, can be more emotionally compelling than the dry recitation of the truth." In 2005, Comedy Central's Stephen Colbert introduced the word *truthiness* to describe emotional appeals that sidestep the facts. "Truthiness is what you want the facts to be as opposed to what the facts are," says Colbert. "What feels like the right answer as opposed to what reality will support." He might have coined the term for Crichton.

Although a work of fiction, *State of Fear* has a clear political agenda, as evidenced by Crichton's December 7, 2004, press release:

> STATE OF FEAR raises critical questions about the facts we believe in, without question, on the strength of esteemed experts and the media. Although the story is fiction, Michael Crichton writes from a firm foundation of actual research challenging common assumptions about global warming.

In an appendix titled "Why Politicized Science Is Dangerous," Crichton draws a direct and lengthy analogy between climate science and eugenics and Soviet biology under Lysenko, where all dissent to the party line was crushed and some Soviet geneticists were executed. With no evidence whatsoever, he claims that in climate science, "open and frank discussion of the data, and of the issues, is being suppressed." With this he is using an old trick—accuse your opponent of the same nefarious thing you yourself are doing.

Modern science is by nature open and frank. Any country and any laboratory can conduct any research it wants, and can publish it in one of hundreds of serious journals around the world. The scientific community conducts peer reviews of arguments on their merits—that's the gold standard. Just before the mistake-riddled, global-warming-will-cause-an-ice-age movie *The Day After Tomorrow* came out, the journal *Science* published an article by two environmental scientists that concluded, "In light of the paleoclimate record and our understanding of the contemporary climate system, it is safe to say that global warming will not lead to the onset of a new ice age." I have yet to see a critique of Crichton's book by the global warming Denyers and Delayers, even though it is seriously flawed, as we will see.

Crichton's book deserves a brief review here, since it has become a rallying cry for the Denyers and Delayers. On TV, in interviews, and in talks around the country, Crichton continues to cast doubt on the seriousness and urgency of global warming. He thinks the scientific and environmental communities have fabricated the threat and that efforts to manage the emissions of greenhouse gases are misguided. To make his case, Crichton accuses the scientific community of bad faith, as noted, and he distorts the science. He creates a scientist-hero, Dr. John Kenner, who outdebates the book's environmentalists.

Kenner says that real-life climatologist Jim Hansen manipulated the media in a 1988 congressional hearing, and that he's discredited because "Hansen overestimated [global warming] by three hundred percent." Had Crichton checked primary sources, he would have found Hansen's prediction came very close to being exactly accurate. The smear Crichton now cites was created ten years later, when global warming Denyer Pat Michaels shamefully misrepresented Hansen's testimony. Michaels is a visiting scientist with the Marshall Institute and a senior fellow at the Cato Institute—organizations that receive funds from ExxonMobil to advance the Denyers/Delayers agenda.

A full factual debunking of the book can be found on real climate.org. It's a fascinating tale of how misinformation is spread. Crichton even spreads truthiness in his bibliography, mischaracterizing the landmark 2002 National Research Council report, *Abrupt Climate Change*, as follows: "The text concludes that abrupt climate change might occur sometime in the future, triggered by *mechanisms not yet understood*." This is simply not true. The report concludes plainly, "Abrupt climate changes were especially common when the climate system *was being forced to change most rapidly*. Thus, greenhouse warming . . . may increase the possibility of large, abrupt, and unwelcome regional or global climatic events" (emphasis added).

Why would Crichton mischaracterize the report in his bibliography? Because one of his main goals in the book is to undermine the case that global warming causes *abrupt* climate change and *extreme* weather events. In his story, a mainstream environmental group is plotting to create extreme weather events that will cause the deaths of thousands of people timed to coincide with a conference on abrupt climate change in order to trick the public into accepting global warming as truth. In a bizarre coincidence, the book's climax has the evil environmentalists carefully plan a seismic tsunami—just weeks before an actual tsunami devastated Southeast Asia.

But the truth is stronger than fiction. Seismic tsunamis are caused by earth tremors. *They are not caused by global warming*. Any climate scientist knows that. This is a stunning blunder by Crichton, calling into question his claim to have any understanding of global warming.

Senator Inhofe, Michaels, and other Denyers have actually accused the environmental community of blaming the Indian Ocean tsunami on global warming. The environmentalists did nothing of the kind. "I am appalled that environmentalists are trying to ride on the backs of 160,000 dead people to push their global-warming agenda without any factual basis," Pat Michaels told the online magazine *Grist* in January 2005. He issued his own press release, saying, "Michael Crichton should sue environmentalists who blame the massive death toll from the Indian Ocean's tragic tsunamis on sea level rise for plagiarism."

In a January 2005 piece titled "The Tsunami Exploiters," columnist James Glassman said that Tony Juniper of Friends of the Earth in Britain had said of the tsunami, "Here again are yet more events in the real world that are consistent with climate change predictions." In fact, Juniper was talking about an increase in 2004 of *other kinds* of natural disasters that may be related to global warming. He had already put out a press release explaining that his remarks were made *before* the tsunami had even hit.

A few environmentalists had pointed out that rising sea levels (caused by global warming) coupled with the decline in natural barriers such as coral reefs (caused at least in part by global warming) had made the area more susceptible to the ravages from a seismic tsunami (caused by earthquakes). They had also pointed out that current climate trends could make future tsunamis even more deadly. Every one of those statements is, unfortunately, true. A *Grist* headline summed up the phony attack with biting rhetoric: "Right-Wingers Exploit Tsunami by Accusing Enviros of Exploiting Tsunami."

The smear about the tsunami is part of a systematic, decade-long effort by the Denyers to change the discourse in the media and the environmental community about the connection between extreme weather events and climate change—and to keep advocates of strong action on the rhetorical defensive. Tragically, their efforts have been all too successful.

THE DEATH OF ENVIRONMENTAL MESSAGING

When a group is so thoroughly beaten rhetorically, its members begin to bicker internally, often self-destructively. In 2004, two environmental strategists, Michael Shellenberger and Ted Nordhaus, released a bombshell essay, "The Death of Environmentalism: Global Warming Politics in a Post-Environmental World," based in part on interviews with twenty-five environmental leaders. Their essay started a virulent debate. Anybody who cares about the environment and global warming should hear both sides.

The original essay is passionately argued but supremely misguided. Interestingly, one of the authors' central arguments concerns rhetoric at its most basic.

> Most environmentalists don't think of "the environment" as a mental category at all—they think of it as a real "thing" to be protected and defended. They think of themselves, *literally*, as representatives and defenders of this thing. Environmentalists do their work as though these are *literal* rather than *figurative* truths. They tend to see language in general as representative rather than constitutive of reality. This is typical of liberals who are, at their core, children of the enlightenment who believe that they arrived at their identity and politics through a rational and considered process. They expect others in politics should do the same and are constantly surprised and disappointed when they don't.
>
> The effect of this orientation is a certain *literal-sclerosis*—the belief that social change happens only when people speak a *literal* "truth to power." *Literal*-sclerosis can be seen in the assumption that to win action on global warming one must talk about global warming instead of, say, the economy, industrial policy, or health care.

Had the authors gone on to make a compelling case that a figurative approach to global warming was superior to a literal approach, these paragraphs might have been a powerful launching point. But ironically, they instead play right into the hands of the political masters of figurative language, the global warming Denyers and Delayers. While figurative language certainly makes for more persuasive messaging—a central point of this chapter—wise public policy, at least in the environmental realm, *must* be based on scientific literalism.

Their thirty-page paper argues three main points:

1. Environmentalists, even after spending "hundreds of millions of dollars" in the previous decade and a half "combating global warming," have "strikingly little to show for it."
2. Environmentalists' efforts to enact policy measures to reduce greenhouse gas emissions through regulation (caps on greenhouse gas emissions and higher fuel-economy standards for cars) have failed and are therefore wrongheaded.
3. Environmentalists are mired in group think and "policy literalism," which makes them unable to see that the true solution to global warming is a visionary technological fix, the New Apollo Project, a proposal to spend $30 billion a year for ten years on clean-energy technologies, developing and deploying renewable energy and hydrogen cars.

The first point is self-evidently true. The authors, however, spend virtually no time trying to analyze *why* the message has failed. They simply assume that the message was wrong. They do not discuss at all the brilliant rhetorical seduction by the Denyers and Delayers. This is like trying to understand why John Kerry lost without examining the Bush team's strategy.

The authors also do not notice that global warming has a key difference compared with previous issues on which the environmental community has been successful—clean air and clean water, for instance. Those issues were dramatically visible (terrible smog in our big cities, Lake Erie catches fire), directly affected people's health at the time, and the solutions, though costly, could be put into place relatively quickly with very visible results. The signs of global warming are less visible (especially since much of the environmental community and media stopped talking about those signs, such as extreme weather, until recently), the major impact is a few decades away, and strong action now will not provide quick visible results. What strong action in the next decade will do—and only strong action can do it—is avoid catastrophic climate change. But that is hardly as sellable—with literal or figurative language—as avoiding tens of thousands of deaths next year by cutting smog.

On the second point, environmentalists have indeed utterly failed to get the United States to put even the mildest cap on greenhouse gas emissions or establish stronger fuel-economy standards. Does the failure to achieve these policies prove they are the wrong policies? Not at all.

The fact that the environmental community is bad at messaging should not be mistaken for proof that its message is bad—particularly in the case of an environmental problem unprecedented in human history and in the face of opponents with vastly superior language intelligence and resources. The industrialized nations, including all of Europe, have made serious commitments to reduce greenhouse gas and are putting into place a cap on carbon dioxide emissions. Those countries all have tougher fuel-economy requirements or much higher gasoline taxes or both than does the United States.

America absolutely needs an aggressive technology strategy similar to the New Apollo Project (minus the push for hydrogen cars). Mandatory reduction targets, such as a cap on carbon dioxide emissions, without aggressive technology programs will slow economic growth. But technology programs without mandatory targets won't solve our climate problem. They are a seductively attractive false hope. That's why the Denyers and Delayers are among the biggest supporters of technology programs without mandatory targets.

CHAPTER SIX

THE TECHNOLOGY TRAP AND THE AMERICAN WAY OF LIFE

There is no doubt that the time to act is now. It is now that timely action can avert disaster. It is now that with foresight and will such action can be taken without disturbing the essence of our way of life, by adjusting behaviour, but not altering it entirely.
—Tony Blair, 2005

It's important not to get distracted by chasing short-term reductions in greenhouse emissions. The real payoff is in long-term technological breakthroughs.
—John H. Marburger III,
president's science adviser, 2006

The mantra of the Delayers is "technology" and "technology breakthroughs." Their technological fix to the greenhouse gas problem is, unsurprisingly, not imminent. It is "long-term." But as we have seen earlier, failing to act in the near term—now—will bring about such drastic conditions that soon our only choice will be to react with extremely onerous government policies.

In 2005, British prime minister Tony Blair described the crucial two-prong strategy we must adopt: "We need to invest on a large scale in existing technologies *and* to stimulate innovation into new low-carbon technologies for deployment in the longer term." Future technology will be able to help preserve our way of life in the long term *if and only if* we have already moved "on a large scale" to technologies that already exist. Over the next few decades, we must rapidly deploy available technologies that stop global carbon dioxide emissions from rising. *Then,* in the second half of this century, we must sharply reduce global greenhouse gas emissions by deploying all the new technologies we have developed.

The time to act is now.

VOLUNTARY WARMING

It is hard to imagine that people will use low-carbon technologies on the vast scale needed until they see a financial return for cutting carbon, and that will not happen until spewing out carbon has a significant financial cost. But for carbon to have a cost, the government must either tax carbon dioxide emissions or create a market that establishes a price for emitting carbon dioxide. This second approach would be similar to the system used to trade emissions of sulfur dioxide under the Clean Air Act administered by the EPA. I prefer the trading system. The Bush administration strongly opposes both.

During the 2000 presidential campaign, George W. Bush promised to regulate greenhouse gas emissions in the electric-utility sector by putting a mandated cap on carbon dioxide emissions that would be modeled on what his father put into place in 1990 regarding sulfur dioxide emissions. This helped blur the distinction between Bush and his opponent, Al Gore, who was well known for advocating action on global warming. Many thought this was a sign that Bush was a moderate on the environment, like his father. Not surprisingly, he has not carried through on this promise, and there have been no regulations of any kind on greenhouse gas emissions during his presidency.

"What will never fly is a mandatory cap on carbon," said James Connaughton in a February 2004 briefing. He is the chair of the White House Council on Environmental Quality and thus is supposed to be one of the administration's *advocates* for the environment. In December 2004 the *Financial Times* reported that U.S. climate negotiators had actually worked "to ensure that future additions to the Kyoto protocol on climate change should avoid committing nations to reducing their carbon dioxide emissions." This must be the first time in U.S. history that a presidential candidate promised a particular environmental remedy and four years later his aides had not only ruled it out but were actively undermining other countries' efforts to adopt it.

Conservative message makers such as Frank Luntz realized that it could be politically dangerous to oppose *any* action on global warming, even if their efforts to obfuscate the climate science were successful. Luntz lays out a clever solution to this conundrum in his 2002 "Straight Talk" memo on climate-change messaging:

Technology and innovation are the key in arguments on both sides. Global warming alarmists use American superiority in technology and innovation quite effectively in responding to accusations that international agreements such as the Kyoto accord could cost the United States billions. Rather than condemning corporate America the way most environmentalists have done in the past, they attack us for lacking faith in our collective ability to meet any economic challenges presented by environmental changes we make. This should be our argument. We need to emphasize how voluntary innovation and experimentation are preferable to bureaucratic or international intervention and regulation.

This pro-technology pitch is quite a reversal for conservatives. In the early 1980s the Reagan administration cut funding for energy efficiency and renewable-energy technology and innovation programs by 70 to 90 percent. The Clinton administration began reversing some of those cuts, but in 1995 the conservative Congress under House Speaker Newt Gingrich refused to fund any increases. In fact, the House of Representatives even pursued legislation that tried to shut down all applied research into low-carbon energy technologies. In April 1996, Deputy Energy Secretary Charles Curtis and I wrote "Mideast Oil Forever," an article for *The Atlantic* explaining "how the congressional attack on energy research is threatening the economy, the environment, and national security."

Ultimately, we were able to stave off the worst of the cuts by demonstrating that the Department of Energy's technology-development efforts had achieved a remarkable payback for the country. My old office at the Department of Energy (DOE) is exceedingly good at developing clean-energy technologies and then getting people to use more efficient versions of existing technology (lighting, motors, heating and cooling). Those energy-efficiency efforts, which cost taxpayers a few hundred million dollars, were verified by the National Academy of Science as having saved businesses and consumers $30 billion in energy costs. But, tragically, while we were able to beat back the most brutal cuts, we did not meet our goal of significantly increasing funding for low-carbon and oil-reducing technologies.

By the time Bush took office, Luntz and other conservative strategists realized that since they opposed genuine action on global warming, they needed a way to sound like they were doing something. The result was the dual strategy of advocating voluntary action and touting new technology.

Luntz counsels conservatives that while the wait-for-new-technology strategy is important, "you will still fall short unless you emphasize the voluntary actions and environmental progress already underway." In February 2002, after a year of sustained criti-cism from Democrats and others for failing to take any action on global warming, the Bush administration set a voluntary target for the nation to reduce greenhouse gas *intensity* by 18 percent by 2012.

The word *intensity* is often dropped in media coverage, because it is a complex concept that means little to most people. But without the word *intensity*, it sounds like the Bush administration actually made a commitment to *reduce* total U.S. greenhouse gas emissions, rather than to *increase* them, which in fact is what they did. Even with the word *intensity*, U.S. emissions are permitted to increase enormously. *Intensity* here means "the amount per unit of economic activity, as measured by gross domestic product (GDP)." Bush's double-talk committed the nation to reduce greenhouse gas emissions per dollar of GDP by 18 percent over a ten-year period, which by the administration's own calculation would lead to an *in-crease* in total emissions of 14 percent during that ten-year period—since GDP was projected to rise about 32 percent.

The intensity rhetoric also allowed the administration to say that it was trying to do something when it wasn't. The nation's "greenhouse gas intensity" had been dropping at a faster rate than in the Bush proposal (while absolute emissions kept rising). So the administration was able to generate positive public relations for a commitment that actually allowed greater growth in greenhouse gas emissions than would otherwise have occurred.

Greenhouse gas intensity is a misleading metric because what threatens us is the total amount of greenhouse gases in the atmo-sphere, not the amount of gases relative to our GDP. Greenhouse gas intensity can drop every year forever, and concentrations will still increase enough to raise sea levels 80 feet.

At negotiations in Montreal in November 2005 to develop a follow-up to the Kyoto Protocol, the chief U.S. negotiator, Harlan Watson, continued the administration's steadfast opposition to mandatory controls. He shamelessly claimed that Bush's strategy had led to genuine environmental progress and had cut emissions from the year 2000 to 2003. But that period includes a recession and 9/11, which severely reduced economic activity and travel-related emissions. Also, Bush did not begin his presidency until 2001 and didn't start his "voluntary" strategy until 2002. Since 2002, U.S. emissions have *risen* at a rate of 1 percent per year.

As compelling as voluntary innovation and experimentation may sound, they simply do not bring about an absolute reduction in emissions, although well-designed efforts funded at high levels *can* slow the growth rate, as discussed below. I know this all too well because for five years in the 1990s I helped develop, oversee, and run the DOE programs aimed at technology development and voluntary greenhouse gas reductions.

In 1992, President George H. W. Bush signed an agreement saying that the United States would adopt policies that would return greenhouse gas emissions to 1990 levels by 2000. The so-called Rio climate treaty came into force in March 1994. In its early days, the Clinton administration thought that an aggressive set of voluntary programs, combined with an energy tax, would stop emissions growth. Personally, I didn't like the energy tax, because energy is not the problem, greenhouse gas emissions are. Congress didn't like the energy tax either and killed it.

After the 1994 midterm elections, the Gingrich Congress began canceling or cutting the funds for most of the voluntary programs. By "voluntary programs" I am referring to efforts that were aimed not at developing new technologies but at accelerating their deployment into the U.S. market. Such market-entry programs involve public education or working with businesses, cities, and states to lower the many barriers to new technology. This key distinction between technology *development* and technology *deployment* may seem mundane, but it is one that will prove critical to whether or not this nation can avoid catastrophic global warming without devastating its economy.

TECHNOLOGY AND THE DELAYERS

"The United States is neither ashamed of its position on Kyoto nor indifferent to the challenges of climate change," then secretary of energy Spencer Abraham said in 2003. "The United States is investing billions of dollars to address these challenges." Following the Luntz script, Abraham continued:

> Either dramatic greenhouse gas reductions will come at the expense of economic growth and improved living standards, or breakthrough energy technologies that change the game entirely will allow us to reduce emissions while, at the same time, we maintain economic growth and improve the world's standards of living.

His Energy Department further reported, "Abraham said no technologies currently exist to significantly cut emissions of gases linked to global warming."

Astonishing double-talk, especially considering that Abraham made it in Berlin to a group of European climate-policy experts, and every single European country had already agreed to dramatic greenhouse gas reductions under Kyoto.

Luntz's memo states that the "scientific breakthroughs" argument works best for the Delayers. He recommends saying that "as a nation, we should be proud. We produce . . . virtually all the world's health and scientific breakthroughs, yet we produce a fraction of the world's pollution." A very large fraction—we Americans produce one-quarter of the world's greenhouse gases, which is presumably more than what he means by "a fraction."

Luntz urges politicians to say, "America has the best scientists, the best engineers, the best researchers, and the best technicians in the world." When Bush launched his hydrogen-car proposal during his 2003 State of the Union address, he said, "With a new national commitment, our scientists and engineers will overcome obstacles to taking these cars from laboratory to showroom, so that the first car driven by a child born today could be powered by hydrogen, and pollution-free."

A hydrogen car available for a child born in 2003 will not be available in time to stop the climate crisis, even if hydrogen cars actually could help reduce greenhouse gas emissions in the 2020s, which they cannot.

Luntz recommends that when supporters of environmental regulations argue, "We can do anything we set our sights on" and "American corporations and industry can meet any challenge," Denyers and Delayers should "immediately agree" but then argue that we don't need "excessive regulation" or an "international treaty with rules and regulations that will handcuff the American economy" (Luntz's favorite metaphor). Republicans, he says, should argue that we can achieve environmental goals with good old American technology alone.

A 2005 Luntz strategy document, "An Energy Policy for the 21st Century," again argues "*Innovation and 21st-century technology should be at the core of your energy policy,*" repeating the word *technology* thirty times. In an April 2005 speech describing his proposed energy policy, Bush repeated the word *technology* more than forty times. This time *Business Week* recognized that Bush was following Luntz's script and noted, "What's most striking about Bush's Apr. 27 speech is how closely it follows the script written by Luntz earlier this year." The article also pointed out "the President's failure to propose any meaningful solutions."

In his 2006 State of the Union address, Bush announced that America was addicted to oil and the solution was a push for breakthrough technologies, especially in advanced batteries for cars, bio-fuels, and renewable energy. He proposed his "Advanced Energy Initiative—a 22-percent increase in clean-energy research." But the 2005 federal budget had actually *cut* energy R&D by 11 percent compared with that of the year before. And three years earlier, in his 2003 address, Bush had said the answer to our energy and environmental problems was hydrogen cars, and he *cut* the budget for renewable energy and bioenergy to pay for that unjustifiable program.

At a February 2006 speech at the National Renewable Energy Laboratory in Colorado, Bush repeated the word *technology* two dozen times. A few reporters noted that two weeks earlier, the lab had laid off a number of people, including top researchers in areas that the president said were now a priority. Bush blamed this on "a budgeting mix-up," saying, "Sometimes, decisions made as the result of the appropriations process, the money may not end up where it was supposed to have gone." A more reasonable explanation: Technology rhetoric is nothing more than rhetoric.

For the Delayers, the technology pitch is win-win-win. It makes them sound like they're doing something, even while global-warming emissions keep rising. The strong pitch for developing new technology leaves the false impression that existing technology cannot solve our problems—the absurd point former energy secretary Abraham made in the 2003 Berlin speech. And the Delayers can even reap the rhetorical rewards of touting technology as our solution to global warming without actually spending more money on the key technologies.

The technology mantra seductively plays to the American people's optimism, while stealing the argument from optimists who believe, as I do, that our technology is precisely the reason why we *can* agree to cap greenhouse gas emissions. The pitch has boxed progressive politicians (and scientists and environmentalists) into a corner. Both sides—those who want to delay on global warming and those who want action now—say they advocate technology, but in this narrative only the stick-in-the-mud progressives want onerous rules and regulations. No wonder those pursuing action today have had so much difficulty getting political traction—and no wonder the Delayers repeat their mantra so much.

Like the best seductions, the technology pitch contains a half-truth: We *do* need to invest in technology—but we *must* couple that investment with mandatory emissions-reduction targets or else global-warming pollution will continue its dangerous rise.

It is not just delaying politicians who use the technology trap as a strategy—corporate Delayers love it too. One of the biggest funders of efforts to convince the public that global warming is not occurring has been ExxonMobil. Since the president announced his hydrogen-car initiative, the oil and gas company has also funded significant advertising about its research into hydrogen-related technologies. It also helped fund a $100 million clean-technology research program at Stanford University. In an April 2005 *Washington Post* ad, ExxonMobil proclaimed:

> We're now making the largest ever investment in independent climate and energy research that is specifically designed to look for new breakthrough technologies. The world faces enormous energy challenges. There are no easy answers. It will take straightforward, honest dialogue about the hard truths that confront us all.

Sounds so reasonable, except ExxonMobil has been as much a champion of "honest dialogue" as the Luntz memo is about "Straight Talk." ExxonMobil has pumped more than $8 million into think tanks, media-outreach organizations, and consumer and religious groups that advance the Denyer and Delayer agenda, including the Competitive Enterprise Institute, the Hoover Institution, the Hudson Institute, the George C. Marshall Institute, the Tech

Central Science Foundation, and the Center for the Study of Car bon Dioxide and Global Change, which calls CO_2 emissions "a force for good." Exxon also participated in discussions involving a 1998 fossil fuel industry proposal "to depict global warming theory as a case of bad science."

The leading opponent of fuel-economy standards is General Motors. It has spent millions lobbying Congress to make sure the company is not required to build more fuel-efficient vehicles—cars that competitors like Toyota are selling briskly today because they saw the inevitability of rising oil prices and growing customer concern about the environment. GM is also the leading U.S. car company that advocates hydrogen cars, and it spends millions on ads asserting that these cars are right around the corner—absurdly claiming in April 2005 that we are actually at the "endgame" of GM's hydrogen strategy. What a pity that GM's promises ring hollow, and not just because hydrogen cars are decades away from being a plausible greenhouse gas reduction strategy.

When I was at the U.S. Department of Energy in the 1990s, we partnered with GM, Ford, and Chrysler to speed the introduction of hybrid gasoline-electric cars, since increased fuel efficiency was (and remains) clearly the best hope for cutting vehicle greenhouse gas emissions by the year 2025. This partnership was part of an informal deal between the Clinton administration and the car companies in which we did not pursue fuel-economy standards and in return the car companies promised to develop a triple-efficiency car (80 mpg) by 2004. Ironically, in the mid-1990s, the car companies were actively lobbying to *cut* funding for hydrogen-car development and to shift that money into near-term technologies such as hybrids. Even more ironically, the main result of our government-industry partnership (which had excluded foreign automakers) was to motivate the Japanese car companies to develop and introduce their own hybrids first.

In one of the major blunders in automotive history, GM walked away from hybrids as soon as it could—when the Bush administration came in—after taxpayers had spent $1 billion on the program. The result: Toyota and Honda walked in. *GM, which had had a technological lead in electric drives, let its number one competitor, Toyota, achieve a stunning 7-year head start* in what will likely be this century's primary drivetrain. GM was publicly criticizing the future of hybrid technology as late as January 2004, and finally announced later in that year a halfhearted effort to catch up to Toyota.

Let this history give pause to anybody who promotes a purely technology-based solution to greenhouse gas emissions (and gasoline consumption) in the transportation sector. GM and President Bush have it exactly backward. It's not, as they have argued incessantly, fuel-economy standards that cost American jobs and market share. It's the lack of them. And because the future is one of constrained oil supplies, inevitable oil price shocks, and the urgent need to reduce greenhouse gases in the transportation sector, the car companies that will have the most success are the ones that can deliver a practical, fuel-efficient vehicle, especially efficient dual-fuel vehicles that can run on low-carbon alternatives to petroleum. Toyota and Honda figured this out, but GM insists on fighting the future. As a result, it has been hemorrhaging cash and market share, both of which are being claimed by smarter competitors.

Yes, joint government–auto industry research and development makes sense, and yes, perhaps even a subsidy to support switching automakers' manufacturing base to hybrids is warranted, but *only* together with legislation that sharply tightens fuel-economy standards and caps carbon dioxide emissions.

BREAKING THE BREAKTHROUGH MYTH

What technology breakthroughs in the past three decades have transformed how we use energy today? The answer: There really haven't been any. We use energy today roughly the same way we did

30 years ago. Our cars still run on internal combustion engines that burn gasoline. Alternatives to gasoline such as corn ethanol make up under 3 percent of all U.S. transportation fuels—and corn ethanol is hardly a breakthrough fuel. Fuel economy did double from the mid-1970s to the mid-1980s, *as required by government regulations*, but in the last quarter-century, the average fuel economy of American consumer vehicles has remained flat or even declined slightly.

The single biggest source of electricity generation, by far, is still coal power, just as it was 30 years ago. The vast majority of all power plants still generate heat to make steam turn a turbine, and the average efficiency of our electric power plants is about what it was 30 years ago. We did see the introduction of the highly efficient natural gas combined-cycle turbine, but that was not based on a breakthrough from the past three decades—and constrained natural gas supply in North America severely limited growth in gas-fired power, so the share of U.S. electricity generated by natural gas has grown only modestly in 30 years. Nuclear power was about 10 percent of total U.S. electric power 30 years ago, and now it's about 20 percent. But the nuclear energy "breakthrough" occurred long before the 1970s, and we haven't built a new nuclear power plant in two decades, in large part because that power has been so expensive.

We do have many more home appliances, but they still haven't fundamentally changed *how* we use energy. Interestingly, home energy use per square foot has not changed that much even with all those new electronic gadgets, for two reasons. First, my old office at the DOE developed major advances in key consumer technologies, including refrigeration and lighting. Second, efficiency standards for appliances have made the use of those efficient technologies widespread. From the mid-1970s until today, refrigerator electricity use has dropped a whopping three-quarters. Perhaps that should be called a breakthrough, especially because some of the savings came from remarkable improvements in the guts of the refrigerator from

Oak Ridge National Laboratory. But we still use refrigerators pretty much as we did, so in that sense these breakthroughs didn't change how we use energy.

One of the most widely publicized energy-technology breakthroughs occurred in 1986 when researchers at IBM Zurich Research Laboratory discovered a material that conducted electricity with no resistance at considerably higher temperatures than previous conductors. Over the next few years a series of breakthroughs in these high-temperature superconductors were announced. This technology generated great excitement because it held the promise of superefficient electric motors and loss-free long-distance electric transmission lines. Yet all these years later, you may ask, where are all the high-temperature superconductors? They have had very little impact on either electric motors or power transmissions.

"Typically it has taken 25 years after commercial introduction for a primary energy form to obtain a 1 percent share of the global market" (emphasis added). So noted Royal Dutch/Shell, one of the world's largest oil companies, in its 2001 scenarios for how energy use is likely to evolve over the next five decades. Note that this tiny toehold comes 25 years after *commercial* introduction. The first transition from scientific breakthrough to commercial introduction may itself take decades. Consider fuel-cell cars, which get a lot of hype today. Yet fuel cells were invented in 1839, and more than 165 years later we still don't have a single commercial fuel-cell car. We barely have any viable commercial fuel cells for stationary electric power generation.

I tend to think that Shell's statement is basically true, although I believe we could in some instances speed things up—but only with the kind of aggressive technology-deployment programs and government standards that conservatives do not like. Given that we must dramatically reverse greenhouse gas emissions trends over the next 25 years, we *must* focus on technologies that are either commercial or nearly commercial *today.*

Why don't never-been-seen-before breakthroughs change how we use energy? Why don't breakthrough energy technologies enter the market the way breakthroughs in consumer electronics and telecommunications seem to? If we focus on the two most important sectors for global warming, transportation and electricity generation, the answer is fairly straightforward: The barriers to market entry for new technologies are enormous. The entire electric grid— from power plant to transmission line to your house—represents hundreds of billions of dollars in investment, much of which has long since been paid off. We have coal plants and hydropower plants that are several decades old and still running. This keeps electricity widely available, and much lower in price here than in almost any other industrialized country. And it keeps competing technologies at a permanent disadvantage.

The entire gasoline-fueling delivery infrastructure—refineries, pipelines, gasoline stations, and the like—also represents hundreds of billions of dollars of investment that assures widespread availability, low price, and very tough competition for any potential alternative fuel. A comparable investment has been made in automobile manufacturing plants, a key reason why we have not seen a new American car company successfully launched for a very long time.

Perhaps the best example of a breakthrough that is changing the vehicle market is the nickel metal hydride battery currently being used in virtually every hybrid gasoline-electric car today. The key to making hybrids work is the battery. Research on nickel metal hydrides began in the 1970s. In the early 1980s, a U.S. company, Ovonics, introduced nickel metal hydride batteries into the market for consumer electronics. At the DOE we were interested in hybrids in the mid-1990s because a few years earlier Ovonics had developed a version of the battery for cars under a partnership with the government in the U.S. Advanced Battery Consortium.

Hybrids were introduced into the U.S. car market by the Japanese car companies Toyota and Honda in 1997. Sales began to soar after 2000, thanks to improved engineering, high gasoline prices, and government incentives. Even so, in 2005, 8 years after they were introduced, hybrids were only slightly more than 1 percent of new-car sales in the United States. But here we want to know how long before a breakthrough significantly affects how we use energy or how much energy we use. So the question is, How long before hybrids reduce U.S. gasoline consumption?

Consider first that the average car now lasts for nearly 20 years, making it difficult for any breakthrough technology to have a rapid impact on the market. Second, consider that engine technology has gotten dramatically more efficient in the past two decades, but the average vehicle on the road has not. Why not? The efficiency gains have been offset by increased performance (faster acceleration) and the increased weight of the average car (thanks to the growing popularity of sport-utility vehicles and light trucks).

How soon will hybrids begin reducing U.S. gasoline consumption? The best answer is, "Maybe never." Why should hybrids increase the average efficiency of the U.S. cars and light trucks any more than the steady advances in engine efficiency of the past two decades did? The good news is that hybrid drivetrains provide enough efficiency improvement and their electric motors develop such high acceleration that automakers have used the technology to raise both horsepower and fuel economy simultaneously. But a number of hybrid models have been introduced that achieve only a very modest efficiency gain. Moreover, vehicle efficiency must rise significantly over the next two decades just to keep gasoline consumption—and hence greenhouse gas emissions—constant, simply to make up for the increases that would otherwise come from more and more people buying more and more cars and driving farther and farther.

If we want to reduce U.S. oil consumption and greenhouse gas emissions from cars, the most obvious strategy is the one that we already employed successfully to double the fuel economy of our cars from the mid-1970s to the mid-1980s—tougher government mileage standards. No other strategy has ever worked for this country.

The Denyers and Delayers remain tragically stuck with their "we must wait for new technology" rhetoric. Perhaps the most egregious example of this came in January 2006, after six former EPA administrators—five of them Republican, including EPA chiefs for Nixon, Ford, and Reagan—urged the Bush administration to impose mandatory greenhouse gas emissions controls as a way to address global warming. In response, EPA's administrator, Stephen Johnson, said the administration policy is to pursue voluntary programs and technological innovation, rather than mandates and standards. He then said: *"Are we going to tell people to stop driving their cars, or do we start investing in technology [to cut emissions]? That's the answer, investing in those technologies"* (emphasis added).

This astonishing false choice—invest in technology or force people to stop driving their cars—comes from our country's top person for protecting the environment. Johnson can't seem to grasp that today's *existing* technology was yesterday's new technology. Hybrids were once new; now they aren't. They can substantially reduce U.S. greenhouse gas emissions if government standards require them to do so. Technology is no substitute for standards. Technology is what makes standards practical and affordable.

The Delayers don't believe in technology—they believe only in *new* technology, that is, until it is no longer new. The Bush administration not only opposes significantly higher national mileage standards for cars, it is even opposing in court a law passed by the state of California requiring that car companies use existing technologies to cut carbon dioxide emissions per vehicle by 30 percent. The administration argues that carbon dioxide is not a pollutant California can regulate and that this law illegally preempts federal authority in setting mileage standards for cars.

If the Delayers were truly serious about new technology offering the only possible strategy for dealing with global warming, they would propose a far larger budget to develop it. Yet the Bush administration has never increased the total energy R&D budget for the federal government. And worse, when we take out programs that offer little hope in the first half of this century (such as the hydrogen car program), and we subtract the notorious congressional earmarks that have run rampant since 2000 (which often divert funds from well-designed technology programs to pork-barrel projects), we have seen a substantial decline in money for development of clean-energy climate solutions.

Our bill for *imported* oil alone now exceeds $250 billion a year. In total, Americans spend nearly $1 trillion a year on energy. The global-warming damages this country will sustain could run into the trillions of dollars. The core of any strategy to reduce greenhouse gas emissions and oil consumption is energy efficiency and renewable energy. The R&D budget for those technologies (minus hydrogen and earmarks) is a paltry few hundred million dollars a year and has dropped steadily since 2000. The federal government is spending less than $2 per American per year on the best technologies for avoiding 80-foot sea-level rise.

The scale of the global-warming problem warrants spending equivalent to that of the Manhattan Project or the Apollo program or even the Pentagon's current technology program for developing a missile defense. That would give us an advanced energy-technology program of about $10 to $20 billion per year. One way we know that the Delayer "technology only" strategy is empty rhetoric: The funding levels they suggest cannot deal with the problem—and they block all efforts to increase funding.

ADAPTATION AND GEO-ENGINEERING

Two other technology-based strategies for dealing with global warming—or, rather, not dealing with it—are adaptation and geo-engineering. I haven't written much about how we would adapt to Hell and High Water, for several reasons.

For the foreseeable future, the primary focus of our climate policy today must be avoiding that grim outcome. Also, making adaptation a major focus of U.S. climate policy presupposes a political consensus that climate scientists are correct about current and future impacts. Otherwise, how could politicians agree to spend hundreds of billions of dollars adapting to a large rise in sea levels or an increased number of super-hurricanes or the growing risk of mega-droughts? But if we had such a consensus, then the only moral choice would be to direct the vast majority of our resources to avoiding this catastrophe in the first place.

Many Delayers use the idea of adaptation to argue against action now, to create the false hope that global warming will be of a pace and scale that our children and their children can deal with—which, ironically, would be true only if we ignored their advice and took aggressive mitigation action now. After all, how do you adapt to sea levels rising a foot or more a decade until oceans are 80 feet higher or more? How do you adapt to widespread, ever-worsening global mega-droughts—especially in a world that will need as much water and arable land as possible by midcentury to feed perhaps 9 billion people and grow vast amounts of zero-carbon energy crops?

Of course we should develop drought-resistant crops and new levee technology and better desalinization technology. But for the foreseeable future, avoiding global warming should receive ten to one hundred times the funds of any adaptation effort.

Interestingly, when I was at the Energy Department, we tried to launch an effort aimed at both mitigation *and* adaptation, called "Cool Communities." Most cities have dark surfaces and less vegetation than their surroundings, making them as much as 5°F warmer. Reducing this "heat island" effect would cut greenhouse gas emissions from air-conditioning and offset some of the increase in

urban temperatures from global warming—and it would even reduce smog formation.

Cooling a city means planting shade trees for buildings and
putting light-colored surfaces on buildings, roads, and parking. The
government has a key role to play in research and testing to help
identify and develop the best roofing and paving materials, in funding computer models for determining the optimal approach to
cooling a city, and in disseminating information. Yet even though
Cool Communities was probably the most cost-effective adaptation
program ever devised, the Republican Congress killed it because it
was part of Clinton's plan to reduce global-warming emissions.

I also don't plan to devote much discussion to how we might
geo-engineer our way out. Geo-engineering is "the intentional
large-scale manipulation of the global environment" to counteract
the effects of global warming. Such a strategy presupposes a political consensus that climate scientists are correct about current and
future impacts. How else could politicians agree to spend the vast
sums of money needed to, say, put in place thousands of satellites
around the earth with mirrors to reflect the sunlight, as some have
proposed?

Geo-engineering also presupposes that politicians and scientists and the public share a high degree of certainty about all aspects
of climate science. Any human-induced engineering project large
enough to affect Earth's climate, such as seeding the upper atmosphere with massive amounts of aerosols, is just as likely to have
unintended consequences that make things worse. If we had such
certainty and consensus about climate science at any time in the
foreseeable future, it would *still* be better to focus the vast majority
of our resources on reducing emissions, since that strategy carries
far less risk.

"The 'geo-engineering' approaches considered so far appear to
be afflicted with some combination of high costs, low leverage, and
a high likelihood of serious side effects," concluded John Holdren,

director of the Woods Hole Research Center and president of the American Association for the Advancement of Science, in 2006.

Moreover, unlike adaptation, which a country can undertake by itself, geo-engineering is necessarily a planetwide strategy that would certainly require approval and coordination by the United Nations. Yet if the United States has not reversed its energy and climate policy by the 2020s, and joined the world community in an aggressive effort to reduce emissions—if the richest, most polluting nation on earth has refused to devote even 2 percent of its enormous wealth to spare the planet from millennia of misery—we will be a pariah nation. We will hardly be in a position to work with other nations in a desperate gamble to reengineer the planet's climate back to what it was before we engineered it into ruins with our emissions.

One might imagine an internationally sanctioned geo-engineering effort that began with small-scale tests and slowly worked up to planetwide deployment in the second half of this century. If we sharply reverse emissions trends in the next decade, we would minimize both the amount of geo-engineering we might need to do and the speed with which we needed to do it, giving us time to get much smarter and making the effort far less risky. If we hit 500 ppm of carbon dioxide in 2050, however, we will probably be on the verge of crossing a threshold that simply cannot be undone by geo-engineering.

Geo-engineering, like adaptation, might be an important post-2050 strategy, but it seems unlikely to be of much value unless we keep concentrations close to, or, preferably, well below, 550 ppm through 2100. And that requires the aggressive deployment of existing and near-term technology in the electricity and transportation sectors, starting immediately.

CHAPTER SEVEN

THE ELECTRIFYING SOLUTION

This analysis suggests that the United States could reduce its greenhouse gas emissions by between 10 and 40 percent of the 1990 level at very low cost. Some reductions may even be a net savings if the proper policies are implemented.
—U.S. National Academy of Sciences, 1991

What are the winning strategies for avoiding climate catastrophe, for avoiding Hell and High Water? This chapter examines the solutions for the power sector. Amazingly, with the right technology strategy over the next two decades, we could cut U.S. carbon dioxide emissions by two-thirds without increasing the total electric bill of either consumers or businesses.

In previous chapters I have touched on a number of aggressive low-carbon strategies or "wedges" we need to achieve over the next five decades to stabilize concentrations below a doubling. Each wedge ultimately avoids the emission of 1 billion metric tons of carbon a year. These are the ones aimed at reducing emissions from electricity and heavy industry:

1. Launch a massive performance-based efficiency program for homes, commercial buildings, and new construction.

2. Launch a massive effort to boost the efficiency of heavy industry and expand the use of cogeneration (combined heat and power).
3. Capture the CO_2 from 800 new large coal plants and store it underground.
4. Build 1 million large wind turbines (or the equivalent in renewables such as solar power).
5. Build 700 new large nuclear power plants while shutting down no old ones.

The biggest climate threat in the power sector comes from traditional coal plants. That's because coal contains more carbon than any other fossil fuel, and a typical coal plant converts only about one-third of the energy in the coal to electricity. The rest is wasted.

As of 2002, we had nearly 1,000 gigawatts (GW) of coal plants worldwide, which was about 40 percent of total global electricity generation. A typical large coal plant is about one gigawatt, or 1,000 megawatts (MW), in size. By 2030, the world is projected to double that to 2,000 GW of coal electricity.

More than a third of the new coal plants are expected to be built in China, but one in six will be here in the United States. Natural-gas plants had been the preferred new U.S. power plant, in part because they are far more efficient and less polluting than coal plants. But high prices for natural gas have made them much more expensive to operate than coal plants.

The coal plants that will be built from 2005 to 2030 will release as much carbon dioxide as all of the coal burned since the industrial revolution more than two centuries ago. On this emissions trajectory, the world would be emitting 10.5 billion metric tons of carbon (38 billion metric tons of carbon dioxide) in 2030. To stabilize atmospheric carbon dioxide concentrations below a doubling of what they were in preindustrial times, we need to keep *average* annual emissions to only 7 billion metric tons during this century.

So if we build these plants, we need to shut them down within two decades. Considering they represent a capital investment of more than $1 trillion, that doesn't seem likely. The only alternative in 2030 would be to retrofit the plants to capture and store the carbon dioxide they release. But virtually all of the planned coal plants are unsuitable for such retrofits.

CARBON CAPTURE AND STORAGE

Carbon capture and storage (CCS), also called carbon sequestration, is an attractive idea across the political spectrum because it might allow us to continue using a major fossil fuel, coal, but in a way that does not destroy the climate. Everyone from the Natural Resources Defense Council to the Bush administration loves carbon sequestration, although not in quite the same way.

Here's what is involved: To permanently store carbon, to keep it out of our atmosphere forever, the carbon dioxide from all power plants must be removed and stored somewhere forever. The carbon dioxide can be captured either before or after combustion— although capturing it before is far easier and cheaper. Coal can be gasified and the resulting syngas can then be chemically processed to generate hydrogen-rich gas and carbon dioxide. The hydrogen-rich gas can be combusted directly in a combined-cycle power plant. The carbon dioxide can be piped to a sequestration site. The whole process is called integrated gasification combined cycle (IGCC).

IGCC technology costs more than traditional coal plants. The total extra costs for this process, including geological storage in sealed underground sites, are currently quite high, $30 to $80 a ton of carbon dioxide, according to the DOE. As the National Coal Council reported in 2003, "Vendors currently do not have an adequate economic incentive" to pursue the technology because "IGCC may only become broadly competitive with" current coal and natural-gas power plants *"under a CO_2-restricted scenario."* Thus, "power companies are not likely to pay the premium to install today's IGCC designs in the absence of clear regulatory direction on the CO_2 issue." Unless we promptly put into place restrictions on CO_2 emissions, carbon sequestration will be pushed much farther into the future. Before carbon capture and storage can become a significant factor, we must have a government policy that puts a cap on emissions.

In February 2003 the DOE announced the billion-dollar, ten-year FutureGen project to design, build, construct, and demonstrate a 275-megawatt prototype plant that would cogenerate electricity and hydrogen and sequester 90 percent of the carbon dioxide. The goal is to "validate the engineering, economic, and environmental viability of advanced coal-based, near-zero emission technologies that by 2020" will produce electricity that is only 10 percent more expensive than current coal-generated electricity.

The administration's strategy is either doubly pointless or doubly cynical, depending on your perspective. First, by the time this technology is ready to commercialize in the early 2020s, the world will have built or begun construction on more than a 1,000 GW of coal plants, using traditional technology that is not designed for CCS. Second, we will still need a mandatory cap on carbon emissions to make FutureGen plants viable because they will be more expensive than traditional plants even in the 2020s. Since the Bush administration opposes a mandatory cap, the whole R&D effort looks like another delaying action.

People in the energy business call it NeverGen.

Sequestration has another problem, one that must be solved if carbon capture and storage is going to be a major contributor to greenhouse gas reductions any time soon: where to put the carbon dioxide. The largest potential physical reservoir is the deep oceans. But ocean sequestration poses serious environmental risks and is unlikely to be viable. After all, the oceans are already storing a large portion of the CO_2 we have poured into the atmosphere. And their ability to store CO_2 is likely to diminish this century (a bad outcome we do not wish to hasten), and the increased acidification of the ocean is already posing a threat to marine life.

Tens of millions of tons of carbon dioxide have already been injected into oil fields to enhance recovery of oil—that's one reason we know CCS works. But using carbon dioxide to increase recovery of oil does not help reduce net greenhouse gas emissions, since the oil itself is ultimately burned, releasing CO_2.

Research is focusing on pumping highly compressed liquid carbon dioxide, called supercritical CO_2, into huge geological formations, such as deep underground aquifers. A 2003 workshop on carbon management by the National Academy of Sciences noted, "Less dense than water, CO_2 will float under the top seal atop the water in an aquifer and could migrate upward if the top seal is not completely impermeable."

What's the problem here? Even tiny leakage rates undermine the environmental value of sequestration. If we are trying to stabilize CO_2 concentrations at twice preindustrial levels, a mere 1 percent annual leakage rate could add $850 billion *per year* to overall costs by 2095, according to an analysis by Pacific Northwest National Laboratory. If we cannot be certain that leakage rates are well below 1 percent, the study concludes, "the private sector will find it increasingly difficult to convince regulators that CO_2 injected into geological formations should be accorded the same accounting as CO_2 that is avoided," meaning that you would not be able to give the same economic value to CO_2 injected underground as to CO_2 that was never generated (because of technologies such as wind or efficiency). The analysis notes, "There is no solid experimental evidence or theoretical framework" for determining likely leakage rates from different geological formations.

The flow of CO_2 *into* the ground from 800 GW of coal plants would equal the current flow of oil *out* of the ground. If we are going to store that huge amount of CO_2 inside deep underground aquifers, exhaustive testing will have to be done. Each potential site will need intensive monitoring to guarantee it can store CO_2 with no leaks. Very sensitive and low-cost in situ monitoring techniques must be developed to provide confidence that leakage rates are exceedingly low. The geologic stability of storage sites—think earthquakes—is especially important because a massive release of carbon dioxide could suffocate a huge number of people if it hit a populated area.

To start sequestering a significant amount of carbon dioxide in the 2020s, we must immediately begin identifying, testing, and certifying sites. This will not be easy; after spending billions of dollars and conducting more than two decades of scientific study, we have identified only one site in this country as a safe, permanent repository for nuclear waste—Yucca Mountain in Nevada—and even in that case, we have been unable to achieve the consensus needed to start storing waste in it.

If sequestration proves feasible on a large scale, there is a glimmer of good news: Analysis suggests carbon capture and storage could eventually eliminate much of U.S. electric-sector coal emissions for between $20 and $40 a ton of carbon dioxide. If we had such a price today—and a major effort to identify and certify storage sites—we *might* see significant sequestration start by 2020. Absent such policies, it will be delayed a decade or more. In the meantime, we must avoid building traditional coal plants. The best strategy for that is certainly energy efficiency.

THE TECHNOLOGY STRATEGY THAT WILL WORK

Our top two priorities in energy policy should be to minimize the need for new coal-fired power and to free up inefficiently used natural gas for high-efficiency power generation. Energy efficiency remains by far the single most cost-effective strategy for achieving these goals, for minimizing carbon dioxide emissions into the air.

Most buildings and factories can cut electricity consumption by more than 25 percent right now with rapid payback (under four years). I have worked with companies from Johnson & Johnson to IBM to Nike who have demonstrated this over and over again. My 1999 book, *Cool Companies*, describes a hundred case studies of companies that have cut their consumption substantially, making a great deal of money in the process and reaping other, unexpected benefits as well. Many companies that have pursued efficiency have found gains in productivity, because better-designed buildings improve office-worker productivity and redesigned industrial processes typically also reduce waste and increase output. So why doesn't every profit-seeking outfit do likewise? There are many reasons why most companies do not do what the best companies do, including inertia and lack of information. Also, I found that companies tend to be far more aggressive about efficiency when there are comprehensive government programs helping them.

We have more than two decades of broad experience with very successful state and federal energy-efficiency programs. In short, we know what works.

Perhaps the most cost-effective federal strategy would simply be to replicate, nationally and globally, California's myriad energy-efficiency programs and standards for homes and commercial buildings. From 1976 to 2005, electricity consumption per capita grew 60 percent in the rest of the nation, while it stayed flat in high-tech, fast-growing California. This astonishing achievement is shown in figure 4, which compares electricity consumption in California (in megawatt-hours per person) with that in the rest of the country since 1960.

How was California able to keep per capita electricity consumption flat for three decades? By adopting an aggressive, performance-based energy-efficiency strategy. By performance-based I mean one targeted toward efforts that deliver the most bang for the buck.

Most of the money came from California utilities. One key reg-

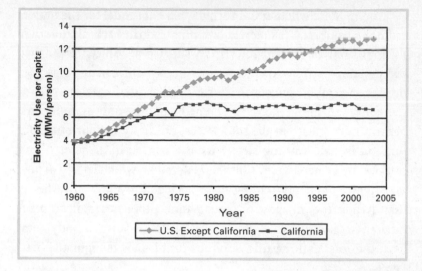

Figure 4. What energy efficiency can really do.

ulatory change was critical. Most utilities in this country can make money only by selling more power, and they lose profits if they sell less. Needless to say, they have little motivation to help their customers cut their electricity bills by using energy more efficiently. California changed the regulations so that utilities' profits are not tied to how much electricity they sell. It has also allowed utilities to take a share of any energy savings they help consumers and businesses achieve. The bottom line is that California utilities can make money when their customers save money.

If it is cheaper to satisfy growing demand with energy efficiency than with new power plants, utilities can still grow their profits. Efficiency strategies today include energy audits, outreach and education, training, technical assistance, and rebates for purchasing energy-efficient products. The California Energy Commission also directly supports efforts to boost energy efficiency, including building codes that specify efficiency requirements for new construction.

You may ask whether California is a good model for the nation, given the troubles it had deregulating its electric-utility industry in the 1990s and the resulting electricity shortages. In fact, the botched deregulation is precisely what convinced Californians that they needed to redouble efforts on energy efficiency.

How had things become botched up? As soon as California began to deregulate in the mid-1990s, utilities cut their efficiency funding in half, causing electricity use per capita to rise. Worse, utilities were forced to sell off their generators, which left them hostage to greedy energy-trading firms such as Enron. Even earlier in that decade, the prospect of deregulation put a near halt to planning and construction of new power plants because nobody knew what the rules and rewards would be in this new deregulated marketplace.

I was at the U.S. Department of Energy at the time, and we warned California that in a deregulated market no one would have an incentive to keep much surplus capacity. Normally, public utility commissions require a lot of spare capacity to ensure that the juice keeps flowing to consumers during the kind of rare long-lasting and widespread heat waves that drive summer air-conditioning demand to extreme levels. Most of the time that spare "peak demand" capacity goes unused, making it relatively unprofitable for companies to maintain. But by the late 1990s, global warming was making those once rare mammoth heat waves commonplace (and in 2006, California would suffer its worst heat wave ever, blanketing the state in 100°F temperature for weeks, killing more than one hundred people and sending electricity demand soaring).

Moreover, California imports a great deal of electricity. In the 1990s, the state failed to anticipate that the rapid growth of neighboring states meant that when the demand crunch came, those imports would dry up. With demand growing faster than expected and supply slowing down, with summers getting hotter and power surpluses shrinking, and with crooked companies like Enron controlling the trade of electricity and natural gas, the day of reckoning was inevitable.

The crisis hit in 1999 and 2000, with shortages and blackouts. The state raised prices and launched a massive efficiency program, the amazing results of which are now in. From 2000 to 2004, California utilities spent $1.4 billion. The average cost of the electricity saved was 2.9 cents per kilowatt-hour—far cheaper than what new peak power generation in the state costs, 16.7 cents per kilowatt-hour, and half the price of building base-load power (generators that run all the time), 5.8 cents per kilowatt-hour. Helping people use electricity more wisely is far cheaper than building new power plants, and that's without even counting the benefits of avoided global-warming pollution and healthier air to breathe.

The utility programs became steadily more effective over time. By 2004, the average cost of the efficiency programs had dropped in half, to under 1.4 cents per kilowatt-hour, cheaper than any form of new power supply in this country—*and far cheaper than any carbon-free power,* including renewable energy and nuclear plants. And it is not just California that has achieved these results. A 2006 report by the Western Governors' Association confirmed that a variety of energy-efficiency programs in western states have delivered savings at similarly low cost.

One of the leaders in California's energy-efficiency push is Dr. Arthur Rosenfeld, the world-class physicist who launched the Center for Building Sciences at Lawrence Berkeley National Laboratory in the 1970s. He helped develop many of the energy-efficiency programs for the state and many of the efficient technologies used around the nation, including windows and lighting. I worked with him at the Department of Energy, and he later became a California energy commissioner, helping guide the state through its crisis.

Rosenfeld told me that California was so satisfied with the efficiency effort that it was going to ramp up funding. Rather than keeping electricity per capita flat, they want to cut it 0.5 percent to 1 percent a year. He notes that the state's efficiency efforts, from the 1970s through 2004, have lowered the energy bill of Californians by $12 billion a year, which comes to a whopping $1,000 a family—even accounting for the extra cost of the efficiency products, services, and programs. The total investment has, on average, paid for itself in energy savings in less than three years and then just keeps generating profits for Californians. *And it is avoiding the emissions of more than 10 million metric tons of carbon dioxide every year.* This is the program to copy—around the country and the world.

I asked Dr. Rosenfeld how much it would cost to duplicate California's program nationwide. His answer: The total effort costs about 2 percent of the revenues of electric utilities, which translates into $6 billion a year nationwide (since the nation's electric bill is about $300 billion). Because parts of United States have more air-conditioning demand than California, he thought the United States might want to invest closer to $9 billion a year, if the goal is to keep electricity consumption per capita flat. Now, that would be a bargain, when America's 100 million households save some $1,000 each year!

Most important, these programs focus on *existing* technology, on getting those technologies into the marketplace, into the homes and offices of consumers and businesses, as quickly as possible. The California Energy Commission has an R&D program to develop new technology, but only so that it can then be sped into the marketplace. In California, efforts to deploy existing energy-efficiency technologies have maintained support through Democratic and Republican administrations alike.

Most conservative politicians do not like energy-efficiency programs, especially ones aimed at accelerating the market entry of new technologies. The Gingrich Congress cut or eliminated most of the deployment programs that the Clinton Energy Department launched in the early 1990s. The Bush administration has sharply cut the funding for the most historically effective efficiency efforts so that they can make room for hydrogen-fuel-cell R&D, which has no realistic prospect of seeing significant marketplace success for several decades.

The Bush administration has relentlessly cut funding for technology deployment. Especially counterproductive is the administration's move to shut down the DOE's regional offices in Boston, Philadelphia, Atlanta, Chicago, Denver, and Seattle. These were set up in the 1970s to help the nation learn how to save energy. They are, or were, the primary national effort to deliver technical and financial assistance to communities, states, industries, and other energy users. The president is shutting them down just when we need them the most.

NATURAL-GAS EFFICIENCY

Since 2000, the United States has suffered through repeated price spikes for natural gas. Between 1999 and 2002 we added some 138 gigawatts in natural-gas-fired capacity, but the increased demand for gas—no surprise—led to a price increase. North American natural-gas supply is limited. Worse, Canadian natural-gas exports to the United States are projected to decline in coming years as Canada uses more and more of the gas for its own purposes, including producing oil from the Alberta tar sands.

High natural-gas prices have driven increases in demand for coal electricity and for new coal plants. High prices have led many politicians to advocate spending tens of billions of dollars on facilities to bring in liquefied natural gas (LNG), even though LNG tankers and terminals are widely seen as a major terrorist target and even though that would increase the nation's dependence on imported energy. About 58 percent of the world's natural-gas reserves are in Iran, Russia, and Qatar—hardly bastions of democracy or stability, hardly the kind of countries we want to be beholden to.

Rather than a major effort to increase our dependence on

foreign-energy supplies, a superior national strategy is more efficient use of our domestic natural gas. As with electricity, most buildings and factories can cut natural-gas consumption by more than 25 percent right now with rapid payback (under four years), after which the savings become profits forever.

A major focus should be on more efficient use of steam, which is crucial for production in energy-intensive industries such as chemicals, food products, plastics, primary metals, pulp and paper, textiles, and petroleum refining. It is generated mainly by natural gas. Steam accounts for $24 billion a year of U.S. manufacturing energy costs and 40 percent of U.S. industrial carbon dioxide emissions. Expanding state and federal efforts to use steam far more efficiently, such as the DOE's Best Practices Steam Program, would cut those numbers sharply.

The energy-intensive industries are not only major consumers of natural gas, they account for 80 percent of energy consumed by U.S. manufacturers and 90 percent of the hazardous waste. They represent the best chance for increasing efficiency while cutting pollution. Many are major emitters of greenhouse gases other than carbon dioxide. A 1993 analysis for the DOE found that a 10 to 20 percent reduction in waste by American industry would generate a cumulative increase of $1.94 trillion in the gross domestic product from 1996 to 2010. By 2010 the improvements would be generating 2 million new jobs, or roughly 1.5 percent of employment in that year.

For these reasons, in the 1990s, the Energy Department began forming partnerships with energy-intensive industries to develop clean technologies. We worked with scientists and engineers to identify areas of joint research into technologies that would simultaneously save energy, reduce pollution, and increase productivity. The Bush administration has slashed funding for this program by 50 percent—and wants to shut it down entirely. This is especially baffling from an administration that opposes environmental regulations, because funding for pollution prevention technology is by far the best way for the nation to minimize the need for such regulations. But that's why it's always important to remember that the new-technology-is-the-only-answer pitch is just empty rhetoric, no matter how many times the administration repeats it.

An important companion strategy to natural-gas efficiency would be a major national effort to encourage the simultaneous generation of both electricity and heat, called *cogeneration,* or combined heat and power. Cogen provides large opportunities to save both energy and carbon dioxide. Right now, fossil fuels burned at large central-station power plants generate most of the electricity used by U.S. companies. These plants are typically quite inefficient, converting *only about one-third* of the energy in fossil fuels into electricity. The waste heat generated by that combustion is literally thrown away, and then more energy is lost transmitting the electricity from the power plant to the factory or building. The total energy wasted by U.S. power generators each year equals the total energy Japan uses each year. More fossil fuels are then burned in our buildings and factories to provide heat, hot water, and steam. The average building boiler converts *only about two-thirds* of its fossil fuels to useful heat or steam.

By generating electricity and capturing the waste heat in a cogeneration system, much energy and pollution can be saved. *Overall system efficiencies can exceed 80 percent.* Total greenhouse gas emissions can be cut in half.

Many studies have shown that the potential market for cogen is enormous. For instance, a 2000 study for the DOE found that the market potential for combined heat and power at commercial and institutional facilities alone was 75,000 megawatts, about one-tenth of current U.S. power-generation capacity. The remaining potential in the industrial sector is about 88,000 megawatts.

Cogen and other *on-site* power systems, such as solar panels, are called distributed energy as opposed to large central-station power plants, like coal or nuclear. Their market penetration is limited by barriers that have nothing to do with their cost or performance—especially the countless obstacles and fees that major utilities can place in their way. In the late 1990s, the DOE launched a study of these barriers, looking at sixty-five distributed-energy projects. The result was a July 2000 report that offered a variety of recommendations we should embrace:

- Adopt uniform standards for interconnecting distributed power to the grid.
- Adopt testing and certification procedures for interconnection equipment.
- Accelerate development of distributed power-control technology and systems.
- Develop tools for utilities to assess the value and impact of distributed power.
- Develop new regulatory principles compatible with distributed-power choices.
- Adopt regulatory tariffs and utility incentives to fit a distributed-power model.

The strategies we need to avoid climate catastrophe are not about imposing the heavy hand of government on the marketplace; rather they are about leveling the playing field and giving an extra push to low-carbon technologies. How much carbon dioxide could an efficiency and cogen strategy save the country? Before answering that, let's look at the potential for renewable power.

THE RENEWABLES REVOLUTION

Energy efficiency can stop the runaway growth of electricity demand. Cogeneration can reduce the carbon emissions of much of the electricity that is generated. Renewable energy can deliver electricity without any carbon emissions. In terms of annual percentage growth, wind and solar energy were the two fastest growing forms of power in the past two decades. I will focus here on wind because it is the renewable that can meet the most large-scale demand at the lowest price.

Modern wind turbines convert the kinetic energy of the wind into electricity. Wind turbines are often grouped together into "farms" to generate bulk electrical power. Electricity from these turbines is fed into the local utility grid and distributed to customers.

America has exceptional wind resources, especially the central United States from the Texas Panhandle up through the Great Plains. North Dakota alone has enough energy from high-wind resources to supply 36 percent of the electricity of the lower forty-eight states. Much of the available wind, however, is not located near the consumer. Therefore, if wind were to become a significant portion of the generation mix, additional investments in transmission and distribution infrastructure would be needed.

Over the past 15 years, major aerodynamic improvements in blade design have cut the cost of electricity from wind power by 10 percent *per year*. New, utility-scale wind projects are being built all around the country today, delivering electricity at prices as low as 4 cents per kilowatt-hour in the best wind sites. Media attention has been focused on the few public disputes over wind-farm locations, such as the offshore wind farm planned near Cape Cod, but most of the country has been embracing wind enthusiastically; aggregated installed wind in the United States is roughly 9,000 megawatts as of the end of 2005—five times the installed capacity of 1999.

The next-generation wind turbine is projected to bring costs down to 3 cents per kilowatt-hour over the next several years (including the wind-production tax credit). Since wind is an intermittent electricity generator and does not provide power on an as-needed basis, it loses some value on a per-kilowatt-hour basis, compared with traditional generation that can provide steady base-load power. On the other hand, wind can more than make up for this lost value by providing benefits in terms of reduced emissions and elimination of fuel risk (such as seen by natural-gas plants).

While wind now provides less than 1 percent of U.S. electricity generation, it represents up to 40 percent of electricity in regions of Germany, Spain, and Denmark. And wind is only one of several renewable technologies that are near-competitive with grid electricity. As a major 2004 report by the International Energy Agency concluded: "Under the best conditions—optimized system design, site and resource availability—electricity from biomass, small hydropower, wind and geothermal plants can produce electricity at costs ranging from 2–5 cents/kilowatt-hour."

Note that geothermal energy made that list. Geothermal power converts the earth's own deep energy into heat and electricity. It remains a very attractive power source. But in 2006, when Bush proposed his "Advanced Energy Initiative—a 22-percent increase in clean-energy research," he needed to find money to fund it. He found it by zeroing out all federal funding for geothermal research.

Renewable-energy power plants typically have high capital costs, but their operating costs are low, because they don't consume fuel on a daily basis. While most forms of renewable energy are not competitive with current wholesale electricity prices, it is well to remember that

1. Many traditional power plants have long since paid off their capital costs, so that their electricity cost comes only from fuel and operating costs. New fossil fuel power plants don't have that price advantage.
2. Many renewables have not yet achieved their ultimate cost reduction from either improvements in technology or manufacturing economies of scale at higher volume.

3. Carbon dioxide emissions have no economic cost to the producer and are never counted in the comparisons of true energy costs.

So new renewables will be increasingly competitive with new fossil fuel plants, especially when we properly account for the real cost of global-warming emissions, which, as we have seen, threatens to bring about almost incalculable damage to the next fifty generations of Americans.

It is then no surprise to learn that by 2005, some two dozen states and more than forty countries had a national target for their own renewable-energy supply, including all twenty-five countries in the European Union. The E.U. has set a target of having 21 percent of its electricity come from renewables by 2010.

Our Congress, however, refuses to adopt a renewable standard that would require even 10 percent of U.S. power to be delivered by renewable energy. Yet a standard requiring *20 percent* of U.S. electricity to be renewable by 2020 has very little net cost to the country, but brings the huge benefit of reducing future natural-gas prices and future greenhouse gas emissions. Under such a standard, electricity prices would be *lower* in 2020 than they are today, according to a 2001 Department of Energy study.

POWER SWITCH

What could this country achieve with an energy policy based on existing technology and the most successful strategies used by states and other countries to get those technologies into the marketplace? In 2003 I coauthored a study on "The Path to Carbon-Dioxide-Free Power," which focused on the three technology areas I have been discussing: energy efficiency, cogeneration, and renewables.

The results were very promising. They showed that with a set of innovative and ambitious policies the U.S. electricity sector could cut CO_2 emissions in half by 2020. The price of carbon dioxide never exceeds about $15 a ton ($55 a ton of carbon), which translates into slightly more than 1.5 cents per kilowatt-hour added to the cost of a traditional coal plant. Electricity rates rise slightly, but at the same time we will be using electricity more efficiently, which will cause bills to drop substantially. The net savings would be about *$20 billion per year* from 2004 to 2020 and would exceed $80 billion a year after 2020.

The country would see only a small increase in electricity generation from current levels, and natural-gas use stays roughly flat, even while the U.S. population rises 20 percent and industrial output increases 75 percent. Yet consumers and businesses would receive the same or better energy services in 2020 than in the business-as-usual case. The power system would become more reliable and less vulnerable to external disruption, including terrorist attack.

As an added benefit, Americans would see a sharp decline in air pollution and a resulting improvement in health. Utility mercury emissions, which threaten the health and developmental ability of children, would drop 90 percent. Emissions of oxides of nitrogen and sulfur dioxide, which are linked to respiratory and other health problems in humans, drop by two-thirds or more.

Many studies before and since this one have shown similar results, including two major studies by our national laboratories. In fact, *Policy Implications of Greenhouse Warming*, a 1991 study by the National Academy of Sciences, concluded, "This analysis suggests that the United States could reduce its greenhouse gas emissions by between 10 and 40 percent of the 1990 level and at very low cost. Some reductions may even be a net savings if the proper policies are implemented."

American conservatives (and many economists) do not believe such emissions reductions are possible without a very high cost. They do not accept that the economy now operates inefficiently, nor do they believe government technology policies would have much value. Their studies typically ignore the possibility of efficiency and cogeneration, and, with tunnel vision, they assume the only way to achieve the proposed reductions is with very high prices for carbon dioxide in electricity.

If we do nothing for the next two decades, U.S. carbon dioxide emissions will rise another 20 percent or more, and we will have invested hundreds of billions of dollars in another generation of inefficient and carbon-intensive technologies and power plants. If we then try to reduce emissions to 60 percent below 1990 levels by 2050, the cost of energy would probably have to double and the government would probably have to simply mandate shutting down most of our coal plants, with devastating consequences for consumers and businesses. The Delayers believe that action on global warming will hurt the U.S. economy and require onerous government mandates. Ironically, their way of thinking could become a self-fulfilling prophecy.

Having worked with dozens of companies to design profitable emissions-reduction strategies, and having carefully reviewed more than a hundred specific case studies of buildings and factories that employed energy efficiency, cogeneration, and renewable energy, I have no doubt that the United States could dramatically reduce its carbon emissions per kilowatt-hour without raising its overall energy bill.

But you don't have to take my word for this. Nor do you have to wade into the dull details of either the technologies or the economics. Just consider California. In 2004 the state consumed about 7,000 kilowatt-hours per person, whereas the rest of the country consumed about 13,000 kWh per person. California's electricity rates (cents per kWh) are about 50 percent higher than the national average, yet its annual electric bill per person is about the same as the rest of the nation because it wastes less electricity. Its rates are higher partly because California is paying for the legacy of its flawed deregulation in the 1990s, and that portion of the extra rate should decrease over time. Its rates are also higher because it has much cleaner power generation, using more renewables and natural gas than the rest of the country. Californians decided that they value the reduction of unhealthful air pollution.

The result is that each kilowatt-hour consumed in California generates only about half the carbon dioxide emissions of the national average. Combine that fact with the more efficient use of electricity, and you get a startling statistic. In terms of electricity consumption, *the average California generates under one-third of the carbon dioxide emissions of the average American while paying the same annual bill.*

NUCLEAR POWER

The lack of knowledge about energy by even the most senior politicians is scary. Consider Senator John McCain's comments in a March 2006 interview, in which he stated he would demand legislation to expand U.S. nuclear power as part of his efforts to reduce greenhouse gas emissions: "It's the only technology presently available to quickly step up to meet our energy needs," he said.

Wrong on both counts: Nuclear is not the only technology, nor is it the quickest. The licensing and construction process for nuclear plants takes many years, and it should, given that the plants are expensive, carry many safety and environmental risks, and have been given limited liability by Congress in case of an accident. An energy-efficiency strategy would be much faster.

McCain's comment reflects a common misconception that some never-named entity is mysteriously holding back the expansion of nuclear power in this country. What has really been holding back nuclear power is the economic and other risks it poses to utilities and financiers—Wall Street.

Nuclear energy is mostly carbon-free power. Yet it is not a slam-dunk solution to global warming. A major 2003 study by MIT, "The Future of Nuclear Power," highlighted many of the "unresolved problems" that have created "limited prospects for nuclear power today." The study found that "in deregulated markets, nuclear power is not now cost competitive with coal and natural gas." The public has significant concerns about safety, environmental, health, and terrorism risks associated with nuclear power. The study also found that "nuclear power has unresolved challenges in long-term management of radioactive wastes." It described possible technological and other strategies for addressing these issues but noted that "the cost improvements we project are plausible but unproven."

Peter Bradford, a former member of the Nuclear Regulatory Commission (NRC), told the *New York Times* in May 2005, "The abiding lesson that Three Mile Island taught Wall Street was that a group of NRC-licensed reactor operators, as good as any others, could turn a $2 billion asset into a $1 billion cleanup job in about 90 minutes."

Nuclear power may well be one important piece of the climate-stabilization puzzle, which is why I have included it as one of the eight wedges. Achieving one nuclear wedge means building a nuclear power plant somewhere in the world every month for the next fifty years, while maintaining current nuclear capacity.

But nuclear power is hardly a fledgling technology that needs even more targeted support from the U.S. government. Nuclear already gets countless subsidies. For instance, the Price-Anderson Act limits liability in the event of a nuclear disaster. And the Energy Policy Act of 2005 gives the industry billions of dollars more in subsidies—even authorizing more than $1 billion to build a nuclear plant solely for the purpose of making hydrogen, an especially pointless subsidy, as we will see in the next chapter.

The nation needs to put into place mandatory carbon dioxide controls. If a significant price for carbon makes nuclear power attractive to utilities and financiers, and if the plants meet the necessary safety and environmental codes, and if the country can finally agree on a place to put the nuclear waste, then new nuclear plants may well make a significant contribution to reducing greenhouse gas emissions in this country. I certainly wouldn't shut down any existing nuclear plants that are run safely. Nor would I discourage other countries from pursuing nuclear power, as long as it is done under the proper international controls to prevent the proliferation of nuclear weapons.

California, however, achieves its remarkably low per capita carbon dioxide emissions from electricity while getting a lower share of its power from nuclear energy than the national average. That's why federal electricity policy should focus on establishing a price for carbon dioxide, promoting energy efficiency, cogeneration, and renewable energy, and accelerating coal gasification together with carbon capture and storage. Those strategies can take us as far as we need to go on emissions reductions in the utility sector for the next few decades.

We will need a similarly aggressive and intelligent set of technology policies to deal with the other major CO_2-producing sector of the U.S. economy—transportation.

CHAPTER EIGHT

PEAK OIL, ENERGY SECURITY, AND THE CAR OF THE FUTURE

We have a serious problem. America is addicted to oil, which is often imported from unstable parts of the world.
—President George W. Bush, 2006

In the absence of revolutionary changes in energy policy, we are risking multiple disasters for our country that will constrain living standards, undermine our foreign-policy goals, and leave us highly vulnerable to the machinations of rogue states.
—Senator Richard Lugar, 2006

Our ever-worsening addiction to oil makes America less secure. Since 1990, we have fought two wars in the Persian Gulf. We suffered a major terrorist attack funded largely by Persian Gulf oil money. Every year we send more than $250 billion overseas because we import most of our oil. Oil prices keep spiking above $70 a barrel, and gasoline above $3 a gallon. The economic lifeblood of our country is held hostage to countries that are antidemocratic and politically unstable—and to terrorists who keep targeting the world's oil infrastructure. Price spikes above $100 a barrel (and $4 a gallon) are all but inevitable in the coming years. And many fear we may be close to seeing worldwide oil production peak and then decline, which will bring an era of steadily rising oil and gasoline prices.

It's no wonder that politicians—even those who don't worry about global warming—keep talking about oil. So why haven't we taken any serious action on oil for decades? The answer is simple— reducing U.S. oil consumption requires a major government-led effort, such as much tougher mileage standards, and our political leaders have rejected such efforts (except for ones that are merely cosmetic).

The astonishing January 2006 statement by President Bush's EPA administrator, Stephen Johnson, bears repeating: "Are we going to tell people to stop driving their cars, or do we start investing in technology? That's the answer, investing in those technologies." This false choice leaves the nation with no oil policy except strong, empty rhetoric suggesting that the cure for our addiction to oil can be found in happy talk about future technology. Here's what President Bush said the next month, in February 2006:

> Our nation is on the threshold of new energy technology that I think will startle the American people. We're on the edge of some amazing breakthroughs—breakthroughs all aimed at enhancing our national security and our economic security and the quality of life of the folks who live here in the United States.

The president has actually misdirected more than a billion dollars toward the development of hydrogen cars, a solution that will not address either our oil or climate problems in our lifetime, as we will see. I also examine in this chapter why the peak in global oil production is less of a threat to our way of life than is widely perceived, and why peak oil won't avert catastrophic climate change.

We will see why the win-win policies needed to avoid Hell and High Water would also make this nation energy-independent by midcentury, even with declining domestic oil supplies. Finally, this chapter describes the car and fuel of the future. Let's start with some background.

TRANSPORTATION AND OIL

About two-thirds of U.S. oil consumption is in the transportation sector, the only sector of the U.S. economy almost wholly reliant on oil. The energy price shocks of the 1970s helped spur growth in natural-gas use for home heating. It also drove the electric utility sector and the industrial sector to sharply reduce their dependence on petroleum. But roughly 97 percent of all energy consumed by our cars, sport-utility vehicles, vans, trucks, and airplanes is still petroleum-based.

Over the past two decades, cleaner engines and reformulated gasoline have worked together to cut vehicular emissions of noxious urban air pollutants, especially the oxides of nitrogen that are a precursor to ozone smog and particulates, the stuff that does so much damage to our hearts and lungs. But the contribution to global warming by cars and light trucks, such as SUVs, has risen steadily. In the 1990s the transportation sector saw the fastest growth in carbon dioxide emissions of any major sector of the U.S. economy. And the transportation sector will generate nearly half of the 40 percent rise in U.S. carbon dioxide emissions forecast for 2025.

Internationally, the situation is equally fearful. As Claude Mandil, executive director of the International Energy Agency (IEA), said in May 2004, "In the absence of strong government policies, we project that the worldwide use of oil in transport will nearly double between 2000 and 2030, leading to a similar increase in greenhouse gas emissions." If by 2050 the per capita energy consumption of China and India were to approach that of South Korea, and if the Chinese and Indian populations increase as predicted, those two supergiant countries *by themselves* would consume more oil than the entire world used in 2003.

"It took us 125 years to use the first trillion barrels of oil," says a Chevron oil-company ad. "We'll use the next trillion in 30." This computes to an average of about 33 billion barrels of oil a year, which is 91 million barrels of oil a day or *A Thousand Barrels a Second*, the title of a 2006 book by energy economist Peter Tertzakian. World demand hit about 84 million barrels a day in 2005, up from 78 million in 2002—a torrid pace of demand growth that slowed only somewhat when prices spiked above $60 and even $70 a barrel in 2005 and 2006.

Since oil is a finite, nonrenewable resource, many analysts have tried to predict when global production will peak and then start declining, just as U.S. oil production in the lower forty-eight states did three decades ago. Some experts believe this peak will occur by 2010. Princeton geophysicist Kenneth Deffeyes wrote in 2001, "There is nothing plausible that could postpone the peak until 2009. Get used to it." Royal Dutch/Shell, a company that has downgraded its own oil-reserve estimates, adds only two or three decades to this forecast. According to Shell, "A scarcity of oil supplies—including unconventional sources and natural gas liquids—is very unlikely before 2025. This could be extended to 2040 by adopting known measures to increase vehicle efficiency and focusing oil demand on this sector." As we will see, Shell's hedges—"unconventional sources and natural gas liquids" as well as "known measures" to increase vehicle efficiency—will largely decide how the peaking of global oil production will affect the climate and our way of life.

"Conventional" oil means the liquid crude petroleum that is extracted from the ground using the traditional method, an oil well. Experts do not agree on how much "ultimately recoverable" oil remains in the ground, in part because they use different definitions for conventional oil and in part because they disagree about how much technology advances will enable more oil to be found and extracted. Also, the peak-oil "pessimists" simply don't believe the claims by some Middle East governments as to how much conventional-oil reserves they have.

Resolving that dispute is beyond the scope of this book, but a few points are critical to understand. The vast majority of the world's conventional-oil reserves are in unstable regions, such as the Middle East, guaranteeing extreme oil-price volatility for decades to come. The rapid growth in demand for oil by developing countries, especially China and India, coupled with the refusal by the United States to adopt strong policies to restrain or reverse our own growing demand, ensure that conventional oil will almost certainly peak and then decline sometime in the next quarter-century. The world is in fact running out of conventional oil. What about unconventional oil?

PEAK OIL AND GLOBAL WARMING

Unfortunately, *most forms of unconventional oil will make global warming worse*—and some of them will make Hell and High Water all but inevitable. Ironically, global warming is making it easier to explore and drill for oil in the Arctic because the sea ice is vanishing at an ever-increasing rate. The amount of undiscovered oil in the Arctic has been estimated at 200 to 400 billion barrels—enough to supply the world for seven to fourteen years at current usage. Let's look at some of the major unconventional sources.

First, we have a number of viscous oils called bitumen, heavy oil, and tar sands (or oil sands). There is more recoverable heavy oil in Venezuela than there is conventional oil in Saudi Arabia, and Canada has even more recoverable oil in its tar sands. Tar sands are pretty much the heavy gunk they sound like, and making liquid fuels from them requires huge amounts of energy for steam injection and refining. Canada is currently producing about a million barrels of oil a day from the tar sands, and that is projected to triple over the next two decades.

The tar sands are doubly dirty. On the one hand, the energy-intensive conversion of the tar sands directly generates two to four times the amount of greenhouse gases per barrel of final product as the production of conventional oil. On the other hand, Canada's increasing use of natural gas to exploit the tar sands is one reason that its exports of natural gas to the United States are projected to shrink in the coming years. So instead of selling clean-burning natural gas to this country, which we could use to stop the growth of carbon-intensive coal generation, Canada will provide us with a more carbon-intensive oil product to burn in our cars. That's lose-lose.

From a climate perspective, fully exploiting the tar-sands resource would make Canada's climate policy as immoral as ours.

Second, even more oil can probably be recovered from shale, a claylike rock, than from the tar sands. Most of the world's shale is found in the United States, and most of our shale, a trillion tons, is found in Colorado and Utah. After the oil shocks of the 1970s, billions were spent exploring the possibility of shale oil, but those efforts were abandoned in the 1980s when oil prices collapsed. Shale does not contain much energy—per pound, it has one-tenth the energy of crude oil and one-fourth that of recycled phone books. Converting shale to oil requires a huge amount of energy—possibly as much as 1,200 megawatts of generating capacity to produce only 100,000 barrels per day. If those were fossil-based megawatts, we would be spewing millions of tons of greenhouse gases into the air every year just to create a fuel that itself would spew more greenhouse gases into the air when burned in a car. But then it would be equally crazy to use renewable energy to make shale, when we critically need that zero-carbon power to displace coal electricity.

We simply must leave the shale in the ground.

Third, the recovery of conventional oil from a well can be enhanced by injecting carbon dioxide (CO_2) into the reservoir. Estimates for potential recovery are 300 to 600 billion barrels. A 2005 study, "Peaking of World Oil Production," led by Science Applications International Corporation (SAIC) explained:

> CO_2 flooding can increase oil recovery by 7–15 percent of original oil in place. Because EOR (enhanced oil recovery) is relatively expensive, it has not been widely deployed in the past. However, as a way of dealing with peak conventional oil production and higher oil prices, it has significant potential.

The SAIC study might also have noted that in a world where carbon capture and storage from coal generation becomes commonplace—which might occur as soon as two decades from now—we may be awash in carbon dioxide that could be diverted to EOR. What a double tragedy it would be if that carbon dioxide were not put into deep underground aquifers (permanently reducing the amount of heat-trapping gas in the atmosphere) but instead was used to extract more fossil fuels from the ground (which would ultimately release carbon dioxide into the atmosphere when burned in internal combustion engines).

Fourth, coal and natural gas can be converted to diesel fuel using the Fischer-Tropsch process. During World War II, coal gasification and liquefaction produced more than half of the liquid fuel used by the German military. America has so much coal, it could replace all imported oil with liquid fuel from coal—and keep generating electricity from coal—for more than 100 years. China has nearly as much coal as we do. The Chinese are launching a huge coal-liquefaction effort and plan to generate 300,000 barrels of oil a day from coal by 2020.

The process is incredibly expensive. You need to spend $5 billion or more just to build a plant capable of producing only 80,000 barrels of oil a day (the United States currently consumes more than 21 million barrels a day). You need about 5 gallons of water for every gallon of diesel fuel that's produced—not a particularly good long-term strategy in a world facing mega-droughts and chronic water shortages. Worse, the total carbon dioxide emissions from coal-to-diesel are about double that of conventional diesel. You can capture the carbon dioxide from the process and store it underground permanently. But that will make an expensive process even more expensive, so it seems unlikely for the foreseeable future, certainly not until carbon dioxide is regulated and has a high price, and we have a number of certified underground geologic repositories.

More important, even if you capture the CO_2 from the Fischer-Tropsch process, you are still left with diesel fuel, a carbon-intensive liquid that will release carbon dioxide into the atmosphere once it is burned in an internal combustion engine. A great many people I have spoken to are confused about this point; they think that capturing and storing the CO_2 while turning coal to diesel is as good an idea as capturing the CO_2 from the integrated gasification combined-cycle process for turning coal into electricity. No. The former process still leaves you with a carbon-intensive fuel, whereas the latter process leaves you with zero-carbon electricity. Worse, some people propose taking the captured CO_2 and using it for enhanced oil recovery, which, as we've seen, is the equivalent of not capturing the carbon dioxide at all.

Coal-to-diesel is a bad idea for the planet. If the United States or China pursues it aggressively, catastrophic climate change will be all but unavoidable. Turning natural gas into diesel is not as bad an idea, at least from the perspective of direct emissions, because natural gas is a low-carbon fuel. But it represents a tremendous misuse of natural gas, which could otherwise be used to displace coal plants and sharply reduce future greenhouse gas emissions.

A 2006 study by the University of California at Berkeley found that meeting the future demand shortfall from conventional oil with unconventional oil, especially coal-to-diesel, could increase annual carbon emissions by 2 billion metric tons (7.3 gigatons of carbon dioxide) for several decades. That would certainly be fatal to any effort to avoid 20 to 80 feet of sea-level rise.

We are simply running out of time, and we no longer have the luxury of grossly misallocating capital and fuels. That's why significantly exploiting unconventional sources of liquid fossil fuel such as coal, tar sands, and shale is the road to ruin. And that's why the Bush administration efforts to push hydrogen-fuel-cell cars make so little sense.

THE HYPE ABOUT HYDROGEN

> *Forget hydrogen, forget hydrogen, forget hydrogen.*
> —Former CIA director James Woolsey, 2006

The promise of hydrogen cars as a simple techno-fix, a deus ex machina to solve our environmental problems painlessly, and without regulations, is a cornerstone of the Bush administration's climate policy. In his January 2003 State of the Union address, the president pledged "$1.2 billion in research funding so that America can lead the world in developing clean, hydrogen-powered automobiles." He then said that "the first car driven by a child born today could be powered by hydrogen, and pollution-free."

The president didn't tell the public that more than 98 percent of the hydrogen made in this country today must be extracted from fossil fuel hydrocarbons—natural gas, oil, and coal—and that process releases huge amounts of carbon dioxide. "It is highly likely that fossil fuels will be the principal sources of hydrogen for several decades," concluded a prestigious National Academy of Sciences panel in 2004. In fact, hydrogen as a transport fuel might even *in-*

crease greenhouse gas emissions rather than reduce them. That was the conclusion of a January 2004 study by the European Commission and European oil companies and car companies.

The only way hydrogen cars could be "pollution-free" is for the hydrogen to be made from pollution-free sources of energy, like wind power. But the administration and Congress won't even pass a law requiring that 10 percent of U.S. electricity be renewable by 2020—so what are the chances that children born in 2003 will be driving a car in 2020 with pollution-free hydrogen?

Making hydrogen for use in cars is a terrible use of pollution-free power. Instead, we should build renewable-power plants to avoid the need to build new coal plants and save *four times as much carbon dioxide at less than one-tenth the cost* of using that same renewable power to make hydrogen to run a car. Study after study has shown that it makes no sense to squander renewable power to make hydrogen for cars until the electric grid is itself virtually greenhouse-gas-free—and that is at least four decades away. That's 40 years from now, even if we are able to reverse our current energy policy the day after Bush leaves office.

And this analysis assumes that hydrogen cars will actually become practical for consumers any time soon. But that is highly unlikely. They simply require too many scientific breakthroughs. For starters, a pollution-free hydrogen car requires a fuel cell for efficiently converting hydrogen into useful energy without generating pollution. Fuel cells are small, modular electrochemical devices, similar to batteries, except that they can be continuously fueled. They take in hydrogen and oxygen and put out only water plus heat and electricity, which runs an electric motor.

Unfortunately, fuel cells for cars currently cost about $2,000 per kW, which is about fifty times greater than the cost of an internal combustion engine. A major breakthrough will be required to make fuel cells affordable and practical.

Yet another major breakthrough is needed to solve the storage problem. Hydrogen is the most diffuse gas there is. No known material can store enough of it in a practical way to give people the kind of driving range they want. A March 2004 study by the American Physical Society concluded that "a new material must be discovered" to solve the storage problem.

Another problem: Currently hydrogen from pollution-free renewable sources would cost the equivalent of $6 to $10 a gallon of gasoline. So we'll need another major breakthrough that will drop the cost by a factor of three.

Hydrogen cars need three major breakthroughs—in fuel cells, storage, and renewable hydrogen—within the next decade or so, in a world where game-changing energy-technology breakthroughs hardly ever happen. And if those three happened, we would still need someone to spend more than $500 billion to build the fueling infrastructure needed to make hydrogen available throughout the country. An analysis in the May 2004 issue of *Scientific American* stated, "Fuel-cell cars, in contrast [to hybrids], are expected on about the same schedule as NASA's manned trip to Mars and have about the same level of likelihood."

When Bill Reinert, the U.S. manager of Toyota's advanced technologies group, was asked in 2005 when fuel-cell cars would replace gasoline cars, he answered, "If I told you 'never,' would you be upset?" A 2004 MIT study concluded that hydrogen-fuel-cell cars would be unlikely to achieve significant market success until the year 2060, far too late to help.

And yet in spite of all this, the Bush administration keeps pumping money into the budget for hydrogen. In its 5-year budget outlook released in 2006, the hydrogen-technology budget rose to a stunning $323 million in fiscal year 2011 (out of $1.13 billion for all energy efficiency and renewable energy) from a requested $196 million in 2007 (out of $1.18 billion). The tragedy of this is a 20 percent drop in funding for technologies that actually hold some promise of helping to reduce greenhouse gas emissions in the first half of this century.

In April 2005, Energy Secretary Samuel Bodman announced that he was disbanding the department's primary independent advisory board on scientific and technical matters, a board that has existed in some form since 1978. Bodman is uninterested in outside scientific advice. A department spokesman claimed Bodman was doing this because he is a chemical engineer by training and "the secretary has an understanding of science and scientific processes." But Bodman's 5-year budget plan grossly misdirects more than a billion dollars of the department's research-and-development funds, suggesting that he doesn't understand at all.

THE WIN-WIN OIL POLICY

> *My message is that the balance of realism has passed from those who argue on behalf of oil and a laissez-faire energy policy that relies on market evolution, to those who recognize that in the absence of a major reorientation in the way we get our energy, life in America is going to be much more difficult in the coming decades.*
> —Senator Richard Lugar, 2006

If neither hydrogen cars nor the peak and subsequent drop in global oil production are going to save us from endlessly rising greenhouse gas emissions, what will?

I have described a variety of aggressive low-carbon strategies or "wedges" we need to achieve over the next five decades. Each wedge ultimately avoids 1 billion metric tons of carbon emissions a year.

The last chapter looked at the five wedges needed to reduce

emissions from electricity, buildings, and heavy industry. The two wedges needed in the transportation sector are:

- Every car and SUV achieves an average fuel economy of 60 miles per gallon.
- Every car can run on electricity for short distances before reverting to biofuels.

How do we ensure that the *average* car on the road in 2060 gets 60 mpg, when the current average is about one-third that? Some push for high gasoline taxes. European countries such as the United Kingdom and Germany have taxes of more than $2 per gallon, which is five times more than the U.S. tax. Yet the average fuel economy of European Union vehicles is nowhere near 60 mpg. Oil and gasoline prices will probably trend higher over the next two decades by themselves as demand continues to grow in the face of supply constraints, and as terrorism and instability cause price spikes and oil-market jitters. When this country gets serious about global warming, we will put in place a carbon-trading system that will increase the price of gasoline somewhat, though far less than European gas taxes do today. I don't think higher gas taxes are the best way to get 60-mpg cars.

Another, more obvious strategy is tougher fuel-efficiency standards. After all, corporate average fuel economy (CAFE) standards, enacted in 1975, were used successfully in this country to double the fuel efficiency of our cars while making them safer, mandating that new cars have a fuel efficiency of 27.5 miles per gallon. In a 2002 report to President Bush, the National Academy of Sciences concluded that automobile fuel economy could be increased by up to 42 percent for large SUVs with technologies that would pay for themselves in fuel savings. That study did not even consider the greater use of diesels and hybrids. The report was ignored.

Studies by the national laboratories, by MIT, and by the Pew

Center on Global Climate Change have concluded that even greater savings could be cost-effective while maintaining or improving passenger safety. In a comprehensive 2005 study of fuel economy and traffic fatalities in industrialized nations, Robert Noland of the Centre for Transport Studies at Imperial College in London found that "average fleet fuel economy has no effect on traffic fatalities." The conclusion: "Policies aimed at improving fuel economy," whether to reduce dependence on imported oil or to reduce carbon dioxide emissions, "will most likely not have adverse safety consequences." Indeed, greater use of hybrid technology should *increase* vehicle safety. *Automotive Engineering International,* which named the Toyota Prius hybrid "Best Engineered Vehicle 2004," explained that the Prius has a variety of safety features, including an electronic brake-by-wire system and a skid-control computer that coordinates with the hybrid system control computers. Hybrid electronics hold the promise of far more controllability, quicker response, and greater safety.

Even with their much higher gasoline prices, the Europeans have still insisted on a voluntary agreement with automakers to further reduce carbon dioxide emitted per mile by about 25 percent from 1996 to 2008 for the average light-duty vehicle, which equates to a vehicle fuel efficiency of about 44 mpg. Japan has a mandatory target with similar goals. Even China has a far tougher standard than we do, plus a 20 percent tax on the most inefficient cars. The car of the future is definitely fuel-efficient.

Our own federal law is a large obstacle—it still requires that the average new car get 27.5 miles per gallon (the same level we had in 1985). The average SUV must get a mere 20.7 miles per gallon (up a tad from 19.5 mpg in 1985). Worse, the National Highway Traffic Safety Administration uses data from unrealistic tests of vehicle efficiency to judge how well car companies have met the CAFE standard. The result is that in 2005, *Consumer Reports* found that the fleet of 2003-model passenger cars they tested averaged only a pitiful 22.7 mpg, far below the 27.5 the law requires (and even farther below the 29.7 mpg that National Highway Transportation Safety Administration had somehow calculated for those models). The light trucks they tested measured a meager 16 mpg, far below the law's 20.7.

We could design the standards more flexibly, and many groups, including the bipartisan National Commission on Energy Policy, have suggested improvements to CAFE. In 2005 the Center for American Progress proposed that the government offer to help U.S. car companies with their legacy health-care costs in return for a commitment to steady improvements in vehicle fuel efficiency. The climate challenge is so enormous that we will certainly need creative deals and bargains like that if we are to have any chance of avoiding catastrophe.

Another worthwhile strategy would be vehicle standards that reduce carbon dioxide emissions from the tailpipe, which in the short run would increase vehicle efficiency but in the long run would include low-carbon alternative fuels. California has put forward just such a carbon dioxide standard, and ten other states have followed. Tragically, those standards have been strongly opposed by both the Bush administration and the auto companies.

In 2006, Bush did slightly increase the fuel-economy standards for SUVs, and included huge gas-guzzling SUVs that exceed 8,500 pounds, such as GM's Hummer H2, which had previously been exempt from such regulations. But the change was minor and left open a huge loophole that exempts large pickup trucks. In the year 2025, the new standards will save the nation about *two weeks' worth of oil.* Hardly a treatment for a serious addiction. Also, the change appears to have been introduced not to have cleaner energy but to allow the administration to better argue in court that its new federal standards preempt California's much stronger proposed standards.

All that said, requiring improved vehicle efficiency, by itself, cannot achieve the greenhouse gas reductions we will need—

because if the world's population and economies continue their rate of growth, the number of cars on the road will triple by mid-century. So we will also need one or more zero-carbon alternative transportation fuels. Those alternative fuels will have to be electricity and biofuels.

THE CAR AND FUEL OF THE FUTURE

With a straightforward improvement to current hybrids, they can be plugged in to the electric grid and run in an all-electric mode for a limited range between recharging. If the initial battery charge runs low, these plug-in hybrids can run solely on gasoline.

We Americans use our cars mainly for relatively short trips, such as commuting—half of American cars travel less than 30 miles a day—followed by extended periods when the vehicle could be re-charged. So an all-electric range of 20 to 30 miles would allow these plug-in hybrid vehicles to replace a substantial portion of gasoline consumption and tailpipe emissions. If the electricity came from CO_2-free sources, these vehicles would dramatically reduce net greenhouse gas emissions.

A conventional car costs about 12 cents a mile to operate, for gasoline costing $2.50 a gallon. In contrast, a plug-in hybrid could run on electrons at 3 cents a mile, using electricity that costs about 8 cents a kilowatt-hour, the current average residential rate. Battery improvement—especially the next generation of lithium-ion batteries that will be available by 2010—will lead to increased functionality for plug-in hybrids. The larger battery of a plug-in hybrid, coupled with a higher-powered electric motor, allows significant downsizing of the gasoline engine and other related mechanical systems. Engineers at the University of California at Davis have built several plug-in hybrid prototypes that can travel 60 miles on electricity alone, with engines that are less than half the size of standard engines.

Plug-in hybrids avoid many of the barriers that have plagued alternative-fuel vehicles and that make hydrogen-fuel-cell cars so impractical. Plug-in hybrids do not have a limited range. They do not have a high fueling cost compared with gasoline. In fact, the per-mile fueling cost of running on electricity is about one-third the per-mile cost of running on gasoline. The key infrastructure dilemma—who will build the new hydrogen-fueling infrastructure until the cars are a success, but who will buy the cars if there aren't thousands of fueling stations already built—is minimized because electricity is widely available and charging is straightforward.

The plug-in hybrid will have a higher first cost, but this will be paid back by the lower fuel bill. One 2006 study found that with gasoline at $3 a gallon—probably the low end of the price range by the time we could begin a broad transition to plug-ins in a decade—the extra cost of the vehicle will be returned in five years, even if electricity prices rise 25 percent from current levels.

The remarkably low fueling cost of the best current hybrids (like the Toyota Prius) and future plug-in hybrids are a major reason why I don't worry as much about peak oil as some do. James Kunstler, for instance, argues in his 2005 book, *The Long Emergency,* that after oil production peaks, suburbia "will become untenable" and "we will have to say farewell to easy motoring." But suppose Kunstler is right. Suppose oil hits $160 a barrel and gasoline goes to $5 a gallon in, say, 2015. That price would still be lower than many Europeans pay today. You could just go out and buy the best hybrid and cut your fuel bill in half, back to current levels. Hardly the end of suburbia. And suppose oil hit $280 a barrel and gasoline rose to $8 dollars a gallon in 2025. You would replace your hybrid with a plug-in hybrid, and those trips under 30 miles that have made suburbia what it is today would actually *cut* your fuel bill by a factor of more than ten—even if all the electricity were from zero-carbon sources like wind power—*to far below what you are paying today.*

I expect commercial plug-in hybrids to be available within a few years. And as battery technology improves and gasoline prices rise in the coming decade, plug-ins will become increasingly popular. Growing concern over global warming will only serve to accelerate the transition.

THE CAR OF THE FUTURE IS CLIMATE-FRIENDLY

Environmentally, plug-in hybrids have an enormous advantage over hydrogen-fuel-cell vehicles in utilizing zero-carbon electricity because of the inherent inefficiency of generating hydrogen from electricity, transporting hydrogen, storing it aboard the vehicle, and then running it through the fuel cell. The overall efficiency of a hydrogen-fuel-cell vehicle's ability to use renewable electricity is a meager 20 to 25 percent. The efficiency of charging an onboard battery and then discharging it to run an electric motor in a plug-in hybrid, however, is 75 to 80 percent.

Replacing half of the U.S. ground-transport fuels (gasoline and diesel) with hydrogen from wind power by 2050, for example, might require 1,400 gigawatts of advanced wind turbines or more. However, replacing those fuels with electricity (for plug-in hybrids) might require less than 400 GW. That 1,000-GW difference is an insurmountable obstacle for hydrogen fuel especially because the United States will need hundreds of gigawatts of wind and other zero-carbon power sources just to sharply reduce greenhouse gas emissions in the electricity sector, as we have seen.

Another advantage of plug-ins is that they hold the potential to make intermittent renewable power, like wind, more cost-effective. Wind delivers power only when the wind is blowing, and this is not as valuable to electric utilities as base-load power plants that provide power available all the time. But most cars stay parked for more than twenty hours a day. We can imagine that an electric utility might lease a plug-in hybrid to a consumer or business willing to leave the vehicle connected when it was not on the road and to permit the utility to control when the vehicle's battery was charged and discharged depending on its generation or voltage-regulation needs. Such an arrangement would help utilities with load balancing. It would also allow utilities to do most of the charging when the wind was blowing, eliminating the need for costly electricity storage that high levels of wind power might otherwise need. One reason the municipal utility Austin Energy has helped launch a national campaign for the plug in hybrid is that they have so much West Texas wind power available at night.

CELLULOSIC ETHANOL

Biomass can be used to make a zero-carbon transportation fuel, such as ethanol, which is now used as a gasoline blend. Today, the major U.S. biofuel is ethanol made from corn, which yields only about 25 percent more energy than was consumed to grow the corn and make the ethanol. A considerable amount of R&D is being spent on producing ethanol that can be made from far less energy-intensive sources. Called cellulosic ethanol, it can be made from agricultural and forest waste and also from dedicated energy crops, such as switchgrass or fast-growing poplar trees, which can be grown and harvested with minimal energy consumption, so that overall net emissions are near zero.

Ethanol's advantage over alternative fuels like hydrogen gas is that it is a liquid fuel and thus much more compatible with our existing fueling system. Existing oil pipelines, however, are not compatible with ethanol, so significant infrastructure spending would still be required before ethanol could become the major transportation fuel. And ethanol production will require technological advances before it can match the price of (untaxed) gasoline on an equivalent energy basis. Carnegie Mellon University researchers note that cellulosic ethanol costs the equivalent of "$2.70 per gallon in order to get as much energy as in a gallon of gasoline."

Thus, if oil prices in, say, 2020 are consistently higher than $70 a barrel, cellulosic ethanol could be a competitive alternative fuel. This is particularly true because by that time we will inevitably have a price for carbon, further improving the cost of cellulosic ethanol relative to gasoline.

Probably the biggest barrier to biofuels, and to biomass energy in general, is that biomass is not very efficient at converting and storing solar energy, so large land areas would be needed to plant enough crops to provide a significant share of transportation energy. One 2001 analysis by ethanol advocates concluded that to provide enough ethanol to replace the gasoline used in the light-duty fleet alone, "it would be necessary to process the biomass growing on 300 million to 500 million acres, which is in the neighborhood of one-fourth of the 1.8 billion acre land area of the lower 48 states" and is roughly equal to the total amount of U.S. cropland in production today. That amount of displaced gasoline represents about 60 percent of all U.S. transportation-related carbon dioxide emissions today but under 40 percent of what is projected for 2025 under a business-as-usual scenario. Given the vast acreage needed, using so much land for fuel would obviously have dramatic effects—environmental, political, and economic.

If ethanol is to represent a major transportation fuel in the coming decades, then U.S. vehicles will need to become far more fuel-efficient. A fleet of 60-mpg cars would substantially reduce the biomass acreage requirements. And putting cellulosic ethanol blends into plug-in hybrids would further reduce acreage requirements, especially since there are plausible strategies for cogeneration of biofuels and biomass electricity.

In the long term, biomass-to-energy production could be exceedingly efficient with "biorefineries" that produce multiple products. Dartmouth engineering professor Lee Lynd described one such future biorefinery where cellulosic ethanol undergoes a chemical pretreatment, then fermentation converts the carbohydrate content into ethanol, as CO_2 bubbles off. The residue is mostly lignin (a polymer found in the cell walls of plants). Water is removed, and the biomass residue is then gasified to generate electricity or to produce a stream of hydrogen and CO_2. The overall efficiency of converting the energy content of the original biomass into useful fuel and electricity would be an impressive 70 percent, even after accounting for the energy needed to grow and harvest the biomass. The CO_2 can be sequestered. Also, this process could be used to generate biodiesel. This is a futuristic scenario, one that is the subject of intense research and that could make ethanol directly competitive with gasoline, and biomass electricity competitive with other zero-carbon alternatives, especially when there is a price for reducing CO_2 emissions.

ENERGY SECURITY AS A SIDE BENEFIT

Because of the abundance of unconventional oil and low-cost alternative fuels, peak oil is not the major energy problem that threatens the American way of life. Yes, if we don't aggressively pursue fuel efficiency and low-carbon alternative fuels *now*, the nation certainly faces oil price shocks and steadily increasing prices over the next quarter-century. But if we fail to pursue those crucial strategies, then Planetary Purgatory and 20-foot sea-level rise becomes all but inevitable, and we face the multidecade struggle to avoid the worst of Hell and High Water. Even if conventional oil peaks within two decades, the growing use of dirty, unconventional oil, along with rapidly rising natural-gas and coal consumption, will generate far too much carbon dioxide.

Global warming is the energy problem that threatens the American way of life. Over the next few decades, we need to triple the efficiency of our cars and SUVs, and have them also be flexible-fuel plug-in hybrids that run mostly on zero-carbon electricity and cellulosic ethanol. Whether your primary concern is peak oil and our energy insecurity or global warming, it is important to recognize that sharply reducing our reliance on oil will not happen with the Bush administration strategy. Their strategy is *rhetoric* about our oil addiction plus the *reshuffling* of some of our federal R&D dollars while at the same time blocking national efforts to boost the use of renewable power and opposing state efforts to boost vehicle fuel efficiency.

Triple-efficiency vehicles will be the norm by 2050 only with much higher mileage standards of the kind that most other countries, including China, are embracing (or with tailpipe-emissions standards for carbon dioxide, as California and ten other states propose). If we fail to embrace such standards nationally, the rest of the world will lead in advanced automotive technology, and GM and Ford will continue to bleed market share and jobs. The standard should be written in such a way as to encourage companies to meet them with hybrid technology, because that will help make cars safer and jump-start the shift to plug-in hybrids.

A successful transition to alternative fuels also requires government standards. Indeed, the only reason Brazil has been so successful in replacing gasoline with ethanol is that the government required minimum levels of ethanol blends and then required all gasoline stations to have at least one ethanol pump. We need such sensible policies in the United States. Here are two from the National Commission on Energy Policy:

- Develop the first six pioneer cellulose-to-energy plants between 2008 and 2012 using production or investment incentives.
- Modify agricultural subsidies to include energy crops without increasing total farm subsidies or decreasing farm income.

We should sharply increase federal investments in biofuels and advanced batteries while cutting the hydrogen program by more than half. We should adopt a renewable-fuels standard whereby 25 percent of our gasoline would be replaced with cellulosic ethanol by 2025. We should also launch a major effort to have at least 10 percent of our new cars be plug-in hybrids by 2025.

These strategies would not only sharply reduce greenhouse gas emissions from cars but would do so without raising the nation's fuel bill for transportation. As huge side benefits, we could achieve genuine energy security, sharply lower our trade deficit, revitalize our domestic auto industry, create countless jobs, and increase our national security, because we would no longer be beholden to undemocratic governments in the Middle East or have our economy repeatedly subject to price shocks from political instability or terrorist attacks.

CHAPTER NINE

THE U.S.–CHINA SUICIDE PACT ON CLIMATE

The "international fairness" issue is the emotional home run. Given the chance, Americans will demand that all nations be part of any international global warming treaty. Nations such as China, Mexico and India would have to sign such an agreement for the majority of Americans to support it.

—Frank Luntz, 2002

We don't need an international treaty with rules and regulations that will handcuff the American economy or our ability to make our environment cleaner, safer and healthier.

—Frank Luntz, 2002

What country's insatiable thirst for oil imports is most responsible for the tightening world market since the mid-1990s? Hint: It's not China. From 1995 to 2004, China's annual imports grew by 2.8 million barrels a day. Ours grew 3.9 million. China now sucks up about 6 percent of all global oil exports. We demand 25 percent, even though China has a billion more consumers.

In what year will China's total contribution to climate change from burning fossil fuels surpass ours? Hint: Climate change is driven by rising atmospheric concentrations of greenhouse gases, and those concentrations have been driven by cumulative emissions since the dawn of the industrial revolution. While China's *annual* CO_2 emissions may well exceed ours by 2025, its *cumulative* emissions might not surpass ours until after 2050.

Not only are we the richest nation in the world, but for many decades to come we will be the one most responsible for global warming. No wonder the Chinese and Indians and others in the developing world expect us to take action first, just as we did to save the ozone layer. No wonder the rest of the industrialized world embraced the Kyoto restrictions on greenhouse gas emissions, even knowing the emissions from developing countries such as China and India were not restricted.

One can only marvel at a strategist like Frank Luntz for his ability to appeal to Americans who "will demand that all nations be part of any international global warming treaty," while, in the same breath, reaching out to Americans who oppose "an international treaty with rules and regulations that will handcuff the American economy." Such a rhetorical flimflam strategy by the global-warming Denyers and Delayers is politically very savvy, but it is the sure road to Hell and High Water.

That said, China's emissions *are* growing at an alarming rate. In 2000 the government walked away from the California-style energy-efficiency effort it had embraced since 1980. For the past few years, it has been building one major dirty-coal plant *almost every week*. The climate problem cannot be solved if China and other rapidly developing countries do not take steps to restrain their emissions growth. But if the United States maintains its position that we will not take strong action until China does, neither country is likely to act in time. This chapter explores how the United States and China might avoid destroying the climate and, with it, our way of life.

A BRIEF HISTORY OF TIMETABLES

> Perhaps the most extraordinary aspect of the Montreal Protocol [on Substances that Deplete the Ozone Layer] was that it imposed substantial short-term economic costs in order to protect human health and the environment against speculative future dangers—dangers that rested on scientific theories rather than on proven facts. Unlike environmental agreements of the past, this was not a response to harmful developments or events, but rather preventive action on a global scale.
>
> —Richard Benedick, former ambassador, 2005

The ozone layer shields life on Earth from the sun's harmful ultraviolet rays. In 1974, climate scientists warned us that chlorofluorocarbons (CFCs) were destroying Earth's ozone layer, threatening to bring about a sharp increase in skin cancer. Within only 5 years, the United States voluntarily banned their use in spray cans, and CFC production began to decline. But other uses for CFCs, as refrigerants and solvents, began driving the demand up again by the early 1980s.

In 1985, scientists discovered a hole in the ozone shield over Antarctica. As the National Academy of Sciences wrote, this was "the first unmistakable sign of human-induced change in the global environment. . . . Most scientists greeted the news with disbelief. Existing theory simply had not predicted it."

Chlorine concentrations had been increasing over Antarctica for decades, up from the natural level of 0.6 parts per billion. Yet as Richard Benedick, President Ronald Reagan's chief negotiator at the Montreal conference, explained in a 2005 Senate hearing, "no effect on the ozone layer was evident until the concentration exceeded two parts per billion, which apparently triggered the totally unexpected collapse." His ominous lesson for today: "Chlorine concentrations had *tripled* with no impact whatsoever on ozone until they crossed an unanticipated threshold." As we have seen repeatedly, Earth's climate system has many such thresholds.

The stunning revelation of an ozone hole drove the world to negotiate the Montreal Protocol. The 1987 agreement called for a 50 percent cut in CFC production by 1999. Significantly, the protocol's targets and timetables *slowed the rate of growth of concentrations only slightly* and would still have led to millions of extra skin cancer cases by midcentury. Further, the protocol allowed developing countries to delay implementing the control measures for about ten years and required rich countries to give them access to alternative chemicals and technologies together with financial aid.

Nevertheless, President Reagan endorsed the protocol, and the Senate ratified it. By the end of 1988, twenty-nine countries and the European Economic Community—but not China or India—had ratified it. The treaty came into effect the next year, but it took many more years of negotiations, continuous strengthening of the scientific consensus, and significant concessions to developing countries in both technology transfer and financial assistance, before amendments to the treaty were strong enough and had enough support from rich and poor countries alike to ensure that CFC *concentrations* in the air would be reduced.

The analogy of the ozone layer and the Montreal Protocol to global warming and the Kyoto Protocol is far from perfect—greenhouse gases are more integral to modern life than CFCs ever were. American politics have changed in two decades, and the terms of the Montreal Protocol would no doubt be viewed today as wholly inadequate and politically unacceptable, especially without ratification by China and India. Yet this small first step by the rich nations jump-started a multiyear process that saved the ozone layer and prevented millions of cases of skin cancer. It also set an example of how the world could come together to tackle the climate problem.

For many decades, scientists have been warning us about the dangers of greenhouse gases. By the late 1970s, the National Academy of Sciences, the nation's most prestigious scientific body, had warned that uncontrolled greenhouse gas emissions might raise global temperatures 10°F and cause sea levels to rise catastrophically. The discovery of the ozone hole in 1985—an unexpected climate impact from an unanticipated emissions threshold—made us more aware of how we have affected the climate and helped push the nations of the world into an international effort to control greenhouse gas emissions.

In 1992, President Bush's father signed the United Nations Framework Convention on Climate Change (UNFCCC), also called the Rio climate treaty, and that year the Senate ratified it unanimously. The convention's goal was to set up an international process to stabilize "greenhouse gas concentrations in the atmosphere at a level that would prevent dangerous anthropogenic [human-made] interference with the climate system." The UNFCCC did not establish what that level was but did establish a nonbinding target that called for developed countries to return their emissions of greenhouse gases to 1990 levels. Perhaps most significant, the signatories to the treaty recognized "that the largest share of historical and current global emissions of greenhouse gases has originated in developed countries, that per capita emissions in developing countries are still relatively low and that the share of global emissions originating in developing countries will grow to meet their social and development needs." The Rio treaty recognized the "common but differentiated responsibilities and respective capabilities" of each nation and established a core principle: "Accordingly, *the developed country Parties should take the lead in combating climate change* and the adverse effects thereof" (emphasis added).

Unfortunately, supporters of action on climate change, including those in the Clinton administration, never fully explained to the American people how and why the rich countries had promised to take the lead in combating climate change. As a result, the U.S. Senate passed a resolution in 1997, offered by Senators Robert Byrd (Democrat) and Chuck Hagel (Republican), with a vote of 95–0, stating a "sense of the Senate" that the United States should not sign any protocol to the UNFCCC that would "mandate new commitments to limit or reduce greenhouse gas emissions for the [industrialized countries], unless the protocol or other agreement also mandates new specific scheduled commitments to limit or reduce greenhouse gas emissions for Developing Country Parties within the same compliance period."

Probably the Clinton administration's biggest political mistake on the climate issue was making no serious effort to stop that 95–0 outcome. This meant that the 1997 Kyoto Protocol, which set targets and timetables only for the emissions of rich countries, was dead before it got to the U.S. Senate—even though it was similar in most important respects to the Montreal Protocol, which had passed the Senate a decade earlier and had saved the ozone layer and the lives of countless Americans.

When you talk to people from China, India, or other developing countries, they don't understand our politics at all. They don't understand how the country that became the richest by spewing greenhouse gases that are now destroying everybody's climate would refuse to use some of that wealth to prevent catastrophic warming. They find it absurd that American politicians argue for delay by saying we must wait for the poorest countries to make commitments at the same time.

In the 1997 Byrd-Hagel amendment that helped kill the protocol, the senators stated their objection: "whereas greenhouse gas emissions of Developing Country Parties are rapidly increasing and are expected to surpass emissions of the United States and other

OECD countries as early as 2015." That language sounds so reasonable. As Luntz wrote, *"The 'international fairness' issue is the emotional home run."*

But remember that the key metric is not *annual* emissions but *cumulative* emissions. Cumulative emissions are what drive up carbon dioxide concentrations, and concentrations are what determine how much the planet warms. Developed countries had four times the cumulative emissions of developing countries from 1850 to 1995. The rich countries' total emissions from fossil fuel consumption would exceed that of the poor countries through midcentury. Even in the year 2000, the average American emitted nine times the carbon dioxide of a typical Chinese and twenty times that of a typical Indian. And, of course, the rich countries were (and still are) far, far, richer, especially on a per capita basis. That's why few developing countries are likely to agree to serious restrictions on their greenhouse gas emissions until and unless the developed countries go first, which is what we agreed to under the Rio treaty. And that's why virtually every developed country (other than the United States) agreed to the terms of the Kyoto Protocol.

THE CHINA SYNDROME

China's energy history can be divided into several phases, as we learn from Dr. Mark Levine, cofounder of the Beijing Energy Efficiency Center. The first phase (1949–1980) was a "Soviet-style" energy policy characterized by subsidized energy prices, no concern for the environment, and energy use that rose faster than economic growth (GDP).

The second phase (1981–1999) was "California on steroids," when the country embraced an aggressive push on energy management and energy efficiency, surpassing the efficiency efforts California has achieved since the mid-1970s. This came about as a result of Deng Xiaoping heeding the advice of leading academic experts who suggested a new approach to energy. Chinese strategies included

- factory energy-consumption quotas and energy-conservation monitoring
- efficient technology promotion and closing of inefficient facilities
- controls on oil use
- low interest rates for efficiency-project loans
- reduced taxes on efficient-product purchases
- incentives to develop new efficient products
- monetary awards to efficient enterprises
- strategic technology development and demonstration
- national, local, and industry-specific technical efficiency service and training centers

During the mid-1990s, China also began dramatic energy-price reforms, which led to higher prices for coal, oil, and electricity. China's policies kept energy growth to a modest level during a time of explosive economic growth. For instance, from 1990 to 2000, its economy more than doubled, but carbon dioxide emissions rose by only one-fourth. Remarkably, *during the 1990s, the United States actually increased its annual emissions of carbon dioxide more than China did.*

Unfortunately, toward the end of the last decade, China scaled back or eliminated many of its efficiency efforts, leading to the third phase of the country's energy history (2000–present), "energy crisis." China's energy demand began soaring again, rising much more rapidly than GDP. Recently, the country has been adding the equivalent of California's entire generating capacity every year. Most of the new power is from traditional coal plants, none of which can be easily retrofitted to capture carbon dioxide. As of 2005, China was burning twice as much coal as the United States. China now con-

sumes more than twice as much steel as the United States and produces nearly as much cement as the rest of the world.

Oil demand has also been exploding, albeit beginning from a
relatively low base. As of 2005, China still used less than one-third
the oil that we do. And it has much higher fuel-economy standards
than we do, as well as a 20 percent tax on the biggest gas-guzzling
vehicles. But China has an exploding middle class, its passenger-car
market increased tenfold in the 1990s, and it has been adding high-
ways so fast that their total length is now second only to that of the
United States. Worse still, China is pursuing several coal-to-diesel
demonstration projects, and plans to replace 10 percent of projected oil imports in 2020 with that most carbon-intensive of liquid
fossil fuels.

A 2005 study by the National Center for Atmospheric Research
looked at our large and growing trade deficit with China. The study
found that if the United States had produced domestically all the
products that it had imported from China, our emissions in 2003
would have been 6 percent higher and China's would have been 14
percent lower. Also, America's rate of growth in CO_2 emissions
would have been nearly 50 percent higher from 1997 to 2003—
which means we are exporting to China a huge fraction of our
growth in greenhouse gas emissions. And since our manufacturing
system is more efficient and less coal-intensive than China's, total
global CO_2 emissions from 1997 to 2003 would have been lower by
a stunning 720 million metric tons had we made the products we
bought from China during that short period.

China, the United States, and the world are at a crossroads.

One path, the current path, leads to catastrophe. In 2004,
China's carbon dioxide emissions rose an alarming 15 percent. If its
recent emissions trend—and ours—continue unchecked, our two
countries alone will be responsible for half of all growth in global
carbon dioxide emissions from 2000 to 2025.

At a 2005 U.S. China conference on coal sponsored by Harvard University, a senior Chinese official told me, "We hope your government will delay action" on climate change since "we benefit from your government policy." America's climate policy gives political cover to those in China who wish to continue their recent explosive growth in carbon emissions.

The Bush administration has not been content merely blocking domestic efforts to cut greenhouse gas emissions but has been actively trying to block international negotiations aimed at developing mandatory reduction targets beyond what Kyoto would require. Worse, the administration has been working hard to woo developing countries away from the UNFCCC Kyoto Protocol effort to develop global mandatory targets. It has launched the Orwellian-named Asia-Pacific Partnership on Clean Development and Climate, which rejects clean development. That partnership, whose members include the United States, Australia, China, India, Japan, and South Korea, explicitly rejects all mandatory efforts to reduce emissions, including caps.

Not surprisingly, the partnership endorses a strategy of voluntary action and technology development. It claims its strategy will reduce annual carbon emissions in 2050 from "reference case" levels of 22 billion tons down to 17 billion tons. But that "reference case" is the most extreme emissions trend line imagined by the Intergovernmental Panel on Climate Change. It represents a world with economic growth that is both very rapid and fossil fuel intensive. If carbon emissions in 2050 are 17 billion tons, we would be on the irreversible path to 80 feet of sea-level rise—even if there were no vicious cycles in the carbon system such as methane released from the melting tundra. *With* those powerful vicious cycles, we must keep global carbon emissions well below 10 billion tons in 2050.

The Asia-Pacific Partnership is a climate suicide pact. It is playing Russian roulette with six bullets in your gun.

America and the world must quickly jump off this path and onto a very different one. China must return to its strong efficiency efforts from the 1980s, while at the same time embracing a low-carbon strategy, including massive amounts of renewable energy and carbon capture and storage. The choking pollution in major Chinese cities, coupled with the energy bottlenecks and frequent blackouts found in most provinces, should be motivation enough—even ignoring the benefits of avoiding catastrophic sea-level rise and climate change that will devastate the country, with so much of its wealth along the coasts, with so much susceptibility to droughts and water shortages.

But as in our country, China's leaders operate under the misguided belief that they can pollute all they want during this time of rapid growth, then use their *future* wealth to solve their environmental problems. While that paradigm has worked in America for polluted rivers and smoggy cities, it is fatally flawed for dealing with the threat posed by irreversible climate impacts, such as the disintegration of the Greenland Ice Sheet or the release of the carbon and methane locked in the frozen tundra.

Most of the rest of the industrialized world is prepared to go down the only effective alternative path and has already made a baby step in the right direction by ratifying Kyoto. But as with restrictions on CFCs and the Montreal Protocol, the developing world will embrace the necessary mandatory restrictions on greenhouse gas emissions if and only if the United States leads the way forthrightly, and only if there is a broad-based strategy for the rich countries to help the poor countries embrace low-carbon development. So the next president of the United States must be a strong leader who makes climate the overriding priority.

In 2009, America must start with very strong domestic actions both to save ourselves and to send a clear signal to the rest of the world that we take moral responsibility for being by far the single biggest contributor to climate change. Second, we must then quickly bring together all the nations of the world to establish appropriate targets and timetables, ones that will distinguish between rich and poor countries, ones that keep atmospheric concentrations of carbon dioxide below 550 ppm. Any other course for this nation is self-destructive.

CHAPTER TEN

MISSING THE STORY OF THE CENTURY

In the end, adherence to the norm of balanced reporting leads to informationally biased coverage of global warming. This bias, hidden behind a veil of journalistic balance, creates ... real political space for the US government to shirk responsibility and delay action regarding global warming.
—Maxwell Boykoff and Jules Boykoff, 2004

This is no time for men who oppose Senator McCarthy's methods to keep silent. We can deny our heritage and our history, but we cannot escape responsibility for the result.
—Edward R. Murrow, March 9, 1954

If we do not avert Hell and High Water, global warming will be the news Story of the Millennium. In a world where sea levels are rising a foot or more every decade for centuries, our coasts are ravaged by superstorms, and we face endless mega-droughts, global warming won't be the most important story—it will be the only story.

If we do avert catastrophe, global warming will still be the Story of the Century. Starting very soon, and for many decades to come, the top news will focus on the country coming together to embrace an aggressive government-led effort to preserve the American way of life by changing everything about how we use energy—on a scale that dwarfs what the nation achieved during World War II.

While the media has begun providing more coverage of global warming, that coverage is still a long way from adequately informing the public about the urgency of the problem and the huge effort needed to avert catastrophe. The media's miscoverage of global warming makes it much less likely that the country will act in time, and it is a key reason why only a third of Americans understand that global warming will "pose a serious threat to you or your way of life in your lifetime," according to a March 2006 Gallup Poll.

We don't have any Edward R. Murrows today, at least not on the climate issue. What we do have is a declining number of science reporters, and only a handful of those are dedicated to covering climate. Worse, the media has the misguided belief that the pursuit of "balance" is superior to the pursuit of truth—even in science journalism. The result is that global warming and its impacts are systematically underreported and misreported.

WHEN BALANCE ISN'T BALANCED

In November 2005, *Meet the Press* with Tim Russert held a remarkable discussion on the threat of avian bird flu. Russert began with a quote from Senate Majority Leader Bill Frist, a physician, who laid out an ominous scenario of "a fast-moving highly contagious disease that wipes out 5 percent of the world population," which the senator said had already happened once, in 1918. The Frist quote ends: "This glimpse into the past might be a preview to our future. An avian flu pandemic is no longer a question of if but a question of when."

Russert then spent a half hour discussing bird flu with Michael Leavitt, President Bush's secretary of Health and Human Services; Michael Ryan, director of the World Health Organization's Epidemic and Pandemic Alert and Response Department; Dr. Julie Gerberding, director of the Centers for Disease Control and Prevention; and Dr. Anthony Fauci, director of the National Institute of Allergy and Infectious Diseases. All four of these experts expressed great concern about avian bird flu and the urgent need for preemptive action.

Russert did not interview anyone who felt that the threat from bird flu had been exaggerated (and such experts do exist). He did not interview anyone who questioned the science of evolution, even though this bird flu can't become a pandemic unless the virus mutates to allow easy human-to-human transmission and even though the Bush administration itself has questioned the teaching of evolution in schools. As one evolutionary biologist wrote in 2005, "If we're unlucky, this virus will give us a nasty demonstration of evolution in action."

Russert asked Fauci how much of a possibility a pandemic flu really was and how worried should people be. Fauci, one of the country's most respected medical experts, pointed out that it wasn't a high-probability event, then added, *"But when you're dealing with preparing for something in which the consequences are unimaginable, you must assume, A, the worst-case scenario, and B, that it's going to happen"*(emphasis added).

That is precisely how we should think about global warming. The threat it poses to our nation and our planet is certainly as grave as that posed by avian flu, and potentially much more devastating. The consequences may be longer-term, but the time to start acting is equally short. And the scientific consensus about global warming is as strong as or stronger than that surrounding the possibility of a bird flu pandemic. Yet there has never been a *Meet the Press* devoted to global warming with four experts all warning the public of the looming danger and the urgent need for action.

I discussed the strong consensus on global warming in chapter 1. To repeat the key point, as *Science* editor in chief Donald Kennedy said back in 2001, "Consensus as strong as the one that has developed around this topic is rare in science." A 2004 analysis of nearly 1,000 peer-reviewed scientific studies concluded that "politicians, economists, journalists, and others may have the impression of confusion, disagreement, or discord among climate scientists, but that impression is incorrect."

This remarkable consensus creates a very large problem for the media when they choose to cover a scientific matter as a political debate and give equal time to "both sides." As long as a handful of U.S. scientists, most receiving funds from the fossil fuel industry, get equal time with hundreds of the world's leading climate scientists, the public inevitably ends up with a misimpression about the state of our scientific understanding. Nor can that ever change as long as the Denyers refuse to alter their views in the face of the evidence and the media keep refusing to weigh the evidence or present the consensus accurately.

This isn't real balance. It is the media putting its thumb on the scale.

Sadly, even the most respected newspapers fall into this trap, as seen in the study "Balance as Bias: Global Warming and the U.S. Prestige Press," which analyzed more than 600 hard-news articles published from 1990 to 2002 in the *New York Times, Washington Post, Los Angeles Times,* and *Wall Street Journal.* The study found that

- 53 percent of the articles gave roughly equal attention to the views that humans contribute to global warming and that climate change results exclusively from natural fluctuations
- 35 percent emphasized the role of humans while presenting both sides of the debate
- 6 percent emphasized doubts about the claim that human-caused global warming exists

■ Only 6 percent emphasized the predominant scientific view that humans are contributing to Earth's temperature increases

The authors found a "significant difference between the scientific community discourse and the US prestige press discourse." As an example of balance as bias, consider these lines from an April 2001 *Los Angeles Times* article:

The issue of climate change has been a topic of intense scientific and political debate for the past decade. Today, there is agreement that the Earth's air and oceans are warming, but disagreement over whether that warming is the result of natural cycles, such as those that regulate the planet's periodic ice ages, or caused by industrial pollutants from automobiles and smokestacks.

Notice how science and politics become merged, and the reader is left with the distinct impression that there is an intense scientific disagreement about whether the warming has a natural or a human-made cause. But there is no such disagreement. Few climate scientists doubt that most of the warming is human-caused and, equally important, that human-caused warming will increasingly dwarf all natural trends.

The media's pursuit of "balance," coupled with their growing desire for drama and entertainment, has left them vulnerable to targeted campaigns of misinformation. To create doubt on any scientific issue, all you have to do is find a few credible-sounding people to present your side, and no matter how many people are on the other side, you've got instant debate. This exploitable flaw in the coverage of science has not gone unnoticed by the global-warming Delayers. As the *New York Times* reported in April 1998, the fossil fuel industry developed a draft plan "to spend millions of dollars to convince the public that the [Kyoto] environmental accord is based on shaky science." Its major strategy was "a campaign to recruit a cadre of scientists who share the industry's views of climate science and to train them in public relations so they can help convince journalists, politicians and the public that the risk of global warming is too uncertain to justify controls on greenhouse gases like carbon dioxide."

The amount of media coverage of global warming has improved in the last few years, likely because the weight of scientific evidence plus the consensus about the dangers of inaction have become too strong to ignore. Yet most articles on climate are still confusing or misleading or both. Let's look at a few 2006 articles from the *Washington Post*, a newspaper that has done some of the media's best reporting on global warming.

Consider a short January 23 article on a *Nature* paper that "suggests that melting mountain glaciers and ice caps, which account for about a quarter of the expected sea level rise, will produce about half the level of sea level rise by 2100 others have predicted." You might expect the article would be balanced with an expert explaining why scientists are far more concerned with observations of accelerated disintegration of the Greenland and Antarctic ice sheets, which contain far more ice and which this study doesn't examine at all. Instead, the article quotes Pat Michaels, of the Marshall and Cato Institutes, both funded by ExxonMobil to advance the Denyers' agenda.

Michaels is quoted saying the *Nature* paper "is one of many recent papers pointing towards reductions in sea level rise in this century due to more refined models of ice balance"—a claim that is best described as the opposite of the truth. Indeed, six days later, on January 29, the *Post* itself got the story straight and published a front-page article noting, "Most scientists agree human activity is causing Earth to warm," so "the central debate has shifted to whether climate change is progressing so rapidly that, within decades, humans may be helpless to slow or reverse" key impacts such as "dramatic sea level rise by the end of the century that would take tens of thousands of years to reverse."

A July 2006 coal-industry memo revealed how the industry is funding Michaels as part of its strategy to stop action on global warming. The Associated Press led its story, "Coal-burning utilities are passing the hat for one of the few remaining scientists skeptical of the global warming harm caused by industries that burn fossil fuels." That article also explained how Michaels misrepresented James Hansen's testimony in an effort to discredit him (see chapter 5).

Consider a May 3, 2006, *Washington Post* article on how the new conservative government in Canada is cutting programs to reduce greenhouse gas emissions. The article explained that in the Kyoto Protocol, countries "pledged to meet quotas to reduce the carbon dioxide emissions that many scientists believe are warming Earth, melting glaciers and brewing more intense storms." Such misleading sentences serve only to confuse the public. The overwhelming majority of scientists believe carbon dioxide emissions are warming the earth and melting glaciers, as the earlier January 29 *Post* article had noted. And the scientific literature is clear that global warming makes storms more intense; the debate on this issue is primarily over *how much* more intense.

The article balances quotes from Canadians who believe the country should take action on climate change with quotes from Morten Paulsen of Friends of Science, a group of Delayers and Denyers with links to the fossil fuel industry. According to Paulsen, "We shouldn't be spending billions of dollars fighting a problem that may not be there." The article states, "He said that arguments that global warming is caused by carbon dioxide are unproven and that 'we believe they are a white elephant.'"

Arguments that global warming is caused by carbon dioxide are *not* unproven. Countless studies have been published on this, all major scientific bodies that have looked at the question acknowledge this as a fact, and it would be hard to find 1 scientist in 10,000 who would agree with Paulsen's claim. Would the *Post* quote someone denying that we had landed on the moon? Would the *Post* quote a tobacco-company lobbyist saying, "Arguments that cancer is caused by cigarette are unproven"?

Consider another *Washington Post* article from the same day, May 3, on a major government study that "undermines one of the key arguments of climate change skeptics, concluding that there is no statistically significant conflict between measures of global warming on the earth's surface and in the atmosphere." For more than a decade the Denyers have argued that global warming could not be happening because the measured warming of the earth's surface was apparently not matched by the satellite measurements of the atmosphere's temperature —measurements first analyzed and reported by University of Alabama researchers led by John Christy. Christy's analysis had suggested a temperature *decrease* in the satellite data. As one encyclopedia notes, however, other scientists "over the years have shown errors in his interpretation of the data which has slowly and consistently increased his results."

Christy, like Michaels, is among a handful of scientists regularly quoted by the media for "balance." While the number of scientists reporting evidence of human-induced climate change multiplies with each passing year, the "balancers" remain a group small enough to fit into a typical home bathroom. Or even its shower. Christy contributed to a 2002 book called *Global Warming and Other Eco-Myths*, published by the Competitive Enterprise Institute, which is funded by ExxonMobil.

Science magazine begins its article on that same 2006 government study: "Global warming contrarians can cross out one of their last talking points." *Science*'s headline trumpets the news: "No Doubt About It, the World Is Warming." Such a stunning vindication for climate scientists needs no quote from Denyers for phony balance. The *Post,* however, spends nearly half the article quoting James Inhofe and John Christy dismissing the relevance of the blockbuster report. Inhofe's spokesman repeats the discredited natural-cycles argument, which the *Post* article does not rebut. Christy claims the earth isn't heating up rapidly enough for him to be very worried, an assertion the article also chooses not to rebut. So an article that should read as a crushing blow to global-warming Denyers instead becomes a vehicle for them to rehash dubious and discredited arguments, with little or no check by the newspaper.

The *Science* article isn't quite perfect. It says the new report, though commissioned by the Bush administration, "will not change White House policy." It then paraphrases a White House spokesperson: "President George W. Bush believes that greenhouse gas emissions can be brought down through better use of energy while the understanding of climate science continues to improve." If Bush really believes that, he has never publicly stated it, nor has he pursued a single policy to achieve reductions in emissions through better use of energy. The spokesperson, or the reporter, may have been confused or mistaken—or meant that Bush believes greenhouse gas emissions *intensity* (per unit GDP) can be brought down through better use of energy. Either way, someone reading the article would be left with the mistaken impression that Bush is actually pursuing energy strategies that reduce emissions.

I can't see why serous news outlets would quote Michaels or Christy on climate science. Those that do quote Michaels should follow AP's lead in explaining that he has been intentionally misleading and is heavily subsidized by the coal industry. Those that quote Christy should explain how he consistently misanalyzed key data and then trumpeted his mistaken conclusions as proof that global warming wasn't happening, long after other scientists explained that he was wrong.

Then there is meteorologist Bill Gray, who testified at a 2005

Senate hearing that we will be headed back into a period of global cooling in a few years and that climate science is just a hoax created by the scientific community to get more funding. Gray is typically described as a great hurricane forecaster, as in a 2006 *Washington Post Magazine* cover story. You would never know from such coverage that shortly after the 2004 hurricane season, he predicted, "We probably won't see another season like this for a hundred years." He was off by only 99 years.

How consistently wrong do you have to be before the media stops quoting you as an expert?

"If your mother says she loves you, check it out" was the adage journalists like my father were schooled on. Be skeptical of even the most obvious truths and check your facts, yes, but nowhere does the motto say to ignore the truth or assume there is none. Today the media's motto seems to be "If your mother says she loves you, get a quote from the neighborhood bully."

EVERYBODY TALKS ABOUT THE WEATHER

One area of media miscoverage in this country deserves particular mention. The key message about what is happening has been muffled. That message is: Climate change is a driving force behind the increasing amount of extreme weather we are experiencing.

Consider a *New York Times* article from July 2003, "Records Fall as Phoenix All but Redefines the Heat Wave," highlighting daytime temperatures of 117°F and nighttime temperatures of 96°F—"the hottest night in Phoenix history." The article never suggests even the possibility that global warming has contributed to redefining the heat wave or that scientists expect such heat waves to become not only more commonplace but more severe.

Consider a *Washington Post* article from the same month, "Coastal Louisiana Drowning in Gulf: Encroaching Salt Water Is

Threatening the State's Economy and Homes." The article discusses a variety of reasons Louisiana annually loses more than 25 square miles of coastland to the Gulf of Mexico, such as efforts to control the flow of the Mississippi River. Nowhere does the article mention even the possibility that climate change has contributed to the problem or that future sea-level rise, left unchecked, may undermine all efforts to find a long-term solution.

Consider a January 2006 NBC News report on extreme weather titled "Meltdown." The report starts in New York, which in midwinter was experiencing springlike weather with temperature in the 50s. It shows reporter Mike Taibbi hitting golf balls in a short-sleeve shirt and getting advice from a golfing pro. After jumping to footage of unusual weather around the country and the world, Taibbi talks to NBC meteorologist Jeff Ranieri:

> TAIBBI: But the unseasonable weather isn't restricted to the Northeast. With twenty-five straight days of downpour, Seattle and the Pacific Northwest are approaching rainfall records. Extreme heat and lack of rain have fed the wildfires tormenting parts of Oklahoma and Texas. Rare ocean tornadoes have been seen off the Florida coast. And in usually frigid Chicago, kids eating ice cream cones watch flamingos and giraffes take the sun. . . . Around the world, more extreme weather; the snowiest winters in generations in parts of Japan and China. The cause of all this?
>
> RANIERI: *I wouldn't say that this is, uh, a long-term pattern that we're stuck in. It's just . . . it's Mother Nature and it's just how it's working in the beginning of January.*
>
> TAIBBI: Back to the *thoroughly enjoyable extreme weather* in New York . . . [Emphasis added.]

Wrong, wrong, and wrong. As the chapter 2 discussion of the U.S. Climate Extremes Index makes clear, it *is* a long-term pattern.

The pattern is *not* what we expect from Mother Nature, but it is precisely what we *do* expect from global warming. And while it may be enjoyable in wintertime for New Yorkers, it is catastrophic for those suffering from flooding and wildfires.

If the media's coverage of weather extremes does not improve in the next few years, we will have no chance of avoiding the disintegration of the great ice sheets. Ironically—and as we have seen throughout the book, irony is the defining characteristic of the global-warming debate—the only truly prophetic element of the NBC story was its title, "Meltdown."

Such bad coverage has consequences: Even sophisticated people are left uninformed. Consider Lisa Murkowski, Republican senator from Alaska, the state most strongly hit by the effects of climate change, who sits on the Senate Environment Committee and casts votes that determine the nation's climate policy. Near the end of a September 2005 hearing on climate science, she pointed out that Alaska had experienced "continuous erosion of our coastal villages" and the "warmest summer that we've seen in 400 years." What does she think of all this? "I'm sitting up in Alaska where I can see that we're experiencing climate change. *I'm not going so far as to say it is global warming. But we see climate change*" (emphasis added).

Why take any serious action now if it all might just be a natural event, purely a coincidence that it is occurring at the same time that we're putting into the atmosphere massive amounts of greenhouse gases that scientists predicted would cause these exact changes?

How did the media coverage get so bad? The story should be as simple and logical as the story about avian flu. We have an overwhelming consensus among our leading scientists that global warming is happening and humans are the primary cause. We know that one of the earliest expected impacts of global warming is an increase in extreme weather events. We have a painfully obvious increase in extreme weather.

We even have the federal agency in charge of climatic data, the

National Climatic Data Center, with a comprehensive statistical measure showing that the weather has actually gotten more extreme—and which explained more than ten years ago that the chances that this increase was due to factors *other* than global warming, such as "natural climate variability," was statistically very small.

Yet my guess is that you've never heard of the U.S. Climate Extremes Index, even though it was explicitly created to take a complicated subject ("multivariate and multidimensional climate changes in the United States") and make it more easily understood by American citizens and policy makers. I follow this subject of the connection between climate change and extreme weather very closely, and yet, until 2006, I had not seen a single mention of the index in the media or even in a scientific paper since its original introduction back in 1995.

Story after story in the media appear with no link whatsoever between extreme weather and global warming, no link to the human-made trend that will ultimately transform all our lives. Even the monster U.S. heat wave at the end of July and early August 2006 generated few stories that mentioned global warming. I was actually interviewed by a major national news outlet about this heat wave. They were interested in my work on urban heat islands, whereby dark roofs and asphalt pavement and the loss of shade trees have made cities much hotter than they would otherwise be (see chapter 6). Although I discussed how global warming is making this kind of devastating heat wave more likely and more intense—and combining with the heat-island effect to make cities increasingly inhospitable in the summer—they did not use any of these comments. They wanted only a story on how heat islands affect heat waves.

What are the reasons for this flawed and incomplete reporting?

One reason is that the Delayers have been hard at work criticizing the media for making the link between extreme weather and climate change—and they've succeeded in intimidating them. In his 2004 book, *Boiling Point*, Pulitzer Prize winning journalist Ross Gelbspan wonders why journalists covering extreme weather events don't use the statement "Scientists associate this pattern of violent weather with global warming." He reports that a few years earlier he had asked "a top editor at a major TV network" why they didn't make this link. The reply was: "We did that. Once. But it triggered a barrage of complaints from the Global Climate Coalition [then the major anti-global-warming lobbying group of the fossil fuel indus-try] to our top executives at the network."

The lobbyists argued then, as they do now, that you can't prove that any individual weather event is caused by climate change. But that is irrelevant to the two key points: The pattern is exactly what we expect from climate change, and we can expect to see more vio-lent weather events in the future if emissions trends are not reversed soon.

Another reason the media gets the climate extreme-weather link wrong: Most meteorologists in this country, including virtually every TV meteorologist, are not experts on global warming. As one climate scientist explained to me:

> Meteorologists are not required to take a course in climate change, this is not part of the NOAA/NWS [National Oceanic and Atmospheric Administration/National Weather Service] certification requirements, so university programs don't re-quire the course (even if they offer it). So *we have been educat-ing generations of meteorologists who know nothing at all about climate change.* [Emphasis added.]

Asking a meteorologist to explain the cause of recent extreme weather is like asking your family doctor what the chances are for an avian flu pandemic in the next few years or asking a Midwest sheriff about the prospects of nuclear terrorism. The answer might be interesting, but it wouldn't be one I'd stake my family's life on.

A final reason you don't see the link made here in this country as much as you should is that the environmental community itself decided in the mid-1990s to *deemphasize* it. Yes, you read that right. Many environmentalists actually made a conscious decision to stop talking about what are arguably the most visible and visceral signs of warming for most people. A number of senior environmentalists, including those involved with media outreach, told me at the time that they were tired of being beaten up by the other side on this issue. I thought that was a blunder then, and I still do today.

Peter Teague, Environment Program director for the Nathan Cummings Foundation, wrote about this problem in the summer of 2004 after "the fourth in a series of violent hurricanes [had] just bombarded the Caribbean and Florida." He pointed out "no prominent national leader—environmental or otherwise—has come out publicly to suggest that the recent spate of hurricanes was the result of global warming."

But the ever-worsening reality of climate change together with the diligence of leading climate scientists brought the hurricane-warming link roaring back. As noted in chapter 2, leading scientists from MIT, the Georgia Institute of Technology, and the National Center for Atmospheric Research (NCAR) published a series of scientific articles on the rise of intense hurricanes—in what turned out to be the most devastating hurricane season in U.S. history, 2005. And in the months following Katrina, the scientific basis for the connection between global warming and intense hurricanes has grown even stronger.

The media still do not cover the story well. In a major article on climate change in April 2006, the *New York Times* actually claimed, "Few scientists agree with the idea that the recent spate of potent hurricanes, European heat waves, African drought and other weather extremes are, in essence, our fault." Few? That doesn't gibe with the dozens of climate scientists I talked to while researching this book. They all told me what climate scientists have been telling us so many times before—global warming makes extreme weather events more likely and more destructive.

Again, the story is fairly straightforward. Global tropical sea-surface temperature is increasing as a result of greenhouse warming. Average hurricane intensity increases with increasing tropical sea-surface temperature. The frequency of the most intense hurricanes is increasing globally. So greenhouse warming is causing an increase in global hurricane intensity. True, not every scientist agrees with that conclusion, but fewer and fewer are disagreeing, while more and more are speaking out bluntly. "The hurricanes we are seeing are indeed a direct result of climate change, and it's no longer something we'll see in the future, it's happening now," Greg Holland, an NCAR division director, told the American Meteorological Society's 27th Conference on Hurricanes and Tropical Meteorology in April 2006.

That is what I told my brother, to aid in his decision about whether to rebuild or relocate from the Gulf Coast. That is what everyone making such decisions needs to hear to make an informed choice.

THE STORY OF THE CENTURY: BE *VERY* WORRIED

Most of the media do not get global warming—yet. And that extends from TV and radio to newspaper to magazines to even the most sophisticated policy journals such as *Foreign Affairs,* which routinely publishes major articles on subjects like China and energy with virtually no mention of global warming. One publication, however, has consistently delivered timely and powerful stories on global warming, largely unfettered by faux balance—*Time* magazine.

In April 2006, *Time* published a powerful special report on global warming with a warning on the cover in huge letters, "BE WORRIED. BE *VERY* WORRIED. Climate change isn't some vague future problem—it's already damaging the planet at an alarming pace." One of the most interesting things in the issue was a poll in which 1,000 Americans were asked, "Do you think most scientists agree with one another about global warming, or do you think there is a lot of disagreement on this issue?" Only 35 percent said, "Most agree," while 64 percent said, "A lot of disagreement." As *Time* noted, "Most people aren't aware of the broad scientific consensus on warming." But then how could they be, with other media continually misreporting the subject, insisting that as long as there is one global-warming Denyer, that Denyer deserves equal time with the entire rest of the scientific community?

In a fascinating example of intramedia "balance," *Time*'s rival, *Newsweek,* also published an article on global warming that week. Unlike *Time, Newsweek* devoted almost half of its article to quoting various Denyers and Delayers, claiming, "To be fair, neither side has a monopoly on hot air in this debate," falsely equating one or two mild overstatements by advocates of action on global warming with major campaigns to deny the science entirely and delay action indefinitely.

The *Newsweek* article seeks to downplay the growing concern over warming: "But both the [Elizabeth] Kolbert and [Tim] Flannery books are sober, detailed and alarming without being alarmist." Yet Kolbert's book is titled *Field Notes from a Catastrophe,* and the final sentence is "It may seem impossible to imagine that a technologically advanced society could choose, in essence, to destroy itself, but that is what we are now in the process of doing." Flannery's book warns that if we don't act fast enough to limit greenhouse gas emissions, we will "destroy Earth's life-support systems and destabilise our global civilisation." The result: "Humans are thrust into a projected Dark Ages far more mordant than any that has gone before. . . . These changes could commence as soon as 2050."

Both Kolbert's and Flannery's books strike me as alarming *and* alarmist—as befits any sober and detailed examination of the facts.

The subhead on the *Newsweek* article is "Books, Films and a Slick Ad Campaign Make Global Warming the Topic *Du Jour*." No. Global warming is the topic *du siècle*. And if we don't get a lot more stories, and a lot better stories, on the threat and how to stop it, global warming will be the only story that matters to the next fifty generations of Americans.

CONCLUSION

THE END OF POLITICS

The hottest places in Hell are reserved for those who in time of great moral crises maintain their neutrality.
—attributed to Dante

America is great because she is good. If America ceases to be good, America will cease to be great.
—attributed to Alexis de Tocqueville

G lobal warming will change American life forever and end politics as we know it, probably within your lifetime. How might this play out?

In the best case, we immediately start changing how we use energy in order to preserve the health and well-being—the security—of the next fifty generations. The nation and the world embrace an aggressive multidecade, government-led effort to use existing and near-term clean-energy technologies.

The enabling strategy is energy efficiency—since that generates the savings that pays for the zero-carbon energy sources, like wind power and coal with carbon sequestration. Efficiency keeps the total cost low to consumers and businesses. For utilities, we need a California-style energy-efficiency effort nationwide. For cars and light trucks, we need serious federal standards for high-mileage hybrids that can be plugged in to the electric grid. The goal of all these efforts: keeping global emissions at or below 29 billion metric tons of carbon dioxide (8 billion tons of carbon) for the next several decades—and keeping concentrations well below 550 ppm (a doubling of preindustrial levels) this century.

I have called this scenario Two Political Miracles because it would require a radical conversion of American conservative leaders—first, to completely accept climate science, and second, to strongly embrace climate solutions that they currently view as anathema. I have spent nearly two decades working to achieve this clean-energy future and will continue doing so, because it is the best way to preserve the health and well-being of future generations and to boost energy security while creating millions of clean-energy jobs here at home. Yet none of the more than one hundred people I interviewed for this book considers this in the least bit plausible.

They may be right. Tragically, in the face of the stunning recent evidence that climate change is coming faster and rougher than scientists have expected, many conservatives have chosen to redouble their efforts to deny the science and delay serious action. Consider the words of President Bush in May 2006: "In my judgment, we need to set aside whether or not greenhouse gases have been caused by mankind or because of natural effects." That statement is reminiscent of leaders like Herbert Hoover and Neville Chamberlain who were blind to their nation's gravest threats.

President Bush misspoke. The massive surge in greenhouse gas emissions is clearly caused by humankind—that is not even in dispute. What Bush may have meant to say is "climate change" rather than "greenhouse gases," which is the standard rehashing of the long-discredited "climate change is all just natural cycles" argument. We cannot, however, set aside the overwhelming evidence and solid scientific consensus that humankind is to blame for virtually all of recent climate change because that would mean setting aside the possibility of any serious effort to prevent future catastrophic climate change from human emissions.

Consider two ads launched in May 2006 by the Competitive Enterprise Institute, an oil-industry-funded think tank. One claims that the Greenland and Antarctic ice sheets are increasing in mass due to increased snowfall. The ad conveniently ignores the evidence that both ice sheets are now losing ice at the edges faster than they are gaining mass in the center—and doing so much faster than predicted. As recently as 2001, the international scientific community thought that the great ice sheets would not contribute significantly to sea-level rise this century. But as climatologist Richard Alley warned, also in May 2006, "The ice sheets seem to be shrinking 100 years ahead of schedule."

Both ads end with a rhetorical tagline that would be funny if the stakes weren't so deadly serious: "Carbon dioxide—they call it pollution, we call it Life!" Yes, carbon dioxide is needed for life, as is water. But too much of either can be fatal. Just look at New Orleans and the Gulf Coast. The Competitive Enterprise Institute might just as well have ended its ads, "Après nous le deluge" (*After us, the deluge*)—literally. Under the Competitive Enterprise Institute's banner, we would never take any action whatsoever to reduce carbon dioxide emissions, even to avoid a tripling or quadrupling of preindustrial concentrations. Does the conservative movement really want to side with global-warming pollution over the health and well-being of the next fifty generations?

The conservative Denyers and Delayers are not the only reason America has failed to take up the fight against climate change. "Scientists present the facts about climate change clinically, failing to stress that business-as-usual will transform the planet," leading to as much as 80-feet-higher sea levels, rising "twenty feet or more per century," as NASA's Jim Hansen wrote in 2006.

Progressive politicians have been slow to grasp the overwhelming urgency of the problem. But that is starting to change. Al Gore has launched a major effort to mobilize action, built around his 2006 movie, *An Inconvenient Truth*. Also in 2006, Democrats in both the House and Senate have for the first time introduced legislation that would require reductions in greenhouse gas emissions sufficient to avert catastrophe.

Some major groups that have been on the sidelines, such as evangelical Christians, have begun reconsidering their position on climate. In February 2006, the Evangelical Climate Initiative, a group of more than 85 evangelicals, issued a statement saying, "Human-induced climate change is real," the "consequences of climate change will be significant," and government should immediately pass legislation reducing U.S. carbon dioxide emissions. In response, however, key conservative evangelicals launched the Interfaith Stewardship Alliance, "which has aligned itself with prominent global warming skeptics, including John Christy and . . . Patrick Michaels," as an April 2006 news story explained. In July 2006, the Heritage Foundation hosted an event at which the alliance released a letter, signed by more than 100 evangelicals, questioning the science of climate change; the letter claimed that global warming will have mild and possibly "helpful" consequences and opposed any "government-mandated carbon dioxide emissions reductions," saying they "would cause greater harm than good to humanity."

So I do believe that for all of the failings of the groups seeking strong action on global warming, the conservative Denyers and Delayers are the main reason America lacks the consensus and the political will to take up the fight against catastrophic climate change. They actively spread misinformation. They block those seeking to take action at a state, national, and global level. We will not be able to prevent catastrophic warming without conservatives embracing a dramatically different view of energy policy, international negotiations, and the role of government.

For now, the political success of the global warming Delayers must be acknowledged. No proposal to reduce U.S. greenhouse gas emissions has ever achieved a majority vote in either chamber of Congress. America will almost certainly take no serious action on climate under President Bush, and he may very well block any serious efforts by other nations. Long after Bush leaves office, conservatives in Congress will hold enough strength to block significant action on climate, should they so choose. This suggests that America will at best take some half measures to slow our emissions growth in the next decade, while China and other developing nations continue their breathtaking emissions growth largely unchecked. That will put us on the brink of disaster.

THE RECKONING

Soils, tundra, tropical forests, and oceans currently serve as sinks that absorb nearly half the carbon we are spewing into the atmosphere. The tundra by itself today contains about as much carbon as the atmosphere, much of it in the form of methane, which is more than twenty times as potent at trapping heat as carbon dioxide. At 550 parts per million of atmospheric carbon dioxide concentrations, a doubling of preindustrial levels, we are likely to lose most of the tundra and most of the Amazon rain forest, and with them any hope of avoiding a tripling, which would ruin this planet for the next fifty generations.

But barring the Two Political Miracles, global emissions will hit 37 billion metric tons of carbon dioxide a year in the early 2020s, while global concentrations hit about 430 ppm, rising 3 ppm a year. We will have vastly overshot a safe level of carbon emissions, and misallocated trillions of dollars in capital constructing conventional coal plants, producing unconventional oil, and manufacturing inefficient vehicles. At that point, if we wanted to avoid climate catastrophe while avoiding economic collapse, we would have no choice but to scrap most of this polluting capital long before the end of its natural life, while replacing it with clean, efficient capital at a rapid rate.

This national (and global) reindustrialization effort would be on the scale of what we did during World War II, except it would last far longer. "In nine months, the entire capacity of the prolific automobile industry had been converted to the production of tanks, guns, planes, and bombs," explains Doris Kearns Goodwin in her 1994 book on the World War II home front, *No Ordinary Time.* "The industry that once built 4 million cars a year was now building three fourths of the nation's aircraft engines, one half of all tanks, and one third of all machine guns."

The scale of the war effort was astonishing. The physicist Edward Teller tells the story of how Niels Bohr had insisted in 1939 that making a nuclear bomb would take an enormous national effort, one without any precedent. When Bohr came to see the huge Los Alamos facility years later, he said to Teller, "You see, I told you it couldn't be done without turning the whole country into a factory. You have done just that." And we did it all in less than 5 years.

But of course we had been attacked at Pearl Harbor, the world was at war, and the entire country was united against a common enemy. This made possible tax increases, rationing of items such as tires and gasoline, comprehensive wage and price controls, a War Production Board with broad powers (it could mandate what clothing could be made for civilians), and a Controlled Material Plan that set allotments of critical materials (steel, copper, and aluminum) for different contractors.

Such desperate and undesirable national actions are a long, long way from mandated controls on carbon dioxide emissions or requiring that 20 percent of all power come from renewable sources—neither of which conservatives currently support. The ultimate irony would be if conservative disdain for straightforward government-led solutions *today* forced the country into far more intrusive and onerous government solutions *tomorrow.*

And what happens if the nation and the world fail to take serious action in the 2020s? In the 2030s, record-breaking heat waves and searing droughts will be the norm. Relentless super-hurricane seasons, coupled with the reality of accelerating sea-level rise, will change the landscape of the Gulf Coast and the eastern seaboard. We will simply stop rebuilding most coastal cities destroyed by hurricanes. In this Planetary Purgatory, everyone will realize that the world has but one great task—stopping Greenland and the West Antarctic Ice Sheet from melting, avoiding runaway growth in greenhouse gas concentrations.

Politics as we know it will end. Nonessential efforts, such as the manned space program, will be shut down as politicians direct most of the nation's vast resources toward dealing with the climate. The problem with waiting until the 2030s is that carbon dioxide concentrations are likely to be over 450 ppm and climbing more than 3 ppm a year. At that point, our fate will be largely out of our hands and in the hands of the vicious carbon cycles. Most likely we will be headed irrevocably toward Hell and High Water—a tripling of concentrations or worse, warming of the inland United States of 10°F or worse, sea-level rise exceeding 1 foot a decade, widespread ecosystem collapse, and mass extinctions.

The suffering that my brother and his family and the hundreds of thousands of victims of Hurricane Katrina experienced will be magnified a thousandfold in a world with half a billion environmental refugees, water and food shortages affecting a billion or more people, and worldwide civil strife.

We must pay any price and bear any burden to avoid this fate.

What would have to happen in the next decade to create the political will needed to transform the entire country into a carbon-reducing factory? I see two possibilities. The first requires that a major climatic event or series of events occur. A portion of the West Antarctic Ice Sheet could disintegrate rapidly, raising sea levels 20 inches. Or the country could be hit by the kind of murderous heat wave that overwhelmed Europe in 2003. Or we could experience several more hurricane seasons like 2005. Or, more likely, all of those, since the national and global heat wave of 2006 does not appear to be changing U.S. climate politics.

Second, the public—you—could simply demand change. This is vastly preferable to waiting for multiple disasters. Global warming is the gravest threat to our long-term security. More and more people are coming to this realization every day. When people ask me what they should do, I reply, "Get informed, get outraged, and then get political." I think it is a good idea to take steps to reduce your own greenhouse gas emissions, purchasing a hybrid vehicle, buying Energy Star home appliances, buying renewable power, encouraging your workplace to take action—mainly so that you can see that taking action is not that hard.

You must become a climate champion, a single-issue voter. You must take whatever action you can. You must use whatever influence you have wherever it would make a difference, even if it is only to educate the people around you.

I do believe that if we fail to act in time, it will be the single biggest regret any of us has at the end of our lives.

So you can see why my hair *is* on fire. I hope yours is, too.

ACKNOWLEDGMENTS

While the final judgments in the book are my own, I am exceedingly grateful to everyone who shared their ideas with me: Richard Alley, John Atcheson, Peter Barrett, Bill Becker, Dan Becker, Alec Brooks, Brian Castelli, Joseph Cirincione, Ana Unruh Cohen, Jon Coifman, Bob Corell, Judith Curry, Noah S. Diffenbaugh, Kerry Emanuel, Alex Farrell, Tim Flannery, Louis Fortier, Peter Fox-Penner, Andrew Frank, S. Julio Friedmann, Tore Furevik, David Gardiner, Dean Grodzins, Jason Grumet, Hank Habicht, David Hamilton, Kate Hampton, James Hansen, David Hawkins, Bracken Hendricks, John Holdren, Roland Hwang, Andrew Jones, Chris Jones, Tina Kaarsberg, Dan Kammen, Thomas Karl, David Keith, Henry Kelly, Melanie Kenderdine, Felix Kramer, Kalee Kreider, David Lawrence, Mark Levine, Lee Lynd, Jerry Mahlman, Wieslaw Maslowski, Jan Mazurek, Alden Meyer, Ron Minsk, Ernest Moniz, Philip Mote, Walter Munk, Joan Ogden, Michael Oppenheimer, Jonathan Overpeck, John Passacantando, John Podesta, Arthur Rosenfeld, Doug Rotman, Gavin Schmidt, Stephen Schneider, Dan Schrag, Laurence Smith, Robert Socolow, Kevin Trenberth, Peter Webster, Robert Williams, James Woolsey, Paul Wuebben, and Jay Zwally.

I am grateful to James Fallows for suggesting that I write this book. Special thanks go to those who reviewed all or part of it: Ana Unruh Cohen, Judith Curry, Jay Gulledge, Greg Kats, and Steve Silberstein. I would particularly like to thank Pete O'Connor for his help on research and references, and John Atcheson for his help and support. I would like to thank the Hewlett Foundation for its support of my work.

I owe a permanent debt to my mother for applying her unmatched language and editing skills to innumerable drafts. I am exceedingly grateful to Peter Matson, my agent, for his unwavering efforts on behalf of my work and my writing. He found this book the perfect home.

Henry Ferris, my world-class editor at William Morrow, improved the book tremendously. I would like to thank him and the rest of the staff at William Morrow for their enthusiastic support of this book from the very beginning.

Finally, special thanks go to my wife, Patricia Sinicropi, whose unconditional love and support provide me unlimited inspiration every day. Words cannot express what a remarkable person she is.

NOTES

INTRODUCTION

1 *"We are on"*: James Hansen, "Is There Still Time to Avoid 'Dangerous Anthropogenic Interference' with Global Climate?" (paper presented at the American Geophysical Union, San Francisco, December 6, 2005).

1 *"The ice sheets"*: Richard Alley, American Meteorological Society seminar, Washington, D.C., May 3, 2006.

2 *March 2006 Gallup Poll*: Gallup Poll, March 13–16, 2006, available online at http://www.pollingreport.com/enviro.htm.

5 *advanced acoustic techniques*: Joseph Romm, "Applications of Normal Mode Analysis to Ocean Acoustic Tomography" (Ph.D. diss., Massachusetts Institute of Technology, researched at the Scripps Institution of Oceanography, 1987).

6 *"straw that breaks"*: Kevin Trenberth (American Meteorological Society seminar, Washington, D.C., October 25, 2005).

7 *National Academy of Sciences*: Walter Sullivan, "Scientists Fear Heavy Use of Coal May Bring Adverse Shift in Climate," *New York Times,* July 25, 1977.

CHAPTER ONE: THE CLIMATE BEAST

11 *"The paleoclimate record"*: Wallace S. Broecker, "Cooling the Tropics," *Nature* 376, no. 6357 (July 20, 1995): 212–13.

11 *"The ongoing Arctic"*: Louis Fortier, "The Arctic as a Bellwether for Climate Change" (paper presented at the Arctic Climate Symposium, Washington, D.C., June 15, 2006).

11 *"hypertext history"*: American Institute of Physics website, www.aip.org/history/climate/.

12 *"the stated degree"*: National Research Council, *Climate Change Science: An Analysis of Some Key Questions* (Washington, D.C.: National Academies Press, 2001).

12 *"Consensus as strong"*: Donald Kennedy, "An Unfortunate U-Turn on Carbon," *Science* 291, no. 5513 (March 20, 2001): 2515. See also S. Fred Singer, "Editor Bias on Climate Change?" and Donald Kennedy's response, *Science* 301, no. 5633 (August 1, 2003): 595–96.

12 Science *published:* Naomi Oreskes, "Beyond the Ivory Tower: The Scientific Consensus on Climate Change," *Science* 306, no. 5702 (December 3, 2004): 1686.

13 *"Evidence of global"*: Robert Kunzig, "Turning Point," *Discover*, January 2005: 26–28.

13 *"There can no longer"*: James Hansen, "Answers About the Earth's Energy Imbalance," Earth Institute at Columbia University, 2005, available online at www.earthinstitute.columbia.edu/news/2005/story11-04-05_html; James Hansen et al., "Earth's Energy Imbalance: Confirmation and Implications," *Science* 308, no. 5727 (June 3, 2005): 1431–35.

13 *a joint statement:* "Joint Science Academies' Statement: Global Response to Climate Change," June 7, 2005, available online at http://nationalacademies.org/onpi/06072005.pdf.

14 *heat, infrared radiation:* Wikipedia, s.v. "greenhouse effect," http://en.wikipedia.org/wiki/Greenhouse_effect.

15 *ideal for us humans:* Glass greenhouses achieve most of their enhanced warming by physically stopping hot air from leaving the enclosure. The atmospheric greenhouse effect is thus a different type of process, since it relies on gases such as carbon dioxide trapping infrared radiation.

16 *Figure 1:* Jean-Rubert Petit et al., "Historical Isotropic Temperature Record from the Vostok Ice Core," January 2000, Carbon Dioxide Information Analysis Center, Oak Ridge National Laboratory, available online at http://cdiac.esd.ornl.gov/trends/temp/vostok/jouz_tem.htm, and based on the following studies: Jean Jouzel et al., "Vostok Ice Core: A Continuous Isotope Temperature Record Over the Last Climatic Cycle (160,000 Years)," *Nature* 329, no. 6138 (October 1, 1987): 403–8; "Extending the Vostok Ice-Core Record of Palaeoclimate to the Penultimate Glacial Period," *Nature* 364, no. 6436 (July 29, 1993): 407–12; "Climatic Interpretation of the Recently Extended Vostok Ice Records," *Climate Dynamics* 12, no. 8 (June 1996): 513–21; and Jean-Rubert Petit et al., "Climate and Atmospheric History of the

Past 420,000 Years from the Vostok Ice Core, Antarctica," *Nature* 399, no. 6735 (June 3, 1999): 429–36.

16 *"Recent scientific"*: National Research Council, *Abrupt Climate Change: Inevitable Surprises* (Washington, D.C.: National Academies Press, 2002). See also Jonathan Adams et al., "Sudden Climate Transitions During the Quaternary," *Progress in Physical Geography* 23 (March 1999): 1–36.

17 *"in periods as short"*: Ibid.

17 *"Abrupt climate changes"*: Ibid.

18 *white summer ice cap:* Andrew C. Revkin, "Arctic Ice Cap Shrank Sharply This Summer, Experts Say," *New York Times,* September 28, 2005.

18 *2005 study:* Brian Soden et al., "The Radiative Signature of Upper Tropospheric Moistening," *Science* 310, no. 5749 (November 4, 2005): 841–44.

18 *this is precisely:* Petit et al., "Historical Isotropic Temperature."

18 *The warming appears:* Nicholas Caillon et al., "Timing of Atmospheric CO_2 and Antarctic Temperature Changes Across Termination III," *Science* 299, no. 5613 (March 14, 2003); 1728–31.

19 *Figure 2:* Temperature variation from Petit et al., "Historical Isotropic Temperature Record." CO_2 concentrations from Jean-Marc Barnola et al., *Historical CO_2 Record from the Vostok Ice Core,* January 2003, Carbon Dioxide Information Analysis Center, Oak Ridge National Laboratory, available online at http://cdiac.esd.ornl.gov/ftp/trends/co2/vostok.icecore.co2.

19 *a 2-mile-long:* Urs Siegenthaler et al., "Stable Carbon Cycle–Climate Relationship During the Late Pleistocene," *Science* 310, no. 5752 (November 25, 2005): 1313–17.

19 *"That a number of":* Gavin Schmidt, post on RealClimate website, November 24, 2005, www.realclimate.org/index.php?p=221.

20 *Carbon dioxide levels:* Richard Black, "CO_2 'Highest for 650,000 Years,'" BBC News, November 24, 2005, available online at http://news.bbc .co.uk/2/hi/science/nature/4467420.stm.

20 *Eemian interglacial:* James Hansen, "A Slippery Slope," *Climate Change* 68, no. 3 (February 2005): 269–79; and "Is There Still Time."

20 *The last time Earth:* Hansen, "A Slippery Slope."

21 *1,100 billion tons:* Gregg Marland, Thomas A. Boden, and Robert I. Andres, "Global, Regional, and National CO_2 Emissions," in *Trends: A Compendium of Data on Global Change,* Carbon Dioxide Information Analysis Center, Oak Ridge National Laboratory, U.S. Department of Energy, available online at http://cdiac.esd.ornl.gov/trends/emis/tre_glob.htm.

21 *more than 26 billion tons:* An additional 4 billion tons of carbon dioxide is released annually from land-use changes (mainly burning and decomposition of forest biomass). See Stephen Bernow et al., *The Path to Carbon Dioxide–Free Power* (Washington, D.C.: Tellus Institute and the Center for Energy and Climate Solutions, for the World Wildlife Federation, June 2003).

21 *2 ppm a year:* National Oceanic and Atmospheric Administration ESRL Global Monitoring Division website, http://www.cmdl.noaa.gov/ccgg/trends/co2_data_mlo.php. Based on Charles David Keeling et al., "Atmospheric Carbon Dioxide Variations at Mauna Loa Observatory, Hawaii," *Tellus* 28 (1976): 538–51; and Kirk W. Thoning, Pieter Tans, and Walter D. Komhyr, "Atmospheric Carbon Dioxide at Mauna Loa Observatory 2: Analysis of the NOAA GMCC Data, 1974–1985," *Journal of Geophysical Research* 94 (1989): 8549–65.

21 *another 0.6°C:* James Hansen et al., "Earth's Energy Imbalance: Confirmation and Implications," *Science* 308, no. 5727 (June 3, 2005): 1431–35, originally published online by *Science* Express, April 28, 2005, www.sciencemag.org/scienceexpress/recent.dtl.

21 *nearly 60 percent:* Hansen, "Is There Still Time."

22 *more than 50 percent:* U.S. Department of Energy, Energy Information Administration, *Annual Energy Outlook 2006*, DOE/EIA 0383 (2006): 71–79, available online at http://www.eia.doe.gov/oiaf/index.html.

22 *2004* Science *magazine article:* Stephen Pacala and Robert Socolow, "Stabilization Wedges: Solving the Climate Problem for the Next 50 Years with Current Technologies," *Science* 305, no. 5686 (August 13, 2004): 968–72.

23 *store that* CO_2 *underground:* Robert Socolow, "Stabilization Wedges: Mitigation Tools for the Next Half-Century" (paper presented at the Global Roundtable on Climate Change, New York, November 14, 2005).

24 *"humanity already possesses":* Pacala and Socolow, "Stabilization Wedges."

26 *climate could be even:* Richard A. Kerr, "Climate Change: Three Degrees of Consensus," *Science* 305, no. 5686 (August 13, 2004): 932–34.

CHAPTER TWO: 2000–2025: REAP THE WHIRLWIND

27 *"I don't see any":* Richard Bradley, "Rain Man," *Plenty*, February/March 2006: 33.

27 *"On our current":* Judith Curry, personal communication, 2006.

28 *On August 28:* The description of Hurricane Katrina in this section is from

Axel Graumann et al., *Hurricane Katrina: A Climatological Perspective*, Technical Report 2005–01, National Climatic Data Center, October 2005, update January 2006; and Richard D. Knabb, Jamie R. Rhome, and Daniel P. Brown, *Tropical Cyclone Report: Hurricane Katrina, 23–30 August 2005*. National Hurricane Center, December 20, 2005.

28 1930s dust bowl: Spencer S. Hsu, "2 Million Displaced by Storms," *Washington Post*, January 13, 2006.

30 *"largely false"*: Kerry Emanuel, personal communication, 2006.

30 *Hurricane seasons:* Here I am defining a super-hurricane as any category 4 or 5 hurricane. This is different from the official term *super-typhoon* for typhoons with winds of 150 mph or higher.

31 *extreme events:* World Meteorological Organization, press release, WMO-no. 695, Geneva, July 2, 2003.

31 *"weather is going haywire":* "Reaping the Whirlwind," *Independent* (London), July 3, 2003.

31 *35,000 deaths:* Shaoni Bhattacharya, "European Heatwave Caused 35,000 Deaths," NewScientist.com news service, October 10, 2003, http://www.newscientist.com/article.ns?id=dn4259.

31 *Goddard Institute:* NASA says 2005 just edged out 1998, which it calls "notable" because 1998's temperature was "lifted 0.2°C above the trend line by the strongest El Niño of the past century." See "Global Temperature Trends: 2005 Summation" available online at http://data.giss.nasa.gov/gistemp/2005/.

31 *Mumbai:* Steve Connor, "The Worst Weather Ever? At $200bn, It's Certainly the Costliest," *Independent* (London), December 7, 2005.

31 *"the eight months":* National Oceanic and Atmospheric Administration Satellite and Information Service website, http://lwf.ncdc.noaa.gov/oa/climate/research/2006/jun/hazards.html.

31 *worst wildfire season:* Seth Borenstein, "America's Weather Went Wild in 2005," Knight Ridder newspapers, December 30, 2006; and Wikipedia, s.v. http://en.wikipedia.org/wiki/Northeast_Flooding_of_October_2005.

32 *and more intense—precipitation:* Thomas Karl et al., "Trends in U.S. Climate During the Twentieth Century," *Consequences* 1, no. 1 (Spring 1995).

32 *"precipitation, temperature":* Pavel Ya. Groisman et al., "Contemporary Changes of the Hydrological Cycle over the Contiguous United States: Trends Derived from In Situ Observations," *Journal of Hydrometeorology* 5 (February 2004): 64–85.

32 *precisely what is predicted:* Gabriele Hegerl et al., "Detectability of Anthro-

pogenic Changes in Annual Temperature and Precipitation Extremes," *Journal of Climate,* provisionally accepted.

32 *Washington, D.C.:* Capitalweather.com, June 27, 2006, www.capitalweather. com/2006/06/historic-june-2006-flood-day-three.php.

32 *45 percent:* Sarah Goudarzi, "Scorching U.S.: First Half of 2006 Sets Heat Record," livescience.com, July 14, 2006, www.livescience.com/environment/ 060714_record_heat.html.

32 *Climate Extremes Index:* U.S. Climate Extremes Index, available online at www.ncdc.noaa.gov/oa/climate/research/cei/cei.html.

33 Half or more: *Alaska Native Villages,* General Accounting Office, December 2003, GAO-04-142.

33 *Valdez, Alaska:* Borenstein, "America's Weather Went Wild."

34 *Judith Curry and others:* Judith L. Curry et al., "Mixing Politics and Science in Testing the Hypothesis That Greenhouse Warming Is Causing a Global Increase in Hurricane Intensity," *Bulletin of the American Meteorological Society,* August 2006. See also Judith Curry, "Global Warming and Hurricanes," testimony, U.S. House Committee on Government Reform, *Climate Change Hearing,* July 20, 2006.

34 *"There has been":* Graumann et al., *Hurricane Katrina.*

34 twenty times: Sydney Levitus et al., "Warming of the World Ocean," *Science* 287, no. 5641 (March 24, 2000): 2225–29.

34 *matches the predicted warming:* See also James Hansen et al., "Earth's Energy Imbalance: Confirmation and Implications," *Science* 308, no. 5727 (June 3, 2005): 1431–35.

35 *"A warming signal":* Tim P. Barnett et al., "Penetration of Human-Induced Warming into the World's Oceans," *Science* 309, no. 5732 (July 8, 2005): 284–87.

35 *2006 analysis:* James Hansen et al., "Dangerous Human-Made Interference with Climate: A GISS ModelE Study," 2005, submitted to *Journal of Geophysical Research.* See also Nathan P. Gillett and Peter A. Stott, "Detecting Anthropogenic Influence on Tropical Atlantic Sea Surface Temperatures," *Geophysical Research Abstracts* 8, no. 03698 (2006).

36 *"By trapping heat":* Kerry Emanuel, *Divine Wind: The History and Science of Hurricanes* (New York: Oxford University Press, 2005), p. 23.

36 *2006 report on Katrina:* Graumann et al., *Hurricane Katrina.*

37 *"a methodology":* Carlos D. Hoyos et al., "Deconvolution of the Factors

Contributing to the Increase in Global Hurricane Intensity," *Science* 312, no. 5770 (April 7, 2006): 94–97.

37 *the first, in* Science: Kevin Trenberth, "Uncertainty in Hurricanes and Global Warming," *Science* 308, no. 5729 (June 17, 2005): 1753–54.

38 *at least 74 mph:* For a good discussion of the various terminology used around the world, see Emanuel, *Divine Wind*, 23.

38 *Kerry Emanuel:* Kerry Emanuel, "Increasing Destructiveness of Tropical Cyclones Over the Past 30 Years," *Nature* 436, no. 7051 (August 4, 2005): 686–88.

38 *Georgia Tech:* Peter Webster et al., "Changes in Tropical Cyclone Number, Duration, and Intensity in a Warming Environment," *Science* 309, no. 5742 (September 16, 2005): 1844–46.

39 hypothesis: Dave Wilton, "Theories and Intelligent Design," *A Way with Words: The Weekly Newsletter of Word Origins* 4, no. 12 (June 17, 2005), available online at www.wordorigins.org/AWWW/Vol04/AWWW061705 .html.

39 *National Oceanic and Atmospheric Administration: Climate of 2005: Atlantic Hurricane Season,* National Climatic Data Center, National Oceanic and Atmospheric Administration website, www.ncdc.noaa.gov/oa/climate/ research/2005/hurricanes05.html.

41 *first major critique:* Roger Pielke Jr. et al., "Hurricanes and Global Warming," *Bulletin of the American Meteorological Society,* November 2005. A note indicates "in final form 24 August 2005."

43 *"specifically shows":* Richard Anthes et al., "Hurricanes and Global Warming: Potential Linkage and Consequences," *Bulletin of the American Meteorological Society* May 2006: 623–28.

44 *recent modeling studies:* See, for instance, Hansen et al., "Dangerous Human-Made Interference"; Peter A. Stott et al., "External Control of 20th Century Temperature by Natural and Anthropogenic Forcings," *Science* 290, no. 5499 (December 15, 2000): 2133–37; and Gareth Jones et al., "Sensitivity of Global-Scale Climate Change Attribution Results to Inclusion of Fossil Fuel Black Carbon Aerosol," *Geophysical Research Letters* 32, no. 14 (July 16, 2005).

45 *six major volcanoes:* Alan Robock, "Volcanic Eruptions," in *The Earth System: Physical and Chemical Dimensions of Global Environmental Change,* vol. 1 of *Encyclopedia of Global Environmental Change,* Andrew S.

Goudie and David J. Cuff, eds. (New York: Oxford University Press, 2002), 738–44.

46 *"produced the largest"*: Ibid.

46 *Lawrence Livermore National Laboratory:* Peter Gleckler et al., "Volcanoes and Climate: Krakatoa's Signature Persists in the Ocean," *Nature* 439, no. 7077 (February 9, 2006): 675.

47 *"It would appear"*: Kerry Emanuel, personal communication, 2006. He pointed out that the "tropical North Atlantic ocean temperature follows the whole northern hemisphere rather closely," which argues against any "regional influence," such as the AMO.

47 *"there is no evidence"*: Michael E. Mann and Kerry A. Emanuel, "Atlantic Hurricane Trends Linked to Climate Change," *EOS* 87, no. 24 (June 13, 2006): 233–44. Interestingly, the study notes that the positive or peak phase of the AMO corresponds with the strengthening of the Atlantic's thermohaline circulation, which takes warm and salty water to the coast of western Europe, keeping the continent's climate relatively mild. Some recent evidence suggests that the circulation is weakening, which would mean the AMO is not making a positive contribution to sea-surface temperatures. And that would mean hurricanes are intensifying in spite of—not because of—the AMO.

47 *meteorologist Eric Blake:* Mark Schleifstein, "Katrina Bulks Up to Become a Perfect Storm," *New Orleans Times-Picayune,* August 28, 2005.

47 *"The warmer"*: Chris Carroll, "In Hot Water," *National Geographic,* August 2005, 79.

48 *"We think the best"*: Rush Limbaugh Show, September 26, 2005, transcript, available online at www.rushlimbaugh.com/home/eibessential/enviro_wackos/max_mayfield_shouts_it_s_not_global_warming.guest.html.

48 *"The increased activity"*: Max Mayfield, testimony, *Oversight Hearing on the Lifesaving Role of Accurate Hurricane Prediction,* Senate Committee on Commerce, Science and Transportation Subcommittee on Disaster Prevention and Prediction, 109th Cong., 1st sess. September 20, 2005, available online at www.legislative.noaa.gov/Testimony/mayfieldfinal092005.pdf. See also "NOAA Attributes Recent Increase in Hurricane Activity to Naturally Occurring Multi-Decadal Climate Variability," *NOAA Magazine,* November 29, 2005, available online at www.magazine.noaa.gov/stories/mag184.htm.

48 *a major 2006 study:* Hansen et al., "Dangerous Human-Made Interference."

48 *"a trend in landfalling"*: Kerry Emanuel, "Emanuel Replies," *Nature* 438, no. 7071 (December 22, 2005): E13.

49 *"More than half"*. Emanuel, personal communication.

49 *"threshold"*: Patrick J. Michaels, Paul C. Knappenberger, and Robert E. Davis, "Sea-Surface Temperatures and Tropical Cyclones in the Atlantic Basin," *Geophysical Research Letters* 33, no. 9 (May 10, 2006).

50 *"I don't see"*: Kerry Emanuel quoted in Richard Bradley, "Rain Man," *Plenty*, February/March 2006, 33.

50 *Super Typhoon Tip*: National Weather Service Southern Region website www.srh.weather.gov/srh/jetstream/tropics/tc_structure.htm.

50 *Ultimately*: Bill Blakemore, "Category 6 Hurricanes? They've Happened," ABC News, May 21, 2006, available online at http://abcnews.go.com/GMA/ print?id=1986862.

51 *Zeta*: "Tropical Depression Zeta Discussion Number 30," National Weather Service Tropical Prediction Center at the National Hurricane Center, Miami, 4 P.M. EST, January 6, 2006. See www.nhc.noaa.gov/archive/2005/ dis/al302005.discus.030.shtml.

51 *1°F increase*: Judith Curry and Peter Webster, "Hurricanes & Global Warming" (paper presented at the EESI Symposium *How Changes in the Arctic Are Affecting the Rest of the World*, Washington, D.C., June 15, 2006).

CHAPTER THREE: 2025–2050: PLANETARY PURGATORY

53 *"Obviously"*: David Rind, quoted in Elizabeth Kolbert, "The Climate of Man," *The New Yorker*, May 2, 2005.

53 *"We're showing"*: Thomas Swetnam, quoted in Tony Davis, "Study: Wildfire Increase Due to Climate Change," *Arizona Daily Star*, July 7, 2006.

53 *Mega-droughts and widespread wildfires*: "NOAA Reports Warmer 2005 for the United States, Near-Record Warmth Globally Hurricanes, Floods, Snow and Wildfires All Notable," *NOAA Magazine*, December 15, 2005, available online at www.noaanews.noaa.gov/stories2005/s2548.htm.

54 *nearly 1°F per decade*: James Hansen et al., "Dangerous Human-Made Interference with Climate: A GISS ModelE Study," 2005, submitted to *Journal of Geophysical Research*.

54 *The oppressive heat*: Shaoni Bhattacharya, "European Heatwave Caused 35,000 Deaths," and "French Heat Toll Tops 11,000," CNN.com, August 29, 2003, www.cnn.com/2003/WORLD/europe/08/29/france.heatdeaths/.

55 *human influence:* Peter Stott et al., "Human Contribution to the European Heat Wave of 2003," *Nature* 432, no. 7017 (December 2, 2004); 610–14.

55 *"These results":* Aiguo Dai et al., "A Global Dataset of Palmer Drought Severity Index for 1870–2002: Relationship with Soil Moisture and Effects of Surface Warming," *Journal of Hydrometeorology* 5 (December 2004): 1117–30.

55 *Every decade:* Millennium Ecosystem Assessment, ed., *Ecosystems and Human Well-Being: Current Status and Trends* (Washington, D.C.: Island Press, 2005), figure 16–8, 449.

55 *"The period since":* Kirk Johnson and Dean Murphy, "Drought Settles In, Lake Shrinks and West's Worries Grow," *New York Times,* May 2, 2004.

56 *Phoenix:* Michael Wilson, "In Phoenix, Even Cactuses Wilt in Clutches of Record Drought," *New York Times,* March 10, 2006. See also "Climate of 2006—June in Historical Perspective," National Climatic Data Center, National Oceanic and Atmospheric Administration website, www.ncdc.noaa.gov/oa/climate/research/2006/jun/jun06.html.

56 *wildfires destroyed:* "Climate of 2005 Wildfire Season Summary" and "Climate of 2006 Wildfire Season Summary," National Climatic Data Center, National Oceanic and Atmospheric Administration website, www.ncdc.noaa.gov/oa/climate/research/2005/fire05.html and www.ncdc.noaa.gov/oa/climate/research/2006/fire06.html.

56 *A 2005 study:* "Regional Vegetation Die-Off in Response to Global-Change-Type Drought," *Proceedings of the National Academy of Sciences* 102, no. 42 (October 18, 2005): 15144–48. The recent drought had trees dying at rates reaching "90 percent or more" at upper-elevation sites in Colorado and Arizona, whereas the trees that died in the 1950s drought did so mostly at lower elevations.

57 *"We're seeing changes":* Michelle Nijhuis, "Global Warming's Unlikely Harbingers," *High Country News,* July 19, 2004.

57 *thanks in large part:* Kim McGarrity and George Hoberg, "Issue Brief: The Beetle Challenge: An Overview of the Mountain Pine Beetle Epidemic and Its Implications," Department of Forest Resources Management, University of British Columbia, 2005, available online at www.policy.forestry.ubc.ca/issuebriefs/overview%20of%20the%20epidemic.html.

57 *winter death rate:* "Pine Beetles at 'Epidemic' Levels in Northwest Forests," Associated Press, March 23, 2006, available online at www.signonsandiego.com/news/science/20060323-1411-wst-forestbeetles.html; and The Center

for Health and the Global Environment, *Climate Change Futures* (Harvard Medical School, 2005), available online at www.climatechangefutures.org/pdf/CCF_Report_Final_10.27.pdf.

57 *February 2006 speech:* Senator Lisa Murkowski, "Climate Change: An Alaskan Perspective" (address to Catholic University Law School, Washington, D.C., February 13, 2006), available online at http://murkowski.senate.gov/pdf/Catholic%20U.%20Law%20School.pdf.

57 *Half of the wildfires:* "U.S. Climate Agency Ranks 2005 Near Record for Heat," U.S. Department of State USINFO service, December 16, 2005, available online at http://usinfo.state.gov/gi/Archive/2005/Dec/16-239160.html.

57 *grim reality:* Marvin Eng et al., *Provincial-Level Projection of the Current Mountain Pine Beetle Outbreak: An Overview of the Model (BCMPB v2) and Results of Year 2 of the Project,* for the Mountain Pine Beetle Initiative of the Canadian Forest Service and the British Columbia Forest Service, April 2005, available online at www.for.gov.bc.ca/hre/bcmpb/BCMPB_Main Report_2004.pdf.

57 *"it has become apparent":* McGarrity and Hoberg, "The Beetle Challenge."

57 *"Harvest levels":* Ibid.

58 *"super-interglacial drought":* Jonathan Overpeck, "Warm Climate Abrupt Change—Paleo-Perspectives" (paper presented at the Third Trans-Atlantic Co-operative Research Conference, *Climate, Oceans and Policies—Challenges for the 21st Century,* Washington, D.C., November 1, 2005).

58 *predicted back in 1990:* David Rind et al., "Potential Evapotranspiration and the Likelihood of Future Drought," *Journal of Geophysical Research* 95 (1990): 9,983–10,004 available online at http://pubs.giss.nasa.gov/abstracts/1990/Rind_etal_1.html.

58 *"The development of":* Kirk Johnson et al., "Drought Settles In, Lake Shrinks and West's Worries Grow," *New York Times,* May 2, 2004—through the article makes no mention of global warming.

58 *California's Sierra Nevada:* Robert Service, "As the West Goes Dry," *Science* 303, no. 5661 (February 20, 2004): 1124–27.

59 *2006 study:* Anthony Leroy Westerling, "Warming and Earlier Spring Increases Western U.S. Forest Wildfire Activity," *Science* Express, July 6, 2006, available online at 10.1126/science.1129185.

59 *West is likely:* Steven W. Running, "Is Global Warming Causing More, Larger Wildfires?" (*Science* Express), July 6, 2006, available online at 10.1126/science.1130370.

59 *"the area burned":* Donald McKenzie et al., "Climatic Change, Wildfire, and Conservation," *Conservation Biology* 18, no. 4 (August 2004): 890–902.

60 *2002 study:* John D. Sterman and Linda Booth Sweeney, "Cloudy Skies: Assessing Public Understanding of Global Warming," *System Dynamics Review* 18, no. 2 (Summer 2002): 207–40.

61 1 ton carbon: The fraction of carbon in carbon dioxide is the ratio of their weights. One ton of carbon, C, equals $44/12 = 11/3 = 3.67$ tons of carbon dioxide, CO_2. The atomic weight of carbon is 12, while the weight of carbon dioxide is 44, because it includes two oxygen atoms that each weigh 16. So, to switch from one to the other, use the formula: 1 ton carbon, C, equals $44/12 = 11/3 = 3.67$ tons carbon dioxide, CO_2.

62 *In 2005, the U.S. Department:* U.S. Energy Information Administration, *Annual Energy Outlook 2006,* DOE/EIA 0383 (2006), available online at www .ela.doe.gov/oiaf/index.html.

65 *"positive feedbacks":* The climate system does have negative feedbacks loops, whereby a little warming causes a change that slows down warming. For instance, as sea ice retreats, more ocean area is exposed directly to the atmosphere, which could increase the rate at which the ocean takes up carbon dioxide, thereby slowing the rate at which atmospheric concentrations would otherwise have risen. But as the text indicates, scientific observation and analysis strongly suggests the vicious cycles or positive feedbacks dominate the climate system's response to the kind of greenhouse gas forcings it is now experiencing.

65 *"widespread, extreme climatic":* Appy Sluijs et al., "Subtropical Arctic Ocean Temperatures During the Palaeocene/Eocene Thermal Maximum," *Nature* 441, no. 7093 (June 1, 2006): 610–13.

65 *Middle Ages:* Martin Scheffer et al., "Positive Feedback Between Global Warming and Atmospheric CO_2 Concentration Inferred from Past Climate Change," *Geophysical Research Letter* 33, no. 10 (May 26, 2006).

66 *third study:* Margaret Torn, "Missing feedbacks, asymmetric uncertainties, and the underestimation of future warming," *Geophysical Research Letters* 33, no. 10 (May 26, 2006).

67 *2005 report:* "Oceanic Acidification Due to Increasing Atmospheric Carbon Dioxide," Royal Society (London), June 2005, 7.

67 *more CO_2 would stay:* Jef Huisman et al., "Reduced Mixing Generates Oscillations and Chaos in the Oceanic Chlorophyll Maximum," *Nature* 439, no. 7074 (January 19, 2006): 322–25.

67 *2002 study of Texas:* Richard A. Gill, "Nonlinear Grassland Responses to Past and Future Atmospheric CO_2," *Nature* 417, no. 6886 (May 16, 2002): 279–82.

68 *enlightened energy policies:* John Pickrell, "Soil May Spoil UK's Climate Efforts," *New Scientist* news service, September 7, 2005, available online at http://www.newscientist.com/channel/earth/dn7964-soil-may-spoil-uks-climate-efforts.html; and Pat H. Bellamy et al., "Carbon Losses from All Soils Across England and Wales 1978–2003," *Nature* 437, no. 7056 (September 8, 2005): 245–48.

68 *"locker of carbon":* Laurence Smith, American Meteorological Society seminar, Washington, D.C., February 20, 2006.

68 *nearly 1,000 billion metric tons:* Sergey A. Zimov et al., "Climate Change: Permafrost and the Global Carbon Budget," *Science* 312, no. 5780 (June 16, 2006): 1612–13.

68 *recent degradation:* M. Turre Jorgenson et al., "Abrupt Increase in Permafrost Degradation in Arctic Alaska," *Geophysical Research Letters* 33 (January 24, 2006).

69 *"a mass of shallow lakes":* Fred Pearce, "Climate Warning as Siberia Melts," *New Scientist,* August 11, 2005.

69 *Some 600* million: Wikipedia, s. v. "methane," http://en.wikipedia.org/wiki/Methane.

69 *20 to 60 percent increase:* Torben Christensen et al., "Thawing Sub-Arctic Permafrost: Effects on Vegetation and Methane Emissions," *Geophysical Research Letters* 31 (February 20, 2004).

69 *"the gas was bubbling":* Ian Sample, "Warming Hits 'Tipping Point,'" *Guardian* (London), August 11, 2005.

70 *If concentrations hit 690:* David M. Lawrence and Andrew G. Slater, "A Projection of Severe Near-Surface Permafrost Degradation During the 21st Century," *Geophysical Research Letters* 32 (December 17, 2005); and David Lawrence (American Meteorological Society seminar, Washington, D.C., February 20, 2006). See also Karen E. Frey and Laurence C. Smith, "Amplified Carbon Release from Vast West Siberian Peatlands by 2100," *Geophysical Research Letters* 32 (May 5, 2005).

71 *"at the higher end":* Simon L. Lewis et al., "Tropical Forests and Atmospheric Carbon Dioxide: Current Conditions and Future Scenarios," chapter 14 in *Avoiding Dangerous Climate Change,* eds. Hans Joachim Schellnhuber et al. (Cambridge: Cambridge University Press, 2006).

71 *a 2003* Nature *article:* Mark A. Cochrane, "Fire Science for Rainforests," *Nature* 421, no. 6926 (February 27, 2003): 913–19.

71 *more than 60 feet deep:* Susan E. Page et al., "The Amount of Carbon Released from Peat and Forest Fires in Indonesia During 1997," *Nature* 420, no. 6911 (November 7, 2002): 61–65.

72 *the Amazon was suffering:* Larry Rohter, "A Record Amazon Drought, and Fear of Wider Ills," *New York Times,* December 11, 2005.

72 *Dr. Dan Nepstad:* Fred Pearce, "Amazon Rainforest 'Could Become a Desert,'" *Independent* (London), July 25, 2006.

72 *Models suggest:* Geoffrey Lean, "Dying Forest: One Year to Save the Amazon," *Independent* (London), July 23, 2006.

72 *feedback loop at work:* Peter M. Cox et al., "Amazonian Forest Dieback Under Climate-Carbon Cycle Projections for the 21st Century. *Theoretical and Applied Climatology* 78, no. 1–3 (June 2004): 137–56. See also Richard Betts et al., "The Role of Ecosystem-Atmosphere Interactions in Simulated Amazonian Precipitation Decrease and Forest Dieback Under Global Climate Warming," *Theoretical and Applied Climatology* 78, no. 1–3 (June 2004): 157–75. Tim Flannery, *The Weather Makers: The History & Future Impact of Climate Change* (New York: Atlantic Monthly Press, 2006).

73 *the United States and the world:* Chris D. Jones et al., "Strong Carbon Cycle Feedbacks in a Climate Model with Interactive CO_2 and Sulfate Aerosols," *Geophysical Research Letters* 30 (May 9, 2003): 1479.

73 *important study:* Chris D. Jones et al., "Impact of Climate-Carbon Cycle Feedbacks on Emissions Scenarios to Achieve Stabilisation," chapter 34 in Schellnhuber et al., *Avoiding Dangerous Climate Change* (Cambridge: Cambridge University Press, 2006). This study modeled tundra as if it were any other kind of soil, whereas in fact, as we have seen, it is quite different, especially in its ability to release large amounts of carbon as methane, a far more potent greenhouse gas than carbon dioxide.

CHAPTER FOUR: 2050–2100: HELL AND HIGH WATER

75 *"We could get":* Bob Corell, personal communication.

75 *"The peak rate":* James Hansen, "Defusing the Global Warming Time Bomb," *Scientific American* 290, no. 3 (February 2004): 68–77.

76 *polar amplification:* According to the December 2004 *Arctic Climate Impact Assessment,* a comprehensive report by the leading scientist of the nations that border the Arctic Circle, including ours, over the past 50 years it is

probable, with a confidence level of 66 to 90 percent, that polar amplification has occurred. See also RealClimate website, www.realclimate.org/index.php?p=234.

77 *"solar heat absorbed"*: International Arctic Science Committee (IASC), *Impacts of a Warming Arctic* (Cambridge: Cambridge University Press, 2004), 15.

77 *more than 25 percent*: Andrew Revkin, "In a Melting Trend, Less Arctic Ice to Go Around," *New York Times*, September 29, 2005.

77 *"At the present rate"*: Jonathan Overpeck et al., "Arctic System on a Trajectory to New, Seasonally Ice-Free State," *Eos* 86, no. 309 (2005): 312–13.

78 *"The recent sea-ice"*: Tore Furevik, "Feedbacks in the Climate System and Implications for Future Climate Projections" (presented at "Climate, Oceans, and Policies," the Embassy of Norway's Third Annual Forum Transatlantic Climate Research Conference, Washington, D.C., November 1, 2005).

78 *Most models suggest*: Ola M. Johannessen et al., "Arctic Climate Change—Observed and Modeled Temperature and Sea Ice Variability," *Tellus* 56A, no. 4 (2004): 328–41.

78 *"0.3° to 0.4°C"*: Jonathan A. Foley, "Tipping Points in the Tundra," *Science* 310, no. 5748 (October 28, 2005): 627–28.

78 *A 2005 study*: F. S. Chapin et al., "Role of Land-Surface Changes in Arctic Summer Warming," *Science* 310, no. 5748 (October 28, 2005): 657–60.

79 *"If this trend persists"*: Dr. Wieslaw Maslowski, "Causes of Changes in Arctic Sea Ice" (paper presented at the American Meteorological Society ESSS seminar, Washington, D.C., May 2006).

80 *when the planet warms*: Jonathan M. Gregory and Philippe Huybrechts, "Ice-Sheet Contributions to Future Sea-Level Change," *Philosophical Transactions of the Royal Society* 364, no. 206: 1709–31. Note that some studies project a faster rate of growth of the Greenland temperatures compared to global ones. See, for instance, Petr Chylek and Ulrike Lohmann, "Ratio of the Greenland to Global Temperature Change: Comparison of Observations and Climate Modeling Results," *Geophysical Research Letters* 32, no. 14 (July 21, 2005).

80 *another vicious cycle*: Jonathan Gregory et al., "Threatened Loss of the Greenland Ice-Sheet," *Nature* 428, no. 6983 (April 8, 2004): 616.

80 *NASA and MIT*: Jay Zwally et al., "Surface Melt-Induced Acceleration of Greenland Ice-Sheet Flow," *Science* 297, no. 5579 (July 12, 2002): 218–22.

81 *review article in* Science: Julian A. Dowdeswell, "The Greenland Ice Sheet and Global Sea-Level Rise," *Science* 311, no. 5763 (February 17, 2006): 963–64.

81 *1950 to 1996:* Hong-Gyoo Sohn, Kenneth Jezek, and C. J. van der Veen, "Jakobshavn Glacier, West Greenland: 30 Years of Space-Borne Observations," *Geophysical Research Letters* 25, no. 14 (July 15, 1998).

81 *"in October 2000":* Ian Joughin et al., "Large Fluctuations in Speed on Greenland's Jakobshavn Isbrae Glacier," *Nature* 432, no. 7017 (December 2, 2004): 608–10.

81 *A 2006 study:* Adrian Luckman et al., "Rapid and Synchronous Ice-Dynamic Changes in East Greenland," *Geophysical Research Letters* 33 (February 3, 2006). See also "Glacial Change," *Science News* 168 (December 17, 2005): 387.

82 *14 kilometers per year:* "Glacial Change," *Science News* 168 (December 17, 2005): 387.

82 *"accelerated ice discharge":* Eric Rignot and Pannir Kanagaratnam, "Changes in the Velocity Structure of the Greenland Ice Sheet," *Science* 311, no. 5763 (February 17, 2006): 986–90.

82 *"In the next 10 years":* Eric Rignot quoted in Michael D. Lemonick, "Has the Meltdown Begun?" *Time* (February 27, 2006): 38–39.

83 *NASA's Jay Zwally:* "NASA Survey Confirms Climate Warming Impact on Polar Ice Sheets," NASA press release, March 8, 2006.

83 *"The last IPCC report":* Chris Rapley quoted in Matt Weaver, "PM Issues Blunt Warning on Climate Change," *Guardian* (London), January 30, 2006.

83 *eight times as much:* Chris Rapley, "The Antarctic Ice Sheet and Sea Level Rise," in chapter 3 in *Avoiding Dangerous Climate Change,* eds. Hans Joachim Schellnhuber et al. (Cambridge: Cambridge University Press, 2006).

83 *90 percent of Earth's ice:* "Antarctic Ice Sheet Losing Mass, Says University of Colorado Study," ScienceDaily.com, March 2, 2006.

84 *"in the last decade":* ISMASS Committee, "Recommendations for the Collection and Synthesis of Antarctic Ice Sheet Mass Balance Data," *Global and Planetary Change* 42 (2004): 1–15.

84 *The Antarctic Peninsula:* Hamish Pritchard and David G. Vaughan, "Warmer Summers and Faster Glacier Flow on the Antarctic Peninsula" (poster presentation at the Second ENVISAT summer school, Frascati, Italy, August

2004). See also David G. Vaughan et al., "Recent Rapid Regional Climate Warming on the Antarctic Peninsula," *Climatic Change* 60 (2003): 243–74.

84 *lost an area larger:* "Larsen B Ice Shelf Collapses in Antarctica," National Snow and Ice Data Center, March 18, 2002, available online at http://nsidc .org/iceshelves/larsenb2002/.

84 *One glacier's surface:* Eric Rignot et al., "Accelerated Ice Discharge from the Antarctic Peninsula Following the Collapse of Larsen B Ice Shelf," *Geophysical Research Letters* 31, no. 18 (September 22, 2004); and Ted Scambos et al., "Glacier Acceleration and Thinning After Ice Shelf Collapse in the Larsen B Embayment, Antarctica," *Geophysical Research Letters* 31, no. 18 (September 22, 2004).

84 *"the cumulative loss":* Alison Cook et al., "Retreating Glacier Fronts on the Antarctic Peninsula over the Past Half-Century," *Science* 308, no. 5721 (April 22, 2005): 541–44.

85 *"due to an imbalance":* Andrew Shepherd et al., "Warm Ocean Is Eroding West Antarctic Ice Sheet," *Geophysical Research Letters* 31, no. 23 (December 9, 2004); and Fred Pearce, "Antarctic Glaciers Calving Faster into the Ocean," *New Scientist,* October 18, 2005.

85 *A major 2004 study:* Robert Thomas et al., "Accelerated Sea-Level Rise from West Antarctica," *Science* 306, no. 5694 (October 8, 2004): 255–58.

85 *University of Colorado:* "Antarctic Ice Sheet Losing Mass, Says University of Colorado Study," University of Colorado at Boulder, press release, March 2, 2006.

85 *NASA's Zwally:* NASA press release, March 8, 2006.

86 *it is fundamentally:* "Sea Level, Ice, and Greenhouses—FAQ" available online at http://www.radix.net/~bobg/faqs/sea.level.faq.html.

86 *2004 NASA-led study:* Thomas et al. 2004, "Accelerated Sea-Level Rise."

86 *A 2002 study in* Science: Eric Rignot and Stanley S. Jacobs, "Rapid Bottom Melting Widespread Near Antarctic Ice Sheet Grounding Lines," *Science* 296, no. 5575 (June 14, 2002): 2020–23.

86 *another vicious cycle:* As Rapley put it in a 2006 paper, "A combination of accelerated flow and hydrostatic list might cause a runaway discharge." Rapley, "The Antarctic Ice Sheet."

86 *Pine Island and Thwaites:* Pearce, "Antarctic Glaciers."

87 *"A warming of this":* Peter Barrett, "What 3 Degrees of Global Warming Really Means," *Pacific Ecologist* 11 (Summer 2005/06): 6–8.

88 *A 1991 study:* James G. Titus et al., "Greenhouse Effect and Sea Level Rise: The Cost of Holding Back the Sea," *Coastal Management* 19 (1991): 171–204.

88 *The first 1 meter:* James E. Neumann et al., "Sea-Level Rise and Global Climate Change: A Review of Impacts to U.S. Coasts" (prepared for the Pew Center on Global Climate Change, February 2000).

89 *One 2001 analysis:* James G. Titus and Charlie Richman, "Maps of Lands Vulnerable to Sea Level Rise: Modeled Elevations Along the U.S. Atlantic and Gulf Coasts," *Climate Research* 18 (2001): 205–28.

89 *they don't consider the impact:* Stephen Schneider and Robert S. Chen, "Carbon Dioxide Warming and Coastline Flooding: Physical Factors and Climatic Impact," *Annual Review of Energy* 5 (November 1980): 107–40.

89 *a world where sea levels:* Peter Whoriskey, "Post-Katrina Rebuilders Hug Ground, Trust Levees," *Washington Post,* February 26, 2006.

90 *2005 study:* Robert J. Nicholls, Richard S. J. Tol, and Nassos Vafeidis, "Global Estimates of the Impact of a Collapse of the West Antarctic Ice Sheet," January 6, 2004, available online at www.uni-hamburg.de/Wiss/FB/15/Sustainability/annex6.pdf.

90 *A 1980 paper:* Schneider and Chen, "Carbon Dioxide Warming."

CHAPTER FIVE: HOW CLIMATE RHETORIC
TRUMPS CLIMATE REALITY

99 *"The scientific debate":* Frank Luntz, "Straight Talk" memo (Luntz Research Companies, Washington, D.C., 2002), 131–46, available online at http://www.politicalstrategy.org/archives/001330.php.

99 *"Global warming":* David Brooks, "Running Out of Steam," *New York Times,* December 8, 2005.

100 *Kyoto Protocol:* Different countries have different targets. The 5% figure is the average. See Wikipedia, s. v. "Kyoto Protocol," http://en.wikipedia.org/wiki/Kyoto_Protocol.

100 *"It is clear":* Tony Blair, speech on sustainable development, February 2003, available online at www.number-10.gov.uk/output/Page3073.asp.

101 *"And by long-term":* Tony Blair, speech on climate change, London, September 14, 2004, available online at www.number10.gov.uk/output/page6333.asp.

101 *"squandering the chance":* "UK Must Lead on Climate Change," BBC News, September 13, 2004, available online at http://news.bbc.co.uk/1/hi/uk_

politics/3651052.stm. Also see "UK: PM Gives Dire Warning on Climate," BBC News, September 15, 2004, available online at http://news.bbc.co .uk/1/hi/uk_politics/3656812.stm.

101 *major Senate bill:* McCain-Lieberman climate bill roll-call vote is available online at www.senate.gov/legislative/LIS/roll_call_lists/roll_call_vote_cfm .cfm?congress=109&session=1&vote=00148.

102 *"You need 60":* "US Senate Likely to Reject Future UN Climate Deal—Interview," EurActiv.com, February 15, 2006.

102 *"It is clear":* Tony Blair, Foreword, in *Avoiding Dangerous Climate Change,* eds. Hans Joachim Schellnhuber et al. (Cambridge: Cambridge University Press, 2004).

102 *"Though he didn't":* Fred Barnes, *Rebel-in-Chief: Inside the Bold and Controversial Presidency of George W. Bush* (New York: Random House, 2006).

103 *"a compelling presentation":* Senator James M. Inhofe, "Climate Change Update," Senate floor statement, 109th Cong., 1st sess., January 4, 2005, available online at http://inhofe.senate.gov/pressreleases/climateupdate.htm. See also http://epw.scnate.gov/hearing_statements.cfm?id=246814.

103 *"Scientists agree":* John Tierney, "And on the Eighth Day, God Went Green," *New York Times,* February 11, 2006.

105 *"Un-Journalism":* Jude Wanniski, "Un-Journalism at the New Yorker," May 9, 2005, available online at www.wanniski.com/showarticle.asp?articleid= 4350. See also wanniski.com/PrintPage.asp?TextID=3550.

105 *"There is no relationship":* Charles Krauthammer, "Where to Point the Fingers," *Washington Post,* September 8, 2005.

106 *the recent scientific evidence:* "Will Railed About Global Warming-Hurricane Link Claim; Ignored Actual Scientific Data on Hurricane Intensity," *Media Matters for America,* September 26, 2005, available online at http://media matters.org/items/200509260004.

106 *"phony theory":* Charles Krauthammer, "Phony Theory, False Conflict," *Washington Post,* October 18, 2005.

106 *"But it is":* George F. Will, "Grand Old Spenders," *Washington Post,* November 17, 2005.

107 *"Crichton's subject":* George F. Will, "Global Warming? Hot Air," *Washington Post,* December 23, 2004.

108 *"Of all the talents":* Winston Churchill, "The Scaffolding of Rhetoric," unpublished essay, 1897.

108 *"Aptness of language"*: Aristotle, *Rhetoric,* cited in Brian Vickers, *Classical Rhetoric in English Poetry* (Carbondale: Southern Illinois University Press, 1970), 94.

108 *"constitute basic schemes"*: Raymond W. Gibbs, Jr., *The Poetics of Mind* (Cambridge: Cambridge University Press, 1994), 1.

109 *"All the speeches"*: Churchill, "Scaffolding."

109 *"There's a simple"*: Frank Luntz, interview on PBS's *Frontline,* November 9, 2004, available online at www.pbs.org/wgbh/pages/frontline/shows/per-suaders/themes/citizen.html.

110 *"Scientists have"*: Mark Bowen, *Thin Ice Unlocking the Secrets of Climate in the World's Highest Mountains* (New York: Henry Holt, 2005), 21.

111 *Words alone:* Royal Society website, www.royalsoc.ac.uk/page.asp?id=1020.

111 *"Scientists who do"*: Jared Diamond, "Kinship with the Stars," *Discover* 18 (May 1997): 44–49.

111 *"For a scientist"*: Judith Curry et al., "Mixing Politics and Science in Testing the Hypothesis That Greenhouse Warming Is Causing a Global Increase in Hurricane Intensity," *Bulletin of the American Meteorological Society,* August 2006.

112 *does not melt:* "Governor Schwarzenegger Announces Landmark GHG Reduction Goals," June 2005, available online at www.climateregistry.org/Default.aspx?TabID=3423&refreshed=true.

112 *"one who takes"*: Answers.com. s.v. "contrarian," www.answers.com/topic/contrarian.

113 *"If you just"*: Michael Crichton, in Michael Crowley, "Michael Crichton's Scariest Creation: Jurassic President," *New Republic,* March 20, 2006.

113 *2002 memo:* Luntz, "Straight Talk."

114 *emphasis in original throughout:* I use italics here and throughout to signify emphasis for Luntz, but he often uses multiple emphases combining italics with boldface, and sometimes combining both of those with underlining.

114 *the phrase "climate change"*: Andrew C. Revkin, "Call for Openness at NASA Adds to Reports of Pressure," *New York Times,* February 16, 2006.

115 *For Luntz and a large:* In 2006, Luntz was asked by the BBC about the memo and replied, "It's now 2006. Now I think most people would conclude that there is global warming taking place, and that the behavior of humans are affecting the climate." But that was true in 2002. And in any case his cynical lines—"The scientific debate is closing (against us) but not yet closed. There is still a window of opportunity to challenge the science."—imply

that he knew he was on the losing side of the issue scientifically but believed the issue could still be won rhetorically. See "Luntz Converts on Global Warming, Distances Himself from Bush," available online at http://think progress.org/2006/06/27/luntz-gw/.

116 *"Doubt is"*: Tobacco memo available online at www.prevention.ch/doubt-is-our-product.pdf.

116 *"how much warming"*: Will, "Global Warming?"

117 *"We must not rush"*: Luntz, "Straight Talk."

117 *"Science tells us"*: Paula Dobriansky, remarks to "The Convention After 10 Years: Accomplishments and Future Challenges," *Tenth Session of the Conference of the Parties (COP) to the U.N. Framework Convention on Climate Change*, Buenos Aires, Argentina, December 15, 2004, available online at www.uspolicy.be/Article.asp?ID=C4A8C67B-E36F-45EA-B557-EEF 7F9A6EB4A.

118 *stunning conclusion*: Government Accountability Office, *Climate Change Assessment: Administration Did Not Meet Reporting Deadline*, report to Senator John McCain and Senator John Kerry, April 14, 2005. See also Andrew C. Revkin, "Climate Research Faulted Over Missing Components," *New York Times*, April 22, 2005.

118 *White House had secretly*: "Group Sues to Enforce Sound Science Law," Competitive Enterprise Institute, press release, August 6, 2003. See also Ross Gelbspan, *Boiling Point: How Politicians, Big Oil and Coal, Journalists and Activists Are Fueling the Climate Crisis—and What We Can Do to Avoid Disaster* (New York: Basic Books, 2004), 56–58.

118 *White House heavily*: "White House Guts Global Warming Study," CBS News, June 19, 2003, available online at www.cbsnews.com/stories/2003/07/24/politics/main564873.shthml; and Andrew C. Revkin and Katharine Q. Seelye, "Report by the E.P.A. Leaves Out Data on Climate Change," *New York Times*, June 19, 2003.

119 *His documents showed*: Climate Change Research Distorted and Suppressed," Union of Concerned Scientists website, at www.ucsusa.org/scientific_integrity/interference/climate-change.html. This page contains excerpts from *Scientific Integrity in Policymaking*, Union of Concerned Scientists, 2004.

119 *More recently*: Andrew C. Revkin, "Climate Expert Says NASA Tried to Silence Him," *New York Times*, January 29, 2006. See also John B. Judis, "The Government's Junk Science: NOAA's Flood," *National Review*, February 20,

2006; and "Rewriting the Science," *60 Minutes,* CBS News, July 30, 2006, available online at www.cbsnews.com/stories/2006/03/17/60minutes/main 1415985.shtml.

120 *"Scientists who don't"*: Judis, "The Government's Junk Science."

120 *"I do believe"*: Conrad Lautenbacher, quoted in ibid.

121 *"People have hunches"*: Conrad Lautenbacher, quoted in Bill Lambrecht, "Missourians Should Heed Storm Lesson, Experts Say," *St. Louis Post-Dispatch,* August 31, 2005.

121 *"a few recent"*: "Former NOAA Lab Director: 'Climate Scientists Within NOAA Have Been Prevented from Speaking Freely,'" ClimateScienceWatch post, March 10, 2006, available online at www.climatesciencewatch.org/index.php/csw/details/mahlman-lautenbacher/.

121 *"Contrary to Dr. Lautenbacher's"*: Jerry Mahlman, personal communication, 2006.

122 *"With all of the"*: Chris Mooney, "Earth Last," *American Prospect,* May 4, 2004.

122 *A 1977 report:* Walter Sullivan, "Scientists Fear Heavy Use of Coal May Bring Adverse Shift in Climate," *New York Times,* July 25, 1977. The rest of the history is available online at www.aip.org/history/climate/Govt.htm.

123 *"In the 1970s"*: Michael Crichton, *State of Fear* (New York: HarperCollins, 2004), 315.

123 *George Will picked:* Will, "Global Warming?"

124 *"The Global Cooling Myth"*: RealClimate website, http://www.realclimate.org/index.php?p=94. One quote that Will ascribes to the prestigious peer-reviewed journal *Science* actually came from the non-peer-reviewed magazine *Science News.* For a detailed debunking of the notion that scientists were predicting an imminent ice age in the 1970s, see www.wmconnolley.org.uk/sci/iceage/.

124 *A spring 2003 workshop:* Fred Pearce, "Global Warming's Sooty Smokescreen Revealed," *New Scientist,* June 4, 2003.

124 *A 2005 study:* Thomas L. Delworth et al., "The Impact of Aerosols on Simulated Ocean Temperature and Heat Content in the 20th Century," *Geophysical Research Letters* 32 (December 21, 2005).

125 *"Truthiness"*: "The Colbert Report," *60 Minutes,* CBS News, April 30, 2006, available online at www.cbsnews.com/stories/2006/04/27/60minutes/main 1553506.shtml.

125 *"STATE OF FEAR"*: "State of Fear," Marich Communications, press release,

December 7, 2004, available online at www.michaelcrichton.com/press/
index/html.

125 *geneticists were executed:* Wikipedia, s.v. "Lysenkoism," http://en.wikipedia.
org/wiki/Lysenkoism.

126 *"In light of":* Science 304, no. 5669 (April 16, 2004): 400–402.

126 *"Hansen overestimated":* James Hansen, "The Global Warming Debate,"
NASA website, January 1999, available online at www.giss.nasa.gov/edu/
gwdebate.

126 *Michaels is:* Cato Institute website, www.cato.org/people/michaels.html.

128 *The environmentalists did:* "Contextomy Tsunami" at http://www.fallacy
files.org/archive012005.html; and Bill McKibben, "Stranger Than Fiction,"
Mother Jones, May/June 2005.

128 *"The Tsunami Exploiters":* James Glassman, "The Tsunami Exploiters," Tech
Central Station, January 14, 2005, available online at www.techcentral
station.com/011405C.html.

129 *"The Death of Environmentalism":* Michael Shellenberger and Ted Nordhaus, "The Death of Environmentalism," September 2004, available online
at www.thebreakthrough.org/images/Death_of_Environmentalism.pdf.

CHAPTER SIX: THE TECHNOLOGY TRAP AND THE AMERICAN WAY OF LIFE

133 *"There is no doubt":* Tony Blair, "The Prime Minister's Speech to the Business and Environment Programme," September 14, 2004, available online
at www.g8.gov.uk/servlet/Front?pagename=OpenMarket/Xcelerate/Show
Page&c=Page&cid=1078995903270&aid=1097485779120.

133 *"It's important":* Mark Hertsgaard, "While Washington Slept," *Vanity Fair,*
April 17, 2006.

135 *"What will never fly":* Shankar Vedantam, "Senate Impasse Stops 'Clear
Skies' Measure," *Washington Post,* March 10, 2005.

135 *"to ensure that":* Fiona Harvey, "U.S. Is Accused of Undermining Kyoto
Principles on Emissions," *Financial Times,* December 17, 2004.

138 *"voluntary programs":* Conservatives often use the phrase "voluntary programs" to mean efforts to get industry to make voluntary pledges to reduce
emissions.

139 *"The United States is":* Spencer Abraham, quoted in "U.S. Energy Secretary
Says New Technologies Needed to Achieve Global Climate Goals," U.S.

Newswire September 17, 2003, available online at http://releases.usnews wire.com/GetRelease.asp?id=20881.

140 *"With a new"*: George W. Bush, State of the Union address, January 28, 2003.

140 *A hydrogen car:* Joseph Romm, *The Hype About Hydrogen: Fact and Fiction in the Race to Save the Climate* (Washington, D.C.: Island Press, 2005).

140 *A 2005 Luntz:* Frank Luntz, "An Energy Policy for the 21st Century," *A New American Lexicon*, March 2005, available online at www.politicalstrategy. org/archives/001207.php#1207.

140 *"What's most striking"*: "President Discusses Energy at National Small Business Conference," White House press release, April 27, 2005; and John Carey, "Bush Is Blowing Smoke on Energy," *Business Week*, April 28, 2005.

141 *"Sometimes, decisions"*: "Bush Blames 'Mixed Signals' for Energy Lab Layoffs," *USA Today*, February 21, 2006.

143 *"force for good"*: "Put a Tiger in Your Think Tank," *Mother Jones*, May/June 2005, available online at www.motherjones.com/news/featurex/2005/05/ exxon_chart.html.

143 *"to depict global"*: "Industrial Group Plans to Battle Climate Treaty," *New York Times*, April 26, 1998.

146 *Over the next few years:* "High Temperature Superconductors," available online at www.eapen.com/jacob/superconductors/chapter5.html.

146 *"Typically it has"*: Global Business Environment, *Energy Needs, Choices and Possibilities: Scenarios to 2050* (London: Shell International, 2001), 22.

146 *We barely have:* Romm, *Hype*.

147 *Research on nickel:* Battery University.com, www.batteryuniversity.com/ partone-4.htm.

149 *"Are we going"*: Stephen Johnson, quoted in Juliet Eilperin, "Ex-EPA Chiefs Agree on Greenhouse Gas Lid," *Washington Post*, January 19, 2006.

150 *$10 to $20 billion per year:* Daniel N. Kammen and Gregory F. Nemet, "Reversing the Incredible Shrinking Energy R&D Budget," *Issues in Science and Technology* (Fall 2005): 84–88. Missile Defense funding numbers from Missile Defense Agency FY07 budget estimate, available online at www.cdi .org/pdfs/Final%20Budget%20Overview%20FY%202007%20MDA.pdf.

152 *"the intential large-scale manipulation"*: David Keith, "Geoengineering Climate," *Elements of Change*, S. J. Hassol and J. Katzenberger, eds. (Aspen, Colo.: Aspen Global Change Institute, 1998), 83–88.

152 *"The 'geo-engineering' "*: John Holdren, "The Energy Innovation Imperative," *Innovations* 1, no. 2 (Spring 2006): 3–23.

CHAPTER SEVEN: THE ELECTRIFYING SOLUTION

154 *"This analysis suggests"*: National Academy of Sciences, *Policy Implications of Greenhouse Warming: Mitigation, Adaptation, and the Science Base* (Washington, D.C.: National Academies Press, 1991).

155 *The coal plants that will:* David G. Hawkins, testimony, U.S. House Committee on Energy and Commerce, Subcommittee on Energy and Air Quality, *Hearing on Future Options for Generation of Electricity from Coal*, 108th Cong., 1st sess., June 24, 2003, available online at www.nrdc.org/global Warming/tdh0603.asp. The new plants amount to some 1,400 GW, which includes 400 GW of plants to replace existing ones that have reached the end of their lifetime.

156 *The total extra costs:* U.S. Department of Energy, Office of Fossil Energy, *Carbon Sequestration R&D Overview*, available online at www.fe.doe.gov/ programs/sequestration/overview.html. This is the cost for large-scale sequestration in places like deep underground aquifers. Small-scale seques tration for enhanced oil and gas recovery is far less expensive.

156 *"Vendors currently"*: *Coal-Related Greenhouse Gas Management Issues*, National Coal Council, Washington, D.C., May 2003.

157 *FutureGen project:* U.S. Department of Energy, Office of Fossil Energy, *FutureGen Fact Sheet*, available online at www.fossil.energy.gov/programs/ powersystems/futuregen/.

158 *"Less dense"*: National Research Council, *Novel Approaches to Carbon Management*, Workshop Report (Washington, D.C.: National Academies Press, 2003), 3.

158 *Pacific Northwest National:* James Dooley and Marshall Wise, "Why Injecting CO_2 into Various Geologic Formations Is Not the Same as Climate Change Mitigation: The Issue of Leakage," Joint Global Change Research Institute (Battelle Pacific Northwest National Laboratory), 2002. See also David Hawkins, "Passing Gas: Policy Implications of Leakage from Geologic Carbon Storage Sites," Natural Resources Defense Council, Washington, D.C., 2002.

159 *Analysis suggests:* See, for instance, Keith and Farrel; and Timothy Johnson and David Keith, "Fossil Electricity and Carbon Dioxide Sequestration," *Energy Policy* 32, no. 4 (March 2004): 367–82. See also Howard Herzog,

"The Economics of CO_2 Separation and Capture," *Technology* 7, supp. 1 (2000): 13–23.

159 *Energy efficiency remains:* See, for instance, Arthur H. Rosenfeld, "Sustainable Development—Reducing Energy Intensity by 2 percent Per Year" (PowerPoint presentation at the International Seminar on Planetary Emergencies, Erice, Italy, August 19, 2003).

160 *This astonishing achievement:* The chart is derived from "Consumption, Physical Units, 1960–2002" for electricity consumption (kWh) and from "Appendix C: Resident Population" of U.S. Department of Energy, "Data Sources and Technical Notes," available online at http://www.eia.doe.gov/emeu/states/_seds.html.

163 *California utilities:* Cynthia Rogers et al., "Funding and Savings for Energy Efficiency Programs for Program Years 2000 through 2004," paper, California Energy Commission Staff, July 2005.

163 *2006 report:* Western Governors' Association, "Energy Efficiency Task Force Report," January 2006, available online at www.westgov.org/wga/initiatives/cdeac/Energy%20Efficiency-full.pdf.

164 And it is avoiding: Personal communications with Art Rosenfeld. See also Audrey Chang, "California's Sustainable Energy Policies Provide a Model for the Nation," Natural Resources Defense Council, Washington, D.C., May 2005. Available online at http://www.e2.org/ext/doc/CASustEnergy Policies.pdf.

165 *increased demand for gas:* Energy Information Administration, *Annual Energy Outlook 2003*, DOE/EIA-0383 (2006): 67.

166 *Steam accounts:* "BestPractices Steam," Alliance to Save Energy website, www.ase.org/section/program/bpsteam. See also Joseph Romm, *Cool Companies: How the Best Businesses Boost Profits and Productivity by Cutting Greenhouse Gas Emissions* (Washington, D.C.: Island Press, 1999).

166 *2 million new jobs:* Joseph Romm and Charles Curtis, "Mideast Oil Forever?" *Atlantic Monthly,* April 1996. According to the study, this is "a relatively large impact considering that the investments driving it were assumed to be made for purposes other than increasing employment."

167 *about 88,000 megawatts:* "The Market and Technical Potential for Combined Heat and Power in the Commercial/Institutional Sector," prepared by Onsite Sycom Energy Corp. for the U.S. Department of Energy, Washington, D.C., January 2000, available online at www.eere.energy.gov/de/pdfs/chp_comm_market_potential.pdf.

168 *July 2000 report:* R. Brent Alderfer et al., *Making Connections: Case Studies of Interconnection Barriers and Their Impact on Distributed Power Projects* (Golden, Colo., National Renewable Energy Laboratory, July 2000).

169 *9,000 megawatts.* John Douglas, "Putting Wind on the Grid," *EPRI Journal* (Spring 2006): 6–15.

170 *"2–5 cents/kilowatt-hour":* Renewables 2005 Global Status Report: Notes and Reference Companion Document, Renewable Energy Policy Network for the 21st Century (REN21), October 20, 2005, available online at www.ren21 .net/globalstatusreport/RE2005_Notes_References.pdf.

171 *The E.U. has set:* Ibid, pp. 19–24.

171 *Department of Energy study:* U.S. Department of Energy, Energy Information Administration, *Analysis of Strategies for Reducing Multiple Emissions from Electric Power Plants: Sulfur Dioxide, Nitrogen Oxides, Carbon Dioxide, and Mercury and a Renewable Portfolio Standard,* SR/OIAF/2001–03, July 2001. Electricity prices in 2020 under a 20 percent RPS would be about 4 percent higher than the EIA projects they would be in a business-as-usual scenario, but 2 percent lower than they are today.

171 *"The Path to":* Alison Bailie et al., *The Path to Carbon-Dioxide-Free Power: Switching to Clean Energy in the Utility Sector* (Washington, D.C.: Tellus Institute and Center for Energy and Climate Solutions, Report for the World Wildlife Federation 2003), available online at http://assets.panda .org/downloads/powerswitchfinalusa.pdf.

172 *The net savings:* Net savings included the costs for more energy-efficient equipment and additional cogeneration (plus transfers of revenue from the CO_2 cap and trade program back to the consumers).

174 *"It's the only":* Darren Samuelsohn, "McCain Says White House Run Would Not Change Commitment to Emission Curbs," *E&E News,* March 15, 2006.

174 *Nuclear energy is:* Notwithstanding the fact that uranium enrichment in this country makes use of a highly electricity-intensive process that is almost exclusively powered by coal plants.

175 *2003 study by MIT:* John Deutch et al., *The Future of Nuclear Power* (Cambridge: Massachusetts Institute of Technology, 2003).

175 *"The abiding lesson":* Matthew L. Wald, "Interest in Building Reactors, but Industry Is Still Cautious," *New York Times,* May 2, 2005.

176 *California, however:* Energy Source, CA Total Electric Power Industry Net Generation, U.S. Department of Energy, Energy Information Administra-

tion data table, available online at www.eia.doe.gov/cneaf/solar.renewables/ page/state_profile/rsp_ca_table3.html.

CHAPTER EIGHT: PEAK OIL, ENERGY SECURITY, AND THE CAR OF THE FUTURE

177 *"We have a serious"*: George W. Bush, State of the Union address, January 31, 2006.

177 *"In the absence"*: Senator Richard Lugar, "Energy: The Albatross of National Security," submitted to *Conservative Environmental Policy—Quarterly*, spring 2006, available online at http://lugar.senate.gov/energy/press/articles /060301cepquarterly.html.

178 *"Our nation"*: George W. Bush, quoted in "Bush Pushes Alternative Energy Proposals," Associated Press, February 20, 2006, available online at www .msnbc.msn.com/id/11465801/.

179 *And the transportation sector:* U.S. Department of Energy, Energy Information Administration, *Annual Energy Outlook 2003*, Table A19, DOE/EIA= 0383 (2003). Available online at www.eia.doe.gov/oiaf/archive/aeo03/index .html.

179 *"In the absence"*: "Biofuels for Transport: An International Perspective," International Energy Agency, press release, May 11, 2004, available online at www.iea.org/Textbase/press/pressdetail.asp?PRESS_REL_ID=127.

180 *more oil than the entire world:* Romm and Curtis, "Mideast Oil Forever?" *Atlantic Monthly,* April 1996.

180 *when prices spiked:* Energy Information Administration, *International Petroleum Monthly,* March 2006.

180 *"There is nothing"*: Kenneth Deffeyes, *Hubbert's Peak: The Impending Oil Shortage* (Princeton, N.J.: Princeton University Press, 2001), 158. For the opposing view, see Leonardo Maugeri, "Oil: Never Cry Wolf—Why the Petroleum Page Is Far from Over," *Science* 304, no. 5674 (May 21, 2004): 1114–15.

180 *"A scarcity of oil"*: Global Business Environment, *Energy Needs, Choices and Possibilities: Scenarios to 2050* (London: Shell International, 2001), 18.

181 *200 to 400 billion:* International Energy Agency, *Resources to Reserves,* Paris, September 2005; and David Adam, "Global Warming Sparks a Scramble for Black Gold Under Retreating Ice," *Guardian* (London), April 18, 2006.

181 *heavy oil in Venezuela:* Manik Talwani, "The Orinoco Heavy Oil Belt in Venezuela (or Heavy Oil to the Rescue?)," Rice University, Houston, Texas, September 2002, available online at http://cohesion.rice.edu/natural

sciences/earthscience/research.cfm?doc_id=2819; and *Alberta's Oil Sands 2004*, Government of Alberta, Ministry of Energy, available online at www.energy.gov.ab.ca/docs/oilsands/pdfs/PUB_osgenbrf.pdf.

182 *Canada's increasing:* The U. S. Energy Information Administration projects a sharp decline in net imports of Canadian natural gas by 2020. EIA, U.S. Department of Energy, Energy Information Administration *Annual Energy Outlook 2006*, DOE/EIA (2006). See also U.S. DOE, EIA, *Annual Energy Outlook 2004* DOE/EIA (2004), p. 50.

182 *Colorado and Utah:* James R. Udall and Steven B. Andrews, "The Illusive Bonanza: Oil Shale in Colorado," *Energy Bulletin* (October 3, 2005).

183 *"CO_2 flooding":* Robert Hirsch et al., *Peaking of World Oil Production*, Science Applications International Corp., February 2005.

184 *21 million barrels:* Northern Plains Resource Council, *Montana's Energy Future*, 2006; available online at http://www.worc.org/pdfs/Synfuel_Briefing_Paper.pdf; and David Garman, "Unconventional Liquid Fuels" (PowerPoint presentation to Defense Science Board, U.S. Department of Energy, Washington, D.C., June 2006).

184 *Worse, the total:* Adam Brandt and Alexander Farrell, "Scraping the Bottom of the Barrel: Greenhouse Gas Emission Consequences of a Transition to Low-Quality and Synthetic Petroleum Resources," submitted to *Climatic Change.*

185 *2 billion metric tons:* Ibid.

185 *"Forget hydrogen":* James Woolsey, remarks at Plug-in America press conference, National Press Club, Washington, D.C., January 2006, available online at www.connectlive.com/events/austinenergy/.

185 *"$1.2 billion":* George W. Bush, State of the Union address, 2003, available online at www.whitehouse.gov/news/releases/2003/01/20030128-19.html.

185 *"It is highly likely":* National Research Council and National Academy of Engineering, *The Hydrogen Economy: Opportunities, Costs, Barriers, and R&D Needs* (Washington, D.C.: National Academies Press, 2004).

186 *January 2004 study: Well-to-Wheels Analysis of Future Automotive Fuels and Powertrains in the European Context*, European Commission Center for Joint Research, EUCAR, and Concawe, Brussels, January 2004.

186 *save four times:* For a longer discussion of hydrogen cars and plug-in hybrids, see Joseph Romm, *The Hype About Hydrogen: Fact and Fiction in the Race to Save the Climate* (Washington, D.C.: Island Press, 2005).

186 *a pollution-free:* Internal combustion engine cars can also be modified to run on hydrogen, although they are considerably less efficient than fuel-cell vehicles and thus have much shorter range and even higher annual fuel bills.

186 *currently cost about $2,000:* U.S. Department of Energy, *Basic Research Needs for the Hydrogen Economy* (Washington, D.C.: Office of Science, 2003).

187 *"a new material":* American Physical Society, "The Hydrogen Initiative," March 2004.

187 *more than $500 billion:* Marianne Mintz et al., "Cost of Some Hydrogen Fuel Infrastructure Options" (Argonne National Laboratory, presentation to the Transportation Research Board, Washington, D.C., January 16, 2002).

187 *"Fuel-cell cars":* Matt Wald, "Questions About a Hydrogen Economy," *Scientific American* 290, no. 5 (May 2004): 66–73.

187 *"If I told you":* Bill Reimert, quoted in Jamie Butters et al., "Fuel-Economy Technologies," *Detroit Free Press,* January 10, 2005.

187 *2004 MIT study:* Nancy Stauffer, *New Vehicle Technologies: How Soon Can They Make a Difference?* (Cambridge: MIT Laboratory for Energy and the Environment, 2005). Available online at http://esd.mit.edu/esd_reports/summer2005/new_vehicle_technologies.html.

187 *5-year budget:* Daniel Whitten, "Barton Rails at Budget Request for Shorting EPACT," *Inside Energy,* March 13, 2006.

188 *Samuel Bodman announced:* Geoff Brumfiel, "Energy Secretary Ditches Science Advisers," *Nature* 440, no. 7085 (April 6, 2006): 725.

188 *"My message":* Lugar, "Energy: The Albatross."

189 *European countries: Transportation Energy Data Book,* edition 22 (Oak Ridge, Tenn.: Oak Ridge National Laboratory, 2002), 5-2, 5-3.

189 *nowhere near 60 mpg:* Feng An and Amanda Sauer, *Comparison of Passenger Vehicle Fuel Economy and Greenhouse Gas Emissions Standards Around the World* (Arlington, Va.: Pew Center on Global Climate Change, December 2004). As of 2002, the average fuel economy of European Union vehicles was 37 mpg, and some of that fuel-economy improvement was achieved not just with high fuel prices but with strong tax incentives to promote diesel vehicles, which are typically more fuel-efficient.

189 *In a 2002 report:* National Research Council, *Effectiveness and Impact of Corporate Average Fuel Economy (CAFE) Standards* (Washington, D.C.: National Academies Press, 2002).

189 *Studies by the national:* Interlaboratory Working Group, *Scenarios of U.S. Carbon Reductions,* Lawrence Berkeley National Laboratory and Oak Ridge National Laboratory, prepared for the Office of Energy Efficiency and Renewable Energy, U.S. Department of Energy, September 1997, pp. 5.44–5.48, David Greene and Andreas Schafer, *Reducing Greenhouse Gas Emissions from U.S. Transportation* (Arlington, Va.: Pew Center on Global Climate Change, May 2003), 13–18; and Malcolm Weiss et al., "On the Road in 2020: A Life-Cycle Analysis of New Automobile Technologies" (Cambridge: MIT, October 2000), tables 5.3 and 5.4.

An Oak Ridge National Laboratory study found that "based on a comparison of fatality data for SUVs to other vehicles, the registered-vehicle-fatality rate (defined as number of fatalities per number of registered vehicles) for SUVs is higher than the registered-vehicle-fatality rate for other vehicles." Stacy Davis and Lorena Truett, *An Analysis of the Impact of Sport Utility Vehicles in the United States,* ORNL (Oak Ridge, Tenn.: Oak Ridge National Laboratory, 2000), 24.

190 *"Policies aimed":* Robert Noland, "Fuel Economy and Traffic Fatalities," *Energy Policy* 33 (2005): 2183–90.

190 *Toyota Prius hybrid:* "Toyota Prius: AEI Best Engineered Vehicle 2004," *Automotive Engineering International,* March 2004: 58–68.

190 *Europeans have still:* An and Sauer, *Passenger Vehicle Fuel Economy.* I have used their normalization so that European mpg can be directly compared with mpg calculated under CAFE.

190 Consumer Reports *found:* "Fuel Economy: Why You're Not Getting the MPG You Expect," *Consumer Reports,* October 2005.

191 *Center for American Progress:* Bracken Hendricks et al., "Strengthening America's Auto Industry," Center for American Progress, Washington D.C., September 13, 2005. Report available online at www.americanprogress.org/autos.

191 two weeks' worth of oil: www.hybridcars.com/blogs/brain/fuel-econ-raised.

192 *So an all-electric:* Joseph Romm and Andrew Frank, "Hybrid Vehicles Gain Traction," *Scientific American* 294, no. 4 (April 2006): 72–79.

192 *8 cents a kilowatt-hour:* Ibid.

193 *The plug-in hybrid will: Reducing California's Petroleum Dependence,* Joint Agency Report, California Energy Commission and California Air Resources Board, Sacramento, August 2003.

194 *overall efficiency:* Romm and Frank, "Hybrid Vehicles"; and Alec Brooks,

"CARB's Fuel Cell Detour on the Road to Zero Emission Vehicles," Evworld .com, May 2004.

194 *The efficiency of charging:* Ibid.

194 *1,400 gigawatts:* Joseph Romm, "The Car and Fuel of the Future," Report for the National Commission on Energy Policy, Washington, D.C., June 2005.

194 *less than 400 GW:* Ibid.

195 *overall net emissions:* Lester Lave et al., "The Ethanol Answer to Carbon Emissions," *Issues in Science and Technology* (Winter 2001). See also Lester Lave et al., "Life-Cycle Analysis of Alternative Automobile Fuel/Propulsion Technologies," *Environmental Science and Technology* 34 (2000): 3598–3605.

195 *Existing oil pipelines:* Michael Bryan, "The Fuels Market—Biofuel Penetration and Barriers to Expansion" (paper presented at the Conference on National Security and Our Dependence on Foreign Oil, CSIS, Washington, D.C., June 2002), 13–15.

195 *"$2.70 per gallon":* Lave et al., "Ethanol Answer." This calculation includes a 20-cents-a-gallon tax on ethanol. See also Greene and Schafer, *Reducing Greenhouse Gas Emissions,* 30.

196 *One 2001 analysis:* Lave et al., "Ethanol Answer."

196 *Lee Lynd described:* Personal communications with Lynd.

198 *National Commission:* National Commission on Energy Policy, *Ending the Energy Stalemate: A Bipartisan Strategy to Meet America's Energy Needs,* Washington, D.C., 2004.

CHAPTER NINE: THE U.S.-CHINA SUICIDE PACT ON CLIMATE

200 *"The 'international fairness' issue"* and *"We don't need":* Frank Luntz, "Straight Talk."

200 *2.8 million barrels a day:* Kenneth Lieberthal and Mikkal Herberg, "China's Search for Energy Security: Implications for U.S. Policy," *NBR Analysis* 17, no. 1 (April 2006), available online at www.nbr.org/publications/analysis/ pdf/vol17no.1.pdf.

202 *"Perhaps the most":* Richard Benedick, testimony, "The Case of the Montreal Protocol: Science Serving Public Policy," *Hearing on "The Role of Science in Environmental Policy-Making,* U.S. Senate Committee on Environment and Public Works, 109th Cong., 1st sess., September 28, 2005, available online at epw.senate.gov/109th/TestimonyBenedick.pdf.

202 *But other uses:* The history in this section is based on Stephen O. Anderson and K. Madhava Sarma, *Protecting the Ozone Layer* (London: Earthscan, 2002); and Benedick, "Case of the Montreal Protocol."

202 *"first unmistakable sign":* Cheryl Silver with Ruth DeFries (for the National Academy of Sciences), *One Earth, One Future: Our Changing the Global Environment* (Washington, D.C.: National Academies, Press, 1990).

202 *"no effect":* Benedick, "Case of the Montreal Protocol."

204 *National Academy of Sciences:* Walter Sullivan, "Scientists Fear Heavy Use of Coal May Bring Adverse Shift in Climate," *New York Times*, July 25, 1977.

204 *"greenhouse gas concentrations":* U.N. *Framework Convention on Climate Change*, May 1992, full text available online at http://unfccc.int/essential_background/convention/background/items/1349.php.

204 *"Accordingly":* Ibid.

205 *"mandate new commitments":* Byrd-Hagel Resolution, Sen. Res. 98, 105th Cong., 1st sess., *Congressional Record* 143, no. 107 (July 25, 1997): S8113–S8139. Resolution text available online at www.nationalcenter.org/Kyoto Senate.html.

205 *"whereas greenhouse gas":* Ibid.

206 *especially on a per capita basis:* Duncan Austin, José Goldemberg, and Gwen Parker, *Contributions to Climate Change: Are Conventional Metrics Misleading the Debate?* (Washington, D.C.: World Resources Institute, October 1998).

206 *Beijing Energy Efficiency Center:* The discussion of China's energy history is based on Mark D. Levine, "Energy Efficiency in China: Glorious History, Uncertain Future" (remarks at University of California at Berkeley, April 28, 2006); and personal communications with Mark D. Levine.

208 *A 2005 study:* Bin Shui and Robert C. Harriss, "The role of CO_2 Embodiment in U.S.-China Trade," *Energy Policy* (in press).

209 *down to 17 billion tons:* Fiona Harvey and Leora Moldofsky, "U.S. and Australia pledge $128m for climate accord," *Financial Times*, January 12, 2006; and Brian Fisher et al., "Technological Development and Economic Growth, ABARE Research Report" (prepared for the Inaugural Ministerial Meeting of the Asia-Pacific Partnership on Clean Development and Climate, Sydney, January 2006), ABARE, Canberra, available online at www.abare.gov.au/publications_html/climate/climate_06/06_climate.pdf.

CHAPTER TEN: MISSING THE STORY OF THE CENTURY

212 *"In the end"*: Maxwell T. Boykoff and Jules M. Boykoff, "Balance as Bias: Global Warming and the U.S. Prestige Press," *Global Environmental Change* 14 (2004): 125–36.

212 *"This is no time"*: Edward R. Murrow, *See It Now*, March 9, 1954, available online at http://www.spartacus.schoolnet.co.uk/USAmccarthy.htm.

213 *In November 2005: Meet the Press*, MSNBC, November 20, 2005, transcript available online at www.msnbc.msn.com/id/10042399/.

214 *"If we're unlucky"*: Olivia Judson, "Evolution Is in the Air," *New York Times*, November 6, 2005.

215 *"Balance as Bias"*: Boykoff and Boykoff, "Balance as Bias." See also www.fair.org/extra/0411/global-warming.html.

216 *To create doubt*: David Michaels, "Doubt Is Their Product," *Scientific American* 292, no. 6 (June 2005): 96–101.

216 *"to spend millions"*: John Cushman, "Industrial Group Plans to Battle Climate Treaty," *New York Times*, April 26, 1998.

217 *"suggests that melting"*: Juliet Eilperin, "Another Look at Sea Level Rise," *Washington Post*, January 23, 2006.

217 *"is one of many"*: Ibid.

217 *"Most scientists agree"*: Juliet Eilperin, "Debate on Climate Shifts to Issue of Irreparable Change," *Washington Post*, January 29, 2006.

218 *action on global warming*: The memo is available online at http://desmogblog.com/vampire-memo-reveals-coal-industry-plan-for-massive-propaganda-blitz.

218 *"Coal-burning utilities"*: Seth Borenstein, "Utilities Give Warming Skeptic Big Bucks," Associated Press, July 27, 2006. Available online at www.forbes.com/business/feeds/ap/2006/07/27/ap2910768.html.

218 *May 3, 2006, Washington Post*: Doug Struck, "Canada Alters Course on Kyoto," *Washington Post*, May 3, 2006.

219 *"undermines one of"*: Juliet Eilperin, "Study Reconciles Data in Measuring Climate Change," *Washington Post*, May 3, 2006.

219 *"over the years"*: Wikipedia, s.v. "John Christy," http://en.wikipedia.org/wiki/John_Christy.

219 *"Global warming contrarians"*: Richard Kerr, "No Doubt About It, the World Is Warming," *Science* 312, no. 5775 (May 12, 2006): 825.

221 Washington Post Magazine: Joel Achenbach, "What Global Warming?" *Washington Post Magazine*, May 30, 2006.

221 *"We probably won't":* "2004 U.S. Hurricane Season Among Worst on Record," *National Geographic News,* November 30, 2004, available online at http://news.nationalgeographic.com/news/2004/11/1130_041130_florida_ hurricanes_2004_2.html.

221 *Consider a* Washington Post *article:* Lee Hockstader, "Coastal Louisiana Drowning in Gulf," *Washington Post,* July 13, 2003.

222 *Mike Taibbi:* NBC News, "Meltdown," available online at www.dailykos. com/storyonly/2006/1/13/03957/2447; and "January Could Be Warmest on Record in U.S.," Reuters, January 31, 2006, available online at www.msnbc .msn.com/id/11112822/from/RSS/.

223 *"continuous erosion":* Senator Lisa Murkowski, statement, *The Role of Science in Environmental Policy Making,"* Hearing, U.S. Senate Committee on Environment and Public Works, 109th Cong., 1st sess., September 28, 2005, available online at http://epw.senate.gov/hearing_statements.cfm?id= 246814.

224 *Climate Extremes Index:* U.S. Climate Extremes Index available online at www.ncdc.noaa.gov/oa/climate/research/cei/cei.html.

224 *They wanted only:* See, for instance, Don Babwin, "Heat Taxes Utilities, Human Endurance," ABC News, August 1, 2006, available online at http:// abcnews.go.com/US/Weather/wireStory?id=2261076; and Jennifer Steinhauer, "In California, Heat Is Blamed for 100 Deaths," *New York Times,* July 28, 2006.

225 *"Scientists associate":* Ross Gelbspan, *Boiling Point: How Politicians, Big Oil and Coal, Journalists and Activists, Are Fueling the Climate Crisis—and What We Can Do to Avoid Disaster* (New York: Basic Books, 2004), 79–80.

225 *"Meteorologists are not":* Judith Curry, person communications.

226 *"no prominent national":* Peter Teague, quoted in Michael Shellenberger and Ted Nordhaus, "The Death of Environmentalism."

226 *"Few scientists agree":* Andrew C. Revkin, "Yelling 'Fire' on a Hot Planet," *New York Times,* April 23, 2006.

227 *"The hurricanes we":* Thom Akeman, "Global Warming Behind Record 2005 Storms—U.S. expert," Reuters, April 25, 2006, available online at www .climateark.org/articles/reader.asp?linkid=55586.

227 *"BE WORRIED":* Time 167, no. 14 (April 3, 2006): cover.

228 *"To be fair":* Jerry Adler, "The New Hot Zones," *Newsweek,* April 3, 2006.

CONCLUSION: THE END OF POLITICS

230 *"America is great"*: www.bartleby.com/73/829.html.

231 *"In my judgment"*: President Bush (remarks at McCormick Place, Chicago, May 2006), available online at www.whitehouse.gov/news/releases/2006/05/20060522-1.html.

232 *"Scientists present"*: James Hansen, "The Threat to the Planet," *New York Review of Books*, 53, no. 12 (July 13, 2006): 12–16.

233 *Evangelical Climate Initiative*: Christians and Climate website, www.christiansandclimate.org/statement.

233 *April 2006 news story*: Lauren Morello, "Evangelical Leaders Take Debate to Capitol Hill," *Greenwire*, April 25, 2006.

233 *"government-mandated"*: Interfaith Stewardship Alliance website, www.interfaithstewardship.org/pdf/OpenLetter.pdf.

235 *"In nine months"*: Doris Kearns Goodwin, *No Ordinary Time: Franklin and Eleanor Roosevelt: The Home Front in World War II* (New York: Simon & Schuster, 1994), 362.

235 *"You see, I told you"*: Edward Teller story told in Richard Rhodes, *The Making of the Atomic Bomb* (New York: Simon & Schuster, 1986), 500.

INDEX